Negligence

Comparative Studies
in Continental and Anglo-American Legal History

Vergleichende Untersuchungen zur kontinentaleuropäischen
und anglo-amerikanischen Rechtsgeschichte

Herausgegeben von

Helmut Coing (†), Richard Helmholz, Knut Wolfgang Nörr
und Reinhard Zimmermann

Band 22

Negligence

The Comparative Legal History
of the Law of Torts

Edited by

Eltjo J. H. Schrage

Duncker & Humblot · Berlin

Gedruckt mit Unterstützung der Gerda Henkel Stiftung, Düsseldorf

Die Deutsche Bibliothek – CIP-Einheitsaufnahme

Negligence : the comparative legal history
of the law of torts / Hrsg.: Eltjo J. H. Schrage. –
Berlin : Duncker und Humblot, 2001
(Comparative studies in continental and Anglo-American
legal history ; Bd. 22)
ISBN 3-428-10516-8

Fremddatenübernahme: Klaus-Dieter Voigt, Berlin
Druck: Berliner Buchdruckerei Union GmbH, Berlin
Printed in Germany

ISSN 0935-1167
ISBN 3-428-10516-8

Gedruckt auf alterungsbeständigem (säurefreiem) Papier
entsprechend ISO 9706 ♾

Inhaltsverzeichnis

ELTJO J. H. SCHRAGE

Negligence. A comparative and historical introduction to a legal concept*

I. Introduction

In their inauguration of this series of publications the general editors, Prof. H. Coing and Prof. K. W. Nörr stated that their intention was to give rise to a continuation of that tradition of learned scholarship which from a historical point of view kept an eye open for the common features that linked the common law and the civil law – notwithstanding the obvious distinctions. In line with previous volumes this book compares the legal history of *Negligence*, in other words: this collection of essays is devoted to the comparative legal history of liability for unintended harm from the Middle Ages onwards.

In this phrase the words *from the Middle Ages onwards* indicate the framework and the limitations to this volume. Roman law in the narrow sense of the word plays a role only in so far as it is indispensable for the understanding of the medieval and later legal history. Consequently the method of this volume is different from that developed by Buckland and Mc Nair for comparing the Roman law of Antiquity on the one hand and modern English law on the other. This work aims at a dynamic comparison of the similar legal problems concerning negligence and the different solutions given to those problems in the various legal systems. Therefore the contributions covering similar periods should be read together.

---

* The author wants to express his profound gratitude to Tony Weir, fellow of Trinity College Cambridge, for his unrivalled hospitality and his willingness to share his longstanding knowledge. Without his continuous encouragement this article could not have been written. Tony Weir furthermore translated the contribution by Mme Auzary-Schmaltz which was originally in French and he corrected the language of several other contributions. The author also wants to thank the Master and Fellows of the aforementioned Trinity College, who elected him as a visiting fellow during the course of 1998.

I am also under particular obligations to my colleague and friend Dr. Waibel (University of Tübingen) who has undertaken the tedious and thankless duty of reducing the conventions employed by an assortment of writers of different nationalities to uniformity for the benefit of the printer, and has discharged it with admirable diligence and accuracy.

The first question to be raised is a terminological one. The danger of an over-simplification lies around the corner. "It is all too easy" Professor Baker writes right at the beginning of his paper, "to assume that words have always meant the same as they do today, and in particular that words which have become part of the lawyer's stock-in-trade represent eternal legal ideas or categories". In early English law the word *negligence* (*negligencia* in Latin) cannot be regarded as a term of art describing conduct of particular kind. Equivalent words were freely used to describe careless acts or omissions, without any sense that there was a general legal concept of negligence, from which answers could be deduced in specific situations. John Baker found even a number of cases dating back to as early as 1662 and 1671, in which the word *negligent* does not seem to have imported fault in the sense of carelessness, but rather the failure to discharge a strict liability.

But the student of the legal history of the 17th century is mainly concerned with causes of actions. In the 17th century, however, there did not exist a form of action called Negligence. The common law was dealing with actions for Trespass and trespass on the Case, while on the continent notably the *actio legis Aquiliae* and the *actio iniuriarum* played a dominant role in legal teaching. But there is a long way to go from these actions as they were used in the early days of the legal history to the general tort of Negligence of to day and the general remedy for unlawful acts, as codified in art. 1382 of the French Code civil of 1804,[1] and then was taken over from there into numerous other continental codifications.[2]

Admittedly the Common Law's Tort of Negligence as such is essentially a creation of the 19th century, though its tendrils reach back to an earlier usage of the word (Ibbetson). Professor Birks is of the opinion that the action on the case for unintentional harm had the potential to reach the 1932-position as early as 1732. Professor McQueen and Mr Sellar state that the case of *Gardner* v. *Ferguson* (1795) is generally regarded as the first case in the modern Scots law of negligence. G. Rotondi writes in 1917, that already the medieval canon lawyers took the first three steps on the road to the general remedy for unlawful acts by categorizing the *actio legis Aquilia* not so much as an *actio poenalis*, but as an *actio poenabilis*, first of all by understanding the sum to be paid by the defendant rather as damages than as a *poena*, secondly by considering the action as passively

[1] Art. 1382 Code civil: Tout fait quelconque de l'homme qui cause à autrui un dommage, oblige celui par la faute duquel il est arrivé, à le réparer. The text of the German Bürgerliches Gesetzbuch § 823 is quoted *infra*, footnote 22.

[2] *P. Catala, J. A. Weir,* Delict and Torts: A Study in Parallel, in Tulane Law Review XXXVII (1963), p. 573–620; XXXVIII (1964), p. 221–278; 663–716; XXXIX (1965), p. 701–783.

transmissible and thirdly by enlarging the scope of the action to almost every unlawful act or omission.[3] The final step towards a general remedy, however, is ascribed by Professor Feenstra and the great majority of the modern scholars (among whom Rotondi) to Hugo Grotius. Feenstra criticizes a remark made by Kiefer, that the *Usus modernus* had already developed *eine deliktische Generalklausel* before Grotius.[4]

And this leads into the central question of this book. The legal history of the tort of Negligence started off with two actions and similarly so did the law of torts on the continent. Both traditions generalized their initial concepts of specific torts into the universal modern notions, and it is essentially that concept of *generalisation* which makes it possible to compare the legal history of the Civil with that of the Common law. In the Common law the decisive step was made with the ruling that

> "you must take reasonable care to avoid acts or omissions which you can reasonably foresee would be likely to injure your neighbour. Who then, in law is my neighbour? The answer seems to be: persons who are so closely and directly affected by my act that I ought reasonably to have them in contemplation as being so affected when I am directing my mind to the acts or omissions which are called in question",

as Lord Atkin put it in *Donoghue* v. *Stevenson*.[5] There are, however, a few earlier landmarks in the law, such as the case of the unruly horses brought into Little Lincoln's Inn Fields, *Mitchil* v. *Alestree* (1676).[6] The last quarter of the 17th century saw the quiet, gradual emergence of a new species of liability that was to provide one of the two streams that merged in the early 19th century to produce the tort of negligence, the running–down actions, which were the start of a liability in negligence that was independant of trespass, the other stream being the development of an action on the case in tort for negligence in the performance of an undertaking or calling.[7] In 1768 Buller's *Nisi Prius* stated that *Every man ought to take reasonable care that he does not injure his neighbour*, and Prof. Birks points at Sir William Jones who – in his opinion – was in 1781 "the true inventor of the standard of the reasonable man." Tony Weir describes for the time being the importance of the tort of negligence in the common law of today: "announced in hieratic terms in 1932, its principle of liability has become

---

[3] *G. Rotondi,* Dalla "Lex Aquilia" all. Art. 1151 Cod.civ. Ricerche storico-dogmatiche, in Rivista di diritto commerciale 14 (1916), p. 942–970, and 15 (1917), p. 236–295; also in his Scritti Giuridici II (1922), p. 465–578 § 1.

[4] *R. Feenstra, infra,* at footnote 104; cf. the text at footnote 78.

[5] *Donoghue* v. *Stevenson*, [1932] A.C. 562.

[6] *M. J. Prichard, Scott* v. *Shepherd* (1773) and the Emergence of the Tort of Negligence [Selden Society Lecture delivered in the Old Hall of Lincoln's Inn, July 4th, 1973], London 1976, p. 16.

[7] *Prichard,* p. 22.

so dominant that sixty years later Lord Goff cout state that "the law of tort is the general law, out of which the parties can, if they wish, contract"."[8]

On the Continent the decisive step was made in the French codification, although Hugo Grotius is an early landmark in the continental legal development and there are a few more to be found alongside the road to generalization, among whom Buller's contemporary Samuel Coccejus, who likewise reasoned that every man is naturally obliged to apply the utmost duty of care vis à vis his fellowman.[9] It follows from the contributions by Mossler and Ernst, that the German lawgiver intentionally departed from the Prussian, Austrian, French example and stuck to the Usus modernus Pandectarum which started from the (albeit in the course of the ages: extended) use of the Roman actions. For that reason the German lawgiver (*Zweite Kommission*) enumerated a number of rights, the unlawful infringement whereof would make the tortfeasor liable, although the committee knew of the French example. In short: the civil law is divided into two mainstreams: one which in principle sticks to a limited enumeration of different conceptual pigeonholes under which the actual cases have to be subsumed (the German system) and one in which an open norm in principle covers any actual case. It may be true (and Von Caemmerer in particular drew the attention to that phenomenon) that the eventual results in these two legal systems may not be too different. The German enumeration is necessarily enlarged via an analogous interpretation of its component elements, whereas the expression: *sonstige Rechte* gives the codified norm already an open character; the French open norm is entrenched via the classical methods of refinement and distinctions. Notwithstanding these remarks it remains true, that the civil law shows a varied image. In Scotland, Stair, strongly influenced by Grotius' de iure belli ac pacis, drew on "the general moral principle *Quod tibi fieri non vis, alteri non feceris*" (Inst. 1.1.6).

This is our point of departure: which hurdles had the pilgrims to overcome underway to the generalization and the conceptualization of the rea-

---

[8] *Tony Weir*, The Staggering March of Negligence, in P. Cane, J. Stapleton, The law of Obligations. Essays in Celebration of John Fleming, Oxford 1998, p. 97. The quotation of Lord Goff refers to *Henderson* v *Merret Syndicates* [1994] 3 All ER 506, 532.

[9] *Samuel Coccejus,* Jus civile controversum, Lib. XIII, Tit. VI, Qu. X: Ex rigore naturali ergo homo ad omnem etiam exactissimam diligentiam, quae ab humano intellectu proficisci tenetur, l. 21 C. Mand. [C. 4,35,21]; Coccejus ad D. 9,2, qu. 3: At ratio, cur in l. Aquilia levissima culpa praestetur, adeo evidens non est, sed primus e visceribus juris gentium eam eruit, B. Parens in tract. De Culp. Disp. 3, th. 18, junct. Th. 24.n6 et Collat. Ad Struv. Coll. 2, th. 15.: Probavit enim ille ex rigore naturali hominem obligari ex omni eo quod intellectu suo providere potuit (dict. Coll. 1.2.3.4), ideoque teneri eum naturaliter ad exactissimam diligentiam: hunc vero rigorem naturalem remansisse circa legem Aquiliam.

sonable man? And we know on the authority of Chaucer that pilgrims may be rewarding companions, when we can overhear their conversation …

From a theoretical point of view it would be possible to approach these hurdles according to the nature of the interest for which the plaintiff claims protection or damages. Support for this approach can be found on both sides of the Channel. From the continental side, since the *actio legis Aquiliae* at first glance seemed to pertain only to specific harm done; the English side, since around 1500 the forms of action were predicated on the kind of harm done rather than the degree of fault required to impose liability. And similar reasoning applies to German law which in §§ 823 and 826 BGB sets out three in principle limited heads of tortious liability in order to limit liability in respect of both the class of claimants and the kinds of damage eligible for compensation. § 823, Abs. 1 BGB (the litteral text is to be found in footnote 22) enables recovery only for injury either to one of a restrictive list of rights enumerated therein (life, body, health, freedom, ownership) or to another right (*sonstige Rechte*), provided that the injury to the victim was caused intentionally or negligently (*vorsätzlich oder fahrlässig*).

Nevertheless such an approach fits ill with the developing open ended concept of negligence, which essentially puts its emphasis on the injurer's conduct and sanctions the behaviour of the man who fails to attain the requisite standard of behaviour or (if we may borrow a 19th century definition by Alderson B.) failed to live up to the standards of the prudent and reasonable man. Any consideration of the development of liability for causing unintended harm must take account of the nature of the conduct, the kind of harm caused and the manner in which it is caused. The three may run together, since in any case the question will be whether the defendant who acted in *this* manner is to be made liable for causing *this* harm in *this* way, but we shall in this introduction deal with them in the following order: (a) the test of actionable conduct, (b) the nature of the compensable harm, (c) the necessary causal link. We shall consider damage done to property and person, and then liability for the death of a free person. A separate section will be devoted to the vicarious liability. Finally the effect of procedure on the development of the substantive law will be pondered. There is perhaps little point in comparing the style of pleadings in the different jurisdictions at different times, since attorneys everywhere are ever equally wordy and concerned with wording, but readers can see an example of the English style in Professor Birks's contribution at p. 103, and can compare it, to the latter's advantage, with the statement of claim in a Scottish wrongful death case in MacQueen p. 290. The form of pleadings before the Parlement de Paris in the 14th century, as discussed by Mme. Auzary-Schmaltz, is strikingly comparable with the pleadings instanced by Thomasius as a bad example from Schacher's practical handbook: "... and he was unable to eat for so long that he would rather have lost 200 Reichsthaler than have to forego so much food ...".

But before doing so, we will have to face the separation of the civil liability from criminal responsibility and compensation. Before the general principle of liability for harm unintentionally caused could develop, civil liability had to be separated from criminal responsibility and compensation distinguished from punishment. It is true that criminal liability characteristically attaches to deliberate conduct rather than unintended harm, that *culpa* is wider than *dolus*: but the *lex Aquilia* covered intentional conduct as well as conduct which was merely negligent, so the overlap was considerable. After all, the BGB imposes liability for harmful invasions of protected interests which are *vorsätzlich oder fahrlässig* (§ 823 BGB), even if the Code civil has to make the point separately that reparation is due for imprudence and negligence as well as for one's own act.

1. Crime and tort; compensation and punishment

a) At Common law

The distinction between the criminal prosecution and the private action against the wrongdoer has had a remarkably similar evolution in Roman, Germanic and English law. The laws of tort and crime had a common origin in revenge and deterrence, but at quite an early stage they parted company and assumed distinctly separate functions. A crime is nowadays considered to be an offence against the State, as representative of the public, which will vindicate its interests by punishing the offender. A criminal prosecution is not concerned with repairing an injury that may have been done to an individual, but with exacting a penalty in order to protect society as a whole. Tort liability on the other hand, exists primarily to compensate the victim by compelling the wrongdoer to pay for the damage done.[10] Speaking of trespass, Holdsworth says that this action was in Edward I's reign a quasi-criminal proceeding, i.e. though it was a proceeding begun at the suit of the injured individual, it was aimed at serious wrongs and breaches of the king's peace, and it ended in the punishment of the defendant as well as in compensation to the plaintiff.[11] Once the criminal law had developed and convicted felons no longer became incapable of holding property, English lawyers, like their civilian counterparts earlier, had to face the question whether criminal proceedings simply suspended or

---

[10] *J. G. Fleming,* The law of Torts, Sidney 1992, p. 1.

[11] *Holdsworth,* History of English Law II, 364.

wholly barred a civil action, and they opted for suspension.[12] In cases of homicide, however, it was different, with the result that there was no civil liability for killing a person. There was, however, until 1819, the criminal appeal of murder, which could be brought by relatives whatever the result of the criminal proceedings,[13] and the threat of which could be used by them to force a composition.

Although nowadays the distinction between tort and crime is fairly clear, the civil consequences of criminal conduct still present a perplexing picture. In France the strength of the links between the two is stronger than elsewhere. The very word "délit" implies criminality; all punishable conduct is automatically a basis for civil liability for resulting harm, and to cause personal injury by negligence is criminal in itself; very generally the victim can claim compensation in the criminal process, which he is empowered to require to be undertaken (subject to the risk that acquittal will bar a civil claim based on the incriminated conduct, though not one based on breach of contract or on the strict liability for damage done by things under the defendant's control).

In Germany, if we leave aside the extensive liability for harm intentionally caused by revolting conduct (§ 826 BGB), there is liability for other breaches of the law only if the law is "protective" (as many of the offences in the Criminal Code are) and the defendant cannot exculpate himself from the inference of negligence in committing the breach. In England today the mere fact that the plaintiff's harm resulted from conduct for which the defendant could be or has been punished is no indicator of civil liability. Most common law crimes are also tortious, but offences created by statute rarely confer a civil action on the victim. If, exceptionally, it is held otherwise, negligence need not be shown in addition to the breach. In other words, the negligent breach of a statutory duty usually involves liability only if it also constitutes a breach of a duty at common law.

b) At Civil law

The distinction between the criminal prosecution and the private action against the wrongdoer finds the peg, on which the Glossators draped their vestments in Inst. 4.4.10: In summa sciendum est de omni iniuria eum qui passus est posse vel criminaliter agere vel civiliter. According to the Accursian Gloss *agere* to this text the two remedies could not be brought by the same plaintiff against the same defendant *cum utrumque iudicium sit proditum ad vindictam.*[14] Only when the wrong surpassed the threshold of the

---

[12] *Smith* v. *Selwyn* [1914] 3 KB 98.

[13] *Holdsworth,* History of English Law II, 363.

atrox iniuria could the plaintiff bring both the *actio legis Aquiliae* and the *actio iniuriarum* simultaneously against the same defendant, the former action pertaining to the recovery of damages, the latter one being the remedy which originated from the *Lex Cornelia de iniuriis* and which covers the injustice suffered. See the gloss *Agere* ad Inst. 4.4.10: Et ideo si de atroci iniuria actum est iniuriarum, nihilominus potest agi lege Aquilia ad damnum, et econverso, nec enim actione iniuriarum agitur ad damnum ut ad damnum sed ut ad contumeliam, ut ff. eod. l. Item apud Labeonem § Si quis servo verberato [D. 47.10.15.46].

It goes without saying that the glossators initially could not deny the penal character of the *actio legis Aquiliae*, nor did they want to deny it, given the features of the remedy (*infitiando lis crescit in duplum*, passively intransmissible, etc.). But already in the works of the medieval canonists there is a certain tension to be felt between the adjudication of a fixed amount of money in delict on the one hand (the highest value in the preceding year, the value in the nearest 30 days …; two, three or four times the value of the asset stolen) and the amount of requisite restitution on the other hand. And exactly that tension gave shape to the modern doctrines of indemnification, or at least to one root thereof. Simultaneously with the canonists the glossators too definitely tried to soften the consequences of the penal character of the *actio legis Aquiliae*. Odofredus distinguishes between *actiones poenales* and *actiones poenabiles*. The *actio furti* is a true *actio poenalis*, since that remedy covers nothing but a penalty; the *actio legis Aquiliae*, however, is only potentially a penalty (namely in the unanticipated circumstance the wrongdoer dies), but it is in their opinion an *actio reipersecutoria* in as far as it pertains to compensation for actual harm suffered, e.g. when co-wrongdoers commmitted the damaging act: Si plures damnum dederunt et agitur cum uno et solvit, non liberat alium quia poena est … sed quantum est persecutoria solvendo unus alios liberat.[15] Explicit texts like D. 9.2.2 (or C. 4.17.1) prevented Odofredus and Accursius from categorizing the *actio legis Aquiliae* unreservedly as an action for damages, but there were certain consequences inherent in their view that by way of this action the plaintiff could claim damages. Pillius is already of the opinion that against the builder of a new mill which corrupts the old one which stood on the side taking its water for more than 30 years the *actio legis Aquiliae*, be it in the shape of the *actio legis Aquilia utilis*, could lead to a *restitutio in integrum*.[16] For Baldus already the *actio legis Aquiliae*

---

14 The interpretation given in the Accursian Gloss is generally accepted in later ages. See e.g. *Perezius*, Praelectiones, ad C. 9.25; *Grotius*, Inl. III.32.2. *in fine*.

15 *Odofredus* ad. D. 9.2.11; Inst. 4.3.9.

16 *Pyllius*, Quaestiones, ed. Roma 1560, p. 20, quoted by *Rotondi*, p. 242, footnote 2.

constitutes the civil claim for damages, whereas the *actio iniuriarum* makes up for the penalty.[17]

The same reasoning holds true for the canonists.[18] Canon law also for the most part maintained the specific features of the Roman actions in much the same way as civil law. Each action presupposed specified behaviour of the defendant. The reach of these various actions was extended in a similar way as happened in the civil law, namely not so much by way of an extensive interpretation of the various terms in the wordings of the actio, but rather by the creation of an *actio utilis* or an *actio in factum.* This was true both in the *actio legis Aquiliae* and in the *actio iniuriarum,* as the canonists generally derived both from Roman law and from the decretal *Olim* (1215–1216) of pope Honory III. It is only by the end of the 13th century that the canonists came to the conclusion that a distinction had to be made between the compensation of damages and the payment of a private penalty as punishment. This distinction follows remarks made by Augustine and by Thomas Aquinas who differentiated the restitution of what had wrongfully been taken from another and the reparation of the injustice suffered by the victim. *Restitutio* was understood as including the compensation for personal damages caused by injuring or killing, sometimes even for the suffering undergone by the victim. *Satisfactio*, moreover, was also essential. The perpetrator had at least to ask the victim for forgiveness for the injustice caused. Consequently, the canonists laid the foundations for a distinction between a reaction to unintentionally inflicted harm in the sphere of the private law (*restitutio*) and in the realm of the criminal law (*satisfactio*). However, the traditional view according to which it was not until the 16th century that the formulation was reached that any person convicted of a crime could also be held liable in damages, needs to be reviewed, since earlier traces of the same doctrine are to be found in the works of Bartolus and Angelus Aretinus, as Hallebeek and Feenstra show.

For the latter purpose (the general doctrine that any person convicted of a crime could also be held liable in damages) the *actio legis Aquiliae* served. Already with Baldus this action had lost its characteristics of being exclusively penal and it had become mainly a remedy for damages, which could be brought for any harm done *per corruptionem rei.* It seems as if Baldus was the first to draw this conclusion, (although it seems as if Lauterbach was the first to coin the phrase: *per corruptionem rei*).[19] Also Stryk emphasizes this aspect of the *actio legis Aquiliae*: in the first paragraph of his commentary on Digest 9.2 Stryk says: Tituli praesentis usus

---

[17] *Baldus,* Consilia 249.

[18] *Dondorp, infra* at footnote 30.

[19] *Lauterbach,* Collegii theoretico-practici ad D. 9,2, nr. 2.

amplissimus est, cum omnium damnorum reparatio ex hoc petatur, si modo ulla alterius culpa doceri possit.[20]

II. Actionable types of conduct

1. Positive Acts

a) At Common law

The legal history of the tort of Negligence started off with two actions, the actions of trespass and the action on the case. There was no form of action called negligence. The action of trespass lay for invasive interference with land, goods, or the person; the action on the case covered a wider range of situations where loss had been wrongfully caused. Writers as late as Winfield and even Plucknett stated, that liability in case was often or usually based on negligence, whereas in trespass liability was strict and negligence irrelevant. In this volume, however, Professor Baker will show that there is no contemporary evidence that trespass and case were separated by differing standards of liability. In so far as differing standards may be discerned at all, it seems most likely that they varied according to the types of situation in which liability arose rather than the form of action through which the remedy had to be sought. And Baker identifies than four main kinds of situation where liability may be imposed (in actions of Trespass and Case) for harm caused by negligence in the sense of carelessness:

- (1) Negligence in performing an undertaking which expressly or impliedly requires the exercise of due care.
- (2) Negligence in looking after someone else's property, in the absence of or without regard to any legally enforceable contract requiring careful custody.
- (3) Negligence in the custody or control of something dangerous.
- (4) Negligence in carrying on one's own activities.

Under these four headings he analyzes innumerable cases in which adverbs were used like: 'negligently' (*negligenter*), 'improvidently' (*improvide*), 'in an unworkmanlike manner' (*inartificialiter*) and several others, which have a more or less similar meaning. As we shall see when considering the effect of procedure, it is extremely difficult to tell in the early common law what standards were actually applied to the defendant's conduct, because the wording of the writs was simply a fiction and the

---

[20] *Stryk,* Continuatio usus moderni Pandectarum a libro VI usque ad XII, Hallae 1704, p. 146–147; cf. *Feenstra, infra* at footnote 198.

decision of the jury was shrouded in silent obscurity. But Baker shows that it is possible to penetrate a little way beneath the Common law forms by making use of the records of the different courts and this leads him to the conclusion that by 1700 judges and practitioners were beginning to find a new general principle, that 'a man must always use his own so as to do no harm to his neighbour' and was answerable for all mischief proceeding from his neglect or his actions, unless they were of unavoidable necessity'.

The words "were beginning to" are significant. The meaning, the reach and the effects of the formulation of such general principles remains quite problematic in the centuries to come. It was not until 1932 that Lord Atkin in London said: "... there must be, and is, some general conception of relations giving rise to a duty of care of which the particular cases found in the books are but instances." Although in certain areas it has seemed possible to discern a move towards principle, or, what comes to the same thing, the abolition of narrow distinctions at the factual level (the action on the case seemed to have some procedural benefits over the action of trespass, which in its turn, however might have been counterbalanced by the substantive benefits of the action of trespass (which did not raise any question of the defendant's fault), in others the courts seem to commit themselves to pragmatic and gradual development; recent cases in negligence, one judge has said, "signalled the retreat from high principle and the resurgence of pragmatism."[21]

On the Continent the situation is similarly complex. The law of delict in the French Code civil consists of a mere five short articles, of which the first one codifies one general principle: "Every act whatever of man which causes damage to another binds the person whose fault it was to repair it". Similarly the (admittedly: older) Prussian Code, the Saxonian, Austrian, Dutch and Italian Codes (both the 1865 and the 1942 Code) as well as the Suiss Obligationenrecht (1911). The German civil code, however is less general and so more extensive and it deals with the law of unlawful acts in 31 brief sections. The main one reads: "A person who deliberately or carelessly injures another contrary to law in his life, body, health, freedom, property or other right is liable to compensate that other for the resulting damage."[22]

---

[21] *White* v. *Jones* [1993] 3 All E.R. 481, 501, *per* Steyn L. J.

[22] § 823 Bürgerliches Gesetzbuch: [Schadenersatzpflicht] (1) Wer vorsätzlich oder fahrlässig das Leben, den Körper, die Gesundheit, die Freiheit, das Eigentum oder ein sonstiges Recht eines anderen widerrechtlich verletzt, ist dem anderen zum Ersatze des daraus entstehenden Schadens verpflichtet. See footnote 1 for the text of art. 1382 Code Civil.

b) At Civil law

On the Continental side the *actio legis Aquiliae* and the *actio iniuriarum* deserve special attention. Interdependence of the type of conduct and the type of harm is obvious, since the first chapter of the *lex Aquilia* deals with a type of actionable conduct qualified by the effect. The history of the *actio legis Aquiliae,* analogously in Antiquity and in the Middle Ages, is characterized by a continuous extension of the interpretation of the requirements for this action. This process had started already in the days of the classical Roman law. Although the first chapter of the *Lex Aquilia* related to the tortfeasor's own act, which immediately and directly caused the death of the victim (*occidere*), and whereas the third chapter required the tortfeasor to have inflicted the damage with his own hands (*corpore corpori datum,* if we may borrow the 16th century expression in this context), it was apparently arguable that in other cases of lesion or damage done to slaves, animals or chattels an action was given which was not so much the *actio legis Aquiliae* itself, but rather an ancillary action, *actio utilis* or *actio in factum).* The classical Roman lawyers distinguished the primary civil action on the *lex* from ancillary actions granted by the praetor to deserving plaintiffs on deserving facts when one or both fell outside the purview of the statute, but we really do not know whether the civil and praetorian claims differed as to any of their incidents, and in any case the distinction became irrelevant when proceedings ceased to be formulary. Justinian preserved the distinction, however, and the conservatism of scholars ensured that it was nominally retained in continental doctrine until quite a late stage, although by that time it was purely theoretical, without any practical consequences. The most that can be said is that the further the facts diverged from the heartland of the principal claim the more reluctant the courts might be to extend liability, although the actio *in factum* was available to them. Procedure did not, however, stand in the way of generalisation as it did in England.

In the sources we find examples of such ancillary actions, e.g. the imprisonment of another person's slave or cattle in such a way that the slave or cattle came to starve. Other examples are the situation in which the defendant drove an animal so hard, that it collapsed and died, or when the defendant had persuaded the plaintiff's slave to climb into a tree or to descend into a well. If this slave got wounded or killed during this expedition the owner could not bring the *actio legis Aquiliae* itself, but he could bring the *actio utilis*, modelled after this remedy.

The interpretation by the medieval jurists of this action concentrated firstly upon the manner of perpetrating the harm, namely as to the object of the attack and the question of causality. The glossators followed almost literally the text of the Corpus iuris civilis, but they systematised these three variants of the *actio legis Aquiliae* in this way, that they maintained for the *actio legis Aquiliae* itself the old requirement that the death or the wounds were caused directly by a violent (*adhibita vi*) and direct (*quasi manu*) corporeal act of the tortfeasor himself (*damnum corpore corpori datum*)[23]; if the direct relation between the acts of the tortfeasor himself and the occurrence of the damage was less obvious (e.g. the damage was not inflicted *corpore*), then they were of the opinion that an *actio utilis* would lie; was – eventually – the damage not directly inflicted to the slave, the animal or the chattel, then the *actio in factum* was to be considered. An example of this situation occurred when a person liberated a slave from his manacles so that he could run away. It was not until the *Usus modernus* before any distinction between these three varieties of the *actio legis Aquiliae* came to disappear, and the action as such became the remedy for every harm *per corruptionem rei.*[24]

Prof. Hallebeek stresses the point that the Glossators showed a strong tendency to classify the different actions in Roman law according to four different standards, which he calls: *degrees of liability*. In cases of specified contractual relations the plaintiff may bring an action when the defendant did not meet the required *diligentia quam in suis*. In other contractual or delictual situations actions may require *culpa lata* (foolishness), *nimia (magna) negligentia*, or *dolus* (fraud). More severe as a degree of liability is the standard of *culpa, culpa levis, negligentia*, whereas the standard of the *diligentissimus pater familias* is synonymous to *culpa levissima.*[25] It depends on the specifications of each action, which degree exactly founds the cause of action, but for the Glossators the *actio legis Aquiliae* presupposes at least *culpa levissima* on the part of the defendant: *In lege Aquilia et levissima culpa venit* (D. 9.2.44*pr.*). It goes without saying that the action also lies in case of *dolus* or *culpa.*[26]

Thus already the glossators took a number of important steps on the road to generalization of this remedy by redefining the type of conduct that con-

23 D. 9.2.7.1 (Ulpian): explains the direct and violent qualification of the inflicted death: occisum autem accipere debemus sive gladio sive etiam fuste vel alio telo vel manibus – si forte strangulavit eum – vel calce petiit vel capite vel qualiter qualiter.

24 If we may borrow the words of *Lauterbach,* Collegii theoretico-practici ad D. 9.2. nr. 2. See also *supra*, at footnote 19.

25 *Rotondi,* p. 245 at footnote 4 quotes a text taken from the 16th century scholar Tiberius Decianus, in which he defines *culpa levissima* as *aliqualis negligentia post factum cognita, quam etiam diligens pater familias non evitasset.*

26 D. 9.2.32.2: In hac quoque actione dolus et culpa punitur, where culpa in the footsteps of D. 9.2.31 is defined as: quod cum a diligente provideri poterit non esset provisum.

stitute the cause of action, the degree of culpability and the causality. From the point of view of the common lawyer the *actio legis Aquiliae* came to apply in some of the ground which is nowadays covered by the common law of negligence.[27] There were, however, a few more hurdles to overcome. Another important step was the extension to another type of harm than the killing and wounding of cattle and slaves, namely the killing or wounding of free persons. We shall return to that aspect shortly, but first we have to face the *actio iniuriarum.* The *lex Aquilia* referred originally to damages inflicted upon property, cattle or slaves. Wounding of free persons remained, at least originally outside the reach of this action.[28]

The medieval interpretation of the *actio iniuriarum* as found in the Corpus iuris civilis is interesting for several reasons. Some modern authors have drawn attention to the fact that this *actio iniuriarum* is narrowly correlated to the natural feelings of the late-medieval man for whom the feudal ideals of courtesy and chivalry found expression in the values of honesty and reputation. No violation of honour and good fame could be left without revenge. The Christian church tried to canalize this revenge and it firmly resisted taking the law into one's own hand, being opposed also against duels.[29] The duel was seen as an ordeal (more specifically, a two sided ordeal) and already on the fourth Lateran Council (1215) the servants of the church were forbidden to be present at ordeals. The church pleaded for more peaceful methods of conflict solution and found the necessary remedy in this very action, on the one hand since the procedural estimation of the amount to be adjudicated to the victim had the character of a penalty to be paid to the victim, on the other hand since the indigenous law of Northern Italy offered remedies similar to that *actio iniuriarum.*

The concept of *iniuria* was even further defined. To begin with the concept itself, the medieval scholars maintained assault, battery and insult as specifications of *iniuria*. This is rather obvious against the background of the sources in which flagellation or punching (*verberare, pulsare*) or the unlawful entrance to a dwelling were qualified as *iniuria*. But on the basis of several texts taken from the Corpus iuris civilis the medieval scholars distinguished between written, oral and real infringements of the honour,

---

[27] See D. 9.2.31 for the case of the negligent pruning of the tree; D. 9.2.52.1 for the liability in case of consecutive (serial) lethal wounds; Inst. 4.3.16 for false emprisonment; D. 9.2.27.10 and 29.1–2 for trespass to goods and nuisance.

[28] But see D. 9,2,13*pr* and parallel texts.

[29] See also *B. Schwentner,* Die Stellung der Kirche zum Zweikampfe bis zu den Dekretalen Gregors IX, in Theol. Quartalschrift 3 (1930), p. 190–234. *V. G. Kierman,* The duel in european history (1988), p. 185 ff. is of a different opinion. The latter author places the origins of the anti-duel movement in the second half of the 16th century, notably in Saxony.

honesty, integrity or reputation,[30] the written including libels, the oral insults in the face of the victim, and also slander as well. It is the real ones, however, which are the most interesting. Real insults give us an insight into the value patterns of the medieval and later society. Trespass to another person's field by a hunting company was (at least on the Continent) valued as an insult (*iniuria*) even more so, since the trespasser seemed to be asserting a feudal right. Illustrative are also infringements of the rules concerning the seating at the table, the priority in processions, etcetera. Procedures against professors who claimed a more exalted position in the parade than was warranted by their seniority are well known until the 19th century.

In canon law the conditions under which the various actions could be brought were scrutinised on the basis that wrongs should be punished in proportion to the severity of the consequences, provided that some fault could be ascribed to the tortfeasor. What degree of fault? Accidents fall outside the scope of the *actio iniuriarum*, but they could come within the reach of the *actio legis Aquiliae*, which, as we stated above, could be brought even in cases of extremely slight fault, as it is stated above: *In lege Aquilia et levissima culpa venit* (D. 9.2.44*pr.*). Consequently the canon law placed a rather strong emphasis on the tortfeasor's conduct and thus on the distinction between fault and fortuitous events. The blameworthiness or innocence of the offender's conduct, could have different effects in the *forum internum* and the *forum externum*. According to Joannes Andreae the neighbour who confessed to insufficient effort in preventing the spread of a fire from his house to the neighbouring one, could be liable under the *actio legis Aquiliae* for damages even in the case of *culpa levissima*, whereas the priest in the confession-stall could absolve him without requiring him to compensate the neighbour for his damage. This (mainly 19th century) doctrinal development was eventually to lead to a number of canons in the first Codex iuris canonici (1917), in which the notion of *culpa* referred to the element of subjective imputability.

2. *Omissions*

a) At Common law

An original feature of the action of trespass was its concern with the breach of the king's peace. Although this expression says nothing about what a trespass actually was and rather looked to which trespasses would be actionable in the royal courts, it nevertheless required a minimum amount of force. If practically any physical interference could be brought

---

30 E.g. *Angelus Aretinus* ad Inst. 4.4.

within the scope of the action (defamation was hived off into the ecclesiastical courts and breach of contract was rerouted into the action of covenant) the action of trespass was in the 13th and 14th century strongly focused on the liability of the person who had *wrongly caused* harm to another. As a consequence liability was very rarely imposed for simple omissions. Although the distinction between misfeasance (doing something wrong) and nonfeasance (failing to do something right) is only cognate, though not congruent, with the direct/indirect distinction in terms of causation (an omission cannot directly cause anything) it has long been an issue in the development of liability for unintentionally causing or contributing to harm.

Yet even the word "negligence" did not invariably connote omission – in the Limitation Act of 1623 we read in s. 5 of "... accions of trespas quare clausum fregit ... wherein ... the trespas be by negligence, or involuntary ..." – and it is apt to do so only if one starts with the idea of the defendant's duty to take care (though "breach" itself suggests a positive act). But whatever the verbal implications, it was unquestionably positive conduct which, in England as on the continent, most easily rendered a defendant liable: of passive conduct, even in the seventeenth and eighteenth centuries, Winfield could say that "the recorded cases are near as few in this period as in that of the Year books".[31] The truth of the matter is that if the defendant had acted positively the plaintiff could sue in trespass (supposing that the harm was the direct result), and since in that form of action negligence did not have to be alleged and could not usefully be denied, the negligent infliction of damage by a positive act was unquestionably actionable, whereas liability for careless omission was certainly not actionable in trespass ["... for nonfeasance, or negligence, shall never be said to be vi et armis" (id. at 193, per Coke CJ)] and was actionable in case only under certain circumstances, generally when negligence was present.

Here, however, we have to face a terminological problem. In eighteenth century England, according to Professor Birks (p. 176) "it is clear that 'negligence' and 'negligently' primarily indicated inactivity" and he quotes an argument of counsel in 1799: "it does not appear that any act whatever was done by the defendants: on the contrary, it appears that the injury was occasioned by their negligence." (p. 177). John Austin, too, ordained at the beginning of the nineteenth century that "'negligence' should be applied exclusively to 'breaches by omission of positive duties'." [Ibbetson p. 236] though Brian Simpson observes that "There is no reason to suppose that Austin's views on the law of tort, or on any other breach of law, ever had the least influence."[32]

---

31 96 Law Quarterly Review 184, 193.

And indeed, towards the beginning of the nineteenth century plaintiffs who wished to assert that their action was not contractual in nature began to assert that the defendant's conduct had been such as to impose a duty to take care. Here also the emphasis on the positive act, not the mere omission of the defendant is striking. Ibbetson states that it was in the 1860s that the use of the duty of care established itself as an organising device. According to his view as late as 1860 the general principle gets only the briefest mention in the first edition of Charles Addisson's *The law of wrongs and their remedies*. The language of duty had been found already in the writings of the 17th and 18th century Natural lawyers (Pufendorf deserves particular mention in this context as the contributions of Ernst and Mossler will show, since it was he who began to treat the duty of the citizen as an axiom from which inferences of legal liability could be drawn), and it was taken from there into Buller's *Nisi Prius*. There is a tendency to equate 'negligence' with 'neglect' elevated to the role of the duty for just as an omission to act would constitute culpable neglect only if there had been a duty to act, culpable negligence could be defined in terms of a failure to observe a duty of care. The latter concept provided the necessary tool to bring about a more general doctrine of liability for omissions. The notion of the duty of care, combined with the notion of the breach of duty is the defining feature of the English tort of negligence, including both positive acts and omissions. However, this view has not gone uncriticised: Lord Atkin's famous conjunction of misfeasance and nonfeasance in his seminal generalisation: "you must take reasonable care to avoid acts or omissions which you can reasonably foresee would be likely to injure your neighbour" has been disavowed by the House of Lords in a recent judgement: "Omissions ... are notoriously a category of conduct in which Lord Atkin's generalisation ... offers limited help."[33] and the ingrained habit of pleaders of insisting on precautions which the defendant failed to take, even when he was guilty of a positively dangerous act, was criticised by Viscount Simonds: "The accident occurred not through a failure to supply a suitable [tool] – a failure that could result in nothing – but through the supply of an unsuitable [tool].[34]

b) At Civil law

In the Middle Ages, however, neither the glossators nor the canonists extended the *actio legis Aquiliae* far enough to cover liability for mere

[32] *AWB Simpson,* The Elusive Truth about Holmes, 95 Mich L Rev. 2027, 2028 (1997).

[33] *Stovin* v. *Wise* [1996] 3 All ER 801, 818.

[34] *Davie* v. *New Merton Board* [1959] A. C. 604.

omissions: *culpa levissima* presupposed already in Roman law a positive action.[35] The requirement of a direct causal relation between the action and the effect is another test which impedes liability for omissions. The medieval scholars did not want to set these requirements aside.

The substantive distinction between acting and failing to act was found in the texts of the Corpus iuris civilis: in principle a claim under the *lex Aquilia* itself in its technical form lay only if the defendant had caused the harm by a positive act: the *damnum* had to be *datum*. This requirement of a direct causal relation between the positive act and the harm was mitigated in the course of the time: an *actio utilis* or an *actio in factum* could be given when the defendant had locked up another person's slave or animal and the latter came to starve, or when a defendant had so excited another person's beast of burden or pack-animal, that it collapsed and died.

Thus the glossators systematised the three varieties of the actio legis Aquiliae and extended the reach of the claim, although the extension remains rather marginal. Paul's observation on the personal liability of the master who knew that his slave was wounding or killing another slave – (D. 9.2.45.pr. *qui prohibere potuit, teneatur si non fecerit*; – or even Diocletian's observation on the liability of the owner who was unaware of the slave's acts (C. 3,41,4: *ignorante domino.. dominum simpli noxali iudicio convenire potes*) was not carried through, though it pre-echoes Loysel's famous observation, typically Gallic in its epigrammatic exaggeration, "*qui peut et n'empèsche, pèsche.*"

Canon law seems to have contributed relatively little to the doctrinal development. Nevertheless its contribution should not be underestimated. It has at its disposal two pegs on which to hang the developments. The first peg is of C. 14 q. 6 c.1: Non remittetur peccatum nisi restituatur, the principle that sins are only forgiven provided that the stolen object is restored. This was also true for the deceased. From the point of view of the church he was already during his life obliged to restitution; this obligation passed to his heirs (in X 3,28,14 Innocent IV presupposes an implied *stipulatio*; Joannes Andreae takes a tacit *mandatum* for granted). The canonists saw a

---

[35] *Zimmermann*, p. 979 for a number of texts testifying that in classical Roman law the *actio legis Aquiliae* did not cover cases of omissions. In footnote 172 he refers to the requirement of *direct means* for the tort of trespass. *Maitland*, The Forms of Action at Common Law, 1909 (repr. 1962), p. 50 footnote 164. *B. Markesinis*, The German Law of Obligations, vol II The Law of Torts, A. Comparative Introduction, Oxford 1997 at p. 74–5: "From Roman times to today, it has been well known that liability for an omission could be imposed if a previous duty to act could be discovered. In early times, statute and contract were the main progrenitors for duties of affirmative action. Later the areas of liability for omission was widened ... *Verkehrssicherungspflichten* entail liability for snow covered steps or lettuce leaves.

parallel with the Roman texts stating that the passive intransmissibility of the actio legis Aquiliae was subject to an exception in so far as the heir was enriched as a consequence of the delict committed by the deceased. Consequently the doctrine of the confession, the conviction of the canonists and the civilians pointed in the same direction. This resemblance between three intellectual mainstreams contributed to the authority of this this view, which was to become dominant among Natural Law scholars, as Feenstra shows. The second peg is the Decretal *Si culpa tua* (X 5,36,9), issued by Gregor IX in 1234, which blurred the originally strict borderlines between the *actio legis Aquiliae* and the *actio iniuriarum.*[36] The text of the Decretal repeats the famous Roman saying that the perpetrator who caused the conditions for the harm is responsible for the occurrence and therefore liable. The text, however did not take the decisive step towards unlimited liability for omissions.

Rotondi draws attention to a decision of the Rota Romana which states that liability for *culpa levissima* is accepted *praesertim quando culpa consistit in committendo.*[37] He also quotes a text by Matteus de Afflictis who warns that *culpa levissima in omittendo* is insufficient as a cause of action. And indeed, the glossators had already held that Aquilian liability for omissions only existed where the damage had been *committendo et omittendo simul datum* (cf. much later Voet ad D. 9,2 num. 3), or in the words of Lauterbach *si quis circa factum praeteritum culpam committat in omittendo* (Collegiuum theoretico-practicum 9.2. not. 10). In other words: *nur die unechten Unterlassungsdelikte, Kommissivdelikte* are covered by the *lex Aquilia*, certainly not *die echten Unterlassungsdelikte, Omissivdelikte*. A good example is to be found in the gloss *culpae reus* ad D. 9.2.8. The doctor who operates successfully upon a patient but omits the necessary aftercare commits a fault under the *lex Aquilia*, since *culpa* may either precede or follow the action itself.[38] Similar remarks are to be found in the glosses to D. 9.2.27.9: the case of the stoker who took a nap by his furnace seems to have been an important stepping stone for the liability for omissions. It was, of course, the Age of Reason which occluded the distinction between action and inaction, though Newtonian physics might have indicated its importance. For Grotius an obligation of restitution arose from

---

[36] X 5,36,9: Si culpa tua datum est damnum vel iniuria irrogata, seu aliis irrogantibus opem forte tulisti, aut haec imperitia tua sive negligentia evenerunt: iure super his satisfacere te oportet, nec ignorantia te excusat si scire debuisti quod ex facto tuo iniuriam verisimiliter posse contingere vel iacturam ... Sane licet qui occasionem damni dat damnum videatur dedisse, secus tamen est in illo dicendum qui ut non accideret, de contingentibus nil omissit.

[37] *Rotondi,* p. 246 at footnote 1.

[38] Gl. *culpae reus*: culpa quandoque inest facto, quandoque precedit factum, quandoque sequitur factum.

maleficium involving "omnem culpam sive in faciendo sive in non faciendo",[39] and this equiparation is found frequently thereafter. As we shall see, it is most emphatically accepted in France, but it even figured in a draft provision of the BGB. (§ 704 of the Draft; see von Bar p. 22 n. 43). Stryk seems to be have played an influential role among those who were prepared to drop any distinction between faults of commission and omission: sufficit autem, culpa levissima damnum illatum esse, .. sive committendo, sive omittendo (Usus mod. Pandect. 9.2.14).

This view, however, did not immediately become dominant in Germany. After the rejection of the first draft of the Civil Code, the Reichsgericht had recourse to the lex Aquilia when it had to answer the question "Does the BGB envisage noncontractual liability for omissions?" After stating that the modern law could not be more restrictive than ancient Roman law, it gave, rather uncomfortably, a positive answer: "The general objection sometimes raised that noncontractual liability for *omissions* cannot arise under this provision [§ 823 (1) BGB] must be rejected as unjustified."[40] In order to ascertain which omissions gave rise to liability the system devised the notion of *Verkehrs(sicherungs)pflichten:* "everyone who in his affairs creates a source of danger or permits it to continue is bound to take all appropriate precautions to protect other persons and their absolute rights".[41] In the absence of such a duty, however, it remains the law that an omission, though unreasonable, is not actionable. Thus on 16 June 1987 the Bundesgerichtshof, reversing the court below, denied the liability of an employee of a security firm whose somnolence enabled thieves to steal the goods warehoused by the plaintiff with the security firm's customer.[42]

Romanists will note that even Ulpian was ready to grant an actio utilis when a slave fell asleep while watching a fire. (D. 9.2.27.9). In all systems the dormant employee would in principle be liable to his employer: indeed, omission to act is so characteristic a ground of contractual liability that some systems have had problems with positive breaches. There has consequently been some tendency to impose liability in tort not only on those who cause a danger and then fail to defuse it, but also on those who have undertaken to protect the plaintiff or, especially, his property. Indeed it is the concurrence of contractual and delictual liability in many such cases which has provoked discussion about the precise degree of care required of the custodian (including, no doubt, the sleepy employee!). In England the

[39] *Feenstra, infra* at footnote 50.

[40] RG 30 Oct. 1902, RGZ 52, 373f.

[41] BGH 28 April 1952, BGHZ 5, 378, 380–381; *C. von Bar,* Gemeineuropäisches Deliktsrecht I, Die Kernbereiche des Deliktsrechts, seine Angleichung in Europa und seine Einbettung in die Gesamtrechtsordnungen, München 1996, p. 114.

[42] BGH 16 June 1987, NJW 1987, f 510.

liability of the inn-keeper for the safe custody of the goods was based on "the custom of the realm", i.e. the general law, as was, later, that of the carrier. This in turn developed into liability fir failure to perform one's functions properly, though here, too, misfeasance led the way: in the early days "The cases are all of misfeasance rather than nonfeasance." [Baker p. 56]. Characteristic is the rule of the common law, changed only in 1960, that a highway authority was liable only for making the highway worse, not for failure to effect necessary repairs (for which Austrian law still requires gross negligence: ABGB § 1319a).

3. Strict liabily – presumed fault

a) At Common law

Baker draws attention to the forms of pleading as one of the main obstacles to comparison between the substantive medieval common law of torts and the civil law. And indeed, the interplay of procedure and substance, rule and application constitutes the issue on which comparison between continental and English systems on our topic proves most difficult. On the continent we have a plethora of doctrine, primarly Romanist, and very much less evidence of what actually happened in court; in England, by contrast, we have virtually no doctrine at all, and although the cases have been very well studied as compared with historical scholarship on the continent, even they for procedural reasons, barely disclose the reality of decision-making or even the results of litigation. There is perhaps little point in comparing the style of pleadings in the different jurisdictions at different times, since attorneys everywhere are ever equally wordy and concerned with wording, as was stated above (at p. 11).

In the action of trespass, the main action in our field, the claimants simply alleged that they had been injured in their person, land or goods by the forcible act of the defendant. According to Ibbetson the effective boundaries of liability are in fact practically concealed from us by the uniformity of this type of pleading. Whenever issues arose which nowadays we would classify as questions of strict liability – whether an employer should be liable for the wrongs of an employee, for example – these would largely have been determined by the jury, with a minimum of judicial control.

Once the unforthcoming general action of trespass on the case had established itself in the middle of the fourteenth century claimants were able to formulate their claims with a degree of transparency that enables us to penetrate beneath the forms of pleading to the underlying facts. We do know from these pleadings that negligence was never alleged in trespass claims, though it frequently figured in the plaintiff's more extensive pleadings in trespass on-the-case. An example of these seems to be *Broadmeadow* v. *Rushenden*,[43] a case which began by writ in December 1363. An action was brought against a London doctor who had promised to cure an injured woman's arm, claiming that he had carried out the treatment so carelessly, negligently, or maliciously that her hand had been lost. The jury found a verdict for the defendant and in Michaelmas term 1365 judgement was entered accordingly. Ibbetson is of the opinion that this case marks the real watershed in the expansion of trespassory liability, since the writ did not contain the seemingly inappropriate allegation of the breach of the king's peace. This form of writ came to be known as trespass on the case, which was used by claimants who wanted to get the details of their story into the pleadings. Thus a distinction arose between the general action of trespass vi et armis in breach of the king's peace and the action of trespass on the case in which the plaintiff's story was told and the allegations of force and breach of the king's peace omitted. It should be noted that no differences of substance hung on this distinction, but the latter action, freed from the allegation of forcible wrongdoing, turned out to have an inbuilt potential to expand into other areas, both providing remedies in situations that had formerly been remediless and offering an alternative form of action where an existing remedy was thought to be inadequate.

In both actions the plaintiff who had suffered harm caused by the defended sought compensation. Throughout the medieval and early modern periods there is a strong focus on the loss suffered by the plaintiff rather than on the wrongful conduct of the defendant: 'If a man suffers damage it is right that he be compensated'. In fact, plaintiffs in trespass did not allege fault on the part of the defendants, but – what is even more important – defendants hardly ever pleaded that the injury had been caused without their fault or negligence. Defendants simply denied that they were guilty, the matter was referred to the jury, evidence was given (of which we have no record) and the jury came to their conclusion, including the amount of damages, if any, without disclosing why. Approaching the question without the preconception that liability must have been fault-based it is hard to avoid the conclusion that liability in the writs of trespass and trespass on the case was prima facie strict.

This is not to say that liability in trespass was absolute. There clearly existed a number of defences that allowed defendants to admit that they had caused the injury and to explain that their behaviour was justified. In the Limitation Act 1623 § 5 we read: "... in all accions of trespas quare

---

[43] 103 SS 422, case 40.1; ELABD 343 A7e; *D. Ibbetson,* A Historical Introduction to the Law of Obligations, Oxford 1999, p. 54.

clausum fregit ... and the trespas was by negligence or involuntary, the defendant ... shall be admitted to pled a disclaymer, ant that the trespas was by negligence, or involuntary ... [the issue may be found for the defendant or the plaintiff nonsuited ...] (Chapman, Statutes ... p. 358).

Consequently it would be a mistake to exaggerate the contrast between this regime of strict liability qualified by justificatory defences and a regime of fault liability. In law it was neither necessary nor sufficient for liability that the defendant had fallen short of the standard of reasonable care in the circumstances. It is probable that the jury actually acquitted the defendants who had pleaded "not guilty" and then showed that they had not been at fault in causing the harm. There was, of course, no appeal from the jury's inscrutable decision unless, as rarely happened, they found the facts specially. It can be seen that a general principle of liability for harm negligently caused could hardly arise when there were many different forms of action, some of which required negligence and some which did not. Indeed it was nearly a hundred years after the abolition of the forms of action before a semi-general principle was accepted. The real block was the distinction between trespass and trespass-on-the case, and it was all the more a block during the long period when it was held that a claim which could be brought in one of those forms could not be brought in the other and an election had to be made, since until a statute of 1852 joinder was impossible.

What was the criterion of distinction? Pleadings in trespass called for an allegation that force had been used by the defendant, and while that allegation was not traversable, this form of action was obviously uncomfortable where the facts made it manifest that force could not have been used, as where a bailee had damaged goods which the plaintiff had entrusted to him. Nevertheless it was trespass when one's cattle went on to the neighbour's land. Later it was held that trespass was the (only) appropriate form where the injury was the direct result of the defendant's act, trespass on the case where the harm was consequential, including the situation where the act, even if trespassory, was that of the defendant's servant. However, by 1833 it was clear that "where the injury is occasioned by the carelessness and negligence of the defendant the plaintiff is at liberty to bring an action on the case, notwithstanding that the act is immediate, so long as it is not a wilful act." (2 L.J.C.P. (N.S.) 190.)

The tenacity of history is indicated by a decision of the House of Lords in 1993[44] in which it was held that the limitation period applicable to claims for negligence was inapplicable where the personal injury was the result of a wilful act. Therefore it cannot be said, that in medieval law

[44] *Stubbings* v. *Webb* [1993] 1 All ER 322.

there was anything akin to the modern notion of negligence as an external standard according to which the wrongfulness of conduct could be assessed. It would last until the third quarter of the 19th century before the view emerged that a plaintiff could no longer in trespass complain of personal injury unless it be caused by the defendant's intentional aggression or negligent default.

b) At Civil law

The actionable type of conduct that is of special interest here, is also qualified by the presumption of fault. In the Middle Ages foundations were laid for future developments related to the subjective element of the tort, in German the *Verschuldensprinzip*.

In this respect canon law plays an important role on the continent. In the sacrament of the confession the Christian church attributed special importance to conscience. It is still not agreed when exactly this theological notion developed into the legal view reproachability for the act. If it is conscience which whispers into the human ear, that certain acts (or omissions) constitute sins, would not liability at law for one's own acts also depend wholly or partly on conscience? Sin is insolubly connected with the duty to make restitution, which in law is called liability. Can, in short, liability be assumed whenever the sin requires restitution? Should the theological notion be immediately translated into a legal concept?

There is reason enough to suggest a negative answer. For the actions in tort under discussion (*actio legis Aquiliae, actio iniuriarum*) Roman law in principle required a fault, be it intentional or otherwise culpable, distinguishing between *culpa lata, culpa levis* and *culpa levissima.*

This triparte distinction is not completely alien to the Common law since the first person to insist on the necessity in torts of explicit standards of behaviour, Sir William Jones, drew heavily on civilian lawyers, when he in 1781 formulated that *the generality of rational man use the same degree of diligence in the conduct of their own affairs*. This standard of the care, which every prudent man takes of his own property becomes in his vocabulary *ordinary default* or *ordinary neglect*, while different degrees of care stand on either side of this concept, *less neglect* or *slight neglect* at one side of the spectrum, *greater* or *gross neglect* at the other side.[45] In the course of the 19th century, however, this tripartite division was increasingly attacked, both at a theoretical and at a practical level. On the one hand is considered too articificial and alien to the Common law, on the

[45] *Birks, infra*, 195.

other hand it was described as analytically empty. The tripartite division made sense for the degree of care required by the law, variable according to the circumstances, but then negligence need to be defined solely as a failure to live up to the standard of care required by the law. Consequently a single standard of negligence was developed as by Alderson B. in *Blyth* v. *Birmingham Waterworks* in 1856, followed by Sir Alexander Cockburn C. J. in his lenghty (dissenting) opinion in the international arbitration between the United States and the United Kingdom, commonly known as the Alabama-affair.[46] This discussion about the tripartite interpretation of the notion of *culpa* or the desirability of a single standard of behaviour did not touch Scots law. The Scottish understanding of *culpa* was never authoritatively formulated in either text or judicial opinion.[47] But let us return to the continental development, more specifically to the canon law.

The *actio legis Aquiliae* presupposed the lightest degree of *culpa*, the *culpa levissima*. Neither the glossators nor the canonists deviated from that view, although the latter were of the opinion, that the *culpa levissima* did not play any role *in foro interno*.[48] And would not the notion of culpability and the role of the conscience lead to a similar tension between theology and law? It seems not unreasonable. It is obvious that the Corpus iuris civilis contained quite a few texts, from which the medieval glossators could deduce that the Romans recognised a liability for a slight degree of negligence, as e. g. the case of the pruning gardener shows.[49] Texts of this type in which a very slight degree of culpability (*culpa levissima*) nevertheless leads to liability, are apt to lead to a doctrine in which it is specifically the culpability of the tortfeasor which founds his liability. This principle, in German *Verschuldensprinzip*, rose in the 15th and 16 century from this *choc des opinions*. It would be wrong, however, to interprete too narrowly the doctrine in which culpability (*culpa*) is interpreted as a necessary condition for liability. Every legal system, whatever its date, and whether or not it contained a *Verschuldensprinzip* offers examples of strict liability of the owner of an immoveable by way of the *actio de effusis et deiectis* or the strict liability of the owner of an animal via the *actio de pauperie* or the *actio de feris*. The mere fact, that a subject owns a house, gives rise to his liability for the harm caused by a loose roof tile, that the storm deposits on

---

[46] *Ibbetson,* infra, § 2.

[47] *McQueen* and *Sellar, infra,* 291.

[48] *Rotondi,* p. 245 at footnote 3.

[49] A separate problem is posed by D. 9,2,44,1 also a text which is often quoted in this context. D. 9,2,44,1 deals with a specific legal question concerning the liability of the *pater familias* for the torts committed by his son or his slave. When the *pater familias* had knowledge about this tort being about to happen, than his liability is almost absolute, even though the son or the slave are only to a very small extent culpable (D. 9,2,45*pr*; C. 3,41,4).

the head of a passing pedestrian. The quality of possessor of the house or the animal, not his culpability, is at first glance decisive for the liability.

The same holds true for *vicarious liability*. This notion covers the liability of the defendant, who because of a certain quality (parent, guardian, employer, teacher) is liable for the torts committed by his child, pupil, employee or student in the age of a minor. In Roman law this type of liability was known under the heading of the *actio noxalis*: the Roman slave owner was vicariously (though conditionally) liable for the harm inflicted by his slaves. In the Middle Ages slavery as such was hardly a substantial phenomenon. Naturally the texts mentioning the *actio noxalis* could not be interpreted as if they pertained to free labourers, but the writers did not hesitate to deduct from these texts (and analogously from those referring to the strict liability of the owner of an immoveable or animal) the principle of vicarious liability. It is Guillelmus Duranti who took the decisive footsteps,[50] generalizing a Roman statement about the liability of the *pater familias* for the acts of his slaves in the *actio de effusis et deiectis*:

Si servus meus, vel is qui praestabat mihi operas, tibi damnum dedit et ego pro illo damno conveniar, et satisfaciam, ego illud recuperabo ab illo per actionem ex conducto, quia operas suas mihi locavit, et tantundem potero retinere de mercede sua, Quod autem tenear ex delicto famuli mei vel ex damno per eum dato est arg. ff. de his qui effuderint, l. Si vero plures [D. 9,3,5].

It should however be noted, that these penal actions of Roman law were never as such introduced into France, unlike Germany. Criminal procedure there was directed by a public prosecutor and the penalty was forfeited to the public treasury. As a consequence the Roman sanctions as two, three or four times the damage done were meaningless in French law. To the victim who sought compensation a remedy in private law stood open; the access to the judiciary, however, was never canalized along the fixed borderlines of the Roman actions. The French law stood in principle on the standpoint, that in cases where the criminal law provided for the protection of private interests, the victim of the felony should be awarded restitution. This restitutionary clause was generally part of the criminal sentence. Not until the 18th century did the notion (which incidentally already appeared in earlier centuries) that liability for restitution went hand in hand with every felony gain the overhand.[51]

In either case, however, it is possible to reconcile the liability of the defendant with the *Verschuldensprinzip*: the owner of the house can be held to have it maintained insufficiently; the owner of the cattle can be accused

---

50 *Guillelmus Duranti,* Speculum juris, ed. Torino 1578, pars IV, f. 215, nr. 31–32.

51 *Pothier,* Traité des Obligations, Oeuvres II, Paris 1848, nr. 116.

of insufficient maintenance of the fences; the parent of insufficient supervision of his child, etc.

III. Kinds of damage

a) At Common law

Actual damage or injury is nowadays in the common law a necessary element of tort liability for negligence. Unlike assault and battery or defamation where violation of a mere dignitary interest like personal integrity or reputation is deemed sufficiently heinous to warrant redress, negligence is not actionable unless and until it results in actual damage to the plaintiff.[52] What qualifies as actionable damage, however, is for the greater part determined by the history. Specific to the medieval common law of torts is the action of trespass (and the action of trespass on the case) in which the plaintiff alleged that he had been injured in his person, land or goods by the forcible act of the defendant. Consequently the common law of England did not have to contend with the restrictions inherent in the lex Aquilia: the law is not even mentioned by Bracton, though he paraphrases Inst. 4.3.3, and notes that "non tenetur si per infortunium et non anime et voluntate occidendi nec dolus nec culpa eius invenitur ... et de gratia principis cum eo mitius agitur hoc probato."[53] The common law had restrictions of its own. Since the tort of trespass came to cover principally direct forcible invasions of person and property (no negligence needing to be alleged), virtually the equivalent of *corpore corpori*, and although damage was often alleged in vibrant terms no actual damage need be proved: the invasion of the protected interest was enough. Thus *contrectatio* of goods sufficed, as did any complete restriction of liberty, however temporary, and even the mere threat of immediate personal violence.

It will be observed that the interests protected were all physical in nature. There was no problem whatever, as there was on the continent, in giving compensation for personal injury, including compensation for pain and suffering: the award of damages was in the province of the jury.[54] When trespass on the case (the unrelated analogue of the *actio in factum*) emerged, the requirement of directness of invasion was dropped, and allegations of damage became necessary. This opened up the way to compensating for harm arising otherwise than through invasions of interests protected by the tort of trespass. On the whole, however, the extension was

---

[52] *Fleming*, The law of torts, p. 191.

[53] *Bracton* f. 155 in *H. G. Richardson*, Bracton, the Problem of his text (Selden Society, London 1965) 49, 134.

[54] See *Catala and Weir* (footnote 2) at p. 665 for the dentist case in late C19).

towards the same kinds of harm indirectly caused rather than harm of all kinds. There are isolated examples of compensation being granted for purely economic harm,[55] and since economic harm in the absence of physical damage is characteristic of contract claims, and since the form of contract claim at common law, assumpsit, was itself a variant of trespass on the case, it is not too surprising that this tendency to treat trespass on the case as extending to merely economic loss was not uniformly resisted. But in 1861 the House of Lord's indignantly rejected a claim by sureties against the debtor's lawyer who had negligently drafted the document which was designed to protect them from financial loss,[56] and in 1898 put a block on the development of liability for negligently causing financial harm by holding that the addressee of negligently inaccurate information had no claim in the absence of contract or actual deceit.[57]

This block on liability for causing harm which was merely economic was not removed by the generalising opinion of Lord Atkin in the case of the snail in 1932, and it remained until 1963, when the House of Lords decided in the case *of Hedley Byrne* v. *Heller* that there might well be a duty to take care not to cause financial loss to a party with whom one stood in a special relationship "akin to contract", especially if one were an expert or claimed expertise in the matter.[58] This liability has swiftly been extended from cases of negligent misrepresentation to cases of misperformance of tasks undertaken and even now to nonperformance of tasks undertaken for another.[59] It remains true, however, that it is much easier to obtain damages for personal injury or property damage than for mere economic loss.

b) At Civil law

In Roman law different kinds of harm were covered by different delicts: the *lex Aquilia* applied to damage done to property and nothing else; *furtum* covered deliberate interference with moveable property without physical damage necessarily being caused; the *actio iniuriarum* was apt for

---

[55] *Shiells* v. *Blackburne* 126 Eng. Rep. 94 (1789); *Wilkinson* v. *Coverdale* 1 Esp. 74 (1793).

[56] *Robertson* v. *Fleming*, (1861), 4 Macq. 167.

[57] *Allen* v. *Flood* [1898] A.C. 1, discussed by *Fleming,* The Law of Torts, p. 698 under the heading: Unlawful Interference with Trade or Business. *Tony Weir* discusses this case amply in his: Economic Torts [Clarendon Law Lectures], Oxford 1997. It leads him to the conclusion "that a person who deliberately causes economic harm to another should be liable only if he uses wrongful means to effect his object." (a.o. p. 45).

[58] *Hedley Byrne* v. *Heller*, [1963] 2 All ER 575.

[59] *White* v. *Jones* [1995] 1 All ER 691.

outrageous insulting behaviour, which might, but did not necessarily, take the form of actual assault or defacing of property. Since *furtum* and *iniuria* called for intentional conduct and we are interested in unintentional harm, we shall concentrate on the *lex Aquilia* in our consideration of the kinds of harm which called for compensation.

For liability under the lex Aquilia there had to be *damage* to property: manuring another's field led to liability only if it made the field worse (other examples in D. 9,2,27). Furthermore the damage in principle needed to be done *corpori*, the damage must be physical in nature. Where loss of property rather than damage was intentionally caused, slight extensions were made (it would be furtum if it were done with a view to gain). This obscured the distinction between the owner's right to the possession of his property and his right to its physical integrity: the damage suffered by the owner who had lost his property comes close to merely economic loss, and the reluctance to give compensation even when a specific thing was affected can be seen from the fact that the buyer to whom the risk of damage to a chattel had passed under the contract of sale had no claim against the third party who carelessly damaged it and thereby caused the buyer financial loss.

The lex Aquilia did not purport to cover personal injury to free men and although in postclassical times sometimes a claim was given to the *pater familias* in respect of expenditure incurred in treating a wounded *filius familias* (e.g. D. 9,2,5,3), the injured party himself had no claim, the reason given being that no one owned his own body. It followed that there was no Aquilian liability for causing pain and suffering, much less Aquilian liability for purely moral harm unconnected with personal injury.

The inherent limits on the damage compensable under the *lex*, which had to be overcome before a general principle of liability for carelessly causing harm could develop, were accordingly (a) purely economic harm, (b) personal injury and (c) hurt feelings.

The Glossators and the Canonists adhered in principle to the text of the Corpus iuris civilis. Nevertheless they extended the scope of the different actions considerably. Bulgarus still denied the possibility that the *actio legis Aquiliae* could be brought in case of the death of a free man;[60] Azo

60 See the gloss *Gloriae causa* ad D. 9.2.7.4; comp. *R. Feenstra,* L'actio legis Aquiliae utilis en cas d'homicide chez les Glossateurs, in *J. E. Spruit* (éd.), Maior viginti quinque annis, Assen 1979, p. 45–65; repr. (with addenda) in *R. Feenstra,* Le droit savant au moyen âge et sa vularisation [Variorum Collected Studies Series, 236], London 1986, nr. VIII; German translation: *R. Feenstra,* Die Glossatoren und die actio legis Aquiliae utilis bei Tötung eines freien Menschen, in *E. J. H. Schrage* (Hrsg.), Das römische Recht im Mittelalter [Wege der Forschung 635], Darmstadt 1987, p. 205–232.

was of the opposite opinion as far as medical costs were concerned: *sed ad cetera damna sic.* This was also the opinion of Guillelmus Duranti: *licet liberum corpus non recipiat aestimationem, agetur ad mercedes medicorum et alias expensas in curatione factas: veniat etiam aestimationem operarum quibus parens occisi caruit et cariturus est.*[61] And in case of a brutal, immediate death and when there were no expenses for cure: *tunc.. aestimabit haeres operas illas quas amisit et habere potuit tempore vitae suae, puta qui erat cerdo, vel pelliparius, vel mercator vel advocatus.* And these *operae* would be estimated *usque ad tempus quo verisimile est illum occisum vivere potuisse.* Also the decretal *Olim* (1215–1216) of pope Honory III played an important part in the extension of the *actio legis Aquiliae* to cases in which a free person was assaulted, insulted or killed. Not until the 17th century the action came to include not only compensation for medical expenses and lost earnings, but also compensation for immaterial losses and physical deprivations (*pecunia doloris et deformitatis*). Here we must again refer to Grotius who disseminated views on the kinds of interest protected against faulty invasion. He identified as natural rights *vita, corpus, fama, honor, actiones propriae* as well as property. Feenstra notes that he clearly wanted to extend liability "beyond the cases in the Roman texts concerning the *lex Aquilia*" (p. 138).

Vita we deal with elsewhere. Liability for the moral consequences of personal injury was increasingly accepted in the *ius commune*, but *fama* and *honor* were covered by the *actio iniuriarum* which called for intentionally insulting behaviour, and this provided a block on imposing liability for undeliberately offensive conduct.

Damages for pain and suffering are still not straightforward on the continent. In Germany they are available only where the law provides, and most statutes imposing strict liability do not so provide (with the result that most personal injury victims try to sue under the BGB). Even for the moral harm resulting from unreasonable invasions of the *allgemeines Persönlichkeitsrecht* the *Bundesgerichtshof* had to bypass a restrictive provision of the Code. Italy rendered that provision even more restrictive by providing that such damages were available only where the defendant's conduct was criminal, and much trouble has been caused by that. The EU Directive on Liability for Defective Products, though concerned almost exclusively with personal injury and death, leaves it to the member states to decide whether damages for immaterial harm should be awarded.

---

61 *Guillelmus Duranti,* Speculum juris, ed. Torino 1578, pars IV, f. 213, nr. 3–4. Feenstra (in his article cited in the previous footnote on p. 57 and at footnote 93) proved, that Duranti quoted this text from Roffredus.

Notoriously *fama* and *honor* were omitted from the list of interests protected against damaging invasions in § 823 I BGB, and it was not until the Bonn "constitution" of 1949 that under the impact of the totalitarianism of the Nazi regime the *allgemeines Persönlichkeitsrecht* was added in its first two articles. Delictual protection of the personality was eventually introduced by the Federal Supreme Court via the "or other right"clause contained in § 823 I BGB, thereby, as Zimmermann notes, awarding monetary damages for the non-pecuniary harm suffered by the claimant.[62]

Equally importantly, the list contains ownership but not wealth as such, and it remains the law in Germany today that there is no liability in tort for negligently impoverishing another in the absence of an invasion of a protected interest. Here the courts have added, perhaps unwisely, the "right to an established and operating business", and-have had difficulty in containing its range of operation. Of course it is true that contractual liability is more widespread in Germany than in the common law, given (a) the presence of third party rights and the absence of any requirement of consideration, (b) that § 826 BGB can be deployed where the negligence is gross and the harm envisaged, (c) that if a law is designed to protect the plaintiff against financial harm, the party negligently in breach of it may have to make compensation and (d) that actionable invasion of ownership need not involve actual physical damage. Nevertheless, the general principle of liability for harm negligently caused does not, either in Germany or in England, extend fully to harm which is purely economic.

c) Death

Death presents several problems for the tort lawyer: (a) is a person civilly liable for killing a victim, and if so, to whom? (b) is a claim for personal injuries transmissible (i) actively, and (ii) passively? The development on these questions has been complex, and very different on the two sides of the Channel. Significant differences remain between civil systems.

(a) Claims arising from the death of the victim.

The harm resulting from the death of a relative is either purely economic – loss of support, burial expenses – or purely emotional – grief. Loss of support is much more significant in modern times than previously, since nowadays the money that comes into the family home is earnings and the breadwinner's earnings end on his death, whereas free Romans tended to live of their property, slaves or land, and such income continues unabated on the owner's death. It is true that grief is as common as ever, as many

[62] *R. Zimmermann,* The Law of Obligations. Roman Foundations of the Civilian Tradition, Cape Town … 1990, p. 1093.

lapidary inscriptions testify, but the law has never been very interested in making monetary compensation for emotional harms unintentionally caused.

In ancient Roman law the owner could sue the person who killed his slave *iniuria,* because a slave was property, but where the fatal victim was a free man, whether *sui* or *alieni iuris,* there could be no question of liability under the first chapter of the *lex Aquilia,* although penalties were payable by the occupier from whose building things were fatally thrown or poured. Homicide is of course a crime of which the state must take serious note. It was criminally sanctioned in ancient Rome under the *lex Cornelia* (Sulla's own homicides being naturally lawful), but it had no civil compensatory consequences where the victim was a free man. It was, however, to play a role in the Middle Ages. Homicide is often intentional – murder – but even when it was not, the Church, strongly antipathetic to violence, tended to look to the result of the action rather than the attitude of the actor and deployed its monetary sanctions against the person guilty of negligent homicide as well. In addition to the fine which was a sanction for sin, penance might require some payment to survivors, whether heirs or relatives. The development is traced by Professor Dondorp. The position was reached that in the absence of grave fault, sanctioned under the *lex Cornelia,* damages might be due as compensation for negligence. This was reinforced by the view that every public offence was also a private wrong. In the early Middle Ages it was standard for the killer to offer composition to the family of the victim. Mme. Auzary-Schmaltz traces the way in which composition was progressively displaced and the fine payable to the king for the crime became dissociated from the money payable to the family which came to be seen as a kind of compensation capable of taking priority over the criminal consequences.

If Roman law gave no claim to the survivors of persons killed by things thrown or poured from a building, customary law did so, and Grotius – brought it into the learned law, possibly extending its scope (Feenstra p. 138). Stryk, however, is still opposed to the possibility that the heirs may claim compensation for the expenses of the funeral and their lost maintenance, but in his day he turns out to be one of the very few.[63] Under the *Usus modernus Pandectarum* the feeling that *liberi hominis corporis nulla aestimatio* lost its meaning. The position in Germany later was clearly given by Glück: "No claim lies when a free man is unlawfully killed, for no evaluation and consequently no replacement is possible ... The older German laws could make the killer pay *Wehrgeld,* which went as satisfaction to the deprived family. But this is obsolete in most places ... But there is no

[63] Stryk, Usus modernus, ad. D. 9.2 nr. 10.

doubt that to the extent that the orphans and widow are actually deprived by the death and their own means are insufficient they have a right to claim appropriate compensation by means of an *Actio legis Aquiliae utilis* or *in factum*."[64]

Thus the survivors of a person tortiously killed in Germany were better off than in England, where they had no claim at all at Common law, as was emphasised by a judge in the very year of Glück's publication: "In a civil suit, the death of a human being should not be complained of as an injury".[65] Legislation in 1846 was required to give the widow and orphans a claim, a claim which the judges held extended only to net financial loss: nothing could be awarded for grief.

The position in Scotland, as emerges from the contributions of MacQueen and Sellar, was quite different, for Scotland retained a curious common law claim called "assythement" which is not easily disentangled from its criminal origins, and in the late eighteenth century developed a common law claim, known oddly as the *actio iniuriarum.* carrying a right to *solatium* in addition to compensation for patrimonial loss, if any.

Who could sue? The widow and orphans were obvious candidates and first recognised as such. In France, as Mme. Auzary-Schmaltz tells us, the claim of ascendants was regarded as more problematic, but Grotius allowed the claim to parents as being among those whom the deceased was accustomed to aliment *ex officio* (Feenstra p. 139). Scotland originally included siblings, but soon excluded them.

In current German law only those to whom the decedent actually or potentially owed an actual obligation of aliment may claim and then only for what they were entitled to receive, nothing being awarded for grief, unless it produces pathological effects. In England the range of those who may claim is laid down in quite wide terms by statute and the claim lies for what the claimant has in fact lost by way of support or otherwise, not what he was entitled to claim by way of support, a fixed sum being awarded to parents and spouses for "bereavement", but nothing for grief, even pathological, unless resulting from witnessing the death. In France, which required no special text by reason of the width of the notion of "dommage" as covering both purely economic loss and emotional distress, there is no legal restriction on who can claim or what can be claimed, provided that the loss is direct, personal and foreseeable.

---

[64] *F. C. von Glück,* Ausführliche Erläuterung der Pandekten nach Hellfeld, ein Kommentar, vol. 10, Erlangen 1808, p. 340.

[65] *Baker* v. *Bolton*, 170 Eng. Rep. 1033 (1809).

IV. Types of causation – directness required?

a) At Common law

The interplay of procedure and substance, rule and application, constitutes the issue on which comparison between continental and English systems on our topic proves most difficult. On the continent we have a plethora of doctrine, primarily Romanist, and very much less evidence of what actually happened in court; in England, by contrast, we have virtually no doctrine at all, and although the cases have been very well studied as compared with historical scholarship on the continent, even they, for procedural reasons, barely disclose the reality of decision-making or even the results of litigation. We have the pleadings, which were largely fictional, and the arguments, often inconclusive; but hard facts are few and far between.

Ibbetson draws attention to the fact that in medieval times questions of causation were rarely, if ever, explicitly pleaded. Such questions were fundamental to the central question of trespassory liability, whether the defendant caused the harm to the plaintiff, and would have been considered behind the general issue of not guilty. There are a few rather obvious defences like unavoidable necessity, self-defence or the argument, that the damage was the plaintiff's own fault. There is a striking resemblance between the famous case discussed by Alfenus (D. 9.2.52.1) of the innkeeper who, having been struck by the thief from whom he tried to recapt the stolen oil-lamp, retaliated by a blow which blinded the thief, and the case of around 1300 described by Ibbetson: A man who brought an action complaining of a battery lost his case when it was shown that he had first hit an innkeeper's wife over a dispute about a tavern bill, as a result of which the hue and cry had been raised against him: it was his own folly that was the cause of the battery.

The medieval action of trespass was built on a theory of strict liability, subject to a range of justificatory defences.[66] Consequently this strict liability was suffused through and through with ideas of fault, which became more obvious when technical developments gave rise to the defence that the accident was inevitable: "judged utterly without his fault; as if a man by force take my hand and strike you"[67] We do know from the pleadings that negligence was never alleged in trespass claims though it frequently

[66] In the Limitation Act 1623 s. 5 we read: "... in all accions of trespas quare clausum fregit ... and the trespas be by negligence, or involuntary, the defendant ... shall be admitted to pled a disclaymer, and that the trespas was by negligence, or involuntary ... [the issue may be found for the defendant or the plaintiff nonsuited ...] (Chapman, Statutes ... p. 358).

figured in the plaintiff's more extensive pleading in trespass-on-the-case. in neither case, however, did the defendant rehearse the facts which in his view showed that he was not negligent. Indeed, in trespass a denial of negligence was unacceptable as a pleading matter. Defendants simply denied that they were guilty, the matter was referred to the jury, evidence was given (of which we have no record) and the jury came to their conclusion, including the amount of damages, if any, without disclosing why. If the pleadings were delusive, the reality is in a "black box". There was an almost complete mismatch between what was alleged on the pleadings, which we have, and what could be given in evidence, which we do not have.

Even in trespass the incidence of liability depended on societal perceptions of where the blame ought to be laid for an allegedly wrongful injury in individual cases. It was the jury who took that decision; the law did not formulate an explicit theory in terms of the language of causation, blame, fault, guilt or responsibility. We know that in law it was neither necessary nor sufficient for liability that the defendant have fallen short of the standard of reasonable care in the circumstances, it is just a matter of supposition, however probable that the jury actually acquitted the defendants who had pleaded "not guilty" and then showed that they had not been at fault in causing the harm. There was, of course, no appeal from the jury's inscrutable decision unless, as rarely happened, they found the facts specially. It can be seen that a general principle of liability for harm negligently caused could hardly arise when there were many different forms of action, some of which required negligence and some of which did not. Indeed it was nearly a hundred years after the abolition of the forms of action before a semi-general principle was accepted. The real block was the distinction between trespass and trespass-on-the case, and it was all the more a block during the long period when it was held that a claim which could be brought in one of those forms could not be brought in the other and an election had to be made, since until a statute of 1852 joinder was impossible.

b) At Civil law

Another really important extension in canon law to the Roman *actio legis Aquiliae* was to be found in the notion of causality: *Qui occasionem damni dat, damnum dedisse videtur.* This extension is largely founded upon texts taken from the Corpus iuris civilis itself (e.g. D. 9.2.9*pr*), but interpreted against the background of Aristotelian-scholastic concepts. The basis

---

[67] *Weaver* v. *Ward* (1616) Hob. 134; 80 E.R. 284; *Fleming*, p. 20; *Ibbetson*, Historical Introduction, p. 62.

for liability remained *culpa levissima*, which led to disputes concerning liability for omissions. Similar dissension arose as to whether the remedy in tort can or cannot be brought if a contractual remedy is available, yes or no (bailment-cases e. g.).[68]

In the *actio iniuriarum*, however, Covarruvias was the first to state that the victim is not only entitled to indemnification, but also to further compensation. Succeeding canonists initially differentiate between the *forum internum* and the *forum externum*, but from the end of the 15th century it is argued (Angelus de Clavasio), that an obligation to restitution exists in all cases where, according to Roman or canon law, one can be compelled to pay compensatory damages. And this payment is compulsory, when the defendant is to be blamed for *culpa*, be it in the form of *culpa levissima*.

The 17th century Natural law School saw itself faced with the challenge of describing the subject of their studies, the natural law, in categories which would do justice to its predecessors, theology and philosophy, including moral philosophy, canon law, Roman law and indigenous (statutory and customary) law. The extensive interpretation of the *actio legis Aquiliae* is in accordance with the general tendency within the *Ius commune*; it is in conformity with the indigenous legal practice of those days. Consequently the technicalities of the division of the *actio legis Aquiliae* into an *actio directa, actio utilis* and *actio in factum* lost their significance. The natural lawyers called the actio simply after its Roman example *actio legis Aquiliae*, although Thomasius (at the end of the 17th century) was of the opinion that the forensic remedy of his days had little or nothing in common with the Roman action of the same name.[69] As a newly formed remedy in tort and no longer a penal claim, so the ratio for the intransmissability to heirs fell away. In the 19th century no trace of it remains.

V. Conclusion

This was our point of departure: what hurdles did the pilgrims have to overcome on the road to generalisation and the conceptualization of the reasonable man? We have seen the development of the general principle of liability for harm done by fault and its enactment in the Code civil and other early codifications. We have seen, too, that the Common Law also has moved towards a generalisation, though more hesitantly. The question now is whether the generalisation has proved its value in practice.

---

68 Stryk, ad D. 9.2, nr. 14; *Rotondi*, p. 244 ff.

69 Chr. Thomasius, Larva legis Aquiliae detracta actioni de damno dato receptae in foris Germanorum, Halae 1703; *Glück*, Pandekten Bd 10, § 705; see especially *Feenstra, infra*, footnote 179.

The most obvious point is that the draftsmen of the German BGB declined to enact such a general principle because they were aware of its practical consequences. It is true that the restrictions which were adopted have proved in the view of some courts and scholars to be unduly restrictive. Economic losses associated with physical injury have caused least concern. On both sides of the Channel there is the long established practice of allowing recovery not only for the cost of repairing physical damage to persons or tangible property, but also for consequential loss of earnings or profits resulting from such damage during rehabilitation or repair. It remains in several jurisdictions, however, a controversial area as to whether pecuniary loss *standing alone* can be claimed. A comparison of the various limitation to this type of damages deserves a separate survey. In recent years English courts have been reluctant to expand duties of care for pure economic loss[70] against the background of a number of cases in which the liability in negligence was extended very far.[71] As Lord Templeman accurately and acidly observed: "[A] fashionable plaintiff alleges negligence. The pleading assumes that we are all neighbours now, Pharisees and Samaritans alike, that foreseeability is a reflection of hindsight and that for every mischance in an accident-prone world someone solvent must be liable in damages."[72] Such allegations carry generalisation much too far for comfort, especially as they start from the wrong premises.[73]

A similar movement is to be found in Germany: the protection of interests is limited to those which are included in the enumeration of § 823 BGB and this list does not mention the protection of wealth as such. Although the refusal to compensate pure economic loss through the medium of tort rules seems to be a basic premise, there is a certain willingness to allow certain attacks to the system, for instance via an extensive interpretation of the expression: *sonstige Rechte,* which gives the codified norm already an open character or by resort to § 826 BGB (laying down that 'A person is liable in damages if he deliberately causes harm to another in a manner repugnant to good morals').[74] The most famous 'other right' created by the Bundesgerichtshof is 'the general right of human per-

---

[70] E.g. *Banque Bruxelles Lambert SA* v. *Eagle Star Insurance Co. Ltd* [1997] AC 191.

[71] E.g. *Anns* v. *Merton London Borough Council,* [1978] AC 728; *Junior Books* v. *Veitchi Co.,* [1983] 1 AC 520. In *F* v. *Wirral BC* [1991] 2 All ER 648 the notion of all rights being equally protected against invasion is suggested where Ralph Gibson LJ unembarrasedly analogises between the rights of a parent ant the rights of a contractor.

[72] *CBS Songs* v. *Amstrad plc* [1988] 2 All ER 484, 497, quoted by *A. J. Weir,* The Staggering March of Negligence (*supra,* footnote 8), at footnote 213.

[73] *Weir,* Economic Torts [Clarendon Lectures], Oxford 1997, p. 32 enumerates a few fascinating cases.

sonality', better understood as 'personal dignity', which has indeed been used to protect firms against derogatory conduct, but more to our purpose is the 'right to a business as a going concern' created much earlier by the Reichsgericht. One might suppose from this name that any commercial loss would be actionable if unreasonably caused, but the courts have in fact been quite restrictive, and in any case treat it as a subsidiary when the claim is between commercial competitors.[75]

This approach contrasts with the French solution (and that of its derivates, such as the Dutch Code) which to all intents and purposes equates economic loss with physical injury but avoids unduly extensive pecuniary liability by adopting a test of foreseeability. Only damages which are foreseeable at the moment of the tort need to be compensated, but it remains true that the (admittedly: more general than many think beneficial) wording of art. 1382 is applied to conduct of every kind (including behaviour in commercial competition and industrial conflict; even conduct in the exercise of a defined right and not just of a general liberty might involve liability under the subhead of *abus de droit*) and to damage of every kind, including the pure economic loss. Even jurisdictions which followed the wording of the French rule laid down in art. 1382 C.c. have restricted unduly extensive pecuniary liability, despite the absence of clear textual authority, much as the Germans have done, though it is easier for them to deviate. Italy underwent in recent years a spectacular development in the field of the liability for wrongful death. According to the text of the articles 2059 Codice civile and 185 Codice Penale the tortfeasor is in principle only liable for pure economic loss if he committed a crime, whereas art. 2043 Codice civile requires the invasion of a right rather than a mere interest. Apparently while codifying art. 2059 the Italian legislator had notably emotional damages in mind. Also the purely psychical harm is considered to be an economic loss and as a consequence compensation may be claimed in so far as the victim's right has been invaded. A benign interpretation of this requirement was given in a recent decision, in which the court declared that: il danno biologico è risacibile a norma dell' art. 2043 Codice civile in tutti i casi di illecita menomazione dell'integrità psico-fisica della persona.[76] Switzerland has it.

In England no text limited the principle which poked its nose out of the cases when the courts felt expansive, and the extension of liability to cover

---

[74] Note that in BVerfGE 66, 116, 138 = NJW 1984, 1741 the court censured the BGH for failing to make the right to an established and operative business predictable in its application. Ex *Stoll*, The General Right to Privacy in German Law in Markesinis (ed.) Protecting Privacy (Oxford 1999), p. 29, 42 n. 34.1.

[75] *Weir*, Economic Torts, p. 46 ff.

[76] *Von Bar*, p. 569.

pure economic loss has led to difficulties of containment, framed in terms of the existence of non-existence of a "duty of care". Attempts to lay down a presumption of liability for harm done by negligence have been qualified or discountenanced or rejected by subsequent courts, free under the doctrine of precedent to ignore large statements beyond the purview of the facts of the case in which they were uttered. A good instance is provided by *White v. Jones* where the plaintiffs failed to obtain the intended legacy because of the failure of the defendant lawyer to draft the will as instructed by the testator, now deceased.[77]

In other areas of the law of obligations also there is a tension between general principle and narrower category. Even the Code civil had no general principle of liability to disgorge an enrichment obtained at the claimant's expense; it was ordained by the courts, and subsequent views have questioned its wisdom. Whether the clause of the BGB is a general one or not is much doubted, but the Italian Codice civile of 1942 certainly does adopt such a clause, and has been followed in Quebec and Louisiana. It remains to be seen whether or not, as Von Caemmerer seminally suggested, it can be applied only through *Fallgruppen*, a notion which brings to mind the "incremental' approach presently favoured by the courts in England, though not all academics, who like simple formulations and are not exposed to the wide variety of facts presented by our kaleidoscopic world.

[77] *White* v. *Jones* [1995] 1 All ER 691. Weir reproaches Lord Brown-Wilkinson to arrive "at the extremely extensive view that whenever a person does or agrees to do anything which he should realize would benefit another if properly done, he is liable in damages if owing to his failure to do it properly that benefit is not achieved. Weir qulifies this statement as "a proposition which Lord Mustill convincingly depontentiates in his marvellous dissenting judgement in that unhappy decision." *Weir,* The Staggering March of Negligence (*supra*, footnote 8), at footnote 160.

J. H. BAKER

Trespass, Case, and the Common Law of Negligence 1500–1700

In a famous article written in 1926 on the history of negligence in the law of torts, Winfield made the remark:[1]

> If we have started with the age of Bracton, where can we make our next pause in an historical sketch? Not until the nineteenth century. This may seem a breathless course, but till then the history of negligence is a skein of threads, most of which are fairly distinct, and no matter where we cut the skein we shall get little better than a bunch of frayed ends. In fact the tale is from beginning to end almost exclusively a narrative of action upon the case.

Cutting the skein may not be as deft an exercise in historical surgery as separating the threads, but before doing either it is worth pausing to reflect on some of the reasons for Winfield's perplexity. This will involve reviewing some of the historiography; but the excursion seems necessary in view of the continuing difficulties which have beset this topic.

First, there is the matter of vocabulary. It is all too easy to assume that words have always meant the same as they do today, and in particular that words which have become part of the lawyer's stock-in-trade represent eternal legal ideas or categories. When a word is captured by lawyers, it does tend to spend the rest of its life in a kind of conceptual imprisonment; but words are rarely born in legal custody. Certainly the word negligence – which occurs in law Latin as *necgligencia* or *negligentia* – cannot be regarded as having become a term of art until after 1700. Equivalent words were freely used to describe careless acts or omissions, without any sense that there was a general concept of negligence from which answers to legal questions could be deduced in specific situations. Negligence is in any case an ambiguous word, since in medieval and early-modern usage it seems most often to mean 'neglect', focusing on some failure rather than on misconduct.[2] It could include neglect of due care and attention in the course of conduct – that is, our modern notion of carelessness[3] – but it also encom-

---

[1] *P. H. Winfield*, The History of Negligence in the Law of Torts (1926) 42 L.Q.R. 184–201, at p. 185.

[2] This explains the remark in *The Earl of Shrewsbury's Case* (1610) 9 Co. Rep. 46 at fo. 50, 'for nonfeasance, or negligence, shall never be said *vi et armis*'.

passed passive neglect, in the sense of an omission to fulfil a positive duty. Thus, failing to find an allowance of ale for the hundred beadle, as required by local custom, is classified in one eighteenth-century abridgment as a species of negligence.[4] Even the non-payment of money could be a form of negligence in this sense.[5] If we read negligence as meaning 'neglect', it can also, without any affront to common sense or to the English language, include the neglect of what today would be called a strict duty. And this brings us up against a fundamental and potentially very confusing difference from modern usage.

There is evidence that in some kinds of action (for instance, those against innkeepers and carriers) words of negligence and 'fault' (if we may so translate L. *defectum*) did indeed conceal strict liability. And the same might be true in other contexts. For instance, in *Herbert* v. *Pagett* (1662), an action was brought against the custos brevium of the King's Bench for 'so negligently' keeping records that they were altered, and it was explicitly held that liability was strict in the sense that proof of actual carelessness was not required.[6] Likewise in *Mors* v. *Slue* (1671),[7] where an action was brought against the master of a ship for 'so negligently' keeping a cargo of silk that it was totally lost, it was held that the master was liable even though 'the defendant proved that there was no carelessness nor negligent default in him'.[8] These were both cases where the court was inclined to favour the defendant on the merits, but nevertheless felt that as a matter of law each of them was answerable for 'negligence'. So there was no question of stretching the ordinary meaning of the word in order to achieve a desired result. The word simply did not mean what we understand by it today. This is further borne out by Holt C. J.'s dissenting opinion in *Lane*

---

3 E.g., Holt C. J. refers in 1697 to a 'duty to take care': *Turbervile* v. *Stamp* (1697) 1 Comyns 32.

4 Com. Dig. 'Action upon the Case for Negligence', (A.3). For a similar example (failing to find a chantry chaplain), see *J. H. Baker*, Introduction to English Legal History (3rd ed., 1990), p. 463, n. 39.

5 See *Crisp* v. *Fryer* (1596) Cro. Eliz. 505 ('a negligent non-payment'); *Stevenson* v. *Powell* (1612) 1 Buls. 182, 183 ('negligence in not paying his rent').

6 1 Lev. 64; 1 Keb. 288, 346; 1 Sid. 77. Cf. 1 Lord Raym. 653, where it is said that the court inclined for the defendant.

7 1 Vent. 190, 238 (repr. in *C. H. S. Fifoot*, History and Sources of the Common Law (1949), pp. 171–3); 2 Lev. 69; 2 Keb. 866; 3 Keb. 72, 112, 135; 1 Mod. Rep. 85; T. Raym. 220; Heath's MS. reports in Middle Temple Library, ff. 6, 9 (arguments only). According to Ventris, the action was eventually settled.

8 1 Mod. Rep. 85. It was found by special verdict that the usual watch was set on the ship while in the Thames, and that it was robbed by men pretending to be a press-gang. The court at first 'inclined strongly for the defendant, there being not the least negligence in him'; but after argument gave judgment for the plaintiff.

v. *Cotton* (1700–01), where he held a postmaster-general liable for the unexplained loss of a postal packet:[9]

> this case is within the same reason with those cases that make men responsible for negligent keeping, viz. that if they could not be charged without assigning a particular neglect, they might cheat any man living, and it would not be in his power to prove it ... It would be hard in this case to put the plaintiff to prove a particular neglect amongst such a multitude of under-officers; ergo, the postmaster is charged with it.

In all these cases, the words 'neglect', 'negligent' and 'negligently' do not seem to have imported fault, in the sense of carelessness, but rather the failure to discharge a strict responsibility. Although only Holt C. J. made the point explicitly, they seem all to have involved an element of vicarious liability as well,[10] and the essence of such liability is that no specific fault in the master should have to be proved. Someone must have been negligent for the losses to have occurred at all, and it was convenient to make masters answerable for it, because they at least were in a position to take steps to keep their employees vigilant. We must therefore face the possibility that the negligence alleged in these cases was merely fictitious. Nevertheless, the language of the judges suggests that they saw a factual distinction between 'particular negligence', or special negligence,[11] meaning demonstrable fault proved by evidence, and what was presumably classified as the 'general negligence' of someone with overall responsibility for a state of affairs. Even at the conclusion of our period, then, there was no necessary equation of negligence with fault as we understand it.

Negligence can also operate negatively, for instance to bar a claim:[12] what is nowadays more usually called laches (*laxitas*).[13] However, we are at present concerned only with causes of action; and in the common-law system that brings us at once to the available forms of action and their workings. There was no form of action called Negligence, and so it is a matter of rummaging through the register of writs to see where carelessness might have been an ingredient in the plaintiff's cause of action. The most obvious areas of enquiry are Trespass and Case, since they are concerned with the recovery of damages for harm, and Detinue, which is concerned with the failure to return goods to the owner, though there are other corners

---

9 1 Salk. 18. See also 1 Ld Raym. 652; Pengelly's reports, BL MS. Add. 6724, ff. 61–65 (Pas. 1701).

10 Likewise the fire case of *Turbervile* v. *Stamp* (1697), discussed below at p. 61. And see *Anon.* (*c.* 1698) 1 Ld Raym. 739, 2 Salk. 441 (running down).

11 *Turbervile* v. *Stamp* (1697) 1 Comyns 32, per Holt C. J.

12 This is the only sense noted in Vin. Abr., 'Negligence'.

13 For 'negligence or laches', see Plowd. 375; 7 Co. Rep. 16b; 10 Co. Rep. 111b; 3 Buls. 41.

of the register (for instance, Waste or Replevin[14]) in which carelessness might have been a relevant factor in imposing liability. Obviously, if we were to reassemble these actions into a category called Negligence, it would be a category of our own making. But here we hit another of the problems which bedevilled Winfield. The only actions in which words of negligence were explicitly set out in the writ or declaration were actions on the Case. If the words of writs were taken at face value, it might indeed seem – as it seemed to Winfield – that the history of negligence was a subdivision of the history of Case. However, it was the peculiar property of actions on the case that they were the only personal actions in which the plaintiff was allowed to state with any sort of particularity what he alleged had actually happened. That statement of detail is what the eponymous 'special case' was. In contrast to the verisimilitude of a declaration in Case there was the bald narrative of Trespass. We know that it was not only bald but unconvincing, because the plaintiff was required to expand the *vi et armis* allegation with a blood-curdling list of weapons (such as swords, staves and knives), even when the only force was that of placid cows munching grass. The formal difference fostered an ingrained notion that Trespass and Case were somehow fundamentally different. It was a mystical difference, because no one could define exactly what it was, or why it was needed; but it seemed part of the natural order of things that there should be two quite separate categories of remedy. This problem has evaporated since Milsom: the distinction now seems to be little more than an accident of jurisdiction. But lawyers in our period had not read Milsom.

One later consequence of this optical illusion was a deep-rooted mistake about standards of liability. We see negligence frequently alleged in actions on the case, but never – or hardly ever[15] – in trespass *vi et armis*. It was deduced from this, and not only by Winfield, that in Case liability was often or usually based on negligence, whereas in Trespass liability was strict and negligence irrelevant. This view is found as late as Plucknett.[16] It

---

[14] E.g., *Peperell* v. *Wyllyam* (1488) CP 40/905, m. 448 (defendant justifies taking a horse as a stray; plaintiff replies that the defendant tied the horse with a rope round its neck and a running knot – *nodo currente non habente aliquem nodum securum* – and so negligently tied it in that way to a tree that the horse was strangled and died, in default of the defendant; the defendant rejoins that the horse was sick with glanders and 'bottys', from which it died, and traversed the fault; no verdict is recorded). It is not clear how replevin was brought for a dead horse.

[15] Professor Kiralfy found a few stray precedents where plaintiffs in trespass combined an allegation of negligent driving with 'force and arms', but these were rare: *A. K. R. Kiralfy*, The Action on the Case (1949), pp. 102–3; *Colan* v. *West* (1367) B. & M. 303.

[16] *T. F. T. Plucknett*, Concise History of the Common Law (5th ed., 1956), pp. 461–2, 468. See also *T. A. Street*, Foundations of Legal Liability (1906), i. 74,

was an ancillary part of this story – and this much survived in the first edition of Baker[17] – that in Case liability for negligence could only be imposed if there was some other factor giving rise to a duty of care: usually an undertaking (*assumpsit*), sometimes a 'custom of the realm'.[18] According to a widely held view,[19] the first case in which the common law recognised negligence *per se* – that is, liability attaching to someone who was negligent in carrying on his own projects and undertakings – was *Mitchell v. Allestry* (1676), to which we shall return. The modern tort of negligence on this view dates from somewhere between 1760 and the 1820s and 1830s, when Case began to be used instead of Trespass for road accidents.[20] Before then people either kept their grievances to themselves, or resorted to local courts.[21] Some have attributed the change to the industrial revolution, which undoubtedly brought new risks and new kinds of accident.[22] There have been some amazing embellishments on this theme: for instance, one writer in 1970 even hazarded the conclusion that in medieval times most harm was inflicted intentionally.[23] Accidents are, perhaps, themselves a result of industrialisation.

189–90; *P. H. Winfield*, 'The Myth of Absolute Liability' (1926) 42 L.Q.R. 37–51 (where he distinguished absolute from strict liability).

[17] *J. H. Baker*, Introduction to English Legal History (1971), p. 227. The proposition was supported by an Elizabethan judge (Walmsley J.): *Bradshaw* v. *Nicholson* (1601) ibid.; cf. B. & M. 609.

[18] Cf. *Turbervile* v. *Stamp* (1697) Pengelly's Reports, BL MS. Add. 6722, fo. 78 ('Serjeant Gould moved in arrest of judgment: actions of the case are grounded either on Negligence or Malfeasance; those on Negligence are either where there is a speciall trust or else on the common custom of the realme ...').

[19] *Street*, Foundations of Legal Liability, i. 189; *W. S. Holdsworth*, History of English Law, viii. 453; *H. Potter*, Historical Introduction to English Law and its Institutions (4th ed., 1962), p. 387 ('The modern tort of negligence probably stems from this case of the unruly horse ...').

[20] *P. H. Winfield* and *A. L. Goodhart* dated the action on the case for negligence to 1762, when it was mentioned in Comyn's *Digest*: 'Trespass and Negligence' (1933) 49 L.Q.R. 359–78, at p. 364. *J. H. Wigmore*, 'Responsibility for Tortious Acts: Its History' in Select Essays in Anglo-American Legal History (1908), iii. 474–537, at p. 517, suggested a date after 1800 (distinguishing *Mitchell* v. *Allestry*); and *G. L. Williams*, Liability for Animals (1939), p. 340, suggested the early nineteenth century (noting *Mitchell* v. *Allestry* as an earlier stray).

[21] The latter was Winfield's explanation: 'The History of Negligence', at p. 185.

[22] E.g. *Potter*, Historical Introduction to English Law, p. 390 ('The growth of a mechanical civilization beginning with the industrial revolution and the development of railways emphasised the need for care towards persons generally in many departments of life').

[23] *W. S. Malone*, 'Ruminations on the Role of Fault in the History of the Common Law of Torts' (1970), 31 Louisiana Law Review 1–44, at p. 24 ('It is important to bear in mind that in an earlier society most harms were inflicted intention-

Some of us have moved away from these positions in the last few decades, and they are no longer orthodox. The subject seemed messy to the older writers partly as a result of projecting back modern problems in an anachronistic way. Winfield was really concerned to establish whether negligence was an 'independent tort' in 1926, and thought an answer could be found from its history. One of the noble few who detected the anachronism in this approach was Wigmore, who alone of the earlier writers considered that the vague language of the older cases had been misunderstood when taken out of the context of pleading practice.[24]

We now make a primary distinction of obligations into Contract and Tort, and then subdivide Tort into Negligence, Strict Liability, and Miscellaneous Torts. It is as well to remember that Contract also has a Negligence division; but it does not raise as many legal problems, since the duty and standard of care rest on the interpretation of the particular contract. However, in 1500 these juristic categories did not exist. The forms of action were predicated on the kind of harm done rather than the degree of fault required to impose liability. There is no need to assume that lawyers or ordinary people thought laterally across these forms and saw a single standard of care or a definite scale of degrees of fault to be used in different contexts. Nor is there any need to suppose that the standard of care, or the existence of a duty to take care, was a technical requirement of each specific form of action. These are questions which seem so basic to us that we may be surprised not to find more guidance upon them in the law reports. But these were not questions for the court in banc, or the law school. In most cases, they would not have been questions for lawyers at all, except as trial advocates, because they were considered to be questions of fact for the jury.

This has perhaps been the most hazardous stumbling block, for obstacles are most likely to do us harm when we cannot see them. It is all too easy to assume that questions which occur to us as questions of law would have occurred to our forebears as questions of law. In consequence, where we do not find legal discussion of fault in the books, we naturally assume that liability must have been strict. But this is to overlook the radical shifts which have taken place in the boundary between judge and jury.

Perhaps it is not surprising that lawyers seeking the origins of negligence looked only at Case, because we need facts to tell history and only in Case do we find the facts set out. But there is no contemporary evidence that Trespass and Case were separated by differing standards of liability. In so

---

ally'). If evidence be needed in refutation, it is furnished in abundance by the coroners' records.

[24] *J. H. Wigmore*, Tortious Liability, at pp. 505–7.

far as differing standards may be discerned at all, it seems most likely that they varied according to the types of situation in which liability arose rather than the form of action through which the remedy had to be sought. For the sake of exposition, we may identify four main kinds of situation where liability may be imposed (in actions of Trespass and Case) for harm caused by negligence in the sense of carelessness:[25]

1. Negligence in performing an undertaking which expressly or impliedly requires the exercise of due care.
2. Negligence in looking after someone else's property, in the absence of or without regard to any legally enforceable contract requiring careful custody.
3. Negligence in the custody or control of something dangerous.
4. Negligence in carrying on one's own activities.

1. Negligence in performing an undertaking

In the pleading formula known as *assumpsit* for misfeasance, the defendant was alleged to have undertaken to perform some specified labour or service, and then to have performed it so carelessly that some specified damage followed. It was rare for the declaration to allege an undertaking to use skill and care; the undertaking as laid was only to perform the task. To that extent the liability may therefore have been closer to what we call tort than to contract, the undertaking being subsidiary and explanatory, and the duty of care implied by law – a duty to take care in carrying out undertakings.

In cases noted in the King's Bench rolls between 1490 and 1540, the adverbs used to describe the defendant's fault in carrying out his undertaking were (in descending order of frequency): 'negligently' (*negligenter*), 'improvidently' (*improvide*), 'in an unworkmanlike manner' (*inartificialiter*), 'unduly' (*indebite*), 'imprudently' (*indiscrete*), 'carelessly' (*incaute*), 'unwittingly' (*inscienter*), and 'unskilfully' (*absque arte*). Whatever it was that they expressed could only, it seems, be expressed negatively. The cases are all of misfeasance rather than nonfeasance; that is, there was either positive misconduct or a failure to exercise skill in performing a positive act. The actions were most commonly brought against tradesmen whose callings raised an expectation of skill – for instance, the barber, the surgeon, the blacksmith, the scrivener, the builder, or the painter – or against manufacturers who met orders with defective goods. In these latter

---

[25] This is the writer's own classification scheme, but seems to reflect different currents of pleading practice and judicial authority.

cases we cannot be sure – and we do not know that it mattered – whether the defendant was thought to be liable for supplying an imperfect product or for not supplying a perfect product; the same harm was done to the plaintiff. These professional and business cases are the common types; but there was no theoretical objection to bringing similar actions against mere labourers who caused damage by negligent work.

In most of the cases there was no pleading at all, because the defendant never appeared. Where the defendant did appear, he usually pleaded Not Guilty or *Non Assumpsit* and so we learn no more of the substance of his defence. No case has yet been found in which a special plea throws any light on the standard of liability. However, there are two cases in the sixteenth century in which surgeons sued for failing to effect cures pleaded that they had not given an undertaking to cure but had only promised to give treatment according to the best of their skill and ability.[26] These were cases of nonfeasance rather than negligent misfeasance, though the distinction is not altogether meaningful in medical cases and the pleas suggest that, in the absence of a special agreement, the liability of a surgeon was not thought to be strict. There is, however, a genuine factual difference between a contract guaranteeing a cure and a contract to do one's best for a patient. What we cannot tell is how far the supposed terms of such contracts could be implied from social usage. Generalisation from these cases is therefore unwise. It would not be altogether surprising if the standard of liability in *assumpsit* for negligence turned at least in part on the construction of the contract in question.[27]

We should, in any case, be wary of equating *assumpsit* in these cases with contract in the modern sense. Although the alleged 'undertaking' betokened some prior relationship between the parties, it was not necessarily part of a contract supported by consideration,[28] and therefore we can – at any rate, by the seventeenth century – find precedents of declarations for negligence against tradesmen in which the relationship is set out in some other way, without an *assumpsit*.[29] However, all or most of these cases

---

26 *Roggers* v. *Walssh* (1532) CP 40/1074, m. 505 (verdict for plaintiff); *Reade* v. *Porter* (1553) KB 27/1167, m. 118. Cf. CP 40/1079, m. 518 (pleads tender of medicine and refusal to take it).

27 See *Williams* v. *Lloyd* (1628) W. Jones 179, where the natural death of a bailed horse was said to discharge the bailee, either because there was no negligence or because it was an act of God (what we would call frustration). It seems that only an act of God provided a discharge from a specific promise to return the horse, whereas the implied duty arising from the bailment alone was merely to take care. Cf. *Southcote* v. *Bennett* (1601) Fifoot 169.

28 *Powtney* v. *Walton* (1597) in *J. H. Baker* and *S. F. C. Milsom*, Sources of English Legal History: Private Law to 1750 (1986) [hereafter B. & M.], p. 370; *Coggs* v. *Barnard* (1703) B. & M. 370.

overlap with the next category, because they involve damage to chattels entrusted to the defendant.

2. *Negligence in looking after another's property*

Rather more information is available concerning the liability of carriers and innkeepers, probably because they were subjected to a stricter standard of care than ordinary bailees. The liability of a bailee was not necessarily contractual, because even when he was sued in an action on the case upon *assumpsit* the word might denote the physical undertaking of a task, or of custodial responsibility, rather than a contract supported by consideration.[30] Indeed, bailees could be sued without any *assumpsit* at all, by an action on the case alleging that the goods were delivered on terms that they were to be redelivered in good order, and that the bailee had negligently damaged them.

A bailee could be made strictly liable by a contractual undertaking to that effect, but if he only agreed to look after the goods with the same care as his own he might have an excuse for loss or damage, though it was controversial which of these was the reasonable everyday understanding of an ordinary or non-contractual bailment.[31] He might also have been excused if the goods were stolen from him rather than merely taken by way of trespass, on the ground that the felony changed the property. On the other hand, he may not have been entitled to this defence if he had deviated from the bailment by leaving the goods with a third party. In 1556, the Common Pleas entertained an action of detinue against a Norfolk esquire for a horse and bridle; the defendant had borrowed it to ride to Norwich, and was to

---

[29] E.g., two precedents from a book of entries: *T. H.* v. *R. S.* (1602), in BL MS. Lansdowne 1149, fo. 28, citing Trin. 44 Eliz., rot. 604 (H lent S a horse, three geldings and a chariot (*currus*) for carrying timber; S so negligently drove them that the cart fell on one of the geldings and killed it, and was completely broken); *Cockaine* v. *Holland* (1636), ibid., fo. 22 (C delivered to H, a watchmaker, a crystal watch garnished with gold, to polish and mend and return whole and safe; 'tamen [H] tam negligenter, inartificialiter et improvide predictum horologium tractavit et custodivit quod horologium et christallum predictum fregit et spoliavit, per quod horologium predictum nullius valoris eidem [C] devenit'). See also *Best* v. *Yates* (1675) 3 Keb. 449; 1 Vent. 268 (action against a tailor for negligently making a coat that was of no use; declaration held bad on demurrer, because it did not allege that the plaintiff had delivered his cloth to the tailor).

[30] *Powtney* v. *Walton* (1597) B. & M. 370; *Coggs* v. *Barnard* (1703) ibid.

[31] In *Southcote* v. *Bennet* (1601) 4 Co. Rep. 83; Cro. Eliz. 815; Co. Litt. 89; the Queen's Bench, in an action of Detinue, held a general bailment to be strict, and that a bailment to look after as one's own, or as best one could, was a special arrangement. As a general position, that was overturned, relying on civilian learning taken from Bracton, in *Coggs* v. *Barnard* (1703) B. & M. 370; 2 Ld Raym. 909.

keep it there to the plaintiff's use until the plaintiff came to collect it; but the defendant left it in another person's house, whence it was taken by Kett and his rebels, who rode it to death. On demurrer, this was held not to be a good plea.[32]

In the case of innkeepers, the action was founded on the 'custom of the realm', following a standard form introduced in the fourteenth century. In later times the carrier also would be brought under a custom of the realm, though there is no mention of such a custom before the seventeenth century.[33] The common link is that both the innkeeper and the carrier were made responsible for the property of another as part of their business, and it seems likely that a higher standard was expected of them than of ordinary bailees. Indeed, it may have been the general understanding, in the absence of special terms, that they should insure the customer against loss or damage. Thus, in an Inner Temple discussion of the 1530s, it was said that a carrier could not plead that he was robbed of the goods, because he had undertaken the risk; it was different if a servant was robbed, because he was merely carrying out the master's orders and the risk remained with the master.[34] Likewise, an innkeeper was responsible for the theft of goods by strangers; indeed, this was the usual ground of complaint in actions against innkeepers. His own remedy, in theory, was to sue the thieves.[35] There was therefore a chain of responsibility in which fault in the modern sense would have had no place. It is not easy to find real examples of successive actions, but there is one in the King's Bench rolls for 1555. A carrier was sued on an undertaking, in return for 12*d.*, to carry goods to Birmingham, on the grounds that through his negligence they were taken from him by persons unknown. The carrier confessed the action, but immediately sued the innkeeper of the Rose at Dunchurch for loss of the goods on the journey.[36] Both actions rested formally on an allegation of negligence or fault, but the implication of the confession may be that the carrier was considered responsible for the loss of goods whatever precautions he might have taken,[37] and that he and the innkeeper each insured his own customer. This is confirmed by an entry two years later, when an attempt by a

---

32 *Barlee* v. *Corbett* (1556–7) CP 40/1168, m. 1005 (judgment for plaintiff).

33 Until then the appropriate action against a negligent carrier was still *assumpsit*.

34 BL MS. Harley 1691, fo. 105. Cf. *Hachard* v. *Wynnals* (1511–12) CP 40/997, m. 503; Rast. Ent. 14 (account against common carrier in respect of a sack of grain; pleads theft in transit; judgment for plaintiff on demurrer).

35 *Osbern* v. *Myller* (1490) Caryll's reports, 115 Selden Soc. 30, *per* Fairfax J. It was agreed that he could plead act of God, such as lightning, because he had no action over in that case. Cf. Trin. 10 Hen. VII, fo. 26, pl. 3, *per* Fisher sjt (denies that a common innkeeper has a remedy over when goods are robbed).

36 *Colimer* v. *Arrowsmyth* (1555) KB 27/1174, m. 96 (*assumpsit*, says *non potest dedicere*); *Arrowsmyth* v. *Carter* (1555) ibid., m. 96d (innkeeper pleads Not Guilty).

common carrier to shift liability on to an innkeeper met with a demurrer.[38] The law was not finally settled in the sixteenth century, because the Common Pleas judges apparently took the view that since the common carrier was compellable to receive goods for carriage he was not strictly liable for their loss by theft.[39]

To the extent that strict liability was regarded as the normal regime for professional bailees, the best means of escape was to plead a special agreement excluding or limiting liability. The normal position of a carrier was that he undertook to deliver safely; at least, that is how it was expressed in *assumpsit* declarations. But the law did not forbid a carrier, any more than a surgeon, to make other arrangements, at any rate if they were reasonable.[40] Thus, a carrier of goods by sea could plead that he had not undertaken absolutely to deliver, but had only undertaken to carry the goods safely to the best of his ability and on condition that the goods were not damaged 'by tempest of wind and sea' in the mean time.[41] In other words, he could rely on an exclusion clause which would leave some of the risk with the shipper. A more remarkable example of special pleading, which must be regarded as an aberration by an inexperienced pleader, is provided by a King's Bench entry of 1528.[42] The plaintiff, in an unusually full declaration, complained that the defendant – for a sum of 2*d.* agreed – had undertaken safely to carry a butt of malmsey in his wagon from Maidstone to Sutton Valence, in Kent, that he had so carelessly loaded it on to the wagon that the wagon overturned and the hoops of the butt were broken, and that on arrival he had so carelessly unloaded the damaged butt that one hundred gallons of malmsey gushed out and were lost. The defendant

---

37 A carrier could therefore be sued in *assumpsit* without alleging negligence: e.g., *Aylmer* v. *Dene* (1503) KB 27/969 m. 6d (*warrantizando assumpsit* to carry tun of sugar safely from London to Norwich, but wholly lost it).

38 *Hatche* v. *Thorne* (1557) KB 27/1183, m. 193 (trover for clothing; pleads he is a common carrier and the goods were taken from him in the Catharine Wheel in Egham through the negligence of the innkeeper; demurrer; c. a. v.).

39 *Anon.* (1553) Dal. 8, pl. 1 (sim. to last; held that the consignor should sue the innkeeper and not the carrier, '(tr.) for they are not the carrier's goods, and he is not liable for them inasmuch as he is compellable by law to carry them, and it is not like where someone undertakes goods to carry generally,' in which case robbery was no defence).

40 *C. St German*, Doctor and Student, 91 Selden Soc. 261, denied that a common carrier could exclude liability for negligence, 'for it were against reason and against good manners' (*sp. mod.*). Cf. Co. Litt. 89, written a century later.

41 *Jekeler* v. *Newgate* (1537) KB 27/1103, m. 9 (pleads undertaking to carry fish 'pro posse suo ... si iidem pisces per ventus et maris tempestates medio tempore deteriorati non essent').

42 *Terry* v. *White* (1528) KB 27/1067, m. 34d. It is not recorded that the action was ever tried.

matched this narration of events with an even more detailed plea. Denying the undertaking by protestation, he said that he happened to be in Maidstone when the plaintiff's agent approached him and asked him to take the butt to his house in Sutton; he had agreed, and on arrival at the house the agent had directed him to unload; the defendant had declined to do so, because the weather was stormy and night was approaching, and said he would leave it till the morning; the agent had thereupon urged him to unload at the plaintiff's own risk, promising to support the tail of the wagon while he did so; then, while the butt was being unloaded, the agent had carelessly let go of the tail so that the butt had fallen on the ground; and finally, apparently in an attempt to hammer the hoops back into position, the agent had smashed the butt with an axe so that the wine had been spilt. The plea concluded by traversing (with an *absque hoc*) the breaking of the butt by the defendant's negligence; to which the plaintiff replied that it was broken by the defendant's negligence, through the defendant's fault. Now, it would have been more regular for the defendant in such a case to plead the general issue (Not Guilty) and tell this story to the jury, since the essence of the defence was a denial of negligent conduct rather than a justification. The core of the defence was contributory negligence, but the language of risk transference is revealing. Even if the contract for carriage was in standard form, it was open to the defendant to show that the consignor had accepted the risk of a particular mode of performance. Although it is inappropriate to read too much law into such an unusual case, especially since there is no indication that it ever came before the judges, the pleadings do at least show the level of sophistication of the questions which might normally be left to juries. In the seventeenth century it became common to sue carriers upon a custom of the realm which made them more strictly liable,[43] rather than upon a special assumpsit; but it was nevertheless held that an action on the custom sounded not in tort but in contract.[44]

The common defences open in an action on the case against an alleged innkeeper were that the goods were not taken from the inn, or that the defendant returned them to the plaintiff or at his order, or that the defendant was not a common innkeeper at all. Insanity was no defence.[45] Where goods were indisputably taken from an inn, the best line of defence was to

---

[43] The first known case is *Rich* v. *Kneeland* (1613) Cro. Jac. 330; Hob. 17; B. & M. 561. The analogy with innkeepers was no doubt suggested by the circumstance that both were under a duty to accept customers.

[44] *Dalson (or Dalston)* v. *Janson (or Iveson)* (1695) 1 Ld Raym. 58 ('though this action upon the case against the carrier be founded on a wrong, yet it sounds in contract'); 3 Ld Raym. 115; 5 Mod. Rep. 90; 12 Mod. Rep. 73; 1 Salk. 10; 3 Salk. 204; Comb. 333. Cf. *Mathew* v. *Hopkins* (1665) 1 Keb. 870; 1 Sid. 244; 1 Vent. 365.

show that the risk had not been assumed by the innkeeper. This was usually a matter of showing that the plaintiff had been given the key to his own room, but it could also be achieved by showing that the plaintiff had himself agreed to the method of storage which had proved defective. In the 1550s the judges approved a defence that when the inn was full the innkeeper had admitted the plaintiff at his own risk to share a room with others,[46] and another that the plaintiff had asked for a stable for his horses, saying he would take upon himself the responsibility (*caperet super se onus custodie*), and had taken the key to the stable door and left his servant in the stable.[47] It seems, therefore, that in the absence of such a special agreement for the guest to deposit goods at his own risk, the risk of loss would have fallen on the innkeeper.

3. *Negligent custody or control of hazards*

Liability for negligence was not confined to those who misperformed undertakings and bailments, but extended to those who failed to keep animals, fire, or water, under proper control with the result that another person was injured. In the case of fire and animals, use was still made of special forms of action of medieval origin, but the gaps could be filled by new actions on the case.

The usual action for damage done by animals was the species of trespass for knowingly retaining an animal with mischievous propensities – the *scienter* action, used since 1358[48] – though at least one early Tudor attorney made the understandable mistake of supposing this to be founded on a custom of the realm.[49] It long remained uncertain whether the plaintiff in such an action should allege force and arms; but most Tudor plaintiffs did, unperturbed by the notion of keeping something with force.[50] The *scienter* action did not expressly mention negligence, though the requirement of

---

[45] *Cross* v. *Andrews* (1598) Cro. Eliz. 622, Rolle Abr. i. 2, line 38. However, it was said in that case that infancy was a defence, at any rate where an infant inherited an inn: Rolle Abr. i. 2.

[46] *Dey* v. *Ungor* (1551) KB 27/1157, m. 67; *White's Case* (1558) Dyer 158b

[47] *Hatcher* v. *Shakelforth* (1555) CP 40/1164, m. 817 (judgment for plaintiff after verdict by default).

[48] *Beneyt* v. *Brokkere* (1358), cited in *R. C. Palmer*, English Law in the Age of the Black Death (1993), pp. 239, 371.

[49] *Orenge* v. *Haywarde* (1535) CP 40/1086, m. 325 (custom of the realm to keep animals from doing harm to neighbours, and *scienter retinuit* dog accustomed to biting sheep; general issue).

[50] For exceptions, see 94 Selden Soc. *228* n. 11. Earlier declarations omit the *vi et armis* clause, and it has been suggested that confusion later arose with the action for sheep-chasing: *Williams*, Liability for Animals, pp. 280–1.

knowledge – held by all the justices of the Common Pleas in 1537 to be essential[51] – shows that liability was not absolute. Moreover, it was arguable that the owner was not liable if the animal was encouraged into mischief by a third person, such as a servant acting without authority.[52] Cattle trespass was a different legal category: since all cattle are accustomed to munch grass, there was no need to prove *scienter*, and it is likely that the owner was held liable even in the absence of fault.[53] This, however, is not really a form of accident litigation; the cattle were injuring the freehold, and the question would often be one of title to land.

The action on the case for losing control of a domestic fire, which is first found in 1401, set out a custom of the realm requiring everyone to keep their fires so as not to injure their neighbours.[54] Little is known about the standard of liability imposed by the custom of the realm,[55] because the standard plea was either the ambiguous 'Not burned for want of due custody of the fire' or the general issue Not Guilty. There is, however, a precedent of the former plea with the inducement that the fire happened by misfortune and act of God (*ex infortunia et actu Dei*), which suggests that liability may not have been regarded as strict.[56] If a fire started by accident, so that the action on the custom of the realm was unavailable, it became possible in the sixteenth century to bring an action on the case for negligence;[57] this was useful to lessors who for some reason could not bring waste,[58] though in the time of Elizabeth I the Queen's Bench began to doubt whether such an action lay against the lessee.[59] It was decided in

51 *Anon.* (1537) Dyer 25b, §162; BL MS. Harley 1691, fo. 133.

52 Hil. 13 Hen. VII, fo. 15, pl. 10 (query by reporter).

53 See *Anon.* (1480) Mich. 20 Edw. IV, fo. 10, pl. 10, *per* Bryan C. J. (owner liable even if cattle driven on to land by a third party's dogs); *Anon.* (1481) B. & M. 315, *per* Catesby J.; *Anon.* (1486) Caryll's reports, 115 Selden Soc. 2, pl. 2 (owner liable even if cattle strayed because third party neglected to mend fence); *Anon.* (1496) ibid. 303, pl. 209; Hil. 13 Hen. VII, fo. 15, pl. 10 (owner liable for cattle which broke close of their own wrong, against his will and without his knowledge, but not if they are put in by a wife or servant acting without his knowledge).

54 *Beaulieu* v. *Finglam* (1401) B. & M. 557.

55 It was held in *Shelley* v. *Burr* (1625) Rolle Abr. i. 2, line 1, that the action on the custom lay only against the *paterfamilias*, and not against a wife or servant whose negligence caused a fire.

56 *Pryst* v. *Belche* (1510) KB 27/994, m. 47. Cf. the precedent in *Anon.* (1416) entry in CUL MS. Add. 8141, fo. 7, citing Trin. 4 Hen. V, ro. 443 (pleads that '*quidem ignis subitaneus per infortunium desuper flaute vento vehementi in gallicantum issuit super domus orrei* [of the defendant] *per infortunium*').

57 *Anon.* (1582) Cro. Eliz. 10; B. & M. 569.

58 *Critoft* v. *Emson* (1506) CP 40/978, m. 320 (B. & M. 566 n. 13); *Gravener* v. *Squyer* (1522) CP 40/1037, m. 452d (defendant shows in evidence a lease for 40 years and possession; plaintiff demurs because he is tenant by the curtesy and cannot bring waste); *Castell* v. *Browne* (1541) CP 40/1109, m. 121 (plaintiff declares

1600 that it did not against a mere tenant at will,[60] but it was established as a remedy against tenants for years and under-lessees.[61] A special action on the case could also be brought for an outdoor fire.[62] A less clear extension is found in a precedent of 1507, when case was brought in respect of a shooting accident; the declaration stated that the defendant had presumed to shoot with a hand-gun, and that for want of proper control of the gun a spark had flown out and burned the left eye of the plaintiff's apprentice, so that he had to abandon his apprenticeship; but the main reason here for framing the action in Case was that it was brought by the master for loss of services.[63] The matter was discussed in *Turbervile* v. *Stamp* (1697), where an outdoor fire had spread by accident and the defendant was held liable in an action on the custom of the realm.[64] Holt C. J. said in that case, 'he must at his peril take care that it does not, through his neglect, injure his neighbour: if he kindle it at a proper time and place, and the violence of the wind carry it into his neighbour's ground, and prejudice him, this is fit to be given in evidence'.[65] It therefore seems that, even in actions notionally strict, it was considered proper for the jury to exculpate those who were not at fault.

Liability for harm caused by the negligent control of water was also imposed by an action on the case. Although legal historians are wont to categorise such actions as 'nuisance', because of the damage to real property, the declarations often rested on negligence. In these cases it was apparently necessary to allege a duty to control the water, though the source of the duty of care is not always clear.[66] No indications of the standard of care have been found.

---

on seisin of house according to custom of manor though someone else lived there). See also Fitz. Abr., 'Action sur le case', pl. 43.

59 *Anon.* (1580) BL MS. Add. 35949, fo. 14v (case adjourned for advisement). Cf. *Jeremy* v. *Lowgar* (1596) Cro. Eliz. 461, where two judges were in favour of such an action, but the other two were absent.

60 *Countess of Shrewsbury* v. *Crompton* (1600) 5 Co. Rep. 13; Cro. Eliz. 777, 784; B. & M. 565.

61 *Cudlip* v. *Rundall* (1691) KB 27/2080, m. 646; 4 Mod. Rep. 12; 12 Mod. Rep. 14; 1 Show. 310; Carth. 202; Comb. 177; 3 Salk. 156; *Hicks* v. *Dowling* (1696) 12 Mod. Rep. 100; 1 Ld Raym. 99.

62 *Kytt* v. *Dovell* (1522) CP 40/1037, m. 158d.

63 *Clerk* v. *Terrell* (1507) KB 27/985, m. 42d.

64 Skin. 681 says the plaintiff counted alternatively in a special action on the case. For other reports, see 1 Ld Raym. 264; 12 Mod. Rep. 152; 1 Salk. 13; 1 Comyns 32; Carth. 425; Comb. 459; Holt 9. According to Comyns, Holt C. J. said 'The only question is whether the plaintiff ought not to have shewn a special negligence in the defendant'.

65 12 Mod. Rep. 152.

If we may count gravity as a hazardous force, here was another area where liability was imposed for negligence in the absence of an undertaking or custom of the realm. Actions on the case were brought for such hazards as creating a dangerous structure which fell on someone,[67] or making a dangerous cavity into which someone fell.[68] Since it seems not to have occurred to anyone before Victorian times to impose liability on occupiers of private premises towards visitors encountering such hazards, the cases all concern highways. Instances are few and far between, and nothing is known of the standard of liability.

4. Negligence in carrying on one's own activities

It is in the sphere of accidents occurring between strangers,[69] in the course of ordinary activities in public places, that actions on the case are little in evidence before 1676. But can it really be that in medieval times there were no serious accidents of this kind, or that (if there were) the law was too primitive to take notice of them? Was there a sudden wave of careless abandon in Restoration England? Since we know that the swords, staves and knives of trespass declarations are not to be taken literally, can we safely rely on the other outward forms as a true guide to the facts?

The suggested solution to this puzzle is that the records have indeed deceived our eyes, and that there was no sudden change in the extent of carelessness or in the scope of negligence actions. An increase in the frequency of accident litigation because of improvements in technology, and

---

66 *Constable* v. *Garton* (1508) KB 27/988, m. 48 (duty of mill-keeper 'by reason of office' to control sluice); *Colles* v. *Tevy* (1514) KB 27/1013, m. 58 (accustomed to clean ditch); *Guybon* v. *Palmer* (1516) CP 40/1013, m. 106 (accustomed to repair sea-dyke to prevent flooding); *Fynamore* v. *Clyfford* (1520) CP 40/1029, m. 161 (duty of mill-keeper 'by reason of office' to control sluice; so negligently controlled it that water flooded plaintiff's land); *Abbot of Stratford* v. *Hubbulthorn* (1529) CP 40/1062, m. 521 (duty to open lock, which defendant controlled, when water rose to a high level).

67 *Loghton* v. *Calys* (1473) B. & M. 567 (pile of logs collapsing into road); *Frankessh* v. *Bokenham* (1490) Caryll's reports, 115 Selden Soc. 27 (mill-stone falling off wall onto road). Cf. B. & M. 571.

68 E. g., anonymous reading (late 15th or early 16th cent.) on Westminster II, c. 13, in BL MS. Hargrave 87, fo. 375 (transl., 'If someone ... digs a ditch or pit whereby a man is damaged, he shall have an action on the case and recover damages, though he may not reform it by way of presentment'); *Blyth* v. *Topham* (1607) B. & M. 570 (pit in common); *Anon.* (1621) ibid. 571n (concealed mine-shaft); *Drake* v. *Hall* (C.P., Hil. 1669) Girdler's entries, CUL MS. Add. 9430(3) (pit in highway). Note also *Fowler* v. *Sanders* (1617) Cro. Jac. 446, where the defendant pleaded negligence in the plaintiff.

69 I. e. where there is no privity or prior relationship between the parties.

road surfaces, or even in medical care, there may well have been; but there was no need for new categories. There had always been actions for compensation in respect of accidents, but they had mostly taken the form of general *vi et armis* writs, which we know to have been used in the seventeenth century in cases where harm was caused directly, such as shooting or running-down accidents.[70] The fictional swords, staves and knives which represented force and arms could in contemplation of law include the flesh and bone of a wayward horse as well as a human fist or the molars of a stray ruminant. The question of legal history is, therefore, whether we can find out anything about the standard of liability in trespass *vi et armis*. The words of the writ do not help, and in the vast majority of cases the pleadings do not help either, because the wise defendant always pleaded Not Guilty and kept his story for the jury.

The legacy of the *Case of Thorns* (1466)[71] was that lack of intention was no defence in a civil action; but it was left open how far a defendant could excuse himself in respect of unintentional harm by showing that he had not, in an objective sense, been at fault.[72] Choke J., at any rate, was in favour of a plea that the defendant had done what he could to prevent the accident; but said it would be necessary for him to set out the relevant facts. Such pleas are almost impossible to find in the rolls,[73] but another attempt was made in a case of 1534. A member of Clement's Inn was injured in a shooting accident in St Clement's Field,[74] and brought a common action of battery.[75] The defendant pleaded that the field contained archery butts – 'le crosse pryckes' – where the king's lieges were wont to

---

[70] For examples where the truth came out, see *Weaver* v. *Ward* (1616) B. & M. 331; *Angell* v. *Satterton* (1663) ibid. 464; *Burford* v. *Dadwel* (1669) ibid. 334; *Dickinson* v. *Watson* (1682) ibid. 334; *Gibbon* v. *Pepper* (1695) ibid. 335.

[71] *Hulle* v. *Orynge* (1466) B. & M. 327.

[72] *S. G. Gilles*, Inevitable Accident in Classical English Tort Law (1994) 43 *Emory Law Jnl* 575–646, at pp. 599, 600, criticises this interpretation on the grounds that 'against his will' is different from 'without his will', and only the latter means 'unintentional'. But *ipso invito*, the words used in the plea (literally 'him unwilling'), might just as well, if not better, be rendered as 'without his will'.

[73] Note, however, *Hampden* v. *Doyly* (1443) B. & M. 325 (pleads he did all he could to stop his greyhounds entering the plaintiff's park; undetermined demurrer). An anonymous reader, putting this same case a few years later, held that 'it would be against all reason if he were to be punished, since there was no fault in him': ibid. n. 4.

[74] The membership of Clement's Inn is not stated in the record. William Ustwayt was sued for dues by the principal of the inn in 1538: CP 40/1096, m. 662d. (He was still being pursued by the inn in 1554, when he was reportedly living in Boston, Lincs.: CP 40/1159, m. 773.) John Alyngton was later of the Middle Temple and may have been a fellow student.

[75] *Ustwayt* v. *Alyngton* (1534) CP 40/1083, m. 323.

shoot, that he fired an arrow at the target, and that while the arrow was in flight the plaintiff negligently ran across the butts and was struck, without the defendant willing it (*se invito*).[76] The plaintiff denied this generally, and a jury was summoned, though no outcome is recorded. Our injured inn of chancery student was unlikely ever to have heard such a case mooted, and (since he did not object to *se invito*) he may not even have read the *Case of Thorns*;[77] but, given that he was not stirred to demur, we can hardly doubt that the defence was considered good in substance. The defence was not, of course, standard pleading, because it amounted to Not Guilty. The plaintiff had caused his own misfortune, and broken (as we now say) the chain of causation necessary in an action *vi et armis*.

The famous case of *Weaver* v. *Ward* (1616)[78] is often taken to have sanctioned a strict standard of liability in trespass, though the issue of law raised upon the pleadings was the same as in the *Case of Thorns*. In an action for battery ('with swords, clubs and knives'), the defendant set out that he had accidentally and against his will shot the plaintiff while they were skirmishing with muskets as members of one of the 'trained bands'. Upon demurrer, it was held that the plea was bad. But there was nothing in the plea to show whether the defendant had taken proper steps to ensure against unnecessarily endangering his fellow musketeers. His plea was doubtless meant to show that he was merely carrying out his public duty as a good citizen; and yet, consistently with the facts as pleaded, he might have ignored all the safety drill of the period. All he had said in direct answer to the battery was that it was an accident, against his will; and the principle laid down in 1466 required the court to reject a defence based merely on the lack of intention to cause harm. The notion of a relatively strict standard of liability has arisen from an interpretation placed upon some remarks in the report of the case by the presiding judge, Hobart C. J.[79] There are two general propositions embedded in his report: first, that 'no man shall be excused of a trespass ... except it may be adjudged utterly without his fault', and, second, that for a plea to be valid it would have to 'set forth the case with the circumstances so as it had appeared to the court

---

76 Cf. the similar plea in *Reygnesbury* v. *Croyle* (1397) 100 Selden Soc. 30 (which also alleges foolishness and fault in the plaintiff). Another, undated, precedent is to be found in *R. Brownlow*, Declarations and Pleadings in English (1652), p. 188 (pleads he was shooting a long bow in a field for a wager, and the plaintiff negligently and unawares passed across the line of fire and was struck with an arrow).

77 The report was first printed by Pynson in 1496, and Choke J.'s remark had been abridged by Fitzherbert in 1516: Fitz. Abr., 'Trespas', pl. 110.

78 B. & M. 331.

79 Hob. 134; B. & M. 333. Hobart does not mention that Warburton J. dissented: Harvard Law School MS., translated in B. & M. 332.

that it had been inevitable, and that the defendant had committed no negligence to give occasion to the hurt'. The second of these propositions gave rise to the so-called defence of 'inevitable accident', which has been considered a much more restricted defence than a mere denial of fault.[80] And yet both passages mention fault as a requirement.[81] Whatever 'utterly' meant, it was a defence that an injury occurred without the defendant's fault. And whatever 'inevitable accident' meant, it was coupled with a requirement that 'the defendant committed no negligence'.[82] On no reasonable reading, therefore, could it be maintained that Hobart C. J. was ruling fault to be irrelevant. What precisely amounted to fault was not necessary to be decided, because the relevant facts were never put before the court.[83] Indeed, as in 1466, that was the ratio decidendi: unless a defendant pleaded sufficient facts to show that he had committed no negligence, the court could not adjudicate upon the defence as a matter of law. On this view, the facts necessary to be shown, in the case of a sudden accident, would be such as would enable the court to decide whether a reasonable defendant would have done something to avoid the accident; and that, surely, is all 'inevitable' means in these cases.[84] Of course, there are degrees of avoidability. An unavoidable accident may be one 'which by no foresight, or diligence, or possibility, could be avoided',[85] or it may simply be one which due care would not have averted.[86] But such gradations were for the jury, not the court.

---

[80] See now the full discussion in *Gilles*, 'Inevitable Accident', who argues for a meaning somewhere between liability for negligence and strict liability.

[81] Even Gilles recognises (ibid., pp. 587–8) that inevitable accident cannot mean more than that it was reasonably practicable to avoid the accident; one can hardly be required to avoid road accidents by staying indoors all the time. His position is not therefore radically different from that of the present writer.

[82] It has been suggested that negligence here refers to 'antecedent negligence': *R. J. Kaczarowski*, The Common-Law Background of Nineteenth-Century Tort Law (1990) 51 Ohio State Law Jnl 1127 at p. 1171; but cf. *Gilles*, Inevitable Accident, at p. 592.

[83] The effect of the demurrer was that the court could only consider the facts as pleaded: namely, that the defendant shot the plaintiff against his will.

[84] Consistent with this are the ways the word is used in *Dickenson* v. *Watson* (1682) and *Gibbon* v. *Pepper* (1695), below; and see *Wigmore*, Tortious Liability, at p. 506.

[85] *Reniger* v. *Fogossa* (1550) Plowd. 1, 9. The phrase 'unavoidable accident' occurs in the 1761 translation. But the original text reads, 'un *chaunce* que per nul providence, per nul diligence, ne per nul possibilitie poet este eschewe'. Cf. Co. Litt. 89b ('shipwreck by sea, fire by lightning, and other like inevitable accidents').

[86] See *Ratcliffe* v. *Goodcheap* (1742) 7 Mod. Rep. 458, where 'unavoidable accident' is contrasted merely with 'want of care'.

Nothing significant is added by the third case in the trilogy, *Dickenson* v. *Watson* (1682), which is very poorly reported.[87] Trespass, we are told, 'shall not be excused without unavoidable necessity'. But this is merely a paraphrase of the passage in Hobart's report of 1616, which is cited. As in the previous case, the defendant had failed to set out the facts which bore on the question of objective fault. He was, he said, a tax-collector in Yorkshire, and needed a pistol to safeguard the moneys which he had collected, not to mention his own person. So far, as in the 1616 case, he was merely setting out the context and explaining why he had the offending weapon in his possession. He then said that on the day in question he had fired the pistol, not intending to harm anyone, no-one being in sight; that the plaintiff had accidentally wandered across the line of fire and been shot; and that this was 'inevitable' and against the defendant's will. The plea was held bad. It is noteworthy that the court held it no plea merely to say that the accident was inevitable. The gist of the decision, as in the cases of 1466 and 1616, must therefore have been that the defendant ought to have pleaded what steps he took to avoid the harm. But our tax-collector had really said little more than that he had not wanted the accident to happen. He might have been blazing away with undue abandon at night, when no one was visible. The plea was therefore no more successful than those of 1466 and 1616 in putting before the court facts which showed the defendant not to have been negligent.[88]

When such a plea was finally framed in 1695,[89] the court was obliged to announce what all good pleaders had known for centuries.[90] It was not the done thing to plead details of the lack of negligence, in the form of a special plea, because lack of fault was not a justification for harming someone.[91] It was not like a sheriff pleading that he did indeed lay hands on the

---

[87] B. & M. 334. The only known report is in T. Jones 204.

[88] A similar explanation will account for the decision, in the following year, that a boundary mistake was no defence in trespass to land, the defendant having voluntarily committed the act complained of: *Basely* v. *Clarkson* (1682) 3 Lev. 37; record in *A. K. R. Kiralfy*, Source Book of English Law (1957), p. 136. However, a trespasser could bar such an action by disclaiming title and tendering amends, provided the trespass was 'by negligence or involuntary': Limitation Act 1623, 21 Jac. I, c. 16, s. 5. The wording of the statute seems to imply that even an involuntary trespass to land was actionable; but trespass to land may be a special case, since it was often used to try title.

[89] *Gibbon* v. *Pepper* (1695) B. & M. 335. The plaintiff is 'Gibbons' in the report, but 'Gibbon' in the record.

[90] *S. F. C. Milsom*, Historical Foundations of the Common Law (2nd ed., 1981), pp. 298–9. Cf. *Gilles*, Inevitable Accident, at pp. 583–4, 616–17, where it is contended that the 1695 decision did not reflect long-standing practice.

[91] A special plea had to be worded either as a denial ('traverse') or as an admission of all the facts alleged coupled with new facts which took away their effect

plaintiff, but that he had done so in the course of effecting a lawful arrest. The man who accidentally shot someone else, or was riding or driving an unruly horse when it ran out of control, was not claiming a right to shoot someone or run them over, and was therefore supposed to plead by way of a denial that he had committed any battery at all. That was most properly done by a general plea of Not Guilty. Any special plea would have to set out the facts by way of excuse, rather than justification, and it was not altogether clear how that could be achieved.[92] It was also practically ill advised, since the plea of Not Guilty was proof against technical objections going to the substance of the defence. It was hardly possible to set out specific facts in support of a negative, such as the absence of negligence, and almost as difficult to demonstrate that the defendant had taken all appropriate steps to avoid the accident, since that would logically require a demonstration not only that he had acted sensibly but also that he could not practicably have done anything else. The pleader's mind might well have boggled at such a prospect. Such matters were best dealt with by evidence at the trial. And this, of course, explains why there are so few visible examples in the plea rolls of special pleas going to fault. Nevertheless, the judges in 1695 were quite clear about the substance of the no-negligence defence. There was no question, they said, but that the lack of fault, as shown by the conduct of the defendant in attempting to avoid the accident – where a horse suddenly ran away with its rider, and the rider called out warnings to those in the way[93] – would have been accepted by the jury as a defence.

It is suggested that each of these cases is more consistent with liability resting on some kind of fault than with strict liability. But in none of them did the defendant manage to plead lack of fault effectively, and so we are left in doubt not only as to the legal permissiblity of a special plea but also as to the substantive standard of liability. The facts which exculpated the defendant were not placed on the record in trespass, because they amounted

('confession and avoidance'). A justification was a form of confession and avoidance, while 'Not Guilty' (the usual plea in Trespass) was a 'general' traverse.

92 Clearly Choke J. in 1466, and Hobart C. J. in 1616, were prepared to countenance some kind of special plea, and Gilles ('Inevitable Accident', pp. 615–28) deduces from their dicta – fortified by the opinion of Mr Serjeant Stephen in the 1830s – that the defence of inevitable accident could always have been pleaded by way of confession and avoidance, on the analogy of act of God. But the precedents of the latter are mostly from the fourteenth century, when pleading was in a nascent state. Despite reading many thousands of trespass entries in the plea rolls, the example of 1534 is the only one we have seen after 1450 which was not challenged; and it is far from clear whether it is a confession and avoidance or a traverse.

93 These facts, incidentally, were said by Serjeant Darnall to show that the accident was 'inevitable'.

to Not Guilty. There are thousands of pleas of Not Guilty in the plea rolls, and they presumably encompassed a wide spectrum of factual defences; but in the vast majority of cases we shall never know what they were. What we do know for sure is that questions of fault – which encompassed both questions of causation and questions relating to any action which should have been taken to avoid mishap – were matters for the jury and were therefore never in our period analysed with legal precision.

If this explanation is right, the next question is why plaintiffs in collision cases and the like should have transferred their allegiance to Case in the eighteenth century. A convenient starting point is *Mitchell* v. *Allestry and Scrivener* (1676),[94] the case singled out by Street and Holdsworth as marking a new form of liability. The plaintiff complained that his wife had been kicked and injured by unruly horses which were being taught to pull a coach in Little Lincoln's Inn Fields, where many people were walking about. This is indeed the first fully reported case where liability seems to rest on negligence alone. But its novelty has been unduly exaggerated.[95] No one has searched the plea rolls of the seventeenth century, though it is clear that actions on the case had already been brought in the 1660s and 1670s in respect of negligent collisions on water.[96] In the next place, the 1676 case was not an action for negligence in the way the activity in question was performed, for we know that Mitchell had brought an earlier action for negligent governance of the horses and it had been thrown out at the trial.[97] It was not quite a *scienter* action either, since the animals were behaving normally for horses which had not been broken in.[98] The complaint was that the defendant should not have brought untamed horses into a public square to train them. It was really a case of public nuisance. But the most interesting feature of the case is that it never occurred to an increasingly desperate counsel for the defendant to argue that negligence was not actionable *per se*. No floodgates were visible at the time, no great

---

[94] B. & M. 572.

[95] Much earlier examples can be found: see, e.g., *Whitlok* v. *Wherwell* (1398) in *M. S. Arnold*, Select Cases of Trespass from the King's Courts 1307–99 (103 Selden Soc., 1987), p. 412. But these had probably been forgotten long before 1600.

[96] See, e.g., *Gutteridge* v. *Pilgrim* (Pas. 1668), Girdler's entries, CUL MS Add 9430 (3), p. 523; *Stanton* v. *Elmes* (C.P., Trin. 1669), ibid., p. 525 (both cases of negligent driving by bargemen). Cf. also *Martin* v. *Green* (1664) 1 Keb. 730 (availability of action noticed); *Anon.* (1679) in *Kiralfy*, Action on the Case, p. 103; *Mustard* v. *Harnden* (1680) T. Raym. 390 (hoy).

[97] *Mitchell* v. *Allestry* (No. 1) B. & M. 574. See also *Wigmore*, Tortious Liability, at pp. 517–18 n. 6.

[98] Cf. *Scotchet* v. *Eltham* (1681) 1 Freem. K.B. 535 (no action lay for negligently keeping a horse which broke the plaintiff's close; a *scienter* allegation was necessary).

issue of principle perceived. Actions had always been allowed for negligently creating dangers; but in the past they had been needed only where the injury was indirect.[99]

The real question is not why Case was available, but why in cases such as this a plaintiff was advised to use Case rather than Trespass. Part of the answer in Mitchell's case may have been that creating a dangerous situation was a case of causing harm indirectly, and that Trespass was only appropriate for activity-negligence. But the principal motive was almost certainly a desire to impose vicarious liability, or something like it, on the owner of the coaches. We learn from one of the reports that the second defendant Scrivener was a servant and that Allestry, described in the record as an esquire, was not even present.[100] It can hardly be believed that esquires would be seen breaking in coach-horses in central London. But they were far more likely to be in a position to pay medical expenses than their coachmen. Whether it was truly a case of vicarious liability is obscure, and – since the case never came to trial – it was no business of the court in banc. It remains unclear from the reports whether Allestry had authorised the activity in London; Keble said he was only liable if he had done so so, Levinz that it would be presumed that he had. But the record conceals all this with the fiction that Allestry was present doing the act himself. Vicarious liability, like so much else in the law of tort, was kept off the record by fiction.

The desire to sue the master as well as the servant probably underlay a good many of the other cases, for obvious economic as well as evidential reasons.[101] But it was not the only possible reason for using Case. Others were the ability to focus the attention of the jury on the negligence in creating a situation rather than on the causation; the availability of a longer limitation period; and the means of evading the statutory rule of 1670 that in Trespass no more costs could be recovered than damages.[102] None of these reasons, it will be noted, had anything to do with substantive thinking; they were all procedural. Lawyers were not thinking in grand terms about how

---

[99] See above, pp. 62–63.

[100] The reports are unclear as to whether Allestry authorised the activity in London (and, since the case never came to trial, it cannot have been judicially known). Keble said he was only liable if he did so, Levinz that it would be presumed that he did so. The record conceals all this with the fiction that Allestry was present doing the act himself.

[101] For the evidential reasons, see the cases mentioned above, p. 49.

[102] For unsuccessful early attempts to evade the Act by framing actions as Case when they should have been Trespass *vi et armis*, see *Thornton* v. *Austen* (1693) cited at 1 Ld Raym. 188, *per* Gould sjt; *Hills* v. *Clerk* (1697) 1 Ld Raym. 188n.

the tort of negligence ought to develop in the age of reason, but about how to achieve the best outcome in the case in hand.

Two features of the movement from Trespass to Case support the thesis advanced earlier, that there was no discernible substantive difference between the two actions. The first is obvious on the face of the change. If liability in Trespass was indeed strict, or at least more strict than in Case, plaintiffs would hardly have preferred actions in which they had to allege and prove negligence. It is therefore reasonable to assume that the choice of form had nothing to do with the standard of liability. The second is a less direct inference from pleading practice. It seems from the limited evidence of books of entries that when the plaintiff's pleader in the later seventeenth century was troubled about the standard of care, and the difficulty of proving negligence, his mind turned not to Trespass but to the old device of the custom of the realm. Indeed, around the time of *Mitchell* v. *Allestry*, there seems to have been a period of experimentation with new customs of the realm imposing duties of care on drivers of carts[103] and masters of ships.[104] These were perhaps conceived of as extensions of the custom of the realm which imposed strict obligations on the common carrier,[105] although in these new cases there was no privity between the parties. The device enabled a plaintiff to particularise both the duty and the standard of care in his declaration. However, the 'custom of the realm' approach seemingly did not long survive, perhaps because in theory such a custom was necessarily common law and did not need to be pleaded.[106] The standard of care was therefore, once again, plunged into juridical darkness.

Our conclusion cannot in the nature of things be very precise. It may be that by 1700 judges and practitioners were beginning to recognise a new general principle, that 'a man must always use his own so as to do no harm

103 *Anon.* (*c.* 1675) B. & M. 562.

104 *Mors* v. *Slue* (1671) above, p. 48, n. 7 (custom of the realm to keep goods safely); *Gore* v. *Arnold* (1685) Girdler's entries, CUL MS Add 9430 (3), p. 315 (custom of the realm as to the use of buoys by ships at anchor; judgment for plaintiff); cf. *Hawbank* v. *Trim* (1697) in *J. Mallory*, Modern Entries, i. 297 (similar custom as to buoys, but intention and malice alleged).

105 Above, p. 58.

106 *Matthews* v. *Hopkin* (1665) 1 Sid. 245. (The court said it was nevertheless better to plead it.) Cf. *Beaulieu* v. *Finglam* (1401) B. & M. 557; *Anon.* (1582) Cro. Eliz. 10; *Rich* v. *Kneeland* (1613) Hob. 17; B. & M. 562 n. 20; Co. Litt. 110b. The same point arose in connection with attempts to plead mercantile customs as customs of the realm: *Vanheath* v. *Turner* (1621) Winch 24, *per* Hobart C. J.; *Woodward* v. *Rowe* (1666) 2 Keb. 105, 132; *Anon.* (1668) Hard. 485, *per* Hale C. B.; *Carter* v. *Downich* (1689) 3 Mod. Rep. 226; Carth. 83; Show. 127. By the mid-19th century, it became the practice in all negligence actions to lay a duty of care and its breach.

to his neighbour',[107] and was 'answerable for all mischief proceeding from his neglect or his actions, unless they were of unavoidable necessity'.[108] What precisely was meant by 'unavoidable necessity' (or 'inevitable accident') remained far from clear, and is still a matter of controversy. Negligence was still an elusive and non-technical notion, because it remained in most cases within the exclusive province of the ordinary laymen who sat on juries. Despite the dimness of our vision, however, the occasional insights provided by the case-law suggest that causation and fault were both treated as relevant factors in most tort actions. Expected standards of care may have varied from one situation to another, from one generation to another, perhaps even from one county to another. But jurymen could not ignore questions of fault when deciding whether to make someone answer in damages for the consequences of an accident.

107 *Turbervile* v. *Stamp* (1697) Pengelly's reports, BL MS. Add. 6722, fo. 78. Cf. above, p. 61.

108 *Mason* v. *Keeling* (1700) 1 Ld Raym. 606 at p. 607. Cf. the report of the same case in 12 Mod. Rep. 332: 'it was said to be part of the excellency of the law of England, that it leaves no man without a remedy, that has suffered a wrong through the fault of another'.

JAN HALLEBEEK

Negligence in Medieval Roman Law

I. Introduction

The Roman law of obligations, as found in the *Corpus iuris civilis* and interpreted and taught during the Middle Ages, certainly displays elements comparable to negligence as a ground of tortious liability in later Anglo-American law[1]. However, as will be shown below, making a selection from these elements in view of such a comparison, is not quite simple. The linguistic equivalent of the word negligence in Latin is *negligentia* and in the *Corpus iuris*, the legislation of Justinian (482–565), this notion *negligentia* sometimes occurs in a sense quite similar to the common law meaning of negligence. It may be used in the sense of 'carelessness' both in contractual and non-contractual contexts. The depositary, for example, is only liable for *culpa* in the sense of *desidia*, neglect, and *negligentia*, carelessness (Inst. 3.14.3). The lessee of a building burnt down is liable for having been *negligens* in selecting a slave to watch over the burning fire or for this slave having performed his duty *negligenter* (D. 9.2.27.9). Moreover, the one burning weeds on a windy day is liable for his *imperitia* or *negligentia* in case the fire spreads and causes damage to adjacent fields (D. 9.2.30.3). Thus, Justinianic law can be said to contain *negligentia* as a technical term in embryo, although it certainly is not the notion most frequently used in the *Corpus iuris* to refer to liability for careless conduct. It is only in later scholarship that some authors appear to adopt *negligentia* as a central

[1] See for contractual and delictual degrees of liability in medieval Roman law: *H. Dilcher*, Die Theorie der Leistungsstörungen bei Glossatoren, Kommentatoren und Kanonisten [Frankfurter wissenschaftliche Beiträge, 19], Frankfurt am Main 1960, *H. J. Hoffmann*, Die Abstufung der Fahrlässigkeit in der Rechtsgeschichte, Unter besonderer Berücksichtigung der culpa levissima [Neue kölner rechtswissenschaftliche Abhandlungen, 54], Berlin 1968, *R. König*, Das allgemeine Schadenersatzrecht im Mittelalter im Anschluss an die Lex Aquilia, Frankfurt am Main 1954 (unpublished dissertation), *H. Lange*, Schadenersatz und Privatstrafe in der mittelalterlichen Rechtstheorie [Forschungen zur neueren Privatrechtsgeschichte, 2], Münster/Köln 1955, *H. J. Wieling*, Interesse und Privatstrafe vom Mittelalter bis zum Bürgerlichen Gesetzbuch [Forschungen zur neueren Privatrechtsgeschichte, 15], Köln/Wien 1970 and *R. Zimmermann*, The law of obligations, Roman foundations of the civilian tradition, Cape Town/Wetton/Johannesburg, 1990.

notion of the law of obligations and use it to describe all kinds of liability according to both canon law and civil law[2]. Indeed the casuistry of the Digest and Codex offers examples of liability for negligence (carelessness) comparable to the several forms of negligence in early common law, such as negligence in performing a task under a contract calling the exercise of due care, negligence in looking after someone else's property, negligence in the custody of something dangerous or negligence in carrying out one's own activities.

However, two major complications arise from adopting this approach. In the first place according to Justinianic law the carelessness which results in liability is not of one kind only: there are a variety of degrees of carelessness: a particular delict gives rise to an obligation only observed and the same is true of each kind of contract. Moreover there were specific forms of liability in Roman law comparable to the strict liability known in contemporary law, i.e. where the defendant's conduct need not be culpable at all. Secondly, Justinianic law had no general remedy for harm unintentionally caused, such as our modern actions for non-performance and tort. Instead there were quite a number of different actions, each applying only to a specific kind of situation.

II. Divergent degrees of liability for careless acting

Negligentia is not the only notion employed in Roman law to describe liability for unintentional harm; other terms used include *culpa*, *diligentia*, *prudentia*, etc. Of all these, the notion *diligentia* appears to be the one most frequently used in the *Corpus iuris*. In later doctrine, however, it was *culpa*, which gradually grew into the most important technical term. As stated above, a simple notion of 'carelessness' cannot be found in the Roman sources, but only differentiations of carelessness; Roman law offers no unequivocal answer to the question how much care is required in social intercourse. The criteria outside the sphere of contract differ from those within it. Within the contractual context much depends on the interest one has in the contract. According to the so-called principle of utility, the party having the greater interest may be expected to observe a greater amount of care, than the party with a lesser interest, whereas parties with no interest at all are generally liable only for intentional harm. If we glance Roman law, and disregard for the moment the traces of pre-Justinianic disputes which are still visible in the Justinianic texts, it becomes clear that the required amount of care depends primarily upon the specific kind of legal

---

[2] See, for example, Andreas Bertoni (1621–1698), De negligentiis et omissionibus tractatus, Ferrara 1704.

relationship between the persons involved and that these various duties to take care can be described according to divergent social standards, phrased either subjectively or objectively. We can broadly distinguish three or four degrees of liability for carelessness[3].

1. *Diligentia quam suis* is a subjective standard, established as a criterion for liability in certain contractual obligations to look after someone else's property. The debtor, e.g. a depositary, is expected to be as careful of the other party's property as he usually is for his own. However, when the depositary's own goods are undamaged, but those entrusted to him cannot be restored, the glossators presume some kind of intent (*dolus praesumptus*), i.e. they here interpret in such a case the subjective criterion as an objective criterion. Apparently the depositary had not been as careful as he had as regards his own things. Thus, he should, as the glossator Azo Porcius († 1220) explains, be presumed to have acted with malicious intention[4]. The commentators make clear that there is a difference between this *dolus praesumptus* and a genuine malicious intent, *dolus verus*, because the presumption of malicious intent may be rebutted by proof. Moreover, according to Bartolus de Saxoferrato (1314–1357) the presumption may be nullified by a second, different presumption: if it is the question to safeguard all the things one is looking after, one may give priority to one's own more valuable things. Thus, the presumption of having acted fraudulently can be neutralized[5]. As a consequence, the lack of *diligentia quam suis* is a criterion for liability for unintentional harm, as long as this standard is not interpreted as a kind of malicious intent.

2. There are several objective standards of liability for carelessness.

[3] See for the tripartite division of culpa into lata, levis and levissima: *M. Talamanca*, Colpa civili (storia), Sez. II Diritto intermedio, in Enciclopedia del diritto, VII (Cir-Compa), Rome 1960, p. 523–534 and *F. Parisi*, Liability for negligence and judicial discretion [Research series, no. 82], Berkeley 1992, p. 84–95.

[4] Azo, Summa super Codicem, Pavia 1506 (reprint Turin 1966) ad C. 4.34 (p. 144a): Praesumitur autem lata culpa dolus circa depositarium, quia licet non sit adeo diligens, ut natura desiderat, uel ut homines consueuerunt esse diligentes, si tamen curam in deposito non prestet ad modum suum, id est, quem obseruat in rebus suis propriis, fraude non caret, nec enim salua fide minorem depositis rebus diligentiam prestabit, quam suis. Abesse enim presumitur bona fides, cum res suas habet saluas et res deposite non apparent, (...). Cf. also Azo, Lectura super Codicem, Paris 1577 (reprint Turin 1966) ad C. 4.65.1 n. 4 (p. 360).

[5] Cf. Bartolus, Opera, Basel 1588, In Secundam Partem Digesti Veteris, D. 16.2.32 n. 4 (p. 320): (...) qui res suas pretiosiores facit saluas et commodatas dimisit non tenetur et sic non adhibuit eam diligentiam in rebus alienis quam in suis. Sol. Eodem modo ibi non potuit omnes saluas facere, tamen sibi licitum fuit suas pretiosiores saluas facere et praeferre propter quod cessat presumptio fraudis. Vna ergo presumptio tollit aliam praesumptionem.

a) First of all, there is the moderate degree of liability which comes close to liability for intentional harm, i.e. that one is only expected to foresee what all people (*omnes*) can foresee. According to this standard one is only liable for *culpa* of a serious kind, which in the *Corpus iuris* is termed *culpa lata* (D. 50.16.213.2, D. 50.16.223pr and D. 22.6.9.2) or *magna* (*nimia*) *negligentia* (D. 50.16.226). During the Middle Ages *culpa lata* or *magna negligentia* is commonly put on a par with *dolus*, especially in contractual or quasi-contractual contexts[6]. The person who leaves the precious thing he borrowed in a public place by night, displays such a *culpa lata*, comparable to *dolus*[7]. The Accursian Gloss (1265) explains that the two are similar, but not identical. *Dolus* is fraud, *culpa lata* is foolishness[8]. The commentators usually employ the term *deviatio* in order to describe the several forms of liability. According to Bartolus *culpa lata* too is a specific kind of *deviatio*. However, in his doctrine *culpa lata* is no longer a merely objective standard. *Culpa lata* is the deviation from the care other people with the same profession (*professio*) and personal circumstances (*conditio*) normally observe[9]. This new definition of *culpa lata* was not generally accepted. Paulus de Castro († 1441), for example, sticks to the more traditional meaning of *culpa lata*[10]. Baldus de Ubaldis († 1400) seems to be inspired by Bartolus' definition. While commenting upon D. 24.3.24.5 he states that *culpa lata* is present, when one acts against what the *ratio* generally recommends to persons of one's own condition. From other passages it appears, however, that according to Baldus *culpa lata* is not a mere subjec-

---

6 The gloss 'late culpe' ad D. 50.16.223pr: quae dolo comparatur, ut supra depositi l. Quod Nerua (D. 16.3.32).

7 See: Odofredus, Lectura super Digesto Veteri, Lyons 1550–1552 (reprint Bologna 1967–1968), ad D. 13.6.5.2 (II fol. 53va): (...) Lata culpa est magna negligentia uerbi gratia commodaui tibi rem meam pretiosam tu credebas de nocte dimittere in publico posse hic fuit lata culpa et magna negligentia que comparatur dolo ut (...). A similar example can be found in Nicolaus de Tudeschis († 1445). Cf. the contribution of Dondorp in this volume p. 122.

8 See the gloss 'dolum esse' ad D. 16.3.32: id est dolo comparari, ut ubi quis de dolo tenetur, ibidem teneatur et de lata culpa; non autem est idem, cum dolus fit ex fraude; et lata culpa ex fatuitate; preterea dicitur similis esse (...) ergo non est idem, cum dicat Aristoteles: nihil est iden cui idipsum simile est. See also Azo (4, Summa) ad C. 4.34 (p. 144a): (...) alias alibi dicitur quod magna negligentia sit dolus ut ff. de uer. sig. l. Magna (D. 50.16.226). Et illud eodem modo expono, ut diximus. Nam si uere esset dolus, ergo ueniret in legem Corneliam quod lex negat ut (...).

9 Bartolus (5) ad D. 16.3.32 n. 17 (p. 322): (...) lata culpa est deuiatio incircumspecta ab ea diligentia quam communiter habent homines, qui sunt eiusdem professionis et conditionis.

10 Paulus de Castro, In Secundam Digesti Veteris Partem, Lyons 1553, D. 16.3.32 n. 4 (fol. 130 rb): Culpa lata est non facere illud quod quilibet alius facit uel facere solet: et sic deuiatio ab eo quod communiter omnes faciunt (...).

tive standard. In his commentary on C. 4.24.6 he interprets the word *omnes* in D. 50.16.223 not literally as 'all people', but as 'the majority, which has a comparable intellect and prudence'. *Culpa lata* is stupidity, gross negligence of a kind one finds in very few people[11]. Subsequently Baldus produces as examples a series of extremely stupid actions, all derived from the *Corpus iuris*: to navigate without a pilot, to set sail during a storm, to err enormously in the earnest money agreed upon, to refuse a cure from a wound, to overload a horse or mule or overexert it, to guarantee what one does not know, to sow out of the season, to keep disorderly accounts out of laziness or to abandon the goats one is tending in a wood.

b) It is a more severe degree of liability, when one is expected to foresee what a sensible person would foresee. This standard is termed *culpa* or *culpa levis* (D. 9.2.31). The glossators always interpret the word *culpa* in the sources as this *culpa levis*, unless this would clash with the principle of utility. *Culpa levis* is sometimes also classed as *negligentia* or described as a duty to observe *diligentia*. Such negligence can exist, for example, in leaving the key in the door when closing the office[12]. When describing *culpa levis*, Bartolus draws a distinction between things belonging to others (*res alienae*) and joint property (*res communes*), i.e. things which are communal either by accident (*incidenter*) or by convention (*ex conventione*). The *culpa levis* one is liable for in looking after another's property, consists in any deviation from the diligence of a careful person, whereas the *culpa levis* one is liable for in looking after communal property, coincides with the subjective standard of *diligentia quam suis*[13]. Baldus, on the con-

---

[11] Baldus, In Quartum et Quintum Codicis Libros Commentaria, Venice 1586, C. 4.24.6 n. 33 (fol. 68rb): (...) Ergo l. Latae culpe (D. 50.16.223) quae dicit quod late culpe finis est non intelligere quod omnes intelligunt, debet intelligi supple omnes uel maior pars, qui sunt similis ingenii uel prudentiae, uel dic quod lata culpa est stultitia et negligentia in qua reperiuntur pauci ita stulti uel ita negligentes, uel est quedam deuiatio a prudentia naturaliter insita (...).

[12] Azo (4, Summa) ad C. 4.37 (p. 150b): Item uenit in hanc actionem bona fides, ut dolus absit. Item culpa, si non prestet eam diligentiam quam in rebus suis adhibere solet (...); Odofredus (7) ad D. 13.6.5.2 (II fol. 53va): (...) Est leuis culpa negligentia ut potest uideri in scholari qui est ita negligens quod claudit scrinium et dimittit clauem in clauatura; unde leuis culpa est negligentia ut supra ad l. aquil. l. Scientiam § Qui cum aliter (D. 9.2.45.4); the gloss *contractus* ad D. 50.17.23: (...) et sic in his decem praestatur diligentia, sed in quibusdam exacta et in quibusdam exactissima (...).

[13] Bartolus (5) ad D. 16.3.32 n. 26 (p. 324): (...) culpa leuis in rebus alienis est deuiatio incircumspecta ab ea diligentia quam adhibent homines diligentes eiusdem conditionis et professionis. (...) Leuis culpa in communibus incidenter est deuiatio incircumspecta ab ea diligentia quam ipse deuians tunc temporis in rebus propriis adhibet. (...) leuis culpa in rebus communibus ex conuentione est deuiatio incircumspecta ab ea diligentia, quam ipse deuians tunc temporis in rebus propriis adhibere solebat, quando contrahebat, seu ante contractum.

trary, rejects the idea that *diligentia quam suis* can be used to determine the scope of *culpa levis* required in looking after communal things, because it is sometimes impossible to establish what a person's *diligentia quam suis* exactly is. If, for example, the person looking after joint property is a pauper with no property of his own, there can be no *diligentia quam suis*, because he has nothing of his own to take care of; yet it would be ridiculous if in consequence he were not liable for *culpa levis*[14].

c) A third and last objective standard exists in the duty to observe the utmost care and to act as a *diligentissimus paterfamilias*. According to this standard there would be liability for leaving borrowed property on the table instead of putting it away in a chest. The Gloss classifies this degree of liability as *culpa levissima*, a term which is used only sporadically in the *Corpus iuris*, mostly within the scope of the *lex Aquilia* (Cf. D. 9.2.44pr)[15]. The commentators define *culpa levissima*, just as the other categories of *culpa*, as a kind of *deviatio*. Also for *culpa levissima* Bartolus allows someone's circumstances and profession to determine the exact quantity of *exactissima diligentia* which may be expected[16]. Unlike Bartolus, Baldus interprets *culpa levissima* in a more objective way, i.e. that what may be expected from a *homo diligentissimus* is determined by what is laid down in the law as *diligentissimus*[17].

Apart from these subjective and objective standards, there are other, more specific degrees of liability for damages, especially in certain contractual relationships, such as *imperitia* (liability for lack of professional skill) and *custodia* (a liability primarely for theft by an outsider). In the sources *imperitia* is considered to be a kind of *culpa*[18], *custodia* is not. No matter how we qualify these standards, they come close to strict liability, i.e. a liability based on a certain capacity of the defendant. This holds also for other forms of liability which, like *imperitia* and *custodia*, exist irrespective

---

14 Baldus (11) ad C. 4.24.6 n. 37 (fol. 68va): (...) pone enim, quod de diligentia in suis nihil constet, uel pone quod est pauper qui nunquam proprium habuit, iam sequeretur quod iste non est in culpa leui, quod est ridiculum dicere.

15 See, for example, the gloss 'hoc ita' ad D. 13.6.18: (...) quod sicut diligentissimus teneatur et sic de leuissima culpa: ut supra in principio legis dixi. Cf. also Odofredus (7) ad D. 13.6.5.2 (II fol. 53va): (...) Leuissima culpa est si debuit esse diligentissimus et non fuit; ipse debebat ponere rem commodatam in archa non dimittere in disco; dimisit in disco leuissima culpa est; unde (...) diligentissimus est qui custodit rem a dolo lata et leui et leuissima (...).

16 Bartolus (5) ad D. 16.3.32 n. 27 (p. 324): Leuissima culpa est deuiatio incircumspecta ab ea diligentia quam habent homines diligentes et diligentissimi eiusdem conditionis et professionis.

17 Baldus (11) ad C. 4.24.6 n. 39 (fol. 68vb): (...) Leuissima culpa est deuiatio a legis dispositione in eo, quod lex disponit esse diligentissimum (...).

18 D. 19.2.9.5.

of any negligence on the part of the defendant, such as the *receptum*-liability of the *caupo*, *nauta* and *stabularius* and the liability for damages caused by animals (*actio de pauperie*). Although strict liability includes liability for carelessness (one liable for *custodia* is also liable for *culpa levis*), strict liability itself falls outside the scope of this volume.

Consequently, for a comparison with negligence we should focus on the subjective standard of *diligentia quam suis* (i.e. apart from the presumption of *dolus*, when the damage must also be presumed to be inflicted intentionally) and the objective standards *culpa levis* and *culpa levissima*; *culpa lata*, because of its resemblance to *dolus*, is comparable rather with intentional harm, than with unintentional harm.

III. The lack of a general legal remedy for unintentional harm

1. Justinianic law

In modern common law negligence is the most generalized form of distinct tortious liability. The requirements are a duty of care, the breach of that duty and a causal connection between this breach of duty and the resulting damage. An equally general tortious liability is known in most of the continental systems of law. However, such a concept is not derived from Roman law, at any rate not directly. In Hugo Grotius (1583–1645) we find a general doctrine of tort, but it still remains to be seen whether the roots of this doctrine can be located anywhere in Roman law[19]. In both classical and Justinianic Roman law compensation for contractual and extra-contractual damage is not generalised: the degree of liability, the assessment of damages and the causal connection to be shown depends greatly on the action specific to the case under dispute. The remedy chosen inevitably depends on the facts of the case as a specific contract or delict within the restrictive system of sources of obligations.

2. Medieval interpretation: the specific delicts are not replaced by a general doctrine

Basically, this was not altered in medieval doctrine. The divergent delictual actions retain their own specific features.

---

[19] See Hugo Grotius, De iure belli ac pacis libri tres (ed. *B. J. A. de Kanter-Van Hettinga Tromp*, Leyden 1939, reprint with additions Aalen 1993) II, cap. 17 (p. 427–434).

a) Justinianic law was characterised by the fact each delictual action had a different standard of liability. For the *actio furti* (theft) a malicious intent (*dolus*) was required as it was for the *actio iniuriarum* (injury of freemen), but for the *actio aedium incensarum* (arson) negligence was sufficient (D. 47.9.9), and for the *actio legis Aquiliae* (damage to property) even the slightest negligence (*culpa levissima*)[20]. These differences are preserved and can clearly be traced in medieval doctrine[21].

b) Given the difference in liability required for the actions of theft and damage to property, we are dealing here with two separate delicts each with a delictual action of its own. The remedy for damages to property does not include the remedy for theft[22].

c) Other specific rules are also preserved. The rule that a wrongdoer who denies that he caused the damage should – if proven culpable – be condemned to pay double the regular compensation[23], applies in the *Corpus iuris* only to *damnum iniuria datum*, not to other delicts. This was not altered during the Middle Ages. Even in late medieval treatises on procedural law, such as that of Johannes Crispus de Montibus (Giovanni Crispo de Monti or Crispomonti, *saec.* XV), liability under the *lex Aquilia* is still subject to litiscrescence[24].

---

[20] D. 9.2.44pr: In lege Aquilia et leuissima culpa uenit.

[21] See the gloss 'dolo' ad D. 9.2.32pr: Furtum autem non fit sine dolo.; Odofredus (7) ad D. 9.2.32 (I fol. 275va): Sed furtum sine dolo non committitur infra pro socio l. Merito (D. 17.2.51) (...). See also the gloss 'criminalem' ad C. 3.35.3, Odofredus (7) ad D. 9.2.44 (I fol. 276va), Odofredus, Lectura super Codice, Lyons 1552 (reprint Bologna 1968–1969) ad C. 3.35.3 (I fol. 178ra–b), Roffredus († after 1243), Libelli iuris ciuilis, Avignon 1500 (reprint Turin 1968), fol. 24va.

[22] See Joannes de Platea († 1427), Super Institutionibus, [s.l.] 1532, ad Inst. 4.3. n. 3 (fol. 81va): Nunc quero an furtum contineatur appellatione damni dati ut actio et pena que datur pro damno dato per legem et statutum, detur etiam pro furto facto. Et respondet hic i. glo. Nota quod large accipiendo damnum, prout est diminutio patrimonii, comprehendit etiam furtum, sed stricte sumendo et proprie aliud est damnum et aliud est furtum. Et ideo pro unoquoque est adinuenta actio et pena scilicet actio legis aquilie et furti, nam damnum est cum rei corruptione, ut dicit glossa in lege Qui occidit § In hac ff. eo (D. 9.2.30.3) et furtum est cum rei amotione ut probatur text. in l. Seruus seruum § Si oliuam ff. ad l. aquil. (D. 9.2.27.25) et tetigi supra de oblig. que ex quasi delict. nascu. in § Furtorum (Inst. 4.1.3).

[23] See the maxim 'infitiando lis crescit in duplum' (D. 9.2.2.1, Inst. 4.16.19 and C. 3.35.4).

[24] Johannes Crispus de Montibus, Tractatus admodum elegans, in Jason, De actionibus, Lyons 1554, n. 170 fol. 175va; Bartolus explains the rule as a punishment for the defendant, because by denying he aggravates the plaintiff's claim with a burdon of proof. Bartolus, Opera, Basel 1588, Consilia, Quaestiones et Tractatus, Quaestio 8 n. 17 (p. 229): Secundum fundamentum est, quod tunc negans punitur, quando per negationem grauabit aduersarium onere probandi, ita quod aduersarius habeat necesse probare per testes, uel aliis legitimis probationibus; alias non puniretur, ut negans, ut (...).

d) The assessment of damages to property according to the chapters I and III of the *lex Aquilia* also remains intact. According to chapter I, which covers the killing of a slave or a grazing animal, the wrongdoer should pay *quanti id in eo anno plurimi fuit* (the highest value in the previous year). According to chapter III, covering the wounding of a slave or a grazing animal and other property damage, the wrongdoer should pay *quanti ea res erit in diebus triginta proximis* (the value in the nearest thirty days)[25]. The glossators see in these methods of determining compensation, especially the assessment of chapter I, a clear trace of the penal character of the *actio legis Aquiliae*. Even in cases where the remedy at first sight seems to be purely reipersecutory and the wrongdoer is not penalized financially, where, for example, the damaged property had only enhanced in value during the period previous to the damaging act, the action still retains its penal character[26] and, in consequence, its passive intransmissibility. The same holds good for cases of physical injury inflicted upon freemen[27], where the civilians were willing to grant the *actio legis Aquiliae utilis*. Here, too, the use of the remedy may seem reipersecutory, because the Gloss speaks only of claiming the expenses for medical care and compensation for lack of income and loss of future support[28].

---

[25] See D. 9.2.2pr, D. 9.2.27.5 and Inst. 4.3.13–14.

[26] Azo (4, Summa) ad C. 3.35 (p. 91): (...) Penalis autem hec actio est sui natura saltem propter repetitionem preteriti temporis, licet quandoque non exigat penam, ut si res plurimi est cum datur damnum quam prius (...).

[27] Literature: *R. Feenstra*, Théories sur la responsabilité civile en cas d'homicide et en cas de lésion corporelle avant Grotius, in Etudes d'histoire du droit privé à Pierre Petot, [Paris] 1959, p. 157–171, reprinted with additions in *R. Feenstra*, Fata iuris romani, Etudes d'histoire du droit [Leidse Juridische reeks, 13], Leyden 1974, p. 323–337, *R. Feenstra*, L'actio legis Aquiliae utilis en cas d'homicide chez les glossateurs, in *J. E. Spruit* (ed.), Maior viginti quinque annis, Essays in commemoration of the sixth lustrum if the Institute for Legal History of the University of Utrecht, Assen 1979, p. 45–65, reprinted in *R. Feenstra*, Le droit savant au moyen âge et sa vulgarisation [Collected studies series, 236] as no. VIII, and translated into German in *E. J. H. Schrage* (ed.), Das römische Recht im Mittelalter [Wege der Forschung, 635], Darmstadt 1987, p. 203–232 and *H. Kaufmann*, Rezeption und usus modernus der actio legis Aquiliae [Forschungen zur neueren Privatrechtsgeschichte, 5], Köln-Graz 1958, p. 19–22.

[28] The gloss 'liber homo' ad D. 9.2.13pr: liber homo habet actionem, ut supra e. Qua actione § Si quis in colluctatione (D. 9.2.7.4.). sed an aget hoc ob futuras operas? Responde non secundum quosdam, ut arg. infra e. Quemadmodum § Idem Labeo (D. 9.2.29.3). Sed hoc cessat in fructu immature collecto, ut infra e. Si servus servum § Si olivam (D. 9.2.27.25) et in servo instituto herede qui occiditur a alio, ut infra e. Inde Neratius in prin. (D. 9.2.23pr), nam habetur ratio futuri comodi. Item in opera etiam videtur idem quod agatur ex futura opera, ut supra ti. i Ex hac. (D. 9.1.3).

The assessment of damages according to the chapters I and III of the *lex Aquilia*, solely applicable to cases of *damnum iniuria datum* and not to one of the other delicts, can still be found in practice-orientated jurists of the fifteenth century such as Baptista de Sancto Blasio (Giovanni Battista de Sanbiagio, 1425–1492)[29] and Johannes Crispus de Montibus[30].

3. Medieval interpretation: the emergence of a general but subsidiary remedy for damages

As we have seen, medieval Roman law did not develop a general action for tort and non-performance in place of the more specific actions of the *Corpus iuris*. It is also clear that Roman law in its Justinianic form did not cover all kinds of extra-contractual damage, but only specific kinds of patrimonial loss. Where the Roman texts offered no satisfactory solution, one could – as a matter of fact – seek safety elsewhere. About the time Roman law was received, a general action for reparation was already developed in the practice of the courts[31], and canon law acknowledged a duty to make compensation wherever the damage was inflicted culpably, either in the *forum internum* or the *forum externum*, for the mere pretext that the defendant fell into sin (*praetextus peccati*) would give the ecclesiastical court jurisdiction. However, to yield openly to the demand for indigenous and canon law remedies would undermine the practicability and authority of Justinian's legislation. So the civilians tried to fill the unwanted gaps of the restrictive Justinianic system of sources of obligation without replacing the delictual actions named in the Roman texts by a general action.

In order to fill the gaps, medieval doctrine extended the use of the *actio legis Aquiliae*, especially in the shape of *actiones utiles* or *actiones in factum*. This could serve as a means of recovery of certain forms of patrimonial loss. The Institutes had allowed an *actio in factum* after the example of the *actio legis Aquiliae* where damage was caused by setting free another man's slave out of pity and the slave subsequently fled[32], and in medieval doctrine the *actio legis Aquiliae utilis* could be used to claim compensation for the lack of income or future support of a freeman who was wounded[33] or killed[34]. However, in the case of setting free a slave the

---

29 Baptista de Sancto Blasio, De actione et eius natura, in Tractatus illustrium iurisconsultorum, Tom. III, Pars II, Venice 1585, fol 43–56, n. 82 (fol. 55vb).

30 Johannes Crispus de Montibus (24) n. 170 (fol. 175va).

31 See *G. Rotondi*, Dalla 'Lex Aquilia' all'art. 1151 Cod. civ., Ricerche storico-dogmatiche, in Rivista di diritto commerciale, 14 (1916), p. 942–970 and 15 (1917), p. 236–295, reprinted in *G. Rotondi*, Scritti giuridici, II, Milan 1922, p. 465–578.

32 See Inst. 4.3.16.

33 See the gloss 'liber homo' ad D. 9.2.13pr.

patrimonial loss still consisted in the loss of a corporeal object, and in the second case, too, the plaintiff was deprived of a corporeal asset resulting from an act comparable to the wounding or killing of a slave. So the extended use of the *actio legis Aquiliae* only reached cases where the loss is related to a specific object owned by the plaintiff or a comparable situation. It did not cover all cases of purely patrimonial loss as such.

There are, however, some texts in Justinian's Digest dealing with recovery of a purely patrimonial loss as such, i. e. not related to a specific corporeal asset of the plaintiff. In D. 48.10.25 the damage results from falsifying documents, whereas in D. 48.10.32.1 it results from tampering with weights and measuring rods. The first text speaks about an *actio poenalis in factum*, the second only mentions a liability for the *duplum* without referring to a specific action. Apparently Roman law offered some kind of protection here. But which Roman action was meant? The Accursian Gloss describes the *actio poenalis in factum* as a remedy for the plaintiff's interest (*ad interesse*) and does likewise for the remedy granted for the *duplum* in the second case[35]. Commenting upon D. 17.2.56 the Gloss qualifies both actions as *actio in factum* and explains that this is a civil remedy resulting from a public delict[36]. In later doctrine the *actio in factum ad interesse* granted in D. 48.10.25 and D. 48.10.32.1, was presented as resulting from a more general rule of law or as a specific application of a more general *actio in factum*. According to Bartolus it is a rule of law that every Roman delict gives rise to a civil *actio in factum* against the wrongdoer[37]. Bartolus' opinion seems to have been generalized by some late medieval jurists: an action, called an *actio in factum*, additional to the state's or the victim's claim for a penalty, is available for every public or private delict found in the Roman sources or laid down in municipal statutes[38].

---

34 See Guillelmus Durantis († 1296), Speculum iudiciale, Basel 1574 (reprint Aalen 1975), Liber IV Part. IV De iniuriis et damno data n. 3 (I p. 512).

35 See the gloss 'penali' ad D. 48.10.25: Ad interesse ut infra eod. Hodie i. (D. 48.10.32.1) (...); the gloss 'condemnatur' ad D. 48.10.32.1: Qua actione? Responde: condictione ex hac lege uel dic actione in factum, quae alias datur pro simplo eius, quod interest ut supra eo. l. Qui nomine (D. 48.10.25) (...).

36 The Accursian gloss 'publicis' ad D. 17.2.56: Ex quibus agitur ciuiliter in factum ut infra de fal. Qui nomine (D. 48.10.25). Further literature: *Lange* (1), p. 12, *Wieling* (1), p. 241 ff.

37 For this opinion Bartolus refers to the texts of D. 48.10.25 and D. 17.2.56. Cf. Bartolus, Opera, Basel 1588, In Secundam Partem Digesti Novi, ad D. 47.8.2 n. 1 (p. 373): (...) Nam cum regula sit quod ex quocunque maleficio potest quis accusari criminaliter, ex eodem potest agi in factum ciuiliter l. Qui nomine infra de fal. (D. 48.10.25) et supra pre soc. l. Nec quicquam (D. 17.2.56). Ergo semper posset proponi ciuilis et criminalis quia ex eadem lege. Cf. also Bartolus (37) ad D. 48.10.25 (p. 508).

This *actio in factum* is much more general than any action in the restricted Roman system, but still not as general as the canon law obligation to make restitution: it still requires an applicable legal provision of some kind, whereas canon law, especially in the *forum internum*, will impose a duty to restore whenever conscience so demands.

However, it is not clear yet whether the *actio in factum ad interesse* of D. 48.10.25 and D. 48.10.32.1 extends to cases of actionable negligence. According to the glossators there must be a public crime or penal action for reprehensible behaviour for this civil remedy in damages to be available. In D. 17.2.56 three actions are mentioned, viz. the *actio iniuriarum* (for insult), the *actio vi bonorum raptorum* (for robbery) and the *actio servi corrupti* (for corrupting a slave). This seems to be an open category, the remedies just mentioned being merely examples, because the text continues by adding 'and in similar actions'[39], but the text of D. 17.2.56 refers explicitly to intentional harm only and it is questionable whether or not liability for negligence would also be covered by the *actio in factum ad interesse*.

However, according to Bartolus, the *actio in factum ad interesse* lies against the magistrate in D. 50.13.6 who pronounced an incorrect judgement and by doing so made the litigation his own[40]. Bartolus speaks here of a magistrate who is *negligens* in upholding the law, whereas according to D. 50.13.6 this magistrate is understood to have committed some kind of offence, albeit out of imprudence (*imprudentia*)[41], which is qualified as

---

38 See, for example, Angelus de Aretino († 1451), De maleficiis tractatus, Lyons 1551, cap. Et querelam n. 11 (fol. 12ra): Nam de unoquoque crimine publico uel priuato oritur duplex actio: una ad commodum iniuriati, que dicitur actio in factum et uocatur actio ciuilis, alia (...) que dicitur criminalis.

39 After all, some actions for outrageous behaviour are nominated (famose), others are not. See this gloss of Azo ad D. 17.2.56, in Bamberg Jur. 11 fol. 206ra, München Clm 3887 fol. 164vb, Paris, BN lat. 4451 fol. 126vb, Paris, BN lat. 4459 fol. 165va, Biblioteca Vaticana, vat. lat. 1408 fol. 193rb: Turpes uocat actiones que famose sunt uel non famose dum tantum ex turpi causa descendant, ut serui corrupti. nec enim omnis turpis actio est famosa ut notantur C. de inoff. t.l. Fratres uel sorores (C. 3.28.27) et de dignitatibus l. Neque sa. (C. 12.1.2). az.

40 This is not justified by the text of D. 17.2.56 itself, but by the fact that such a behaviour is a penal act under the title 'ut differentes iudices audire etc.'. See Bartolus (37) ad D. 50.13.6 n. 2 (p. 683): (...) alias autem regulariter puto, quod iudex negligens facere alteri iustitiam, teneatur actione in factum ad interesse, non per hanc legem et similes, set per tit. in Authent. ut differ. iudic. (Nov. 86 = Aut. 9.10) in quo imponitur iudici neglegenti poena criminalis. Et regula est, quod ubicunque quis potest accusare criminaliter, ex eodem facto datur actio ciuilis ad interesse l. Qui nomine supra de fals. (D. 48.10.25) et supra pro socio l. Nec quicquam (D. 17.2.56) (...).

41 See for the magistrate acting ex imprudentia also Raimundus de Pennaforte († 1275), Summa de poenitentia, II.5.35, p. 511 in the edition by *X. Ochoa* and *A. Diez* (Universa Bibliotheca iuris 1, Tomus B, Rome 1976).

quasi-malificium. Thus, the *actio in factum ad interesse* covers not only cases of damage done *ex turpi causa*, but also of damage *ex imprudentia*. Such imprudence resembles actionable negligence, as becomes clear from the examples of liability *ex imprudentia* given by the Gloss[42]. This leads to the conclusion that liability for unintentional harm was indeed incorporated within the *actio in factum ad interesse*. However, liabitity *ex imprudentia* never during the Middle Ages supplanted the degrees of unintentional harm, such as *diligentia quam suis*, *culpa levis* or *culpa levissma*, and the *actio in factum ad interesse* or the civil *actio in factum* resulting from a public delict never took the place of the specific delictual actions for unintentional harm.

IV. Forms of liability for unintentional damages

If we start from the Justinianic subdivision of the sources of obligation into the several contracts, quasi-contracts, delicts and quasi-delicts, we can ask which of them cover liability for unintentional harm. Since the notion 'unintentional harm' is used here in the sense of 'caused by carelessness', rather than by *dolus* (*culpa lata*), *fraus* or *turpitudo*, we shall not here discuss the delicts of *furtum* (theft) and *iniuria* (injury of freemen) which both require a malicious intent on the part of the wrongdoer.

However, one observation has to be made here. Some kinds of negligence in English common law have no corresponding and comparable action for compensation in Justinianic law. For example, nuisances resulting from smells and the threat of flood or fire may in common law be ascribed to negligence in the custody or control of something dangerous or to negligence in carrying out one's own activities[43]. Here Roman law sometimes offers solutions outside the law of obligations. If the nuisance comes from privately owned property, such as smoke coming from a dairy, one can bring an *actio negatoria* against the wrongdoer in order to force him to admit in court that he lacks a servitude to act in the way he was

---

[42] The gloss 'per imprudentiam' ad D. 50.13.6 gives a number of examples, but the following anonymous pre-Accursian gloss gives much more: the gloss 'per imprudentiam' ad D. 50.13.6 in Paris BN lat. 4455 fol. 170vb: Tenetur quis ex imprudentia ut al. s. de neg. g. Nam et ser. § f. (D. 3.5.20.3) et s. quod quisque iu. l. ii (D. 2.2.2), s. ad l. aquil. Id. iuris § Mulionem (D. 9.2.8.1), s. loc. Si quis fund. § Celsus (D. 19.2.9.5) et l. Item queritur § Si gemma (D. 19.2.13.5), s. como Si ut § Set interdum (D. 13.6.5.7) et s. de offo. pre. Illicitas § Sic. medico (D. 1.18.6.7), s. pro soc. Et quicquid (D. 17.2.21), Ex contrario (D. 17.2.22), De illo (D. 17.2.23), s. loc. Videamus in prin. (D. 19.2.11pr). ad hanc l. facit s. de penis Si quis (D. 48.19.30), Inst. de ob. que quasi ex na. (Inst. 4.5), s. de iudic. Si filius f. (D. 5.1.15), s. de peculio Licet § Id. (D. 15.1.3.11).

[43] Cf. the contributions of Baker, Birks and Ibbetson in this volume.

acting (D. 8.5.8.5). If the nuisance comes from property not privately owned, such as damp coming from a dunghill made on the public road and now penetrating the wall, one can seek an *interdictum* from the praetor, i.e. a prohibition against the unwanted activities (D. 8.5.17.2)[44].

1. Contractual liability for unintentional harm

a) commodatum

The liability of the borrower is not undisputed in the sources. Some texts point towards a *culpa (levis)* liability (D. 13.6.5.3 and D. 50.17.23), whereas other texts seem to be in favour of a more severe liability, i.e. the duty to observe an *exactissima diligentia* (D. 13.6.18pr). The principle of utility enables us to dinstinguish three types of borrowing and so account for difference in liability traceable in the sources. First there is the normal type of contract, i.e. the *commodatum gratia accipientis*, where the borrower's liability is extended to observe an *exactissima diligentia*. Secondly, there is the *commodatum gratia utriusque*, where the borrower is only liable for *culpa levis* (D. 13.6.18pr). In the third place there is the *commodatum gratia tantum dantis*, where the borrower's degree of liability is reduced even more, i.e. to *dolus* (D. 13.6.5.10, D. 13.6.10.1 and D. 13.6.13). Early glossators use the notion *exactissima diligentia* to describe the borrower's liability, later glossators speak about *culpa levissima*[45]. The commentators follow the Gloss, but make a further distinction within the normal type of loan, i.e. in the interest of the borrower, depending on whether the borrower himself had asked for the use of the object or the lender had offered to let him have it. In the first case the borrower is liable for *culpa levissima*, in the latter case only for *culpa lata*[46].

---

44 See for the Roman approach towards casuistry comparable to cases of nuisance also *F. H. Lawson/B. S. Markesinis*, Tortious liability for unintentional harm in the Common law and Civil law, Cambridge 1982, I, p. 38–39.

45 See the gloss 'diligentem' ad D. 13.6.5.5: tenetur enim regulariter omnis commoditarius de lata, leui et leuissima ut plene dices infra ea. l. Interdum (D. 13.6.5.10).

46 See Bartolus (5) ad D. 16.3.32 n. 35 (p. 326): (...) Aut de directa. Et tunc aut commodans ultro se obtulit ad commodandum et commoditarius non tenetur nisi solummodo de dolo et lata culpa ut supra commo. l. Si ut certo § Interdum in fi. (D. 13.6.5.10) secundum ueram lecturam. Aut se non obtulit, sed fuit a commodatario requisitus et tunc uenit leuissima l. Si ut certo § Nunc uidendum (D. 13.6.5.2) et l. In rebus (D. 13.6.18); Baldus, Tomus Secundus in Digestum Vetus, Lyons 1551, ad D. 13.6.5.10 n. 1 (fol. 73ra): (...) commodatarius teneatur de leui et leuissima culpa, oportet quod commodatum fiat rogatum ipsius commodatarius; alias si commodator offert commodatum ipsi commodario et tunc commoditarius non tenetur nisi de dolo, subaudi et lata culpa ut hic. (...).

b) depositum

The liability of the depositary is no less unquestioned in the sources. Some texts speak about *culpa lata* (C. 4.34.1), but according to Justinian's Institutes the depositary is liable for *dolus* only (Inst. 4.1.4.3). The glossators agree he is liable for *diligentia quam suis* and *nimia* (*magna*) *negligentia*. According to Odofredus de Denariis († 1265) the depositary is only liable for *dolus* and *culpa lata*, unless otherwise agreed upon between parties. If he had offered himself as depositary, he would also be liable for *culpa levissima*[47]. The commentators apply the principle of utility more consistently. For the normal kind of the *depositum*, i.e. where the contract was entered into in the interest of the depositor, they assume liability only for *culpa lata*. If the *depositum* took place in the interest of the depositary or if the latter offered himself as such, he is also liable for *culpa levissima*[48]. The outcome is that liability for unintentional harm only occurs in special kinds of *depositum*, not in the usual contract made in the interests of the depositor and at his request[49].

c) pignus

The pledgee is liable for *culpa levis* in looking after the property pledged with him. The *Liber pauperum* of Vacarius († after 1198) relies on D. 13.7.13.1 to impose liability for *culpa levissima*[50], but Azo[51] and the Gloss stick to liability for *culpa levis*[52].

---

[47] Odofredus (21) ad C. 4.34.1 n. 1 (I fol. 238ra): Or segnori, nota quod depositarius tenetur de dolo et lata culpa ut ff. eo. l. Quod Nerua (D. 16.3.32). Aliquando de leui et leuissima tenetur, puta si hoc conuenit ut ff. eo. l. i § Conuenerit (D. 16.3.1.6). Aliquando tenetur de leuissima, puta si conuenit uel obtulit ut ff. eo. l. i § Sepe (D. 16.3.1.35). Cf. also Odofredus (7) ad D. 12.1.4 n. 1 (II fol. 6ra) and ad D. 13.6.5.2 (II fol. 53va) and the Accursian gloss 'contractus' ad D. 50.17.23: (...) sed licet dixerim in deposito solum dolum praestari, secus est quandoque; quia uenit etiam leuissima culpa, ut si se obtulit deposito ut supra depo. l. i § Sepe (D. 16.3.1.35).

[48] Bartolus (5) ad D. 16.3.32 n. 30 (p. 325): Aut de directa: et tunc aut depositarius se obtulit et tenetur de leuissima (...). Secundo casu, quando gratia depositarii tantum depositarius est obligatus actione directa tenetur de leuissima (...).

[49] The Corpus iuris civilis is not clear as regards the question whether in case of culpa levissima the depositary may nevertheless be liable under the lex Aquilia. For medieval law such a liability does not seem to be very likely in view of the increasing importance the civilians attribute to the principle of utility.

[50] *F. de Zulueta* (ed.), The Liber Pauperum of Vacarius, London 1927 [The Publications of the Selden Society, 44], Lib IV tit. 20, gloss ad D. 13.6.5.2 (p. 127): In commodato uenit dolus et culpa leuis et lata et leuissima. In pignore eadem et ideo dicit infra (D. 13.7.13.1): uenit ut in commodo; Lib. IV tit. 21, gloss ad C. 4.24.5

d) emptio/venditio

The vendor is under a duty to provide the purchaser with the possession of the object sold. In performing this obligation he is according to Justinianic law liable for *culpa levis* (see Inst. 3.23.3, D. 18.1.68pr, D. 18.4.3 and D. 19.1.13.16). The glossators base this liability on the principle of utility[53].

e) locatio/conductio

The lessor may be liable for *culpa* if negligent in selecting what he puts at the lessee's disposal (*culpa in eligendo*) or in being unaware of things he should know. The lessor of a muleteer is liable if he selected an inexperienced slave (D. 9.2.27.34) or a slave which could be expected to cause damages (D. 19.2.60.7). The lessor of vessels is liable when he did not know that the vessel he provided was leaky (D. 19.2.19.1)[54]. The lessee and tenant are liable for *culpa levis* if they cannot restore the property in good condition. The tenant, for example, is liable for damage to the land, if he abandons it on seeing soldiers approach (D. 19.2.13.7). Some texts in the *Corpus iuris* may point towards a more severe liability of the *conductor*, viz. for *culpa levissima*. Two texts, D. 19.2.25.7 and Inst. 3.24.5, use the word *dilligentissimus*. The glossators interpret these texts in different ways. Martinus Gosia († after 1157) explains the occurence of the superlative in both texts on the ground that they both deal with the exceptional

(p. 129) sine uitio suo. Quidam dicunt sufficere creditori probare se perdidisse. v. non sufficere nisi sine dolo culpa etiam leuissima probet se amisisse.

51 Azo (4, Summa) ad C. 4.24 (p. 127b): (...) Item uenit in pignoratitiam dolus, et lata culpa et leuis, non leuissima, quia utriusque gratia contrahitur pignus (...).

52 The gloss 'sine vitio' ad C. 4.24.5: idest sine dolo uel lata culpa uel leui, de quibus tenetur creditor ut inst. qui. mo. re contrahi. obl. § fi (Inst. 3.14.4). et ff. e. Si cum uenderet § fin. (D. 13.7.13.1) et l. Ea (D. 13.7.14) et infra de pig. l. Sicut (C. 8.13.19); the gloss 'exactam' ad Inst. 3.14.4: proprie ponitur pro superlatiuo ut supra eod. § At is (Inst. 3.14.2 i.m.) non enim tenetur de leuissima ut ff. de pignoraticia actione l. Si conueniri § Venit (D. 13.7.13.1) et l. seq. (D. 13.7.14).

53 Azo (4, Summa) ad C. 4.48 (p. 158b): (...) quia ex natura contractus uenditor de dolo et lata culpa et leui tenetur non de casu (...). Odofredus (7) ad D. 13.6.5.2 (II fol. 53va): si autem contractus celebratur gratia utriusque ut in emptione indubitanter tenetur quis de dolo et lata et leui culpa ut ibi. sed ubi contrahitur gratia utriusque etc. (D. 13.6.5.2 i.f.) ut infra de reg. iur. l. Contractus (D. 50.17.23); see also Odofredus (7) ad D. 18.6.2.1 (II fol. 104va) and the gloss 'contractus' ad D. 50.17.23.

54 For the interpretation of this lack of knowledge as culpa see the gloss 'in quo herba mala' ad D. 19.2.19.1: (...) quia in doliis ignorare non debuit, in pascuis uero iuste potuit ignorare, nam que facilius sciri possunt, si ignorentur, grauius cohercentur.

case of transport of fragile goods. Consequently the utmost care is required in performing the contract. Two different explanations are given by Azo, first that the superlative is a mistake for the positive, and secondly that the text refers to a person who is *dilligentissimus*, i.e. one who usually takes the utmost care of his own goods[55]. The second solution was adopted in later times by Albericus de Rosate († 1354)[56]. The Accursian Gloss, however, chose to follow Azo's first solution: the superlative 'the most careful' has to be read as the positive 'careful'[57]. Some commentators return to the opinion of Martinus, rejected by the Gloss, and interpret the superlative as a more severe degree of liability, justified by the exceptional circumstances[58].

f) mandatum

The Roman sources are not unequivocal as regards the liability of the mandatory. Some texts point towards *culpa levis* (D. 17.1.22.11, D. 17.1.8.10 and D. 50.17.23), others towards *culpa lata* (D. 17.1.8.10 and C. 4.35.21). There was a dispute amongst early glossators about the interpretation of a text in the Codex. According to C. 4.35.13 the mandatory is liable for all kinds of carelessness (*omnis culpa*). In view of the principle of utility Martinus interpreted this *omnis culpa* as *culpa levis*. However, other glossators, such as Bulgarus de Bulgarinis († 1166), Johannes Bassianus († 1197) and Azo, interpreted the text without regard to the principle of utility and considered the words *omnis culpa* to include *culpa levissima*. The Gloss followed the latter opinion, i.e. that the mandatory in C. 4.35.13 is liable for all negligence[59], while treating the text as dealing with an exceptional case[60], where the principle of utility cannot be decisive,

---

[55] Azo (4, Summa) ad C. 4.65 (p. 171a) (...) Et dixerunt quidam speciale esse in his rebus que portantur, ut ueniat leuissima culpa, uel forte illud superlatiuum diligentissimus ponitur pro positiuo, certum est enim quod iste contractus utriusque celebratur gratia; leuem tamen debet cohercere culpam (...). Vel est intelligendum de eo, qui diligentissimus erat in suis.

[56] Albericus de Rosate, Commentarii in secundam Digesti Veteris partem, Venice 1585 (reprint Bologna 1974) ad D. 19.2.25.7 (fol. 157ra): Qui locat operam tenetur de dolo, lata culpa, leui et non leuissima h.d. et nota glossam hic positam et reproba opinionem Mart. quae est contra tex. qui dicit idem in ceteris rebus. Vel dic quod loquitur in eo qui diligentissimus est in suis ut notat Azo in summa eodem titulo Item adiuuante culpe. etc.

[57] See the gloss 'diligentissimus' ad D. 19.2.25.7 and the gloss 'diligentissimus' ad Inst. 3.24.5.

[58] See Paulus de Castro (10) ad D. 19.2.25.7 (fol. 147rb) (...) Sed certe aliquando fallit hoc, scilicet quando quis asserit se peritum et uidetur asserere se peritum ut quando locat operas tanquam artifex, quia tunc tenetur etiam de leuissima culpa, ut c. man. l. A procuratore (C. 4.35.13) et intelligitur l. Si quis fundum § pen. supra eo. (D. 19.2.9.5) et etiam iste §.

because *mandatum* deviates in many respects from the other contracts[61]. Bartolus, followed by Baldus, maintains that the degree of liability depends on the actual services to be rendered. Some require only little effort, and consequently only a moderate amount of care, such as purchasing something for the mandator or managing his affairs, but other kinds of *mandatum* may require a great effort and the utmost care, such as representing the mandator in court and similar things. In such cases the mandatory will be liable for *culpa levissima*[62].

g) societas

According to some texts in the *Corpus iuris*, the *socii* in a contract of partnership are liable for *diligentia quam suis* (D. 17.2.72 and Inst. 3.25.9), according to other texts for *culpa levis* (D. 17.2.52.2 i.f., D. 13.6.5.2 and D. 17.2.65.9). The glossators take *culpa levis* to be the normal degree of liability, which in certain circumtances can be extended to *diligentia quam suis*[63]. The commentators interpret the *culpa levis* as a lack of the *diligentia quam suis* observed by the parties at the time they entered into the contract of partnership[64].

---

59 See the gloss 'et omnem culpam' ad C. 4.35.13: de dolo et lata culpa et leui tenetur secundum omnes ut hic et ff. eod. Si procuratorem § Dolo (D. 17.1.8.9) et l. Dolus (D. 17.1.44) et ff. de regu. iur. Contractus (D. 50.17.23). Sed secundum Io. et B. et Az. etiam de leuissima tenetur ut hic, nam qui omnem dixit, nihil omisit. sed Ot. et M. contra: ut dicet infra e. In rem (C. 4.35.21). Nec obstat prime opinioni, scilicet de leuissima ff. e. Idemque in princ. (D. 17.1.10pr), ubi dicit nihil amplius quam bonam fidem; nam expone, id est nihil quod sit melius, nam nil melius est bona fide. Vel ibi emerat procurator et omnia fecerat, et sola restabat traditio facienda, in qua sufficit bona fides, que fit in traditione. Item nec obstat ff. de regu. iu. l. Contractus (D. 50.17.23), quia ibi non remouet, quin de leuissima teneatur.

60 See the gloss 'negotia' ad D. 17.1.2.1: (...) sed nos indistincte dicimus eum de omnibus teneri, nisi in casu ut C. e.l. A procaratore (C. 4.35.13) (...); Cf. also the gloss 'contractus' ad D. 50.17.23.

61 The gloss 'iusta causa' ad Inst. 3.26.11: (...) cum hic contractus multum discrepat ab aliis contractibus.

62 Bartolus (5) ad D. 16.3.32 n. 31 (p. 325): Aut in mandato uenit aliquid quod non requirit magnam industriam, sed requirit aliquid diligentiae, ut emere aliquid, gerere negotia et similia, et tunc (quicquid dicat glossa) uenit dolus, culpa lata et leuis (...) Aut in mandato uenit aliquid quod requirit exactissimam diligentiam et industriam, ut in procuratore ad litem et similibus et tunc tenetur de leuissima. Cf. Baldus (11) ad C. 4.24.6 n. 51 (fol. 68vb–69ra): (...) quare concludo quod in mandato semper uenit leuis culpa, in leuissima sto cum Bar.

63 See the gloss 'contractus' ad D. 50.17.23 and Azo (4, Summa) ad C. 4.37 (p. 150b).

64 Bartolus (5) ad D. 17.2.72 (p. 352): In societate culpa leuis est non adhibere eam diligentiam quam in suis adhibere solitus est tempore contractae societatis (...). Baldus de Perusio, Super Institutionibus commentum, Venice 1530, ad Inst. 3.25.9

2. *Quasi-contractual liability for unintentional harm*

a) negotiorum gestio

English common law does not recognize management of another's affairs (unauthorised administration) as a source of obligation. In Roman law, unfamiliar with 'implied contract', *negotiorum gestio* was ranged among the quasi-contracts. Time and again the texts in the *Corpus iuris* attribute divergent standards of liability to the manager: merely *dolus* (D. 3.5.3.9), *culpa lata* (C. 2.18.17), *culpa levis* (D. 50.17.23 and D. 49.14.3.5), *culpa levissima* (Inst. 3.27.1), or even *casus*, liability for fortuitous damage (D. 3.5.10). The glossators and commentators adopted liability for *culpa levis* as the regular standard[65], which could be reduced to *culpa lata* in case of management in an emergency, and extended to *culpa levissima* for cases where another person, observing the utmost care, had been available, and to *casus* for exceptional cases where the remedy for unauthorised administration was used as enrichment action against the principal[66].

b) tutela

The liability of the tutor charged with looking after the property of the ward is normally laid down as *culpa levis* in the Digest (D. 21.1.31.4 and many other texts), in the Codex as *culpa lata* (C. 2.18.17 and many other texts). The glossators and commentators adopt liability for *culpa levis* as the normal standard[67]. Commenting upon D. 26.7.72, however, they give examples of special situations where the liability is reduced to *culpa lata*[68].

(fol. 39vb): In actione pro socio uenit dolus et culpa que non extimatur si non adhibet tantam diligentiam in rebus communibus quantam adhibere solebat in propriis temporis societatis contracte (...). N. B. Maffei ascribes this commentary on the Institutes to Bartolomeo da Novara. Cf. *D. Maffei*, Bartolomeo da Novara († 1408), autore della 'Lectura Institutionum' attribuita a Baldo degli Ubaldi, in Revista di Storia del Diritto Italiano 63 (1990), p. 5–22.

[65] See the gloss 'ad exactissimam' ad Inst. 3.27.1: (...) Quandoque de dolo, lata culpa, et leui et hoc regulariter ut C. eo. Tutori (C. 2.18.20) et ff. eo. l. Si pupilli § fi. (D. 3.5.5.14) (...); Bartolus, Opera, Basel 1588, In Primam Partem Codicis, C. 2.18.20 n. 3 (p. 244): (...) Hic dicitur quod gestor tenetur de leui culpa. Contra ff. eo. l. iii § Interdum (D. 3.5.3.9). Sol. Illud quod hic dicitur est regulare. Fallit in casibus, qui ibi not. (...).

[66] Azo (4, Summa) ad C. 2.18 (p. 38a): (...) Interdum etiam prestatur et a gestore etiam leuissima culpa, si alius diligentissimus erat gesturus, ut Insti. de obl. que ex quasi contrac. § Sicut (Inst. 3,27,1 i.f.) (...); the gloss 'ad exactissimam' ad Inst. 3.27.1: (...) Quandoque de leuissima ut quando alius diligentius uolebat administrare ut hic dicitur et ff. eo. l. Si pupilli § Videamus (D. 3.5.5.14). Quandoque de casu ut in his casibus, ubi agitur in quantum dominus locupletior est ut modo supra diximus in eo. §.

c) precarium

According to the Roman texts the liability of the *precario tenens* is very restricted, i.e. for *dolus* (D. 50.17.23) or *culpa lata* (D. 43.26.8.6). The Gloss assumes a liability for nothing else but *dolus*, because *precarium*, unlike borrowing, is always subject to revocation[69]. The commentators sometimes speak about *culpa lata*[70].

d) dos

The husband has to observe *diligentia quam suis* in looking after the dowry (D. 24.3.24.5, D. 23.3.17pr and C. 5.14.11.4). The Gloss here assumes liability for *culpa levis*, which can be extented to *culpa levissima*, if the husband usually takes the utmost care of his own things. However, he is not allowed to be careless with the dowry just because he is careless with his own property[71]. According to the commentators the husband is liable for *culpa levis*. He is also liable if he, being *diligentissimus* himself, only observes the normal care for the dowry. Bartolus classes this liability as *dolus*, Baldus as *culpa levis*[72].

---

67 Bartolus, Opera, Basel 1588, In Primam Partem Infortiati, ad D. 26.7.33pr (p. 168): Tutor tenetur facere illud, quod diligens paterfamilias facturus esset.

68 See also Azo (4, Summa) ad C. 5.38 (p. 200b): (...) tutores que contingunt eorum dolo culpa, lata uel leui interueniente (...) nisi in eo casu, quando comparuerit predia non idonea. In hac enim parte solam latam negligentiam debent prestare tutores, ut (...), Odofredus (21) ad C. 5.51.2 (I fol. 300vb): In lege ista uidetur poni quidam casus in quo tutor tenetur de dolo et lata culpa (...).

69 See the gloss 'contractus' ad D. 50.17.23: (...) Precarium autem datur sine certi usus praefinitione et ideo passim reuocatur (...) et inde hoc euenire credo, quod in precario dolus tantum praestatur, in commodato autem (quia non licet quandocunque reuocare) et culpa praestatur (...).

70 Bartolus (5) ad D. 16.3.32 n. 36 (p. 326): Precarium potest reuocari, quando libuerit; et sic ab initio et ex postfacto pendet ex liberalitate domini; et sic in hoc grauatur recipiens; ergo releuatur in hoc, ut solum teneatur de culpa lata.

71 See the gloss 'culpanda' ad D. 24.3.24.5: (...) sed tutius est ut omnis leuis culpa ueniat (...), the gloss 'culpam' ad D. 23.3.17: scilicet leuem uel leuissimam si diligentissimus erat in suis et hoc est quod continuat, 'sed etc.', and the gloss 'diligentiam' ad D. 23.3.17: tamen si culpandus erat in suis rebus culpandus erit in dotalibus, si enim minus diligens in suis fuit, non ideo parcendum est sibi in dotalibus ut infra, so. ma. l. Si constante § Si maritus (D. 24.3.24.5).

72 Baldus (11) ad C. 4.24.6 n. 60–61 (fol. 69ra): (...) dicit glosa quod marius qui est in suis diligentissimus in dotalibus non ita, est in culpa, sed Bar. dicit quod est in dolo per l. Quod Nerua (D. 16.3.32); glosa dicit uerum, Bar. errat, quia in rebus communibus uel quasi irregulata diligentia est culpa, non dolus ut ff. fam. ercis. l. Haeredes § Non tantum (D. 10.2.25.16); mitius enim est agendum cum eo qui quodammodo rem suam neglexit. Non obstante l. Quod Nerua (D. 16.3.32), quia ibi loquitur de re prorsus aliena siue fideico.

3. Delictual liability for unintentional harm

a) Damnum iniuria datum

Extra-contractual liability for damage to property under the *lex Aquilia* is comparable with divergent forms of negligence in common law, such as negligence in carrying out one's own activities, but also with negligence in the custody of something dangerous. This rather broad applicability is reflected in the different ways damage can be inflicted as discerned in medieval doctrine. According to the original purport of the *lex Aquilia* compensation was only owed for damages which were caused directly, i. e. *corpore corpori*. However, where damage was caused indirectly the classical jurists were ready to impose liability by means of *actiones utiles* and *actiones in factum* after the example of the *actio legis Aquiliae*[73]. Justinian confirmed this extensive application of the *actio legis Aquiliae*[74]. In medieval doctrine the several cases of damage indirectly caused are classed under two or three different categories. The *Casus Codicis* of Guillelmus de Cabriano (*saec.* XII) offer an example of the *actio utilis* for the case damage was not inflicted *corpore* and an example of the subsidiary *actio in factum* where it was not inflicted *corpori*. Both examples are derived from Inst. 4.3.16[75]. Later generations were to elaborate on this early impetus towards a subdivision of indirectly caused damage into several catagories, but in the main, including the examples given, they stick rather close to the *Corpus iuris*. Apart from damage caused directly (*corpore corpori*), three different categories are distinguished. The damage may be inflicted *a non corpore in corpus*, *a corpore in non corpus* or *a non corpore in non corpus*.

Damage *a non corpore in corpus* is caused, for example, by waving a red rag in order to frighten some cattle which then fall into an abyss[76] or by locking up another man's slave and starving him to death[77]. In such

---

[73] See *P. Rasi*, L'actio legis Aquiliae e la responsibilità estracontrattuale nella 'Glossa', in *G. Rossi* (ed.), Atti del convegno internazionale di studi Accursiani II, Milan 1968, p. 723–775.

[74] See Inst. 4.3.16. Medieval jurists follow Justinian law in this respect and maintain that the adapted actions have the same features as the actio legis Aquiliae itself. They are, for example, also ruled by the maxim 'infitiando lis crescit in duplum'; see Azo (4, Summa) ad C. 3.35 (p. 91), Roffredus (21) fol. 24va.

[75] Guillelmus de Cabriano, Casus Codicis ad C. 3.35 (Hereford P. 5 VI, fol. 128vb and Düsseldorf E 9a, fol. 197vb): Vtilis competit quando quidem leditur, sed non per corpus quia pecus meum inclusisti et studio fame perire permisisti. (...) Ceterum cum corpori nocitum non est, in factum in subsidium habet, puta quia seruum compeditum misericordia ductus soluisti.

[76] Cf. D. 9.2.9.3 and D. 47.2.50.4; see Azo (4, Summa) ad C. 3.35 (p. 89), Roffredus (21) fol. 24rb, Odofredus, De libellis formandis, in Tractatus illustrium iurisconsultorum, Tom. III, Pars II, Venice 1584, fol. 79vb–89vb, I cap. 46 (fol. 82va)

cases an *actio utilis* is granted. Damage *a corpore in non corpus* is caused by knocking a golden ring out of someone's hand so that it falls into a river or the sea[78]. In this case an *actio in factum subsidiaria* or an *actio utilis* is granted. Damage *a non corpore in non corpus* is caused by setting free another man's slave out of pity so that he flees[79]. In this case an *actio in factum subsidiaria* is granted[80].

Such cases of indirectly caused damage, like those where damage was caused *corpore corpori* are comparable to actionable negligence in that the damage was not inflicted intentionally but due to carelessness. Some cases resemble negligence in carrying out one's own activities, some resemble negligence in the custody of something dangerous. The latter can be accounted for on the ground that it is not only culpable acts but also a culpable omission which may lead to Aquilian liability. This has to be explained more fully. In D. 9.2.7.6 (and D. 48.8.15) a distinction is made between 'killing' and 'causing death'[81]. Thereafter one requirement was supposed to be necessary for the causal connection between act and damage. It was derived from D. 9.2.30.3, dealing with the case of burning weeds on a windy day. This Digest text discusses the question of liability in case the fire spreads and causes damage to adjacent fields[82], thereby

and Guillelmus Durantis (34), Lib. 4 Partic. 4 De iniuriis et damno dato § 2, n. 8 (II p. 512).

77 See Inst. 4.3.16, which example is mentioned by Roffredus (21) fol. 24va and Baptista de S. Blasio (29), De actione et eius natura, n. 82 (fol. 55va).

78 D. 9.2.27.21, which example is mentioned by Azo (4, Summa) ad C. 3.35 (p. 89), Roffredus (21) fol. 24va, Odofredus (76) I cap. 46 (fol. 82va) and Guillelmus Durantis (34), Lib. 4 Partic. 4 De iniuriis et damno dato § 2, n. 9 (II p. 512).

79 Inst. 4.3.16, which example is mentioned by Azo (4, Summa) ad C. 3.35 (p. 89), Roffredus (21) fol. 24va, Odofredus (76) I cap. 46 (fol. 82va), Guillelmus Durantis (34), Lib. 4 Partic. 4 De iniuriis et damno dato § 2, n. 10 (II p. 512) and Joannes Crispus de Montibus (24) n. 170 (fol. 175va).

80 As was seen above, the application of the actio legis Aquiliae was also extended in more ways during the Middle Ages. It could be used, for example, to claim compensation in case of physical injury inflicted upon freemen, albeit not for immaterial damages such as pain and suffering.

81 For the latter an actio in factum was granted, which remedy, was according to the Gloss, folowed by Albertus Gandinus (Cremona, † after 1305), considered to have the same features as the actio legis Aquiliae; see *H. Kantorowicz*, Albertus Gandinus und das Strafrecht der Scholastik, Berlin/Leipzig 1926, p. 302: (...) contra uero eum, qui mortis causam prebuit, agitur actione in factum uel utili Aquilia, ut ibidem notatur in apparatu ordinario, licet quantum ad effectum sit idem, quia tantum quis consequitur per actionem directam, quantum per utilem et e contra, ut ff. de negotiis gestis l. Antepen. (D. 3.5.46) et ff. de seruo corrupto l. Vt tantum (D. 11.3.14) et notatur ff. ad l. Aquiliam l. Item Mela § Si alius (D. 9.2.11.1).

82 A comparable case can be found in the decretal 'Si egressus' (X 5.36.5). See for the interpretation of this text the contribution of Dondorp in this volume, p. 119.

introducing *imperitia* and *negligentia* as forms of carelessness. From this text a maxim was derived which was taken as a criterion for the causal connection between the act and the resulting damage: 'one who creates the opportunity is also deemed to have caused the damage' (*et qui occasionem praestat, damnum fecisse uidetur*)[83]. In legal doctrine several examples can be found of what '*occasionem damni praestare*' in practice could be. If someone is subjected to a statutory fine because of the garbage someone else had dumped on the public road outside his house, he is entitled, in his turn, to sue the wrongdoer. Because the latter had created the opportunity of damage (the fine), he is therefore considered to have caused it[84]. In another example, my neighbour had killed his adversary's father and in revenge this adversary set my neighbour's residence on fire; my house was burnt down in consequence. I will have an *actio in factum* against my neighbour[85]. The most extensive interpretation of '*occasionem damni praestare*' may be found in Albertus de Gandino. According to a provision of statutory law, murder should be punished by destroying the murderer's property. However, during the demolition of the murderer's house, the adjacent residence was damaged by a falling wall. Who is liable for this? If the murderer's goods are confiscated, the authorities will be liable, but not because they themselves caused the damage, but only because they are now successor by universal title of the murderer. If the goods are not confiscated, then the murderer himself will be liable for the wall coming down. Though he did not himself demolish the house, he is nevertheless considered to have caused the damage: by committing a murder he created the situation that was eventuelly to result in the damage to his neighbour's residence[86].

Cf. also the action for losing control of a domestic fire in English common law in the contribution of Baker in this volume, p. 60 at footnote 54.

[83] For the reception and the meaning of his maxim in canon law see the contribution of Dondorp in this volume, p. 102. Even after the codification of private law in the Netherlands this maxim did have a certain importance. Cf. the contribution of Schrage in this volume, p. 41 ff.

[84] Guillelmus Durantis (34), Lib. 4, Partic. 4 de iniuriis et damno dato § 2 n. 15 (II p. 513).

[85] Guillelmus Durantis (34), Lib. 4, Partic. 4 de iniuriis et damno dato § 2 n. 16 (II p. 513).

[86] *Kantorowicz* (81) p. 355–356, with a reference to D. 10.3.20: Dum potestas faceret destrui quandam domum cuiusdam homicide secundum formam statuti, accidit quod murus illius domus cecidit super quandam domum vicinam. Queritur quis debeat emendare? (...) Dominus Albertus de Papia dixit potestatem teneri nomine communis secundum primo allegata, cuius opinio locum habet, quando omnia boni dicti malefactoris erant publicata, quia tunc potestas nomine fisci, qui est heres, tenetur resarcire damnum, nam occasione etc. unde fiscus tenetur ut successor (...). Si autem bona non erant publicata, tunc tenetur malefactor (...).

It is questionable whether the *lex Aquilia* also covers liability for damage caused by omissions. Here the sources point towards divergent opinions. According to D. 7.1.13.2 the usufructuary is not liable under the *lex Aquilia* for the deterioration of fields, vines and water pipes. However, according to D. 9.2.8 (the case of a physician who operated well but was negligent in the patient's after-care) and D. 9.2.27.9 (the case of the slave who fell asleep while watching a burning fire) an omission can result in liability. Azo, referring to D. 7.1.13.2, maintains that some act is required: a distinction should be made between damage resulting from the decline of the object itself without any human act and damage not resulting from the damaged goods themselves. Apparently, omissions may lead to liability, if the damage results from human negligence, such as in the case of D. 9.2.27.9, just mentioned, and D. 9.2.27.33 (the case of badly loaded stones) rather than from deterioration in the object itself[87].

b) pauperies

Liability for damage caused by animals is to a certain extent comparable with the common law's negligence in the custody of something dangerous[88]. Here, however, Roman law introduced a more severe degree of liability, and the sources point towards strict liability, as in the *actio de recepto*. As will be shown below, the glossators saw the *caupo*, *nauta* and *stabularius* as having acted with some kind of *culpa levissima*, but such reasoning was untenable for the *actio de pauperie* because of the phrasing in D. 9.1.1.3–4. The idea that the owner must always have acted with some kind of negligence, even of the slightest negligence, was incompatible with the purport of the entire titles on damage by animals in the Digest and Institutes. On the other hand, the owner's liability was limited in that delivery of the animal to the injured party (*noxae deditio*) could take the place of pecuniary compensation. The canonists rejected this restriction of liability when the owner had failed to take precautionary measures[89].

---

87 Azo (4, Summa) ad C. 3.35 (p. 88a–b): According to Bartolus and Baldus the lightest negligence in a non acting is not capable of producing liability. Cf. Bartolus (67) ad D. 24.3.10 n. 16 (p. 27): (...) Culpa uero leuissima in non faciendo non uenit in actione de dolo nec in actione legis Aquiliae ut supra de usufruct. l. Si cuius (alias Si ususfruct.) § Denique (D. 7.1.13.2 i. m.). Et sic culpa in faciendo praeponderat culpae in non faciendo. See also Baldus, Consilia, Venice 1575 (reprint Turin, 1970), Vol. I nr. 441 (fol. 141va): (...) secundo in actione legis Aquiliae, in qua uenit leuissima culpa in committendo non negligendo ut ff. de usufru. l. Si cuius § Denique (D. 7.1.13.2 i. m.) (...).

88 Cf. the contributions of Baker, Birks and Ibbetson in this volume.

89 See X 5.36.9 and the gloss 'animalia tua' ad X 5.36.9.

c) servi corruptio

It is also impossible to treat the degree of liability under the *actio servi corrupti* as one for negligence. D. 11.3.1pr requires that the slave be corrupted with malicious intention.

4. *Quasi-delictual liability for unintentional harm*[90]

The glossators were not sure why the quasi-delicts constituted a separate category in the Roman subdivision of the various sources of obligation. What were the common features of the quasi-delicts and how did they differ from the genuine delicts? It took Jacques Cujas (1522–1590) to draw a clear distinction. In his opinion delicts are based on *dolus* or in case of the *actio legis Aquiliae* on *culpa* causing corporeal damage, whereas quasi-delicts are based on *culpa*[91]. However, the glossators and commentators were not agreed on the basis of quasi-delict as a category.

a) The liability of the magistrate who made the litigation his own, the *iudex qui litem suam facit*, has already been discussed as one of the delicts where the medieval jurists considered the *actio poenalis ad interesse* to be available. This kind of delict, to some extent comparable with negligence by public officials in English law, was ascribed to a lack of prudence or a lack of professional skill (*imperitia*). The latter, in its turn, was rated as carelessness (*culpa*)[92].

b) Liability under the *actio de deiectis vel effusis* in its original Roman shape can hardly be compared with negligence at common law[93]. It was a kind of strict liability, i.e. a liability in one's capacity as occupant of an upstairs apartment, if damage was caused by things and fluids thrown down, regardless of the occupant's actual intent or negligence. In the Middle Ages the jurists incline to dispense with such strict liability. In Roman law payment by one resident, sued by the *actio de deiectis vel effu-*

---

[90] Literature: *R. Hochstein*, Obligationes quasi ex delicto, Untersuchung zur dogmengeschichtlichen Entwicklung verschuldensunabhängiger und rechtspolitische Bewertung [Leipziger rechtswissenschaftliche Studien, 117], Leipzig 1939, p. 34–47 and *P. Stein*, The actio de effusis vel dejectis and the concept of quasi-delict in Scots law, in The International and Comparative Law Quarterly 4 (1955), p. 356–375.

[91] Cf. Stein (90) p. 365–366.

[92] According to the maxim 'imperitia culpae adnumeratur' (Inst. 4.3.7 and D. 50.17.132); Cf. the gloss 'peccasse' ad D. 44.7.5.4: Peccasse alius deliquisse; uere peccauit, quia imperitia culpe annumeratur, quare ergo non ex maleficio tenetur ut in Aquiliana. Respondeo speciale in iudice, aliud in Aquiliana.

[93] Cf. for the liability of bailees and innkeepers in English common law the contributions in this volume of Baker, Birks and Ibbetson.

sis, freed the other residents and the one who paid could bring an *actio pro socio* against the others for a proportion of the judgment (D. 9.3.1.10 and D. 9.3.2–4). This kind of recourse is further developed in medieval doctrine: the party paying is now allowed to sue the actual wrongdoer for the entire amount by means of an *actio utilis pro socio* or an *actio in factum ex hoc edicto*[94].

c) Liability under the *actio de recepto* to some extent resembles liability at common law for negligence in looking after someone else's property, but in fact it was more extensive. Originally it was a kind of strict liability incurred by certain professions, i. e. those of sea carrier (*nauta*), inn keeper (*caupo*) and stable keeper (*stabularius*). Except for cases of *vis maior* these professionals were held liable for the well-being of their clients' possessions, even if they were not themselves at fault (D. 4.9.3.1). However, medieval doctrine rejects the idea of liability without any fault, i. e. for fortuitous damage, a rejection already formulated in the *Corpus iuris* for the *actio legis Aquiliae* (see D. 9.2.52 and C. 3.35). In this form it was sometimes adopted in legal doctrine[95] and was soon regarded as having a more general purport. This explains the inclination, seen above, to dispose of or to mitigate certain forms of strict liability. However, the *nauta*, *caupo* and *stabularius* were not granted recourse against the actual wrongdoer. In the Roman texts, which explicitly hold them liable in spite of their being without fault, they themselves are presumed to have acted with some kind of negligence, however slight. If such *culpa levissima* was obviously lacking, as in case of *casus fortuitus*, liability comes to an end[96].

V. Conclusions

As regards liability for unintentional harm, no major dogmatic developments can be traced in medieval legal doctrine. However, as was shown above, the glossators and commentators do display certain tendencies. The medieval civilians may have found the idea of strict liability hard to take, and the canonists even seem to have rejected it[97]. Whereas Justinianic law

---

94 See Guillemus Durantis (34), Lib. IV partic. 4 § 2 n. 27 (II p. 514).

95 See the Tractatus de diligentia et dolo et culpa et fortuito casu, edited by *G. Dolezalek* in Aspekte europäischer Rechtsgeschichte, Festgabe für Helmut Coing zum 70. Geburtstag [Ius Commune, Sonderhefte 17], p. 87–121; see p. 106–107.

96 See the gloss 'etiam si sine culpa' ad D. 4.9.3.1: Scilicet leui. Leuissima tamen interuenit. Nam si nec leuissima interuenit, ergo fuit casus fortuitus et sic non tenetur ut hic subiicit et infra de admi. re. ad ci. p. l. ii § Si eo (D. 50.8.2.7) et C. de pig. ac. l. Quae fortuitis (C. 4.24.6) (...); see also the gloss 'prestare debet' ad D. 13.6.18pr, Bartolus, Opera, Basel 1588, In Primam Partem Digesti Veteris, ad D. 4.9.3.1 n. 2 (p. 486) and Baldus, Tomus Primus in Digestum Vetus, Lyons 1551, ad 'ex hoc edicto' (D. 4.9.3.1 i. m.) n. 1 (fol. 242va).

acknowledged the strict liability of sea carriers, inn keepers and stable keepers, medieval doctrine inclines to a presumption of negligence, however slight, where the Roman texts impose liability. The party held liable under the *actio de deiectis vel effusis* was given recourse against the actual wrongdoer, but the strict liability of the owner of animals for the damage done by them was preserved because it was impossible to disregard the whole entire title in the sources dealing with the *actio de pauperie*.

Roughly speaking, legal doctrine discerns two degrees of negligence, i.e. one lighter, limited to *culpa levis* or *negligentia*, which may sometimes be extended to *diligentia quam suis*, and one more extensive degree, including *culpa levissima*. Liability for *culpa levis* can be found in obligations resulting from contracts and quasi-contracts, specifically as to parties having only a minor interest in the transaction, such as the pledgee, looking after the pledge in his care, the vendor, who has to put the purchaser in possession of the object sold, the lessor, who has to select what he puts at the lessee's disposal, the lessee, who has to restore the property leased to him, and the mandatory, rendering a service which requires only little effort. Outside the law of contracts also the manager of another's affairs and the tutor, looking after the goods of his ward, are liable for *culpa levis*. Extension of this liability to a duty to observe a *diligentia quam suis* can be found as regards *socii* in a contract of partnership and for the husband looking after the dowry. A liability for *culpa levissima* occurs in obligations resulting from contracts for the party having a major interest (or more interest than the other) such as the borrower (unless the contract was entered into in the interest of the lender or the lender offered him the things for use, because then the borrower is only liable for *culpa lata*), the depositary (not in the normal contract entered into in the interest of the depositor, which results only in a liability for *culpa lata*, but only in the exceptional case where the *depositum* took place in the interest of the depositary or the latter offered himself as such), and the mandatory rendering a service which called for a great effort. Furthermore, this *culpa levissima* may also lead to delictual or quasi-delictual obligations, as in the case of *damnum iniuria datum* and damages to clients of sea carriers, inn keepers and stable keepers.

Civilians in the Middle Ages noticed the similarities between comparable degrees of liability in both contractual and delictual obligations and their mutual coherence. This resulted in an academic and theoretical interest in the degrees of liability as such, an approach quite foreign to the original casuistry of the Roman texts. As early as the middle or second half of the twelfth century, a treatise contains a survey of the Roman remedies and the

[97] For the forum internum the canonists even rejected the idea of a liability for culpa levissima. Cf. the contribution of Dondorp in this volume, p. 120–121.

corresponding degrees of liability[98]. At the beginning of his work *de actionibus* (1256), a commentary on the title *de actionibus* of the Institutes, Johannes de Blanosco (Jean de Blanot) discusses the several degrees of liability under the heading *de culpis et dolo, qualiter diffiniantur*. Because notions such as *dolus* and *culpa* are so frequently brought up when describing the Roman remedies, first a number of definitions is given. Thus, we find here an accurate description of what should be understood by *dolus*, *lata culpa*, *levis culpa* and *levissima culpa*[99]. This dogmatic and systematic treatment of the degrees of liability appears to become common practice. Although many authors formally comment upon the Roman texts *lex* by *lex*, they all find an appropriate place to incorporate a longer treatise on degrees of liability and compare the several Roman contracts and delicts[100]. This doctrinal approach may be seen as a first step towards a more systematic treatment of contractual and delictual liabilities. Given the predominant role of the principle of utility, the medieval civilians could not develop uniform rules for all contracts or a general remedy for non performance. After all, liability was dependent on the debtor's interest in the contract and this interest could only be determined for each specific type of contract individually. Nor did the medieval civilians develop a general doctrine of delict or a generally applicable tortious remedy for damages, although, as shown above, a number of interesting developments took place. The use of the *actio legis Aquiliae* was extented; there was a clear inclination to mitigate the Roman forms of strict liability; and the *actio in factum*, a subsidiary general action for damages resulting from whatever illicit act, was generally accepted. However, we must conclude that Grotius' general doctrine of tort, as presented in *De iure belli ac pacis*, has no clear predecessor in medieval Roman law and that the roots of his teachings must be sought in sixteenth century doctrine, i.e. either in legal humanism or in the late scholastic elaboration of the canon law doctrine of restitution.

---

98 See the Tractatus mentioned in note 95.

99 Johannes de Blanasco Burgundus, De actionibus, in De actionibus tractatus clarissimorum in primis nostrae aetatis iurisconsultorum, Vol. I, Lyons 1596, fol. 222–285, fol. 224rb–224va.

100 See, for example, Odofredus (7) ad D. 13.6.5.2, the Gloss ad D. 50.17.23, Bartolus (5) ad D. 16.3.32 and Baldus (11) ad C. 4.24.6.

HARRY DONDORP

Crime and Punishment

Negligentia for the canonists and moral theologians

I. Introduction

The point of departure in describing the concept of negligence in Medieval canon law and in sixteenth century moral theology is a phenomenon which Kuttner noted as early as 1935. In his study of the "kanonistische Schuldlehre", indispensable also for the history of delict, he comes to the conclusion that Huguccio – one of the most influential canonists of the Middle Ages – in his summa decreti (1188) considers *negligentia* a wrong, to be punished more harshly as the severity of the consequences increases.[1] In this way Huguccio tries to explain why a number of texts in Gratian's Decretum (1139) determine that clerics had to be punished for their actions, if, by accident, these actions led to the death of another.

Why is someone guilty of the death of another person, and therefore punished by the church, if it is certain that it was not his intention to kill the other? Shouldn't the death rather be ascribed to chance? The decretists treat the question of when exactly fault (*culpa*) is to be imputed by considering the example given in D.50 c.37, where a person dies from injuries suffered from being struck by a stone. In such a case the reason why the rock was thrown must first be established. It is, after all, illicit to throw stones at other people, unless there is a particular reason for doing so, such as self-defence. But perhaps the victim was struck by a rock thrown to chase away birds or pigs. If the rock was thus not aimed at a person, the throwing itself did not suffer the taint of impropriety.[2] In such a case fault could not be established from the deed itself, and if the actor had been sufficiently care-

---

[1] Cf. *S. Kuttner*, Kanonistische Schuldlehre von Gratian bis auf die Dekretalen Gregors IX, Systematisch auf Grund der handschriftlichen Quellen dargestellt [Studi e testi 64], Città del Vaticano, 1935, p. 227: "So wird die negligentia, die in Wahrheit eine Schuldform der Herbeiführung des Erfolges ist, für ihn zu einen Sonderdelikt, das wegen eines qualifizierenden Erfolges schwerer bestraft wird".

[2] The canonists also refer to the example of a brick falling from the hands of a bricklayer.

ful and had warned the passers-by, no wrong had been committed if another had been struck.

One is guilty of the death of another person, however, if one is at fault (*culpa*), i.e. if one acted improperly or (though properly) without due care.[3] If one acts with less care than might be expected, this is *negligentia* and is punishable.

In the same way the adage *"Qui occasionem damni dat, damnum dedisse videtur"* (derived from D. 9.2.30.3), was used in the twelfth century to account for punishing accidents with a fatal outcome (*homicidium casuale)*. Ultimately, the reason why anyone was punished was his own illicit act or his negligence, even if it had caused the death of another by chance. There was only a single exception to this rule, as appears from the comments of the decretists on D.50 c.39. This text deals with the case where someone had struck another person, who then fell from his horse and broke his neck.[4] It is clear that the perpetrator was guilty of homicide if the blow itself had killed the victim (*causa directa)*, irrespective of whether the victim fell from his horse or not. If, however, the blow caused the victim to fall from his horse and break his neck in the fall, this was considered an *occasio propinqua*, and the wrongdoer would be punished for *homicidium (casuale)*. If the victim fell from his horse for another reason, such as lack of horsemanship, this was considered an *occasio remota*. In this last case it was not from the blow struck, but through chance (or his own fault) that the victim died.[5]

The decretal *Si culpa* of pope Gregory IX (X 5.36.9), where the adage is codified, must be interpreted in this manner, as Hostiensis remarks in so many words.[6]

---

[3] Cf re. the distinction between *res licita – res illicita Kuttner*, loc. cit. note 1, pp. 200–213.

[4] The interpretation of the decretists and decretalists is discussed by *Kuttner*, loc. cit. note 1, pp. 189–197; The distinction between *occasio propinqua* and *remota* on p. 197.

[5] The example is derived from Huguccio, ad D.50 c.39 (ed. *Kuttner*, loc. cit. note 1, p. 192 nt 2): ... (1) si non cecidit ex percussione nec mortuus est ex ea, fieri debet quod dicitur in prima parte capituli; si vero (2) ex ea cecidit (3) vel non, et tamen ex ea mortuus est; vel (4) si ex ea cecidit et non ex ea est mortuus set ex fractione cervicis quam passus est, cum cecidit, debet fieri quod in ultima parte dicitur. Kuttner (p. 197) wrongly assumes that in the second and third instances given by Huguccio the blow is an *occasio propinqua*. This is the case in the fourth instance, as appears from Huguccio, ad D.50 c.39 s.v. *Qualiacumque percussione* (ibid. p. 193 note 1): sive directo, sive occasionaliter. Directo si percussus fuit ad mortem, occasionaliter si non fuerit percussus ad mortem, set ex percussione cecidit et cervicem fregit.

[6] Cf. Hostiensis, Lectura super X 5.36.9 s.v. *Occasionem*: propinquam, non remotam; Bernardus Parmensis refers to his own commentary ad X 5.12.11 and X 2.20.9.

II. Private poena or compensation of damages

Actio legis Aquiliae

The canonists always assumed that the ecclesiastical judge should apply Roman law if someone had insulted, or assaulted another, or caused him harm. This is already evident in the oldest commentaries on the title *De damno dato* in the *Compilatio Prima* (1188–1191). This title consists almost exclusively of provisions from the laws of Moses (Exodus 21). According to the compiler Bernardus Papiensis the texts from the Old Testament served only for legal comparison and were not to be applied if they deviated from Roman law.[7] Therefore someone who injured another in a fight did not go unpunished, as, according to Roman law, this fell under *iniuria*, assault and insult[8], even if Exodus 21:18–19 (= 1Comp. 5.31.1) provides: "And if men strive together, and one smite another with a stone, or with his fist, and he die not, but keepeth his bed: if he rise again, and walk abroad upon his staff, then shall he that smote him be quit: only he shall pay for the loss of his time, and shall cause him to be thoroughly healed".

The thirteenth century canonists considered the reimbursement of medical costs and loss of income – in the text the verb *restituere* is used – a *poena*, a punishment for injuring another, and not the compensation of damages.[9] In the case of a fight, however, they found the payment of only

[7] Cf. *P. Landau*, Alttestamentisches Recht in der Compilatio Prima, Studia Gratiana 20 (1976), p. 116, 129–133. Cf. also p. 128: The thief caught red-handed need thus not return sevenfold (see Proverbs 6:31), but only fourfold.

[8] Alanus, gloss *Innocens erit* ad 1Comp. 5.31.1 (ed. *Landau*, loc. cit. note 7, p. 130): *Quoad penam homicidii, tenetur tamen de iniuria*. In the commentary of Laurentius and Tancredus (see *Landau*, loc cit note 7, p. 131) the same conception is defended. In the discussion of Alanus's interpretation by Olivier the word "not" has fallen away, where he states that according to Alanus "die *innocens erit* van 1Comp. 5.31.1 slegs van toepassing kan wees, waar die dood op die verwonding volg". Cf. *N. J. J. Olivier*, Die aksie weens die nalatige veroorsaking van pyn en lyding, 'n regshistoriese ondersoek met 'n regsvergelykende ekskursus, [dissertation Leiden], 1978, p. 56. Cf. page 7 for the commentaries on X 5.36.1.

[9] Contra: *T. J. Scott*, Passive transmissibility of delictual actions in old canon law, Acta Juridica (1978), p. 17: "Canon law recognises delictual claims as purely reipersecutory in nature and rejects the possibility of any amount being awarded in excess of actual damages sustained." He does not support his first contention with additional information, and bases his last contention on C.12 q.2 c.11 "*Sed absit ut ecclesia cum augmento recipiat quod de terrenis rebus videtur amittere et lucra de damnis quaerere*". As also Lange (*H. Lange*, Schadensersatz und Privatstrafe in der mittelalterlichen Rechtstheorie, Münster 1955, p. 132) remarks, it appears from the gloss *Cum augmento* of Johannes Teutonicus that this rule was applied *in foro interno*, but was applied as restrictively as possible in legal proceedings. It applied only

the damages too light a penalty. From the existence of the *actio iniurarum* in Roman law,[10] they concluded that the punishment should be more severe; either a combination of corporal punishment and the payment of the damages, or a higher pecuniary fine.[11]

The verb *restituere* is used in another decretal in the same title, namely *Si quis domum* (1Comp. 5.31.6; X 5.36.6), and here, too, is considered as describing the payment of a fine to the victim. Until around 1300 the canonists construed the text as requiring the payment of fourfold damages in the case of arson, as in Roman law, and not only requiring the payment of the damages, as stated in the text itself.[12]

According to these canonists the reimbursement of damages was sufficient punishment only if someone had unintentionally caused another damage or harm. If, by accident, one's action caused damage to another person, or injured him in any way, he was punished for his improper conduct or his negligence. If he had acted illicitly, e.g. by carrying arms, which was forbidden for clerics, and accidentally caused another to injure himself, it was of no consequence whether or not the wrongdoer had exercised due care. If, however, the act was not illicit, e.g. the case where someone burned refuse on his own land and the fire spread to the land of his neighbour, was there also an obligation to pay the monetary equivalent

---

for the church, not to laymen and clerics. Cf. also his glosses *Quadruplum* ad D.18 c.7, *Multiplicatione* ad C.12 q.2 c.7, *Quadruplum* ad C.12 q.2 c.10, *Tripliciter* ad C.17 q.4 c.21, *Per penam* ad 3Comp. 1.25.1, copied by Bernardus Parmensis in his commentary on X 1.43.4. According to Scott, however, "departures from this rule (as in C.12 q.2 c.7) were regarded as rare exceptions". Only later, for example in Archidiaconus (additio ad glosam *Quadruplum)*, can one observe a general rule: "Et litigatoris vero dispensatione seu equitate nec ecclesia, nec alia persona ultra sortem debet recipere, quia nec hoc vellet sibi fieri, quod tibi non vis fieri etc."

10 Cf. re. the *lex Cornelia de iniuriis*, *O. F. Robinson*, The criminal law of ancient Rome, Londen 1995, p. 45–50.

11 It is not clear from their commentary on *Si rixati* (1Comp. 5.31.1; X 5.36.1) whether the canonists were discussing the actio *criminalis* or *civilis*. As the passage from Azo's summa about the possibility of proceeding *criminaliter* is lacking in Hostiensis's summa (ad X 5.31 *(Iniuria)*, no. 8), I conclude that they refer to a civil action. Guillelmus Duranti also only gives the formula for the civil claim, both for where a *poena arbitraria*, as well as for where a *poena pecuniaria* is requested. Cf. Guillelmus Duranti, Speculum iudiciale IV.4.1 (ed. Basel 1574, reprinted Aalen 1975, II, p. 510).

12 This decretal determines that the arsonist *"sublata et incensa omnia restituat et tres annos poeniteat"*. Bernardus Parmensis, Innocentius IV and Hostiensis add: *in quadruplum*. Thus understood this text applies to the *forum externum* only, as the payment of fourfold the damages must be considered a *poena pecuniaria*. Johannes Andreae, Antonius Butrigarius and Panormitanus, on the other hand, consider *restituat* as referring to the compensation of damages by the perpetrator. In their interpretation the text (also) applies to the *forum internum*.

of the crop destroyed by the fire as punishment? It can be concluded from the decretal *Si egressus* (1Comp. 5.31.5; X 5.36.5) that such an obligation indeed rests on the person who lit the fire. Appealing to D. 9.2.30.3, however, the canonists made it a requirement that the person who lit the fire have failed to exercise due care, and that as a consequence the fire had been able to spread to the neighbour's land. If he had intented to destroy the neighbour's crop, they considered a more severe penalty appropriate; if, on the other hand, he had been sufficiently careful, he need not pay anything.[13]

The canonists reasoned in this manner not only when another's goods were damaged, but also when a person was injured or killed. The church opposed the use of violence and punished violence against ecclesiatics particularly severely. The use of violence was illicit unless one acted in self-defence.[14] One who had used violence and had thereby intentionally injured another should, according to thirteenth century standards, be punished more severely than Exodus 21:18–19 provides, even if the victim survived the assault. If the victim succumbed to the injuries, the perpetrator could be banished or executed for homicide *secundum leges*, and be irrevocably excluded from the priesthood *secundum canones*.[15]

While the issue of injuries as a consequence of a fight was extensively dealt with by the canonists, they are practically silent on injuries not resulting from a fight, unless these had a fatal outcome. Their point of reference was a number of texts in Gratian's Decretum about accidents with deadly outcomes (*homicidium casuale*), such as occur while chopping wood and chasing birds or pigs away by throwing stones at them. Should a person then be punished for homicide if a passer-by was accidentally killed? One could defend the idea that there is no reason for punishment. As an argument to this effect Gratian himself had included in his Decretum (D.50 c.46) Codex 9.16.5 where the emperor says that he does not wish to punish such a person.[16] This was, however, already strictly interpreted by the early decretists, by referring to the *lex Aquilia*. Around 1170 Stephanus Tornacensis was the first to do this in his explication of the words *volumus liber-*

[13] Cf. Bernardus Parmensis, gloss *Reddet damnum* ad X 5.36.5; Innocentius IV, gloss *Reddet damnum* ad X 5.36.5; Hostiensis refers to the examples of D. 9.2.30.3 and D. 9.2.27.9. Cf. re. the interpretation of the glossators *J. Hallebeek*, p. 94–95.

[14] Cf. re. necessity and killing in self-defence *Kuttner*, loc. cit. note 1, p. 334–336; 359–367.

[15] Cf. re. *depositio* as punishment for ecclesiastics: *Kuttner*, loc. cit. note 1, p. 227–228; *F. Claes Bouaert*, Deposition in: DDC 4 (1949), 1153–1160; *B. Schimmelpfennig*, Depositio in: LMA III.4 (1984), 708.

[16] C. 9.16.5: Eum qui adseverat homicidium se non voluntate sed casu fortuito fecisse, cum calcis ictu mortis occasio praebita videatur, ..., secundum id quod adnotatione nostra comprehensum est volumus liberari.

ari in D.50 c.46 (= C. 9.16.5): *a poena legis Corneliae, in qua solus dolus venit, nam a lege Aquilia non liberatur.*[17] While indeed in such a case the death penalty (on the grounds of the *lex Cornelia de sicariis*) was excluded, not all penalties were excluded, for if someone accidentally killed a slave[18] – not in a fight, but while chopping wood – the owner had to be paid the highest value of the slave during the preceding year. Huguccio then also comes to the following conclusion in his Summa decreti (circa 1188):

> *Si ergo aliquis insistens operi illicito aut non caute providens, licet in lata culpa comprehendatur et homicidium fecerit, non punitur pena l(egis) Corn(elie) si casu factum est; per legem Aquiliam tamen punitur in qua etiam levissima culpa venit.*[19]

From the Roman *lex Aquilia* the canonists could derive the idea that a person might have to pay for the the damage caused by his negligence, as *punishment*. That a penalty was at issue is apparent, in so many words, from D. 9.2.30.3: *"in hac ... actione ... dolus et culpa punitur"*. If slaves or livestock were killed the highest value during the preceding year had to be paid, according to the first chapter of the *lex Aquilia*. In other cases: if an animal other than livestock was killed through someone's fault, if slaves or animals were injured, or goods damaged, *"quanti ea res erit in diebus triginta proximus"* had to be paid. The sum that had to be paid on the basis of the *lex Aquilia*, "had a dual function", as Zimmermann remarks, "it could be *poena* in the guise of compensation".[20] According to the canonists this meant that the highest value of the slave or animal in the preceding thirty days had to be paid. This amount was thus calculated differently than

---

17 Stephanus Tornacensis, Summa decreti D.50 c.46 s.v. *Liberari* (ed. *Schulte*, p. 74). The canonists use the contrast between the *lex Cornelia de sicariis* and the *lex Aquilia* to justify that someone could be punished for *homicidium casuale* also in canon law. If someone's lack of due care is sufficient reason to require the payment of damages as a means of punishment, then it is also justifiable that the church can expel an ecclesiastic from office (*depositio*), when someone dies through a fault of the ecclesiastic. Cf. *Kuttner*, loc. cit. note 1, p. 214.

18 See Huguccio, Summa decreti D.50 c.46 s.v. *Liberari* (ed. *Kuttner*, loc. cit. note 1, p. 214 note 1): a pene legis Cornelie, scilicet ut conveniatur criminaliter vel puniatur, in qua solus dolus venit et non culpa etiam lata, set a lege Aquilia non liberatur, in qua venit non solum lata, set etiam levis culpa, quia convenitur de dampno dato, si interfecit servum alterius et huiusmodi; ad hoc lege Aquilia conveniatur civiliter.

19 Huguccio, Summa decreti D.50 c.46 s.v. *Liberari* (ed. *Kuttner*, loc. cit. note 1, p. 214 note 1).

20 *R. Zimmermann*, The law of obligations, Roman foundations of the civilian tradition, Cape town 1992, p. 975. Contra: *Kuttner*, loc. cit note 1, p. 186: "Die Digestenfragmente zur *Lex Aquilia* zeigten ein hochentwickelte Lehre von der fahrlässigen Verschuldung, freilich auf dem privatrechtlichem Gebiete des Schadenersatzrechtes".

was the case for the killing of slaves or livestock, and could then be lower, as injuring was a less serious wrong than killing.[21] If goods were damaged, the quantum of damage had to be compensated.[22]

In accidents involving the death of a free person a private poena had to be paid to the family of the deceased as punishment for negligence. For this the jurists of the Middle Ages appealed to the authority of the *actio legis Aquiliae*, as is already evident from the *summa decretalium* (ca 1190) of Bernardus Papiensis:

> *De homicidio casuali potest secundum leges agi lege Aquilia, scilicet ad pecuniariam poenam, ut Dig. ad l. Aquil. l. 2–10.*[23]

Here, too, it is apparent that the canonists at the beginning of the thirteenth century drew no sharp distinction between the compensation for harm and the payment of a fine. For them the pecuniary penalty could encompass compensation. This point of view was derived not only from Roman law, but also from the decretal *Olim* (1215–1216) of pope Honorius III. In Roman law, after all, the amount paid to the owner of a slave killed or injured could encompass compensation as well as a penalty (*quanti id in eo anno plurimi fuit*).[24] The canonists concluded from the decretal *Olim*

---

[21] Cf. Goffredus Tranensis, summa X 5.36 (ed. Lyon 1519, reprinted Aalen 1968, fo. 235vb): Sed si queras quare maior fit aestimatio in primo capite quam in secundo … respondeo, quia in primo capite agitur de occiso, in secundo de rupto, et ideo quia magis peccatur in primo capite quam in secundo maior imponitur poena. Cf. also Hostiensis, summa X 5.36 (ed. Lyon 1537, reprinted Aalen 1962, fo. 267ra), taken from Azo, Summa Aurea C. 3.35 (ed. Turin 1578, reprinted Turin 1964, p. 90).

[22] Cf. Bernardus Papiensis, summa decretalium 1Comp. 5.31 (ed. *Laspeyres*, p. 263: in aliis autem animalibus occisis culpa vel vulneratis, et in servo vel pecude vulneratis, in tantum teneris quanti in xxx diebus retro fuit, ut Dig. ad l. Aquil. Si servus servum § Tertio (D. 9.2.27.5). Si autem in re inanimata damnum dedisti, teneris ad interesse, ratione habita retro plurimi xxx dierum. Cf. also Guillelmus Duranti, Speculum iudiciale IV.4.2 (ed. Basel 1574, reprinted Aalen 1975, II, p. 512): Si autem servus ille melior fuerit retro intra annum, vel res illa intra xxx dies, sic concipitur libellus: Coram etc. conqueror de P. qui T. servum meum occidit. qui retro intra annum valuit quiquaginta unde peto illa quiquaginta … He gives only examples for the cases where slaves or livestock were injured or killed. In the case of injury to livestock Goffredus Tranensis, however, restricts the quantum of the penalty. Cf. Goffredus Tranensis, summa X 5.36 (ed. Lyon 1519, reprinted Aalen 1968, fo. 235rb): Si vero servus fuerit vulneratus tenetur vulnerator domino servi in quantum servum deteriorem fecit. ff. ad l. Aquil. l. Si servum § Rupisse (D. 9.2.27.17).

[23] Bernardus Papiensis, Summa decretalium 1Comp. 5.10 (ed. *Laspeyres*, p. 223). He refers hereto in his commentary on 1Comp. 5.31 (ibid. p. 263). Cf. also Damasus, summa decretalium 1Comp. 5.10 (ed. *Kuttner*, loc. cit. note 1, p. 214): poena homicidii non voluntarii nulla est, nisi quod poterit pro tali homicidio agi civiliter ad poenam pecuniariam.

(5Comp. 5.15.un; X 5.36.7) that this was also the case where a free person was assaulted or insulted. In contrast to the *actio iniuriarum* in Roman law, the private poena for *iniuria* in medieval canon law could encompass both the compensation of damages caused[25] as well as redress for the injustice suffered.[26] As Hostiensis remarks in his *summa*, the quantum of the private poena for *iniuria* increases if compensation for the damage due to assault or insult is claimed in the same action:

Sed et augetur quando expense et damna simul cum iniuria estimantur. infra eod. Olim (X 5.36.7).[27]

The payment of medical expenses and loss of income could thus eventually assume a compensatory character.

Raymund de Pennaforte included Exodus 21:18–19 in the title *De iniuriis et damno dato* in the *Liber Extra* (1234) of pope Gregory IX. Hereby the question of whether someone who injured another in a fight had to pay more than the medical costs and the lost income was raised anew. Did the (estimated) future loss of income also have to be paid? Appealing to D. 9.1.3, D. 9.3.7 and D. 9.2.7.pr. the canonists thought that this was indeed the case.[28] In other words, if an injury meant that a person could no longer

---

24 Cf. Inst. 4.3.9. There is, however, no reference hereto in the commentaries referred to in note 21. For the view of the glossators, see *Lange*, loc. cit. note 9, p. 135–136; *R. König*, Das allgemeine Schadensersatzrecht im Mittelalter im Anschluß an die lex Aquilia (unpublished diss. Frankfurt 1954), p. 46; Azo already (Summa Codicis, C. 3.35. no. 1) restricts the penal character of the *actio legis Aquiliae* to the amount in excess of the actual damages.

25 Bernardus Parmensis, on the other hand, restricts the penalty to this amount. Cf. the end of his gloss *Banniverat* ad X 5.36.7: ... propter hanc iniuriam punitur ad expensas quas propter hoc fecit et damna que pertulit tali occasione, ut patet.

26 Cf. Hostiensis, Lectura super X 5.36.7 (ed. Venice 1581, reprinted Turin 1965, fo. 96) s.v. *Expensas et damna*: sic supra c.i. (X 5.36.1); s.v. *Condemnandum*: potest ergo episcopus agere ad satisfactionem iniuriae sibi illatae, ut hic et in 17 q.4 Si quis deinceps (C.17 q.4 c.22) C. de iniuriis Atrocem (C. 9.35.4), quod verum est quoad poenam civilem, capitalem enim remittere ei sanctitatis gloria dereliquit. Cf. also the gloss of Vincentius Hispanus copied by Johannes Andreae (ad X 5.36.7 nr 1; ed. Venice 1581, reprinted Turin 1963, fo. 118v): Nota quod episcopus agit pro damnis et iniuriis illatis ecclesiis sibi subiectis. de con. di.i. Omnes (De cons. D.1. c.3) de exces. prel. Sicut unire (X 5.31.8) Vin.

27 Cf. Hostiensis, summa X 5.36 no. 7 (ed. Lyon 1537, reprinted Aalen 1962, fo. 265vb). This phrase is lacking in Azo, Summa Aurea C. 9.35 (ed. Turin 1578, reprinted Turin 1966, p. 340), from where Hostiensis derived his commentary on X 5.36.

28 Bernardus Parmensis refers to D. 9.1.3, D. 9.3.7 and D. 9.2.7.pr. in the gloss *Operas eius* ad X 5.36.1. From this it appears that, as Johannes Andreae (ad X 5.36.1) remarks, also future lost income due to the injury would have to be compensated. According to Hostiensis (Lectura super X 5.36.1), in addition *omne aliud interesse* had to be compensated. In so far as necessary – as in the case of future

practise his occupation, more had to be paid. Did the amount also increase if someone suffered disfigurement? The canonists answered this question in the negative. They interpreted this text (X 5.36.1) in the light of the *actio legis Aquiliae* and refused to calculate the "diminution in value of a free person" which had been caused by the disfigurement (*damnum in personam*):[29] a monetary value could not be placed on a person's life and body.

Raymund de Pennaforte had omitted the words "then shall he that smote him be quit" *(innocens erit)* in Exodus 21:18 (1Comp. 5.31.1) when he included this text in the *Liber Extra*. He apparently concurred with Alanus, Laurentius Hispanus and Tancred that, in addition, a sum for *iniuria,* the injustice suffered by the other person, would have to be paid. Similarly Innocentius IV, who explicitly remarks on the different characters of the amounts to be paid: The victim institutes the *actio iniuriarum* regarding the injustice suffered, while the *actio legis Aquiliae (utilis)* is instituted to recover expenses and the damages suffered as a consequence of the injury. This also appears from the references employed: D. 47.10.15.46 and D. 44.7.34. It is apparent that he considers the payment of medical costs and loss of income as compensatory.[30] The action by which these costs are claimed, the *actio legis Aquiliae (utilis)*, thus assumes some reipersecutory characteristics. The action by which redress of the injustice suffered (by assault or insult) is claimed, the *actio iniuriarum*, however, remains strictly penal.[31]

---

lost income – the judge had to estimate the extent of the damages and have the claimant confirm this under oath. Johannes Andreae and Antonius Butrigarius include this in their commentary on X 5.36.1.

[29] Bernardus Papiensis (summa decretalium 1Comp. 5.31, ed. *Laspeyres*, p. 261) defines damages as a *"diminutio vel iactura in rem vel personam data"*. Goffredus Tranensis and Hostiensis define damages as *"diminutio vel ademptio patrimonii"*. Goffredus, however, still distinguishes, just as Bernardus Papiensis, between damage to a (free) person, to an animal, and to a good. Cf. his summa decretalium, X 5.36.

[30] Cf. Innocentius IV, ad X 5.36.1 (ed. Lyon 1548, fo. 205rb): Actio iniuriarum solum iniuriam prosequitur, non interesse nisi in hoc quod propter maius damnum aestimatur magis iniuria. ut ff. ad legem Aquil. Item apud §. Si quis <servo verberato> (D. 47.10.15.46) ff. de act. et obl. Si quis servum (D. 44.7.34), C. de iniur. Dominum (C. 9.35.8), tamen pro damnas et expensis quandocunque datur actio legis Aquiliae ut in predictis legibus vel ad minus act. de do. Cf. also Hostiensis, summa X 5.36 *Iniuria* no. 8 (ed. 265vb), derived from Azo.

[31] Contra: *Scott*, loc. cit. note 9. He generally assumes that delictual actions are reipersecutory in nature: "Canon law recognizes delictual claims as purely reipersecutory in nature ...". This was certainly not true in the Middle ages, neither for the *actio legis Aquiliae* nor the *actio iniuriarum*. For the *actio legis Aquiliae* see note 95. The *actio iniuriarum* remained actively as well as passively hereditarily non transmissible. Cf. Hostiensis, Summa aurea X 5.31 *Iniuria* no. 8 (ed. Lyon 1537, reprinted Aalen 1962, fo. 265vb): *Heredi non datur hec actio nec in heredem, nisi lite*

No dominant theory has yet emerged by the middle of the thirteenth century. The apparatus of Bernardus Parmensis, for example, lacks any reference to the punishment for *iniuria*, the injustice inflicted on someone through assault or insult. He possibly agrees with the author of Exodus 21:18–19 that the payment of damages is sufficient punishment.[32]

From around 1300 the canonists no longer interpreted the word *restituere* in the decretals *Si rixati* (X 5.36.1 = Exodus 21:18) and *Si quis domum* (X 5.36.6) as the payment of a private poena – the punishment for assault or arson – but as compensation for harm, calculated according to the guidelines of the *actio legis Aquiliae (utilis)*. They followed the interpretation of pope Innocentius IV and use the concept *restitutio* in the same way as the theologians. As there can be no return of what another has lost in the case of assault and arson, compensation is due for the damage done, as for medical costs and the loss of income of the injured party,[33] and the value of what was lost in the fire.[34] Moreover, they concluded from X 5.36.6. that penance was required:[35]

---

contestata, nam ad solam vindictam est prodita. Also here Scott does not distinguish between the obligation to compensate the damages and that of paying a private penalty. According to him the heirs were "obliged to fulfil his delictual debts from the moment the inheritance had devolved upon them". Cf. also *Scott*, loc. cit. note 9, p. 19: "Thus it appears from X 3.28.14 that Canon law differs from Roman law in two important aspects. In the first instance, the former system acknowledges the general principle of passive transmissibility of delictual claims.[...]". Thus also *Zimmermann*, loc. cit. note 20, p. 1021: "The canonists had always recognised the passive transmissibility of delictual claims." Innocentius IV, Hostiensis and Johannes Andreae expressly indicate that this is not the case. According to them there is an obligation, based on the guarantee of the deceased on his deathbed, explicitly given to the priest (*stipulatio*), or on the implicitly given order (*mandatum* according to Johannes Andreae), to compensate the damages the deceased had caused. Cf. Innocentius IV, ad X 3.28.14; Hostiensis, Lectura super X 3.28.14, Johannes Andreae, ad X 3.28.14. Only Bernardus Parmensis, who makes no distinction between punishment and compensation, still defends the older conception in the gloss *Sed eius heredes* ad X 3.28.14.

32 Cf. Bernardus Parmensis, Casus X 5.36.1: *Nota hic poenam percutientis secundum veterum legem*. He thus similarly restricts the penalty for *iniuria* also in his commentary on X 5.36.7. See note 25.

33 Cf. Johannes Andreae, ad X 5.36.1, Antonius Butrigarius, ad X 5.36.1; Panormitanus, ad X 5.36.1. Just as Guillelmus Duranti, Panormitanus draws a link between injuring and killing. If the victim survives, the victim has to be compensated for what he would have been able to earn had he not been injured, and if the victim succumbs to his injuries, the same applies: *quinimo dicit Spe(culator) ti. de iniuriis §.ii. post princ. quod mortuo percusso potest pater vel heres eius pro operibus quas iste potuit exercere toto tempore vite sue. et habebitur respectus verisimiliter quanto tempore potuisset vivere*. (ed. Lyon 1509–1510, fo. 101rb).

34 Cf. Johannes Andreae, gloss *Restituat* ad X 5.36.6 (ed. Venice 1581, reprinted Turin 1963, fo. 118va): proprie quo ad sublata, si extant, improprie quo ad incensa, scilicet ibi emendet.

Peccatum ergo non tollitur per emendationem damni, immo necessaria est penitentia post emenda(tione)m.[36]

As Laurentius Hispanus had already remarked in around 1215, the victim could elect to claim only his medical costs and loss of income. The victim was, however, not required to restrict his claim in this manner, and could also claim an amount for *iniuria.*[37] A forgiving person could abandon the *actio iniuriarum*, and could – also in return for payment – formally renounce his claim, but in this event, it was still possible to institute an action for the compensation of damages.[38] Likewise vice versa; even if the perpetrator had paid compensation for the harm done, the victim could claim a poena for the injustice suffered.

III. Private penalty or the compensation of incorporeal damages

Actio iniuriarum

When calculating the sum to be paid to the victim of *iniuria*, an important consideration the judge had to bear in mind[39] was the seriousness of

[35] Cf. note 12.

[36] Johannes Andreae, gloss *Poeniteat* ad X 5.36.6 (ed. Venice 1581, reprinted Turin 1963, fo. 11va); Antonius de Butrio, ad X 5.36.6; Panormitanus, ad X 5.36.6.

[37] Cf. Goffredus Tranensis, Summa decretalium X 5.36 no. 6, Innocentius IV, gloss *Si rixati* ad X 5.36.1; Johannes Andreae, ad X 5.36.1; Panormitanus, ad X 5.36.1.

[38] Cf. Guillelmus Duranti, Speculum I.2.8 (ed. Basel 1574, reprinted Aalen 1975, I, p. 192): Quid si vulneratus remisit iniuriam pecunia recepta, numquid poterit agere lege Aquilia? ... Unde dici potest secundum quosdam quod tollitur actio iniuriarum, non autem actio legis Aquiliae. et facit C. lib. xii. de numer. actuar. l. Nulli (C. 12.49.10). Cf. also Johannes Andreae, gloss *Restituat* ad X 5.36.1; Panormitanus, ad X 5.36.1, Hadrianus VI (see note 59), Covarruvias, Var. resol. 2.10.7 (ed. Opera omnia, Geneve 1734, II, p. 204).

[39] From the formulation *"taxatione iuramento premissa"* in X 5.36.7 it is apparent that the judge first had to estimate the maximum amount which can be awarded against the defendant for *iniuria*; hereafter the plaintiff declared under oath the amount of money which he would have preferred to lose rather than to have suffered the offence (*quod tantum de suo potius amisset quam hanc iniuriam est passus*). Cf. Bernardus Parmensis, gloss *Taxatione* ad X 5.36.7; Goffredus Tranensis, summa decretalium X 5.36 no. 4; Hostiensis, Summa X 5.36 *(iniuria)* no. 7; Guillelmus Duranti, Speculum IV.4.1 no. 5 and 10; Panormitanus, X 5.36.7. Herein they concur with the opinion of Azo. Johannes Andreae (ad X 5.36.1 no. 4), on the other hand, concurs with Accursius. *Olivier* (loc. cit. note 8, p. 79) fails to bear all this in mind, where he restricts himself to the glossators and states: "Die bepaling van die hoogte van die *poena* berus dus in die beheer van die benadeelde". Cf. re. the view of the glossators also *Lange*, loc. cit. note 9, p. 94–96 and *B. Ranchod*, Foundations of the south african law of defamation, [diss. Leiden], Leiden 1972, p. 57–61.

the mutilation. Like the glossators, the canonists distinguished between the *aestimatio damni*, the estimate of the extent of the damages which would otherwise be difficult to prove (for example the aforementioned future loss of income due to injury), and the *aestimatio iniuriae*, the pecuniary valuation of the seriousness of the injustice suffered by someone through assault or insult.[40] This was determined not only by the position and fortune of both parties, but also by the extent and location of the injury, as Hostiensis derived from Azo: "*sed et quantitas vulneris consideratur et locus vulneris, utrum in oculo vel in alio loco*".[41]

Anyone injured in a fight, even a bystander accidentally injured, could claim a private penalty for assault "*quam iniuriam nolle(t) sustinere pro quinquaginta libris*".[42] While there was no intention to injure a bystander, the combatant should have been more careful, even if acting in self defence.[43] According to the canonists *culpa* was sufficient, and this was derived from X 5.36.9:

---

40 Thus, in so many words, according to Guillelmus Duranti, Speculum iudiciale IV,4.1 no. 17 (ed. Basel 1574, reprinted Aalen 1975, II, p. 511); Johannes Andreae, glosses *Damnis et iniuriis* ad VI 1.16.2; Panormitanus refers to this, ad X 5.36.7. The distinction is based on D. 9.2.5.1 and is also drawn in Azo's summa, from where Hostiensis derives the commentary in his Summa Aurea (X 5.36, *iniuria* no. 7 ad *de damno dato* no. 5). Cf. Azo, summa codicis, C. 9.35 (ed. Turin 1578, reprinted Turin 1964, p. 34): *nec enim in actione iniuriarum habetur ratio damni ut damni set ut contumelie, id est ut maior videatur contumelia.* Cf. also Azo, Lectura super C. 9.35.8.

41 Hostiensis, summa X 5.36 no. 8 (ed. Lyon 1537, reprinted Aalen 1963, fo. 265vb).

42 Cf. Guillemus Duranti, Speculum iudiciale IV.4.1 no. 10.

43 The example is taken from Bernardus Parmensis, gloss *Ignorantia* ad X 5.36.9: Hic non excusat ignorantia a culpa, si potuit scire ex facto suo contingere iacturam vel iniuriam, puta mihi licet percutere percutientem me, si vellem eum percutere, alium percussi imputatur mihi. ff. ad legem Aquil. Scientiam §. pen. (D. 9.2.45.4) et ff. eod. Si cum servo (D. 47.10.4). Et illud scias quod iniuria sit aut re aut verbis, re quotiens manus infertur, verbis quotiens convicium dicitur. ... It appears from the references that *error in persona* is meant. Cf. for the view of earlier canonists *Kuttner*, loc cit note 1, p. 179–184. Hostiensis (Lectura super X 5.36.9 s.v. *Posse contingere*) gives the same example. From the warning "And bear in mind that not only assault, but also defamation, can be subsumed under *iniuria*" it appears that the defence 'I thought that the person I was calling a thief was the person who had stolen my property' was of no avail. As those who are struck may strike back in self defence, one may of course charge the other with the delict. Even then, however, one must bear in mind the possibility that one may be accusing the wrong person. Outside the court room, such an allegation is *per se* considered defamatory, and if the person insulted instituted an action of *iniuria*, he thus did not bear the burden of proving that the defendant had the intention to defame. Cf. Hostiensis, Lectura super X 5.36.9 no. 4; adopted by Johannes Andreae (ad X 5.36.9 no. 5) and Antonius Butrigarius (ad X 5.36.9 no. 1). Cf. also Johannes Andreae, additiones super Speculum IV.4.1.1.

Si culpa tua datum est damnum vel iniuria irrogata, seu aliis irrogantibus opem forte tulisti, aut hec imperitia tua vel negligentia evenerunt iure super his facere satisfacere oportet; nec ignorantia te excusat, si scire debuisti ex facto tuo iniuriam verisimiliter posse contingere vel iacturam. ... Sane licet qui occasionem damni dat, damnum videatur dedisse, secus tamen in illo dicendo qui ut non accideret de contingentibus nil omisit.[44]

Not every injury, however, could give rise to an *actio iniuriarum*. Accidents, such as those occurring while chopping wood, fell outside the application of the *actio iniuriarum ex lege Cornelia*, which required that the victim have been struck down or stabbed.[45]

Modern writers have remarked on the different approach of the moral theologians, under the influence of Thomas Aquinas's "aanvaarding van die standpunt dat immateriële skade voortvloeiend uit 'n besering vergoed moet word".[46] Their line of reasoning, however, differs from that of the canonists.

The jurists discuss whether compensation and a penalty can be claimed in an ecclesiastical court, if someone has been killed, injured or insulted, had his goods damaged, or suffered damage in another way. The theologians ask what a person must do to be absolved before God if he has sinned by insulting his neighbour, or by injuring him, or causing him damage. Both jurists and theologians consider the question of whether the damage which resulted from sin had to be compensated. The jurists deal with this issue within the framework of (default and) delict, and the theologians consider it within the framework of the doctrine of (penance and) restitution.

As the jurists obliquely address the *forum internum*, in their commentary on X 5.36, so the theologians obliquely address the *forum externum*. An example of the jurists thus at work is the commentary on the decretal *Si egressus* (X 5.36.6): *"Peccatum ergo non tollitur per emendationem damni, immo necessaria est penitentia post emendationem"*.[47] An example of the

---

[44] X 5.36.9. The middle section concerns the liability for damage caused by animals: Quod si animalia tua nocuisse proponas, nihilominus ad satisfactionem teneris, nisi ea dando passis damnum velis liberare te ipsum. Quod tamen ad liberationem non proficit, si fera animalia vel que consueverunt nocere fuissent, et quam debueras non curasti diligentiam adhibere.

[45] Cf. D. 47.10.5.pr.–1 & 47.10.7.1; Goffredus Tranensis, summa decretalium X 5.36 no. 6; Hostiensis, Aurea, *Iniuria* no. 4; Guillelmus Duranti, Speculum iudiciale IV.4.1 no. 10: iniuria vero que facto irrogatur, puta quia quis verberatur vel pulsatur vel alio modo manu iniuria infertur vel domus sua introita punitur per actione iniuriarum ex lege Cornelia; Johannes Andreae, ad X 5.36.1.

[46] *Olivier*, loc. cit. note 8, p. 87; Similarly *G. Nufer*, Über die Restitutionslehre der spanischen Spätscholastiker und ihre Ausstrahlung auf die Folgezeit [Dissertation Freiburg], 1969, p. 32.

theologians thus at work is the passage in the *Summa Theologiae* (ST II II q.62 art.3), where Thomas Aquinas answers (in the negative) the question of whether more than the value of the goods has to be returned, for example by the thief. While the judge may punish the offence[48] by awarding quadruple the value of the goods to the victim, it was not necessary to pay more than compensation in order to be absolved before God and one's fellow man.[49]

In this line of reasoning there is no obligation in the *forum internum* to compensate the other financially for injustice caused by assault or insult. It is sufficient to beg the other for forgiveness: *quandoque est satisfactio sine restitutione aliqua, ut cum quis se proximo humiliat de aliquibus contumeliis ei dictis.*[50]

According to Thomas Aquinas (1225–1275) justice demands that everyone be restored in that which has been taken against his will.[51] A person is deprived of something not only by the thief who steals his goods, but also by the person who insults, kills or maims him. Thomas Aquinas considers those who injure another so seriously that it results in the loss of use of limbs, or even in the loss of life, as having caused damage to the person. He employs the same term as most canonists in this time; i.e. *damnum in personam.*[52]

While the thief can replace the horse he steals, those who deprive another of life or a hand can obviously not restore the life or the hand or even anything similar. Restitution therefore had to be *"qualis possibilis est, scilicet ad arbitrium bonorum (virorum)"*.[53] Thomas Aquinas fails to mention how a person is to be compensated for the loss of his life.[54] He does,

---

47 According to Johannes Andreae, Antonius Butrigarius and Panormitanus.

48 Cf. for the difference between *peccatum* and *crimen*, *poenitentia* and *poena*: *Kuttner*, loc cit note 1, p. 5–6; *S. Kuttner*, Ecclesia de occultis non iudicat, in: Acta congressus Iuridici Internationalis III, Rom 1936, p. 227–246; *Kaufmann*, Strafe in HRG 32 (1990), 2011; *R. Pahud de Mortanges*, Strafzwecke bei Gratian und den Dekretisten, ZRG Kan 78 (1992), p. 122–123; *R. Kottje*, Buße oder Strafe, Zur Justitia in den Libri poenitentiales, in: La giustizia nell' alto medioevo (secoli 5–8), Spoleto 1995, p. 445.

49 Thomas Aquinas, ST II II q.62 art.3 co (ed. p. 607): antequam sit condemnatus per iuidicium non tenetur plus restituere quam accepit, sed postquam condemnatus est tenetur poenam solvere.

50 Thomas Aquinas 4SN dist.15 q.15 ar5a co. (ed. p. 505).

51 ST II II q.62 art.2 co: *restituere importat redditionem illius rei quae iniuste ablata est.* This definition is directed towards the *acceptio iniuste, ut in furto et iniuriis*, as is apparent from the question Thomas treats here, i.e. whether restitution is necessary if another is deprived of something which cannot be returned: his life or a limb. Cf. Caietanus, ad ST II II q.62 art.2 (Opera omnia, ed. Rome 1897, IX, p. 43).

52 See note 29.

however, discuss the case where someone injures another in such manner that a limb is lost:

> *Puta, cum aliquis alicui abstulit membrum, debet ei recompensare vel in pecunia vel in aliquo honore, considerata conditione utriusque personae, secundum arbitrium boni viri.*[55]

Here Thomas only indicates that restitution can be effected by the payment of money; he does not, however, indicate how the arbitrator should calculate the quantum of the amount.

Later theologians do, however, address this issue. They distinguish four items of loss which qualify for compensation: medical expenses, loss of income for the period in which the victim lay ill in bed, future loss of income due to permanent injury, and finally disfiguring mutilation (*damnum corporis)* and the loss of life itself (*damnum vitae*). By this formulation they seek from Thomas the answer to a question he probably did not ask himself, i.e. whether, in addition to the patrimonial loss resulting from the injury, the incorporeal damage resulting therefrom had to be compensated, i.e. the pain, suffering and disfigurement.

The words *"considerata conditione utriusque personae"* cannot be construed as an argument that Thomas Aquinas is here specifically addressing incorporeal damage: disfiguring mutilation and loss of life. Future loss of income is an example of what Thomas Aquinas calls preventing someone from acquiring a good.[56] Also in that case the sum is established *"pensatis*

---

53 Thomas Aquinas, 4SN dist.15 q.1 art.5b ra2 (ed. p. 505), ST II II q.62 art.2 ar1 (Opera Omnia, ed. Rome 1897, IX p. 43).

54 Duns Scotus, did, however, answer this question. As no one can be financially compensated for the loss of his life, the perpetrator ought to compensate him *in spiritualibus*, by giving alms and dedicating masses to the salvation of the victim. If the perpetrator received the death penalty, however, there was no longer any obligation to make restitution, not even to compensate the patrimonial loss of the heirs of the victim. This reveals that for Duns Scotus the amount paid to the family of the victim still bears characteristics of a private penalty. Cf. Duns Scotus, IV dist.15 q.3 art.2 no.9 (IX.220).

55 Thomas Aquinas, ST II II q.62 art.2 ra1 (Opera Omnia, ed. Rome 1897, IX p. 43).

56 Thus reasons Domingo de Soto, De justitia et iure, 4.6.3 (ed. Antwerpen 1568, fo. 121r): "Idem prorsus dicendum de mutilatione membri, ut qui manum alteri abstulit, tenetur solvere operas medici et damna cessantesque labores in integrum, ad arbitrium tamen sapientum virorum. ... Ex his sit consequens quod non debet aestimari pretium huiusmodi laesionem ad libitum illius qui damnum accepit. ... Non enim est eadem hic habenda ratio que in rebus recuperabilibus. Si furto surripui equum debeo vel ipsum reddere vel simpliciter quantum valet, at quia membra non possunt eadem restitui, non debent tantum aestimari quanti homines faciunt, quando habent; quamvis etiam deformitas quae in mutilo restat, sit etiam repensanda. Sed est tandem adnotandum quod inter illustres istae restitutiones non petuntur, nam

conditionibus personarum et negotii, secundum arbitrium sapientis".[57] While Thomas Aquinas's formulation certainly cannot be construed as denying that incorporeal damage must be compensated, it also does not indicate that it should be. It cannot be established with certainty whether Thomas Aquinas was against or in favour of the compensation of incorporeal damage.

The difference in opinion between the jurists and the theologians can be traced back to Duns Scotus (c. 1260–1308), who does indicate how the quantum of the amount to be paid to the victim should be established.

> *... debet respondere non solum damno quod incurrit quis per mutilationem pro toto tempore futuro quo usurus esset quis membro abscisso, sed etiam expensis appositis in curatione, et hoc dicit capitulum allegatum extra de iniuriis et damno dato (X 5.36.1); et ultra placationi ipsius laesi ... et consolationi ipsius afflicti.*[58]

Following Duns Scotus, Angelus de Clavasio († circa 1495), Gabriel Biel (1410–1495), Hadrian VI (1459–1523) and Luis de Molina (1535–1600) assumed the mutilation itself must also be compensated, without mentioning how this sum has to be estimated.[59] The way it is established can be

damna facile condonant, iniuriae enim sunt quas numquam oblivioni tradunt". He restricts the restitution to *patrimonial* loss. Contra: *P. C. Pauw*, Persoonlikheidskrenking en skuld in die suid-afrikaanse reg, 'n regshistoriese en regsvergelykende ondersoek [diss. Leiden], Pynacker 1976, p. 63; *Olivier*, loc cit note 8, p. 99 and p. 102 note 106; *R. Feenstra*, Théories sur la responsabilité civile en cas d'homicide et en cas de lésion corporelle avant Grotius, in: R. Feenstra, Fata iuris romani, Etudes d'histoire du droit, 1974, p. 160 (implicitly).

57 ST II II q.62 art.2 ra4 (Opera Omnia, ed. Rome 1897, IX p. 43). Thomas gives as example: I bar you from aquiring a prebend. A similar problem arises if someone digs up sown seed. The perpetrator is obliged to compensate more than the equivalent of the seeds but less than the estimated value of the crop thereof, "*tenetur tamen aliquam recompensationem facere, secundum conditionem personarum et negotiorum*". Cf. Thomas Aquinas ST II II q.62 art.4 co (Opera Omnia, ed. Rome 1897, IX p. 50).

58 Sententiae 4.15.3.9

59 Angelus Claretus de Clavasio, Summa angelica de casibus conscientiae, *Restitutio* (see *Olivier*, loc. cit. note 8, p. 90); Gabriel Biel, Collectorium circa quattuor libros Sententiarum, ad IV dist.15 q.15 art.3 co5 (ed. *Werbeck & Hofman*, Tübingen 1979 IV.2, p. 330); Hadrianus VI, Quaestiones de Sacramentis in Quartum Sententiarum, *De restitutione* (ed. Rome 1522, reprinted Ridgewood 1964, fo. 98r): "De mutilantibus vel aliam lesionem inferentibus dico quod tenentur ad reparationem proportionabiliter ad damnum illatum, alias enim negocium deduci non poterit ad aequalitatem iustitiae, immo dicunt doctores Specul(ator) ti. de accu(satore) i. Ioan(nes) Andr(eae) et Panorm(itanus) cap. i. de iniur. (X 5.36.1) quod etiam ubi vulneratus remiserit iniuriam etiam accepta pecunia non ergo intelligitur interesse suum remississe". Luis de Molina, De iustitia et iure, 4 disp. 88; Francisco de Vitoria, ad II II 62 no. 8 (ed. *Beltran*, Salamanca 1934, III, p. 118): ... non solum incommodum temporale ratione amissionis manus vel alterius membri tenetur restituere, sed etiam debet restituere iniuriam factam, ratione iniuriae naturalis factae.

found in the commentary of Francisco de Toledo (1534–1596). If someone confesses to having injured another, he is absolved if he makes restitution in an amount calculated by a wise man, bearing in mind the position and fortune of both parties, the seriousness of the injury, and the level of fault of the perpetrator.[60]

This is a standard which exhibits a strong resemblance to the criteria which the judge had to employ in calculating the private penalty for *iniuria*.

IV. Private penalty or the compensation of incorporeal damage

A compromise: Covarruvias

Around 1270 the canonists came to the conclusion that a distinction had to be made between compensation for harm (*damna et impensas)* and the payment of a private penalty (*poena pecuniaria*) as punishment for e. g. theft, arson, assault, or defamation. Thomas Aquinas had also remarked on the difference between the *restitutio* of what had wrongfully been taken from another, and the *poena* due to the delict. He who had taken something from his neighbour had sinned, and was therefore obliged to restitution (*restitutio*), the return of what had been taken, and *satisfactio (proximi),* asking for forgiveness for the wrong committed.[61]

Olivier, loc cit note 8, p. 91, wrongly groups Sylvester de Prierio († c.1523) with these.

[60] Franciscus de Toledo, In Summam Theologiae S. Thomae Aquinatis Enarratio, q.62 art.2 q.3 (ed. Rome 1869–1870, p. 258): Dices quanti aestimandum est membrum? Ad hoc respondet bene Marsilius, in huiusmodi aestimatione arbitrium viri boni est consulendum, pensatis tribus, puta conditione personarum, percutientis et percussae, rursus quantitate nocumenti ex membri dignitate, et rursus gravitate culpae percussoris. The text he refers to Marsilius d' Inghen († 1395). I could, however, not find the passage he referred to. Cf. Marsilius d'Inghen, Questiones super quattuor libros sententiarum, IV. 3.5.2 (ed. Strassburg 1501, reprinted Frankfurt 1966, fo. 568rb): Sed quandoque res in propria forma nequit haberi, ut si quis domum combussisset, hominem interfecisset vel graviter vulnerasset ... [S]i inveniatur penitens et sint huiusmodi facta publica imponat penitenti ut satisfaciat iuxta arbitrium boni viri vel bonorum virorum qui habebunt ponderare omnes circumstantias aggravantes et alleviantes. Si vero peccatum esset privatum et iniuria ignota, tunc presbyter si sciat omnibus ponderatis aestimare estimet et restituere faciat.

[61] Cf. Thomas Aquinas 4SN dist.15 q.1 ar.5a co (ed. 505): Respondeo dicendam ad primam quaestionem quod inequalitas justitiae duobus modis contingit, uno modo in rebus exterioribus, ut quando unus rem aliam detinet, alio modo in actionibus et passionibus, ut cum quis alium per violentiam reverberat. ... Et secundum hoc reparatio justitiae dupliciter significatur, reparatio enim inequalitatis existentis in rebus restitutio dicitur, reparatio autem inequalitatis existentis in actionibus et

The moral theologians of the fifteenth and sixteenth century concluded from this that the perpetrator of a wrong was obliged to *restitutio* of what had been taken from the other, and to *satisfactio*, the reparation of the injustice (*iniuria*) suffered by the other.[62] The concept *iniuria* is here conceived in a wider sense than is the case for the canonists, who speak of *iniuria* when someone is assaulted or defamed. According to the moral theologians *iniuria* occurred in every wrongdoing: robbers and thieves were also obliged to repair the injustice suffered by their victim, either by asking them for forgiveness, or in another manner.[63] Everyone understood *restitutio* as including the compensation of personal damages caused by killing or injuring, and some also understood it as including financial compensation for the suffering of the other. Everyone, moreover, considered *satisfactio* essential: the perpetrator had at least to ask the victim for forgiveness for the injustice caused. Diego de Covarruvias y Leya (1512–1577), however, assumed that this *satisfactio* preferably consisted not of the asking for forgiveness,[64], but of money:

> *Tenetur item is qui alteri injuriam intulit praeter damna et impensas aliquid arbitrio boni viri injuriam passo retribuere in compensationem injuriae illatae, cum ea haberi non possit pro infecta".*[65]

He did not consider the obligation to compensate the victim of assault for the loss of a limb formulated by Thomas Aquinas (ST II II q.62 art.2 ad1) *"vel in pecunia vel in aliquo honore"* as a form of restitution, but as an example of recompense for *iniuria*, like the obligation formulated by Duns Scotus (IV dist.15 q.3)[66] to dedicate masses to the salvation of the deceased's soul.[67]

---

passionibus satisfactio nominatur. Et ideo quandoque est satisfactio sine restitutione aliqua, ut cum quis se proximo humiliat de aliquibus contumeliis dictis. ...

62 Cf. Domingo de Soto, De iustitia et iure IV.6.1 (ed. Antwerp 1568, 117v): ... Itaque satisfactio non est nisi ubi iniuriosum crimen adsuit, restitutio vero etiam, ubi nulla interfuerit culpa. Hoc autem discrimen ex ipsis vocibus innotescit. Restituere namque est reddere quod ablatum est, satisfactio vero, quia pars est poenitentiae est, iniuriam resarcire.

63 Cf. Domingo de Soto, De jusititia et iure IV.6.1 (ed. Antwerp 1568, fo. 117v): Latrones et fures qui vi aut furto alienam domum compilaverint, tenentur in primis ad restitutionem eorum quae rapuerint et praeterea de illata iniuria satisfacere: puta aut petendo veniam aut alia via.

64 Diego de Covarruvias y Leya, Variae Resolutiones 2.10.7 (ed. Geneve 1734, II, p. 205): ... relinquendum est arbitrio boni viri, qui si videret necessarium petitionem veniae ad honoris restitutionem, eam petendam esse censebit. Quod si aliter possit fieri injuriae compensatio et restitutio, aut si petitio veniae decens non sit nec expediens, non erit veniae petitio deliquenti injungenda.

65 Diego de Covarruvias y Leya, Variae Resolutiones 2.10.7, Opera omnia (ed. Geneve 1734, II, p. 205). This is not taken into account by *Olivier*, loc. cit. note 8, p. 102, who states that according to Covarruvias "daar geen vergoedingsplig vir 'n nie-vermoënsskade voortvloeiend uit so 'n toegebragte *iniuria* is nie."

Covarruvias did not consider disfiguring injury as a harm calling for compensation. The wrongdoing which caused the disfigurement could, however, be a ground for the financial compensation of the injustice. There was no cause for this, however, if the disfigurement was caused by accident.

V. Culpa lata or culpa levissima

Canonists and moral theologians

In practice it would have been of little concern to most victims why they were being compensated for their disfiguring injuries. There is, however, a very important difference between *damnum iniuria datum* and *iniuria* in both Roman and canon law. Accidents, after all, fell outside the reach of *iniuria*, but within the reach of the *lex Aquilia*. If, for instance, a passer-by were to be struck by a brick which had accidentally slipped from the hands of a bricklayer during the construction of a house, the *actio legis Aquiliae utilis* was available. Even extremely slight fault, *culpa levissima*, was, after all, sufficient for the applicability of the *lex Aquilia*. This is apparent from D. 9.2.44.pr. *"In lege Aquilia et levissima culpa venit"*.

Both the canonists and the moral theologians, however, hesitated about whether liability should be assumed so readily. In other words: does the *lex Aquilia* penetrate into the *forum internum?* If there was no intention to harm or cause damage to another, was there, none the less, the obligation to restitution?

In their commentary on X 5.36 the canonists asked this question in the context of the decretal *Si egressus* (X 5.36.5). Not only Exodus 21:18–19 but also Exodus 22:6 was enshrined in both the *Compilatio Prima* and the *Liber Extra.* If a fire consumed a harvested or standing crop, the person who lit the fire had to pay for the harm. The canonists applied this to the case where a fire lit on a person's own property spread to the neighbour's land and damaged the crop there.[68] In their view the person who lit the fire was not by definition obliged to compensate the damages, but only if fault (*culpa*; if he had acted otherwise than was expected of him) could be established. Hostiensis gives the example of someone burning hay on a windy day (D. 9.2.30.3), when even the lighting of the fire displayed lack of proper care. Furthermore, if the fire had been lit in a manner which would

---

66 See note 54.

67 Diego de Covarruvias y Leya, Variae Resolutiones 2.10.7 (ed. Geneve 1734, II, p. 205). *Nufer* (loc. cit. note 46, p. 33,37) wrongly qualifies this as damage (*damnum corporis* and *damnum vitae*).

68 Cf. Bernardus Parmensis, Casus ad X 5.36.5.

cause no harm, one had to heed the fire. One who did not do this, had to compensate the damage caused, as in D. 9.2.27.9, where the slave in charge of the fire fell asleep.[69]

Johannes Andreae (1275–1348)[70] refers here (ad X 5.36.5) to a remark of Innocentius IV and Hostiensis in their commentary on X 5.12.6. There they remark on the difference between the *forum internum* and the *forum externum*. If someone confessed to insufficient effort in preventing the spread of a fire from his house to the house of a neighbour, the priest could absolve him without requiring him to compensate the neighbour's damages. There was an exception in the case of gross negligence, for example where a fire was lit in a house filled with hay.

> *Si autem culpa vel negligentis a sua dedit quis damnum, ut si non bene cohibuit ignem ne ad domos aliorum vagarent, tunc tenentur actione legis Aquiliae, ff ad l. aquil. Qui occidit § in hac (D. 9.2.30.3). Sed tamen in foro pentitentiali non videtur quod teneatur ad emendam damni et pena est ei imponenda de negligentia, non pena de damno. arg. xv. q.ii. Inebriaverunt (C.15 q.2 c.9). Lex autem civilis que intendit circa conservationem patrimoniorum constituit quod etiam ad restitutionem damni tenerentur. Item bene fatemur quod si aliquo modo intenderet per ignem dare damnum, quod etiam tunc in foro penitentiali condemnaretur. Et idem dico, si non intenderet, sed lata culpa esset, ut si ignem proiiceret in domum plenam stipula.*[71]

In the *forum externum*, by contrast, when the neighbour whose house had been burnt down demanded compensation, the person who had lit the fire would be ordered to pay the damages, even if only *culpa levissima* could be ascribed to him.

A century later Panormitanus (1386–1445) also draws attention to this remark of Innocentius IV, not only in his commentary on X 5.36.5, like Johannes Andreae, but also elsewhere. Remarkably enough, the fifteenth and sixteenth century moral theologians refer almost exclusively to the commentary, in which he seems to concur with the viewpoint of Innocentius IV. He states that he sees no reason why there should be a difference between the *forum internum* and the *forum externum*, unless one wishes to posit that the payment of damages to the harmed party is a punishment.[72]

---

69 Cf. Hostiensis, Lectura super X 5.36.5; Johannes Andreae, addditio super X 5.36.5; Panormitanus, ad X 5.36.5.

70 Johannes Andreae, Novellae, ad X 5.36.5 (ed. Venice 1581, Turin 1963, fo. 118va): *Circa hoc capitulum et sequens Dio. et Host(iensis) distinxerunt inter forum iudiciale et poenitentiale in decr. Sicut dignum de homici. (X 5.12.6) ubi vide in magna glosa ultra me. vers. Si autem culpa et seq.* In his commentary on VI 5.12.4 he does not discuss the problem.

71 Innocentius IV, gloss ad X 5.12.6 (ed. Lyon 1548 fo. 193vb); see also Hostiensis, Lectura super X 5.12.6 nr. 11.

From his commentary on X 5.36.9, however, it is apparent that Panormitanus himself rejects Innocent's position.

Et dixi in c. Si egressus supra eod. (X 5.36.5) ut etiam in foro anime teneatur ad emendam, licet ex levissima culpa damnum illatum sit: quia cum hec sit lex principis et valde rationabilis et non sit mera pena ex parte damnum passi deberet observari etiam in foro anime ... Nec obstat c. Inebriaverunt xv. q.i. (C.15 q.2 c.9) super quo fundat se Inno(centius) quia ibi est mera pena, sed hic est interesse ex parte patientis damnum.[73]

In the decretal *Si culpa* (X 5.36.9), no distinction is made between different types of fault, nor is *culpa lata* required.[74] Just like other canonists before him[75], Panormitanus concluded from the parallel with the *actio legis Aquiliae* in Roman law that even extremely slight fault, *culpa levissima,* would be sufficient for a canon law court to order compensation for the harm caused. If the payment of the damages had been a punishment, he would have concurred with Innocentius IV, as in the *forum internum* there is no obligation to pay the fine before the judge has imposed this penalty, as is evident from a gloss of Johannes Teutonicus.[76] Panormitanus, however, regards the payment of the harm caused by fire (as in X 5.36.5) or otherwise (as in X 5.36.9) by someone's improper or negligent action as

---

[72] Panormitanus, ad X 5.36.5 (ed. Lyon 1509–1510, fo. 101vb): Et hoc dictum Inno(centii) est valde singulare, de quo multum dubito. Quare forum anime debeat discrepare a foro contensioso, cum hec lex (D. 9.2.44.pr.) sit vale rationabilis, nisi dicatur quod licet ista estimatio fit interesse respectu damnum passi /si/, respectu tamen inferentis est pena, que in foro anime non debet habere locum ex quo est extra dolum et latam culpam, quinimo ibi subest dolus. Licet in fore anime teneatur ad estimationem, non tamen tenetur ad penam. glo. est singularis in c. Fraternitati xii. q.ii. (C.12 q.2 c.11). Cf. ook Panormitanus, ad X 1.2.1, ad X 2.19.11, ad X 2.20.37.

[73] Panormitanus, ad X 5.36.9 (ed. Lyon 1509–1510, fo. 103ra).

[74] X 5.36.9: Si culpa tua datum est damnum vel iniuria irrogata, seu aliis irrogantibus opem forte tulisti, aut hec imperitia tua vel negligentia evenerunt iure super his facere satisfacere oportet ...

[75] Cf. Bernardus Parmensis, gloss *Si culpa* ad X 5.36.9; Hostiensis, Lectura super X 5.369; Johannes Andreae, ad X 5.36.9 (in prima glosa, ibi *Non tenetur*); They discuss only the *forum externum*, as appears from the beginning of their commentary: "Nota quod ad hoc ut teneatur qui damnum dedit seu iniuriam irrogavit, necesse est culpam intervenire". Instead of the question of whether the damages had to be compensated, the question of who had to give reparation for the damage and *iniuria*, was central. They exclude children under seven and insane people *"quia iudicium animi non habent"*, as well as those who acted out of self-defence or injured other through *vis maior* (*alterius impulsu vel violentia ventorum*). Bernardus Parmensis points out that even *levissima culpa* would frustrate an appeal on necessity, as follows from D. 9.2.44; Hostiensis states the same with reference to the appeal to *vis maior.*

[76] Johannes Teutonicus, gloss *Cum augmento* ad C.12 q.2 c.11. Panormitanus refers hereto in his commentary on X 1.2.1, X 2.19.11, X 2.20.37.

compensatory so that the obligation to make restitution (in the *forum internum*) already results from the fact that one acted differently from the way the most careful people would have acted.[77]

Panormitanus uses the same definition as Bartolus de Saxoferrato (1313–1357) had given in his commentary on D. 16.3.32.[78] One could speak of gross negligence where someone had unintentionally been less careful than anyone of his occupation or under his circumstances would have been, for example when someone leaves a borrowed book in the open. Everyone realizes that the chance of the book being stolen is great. It was sufficient for *culpa levis* and *levissima* to have been less careful than a careful person, and an extremely careful person, would respectively have been.

Their definitions of the concepts *culpa lata, levis* and *levissima* were also used by the moral theologians of the fifteenth and sixteenth centuries,[79] when considering the question of whether Innocentius IV was correct in stating that there was no Natural law obligation to compensate for harm caused by *culpa levis* and *levissima.*

The theologians differ on this issue. Angelus de Clavasio († ca. 1495) is of the opinion that there ought to be no difference in liability between the *forum internum* and the *forum externum.* In his view an obligation to restitution exists in all cases where, according to Roman or canon law, one can be compelled to pay compensation.

---

77 Panormitanus, ad X 5.36.9 (ed. Lyon 1509–1510, fo. 103ra): Nota primo ex tex(tu) quod ex sola culpa seu negligentia tenetur quis ad satisfactionem damni dati etiam de iure canonico quantumcumque non habuit voluntatem damnificandi. Et cum hec littera loquatur indistincte de culpa seu negligentia debet intelligi de qualibet culpa, quia indefinita equipollet universali, ut not. in c. Ut circa de elec. lib. vi. (VI 1.6.4). Infertur ergo quod in hac actione legis aquilie venit levissima culpa de iure cano(nico) sicut de iure civili. ut In lege Aquilia. ff. ad le. aquil (D. 9.22.44.pr.). Et dicitur levissima culpa quando diligentissimus homo scivisset precavere ut not. in c.i. de commo. (X 3.15.u) et in l. Quod nerva. ff. depo. (D.16.3.32).

78 Cf. J. Hallebeek, p. 76.

79 Cf. Gabriel Biel, Collectorium circa quattuor libros Sententiarum, ad IV dist.15 q.10 (ed. *Werbeck & Hofman*, IV.2 p. 215), but for them *negligentia* is an independent category besides intention and gross negligence: Si vero negligens fuerit aut est in dolo vel culpa lata tenetur. Similiter qui dat operam illicitae (ibid., p. 324). Angelus de Clavasio, Summa angelica, *Culpa* no. 1 (ed. Straatsburg 1495, fo. 46va); Sylvester de Prierio, Summa sylvestrina, *Culpa* no. 1 (ed. Antwerp 1623, fo. 143ra); Hadrianus VI, Quaestiones de sacramentis in Quartum sententiarum, *De restitutione* (ed. Rome 1522, reprinted Ridgewood 1964, fo. 73ra). In Angelus de Clavasio and Sylvester de Prierio the words "*eiusdem conditionis*" are lacking. Leonard Leys, De iustitia et iure 2.7.22 (ed. Leuven 1605, p. 69); Franciscus de Toledo, ad II II q.62 art.4 (ed. Rome s.a. p. 281). Martin de Azpilcueta, Enchiridion 17.178 (ed. Antwerp 1608, p. 366) has a more general definition.

Tamen ego credo quod teneatur de omni damno ex quacumque culpa sua de qua teneatur tam de iure civili quam de iure canonico per ea que dicam infra lex §. iiii.

From this it follows that one would have to compensate for the harm caused by one's negligence, even if there was only *culpa levissima*. Angelus de Clavasio derived this from the *glossa ordinaria* on C.2 q.5 c.20 and from the decretal *Si culpa* (X 5.36.9). In the gloss Johannes Teutonicus, after all, explicitly states that he considers the text as implying that even *culpa levissima* is sufficient, not only for liability to pay compensation under the *lex Aquilia*, but also before God. Similarly the decretal *Si culpa* (X 5.36.9) is not restricted to cases where *culpa lata* is at issue.[80]

Sylvester de Prierio († ca. 1523) adopted his arguments, but finally considered it better to follow the dominant doctrine of the canonists. His contemporary Adriaan Boeyens, pope Hadrian VI, (1459–1523), however, came to the same conclusion as Angelus de Clavasio, namely that one is obliged to restitution if one's actions have deprived another of his due, even if only through *culpa levissima*.

Hadrian VI chose as his point of reference not Roman law, but the restitution doctrine of Thomas Aquinas.

In his *Summa theologiae* (1269–1272) Thomas Aquinas defined restitution as the return of whatever another was deprived of against his will, for example by theft.[81] But even if the other was deprived of something which could not be returned (if he had been injured or if he had suffered purely partrimonial loss)[82], an obligation to restitution arose, namely to compen-

---

80 Angelus de Clavasio, Summa angelica, *Culpa* no.6 (ed. Strasburg 1495, fo. 43rb): Et pro hac opinione est glosa cum text. in c. Consuluisti ii. q.v. (C.2 q.5 c.20) que dicit quod tenetur etiam quo ad deum, si diligentiam debitam non adhibuit, ut in d(icto) c(apitulo) Consuluisti (C.2 q.5. c.20) et di.l. Clerico (D.50 c.37) et xxxiiii. q.ii. In lectum (C.34 q.2 c.6). Dic tamen quod non punitur ratione homicidii, sed negligentie, ut xv. q.i. Inebriaverunt (C.15 q.1 c.9) et fac(it) c.fi. de iniur. et dam. dato (X 5.36.9) quod indefinite loguitur.

81 ST II II q.62 art.2 co: ... restituere importat redditionem illius rei quae iniuste ablata est. This definition is directed towards the *acceptio iniuste, ut in furto et iniuriis*, by the question Thomas treats here, namely whether restitution is necessary if the other is deprived of something that cannot be returned: a life or a limb. Cf. Caietanus, ad ST II II q.62 art.2 (ed. Rome, IX, p. 43).

82 ST II II q.62 art.4 co: Respondeo dicendum quod quicumque damnificat aliquem videtur ei aufferre id in quo ipsum damnificat. ... Sed aliquis damnificatur dupliciter, uno modo quia aufertur ei id quod actu habebat, ..., alio modo damnificat aliquis aliquem impediendo ne adipiscatur quod erat in via habendi. Cf also the examples given by Caietanus: arson, libel and dishonest distribution of appointments. Cf. Caietanus, ad ST II II q.62 ar6 (ed. Rome, IX, p. 54): Et extenditur in proposito acceptionis nomen ad omnem actum quo proximum minus habet de suo

sate for the harm. This was also the case if someone destroyed or damaged of another's goods.

In this latter instance Thomas Aquinas had fewer cases in mind than had the canonists when they considered whether the *lex Aquilia* also applied in the *forum internum*. The canonists took the Roman law of delict, where also the damaging of goods received under contract fell under *damnum iniuria datum*, as their point of reference. An *actio legis Aquiliae* was possible, for instance, if a teacher injured a child whom he was teaching (D. 9.2.5.3), if the hired mule driver caused the death of the mule (D. 9.2.27.34), or if a doctor operated unprofessionally on a slave (D. 9.2.7.8).[83] According to Thomas Aquinas, however, the question of whether restitution is necessary is then answered on the basis of the contractual liability between the two parties, and not on the basis of the damage to the other's goods.[84]

---

quam habere debeat, incendium enim, contumelia, iniqua distributio et alia huiusmodi sub acceptione comprehenduntur.

[83] From a number of texts it appears that the disadvantaged person could select either the action based on contract on the ground of *locatio-conductio*, or the action based on delict, the *actio legis Aquiliae*. In the *Corpus iuris civilis* there are no texts, however, where the question whether the *actio legis Aquiliae* is available against someone who damaged something received for safe-keeping, is discussed. In Roman and canon law (X 3.16.2) the safe-keeper was not liable on the grounds of the contract *depositum*, unless the good had been damaged intentionally or by gross negligence. Would the safe-keeper then indeed be responsible for *culpa levissima* if the disadvantaged person instituted the *actio legis Aquiliae*?

[84] He contrasts the *acceptio iniuriosa*, an acquisition against the will of the owner, with the *acceptio* with the permission of the holder of the right, either for own use (as in a loan) or not (as in safe-keeping). On the basis of the *acceptio* he considers the borrower always obliged to restitution if the good cannot not returned (undamaged) for whatever reason. Strictly interpreted this would mean that the borrower would be obliged to restitution if the good could not be returned due to vis maior. Thomas of Aquino probably did not intend this (cf. Caietanus, ad ST II II q.62 ar6; ed. Rome, IX, p. 55). The depositary was, on the other hand, according to Thomas Aquinas, not compelled to restitution *ratione acceptionis*, like the borrower, but only *ratione rei*, because he had the good of another. Cf. ST II II q.62 art.6 co: … alio modo aliquis accipit rem alterius in utilitatem absque iniuria, cum voluntate scilicet eius cuius est res, sicut patet in mutuis, et tunc ille qui accepit, tenetur ad restitutionem eius quod accepit non solum ratione rei, sed etiam ratione acceptionis, etiam si rem amiserit, tenetur enim recompensare ei qui gratiam fecit, quod non fiet si per hoc damnum incurrat. tertio modo aliquis accipit rem alterius absque iniuria non pro suo utilitate, sicut patet in depositis. et ideo ille qui sic accepit in nullo tenetur ratione acceptionis, quinimmo accipiendo impendit obsequium, tenetur autem ratione rei et propter hoc, si subtrahatur res absque sua culpa, non tenetur ad restitutionem. Secus autem esset si cum magna sua culpa rem depositam amitteret.

Thomas Aquinas defined the *acceptio iniuriosa* as an action whereby someone was deprived of something against his will. To judge by the examples given; theft, robbery and assault, it is probable that he had in mind cases where the conduct was intentional. It is, however, not a necessary conclusion, that Thomas required *dolus* or *culpa lata*.

> *... [Q]uandoque enim [acceptio] est iniuriosa, scilicet contra voluntatem existens eius qui est rei dominus, ut patet in furto et rapina. et tunc tenetur ad restitutionem non solum ratione rei, sed etiam ratione iniuriosae actionis, etiam si res apud ipsum non remaneat, sicut enim qui percutit aliquem tenetur recompensare iniuriam passo, quamvis nihil apud ipsum maneat: ita etiam qui furatur vel rapit tenetur ad recompensationem damni illati etiam si nil inde habeat. et ulterius pro iniuria illata debet puniri.*

Is restitution obligatory in all cases where a person's action deprived his neighbour of something against his will? Thomas Aquinas did not explicitly answer this question. Arguments for both sides can be derived from his *Summa theologiae*.

Hadrian VI bases the dominant doctrine (*culpa lata* is required to create an obligation to restitution) on the principle that one is obliged to restitution because one has sinned: *"Obligatio restitutionis solum nascitur ex alieni detentione vel iniuriosa ablatione et hoc dicit peccatum et culpabilem malitiam auferentis"*.[85] If someone's actions harmed another without any intention to do so, no sin had been committed, unless the action itself was illicit or reckless (*culpa lata*). In this latter case it is assumed that the carelessness was voluntary.[86]

According to Hadrian VI the obligation to restitution was not based on the fact that someone had sinned, but on the fact that the actions had led to the injury, harm, or loss of repute of the other.

> *Pro huius solutione ... secundo premitto, quod obligatio restituendi non requirit peccatum cuiuscumque auferentis, sed causalis ablatio alieni, sive culpabiliter et peccaminose fiat, sive etiam sine peccato, inducit obligationem de restituendo.*[87]

He concludes from Exodus 22:6 (X. 5.36.5) that the person who had lit the fire should always pay compensation for the harm caused by fire, even

[85] Hadrianus VI, Questiones de Sacramentis in Quartum Sententiarum, *Restitutione*, (ed. Rome 1522, reprinted Ridgewood 1964, fo. 73ra).

[86] Hadrian does not consider this statement tenable, as one who performs a condoned action and omits to do that which anyone would have done, does not per se sin, like the heir at the distribution of the legacy who forgets to withhold the quarter to which he is entitled by virtue of the lex Falcidia.

[87] Hadrianus VI, Questiones de Sacramentis in Quartum Sententiarum, *Restitutione*, (ed. Rome 1522, reprinted Ridgewood 1964, fo. 73va). He justifies this with an appeal to the fact that the bona fide possessor who had lost the thing is also obliged to restitution.

if only *culpa levissima* was present, and it is true that the text does not state that intention, or gross negligence, was necessary.[88] He also interprets X 5.36.9 and the gloss on C.2 q.5 c.20[89] in this light. He expressly states that restitution is not punishment for negligence, but a result of the fact that the action caused another to be deprived of something:

Obligatio vero restitutionis non est poena proprii peccati, sed aliquid consequens causalem ablationem alieni.

The arguments of Angelus de Clavasio and Hadrian VI convinced Diego Covarruvias y Leya (1512–1577)[90] and possibly also Martin de Azpilcueta (1492–1586). The latter treats the restitution doctrine in the framework of the seventh commandment (*furtum non facies*). In his eyes this commandment was contravened not only by the thief, but by all who deprived their neighbour of something due to him, or in any manner disadvantaged him. There could be many reasons for another's entitlement. Martin de Azpilcueta summed up the reasons for which a person would be obliged to make restitution and would be sinning (would contravene the seventh commandment) if this was not done: contract and quasi contract, statute, testament, judicial order, delict and quasi delict, and collaboration.[91] In delict one who had harmed another was liable, whether he had led the other into evil, had killed, injured, insulted, robbed or defrauded him, or had stolen from him.[92] Martin de Azpilcueta does not mention damage to goods as an example. He does, however, consider the liability of the judge who gives an incorrect

---

88 From their interpretation of the text it follows that the canonist assume that *culpa* is present (see p. 4).

89 Hadrianus VI, Questiones de Sacramentis in Quartum Sententiarum, *Restitutione*, (ed. Rome 1522, reprinted Ridgewood 1964, fo. 73vb): Et est ratio quia causaliter proximo abstulit. Iam, ut supra deduxi, causalis ablatio inducit obligationem restitutionis in foro conscientie.

90 Covarruvias, De sponsalibus 2.6.8 (ed. Opera omnia, Frankfurt 1578, p. 90 (no. 12); Geneve 1734, p. 219 (no. 16): Atque in culpa levis mallem ego tenere opninionem ultimam, quam et in culpa levissima probabilem esse opinor, maxime, ubi natura contractus ex legis dispositione etiam levissimam culpam considerat. Est tamen notandum text. in d. l. In lege procedere in culpa commissa in facto, non in culpa que in omissione commissa fuerit. ... Cf. also his commentary on VI 5.12.4 (ed. Frankfurt 1578 p. 448, Geneve 1734, p. 598: Tenetur quis ablatum restituere ratione acceptionis iniustae, sive ea sit iniusta in injuriam proximi, sive quia lege prohibita.

91 Cf. Martin de Azpilcueta, Enchiridion 17.12 – 17.18 (ed. Antwerp 1608, p. 276–287).

92 Cf. Martin de Azpilcueta, Enchiridion 17.14. It is not ascertainable from the examples given whether *culpa levissima* is sufficient to invoke an obligation to restitution for example where someone was killed or injured. He elsewhere (Enchiridion 17.100) discusses arson. There *culpa levissima* appears insufficient to assume an obligation to restitution: Decimotertio peccat qui non casu sed de industria in aliquam domum aut locum aut segetes ignem immittit, cum restituendi obligatione.

sentence because of his lack of legal knowledge, the owner of a house for what fell from it, the inn-keeper, the boatman, and the carrier, and regards them as obliged to make restitution on the grounds of quasi-delict.

> *Octavo tenetur restituere obligatus ex quasi delicto, ut iudex qui iniquam sententiam tulit ob ignorantiam iuris vel imperitiam, et is ex cuius domo aliquid eiectum damnificavit alium, et tabernarius et institor tabernae, aut magister navis et eius institor de furto aut maleficio in navi per alium facto. Et caupo vel stabilarius de re sibi ab hospite commendata.*

Others adhered to the position that *culpa lata* is required in the *forum internum*. They give a number of arguments in support of this position.

Culpa levissima entails taking less care than extremely careful people would to prevent another suffering damage. It is at most a small sin (*peccatum veniale*) and does not involve an obligation to restitution. In other words, if one acted as anyone else would have acted in the same circumstances, one is not obliged to restitution if damage accidentally results therefrom.[93] Since anyone can be momentarily distracted or careless, it may even be possible for the confessor to treat as a small sin calling for penance an act which would have qualified as gross negligence in the *forum externum*, for example where a fire causes damage because the person who had to heed it fell asleep.[94]

From the fact that in Roman law the *actio legis Aquiliae* could not be instituted against the heirs if the perpetrator died before *litis contestatio*, it apparent to them that whatever had to be paid on the basis of the *lex Aqui-*

---

[93] Francisco de Toledo, In summam theologiae S. Thomae Aquinatis enarratio, ad II II 62 art.4 (ed. Rome 1869–1870, p. 283): Tertia conclusio: Qui per se damnum dedit cum culpa, non tenetur in conscientia de levi aut levissima, sed tantum de lata (culpa) damnum reparare. Istam teneo cum Innocentio et aliis. Et probatur, nam forum conscientiae non damni quantitatem, sed delicti et culpae gravitatem respicit quando ratione culpae restitutio est facienda, at in levi et levissima non est delictum, quum ad summum sit veniale leve: non ergo obligatio est sicut in dolo et lata culpa. Leonard Leys, De justitia et iure 2.7.24 (ed. Leuven 1605, p. 69): Probatur primo, quia nemo tenetur adhibere maiorem diligentiam in suis operibus ne alteri noceat quam eiusdem conditionis homines passim in similibus adhibere solent (nemo enim tenetur esse prudentior et circumspectior hominibus suae sortis) ergo damnum eveniens non debet illi imputari, sed censebitur involuntarium.

[94] Leonard Leys, De iustitia et iure 2.7.26 (ed. Leuven 1605, p. 70): Ex his infero: Si ex facto tuo vel omissione sequutum est alteri damnum et tu nihil in hoc peccaveris ob naturalem inconsiderationem vel oblivionem, non teneri ad restitutionem, quamvis in foro externo hoc lata culpa commissum dicetur. ... v.g. egrediens cubiculum et alia cogitatione abreptus, non clausisti ostium; hinc ingressi fures multi abstulerunt. Habes lucernam iuxta locum pericolusum et quamvis solicite proposueris extinguere tamen aliquid intervenit quo absque culpa oblivisceris; vel in somnum incidis et excitatur incendium. Aperuisti puteum et casu oblitus es tegere vel sepire, ne quis incidat: censetur enim huiusmodi eventis damnum fortuito datum.

lia was not meant to be truly compensatory in character, nor binding in the *forum internum.*[95]

In so far as an obligation to restitution exists if *culpa levissima* causes damage, this obligation is based on the particular duty of care inherent in a contract, like thatof a seller, hirer or borrower, who had to be extra careful with the good to be delivered or returned.

[Q]uando non intercessit aliquis contractus, non oritur obligatio restitutionis ratione damni dati (saltem in foro conscientiae), nisi ex culpa lata; non autem ex levi vel levissima culpa.[96]

---

95 Luis Molina, De iustitia et iure, III/2 disp. 698, (ed. Köln 1614, III/2 156): Eadem vero est ratio quare in foro conscientie non deberetur, ... haec duo mutuo sunt connexa obligationem non transire adversus heredes eius, qui ex iuris dispositione ad id tenebatur et id non debere ante latam sententiam adversus eum. Its character was not truly penal either. If one was to be punished for *culpa levissima*, the *lex Aquilia* would have been an unjust law - unjust laws did not, after all, apply in the *forum internum.* See Luis de Molina, De iustitia et iure, III/2 disp. 698, (ed. Köln 1614, III/2 155): Dico deinde quando cum culpa iuridica coniuncta non est culpa theologica, dispositionem legis aquiliae quod solvatur damnum datum quantum res plus valuit intra triginta dies aut intra annum retro a puncto damni dati, non esse proprie ac vere poenalem, non solum quoad latitudinem valoris damni dati, sed etiam quoad excessum illum ultra valorem damni re ipsa dati, neque esset iusta aut servanda ea lex, si in veram poenam aliquid eorum esset sancitum.

96 Leonard Leys, De justitia et iure 2.7.24 (ed. Leuven 1605, p. 69); cf. also Louis de Molina, De iustitia et iure, III/2 disp. 698, (ed. Köln 1614, III/2 156): Illud etiam addo quando ex contractu, ut ex commodato vel ex locatione aut ex alio mihi teneris curare conservatione rerum mearum, tunc damnum quod eis meis reb(us) me proveniret ex tua culpa iuridica, qua mihi ex eo contractu iurisque dispositione tenereris, etiam si adiunctam non haberet culpam theologicam, resarcire mihi teneris in foro conscientie, nulla expectata sententia.

ROBERT FEENSTRA

Grotius' doctrine of liability for negligence: its origin and its influence in Civil Law countries until modern codifications

In the course of the planning for the present volume on the comparative legal history of the law of torts it was decided that I should write a chapter covering roughly the developments on the Continent during the 16th, 17th and 18th centuries. The original idea was that the chapter should simply be entitled 'Negligence in the doctrines of the Natural Law scholars' and be placed between the chapters on medieval Roman law and medieval Canon law on one side and the chapters on the modern continental codifications on the other. On reflection I preferred the present title, using Grotius (1583–1645) as the peg on which to hang my observations on the developments during the period in question[1]. Of course Grotius is generally considered as the founding father of the so-called Natural Law School and his influence is to a great extent to be sought in the work of later Natural Law scholars. But the importance of his doctrines on private law has also been

[1] I have dealt with Grotius' doctrine of liability for negligence in some previous studies, which constitute the basis of the present contribution. About forty years ago I published two articles: (1) Théories sur la responsabilité civile en cas d'homicide et en cas de lésion corporelle avant Grotius, in Etudes d'histoire du droit privé offertes à Pierre Petot (1959), 157–171, reprinted in my Fata iuris romani, Etudes d'histoire du droit (1974), 323–337 (some corrections and additions on 398–399; this 1974 version will be cited below as "Théories"); (2) Over de oorsprong van twee omstreden paragrafen uit de Inleidinge van Hugo de Groot (III.33.2 en III.34.2), in Acta iuridica 1958 [in memory of Robert Warden Lee, published in 1959] 27–42. I returned to the argument of both articles in a study entitled Das Deliktsrecht bei Grotius, insbesondere der Schadensersatz bei Tötung und Körperverletzung, in Das römisch-holländische Recht, Fortschritte des Zivilrechts im 17. und 18. Jahrhundert (ed. by R. Feenstra and R. Zimmermann; 1992), 429–454 (to be cited as "Deliktsrecht"). As far as the second 1959 article is concerned (Over de oorsprong etc.), the 1992 study is essentially an amended German version which supersedes the original text; this is not the case for the first 1959 article (Théories etc.), although the 1992 study gives the main points and adds some elements. Entirely new in 1992 was the first section, entitled "Die grotianische Generalklausel und ihre Elemente". The basis for this section was already laid in my elementary little textbook Vergelding en vergoeding, Enkele grepen uit de geschiedenis van de onrechtmatige daad (Rechtshistorische cahiers, 6; 1982, 2nd ed. 1993), which contains inter alia some quotations from the main sources.

considerable outside the School of Natural Law; they have been taken over by many jurists whose works were used in legal practice, in the Netherlands as well as elsewhere. On the other hand Grotius was not exclusively inspired by the 16th century Spanish Scholastics; his ideas were also influenced by certain civil law authors from that century, in particular French Legal Humanists.

As far as the history of liability for negligence is concerned, Grotius' name has been put in the forefront by various legal historians. I may mention the fundamental study of Giovanni Rotondi, *Dalla Lex Aquilia all'art. 1151 Cod. Civ.* – first published in 1916–1917 and reprinted in 1922[2] –, whose conclusions have been followed by many others[3]. In a recent collection of studies on our subject, *La responsabilità civile da atto*

---

[2] In *G. Rotondi,* Scritti giuridici, II (1922), 465–578 (this version will be cited below); the study had first been published in Rivista di diritto commerciale 14 (1916), 942–970, and 15 (1917), 236–295. Apart from a number of smaller (printing) errors a text of Pufendorf is erroneously attributed to Grotius on p. 529, see below n. 170 and cf. n. 3.

[3] In Theories 323 n. 2 (on 330) I mentioned *F. H. Lawson,* Negligence in the Civil Law (1950) 28, and the manual of *P. Ourliac* and *J. de Malafosse,* Droit romain et ancien droit, Les obligations (1957) 397. Their statements have been reprinted respectively in *F. H. Lawson* and *B. S. Markesinis,* Tortious liability for unintentional harm in the Common Law and the Civil Law, I (1982) 40, and *P. Ourliac* and *J. de Malafosse,* Histoire du droit privé I (1969) 418 (cf. however also 411, where they call Grotius' doctrine "une synthèse assez timide").

I will not try to give here a full bibliography of authors since 1959 who can be considered as having followed, in principle, Rotondi's conclusions. Apart from the studies of Cerami and Kupisch cited below in notes 4 and 5 I would like to mention in particular *H. P. Benöhr,* Ausservertragliche Schadensersatzpflicht ohne Verschulden? Die Argumente der Naturrechtslehren und -kodifikationen, in Zeitschrift der Savigny-Stiftung für Rechtsgeschichte, Rom. Abt. 93 (1976), 208–252, and *R. Zimmermann,* The Law of Obligations, Roman foundations of the civilian tradition (1990) 1032 and 1035–1036 (the text of 1017–1043 of his book is also to be found in his article Usus modernus legis Aquiliae and delictual liability today, in Stellenbosch Law Review 1 (1990), 67–93; the passages cited are on 81–82 and 85–86). Among manuals see in particular *H. Coing,* Europäisches Privatrecht, I: Älteres Gemeines Recht (1500 bis 1800) 1985), 506 and 512. The detailed survey of *G. P. Massetto,* Responsabilità extra-contrattuale, Diritto intermedio, in Enciclopedia del diritto, vol. 39 (1988) 1099–1186, at 1159–1160 and 1164 (unfortunately there is a confusion in the footnotes 576 and 577), is useful for further documentation in general; the older (short) contribution to the Enciclopedia by *G. Crifò,* Damnum, Premessa storica, in vol. 11 (1962), 615–622, follows Rotondi somewhat too slavishly: Crifò cites only one text as being from Grotius but it is actually the passage of Pufendorf wrongly attributed to him by Rotondi, see above, n. 2. Useful surveys are to be found in *G. Schiemann,* Das allgemeine Schädigungsverbot: "alterum non laedere", in Juristische Schulung, 29 (1989) 345–350, in *E. J. H. Schrage,* Van delict tot onrechtmatige daad (1998), in particular at 37 ff., and in *J. H. Dondorp* (with the collaboration of *J. Hallebeek*), Schuld en boete, Enkele grepen uit de geschiedenis van de onrechtmatige daad (1998), in particular at 59 ff.

illecito nella prospettiva storico-comparatistica, published in 1995, one of the contributions is entitled *La responsabilità extracontrattuale dalla compilazione di Giustiniano ad Ugo Grozio*; according to the author, Pietro Cerami, Grotius, in his *De iure belli ac pacis,* "rappresenta nella storia della responsabilità civile lo spartiacque fra esperienza postgiustinianea ed esperienza precodicistica"[4].

A somewhat different appraisal of Grotius' role is found in another contribution to the 1995 volume: Berthold Kupisch, *La responsabilità da atto illecito nel diritto naturale*[5]. Though recognizing Grotius' importance in the history of liability for negligence Kupisch tends to consider the innovations developed by Pufendorf as more decisive.

Other authors have criticized the Rotondi doctrine in a different way, in particular Thomas Kiefer, *Die Aquilische Haftung im "Allgemeinen Landrecht für die Preussischen Staaten" von 1794*[6], which, contrary to what one might expect from its title, contains many important observations on the law of the 16th and 17th centuries. According to Kiefer the *Usus modernus* had already developed "eine deliktsrechtliche Generalklausel" before Grotius. We will pay special attention to Kiefer's statement after our own analysis of Grotius' text and its sources[7].

The remarks on Grotius in the recent book of *F. Parisi,* Liability for negligence and judicial discretion (2nd ed., International and Area Studies, University of California at Berkeley, Research series 82; 1992), in particular at 140 ff., are not very clear. Parisi relies in part on *A. T. von Mehren* and *J. R. Gordley,* The civil law system, An introduction to the comparative study of law (2nd ed., 1977), 572–573, whose observations on Grotius tend in the direction of the Rotondi tradition, but what Parisi adds, referring inter alia to an article by J. L. M. Elders, would seem rather confused.

A masterly short essay on our subject, with comparative and historical perspectives (but without reference to Grotius), was recently published by *J. H. Nieuwenhuis*: Wat is onrechtmatige daad? Europese perspectieven, in Rechtsgeleerd Magazijn Themis 159 (1998) 242–248.

4 *P. Cerami,* La responsabilità extracontrattuale dalla compilazione di Giustiniano ad Ugo Grozio, in La responsabilità civile da atto illecito nella prospettiva storico-comparatistica, I Congresso internazionale ARISTEC, Madrid 7–10 ottobre 1993, a cura di Letizia Vacca (1995) 103–122, at 107; his interpretation of the Grotian texts on 119–121 is, however, not without some flaws (and there are many printing errors in the quotations on 120).

5 In La responsabilità etc., 123–143. The third contribution in this volume concerning our period, *J. Schröder,* Die zivilrechtliche Haftung für Schadenszufügung im deutschen Usus modernus, 144–167, does not deal with Grotius at all. We will see, however, below (at notes 190 ff.) that some influence of Grotius' Inleidinge tot de Hollandsche rechtsgeleerdheid on the authors of the *Usus modernus Pandectarum* can not be denied.

6 (Reihe Rechtswissenschaft 80; 1989).

7 See below at n. 78 ff.

I. Analysis of the Grotian texts and their sources

Two of Grotius' works must be analysed in the context of liability for negligence[8]. The main work, which certainly had the greatest influence outside the Netherlands, is *De iure belli ac pacis* (1625); it deals, in principle, only with Natural Law. But for our subject his work on Roman-Dutch law, *Inleidinge tot de Hollandsche rechtsgeleerdheid* (Introduction to the Jurisprudence of Holland) is also very important[9]. It was first published in 1631 but written about 1620. In this work he does not confine himself to statements on the law prevailing in the province of Holland (indigenous customary law as well as rules of Roman law "recieved" in that province) but fits them into a "system" that is based on concepts of natural law as developed by 16th century theologians (mainly Spanish, and therefore called the Spanish Scholastic School or the Spanish School of Natural Law) who in their turn commented the *Summa theologiae* of Thomas Aquinas.

The systematic approach Grotius uses in the *Inleidinge* is also present in *De iure belli ac pacis*[10] but it is less evident there to a reader unfamiliar with the concepts of the Scholastic School. I therefore deal first with the *Inleidinge*. Since this work was written before *De iure belli ac pacis*, this working-method will also contribute to a better understanding of the latter.

The *Inleidinge* is divided into three books, dealing respectively with the law of persons, the law of things and the law of obligations[11]. Although the

---

[8] Perhaps some attention should also be given to a third work, *De iure praedae commentarius* (ed. by G. Hamaker; 1868), see *P. Haggenmacher,* Droits subjectifs et système juridique chez Grotius, in Politique, droit et théologie chez Bodin, Grotius et Hobbes (ed. by L. Fousneau; 1997), 71–130, at 79, 85 and 88–89. Haggenmacher's article is also very important for the analysis of Grotius' two other works.

[9] As it is for the doctrine of unjust enrichment, see my contribution Grotius' doctrine of unjust enrichment as a source for obligation: its origin and its influence in Roman-Dutch Law, in Unjust enrichment: The comparative legal history of the law of restitution (ed. by E. J. H. Schrage, Comparative studies in Continental and Anglo-American legal history, 15, 1995), 197–236, reprinted in *R. Feenstra,* Legal scholarship and doctrines of private law, 13th – 18th centuries (Variorum Collected Studies Series, 556; 1996) as no. IX, with a few addenda. Some general statements and references concerning the Inleidinge in the present contribution have been taken over from this article, which will be cited as "Unjust enrichment".

[10] On Grotius' systematic approach in general see my article La systématique du droit dans l'oeuvre de Grotius, in La sistematica giuridica: Storia, teoria e problemi attuali (1991), 333–343, reprinted in *Feenstra,* Legal scholarship (above n. 9) as no.VII, with some addenda. Important new observations are to be found in *Haggenmacher* (above n. 8).

[11] The best and most recent critical edition is by *F. Dovring, H. F. W. D. Fischer* and *E. M. Meijers* (1952); it includes Grotius' handwritten marginal notes in his own copy of the 1636 edition, cf. below n. 42. It is the 1952 edition that I will quote in the footnotes. In the text I will use, with a few corrections, the Eng-

contents correspond, roughly speaking, with the order of Justinian's Institutes, it should be kept in mind that the division of the subjects dealt with in books II and III – things and obligation – is based on a hierarchy of subjective rights, divided into real rights and personal rights[12]. Personal right is defined as "the right of property which one man has over another to obtain from him some thing or some act"[13]. In the first section of book III of the *Inleidinge,* after some preliminary remarks on the concept of duty, Grotius deals with what we would call the sources of obligation (here seen from the active side as "personal right"). He states:

> The law of nature considered in itself exhibits two sources of personal right, namely promise and inequality[14].

"Inequality" is a concept taken from Thomas Aquinas and the Spanish School of Natural Law[15]. Grotius' first statement on inequality as a source of obligation is that

> it is not every kind of inequality which is taken into account, for men cannot be equally rich, but only the inequality which actually profits another, or would profit another, if something were withheld; or which is caused by another person[16].

The two categories – "profits another ..." and "caused by another person" – must be considered as rendering the *inaequalitas ratione rei acceptae* and the *inaequalitas ratione acceptionis* of the theologians. The

---

lish translation by *R. W. Lee,* The Jurisprudence of Holland by Hugo Grotius, I: Text (1926; 2nd ed. 1953, reprint 1977). There also exists a Latin translation, made by Joannes van der Linden (see below at n. 160) about 1830–1835 but published only in 1962 under the title *Hugonis Grotii Institutiones iuris hollandici,* ed. H. F. W. D. Fischer (1962).

12 See my La systématique (above n. 10) 338–339; cf. also my article *Dominium* and *ius in re aliena*: the origins of a Civil Law distinction, in New perspectives in the Roman law of property, Essays for Barry Nicholas (ed. by P. Birks; 1989) 111–122 (reprinted in *Feenstra,* Legal scholarship (above n. 9) as no. III, with some addenda), at 118 and n. 48.

13 Inl. 2,1,59: "Inschuld is 't recht van toe-behooren dat den eenen mensch heeft op den anderen om van hem eenige zake ofte daed te genieten"; for the English translation given in the text see Unjust enrichment 200–201 n. 18 and 19.

14 Inl. 3,1,9: "Wat de aengheboren wet in haer zelve ingehezien zijnde aengaet, de zelve opent ons twee oorsprongen van inschuld: te weten toezegging en onevenheid"; for the English translation see Unjust enrichment 201 n. 28.

15 For Aquinas' doctrine of restitution see lastly *G. Dolezalek,* The Moral Theologians' doctrine of restitution and its juridification in the sixteenth and seventeenth centuries, Acta iuridica 1992 (Essays in honour of Wouter de Vos) 104–114, at 110–112). Earlier studies are mentioned in Unjust enrichment 199 n. 11.

16 Inl. 3,1,14: "Wat onevenheid aengaet, zoo en komt alhier niet in aenmerckinge allerhande onevenheid. Want de menschen en konnen niet even rijck zijn; maer die onevenheid alleen die een ander datelick batet, ofte door onthoudinge baten zoude, ofte die door een ander is veroorzaeckt".

first of these does not concern us in the present context; I have dealt with it at length in my study on Grotius' doctrine of unjust enrichment as a source of obligation[17]. The second category – "inequality caused by another person" – is subdivided in its turn into "caused by the wish of the person affected" and "caused against his wish"[18]. With "by the wish" Grotius refers to what we usually call innominate contracts[19]. "Inequality caused against the wish of the person affected" is the formula which Grotius uses for the source of the obligation which arises

> when one has suffered loss against his will through another's wrongdoing[20].

The Dutch word here translated as "wrongdoing" is "misdaed", which is meant as an equivalent of the Latin term *maleficium*[21]. This appears from the fact that in the section where Grotius deals in detail with the concept of obligation from "misdaed" (*Inleidinge* 3,32) he puts in the margin "*ex maleficio*"[22], for the better understanding of readers accustomed to the Roman law terminology.

In this section Grotius first gives a definition of "misdaed" (3,32,3–6)[23]:

> (3) "Misdaed" is an act or omission which is from its own nature illicit or which is prohibited by some law.
>
> (4) I say "or omission": for failing to do what a man is bound to do is also a "misdaed".

---

17 See above n. 9.

18 Inl. 3,1,16: "Onevenheid door een ander veroorzaeckt geschied ter minne of ter onminne".

19 For more details see Unjust enrichment 202 n. 34; cf. also *Haggenmacher* (above n. 8) 93.

20 Inl. 3,1,18: "Ter onminne wanneer iemand schade heeft geleden jegens sijne wille door eens anders misdaed".

21 In modern Dutch "misdaad" is only used for crime; what Grotius means by "misdaed" would in modern Dutch be called "onrechtmatige daad" (literally: "wrongful act"). As to the Latin term *maleficium* in the Grotian context see the analysis of the passages in *De iure belli ac pacis* below at n. 50 ff., in particular at n. 62 (distinction between *delictum* and *maleficium*).

22 See below at n. 30.

23 "[3] Misdaed is een doen ofte laten, zijnde uit zich zelve ofte door eenige wet ongeoorloft. [4] Ofte laten: want oock het naelaten van 't gunt men ghehouden is te doen, is misdaed. [5] Uit zich zelve: als een ander het sijne te benemen, of een ander jeghens sijn wille schade ofte hinder aen te doen, sijn woord niet te houden, niet te doen 't gunt iemands aengenomen ampt vereischt, ende voorts alles wes strijdende is met de redelickheid, die aengewezen ende bekrachtigt werd door het aengheboren recht. [6] Door eenige wet, 't zy der menschen in 't ghemeen, ofte borgher-wet, land-recht ofte plaetsrecht: want de reden en 't aengeboren recht leeren ons, dat geen gemeenschap en kan bestaen zonder ghemeene rechten, ende daarom doen sy onredelick die haer daer toe niet en voegen".

(5) "From its own nature": as to take from another what belongs to him or to cause to another loss or hindrance against his will, to break one's word, to fail to perform the duties of an office which one has undertaken, and, in a word, whatever offends against the rule of reason which is indicated and confirmed by the natural law.

(6) "By some law": whether it be a law of mankind in general or the civil law, general or local: for reason and the law of nature teach us that no community can exist without laws common to the society as a whole and therefore those who do not conform to those laws act unreasonably.

Grotius then specifies that it can give rise to two obligations: the one to suffer punishment, the other to redress the inequality resulting from it (3,32,7; with long historical explanations). After indicating some differences between penalty and compensation (3,32,8–10)[24] he confines himself to compensation and first discusses in some detail how the duty of making compensation arises from the law of nature (3,32,11–19)[25]; he does this in order to clarify the differences between the natural law and the civil law in this matter (3,32,11). He then states (3,32,20):

The civil law in this matter adheres more closely than usual to the law of nature, except that the assessment of the compensation, which is a matter in itself uncertain, is sometimes ascertained by the civil law, occasionally also increased by adding something of a penal character[26].

After mentioning (in 3,32,21) another secondary difference he continues (3,32,22):

However, the principal thing to notice is that the law of nature has regard only to actual facts; but the civil law, seeing that wrongful acts, even though they have

---

[24] One of them concerns the passive and active transmissibility of this kind of obligations to heirs (3,32,10). Grotius' statements on this subject would not seem to be very original, cf. *Zimmermann* (above n. 3) 1020–1022 and, in particular, *T. J. Scott,* Die geskiedenis van die oorerflikheid van aksies op grond van onregmatige daad in die Suid-Afrikaanse reg (thesis Leiden 1976) 164 ff. For a possible inconsistency in one of Grotius' statements see below at n. 154.

[25] As to the fact that in the Inleidinge Grotius in principle confines himself to compensation and does not deal with penalty see *Haggenmacher* (above n. 8) 95–96, who states inter alia: "Les deux conséquences juridiques du "méfait" ont certes un fondement naturel; en pratique cependant Grotius ravale le régime de la sanction pénale entièrement dans le droit positif, contrairement à la réparation dont il esquisse une théorie naturelle avant de passer aux déterminations positives du droit hollandais". Most of this "théorie naturelle", developed in Inl. 3,32,11–19, finds a counterpart in *De iure belli ac pacis,* 2,17 (compare, in the order of the Inleidinge, *De iure belli* 2,17,6–8; 2,17,11; 2,17,13; 2,17, 4–5; 2,17,22; 2,17,16).

[26] "De burgher-wet volgt hierin enger als in andere zaken het aengheboren recht, doch sulcks dat de schatting vande weder-evening, in haer selve onseecker zijnde, door de burgher-wet by wijlen werd seecker ghemaeckt, altemet oock verhoogt, met by-voeging van iet dat tot straffe streckt".

taken place, are difficult to prove, has, in certain cases, introduced an obligation arising as if it were from wrong[27].

This alludes to the traditional medieval interpretation of Justinianic terminology, viz. the distinction between *delictum* and *quasi delictum*. This follows from the continuation of this text (3,32,23):

So that an obligation which arises against the will of the party bound arises either from actual wrong or from wrong-by-construction-of-law[28].

This terminology refers back to a distinction he had made at the beginning of this section (3,32,2): inequality caused against the will of the party affected is

of two kinds, arising either from evident wrong or from (wrong by) construction of law[29].

Here he puts in the margin "*ex maleficio*" and "*ex quasi maleficio*"[30]. There is no doubt that in his *Inleidinge*[31] he intended to adhere to this (*quasi*) Roman terminology.

In the special chapter he devotes to "wrong-by-construction-of-law" (3,38) he mentions three of the four examples given in the title *De obligationibus quae quasi ex delicto nascuntur* of Justinian's Institutes (4,5) and adds a few cases of vicarious liability[32]. He does not follow those civilian

---

27 "Doch voor al staet te weten dat het aengeboren recht alleen ziet op de waerheid van de zaeck: maer de burgerwet ziende dat eenighe misdaden, oock als de selve zijn geschied, niet wel en zijn te bewijsen, heeft in eenighe zaecken verbintenisse inghevoert, als off het waer door misdaed". Lee's translation of the final formula reads "introduced obligations analogous to obligations arising from crime"; I have replaced this translation by one of my own for several reasons: "misdaad" should not be rendered by "crime" (cf. above n. 21), "verbintenisse" is a singular and the translation of "als off het waer" should be nearer to the Latin "*quasi*", which Grotius certainly had in mind, see below at n. 30.

28 "Zulcks dat verbintenisse ter onminne ontstaet of uit dadelicke misdaed, of uit misdaed door wet-duidinge". It would also be possible to translate – as Lee does – "from what is held to be wrong by construction of law" (*quasi ex delicto*). But from 3,38,1 (see below at n. 32) it is clear that "wrong-by-construction-of-law" is a concept in itself, equivalent to *quasi delictum*.

29 "Deze is ... tweederlei, of door blijckelicke misdaed, of door wetduidinge".

30 Cf. above at n. 22.

31 In *De iure belli ac pacis* Grotius is not particularly clear in this respect. In 2,1,2,1 he mentions *obiter* obligations *ex quasi maleficio* as a species of the obligations *ex lege*. In 2,17,1 – at the beginning of the chapter *De damno per iniuriam dato* – he repeats that *lex* is a source of obligation but in this chapter he does not use the term *quasi maleficium*, even not in 2,17,20 and 21 where he deals with cases of vicarious and noxal liability, cf. below at n. 113. For his concept of obligation *ex lege* in general see below n. 49 and n. 54.

32 He does not mention the *iudex qui litem suam fecit* (Inst. 4,5 pr.). He adds cases of liability of masters for their servants, of owners for their animals and of

authors who use the term *quasi delictum* for all cases of *culpa* or *negligentia,* a doctrine usually referred back to a 13th century Orleans professor, Pierre de Belleperche[33], which, after development in the 16th century, had much success in the 17th and 18th centuries, and even left some traces in the French Code civil[34].

So far as "evident wrongs" are concerned, the *Inleidinge* (3,33,1) states that they are

> conveniently distinguished according to the different character of the things which belong to individuals; these we have said above are life, body, personal liberty, honour and property[35].

Consequently Grotius devotes five sections respectively to "wrongs against a man's life" (3,33), "wrongs against the body" (3,34), "wrongs against personal liberty" (3,35), "wrongs against honour" (3,36) and "wrongs against property" (3,37)[36]. With the exception of the second category – "wrongs against the body" – these categories of wrongs had already

---

masters for their ships (and crew); these cases do not fall under Justinian's *obligationes quasi ex delicto.* For a detailed comment on Grotius' statements in this field see *R. Hochstein,* Obligationes quasi ex delicto, Untersuchungen zur dogmengeschichtlichen Entwicklung verschuldensunabhängiger Deliktshaftung unter besonderer Berücksichtigung des 16. bis 18. Jahrhunderts (Beiträge zur neueren Privatrechtsgeschichte 5; 1971) 99 ff.; cf. also *C. G. van der Merwe,* Erscheinungsformen verschuldensunabhängiger Haftung, in Das römisch-holländische Recht, Fortschritte des Zivilrechts im 17. und 18. Jahrhundert (ed. by R. Feenstra and R. Zimmermann; 1992) 455–484.

33 I hope to show elsewhere that one of Belleperche's predecessors, Jacques de Révigny, may have laid the basis of this doctrine.

34 I intend to provide details elsewhere; cf. provisionally *Hochstein* (above n. 32) 59 ff. and *Yvonne Chastaignet,* Contribution à l'étude historique et critique de la notion de quasi-délit (thesis Bordeaux 1927) passim. See also below at n. 210.

35 "Dadelicke misdaed zal bequamelick afgescheiden werden nae de verscheidenheid van de zaken die byzondere luiden toekomen, die wy voor deze hebben ghezeit te zijn 't leven, 't lichaem, de vrijheid, de eer en de goederen". The text to which Grotius refers is Inleidinge 2,1,41–49, where he distinguishes between "inalienable and alienable things" ("onwandelbare" and "wandelbare zaken"): to the first category belong life, body, personal liberty and honour; to the second property. Grotius uses here the same terminology as in Inleidinge 3,33,1, but Lee's translation is not quite consistent in this respect. We will keep to his translation "property" (used in 3,33,1), although "goods" (used in 2,1,49) would be more literal for Grotius' "goed" or "goederen". For the "inalienable things" of 2,1,42–28 see recently *Haggenmacher* (above n. 8) 91 and n. 3, against Tuck. Cf. also below at n. 56.

36 "Van misdaed tegen 't leven" (3,33); "Van misdaed tegen 't lichaem (3,34); "Van hoon" (3,35); "Van lasteringh" (3,36); "Van misdaed tegens goed" (3,37). It should be noted that the headings of 3,35 and 3,36 – translated by Lee as "Of injury" and "Of defamation" – do not use the terminology mentioned in our text; in 3,35,1 and 3,36,1, however, Grotius gives definitions which make the link with "vrijheid" ("personal liberty") and "eer" ("honour").

been mentioned in his description of the duty of making compensation according to the law of nature (3,32,16–18)[37]. We will see that, in a somewhat different setting, all five categories return in his *De iure belli ac pacis* in his description of the duty of making compensation[38]. When dealing with these passages in his main work we will inquire into sources Grotius may have used in this matter. As to the five sections of the *Inleidinge* it should be emphasized that Grotius is describing what he considers to be the civil law of the province of Holland. The departure from Roman law is striking; for the first category in particular it was not easy to fit the killing of a free man in the interpretation of the *lex Aquilia*. We will return to this aspect later[39]. In the present context I would like to emphasize what the *Inleidinge* says about "wrongs against property".

These wrongs consist in "destroying, taking away or damaging property, against the will of the person interested" (3,37,1)[40]. It is specified (3,37,6) that

> any negligence ("verzuim") entailing liability in the matter of killing or wounding is also effectual to oblige a person to make good damage which a man suffers in his property[41].

This is a clear allusion to the general concept of *culpa,* which – as we will see – Grotius uses as the key concept in *De iure belli ac pacis*. In the margin he puts the term "*damnum culpa datum*"; in a later addition – which was not printed until 1952[42] – he adds in the margin of the heading of the section as a Latin equivalent of "wrongs against property" the term "*ex lege Aquilia*". From the contents of the section it appears, however, that he wants to extend this liability beyond the cases in the Roman texts concerning the *lex Aquilia*[43].

We will now turn to *De iure belli ac pacis*[44]. The systematical order in this work, as far as private law is concerned, is less clear than that of the

---

37 Cf. above at n. 25.

38 See below at n. 56–57.

39 Below at n. 81 ff.

40 "Misdaed jegens goed is goed-verderving, goed-beneming, goed-verargering tegens de wille des geenes die 't goed aengaet".

41 "Alle verzuim waer door iemand werd verbonden in 't stuck van doodslag ofte wonden, is oock krachtig om iemand te verbinden tot vergoedinge van de schade die iemand lijd aen sijn goed". For the interpretation of this paragraph by D. G. van der Keessel see below at n. 155.

42 It is one of Grotius' handwritten notes in his own copy of the 1636 edition of the Inleidinge, discovered by F. Dovring in 1948; on these marginal notes see the preface in the 1952 edition (above n. 11) and cf. Unjust enrichment 204 n. 46.

43 Cf. in particular 3,37,7 and 8 concerning damages to and through ships; they are inspired by non-Roman sources.

Inleidinge[45]. One should start from the wellknown passage at the beginning of the second book (2,1,2,1) in which Grotius states that "the sources from which wars arise are as numerous as those from which lawsuits (*actiones forenses*) spring, for where judicial settlement fails, war begins (*ubi iudicia deficiunt incipit bellum*)"[46]. He then gives a survey of the different actions. They lie "either for wrongs not yet committed or for wrongs already done". The latter type of action lies for restitution[47] (*ut reparetur*) or for punishment (*ut puniatur*). Restitution is concerned either with what is or has been ours, giving rise to *vindicationes* and certain *condictiones* – this is Grotius' way of indicating what we now call unjust enrichment[48] – or what is owed to us *sive ex pactione sive ex maleficio sive ex lege*. These latter three sources of obligation (as we would call them) are elaborated in chapters 11 to 19 of the second book of *De iure belli ac pacis*[49]. Only one of these

---

44 I use the edition: Hugonis Grotii De iure belli ac pacis libri tres, curavit *B. J. A. de Kanter – van Hettinga Tromp,* Lugduni Batavorum 1939, as reprinted in Aalen 1993 with additional notes by *R. Feenstra* and *C. E. Persenaire* (with the collaboration of *E. Arps – de Wilde*); I will cite it as "Djbap". Those to whom this edition is not available can use e.g. the original 1939 edition, the edition by *P. C. Molhuysen* (1919) or the photographic reproduction of the 1646 edition in "The Classics of International Law" (1913).

Those who prefer a translation should use the English translation which forms part of the edition in "The Classics of International Law": De iure belli ac pacis libri tres by Hugo Grotius, II: The translation, by *F. W. Kelsey* (etc.), 3 vol. (1925 [de facto 1927–1928]; reprinted 1964 and 1984). Below, in the footnotes, we will indicate some passages where the translation would seem not quite satisfactory; in the text we will make use of the translation for paraphrasing Grotius' train of thought in parts which need not be cited fully in Latin.

A warning should be given against the use of the English translation by A. C. Campbell, first published in 1814 and republished in 1901 (reprinted in 1979): this is an abridged translation. In any case it is not "a reprint of the first, 1625 edition of the book", as was stated recently by *D. J. Bederman,* Reception of the classical tradition in international law: Grotius' De iure belli ac pacis, in Grotiana, 16–17 (1995–1996), 3–34 (slightly different version in Emory International Law Review, 10 (1996), 1–49), at p. 3 n. 2; needless to say, this mark of complete ignorance of the history of Grotius' text vitiates one of the main points made in Bederman's article.

45 Cf. La systématique (above n. 10) 334 ff., Unjust enrichment (above n. 9) 208 ff. and *Haggenmacher* (above n. 8) 97 ff.

46 For the idea underlying "Ubi iudicia deficiunt incipit bellum" see also Mare liberum cap. 13 in fine (ed. 1609, p. 42 [=66]; cf. ed. 1916, by *R. Van D. Magoffin,* p. 75), with some references; cf. also Djbap Prol. 25.

47 I prefer this translation to "reparation" (as the 1925 translation has); for my reasons see Unjust enrichment 208 n. 71.

48 See Unjust enrichment 209 f.

49 Chapters 11–16 deal with obligations *ex pactione,* chapter 17 with obligations *ex maleficio,* chapters 18–19 with obligations *ex lege*. For chapters 11–16 and 17 no doubt is possible. As far as chapters 18–19 are concerned, *Haggenmacher* (above

chapters is devoted to *ex maleficio*: chapter 17, entitled *De damno per iniuriam dato et obligatione quae inde oritur.* In the first paragraph (2,17,1) we find the wellknown definition[50]:

> Maleficium hic appellamus culpam omnem, sive in faciendo, sive in non faciendo, pugnantem cum eo quod aut homines communiter, aut pro ratione certae qualitatis facere debent. Ex tali culpa obligatio naturaliter oritur si damnum datum est, nempe ut id resarciatur[51].

In the beginning of the next paragraph (2,17,2,1) this definition is elaborated in the following way:

> Damnum forte[52] a demendo dictum[53], est τὸ ἔλαττον, cum quis minus habet suo, sive illud suum ipsi competit ex mera natura, sive accedente facto humano, puta dominio, aut pacto, sive ex lege. Natura homini suum est vita, non quidem ad perdendum, sed ad custodiendum, corpus, membra, fama, honor, actiones propriae …[54]

---

n. 8) 106–107 hesitates: "Faut-il considérer que les deux chapitres consacrés au droit des ambassades et au droit de sépulture répondent à l'obligation *ex lege* circonscrite de la sorte? Ils dépendent en effet tous deux du droit des gens, c'est à dire de la loi positive humaine, mais celle-ci ne fait probablement que spécifier en dernière analyse des normes d'ordre naturel, bien que trop vagues pour s'appliquer telles quelles. Les deux chapitres en question pourraient s'interpréter en ce sens; mais il faut reconnaître que Grotius ne fait rien pour corroborer cette interprétation"; in a footnote Haggenmacher adds inter alia: "il serait étonnant que Grotius, si soucieux toujours de marquer les charnières de son système, reste ici totalement muet sur ce point". In Unjust enrichment 209 n. 74 and 75 I have – criticizing an earlier opinion of myself – defended the opinion now called in question by Haggenmacher and I would like to stay by that opinion: the opening statement in Djbap 2,18 [ed. p. 435] quoted in my n. 74 would seem to be at least a sort of "marquer une charnière"; it is not very outspoken but Grotius does not "marquer une charnière" more clearly as far as the *obligatio quae ex dominio oritur* (heading of Djbap 2,10) is concerned. Cf. also below n. 54.

50 The 1925 translation of this definition is not fully satisfactory. I object in particular to the rendering of *communiter* by "from their common interest"; much better is "generally" (as Lawson has, loc. cit. above n. 3).

51 In 1642 Grotius added in a note some references to this statement: "'Αμελίου δίκη Graecis. Vide in decretalibus titulum de iniuria et damno dato [X 5,36] et digestis ad l. Aquiliam [D.9,2] et vicinas rubricas [D. 9,1; 9,3 and 9,4]". Cf. below at n. 67 f.

52 "Forte" does not occur in the *editio princeps*; Grotius added it in the 1631 edition.

53 To "damnum forte a demendo dictum" Grotius added in 1642 a note stating that this was Varro's etymology but referring to other possible etymologies.

54 Grotius continues with illustrations of the other categories of *suum habere* (apart from *ex mera natura*): "Dominio et pactis quomodo suum quid cuique sit, superior tractatio docuit, tum quoad res, tum quoad ius in actiones alienas. Simili modo ex lege ius suum cuique oritur, quia idem, aut plus lex potest, quam in se ac sua singuli. Sic pupillus ius habet exactam quandam diligentiam exigendi a tutore, respublica a magistratu, nec respublica tantum, sed et cives singuli quoties lex id

We find in these two passages a number of elements which also occur in the *Inleidinge*. I will not go into detail as regards the first passage, with its definition of *maleficium*[55]. In the second passage the most striking element which reminds us of the *Inleidinge* is the enumeration of what belongs to men naturally (*natura homini suum est*). If we take together *corpus* and *membra* on one side and *fama* and *honor* on the other, it is easy to identify "*vita, corpus, membra, fama, honor, actiones propriae*" with life, body, honour and personal liberty, which are mentioned – in a slightly different order – in the *Inleidinge*. The main difference between this work and *De iure belli ac pacis* is that in the latter property is not put on the same level[56] as the four "things" just mentioned, which could be qualified as rights in one's own person; *dominium* occurs only as a thing belonging to men *facto humano*. This is connected with Grotius' doctrine that the rights on one's own person already existed before the "introduction" of *dominium*, as expounded in *De iure belli ac pacis* 1,2,1,5[57].

In the definition of *maleficium* in *De iure belli ac pacis* there is one important element which has no equivalent in the *Inleidinge*: the use of the term *culpa*. It has rightly been observed[58] that in 2,17 – whose heading, by the way, reads *De damno iniuria dato* and not *De damno culpa dato*[59] – no special discussion of the concept *culpa* occurs. What did Grotius mean by *omnis culpa*? The question could be asked whether this alludes also to negligent conduct not sanctioned by punishment. In a previous study I have argued that this is indeed the case; the main argument I used there has, however, been criticized by Kupisch[60] and I think he is right. Fortunately Kupisch himself offers a better argument in favour of a positive answer. He cites two passages from other chapters of *De iure belli ac pacis* which confirm this interpretation. The first is 2,21,1,1 which says inter alia[61]:

---

expresse, aut per sufficientem consequentiam significat". The passage on *ius suum ex lege* is considered by *Haggenmacher* (above n. 8) 106 n. 6 as having no link with the obligation *ex lege* mentioned *obiter* in the opening statement of Djbap 2,17; I would think that such a link exists and that it is of some importance for the question discussed above n. 49.

55 The text is to be compared with Inleidinge 3,32,3–6, quoted above at n. 23.

56 As in Inl. 3,33,1; in Inl. 2,1,41–49, however, property is not quite put on the same level, see above n. 35.

57 "... societas eo tendit ut suum cuique salvum sit communi ope ac conspiratione. Quod facile intelligi potest locum habiturum, etiamsi dominium quod nunc ita vocamus introductum non esset. nam vita, membra, libertas sic quoque propria cuique essent, ac proinde non sine iniuria ab alio impeterentur ..."

58 See *Kupisch* (above n. 5) 137.

59 *Damnum culpa datum* was used, as we have seen (above at n. 42), by Grotius in a handwritten marginal addition to the heading of Inl. 3,37.

60 Loc. cit. (above n. 58).

non tamen semper ubi damni obligatio est etiam delictum est, sed tum demum si qua malitia notabilior accesserit[62], cum ad damni dati obligationem saepe qualiscumque culpa sufficiat.

For an explanation of the term *qualiscumque culpa* – which is reminiscent of *omnis culpa* in 2,17,1 – Kupisch refers first to 3,10,5,1: *Ad restitutionem enim sine dolo culpa sufficit*[63]. The most important passage cited is however 3,11,4,8:

Mera infortunia nec poenam merentur, nec ad restitutionem damni obligant. Iniustae actiones ad utrumque. Culpa media ut restitutioni obnoxia est, ita poenam saepe non meretur, praesertim capitalem.

According to Kupisch *culpa media* in this text would be a sort of technical term like *sine dolo culpa* in 3,10,5,1. In my opinion Benöhr's interpretation[64] is to be preferred: *culpa* is something inbetween ("gebe etwas Mittleres"), viz. between *infortunium* and *iniusta actio*[65].

One important external difference between *De iure belli ac pacis* and the *Inleidinge* is that in the former Grotius mentions some of his sources whereas in the latter he gives no references at all. We will have to see whether he gives all his sources in chapter 2,17 or if some remain unmentioned, deliberately or not.

The main works cited in this chapter are those of Thomas Aquinas, Dominicus Soto, Leonardus Lessius and Covarruvias[66]. The references to

---

61 In 2,21 Grotius deals with *poenarum communicatio*. In an opening statement he mentions first *delicti participes*: "Hi qui sint, ex his quae supra de damno iniuria dato dicta sunt intelligi potest. Ferme enim iisdem modis in delicti partem quis venit, quo in damni dati: [follows the passage quoted here]".

62 Implicitly *delictum* would seem to be opposed here to *maleficium*, which is used specifically as the source of an *obligatio* in case of *damnum datum*.

63 This statement is preceded by "Neque admittendam putem exceptionem quam nonnulli adferunt de his qui aliis operam navant: si modo in ipsis aliquid haereat culpae".

64 *Benöhr* (above n. 3) 210 n. 12, who refers also to the context. In my opinion the statement should be seen in the light of 3,11,4,1–2: "Sed notandum est inter plenam iniuriam et merum infortunium medium saepe aliquid intercedere ... Aristoteles huic generi nomen posuit ἁμάρτημα: Latine culpam aliquam liceat dicere ..." Cf. the Index rerum praecipuarum ac verborum (ed. p. 895): "Culpa media inter iniuriam et infortunium", with reference to 3,11,4,1–2.

65 In this context the question could be asked whether with *omnis culpa* and *qualiscumque culpa* Grotius could be considered as opposing the distinction between *culpa levis* and *culpa levissima*, following in this respect Hugo Donellus. This has recently been suggested by *O. E. Tellegen-Couperus*, Culpa levissima en de onrechtmatige daad, in Tertium datur, Drie opstellen aangeboden aan Prof. Mr. J. A. Ankum (1995) 89–118, at 116. I think she may be right; the texts just cited could give further support to her opinion. For influence of Donellus on Grotius see below, at n. 71 f.

these authors appeared already in the *editio princeps* of 1625, but none are linked to the paragraph containing the definition of the liability for negligence (2,17,1). Only in a later edition[67] did Grotius add references to "*Ex tali culpa obligatio naturaliter oritur*"; these are not to any of the authors mentioned but to the title *De iniuria et damno dato* of the Decretals (X 5,36) and to the title *De lege Aquilia* and subsequent titles of the Digest[68]. Of course these are not his real sources but it looks as if *ex post* he wanted to suggest that the natural law is more or less in accordance with the *ius commune* of his time[69]. To the first number of the following paragraph (2,17,2,1), which elaborates the definition, only one reference is added: it is of a non legal character and concerns "*Damnum forte a demendo dictum*"[70].

Unfortunately no sources are cited for the enumeration of what a man may consider his own: *vita, corpus, membra, fama, honor, actiones propriae*. We have to look for ourselves for his possible source. In my opinion there can be no doubt that his direct source was Hugo Donellus' *Commentariorum de iure civili libri viginti octo*[71], a work which inspired him in other fields as well[72]. Donellus made the following classification of "*quod nostrum est*"[73]: either it is "*vere et proprie nostrum*" or "*nobis debetur*".

---

66 For details see Deliktsrecht 431. Further references include works of Caietanus, Medina, Navarrus and Bodinus.

67 The 1642 edition, in which he inserted a great number of *annotata* at the end of the *capita* of his work; in the 1939 and 1993 editions these additions can easily be distinguished, which is not the case in a number of older editions.

68 See above n. 51. For the canon law background of the Grotian doctrine of liability for negligence cf. below at n. 97.

69 These references are preceded by "'Αμελίου δίκη Graecis" (cf. above n. 51), which is suggesting that already the Greeks had this rule in the form of an action for negligence.

70 See above n. 53.

71 First edition Frankfort 1589–1597; I used the ed. Hanau 1612. Books 12 to 28 were published posthumously: Donellus, born 1527, died 1591. A special treatise by Donellus on the Codex-title ad legem Aquiliam is to be found in his Opuscula posthuma (Hanau 1604) 413–433. Apparently it was part of his lectures in Bourges about 1560. It is of no importance for the subject we are dealing with in the text; Grotius does not seem to have used it.

72 See, apart from La systématique (above n. 10) 342 f., my article Hugues Doneau et les juristes néerlandais du XVIIe siècle: l'influence de son "système" sur l'évolution du droit privé avant le Pandectisme, in Jacques Godefroy (1587–1652) et l'Humanisme juridique à Genève, Actes du colloque Jacques Godefroy (ed. by B. Schmidlin and A. Dufour; 1991), 231–243, reprinted in *Feenstra,* Legal scholarship (above n. 9) as no. IV, with some addenda. Cf. also above n. 65.

73 Commentarii, lib. 2, cap. 8 (ed. p. 44 f.), where also the other quoted definitions can be found. For interpretation of Donellus' system of private rights see the studies by Coing and Waider cited in Deliktsrecht (above n. 1) 434 n. 30.

The former category is defined as "*ita nostrum ... ut nulla ex parte sit alterius et ut nostrum amplius fiat, alterius factum aut traditionem ullam non desiderat*"; this kind of *nostrum* can exist "*in persona cuiusque*" or "*in rebus externis*". The right to one's own person is then given concrete form by the enumeration *vita, corporis incolumitas, libertas, existimatio*[74]. When dealing with *obligationes quae ex maleficio nascuntur,* Donellus returns to this classification, but mentions, apart from *res,* only the latter three concepts which exist *in vivente,* viz. *corporis incolumitas, libertas* and *existimatio*; he leaves out *vita*[75]. As to remedies for the protection of these rights he discusses only those of the Roman law (*actio iniuriarum, actio legis Aquiliae* etc.), interpreted in a humanist way[76].

This is what Donellus is known for: he gives an excellent systematization of Roman law but does not go as far as to modify its rules. Grotius' real merit is to have gone further than the Roman law in working out the obligation arising from homicide (*vita* in the enumeration)[77]. Here he made a very fortunate synthesis of the doctrines of contemporary moral theology and Donellus' systematical approach to Roman law, adding elements from 16th century non-humanistic authors and from customary law. This merit of Grotius is apparently underestimated by Kiefer, who, as we have already mentioned[78], is of the opinion that the *Usus modernus* had already developed "eine deliktsrechtliche Generalklausel" before Grotius; he mentions also a number of specific points in Grotius' chapter on liability for *maleficium* as not going beyond the "Lehren des gemeinen Rechts", including even Grotius' remarks on the obligations arising from homicide[79]. Whatever may be the case as to the other points mentioned by Kiefer, in my opinion Grotius' way of dealing with the case of homicide is the example which best illustrates[80] the different sources that influenced his doctrines on negligence.

---

74 These four concepts had already been mentioned by Donellus at the beginning of his Commentarii (lib. 1, cap. 1; ed. p. 1); he adds: "At haec nusquam ex professo aut aperte in Pandectis tradita reperias".

75 Commentarii, lib.15, cap. 24 in fine and cap. 25 in principio (ed. p. 788); see Deliktsrecht (above n. 1) 435.

76 As far as the *actio legis Aquiliae* is concerned, Donellus does not accept an *actio utilis* in case of homicide.

77 Grotius had also some merit in working out the obligation arising from wounding, but in this respect the Inleidinge is more important than De iure belli ac pacis, see below at n. 106 ff.

78 Above at n. 7.

79 *Kiefer* (above at n. 6) 81.

80 Another example which could be mentioned is his way of dealing with liability for pain and bodily disfigurement, see below at n. 106 ff.

The key text[81] is in *De iure belli ac pacis* 2,17,13:

> ... Homicida iniustus tenetur solvere impensas si quae factae sunt in medicos, et iis quos occisus alere ex officio solebat, puta parentibus, uxoribus, liberis, dare tantum, quantum illa spes alimentorum, ratione habita aetatis occisi, valebat ...[82] Vitae autem in libero homine aestimatio non fit; secus in servo qui vendi potuit.

Both Roman and non-Roman elements may be seen in this text. The mention of medical expenses probably alludes to Roman law, though they occur also rather early in some customary law texts[83]. The principle according to which "life in the case of a freeman is not valued in money" would also seem to be Roman, though there is a slight disparity between valuation of life and valuation of the body. But the obligation to pay a certain sum[84] "to those whom the deceased was accustomed to aliment *ex officio,* for example his parents, his widow[85], his children", is certainly not Roman law[86].

---

[81] This text should be compared to Inleidinge 3,33,2: "... the killer ... is bound to compensate the widow and children and any others, if such there be, who where maintained by the dead man's labour, for loss sustained and profit missed calculated on the basis of an annuity" ("... aen de weduwe, kinderen, oock anderen zoo daer eenighen zijn, die door des nedergeslagens arbeid plagen onderhouden te werden, is den doodslager schuldig te doen vergoedinghe van schade ende winst-derving, ghereeckent by maniere van lijfrente"). For a detailed comparison between the two texts see my Théories and Deliktsrecht (above n. 1).

[82] Grotius gives here in the text two examples taken from Diodorus Siculus and Michael of Ephesus: "sicuti Hercules legitur [reference to Diodorus IV,31] Iphiti a se occisi liberis mulctam pependisse quo facilius expiaretur. Michael Ephesius ad quintum Nicomachiorum Aristotelis [V,2]: ... Sed et qui occisus est accipit aliquo modo. Quae enim uxor eius et liberi et cognati accipiunt ipse quodammodo accipit". Cf. below n. 88.

[83] For the nuances as to medical expenses and the principle "life in the case of a freeman is not valued in money" see Théories 324 and n. 10 ff. on p. 331. In De iure belli ac pacis Grotius does not mention the costs of the funeral, but he does so in the Inleidinge; on this point Grotius may have thought of the customary practice which indeed used to allow these costs but he can also have been inspired by Navarrus, see Théories n. 22 on p. 332 and Deliktsrecht 440.

[84] The formula "quantum illa spes alimentorum, ratione habita aetatis occisi, valebat" reminds us of the formula used in the Accursian Gloss to the effect that the calculation of prospective wages should be made according to a scale contained in the Digest dealing with the capitalized value of a usufruct in connection with application of the *lex Falcidia* (D. 35,2,68). For the history of the latter formula see my article L'actio legis Aquiliae utilis en cas d'homicide chez les Glossateurs, in Maior viginti quinque annis (ed. by J. E. Spruit; 1979) 45–65, reprinted in *R. Feenstra,* Le droit savant au moyen âge et sa vulgarisation (Variorum Collected Studies Series, 236; 1986) as no. VIII, with some addenda; German translation: Die Glossatoren und die actio legis Aquiliae utilis bei Tötung eines freien Menschen, in Das römische Recht im Mittelalter (ed. by E. J. H. Schrage; Wege der Forschung 635, 1987) 205–232.

What were Grotius' sources for this statement? As an indirect source one could perhaps mention the customary practice of giving composition in such a case[87], but it is not probable that in *De iure belli ac pacis* Grotius was simply following customary law. His main source should be found in one of his references. It is evident that the examples taken from Diodorus Siculus and Michael of Ephesus[88] cannot have been the true sources of his statement; they belong to what could be called his "parade of learning"[89]. Noteworthy, however, are two references in the margin of his text[90], mentioning a work of one of Grotius' contemporaries, Leonardus Lessius, a Jesuit from the Southern Netherlands belonging to the Spanish School of Natural Law. His *De iustitia et iure,* which inspired Grotius in many other passages of his *De iure belli ac pacis,* contains the main elements of Grotius' statement[91]. Now Lessius in his turn refers to other authors of the Spanish School; for this particular point Dominicus Soto may have been

---

[85] The plural "uxoribus" is probably a slip of the pen of Grotius or a printing error but all editions have it. Some later authors have corrected it tacitly, e.g. Vinnius (below n. 117) and Pufendorf (below n. 171).

[86] Even the medieval Romanists did not use such a formula, see my L'actio legis Aquiliae utilis (above n. 84).

[87] In particular because the statement occurs already in the Inleidinge (above n. 81). It should, however, be realised that such composition was paid to the "family" of the person killed and that this was not the family in the modern sense but in the sense of the male kinship, which by composition should be prevented from taking vengeance. The church, however, was combating the system of private vengeance, and, although it could not go so far as to abolish the composition, it succeeded in several ways in changing the character of the composition into a reparation – a *restitutio*. Such restitution had to go first to the nearest relations of the victim, his widow and his children. Now the widow was hardly anywhere considered as belonging to the family of her husband, so originally she could get no part of the composition. It is most probable that it was through the influence of the theologians that the original customary ideas were changed, although the concept of community of property with the husband could also have played a part.

[88] Cf. above n. 82. The example taken from Diodorus Siculus (IV, 31) did not occur in the *editio princeps*; it was added by Grotius in the 1631 edition. The quotation from Michael of Ephesus, on the contrary, can – through an earlier work of Grotius – be traced back to Cujacius (Obs. 14,4), who, in this respect, may even to a certain extent have inspired Grotius' statement; for details on this interesting but complicated story see the article by *E. Rabbie,* cited below n. 94.

[89] This would also apply to a note added by Grotius in 1642, which refers to a passage in Baba Qama and to a treaty mentioned by Pontanus. For Baba Qama cf. below n. 173.

[90] They are not placed exactly in the margin of the statement in question but that is of little importance. In any case one should not be confused by the attachment of the notes to the text in the modern editions.

[91] Lessius, De iustitia et iure caeterisque virtutibus cardinalibus libri quattuor, lib. 2, cap. 9, dub. 19–26 (ed. Antwerp 1609, p. 106–111).

the most important. In his work Grotius cites him even more often than Lessius and he may have been inspired by him also where he does not cite him[92]. This would seem to have been the case as regards the present statement[93], although it has been held that Grotius here was inspired mainly by Cujacius[94].

This example taken from the passage on homicide brings us back to the question of the sources which might have inspired Grotius' general definition of liability for negligence[95]. In connection with one of the other examples given by Grotius in the elaboration of his general rule we find a reference to a fundamental text of Thomas Aquinas on *restitutio*. It quotes the famous word of Augustine, also taken over in Gratian's Decretum and the Liber Sextus: "*non dimittitur peccatum nisi restituatur ablatum*"[96]. Canon law as well as moral theology should be taken into account in looking for the background of Grotius' rule[97]. In this context the canon law principle "*omnia crimina publica esse*" should be remembered. It led to the rule that in case of a delict private persons could not claim more than damages, never private penalties, a rule which had been generally accepted in secular law, in particular in practitioners' treatises[98]. On the other hand the idea had developed in secular law that an action for damages should be allowed in all cases in which a public prosecution took place. The principle that besides a public *actio criminalis* there is always an *actio civilis* for the

92 Cf. Soto, De iustitia et iure, lib. 4, qu. 6, art. 6, arg. 3 (ed. Venice 1589, p. 346–349; the most important passages are quoted in Vergelding (above n. 1) 36–38.

93 See Deliktsrecht 437–438 and n. 47 and 48 (in n. 47 insert, at the end of line 2, "mit Recht"; in n. 48 my correction of Théories 326 as to "ex officio" should be deleted, the interpretation in Théories was right).

94 By *E. Rabbie,* Grotius on damages in case of homicide: De iure belli ac pacis 2,17,13 and De satisfactione 2,9, in Tijdschrift voor Rechtsgeschiedenis 57 (1989) 109–116; cf., however, my comments in Deliktsrecht 438–439.

95 See above, before n. 66.

96 Thomas Aquinas, Summa theologiae, Secunda Secundae, Quaestio 62, articulus 2 ad secundum (in Opera omnia, iussu impensaque Leonis XIII P. M. edita, vol. IX, 1897, 42 f.); Decretum Gratiani, C.14, q.6, c.1; Liber Sextus, De regulis iuris, 4.

97 See e. g. Decretales Gregorii IX, 5,36,9; cf. above n. 68.

98 See e. g. Jean Imbert, Enchiridion iuris scripti moribus et consuetudine frequentiore Galliae usitati vel abrogati, in verbo Poenae pecuniariae explosae (ed. Lyons 1558, p. 276 f.); this French author from the 16th century is cited by a well-known jurist of the Southern Netherlands, Petrus Gudelinus (1550–1619), in his Commentariorum de iure novissimo libri sex, lib. 3, cap. 13 (ed. Antwerp 1620, p. 119). Both Imbert and Gudelinus refer to a text of the Decretum Gratiani, C.12, q.2, c.11 (Fraternitas). Cf. below n. 124.

aggrieved person is found in Romanist authors[99] as well as in some records of customary law[100]. The medieval Romanists would call this action an *actio civilis in factum,* a term which also occurs in a 16th century author like Antonius Gomez[101]. Most of the jurists abstained from connecting this *actio civilis in factum* with the *actio legis Aquiliae,* perhaps because of the many restrictions mentioned in the Corpus iuris civilis for that action. But some authors of the socalled "popular literature" of Roman law did not scruple to call this action simply an *actio legis Aquiliae*[102].

Grotius may have been familiar with much of this development[103] but in my opinion it goes too far to say with Kiefer that the *Usus modernus* had already developed "eine deliktsrechtliche Generalklausel" before Grotius[104].

Having dealt with Grotius' observations in *De iure belli ac pacis* concerning *maleficium* in general and the special category of *maleficium*

---

99 See e.g. Bartolus on D.47,8,2,1, num.1, and Angelus Aretinus, Tractatus de maleficiis, cap. Et ad querelam, num. 11, both cited by Hallebeek in his contribution to this volume, above p. 83/84, notes 37 and 38.

100 Georges Chevrier, in an unpublished lecture "Les origines de l'article 1382 du Code civil français" in Amsterdam in 1959, states: "Dans de nombreuses chartes de franchise qui énumèrent une suite souvent confuse de délits, il est déjà posé comme règle que celui qui a souffert du délit a droit à une réparation: *Damnum passo emendatio debetur.* C'est l'amorce du principe général que posera l'article 1382 du Code civil français".

101 Variae resolutiones, 3,3,37 (in ed. Commentariorum variarumque resolutionum iuris civilis communis et regii tomi tres, Frankfort 1597, p. 448).

102 Cf. *Kiefer* (above n. 6) 42 ff.

103 In the context of this development mention should be made of a passage from Jodocus Damhouder, Praxis rerum criminalium, cap. 144 (ed. Antwerp 1555, p. 500–501). *Kiefer* 42–43 quotes a German version of this passage, which was almost literally taken over in the Landrecht des Herzogtums Preussen of 1620 (see *Kiefer* 53). The German version of Damhouder's Praxis was a translation of the Dutch version which was almost completely a plagiarism of Philip Wielant's Practijcke criminele of 1516; this work had already served as the basis of Damhouder's Latin text.

104 In the introduction of his book (p. XLVII) Kiefer states this with reference to *H. Kaufmann,* Rezeption und Usus modernus der actio legis Aquiliae (Forschungen zur neueren Privatrechtsgeschichte 5; 1958), 46 ff. As I have already remarked in Deliktsrecht 430 n. 5, Kaufmann refers mainly to Mevius, whose work is much later than Grotius'; the only author before Grotius cited by Kaufmann is Gaill, whose text is not very convincing in this respect. In the paragraph Kiefer devotes to Grotius he acknowledges: "... wenn Grotius auch oft im einzelnen nur wieder zu den Lehren des Usus modernus gelangt, so ist doch seine Ableitung dieser Lehren aus einem obersten Prinzip der Beginn einer neuen Doktrin des Deliktsrechts" (82–83). But in his interpretation of De iure belli ac pacis 2,17 Kiefer is too much inclined to see influence of "Lehren des gemeinen Rechts": even in 2,17,13 Grotius would not go beyond these doctrines (*Kiefer* 81). Although he cites Inleidinge 3,34,2 for "ein Schmerzensgeld", Kiefer does not pay any attention to the "Generalklausel" in this work of Grotius.

against life, we will not go into the details of the other special categories: wrongs against a man's body, against his honour, against his personal liberty and against his property[105].

As far as liability for pain and bodily disfigurement is concerned[106] we may state that in *De iure belli ac pacis* Grotius remains based on firm Roman ground: he does not mention the interesting deviation from Roman law contained in Inleiding 3,34,2: "Pain and bodily disfigurement, though properly speaking incapable of compensation, are assessed in a sum of money, if such is demanded"[107]. For the sources of this passage and its influence in later times I may refer to my earlier publications[108]. In my opinion we may conclude that, just as in the action of dependants in the case of death of their breadwinner, Grotius was not in the first place inspired by contemporary customary law but mainly and more directly by the authors who had formulated the law to be applied *in foro interiori*.

We have already seen[109] that in *De iure belli ac pacis* "property" is not put on the same level as "life, body, honour and personal liberty". It is not dealt with explicitly in the chapter *De damno iniuria dato* (2,17). Grotius refers there (2,17,2,1) to the chapter *De obligatione quae ex dominio oritur* (2,10), where, however, he does not speak specifically of cases of wrongdoing to property[110]. Nevertheless there are some remarks on wrongs against property in chapter 2,17: e.g. on the liability of *fur* and *raptor* (2,17,16)[111] and on liability for servants, for animals and for things.

---

105 Cf. above at n. 56 and 57.

106 Grotius' remarks on wrongs against honour and personal liberty in Djbap 2,17 would seem of less importance than those in Inl. 3,35 and 3,36.

107 "De smert ende ontciering van 't lichaem, hoewel eighentlick niet en zijn vergoedelick, werden op geld geschat, soo wanneer sulcks versocht werd".

108 Apart from Deliktsrecht 451 ff. see my article Réparation du dommage et prix de la douleur chez les auteurs du droit savant, du droit naturel et du droit romano-hollandais, in La douleur et le droit (ed. by B. Durand, J. Poirier and J. P. Royer; 1997) 411–421, at 417 ff. A correction is to be made as to my interpretation of the text of Dominicus Soto cited in both articles (Deliktsrecht 453, Réparation 419): Soto's remark "inter illustres istae restitutiones non petuntur" applies to *restitutiones* in general, not only to those for *deformitas*; the latter remain, however, the most important category, so that Grotius' interpretation would certainly not be wrong. An additional remark should be made to my statement in Réparation 420 (first two lines) that "dès la deuxième moitié du XVIIe siècle, les juristes allemands ont commencé à accepter le *Schmerzensgeld* du droit coutumier": from the end of the 16th century the courts had accepted the *Schmerzensgeld,* but until Georg Adam Struve the institutional writers had declined it, see *Kiefer* (above n. 6) 70–71 and cf. *Kaufmann* (above n. 104) 30 ff.

109 Above at n. 57.

110 See Unjust enrichment (above n. 9) 209 ff.

111 The mention of the liability of *fur* and *raptor* is followed by an enumeration of cases which Grotius puts in the same category (2,17,16 and 17). Of special inter-

As to these last categories we have already touched the subject when dealing with the *Inleidinge*[112]. Grotius' comment there on "wrong-by-construction-of-law" having been introduced by civil law (3,32,22) has its counterpart in *De iure belli ac pacis,* where he considers the vicarious liability of *reges* and *magistratus* for their *ministri* and the noxal liability for slaves and animals as not belonging to natural law or *ius gentium* but being *ex iure civili*[113]. In this context he also mentions the rule on collision of ships without fault (liability for things): *multorum populorum legibus, ut et nostra, damnum tale dividi solet ob culpae probandae difficultatem*[114].

II. Influence of Grotius' doctrine in the Netherlands

Grotius' doctrine of course exercized most of its influence in the Northern Netherlands, in particular in the province of Holland. We will mainly deal with a few Dutch authors who helped to propagate it, not only in his own country but also elsewhere. Some of them may even have been cited more frequently than Grotius himself by contemporary foreign jurists as well as by foreign legal historians, especially as regards Grotius' opinions in the *Inleidinge tot de Hollandsche rechtsgeleerdheid*[115].

In chronological order the first author to be mentioned is Arnoldus Vinnius (1588–1657). The first edition of his *Commentarius in quatuor libros Institutionum* was published in 1642, even before Grotius' death. He does not refer to Grotius' system of sources of obligation and his definition of *delictum* is: *omne factum illicitum quod lege humana poenam meretur* (ad Inst. 4,1 pr.)[116]. But in his discussion of the *principium* of the title *De lege*

---

est is the liability of "qui contractui aut promissioni causam dedit dolo, vi aut metu iniusto" (2,17,17). He does not refer in this context to the liability of a *promissor negligens ... in re exploranda aut in sensu suo exprimendo* which he had dealt with in his doctrine of *error,* see Djbap 2,11,6,3: if the other party had suffered damage from such negligence, "tenebitur id resarcire promissor, non ex vi promissionis, sed ex damno per culpam dato, de quo capite infra agemus" (it is clear that Grotius refers here to Djbap 2,17; he should have referred back to 2,11,6,3 when mentioning *dolus, vis* and *metus* in 2,17,17). Cf. *Feenstra* in Fata iuris romani (above n. 1) 347.

112 Cf. above at n. 27 ff.

113 See Djbap 2,17,20 and 2,17,21.

114 Djbap 2,17,21 in fine; cf. Inl. 3,32,22, cited above at n. 27.

115 A similar statement, made by me in previous publications, has recently been criticized by *R. Voppel,* Der Einfluss des Naturrechts auf den Usus modernus, Eine Untersuchung anhand der Literatur zum geltenden Recht im 17. und 18. Jahrhundert (Beiträge zur Neueren Privatrechtsgeschichte, 11; 1996), 145: "Vermittlung des Gedankengutes der Inleidinge durch Autoren wie Vinnius oder Voet lässt sich, jedenfalls für Deutschland, nicht bestätigen". I cannot go into details here; perhaps my statement applies more to countries like France, Italy and Spain than to Germany.

Aquilia (Inst. 4,3 pr.), after stating that *occiso homine libero non agitur ex lege Aquilia ... sed legi Corneliae locus est,* he observes that *si de damno sarciendo civiliter disceptetur,* the man who killed *injuste* is liable to pay according to a formula which gives the essence of Grotius' statement in *Inleidinge* 3,33,2, to which he explicitly refers; in translating it into Latin he seems, however, to have been much inspired by the text of *De iure belli ac pacis* 2,17,13, from which he takes over some elements that are not in the *Inleidinge*[117]. He adds some references to 16th and 17th century authors – in part copied from Tuldenus – and refers to his commentary on Inst. 4,3,13 for the rule applicable when a free man is wounded or mutilated[118]. There we find, in Latin, the essence of Grotius' statement in *Inleidinge* 3,34,2[119]. When we consider that these passages occur in the 40-odd edi-

[116] For differences between *delictum* and *maleficium* see above n. 62; many authors, however, use the two terms as equivalent, cf. below n. 153 and n. 162.

[117] Commentarius, ad Inst. 4,3 pr. (ed. Leiden 1642, p. 1215): "... tenetur is qui iniuste occidit solvere impensas funeris et si quae factae sunt in medicos, iisque quos occisus alere ex officio solebat, puta liberis, uxori, parentibus dare tantum quantum illa spes alimentorum ratione habita aetatis occisi valebat, Grot. lib. 3 introd. c.33 [follows – without reference – the phrase of Djbap 2,17,13, with the example taken from Diodorus, which I have quoted above n. 82; Grotius' reference to Michael of Ephesus occurs also in Vinnius but only after other references, see below n. 118]. Cf. *Voppel* (above n. 115) 108–109.

[118] After the text quoted above n. 117 (with the phrase taken from Djbap 2,17,13) Vinnius writes: "atque ita censuit Senatus Dolanus apud Ioan. Grevell. Decis. 25 et Card. Puteus [ed. 1642: Putens] lib. 3, dec. 280. Sed et Cuiac. 14 obs. 4 exemplo Hadriani et Const. Porphyrogennetae probat novum non esse ut pars bonorum addicatur occisi liberis vel patri vel uxori, maxime si paupertate premantur, quamvis caedes citra dolum facta, iniuste tamen. Michael Ephesius ad 5 Nicom. Arist. scribit eum ipsum, qui caesus est, quodammodo capere quae uxor aut liberi aut cognati ex bonis homicidae ferunt. Idque in Gallia obtinere usque ad modum lucri amissi testatur Costal. ad l. 3 si quadr. paup. fec. Adde Gomez. 3 resol. 3 n. 37, Grot. 2 de jur. bell. 17 n. 12 et seq., Tuld. ad tit. 5 cap. 3, Christin. vol. 2 decis. 35 n. 10. Libero homine vulnerato aut mutilato quid iuris sit videbimus inf. § capite tertio".

The references to Grivellius, Card. Puteus, Cujacius and Costalius occur already in Diodorus Tuldenus ad Inst. 4,5, cap. 3 (Ad Institutionum juris civilis Iustiniani libros quatuor, Louvain 1633, p. 426–427; I could not check the first edition of 1628); it is quite likely that Vinnius took the references from Tuldenus, whom he cites after "Adde" together with Gomez, Grotius (de iure belli) and Christinaeus.

In general, for Vinnius one should be very careful to distinguish between what he cites from others and what is his own opinion. An example: *Rotondi* (above n. 2) 519 and *Massetto* (above n. 3) 1157 n. 553 cite Vinnius ad Inst. 4,3,9 for the opinion "Hodie actio legis Aquiliae poenalis non est"; they have not seen that this statement and the long passage that follows it has been taken literally from Gudelinus, the only authority he cites here (in the 1642 ed.). Another example below n. 119

[119] Vinnius, Commentarius, ad Inst. 4,3,13 (ed. 1642, p. 1223–1224): "Moribus harum regionum etiam dolorum et deformationis corporis si quando id petitur, aesti-

tions which followed the *editio princeps* of Vinnius' commentary – most of them published outside the Netherlands – it can certainly be said that Vinnius contributed a great deal to the diffusion of Grotius' opinions on these two aspects of liability for negligence[120].

In 1644 Simon van Groenewegen van der Made (1613–1652) was the first to publish an edition of Grotius' *Inleidinge* with marginal notes[121]. Five years later, in 1649, Groenewegen published his own work, *Tractatus de legibus abrogatis et inusitatis in Hollandia vicinisque regionibus*[122]. For his fundamental statement – on Inst 4,3,15 – that the *actio legis Aquiliae hodie non poenalis est sed rei persecutoria* and that therefore *qui culpa damnum dedit moribus hodiernis ultra veram damni dati estimationem non tenetur* his first references are to three chapters of Grotius' *Inleidinge* (3,32; 3,34; 3,36)[123]. After mentioning a number of other authors he refers

---

matio fit, quamvis proprie haec pecunia sarciri non possunt, neque iuri Romano id conveniat, l. ult. de his qui deiec., l. 3 si quadr. paup. Grot. d. loc." The reference to "Grot. d[icto] loc." is to Inleidinge 3,34, cited just before "Moribus etc.". *Voppel* (above n. 115) 109 is wrong in saying about Vinnius: "Beim Schmerzensgeld bezieht er sich ebensowenig auf Grotius wie auf Naturrecht sondern verweist auf die *mores harum regionum*".

120 For the diffusion and influence of Vinnius' works outside the Netherlands see *R. Feenstra* and *C. J. D. Waal,* Seventeenth-century Leyden law professors and their influence on the development of the Civil Law, A study of Bronchorst, Vinnius and Voet ([Verhandelingen der] Koninklijke Nederlandse Akademie van Wetenschappen, Afd. Letterkunde, Nieuwe reeks, 90; 1975).

121 This first edition was published in Dordrecht 1644 (followed by edd. Amsterdam 1647 and 1652); a revised edition appeared in Delft 1652 (followed by 8 edd. up to and including 1767). For these edd. see B. Beinart, Simon van Groenewegen van der Made: A biographical note including references to his legal opinions and notes on Grotius' Inleidinge, in Tijdschrift voor Rechtsgeschiedenis 56 (1988) 333–340, at 338–339, where also English translations of the Inleidinge including Groenewegen's notes are mentioned. – The notes mainly contain references to authorities (which were completely lacking in the original text of Grotius). As to our subject, the most interesting marginal note is the one on Inleidinge 3,33,2: since the revised 1652 edition it contains also a reference to an opinion of Grotius, published in the socalled Consultatiën van Hollandse rechtsgeleerden III–2 as nr. 168 (ed. Rotterdam 1648, p. 459–460); this opinion concerns compensation in case of homicide.

122 The 1649 edition was published in Leiden, shortly before Groenewegen's death in 1652. It was followed by two posthumous editions, Nijmegen 1664 and Amsterdam 1669 (also Wesel 1669). Only the latter, which according to the title page was revised and augmented by Groenewegen before his death, has new matter and some extensive alterations; it is the basis of the critical edition, with English translation, by B. Beinart and M. L. Hewett (4 vols.; 1974–1987).

123 Ed. vol. 1 (1974) 88. For Inleidinge 3,32 and 3,34 the references are specified by indication of the numbers of Groenewegen's notes (paragraph numbers were only added since the 1727 edition of the Inleidinge); he refers to what in later editions is Inl. 3,32,10 ff. and 3,34,2 (instead of "n. 33" read "n. 3", cf. Beinart's edition). The references to other sources mainly concern French and German authori-

to what he has said on Inst. 4,5,1. There, in a comment on the *actio de deiectis et effusis,* he makes a general statement on homicide: *hodie* there is an action for damages *quantum ob eam rem aequum judici videtur,* for which Groenewegen gives in Latin the formula used by Grotius in *Inleidinge* 3,33, specifying that this action belongs *viduae liberisque etiamsi occisi heredes non sint*[124].

In the same year 1644 Antonius Matthaeus II (1601–1654) published his *De criminibus ad lib. XLVII et XLVIII Dig. commentarius*[125]. In his commentary on homicide he mentions[126] that according to custom (*moribus*) besides a settlement an *actio in factum* is granted to the wife, the children and others whom the deceased was obliged to support; this action is for *id quod interest,* taking into account the number of years which are deemed to have been taken away from the wife, children and others by the killing of their husband and father. This would seem to have been inspired by Grotius, but Matthaeus refers neither to the *Inleidinge* nor to *De iure belli ac pacis.* He continues with a long discussion on the question whether this action *moribus dumtaxat an et jure civili defendi possit.* On a strict interpretation of the Roman texts, says Matthaeus, it seems that the action must be derived *ex moribus nostris, non legibus Romanis*; nevertheless the other view is common and can also be defended quite easily[127]. As to the *mores nostri* mentioned by Matthaeus it should be kept in mind that he is thinking

---

ties on contemporary customary law; those to Matthaeus and Schultz were added only in the 1669 edition.

[124] Ed. vol. 1 (1974) 91; apart from Inleidinge 3,33,2 ff. Groenewegen refers to Clarus, Christinaeus and Sande (Schultz was added only in the 1669 ed.). It should be noted that he limits the action to the widow and the children. Among other passages where Groenewegen touches our subject attention should be paid to his comment on the rubrica of C.9,47 (de poenis; ed. vol. 4 (1987) 119–120): for the abolition of the Roman *poenae pecuniariae* he refers inter alia to cap. Fraternitas (C.12, q.2, c.11), Gudelinus and Imbert, as cited above n. 98.

[125] After the 1644 edition, published in Utrecht, the work was reprinted many times. The 1761 Antwerp edition is reproduced as part of an edition with English translation by M. L. Hewett and B. C. Stoop (4 vols.; 1987–1996). In my short analysis of Matthaeus' observations on our subject I have followed this English translation with a few minor alterations. As to the Latin text of the passages cited below there are no essential differences between the 1644 and the 1761 editions (though a few references to contemporary authorities do not yet occur in the 1644 ed., see below n. 128).

[126] De criminibus 48,5,7,11 (ed. vol. 3 (1994) 398).

[127] De criminibus 48,5,7,12 (ed. 398–399). His main argument is that in the very fragment which seems inimical to the other view – D.9,3,5,5 – Ulpian says that an action for *id quod interest* is granted *ex bono et aequo*; nothing, says Matthaeus, is "bono et aequo magis consentaneum quam actionem in id quod interest dari uxori, liberis, parentibus ut consequantur impendia in curationem facta nec non aestimationem operarum".

in the first place of the customary law of the province of Utrecht. This also appears very clearly from his discussion of the action when a free man is injured by the inflicting of wounds[128], where, however, he also cites *mores* of other countries; for the *mores Belgarum* he refers to Grotius and Zypaeus.

The next of the Dutch 17th century authors to be mentioned is Simon van Leeuwen (1626–1682). In his *Rooms Hollands Regt* (1664)[129] in general he follows the opinions of Grotius in his *Inleidinge* quite closely; this is also the case of his exposition of liability for negligence[130]. In his earlier *Censura forensis theoretico-practica* (1662)[131] he remains nearer to the Roman law, but nevertheless gives Grotius' specific statements on the actions for damages in the case of killing and of wounding[132].

Much more interesting than van Leeuwen is Ulricus Huber (1636–1694), who, like Matthaeus, is from outside the province of Holland; he was a Frisian. His *Praelectiones juris civilis* (1678 for the Institutes, 1689–1690 for the Digest)[133] contain nothing new or very important on liability for

---

[128] De criminibus 47,3,3 and 4 (ed. vol. 1 (1987) 101–102). Some of the marginal references to contemporary authorities do not occur in the 1644 edition.

[129] After the 1664 edition, published in Leiden and Rotterdam, many other editions followed (in which additions were made). There are also English translations; the best is: Simon van Leeuwen's Commentaries on Roman-Dutch Law, revised and edited by C. W. Decker, translated by Sir J. Kotze, 2nd ed. (2 vols., 1921–1923). The work was based on a work of his youth: Paratitula juris novissimi (Leiden 1652), which is earlier than his Censura, cited below at n. 131.

[130] See Rooms Hollands Regt 4, 32–39 (ed. Amsterdam 1732, p. 450–494) and cf. Paratitula 4,3, 1–7 and 4,4,1 (ed. 1652, 313–339). Cf. the short analysis by *Voppel* (above n. 115) 113, mentioning inter alia that van Leeuwen gives a different definition of "misdaad" from Grotius.

[131] The 1662 edition, published in Leiden, was followed by several other editions (the best would seem to be Leiden 1741). There exist partial translations into English; for our subject see Part I, book V, of Censura forensis ... edited and translated by M. Hewett (South African Law Commission, Research series 15; 1991).

[132] For killing see Censura 1,5,11,19 (ed. Amsterdam 1678, p. 506; translation 73). The Latin formula given is essentially a translation of Inleidinge 3,33,2 but here van Leeuwen does not mention Grotius among his authorities; from his citations it would seem that he has in part copied Groenewegen (above n. 124) and Vinnius (above n. 118). – For wounding see Censura 1,5,21,16–17 (ed. 1678, p. 524–525; translation 132–133). Here the Latin formula is also a translation of the Inleidinge (3,34,2), this time with explicit reference to Grotius.

[133] A new edition of the Praelectiones on the Institutes appeared in Franeker in 1687; as *pars prior* it formed a whole with those on the Digest (Franeker 1689 and 1690) as parts 2 and 3. In these three volumes Huber had added – with critical remarks of his own – the Scholia on his Positiones on the Institutes and the Pandects which in 1685 Christian Thomasius had published in his edition of this work (U. Huber, Positiones sive lectiones iuris contractae secundum Institutiones et Pandectas ... in Academia Lipsiensi publice iterum ventilatae ac scholiis nonnullis auctae a

negligence. What he says in his chapter on the *lex Aquilia* in the Institutes is better known for its criticism by Thomasius in his *scholia* on Huber than for its own sake; in general Huber adheres here to the Roman law, which was more strictly applied in Frisia than in other Dutch provinces. No influence of Grotius' doctrine is to be found in this part of his commentaries[134], but some can be discerned in his *Hedendaegse rechtsgeleertheyt soo elders als in Frieslandt gebruikelijk* (1686)[135]. His starting point is different from Grotius'. Huber deals with liability for negligence in the sixth book, treating of "misdaden" (as equivalent of *maleficia*). He begins the first chapter (on "misdaden" in general) with the statement that although in the third book he had said that obligation arises from contract or "misdaedt", it was not necessary to speak of "misdaden" immediately after contracts, since at the present day one citizen can hardly be said to be bound to another by true "misdaden"; the only action which may be brought by private persons is that for damages[136]. He defines "misdaden" as "illicit actions which are punished by the law"[137] and distinguishes private and public "misdaden"[138]. He gives two definitions for each; to us the most interesting is the second one[139] for private "misdaden": those which injure private persons in their property, honour, body, life or otherwise[140]. This is strongly reminis-

---

Chr. Thomasio, Leipzig and Frankfurt [1684–]1685). In all later editions of Huber's Praelectiones these scholia and criticisms thereon occur; as from the Leipzig edition of 1707 replies of Thomasius to Huber's criticisms of the scholia were added.

134 For these statements see Huber's Praelectiones on Inst. 4,3, num. 6–7 (ed. Leipzig 1735, p. 371–374); although he does not refer to Grotius he mentions obiter Pufendorf for some "notabilia Ebraeorum" on estimation in money of *libera corpora* (cf. below at n. 172). In his Praelectiones on D.9,2, num.1 and 18 (ed. 1735, p. 821) Huber refers to what he had said on Inst. 4,3; on D.9,3 (ed. 1735, p. 828–829) he says that Grotius' statement in Inleidinge 3,34,2 on estimation in money of *cicatrices* and *deformitas* does not apply in Frisia (cf. below n. 143). As to Thomasius' criticisms I may in particular refer to his *scholium* (and his *nova additio*) to num. 3 of Huber's commentary on Inst. 4,3 (ed. 1735, p. 368–369): whereas Huber considers *damnum culpa datum* as a *verum delictum,* Thomasius prefers the opinion that it is a *quasi delictum* (cf. above at n. 34 and below at n. 210).

135 After the 1686 Leeuwarden edition four other editions were published. An English translation (by P. Gane) appeared under the title Ulric Huber, The jurisprudence of my time (2 vols.; 1939). The work contains a number of elements already found in Huber's Beginselen der rechtkunde gebruikelijk in Frieslandt (Leeuwarden 1684).

136 Hedendaegse rechtsgeleertheyt 6,1,1–2 (ed. Amsterdam 1726, p. 880; translation (vol. 2, 1939) 381).

137 Idem, 6,1,3 (transl. 381); "Ongeoorlofde feiten die door de wetten gestraft worden" (ed. 1726, p. 880).

138 Idem, 6,1,20–23 (ed. 1726, p. 882–883; transl. 383).

139 The first one is in 6,1,21: "Private crimes are those for which the persons damaged or insulted may institute an action against the doer for their own monetary advantage".

cent of Grotius' doctrine. Indeed, after two other chapters on "misdaden" in general – chapter 2 on "innominate", chapter 3 on "improper" ones[141] – special chapters deal with "misdaden" against property (4–7), against honour (8–12) and against body and life (13)[142]. Although the systematical approach is inspired by Grotius, the details are rather different. The most striking point[143] is that in case of homicide a composition of 1000 guilders is to be paid to the heirs of the person killed, besides a composition of 500 guilders to the country (the province of Frisia)[144]; it is specified that the composition of 1000 guilders can also go to the children when they are not heirs[145].

The last of the great 17th century Dutch jurists we should mention in the present context is Johannes Voet (1647–1713). His best known work[146], whose influence outside the Netherlands has been as important as that of Vinnius' commentary on the Institutes, is his *Commentarius ad Pandectas*[147]. It refers regularly to Grotius as far as the *mores hodierni* are con-

---

140 Idem, 6,1,23: "... Private zijn, die particuliere persoonen quetsen in haer goedt, haer eere, haer lijf, haer leven of anderzins ... ". Cf. 6,2,5 (ed. 1726, p. 883; transl. 384) which has only "in haer goedt, eere ende lichaem" (property, honour and body).

141 As to improper "misdaden" Huber follows Grotius by bringing also vicarious liability under this category.

142 Chapter 14 is devoted to "tover-konst, bedriegery ende landt-looperije" ("sorcery, cheating and vagrancy"); Huber, 6,14,1 (ed. 1726, p. 927; transl. 434) considers these as private "misdaden" which are not against property, honour, body or life, although they tend to the detriment of other persons (cf. "anderzins" in 6,1,23, above n. 140).

143 Another point is that Huber does not accept estimation in money of pain or deterioration of body, see 6,4,20 (ed. 1726, p. 888; transl. 390); cf. above n. 134 and Deliktsrecht (above n. 1) 454 n. 124. A somewhat more elaborate statement on this subject is to be found in his Eunomia Romana sive censura censurae iuris justinianaei, of which the first, posthumous, edition appeared Franeker 1700 (reprint Amsterdam 1724; for this work, based on disputations, cf. Unjust enrichment (above n. 9) 226 n. 181). In the part concerning book 9 of the Digest (ed. 1724, p. 397–424) he makes some interesting observations on D.9,3,7 (ed. 1724, p. 422–423).

144 Hedendaegse rechtsgeleertheyt 6,13,35 (ed. 1726, p. 925; transl. 432).

145 Idem, 6,13,38; emphasis is laid on the blood-relation, so probably nothing goes to the widow.

146 Apart from this also his Compendium iuris juxta seriem Pandectarum (first ed. Leiden 1682; many reprints) should be mentioned here. See the paragraphs on the *mores (hodierni)*, ad D.9,2, num.12, and ad D.9,3, num.5 (ed. 1682, p. 156–158).

147 First edition (2 vols. Leiden 1698–1704). Many later editions, also translations into Italian (1837–1840 and 1846–1853) and into English. Among the latter the most important is The Selective Voet, by Percival Gane (8 vols; 1955–1958); it includes texts from the supplement by J. van der Linden, on which see below n. 161. For details on editions and translations see *Feenstra/Waal* (above n. 120).

cerned (which is not surprising because at Leyden University he taught the *ius hodiernum* in private courses with the *Inleidinge* as textbook[148]). He mentions Grotius' opinions on liability for killing and wounding as the law prevailing in the province of Holland[149], but for Grotius' systematical approach and his general rule on liability for negligence there is no room in Voet's work, which follows the order of the Digest[150].

The tradition founded by Voet of lecturing on Grotius' *Inleidinge* in private courses was continued at Leyden University during the 18th century. The most important of these later commentators[151] was Dionysius Godefridus van der Keessel (1738–1816), whose lectures on the *Inleidinge* were published only in 1961–1967[152]. From his comments on the sections concerning delict[153] two passages may be mentioned here. First his observations on the apparent discrepancy between Grotius' statement on transmissibility to heirs of the obligation *ex delicto* in *Inleidinge* 3,32,10 and his

---

148 See *R. Feenstra,* Dictata van Johannes Voet en Gerlach Scheltinga op de Inleidinge van Hugo de Groot, in Tijdschrift voor Rechtsgeschiedenis 56 (1988) 93–133. The edition of Voet's lecture notes (by *P. van Warmelo* and *C. J. Visser*; 1987) mentioned there contains no observation or reference of any importance for our subject which is not also found in his Commentarius.

149 See Commentarius ad D.9,2, num.11, and ad D.9,3, num.4 (ed. The Hague 1731, vol. I, p. 542 and 552); cf. the passages in his Compendium, cited above n. 146. Apart from some details Voet adds no new elements to Grotius' statements.

150 As far as vicarious liability is concerned Voet would seem to offer a new doctrine ad D.9,4, num. 10 (ed. 1731, p. 557): for delicts committed by servants within the scope of their employment the master was liable for full compensation (not only up to the amount of unpaid wages, as was generally held in the 17th century; cf. inter alia Grotius, Inleidinge 3,38,8); see *Zimmermann* (above n. 3) 1119–1120. For the origins of this doctrine see *T. B. Barlow,* The South African law of vicarious liability in delict (1939) 76–79, suggesting that Voet was mainly elaborating observations of his father, Paul Voet.

151 An earlier commentator was Gerlach Scheltinga (1708–1765), whose lecture notes (in Dutch) have also been published recently (by *W. de Vos* and *G. G. Visagie*; 1986), see *Feenstra,* Dictata (above n. 148) at 112 ff. Also in Scheltinga's comments there is no room for Grotius' systematical approach and his general rule on liability for negligence; Scheltinga's observations on liability for killing are unimportant and he does not say anything on Grotius' statement concerning pain and bodily disfigurement.

152 D. G. van der Keesselii Praelectiones iuris hodierni ad Hugonis Grotii Introductionem ad iurisprudentiam hollandicam, ed. by *P. van Warmelo* and others (5 vols.; 1961–1967).

153 In his comment on the definition in Inleidinge 3,32,3 (above at n. 23) van der Keessel translates "misdaed" as *delictum,* not as *maleficium* (ed. vol. 5, 320–322), cf. above n. 62. He agrees, however, with the definition and states inter alia: "... non addidit Grotius delictum esse quod lege humana poenam meretur, quoniam hanc materiam ... repetiit ex principiis iuris naturalis et haec principia dein cum iure civili comparavit" (322); for the latter definition cf. above at n. 116.

obiter dictum in *Inleidinge* 3,30,3 that in principle this obligation is not transmissible *nisi ad lucri restitutionem*[154]. Secondly his interpretation of the term "verzuim" in *Inleidinge* 3,37,6 as *neglegentia*, "onagtzaamheid" (a term occurring in *Inleidinge* 3,37,2).[155]

A much more distant link with Grotius' ideas is to be found in the writings of another Leyden professor, Johannes Ortwinus Westenberg (1667–1737), whose *Principia iuris secundum ordinem Digestorum* was a much used textbook at Dutch (and German) universitites up to the 19th century[156]; he published it in 1712, when he still was a professor at Harderwijk University. In a passage devoted to the *actio in factum legi Aquiliae accommodata* he states that it is given *ex aequitate* and that therefore it is also available to the children and the widow of the victim in case of homicide[157]. He refers to an earlier treatise of his, *De causis obligationum*, where he speaks of an *actio in factum, quae deficientibus verbis legis Aquiliae et mente legislatoris ob damnum culpa datum ex sola aequitate introducta est*[158]. One of the authorities cited there is the passage of Vinnius ad Inst. 4,3 pr., of which we have seen that it is almost literally copied from Grotius[159].

Johannes van der Linden (1756–1835) should be mentioned in the present context for different reasons. Apart from the fact that at the end of his

---

154 See van der Keessel on Inleidinge 3,32,10 (ed. 334) and cf. above n. 24.

155 "Alle verzuijm etc. Sensus esse videtur, neglegentiam, *onagtzaamheid,* ob quam non minus quam ob dolum in § 2 docuerat Grotius teneri eum qui damnum bonis alienis dederit, hic eodem modo esse explicandam uti fecerat supra in doctrina de delictis adversus vitam vel corpus commissis, nempe in Part. art. 33 § 6–8 et Part. art. 34 § 4" (ed. 378); cf. above n. 41. The cited texts (Inleidinge 3,33,6–8 and 3,34,4) deal with exceptions in case of necessary self-defence and accident without negligence.

156 See my article Ein später Vertreter der niederländischen Schule, Johann Ortwin Westenberg, in Festschrift für Heinz Hübner (1984), 47–62, reprinted in *Feenstra,* Legal scholarship (above n. 9) as no. XV, with some addenda.

157 Principia iuris secundum ordinem Digestorum, ad D.9,2, num. 39–41 (ed. Berlin 1823, p. 238).

158 De causis obligationum was originally published in the form of nine *disputationes* which appeared separately to be defended by Harderwijk students between 13 April 1699 and 5 July 1701; in 1704 they were brought together in a new version, De causis obligationum liber singularis seu dissertationes IX (Harderwijk 1704), cf. *Feenstra,* Ein später Vertreter (above n. 156) 51. For our subject see diss. 5, cap. 4, § 11 ff. (ed. 1704, p. 172 ff.). Westenberg argues that this *actio in factum* is based neither on *delictum* nor on *quasi-delictum*; it belongs to *variae causarum figurae, ex quo ob solam aequitatem conceditur actio* (§ 18, ed. p. 173–174). This should be kept in mind for the *celebris quaestio* whether an action is to be given to the children and the widow of the victim in case of homicide, which he answers in the affirmative (§ 35–36, ed. p. 180–181).

159 Above n. 117. This reference occurs in § 36 (cf. above n. 158).

life he translated Grotius' *Inleidinge* into Latin[160], two of his own publications merit our attention. First his supplement to Voet's *Commentarius ad Pandectas,* published in 1793, in which he seems to allude to the existence of a general action for delict[161]. Secondly his *Regtsgeleerd, practicaal en koopmans handboek* (Manual of law, practice and mercantile law), published in 1806[162], which is to be considered as the last synthesis of Roman-Dutch law; for obligations arising from "misdaden" (I, section 16) he gives a clear summary of Grotius' *Inleidinge,* with some interesting nuances[163]. Shortly afterwards, in 1807/1808, he made a draft for a Dutch civil code, in which as far as these obligations are concerned, we find much of the wording of his *Handboek.* It is, however, interesting that, inspired by art. 1382 of the French Code civil, he gives a general rule for delict which can be seen as a mixture of his French example and Grotius: "Anybody who by an illicit act injures somebody else in his person, honour or property is, apart from the punishment prescribed by statute for such an act, liable for the damage it has caused"[164].

---

[160] See above n. 11.

[161] Johannes Voet, Commentarii ad Pandectas ... tomus tertius ... continens supplementum auctore Joanne van der Linden ... sectio prima [no more appeared], Utrecht 1793, p. 152 (on Voet ad D.9,2, num.6): in cases where there is no *corrumpere* or *deterius facere,* such as *consumere alienum vinum aut frumentum,* the perpetrator "tenetur actione utili [D.9,2,30,2] quam producit publica utilitas ex sententia legis eo pergentis ne quod alteri per alterum damnum injuria inferatur". Although the *actio utilis* mentioned for this case is found in the cited Digest text, the motivation given suggests that van der Linden would make such an action available in all similar cases; Grotius' influence would seem evident. The translation of van der Linden's text by Gane (The Selective Voet (above n. 147) vol.2 (1955) 553 note a) wrongly suggests that van der Linden only deals with Roman law in Antiquity.

[162] The 1806 edition, published in Amsterdam, was reprinted there in 1894, probably for use in South Africa. There exist several English translations; the best known is by H. Juta under the title Institutes of Holland or Manual of law, practice and mercantile law (first ed. 1884; I have used the 3rd ed. 1897). For other translations – and for general comments on van der Linden's works – see *A. A. Roberts,* A South African Legal Bibliography (1942) 190–192 and 322–323.

[163] See ed. 1806, p. 171–175 (transl. 150–154). The most important deviation from Grotius would seem to be that from G.'s definition in Inleidinge 3,32,3 (see above at n. 23) he omits "from its own nature illicit"; in 1,16,1 van der Linden states "Een andere oorzaak der verbintenissen is misdaad, waardoor men verstaat een vrijwillig doen of laten, strijdig met de wet, en uit dien hoofde strafbaar" ("Another source of obligation is "misdaad" – the transl. has "crime", but see above n. 21 – by which is understood a voluntary act or omission contrary to [the] law, and for that reason punishable"). In the last paragraph of 1,16,1 occurs the division of "misdaden" in those against life, against the body, against the reputation and against the property "of our fellow-creatures".

[164] Johannes van der Linden, Ontwerp Burgerlijk Wetboek 1807/1808, ed. *J. Th. de Smidt* (Fontes iuris batavi rariores, 1; 1967) book 3, title 13, art. 1 (ed. p. 119):

In the context of codification it may be added that in an earlier effort to make a Dutch civil code, started in 1798, an older jurist, Hendrik Constantijn Cras (1739–1820), had proposed using Grotius' *Inleidinge* as the general basis[165]. As far as delict is concerned, however, he makes a notable exception: he rejects Grotius' concept of "wrong by construction of law", arguing that nobody can be liable in cases where no "verzuim" (*culpa*) can be found[166].

III. Influence of Grotius' doctrine in Germany

As to Germany we will make a distinction between authors belonging to the School of Natural Law and those who can be seen as representatives of the *Usus modernus Pandectarum*[167].

The first author to be considered is Samuel Pufendorf (1632–1694). His doctrine on liability for negligence has recently been analysed very

"Allen, die door eene ongeoorloofde daad een ander in zijn Persoon, Eer of Goederen beledigen, zijn (behalven de straffe, die de Wet op zoodanige daad stelt,) verbonden tot vergoeding van de schade, daar door veroorzaakt" (the English translation is mine). In the rubrica of title 13 the term "misdaad" is used for what in art. 1 is called "ongeoorloofde daad". In the following paragraphs the different illicit acts are dealt with essentially in the same way as in his Manual (see above n. 163), in spite of the fact that in the general formula of art. 1 "life" and "body" are taken together under the term "person" ("persoon"). The relevant texts of van der Linden's Ontwerp can also be found in my Vergelding (above n. 1) 50–51.

165 For H. C. Cras, president of the codification committee created in 1798, cf. Schrage's contribution to the present volume, where also a draft of J. L. Farjon for the part concerning the law of obligations is mentioned. The relevant sources for this part will be published in the near future in Bronnen van de Nederlandse codificatie sinds 1798, [vol.9:] Verbintenissenrecht, ed. by *M. J. E. G. van Gessel – de Roo* and *Y. M. I. Vreeburg* (Werken der Stichting tot uitgaaf der bronnen van het oud-vaderlandse recht, xxx; 1999). The passages quoted by Schrage are from the socalled "Opstel-Farjon" (I,2 and I,4; cf. also the interesting details in I,8 and I,9); they should be compared to the – later – so called "Ontwerp-Farjon", I,5 and I,8. I thank Mrs. Y. M. I. Greuter-Vreeburg for making this material available to me before its publication.

166 See the socalled "Tweede Memorie van Cras" (1799), in Bronnen van de Nederlandse codificatie sinds 1798, vol. I: Stukken van algemene aard verzameld door H. Aa, ed. by *J. Th. de Smidt* and *A. H. Huussen Jr.* (Werken der Vereeniging tot uitgaaf der bronnen van het oud-vaderlandsche recht, Derde reeks, 22; 1968) 29–47, at 45; the relevant passage also occurs in my Vergelding (above n. 1) 48–49.

167 For the influence of the School of Natural law on the *Usus modernus Pandectarum* see the recent work of *Voppel,* cited above n. 115; it also gives much general information on the authors we will cite below and, in some cases, on their views on the law of delict. As to Grotius' influence on the later Natural Law authors in general cf. *H. Schiedermair,* Hugo Grotius und die Naturrechtsschule, in Einigkeit und Recht und Freiheit, Festschrift für Karl Carstens, I (1984) 477–496.

thoroughly – and in close connection with Grotius – by Berthold Kupisch in his article *La responsabilità da atto illecito nel diritto naturale* already mentioned[168].

In his *De jure naturae et gentium libri octo*[169] Pufendorf starts from the double principle "*Ut ne quis alterum laedat, utque si quod damnum alteri dederit, id reparet*" (3,1,1). He derives from it the general rule (3,1,2):

si cui abs aliquo laesio sit illata damnumque datum ullo modo quod ipsi recte potest imputari, id, quantum eius fieri potest, ab eodem esse sarciendum.

Although the wording is rather different from Grotius' formula, it is generally agreed that the tenor of the statement is not fundamentally at variance, at least when the interpretation given by Pufendorf himself is taken into consideration. Pufendorf's observations have been called clearer and going deeper than Grotius', but there is no doubt that he has been largely inspired by Grotius[170]. After a number of general observations in paragraphs 3,1,3–6 he announces that he will discuss the *exempla* given by Grotius in *De iure belli ac pacis* 2,17, viz. the cases examined there in paragraphs 13 sqq. In each of his own following paragraphs (3,1,7 sqq.) Pufendorf starts out by giving Grotius' formula. In the paragraph on homicide (3,1,7) he has added some elements to the Grotian formula[171], which otherwise he cites literally. In the paragraph on wounding (3,1,8) nothing has

---

[168] See above n. 5. See also *Benöhr* (above n. 3) 213, 214 and 216, *Kiefer* (above n. 6) 78 and 83 ff. and *Zimmermann* (above n. 3) 1032; add *A. Giuliani*, Imputation et justification, in Archives de philosophie du droit 22 (1977) 85–96.

[169] First edition Lund 1672; I have used the ed. Frankfurt and Leipzig 1744 but checked the essential passages in the first ed. Users of the 1744 and other 18th century editions should take care in distinguishing the original text of Pufendorf from later additions (mainly in footnotes); even *Kupisch* 127 n. 11 in fine has fallen victim to confusion in this respect, ascribing to Pufendorf what has been written by Barbeyrac (the passage in question is rightly cited as from the latter by *Massetto* (above n. 3) 1161).

[170] Although the inspiration does not go as far as is suggested by *Rotondi* (above n. 2) 530: "riassumendo la definizione groziana"; the definition which *Rotondi* 529 quotes as occurring in Grotius, Djbap 2,17,22, is in fact taken from Pufendorf, De iure naturae 3,1,3, as has already been stated by *Massetto* (above n. 3) 1160 n. 582. On the other hand it would seem to me that both *Schiemann* (above n. 3) 349 and *Kupisch* 136 – though the latter does not agree with the former – exaggerate in claiming that Pufendorf carried Grotius' doctrine a step farther. The new element he brings in – extension of *alterum non laedere* to non-performance of a contract – cannot be considered as an improvement of Grotius' doctrine. For the rest he copies much from Grotius even where he does not cite him, see below in the text; a parallel could be drawn with his way of dealing with *obligationes ex dominio* (lib. 4, cap. 13), see my Unjust enrichment (above n. 9) 207 n. 66.

[171] E.g. he adds to *ex officio* (cf. above at n. 86) "obligationis perfectae vim habente" and for the valuation of the *spes alimentorum* (cf. above at n. 82) he states "habita ratione non tantum facultatum occisi sed et aetatis tam huius quam alumno-

been added to the literal citation. In this paragraph he continues with long citations from Constantinus L'Empereur's edition of a Hebrew source, Baba Qama, under the title *De legibus Ebraeorum forensibus liber singularis* (1637)[172]. Grotius had already referred to this work in a note added in 1642 to the passage cited by Pufendorf[173]. There is no doubt that the latter was induced to use this book by this Grotian reference. He did it in such a way that it is not always easy to see whether his text stems from the Baba Qama edition or from himself. Kupisch has not taken sufficient account of this problem and ascribes to Pufendorf an observation of L'Empereur[174].

There is one point on which Pufendorf disagrees with Grotius. He does not accept that liability for animals and vicarious liability belong only to civil law. He ascribes these liabilities to *naturalis aequitas*; in his opinion this concept should, however, be distinguished from natural law proper, which only accepts liability based on *culpa*[175].

Later German authors of the School of Natural Law certainly show less direct influence of Grotius than Pufendorf, but indirect influence can be detected in their work to the extent they either follow or criticize Pufendorf.

The most interesting author in this context is Christian Thomasius (1655–1728)[176]. In 1688 he published *Institutionum iurisprudentiae divinae libri tres, in quibus fundamenta iuris naturalis secundum hypotheses Pufendorfii perspicue demonstrantur.* In the chapter *De non laedendis aliis et de damno dato resarciendo* he does not deviate very much from Pufendorf and thus from Grotius: as to the interests protected by the "neminem laede" principle he mentions in the first place *vita, corpus, membra, pudicitia* and

rum"; see ed. p. 306. These additions would not seem to be very fundamental. He corrects "uxoribus" into "uxori", cf. above n. 85.

172 For details on this work and its use by Grotius see my Ius commune et droit comparé chez Grotius, in Rivista internazionale di diritto commune 3 (1992) 7–36, reprinted in *Feenstra,* Legal scholarship (above n. 9) as no. VI, at 10–11.

173 See above n. 89.

174 *Kupisch* 132, see my Réparation (above n. 108) 420 n. 4. Also what *Kupisch* 133 cites as "considerazioni del Pufendorf" is taken over almost literally from the text of L'Empereur (including the citation of Maimonides).

A comparable case of ascribing to Pufendorf what the latter had copied from another author is to be found in *Kupisch* 134 and *Kiefer* (above n. 6) 85: they cite as Pufendorfian text what he quotes literally from Boeclerus, see Réparation 420 and notes 6–9.

175 See 3,1,6 (ed. p. 305).; cf. *Hochstein* (above n. 32) 107 f.

176 For Thomasius' observations on liability for negligence see *Benöhr* (above n. 3) 218 ff., *Kiefer* (above n. 6) 78 and 87 ff., *Kupisch* (above n. 5) 138 ff. and *Zimmermann* (above n. 3), 1018, 1022 and 1032–1033. Cf. also *Rotondi* (above n. 2) 533 ff. and 537, *Giuliani* (above n. 168) 91 f., and *Voppel* (above n. 115) 207.

libertas and for *homicida* he gives essentially the Pufendorfian version of Grotius' rule[177]. In 1705, however, he corrected the views given in his *Institutiones* in a new work, entitled *Fundamenta juris naturae et gentium ex sensu communi deducta*. Here, in an addition to the said chapter *De non laedendis aliis etc.*[178] he mainly refers to a disputation he had written in 1703 under the significant title *Larva legis Aquiliae detracta actioni de damno dato receptae in foris Germanorum*[179]. In this treatise he had not only argued that the mask of the *lex Aquilia* should be torn away from the action concerning damage done as practiced in the German courts but also completely changed the basis of the Pufendorfian (and Grotian) general principle of responsability for wrongs: fault is no longer required, the principle is derived from the need for *tranquillitas* and *aequalitas* among men. Liability is merely based on the fact that one person caused the other damage. Liability for animals and vicarious liability belong to natural law; in this respect Thomasias differs now from Grotius as well as from Pufendorf[180].

The new doctrine of Thomasius would seem to have had no great influence on 18th century natural law treatises as far as his deviation from the fault principle is concerned[181]. This principle is e.g. maintained by his pupil Johann Gottlieb Heineccius (1681–1741), who recently has been called one of the jurists "denen in erster Linie die Verbreitung der Errungenschaften der niederländischen Schule in Deutschland zu verdanken ist"[182]. For four years (1723–1727) he was a professor at the University of Franeker. From this short period date not only his two manuals of Roman

---

177 Institutiones, lib. 2, cap. 5, §§ 12 and 48 (ed. Halle 1730, reprinted Aalen 1963 and 1994, p. 122 and 126).

178 Fundamenta, ad lib. 2, cap. 5 (ed. Halle and Leipzig 1718, reprinted Aalen 1963 and 1979, p. 215–217); in his caput prooemiale (ed. p. 4–5) he mentions Grotius and Pufendorf.

179 The first edition appeared in the form of a *disputatio* under his presidency, with G. M. Arend as a respondent, in Halle 1703; several later editions are in the form of a "tractatio iuridica" under Thomasius' name only, e.g. Halle 1750 (a reprint with an English translation by Margaret Hewett and an introduction by R. Zimmermann has been published Oxford 2000). The few lines which follow in my text are based on *Zimmermann* (above n. 3) 1018 and 1032–1033, but I have read the disputation in the original version; Grotius does not appear among the authors cited, but apart from many German sources and writers (in particular Schilter) we find Dutch authors such as Groenewegen, Matthaeus and van Leeuwen.

180 Cf. above at n. 113 and at n. 175.

181 See *Benöhr* (above n. 3) 222.

182 *K. Luig*, Johann Gottlieb Heineccius als Kritiker des Naturrechts von Hugo Grotius, in Europa in der Frühen Neuzeit, Festschrift für Günter Mühlpfordt, 2 (1997) 31–42, at 42. This article contains much information about Heineccius' life and works; I have used it as the basis for the following lines in the text. Cf. also *Voppel* (above n. 115) 159 ff.

law – his most influential *Elementa iuris civilis secundum ordinem Institutionum* (1725)[183] and his somewhat less successful *Elementa iuris civilis secundum ordinem Pandectarum* (1727) – but also[184] his *Praelectiones academicae in Hugonis Grotii de iure belli et pacis libros III* (first published in Berlin 1744, but probably arising from his teaching in Franeker)[185]. In this work he does criticize Grotius on some points[186], but not fundamentally as far as the fault principle is concerned. The same applies to his main work on natural law *Elementa iruis naturae et gentium,* first published 1737 in Halle[187]. Only in his *Elementa iuris Germanici,* dating from 1735–1737, is he in favour of the new Thomasian doctrine of strict liability[188].

183 The first edition of 1725 was published in Amsterdam; some 150 editions followed, see *Luig* (above n. 182) 33 n. 22, referring to an earlier article where he enumerates them. For our subject see in the first place § 1033 (ad Inst. 4,1; ed. Leiden 1751, p. 324): "Est vero delictum factum illicitum, sponte admissum, quo quis et ad restitutionem, si fieri possit, et ad poenam obligatur ..."; in this context he cites Grotius, Djbap 2,17,22 for the distinction between *poena* and *reparatio,* cf. *Voppel* (above n. 115) 162 and n. 123. Another important passage is to be found in § 1095 (ad Inst. 4,3; ed. p. 341), where he states inter alia: "verissima eorum sententia, qui hodiernam actionem non ex lege Aquilia sed ex iure patrio vel aequitate naturali superesse statuunt". Cf. *Rotondi* (above n. 2) 535–536, who, instead of the original text, cites Heineccius' posthumously edited Recitationes in Elementa iuris civilis secundum ordinem Institutionum (first ed. Breslau 1765) on this paragraph.

184 Apart from his edition of Vinnius' Commentarius (Leiden 1726, reprinted many times, see *Feenstra/Waal* above n. 120) 55 ff.). His additions concerning our subject would not seem to be very important; cf. however his comment on the sources of obligation (ad Inst. 3, 14(13), 2) cited in *Feenstra,* Unjust enrichment (above n. 9) 223 n. 168.

185 See *Luig* 33. On Grotius Djbap 2,8,26 Heineccius refers to some of his *disputationes* published in Franeker.

186 On Grotius' definition in Djbap 2,17,1 he comments e.g. (ed. Berlin 1744, p. 585): "Sed magis perspicue definiri potest, quod sit factum illicitum adversus legem dolo vel culpa admissum"; he explains "dolo vel culpa" by saying: "Si dolose adversus legem agitur, est delictum verum; sin culpa, quasi delictum. Tale delictum etiam est damnum iniuria datum". On the other hand he prefers Grotius' opinion to Pufendorf's as to the question whether liability for slaves or cattle belongs to natural law: "Pufendorf. affirmat, Grotius rectius negat, eamque ex iure civili oriri observat" (on Djbap 2, 17,21; ed. p. 597).

187 See *Benöhr* (above n. 3) 222 n. 101 and *Voppel* (above n. 115) 162–163. See in particular § 211 of Heineccius' work (ed. Halle 1738, p. 166–167; cf. the German translation by P. Mortzfeld: Johann Gottlieb Heineccius, Grundlagen des Natur- und Völkerrechts (1994) 159).

188 Vol. I appeared for the first time in Halle 1735, vol. II in 1737. The passages on our subject are to be found in lib. 2, pars 2, tit. 18, par. 80 ff. (ed. vol. II, Halle 1743, p. 72 ff.); see in particular §§ 93–94, stating that the lex Aquilia is not "recieved", with reference to Schilter's Exercitatio 19 (cf. below n. 195) and to Thomasius' Larva (he mentions, however, that this is not the case in Friesland, with reference to Huber). Cf. *Benöhr* 222 n. 102.

The fault principle is also maintained by Christian Wolff (1679–1754); for his opinions and those of some other 18th century natural lawyers in this repect I may refer to recent studies by German legal historians[189].

It is not, however, only in pure natural law writings that the influence of the Grotian texts in Germany should be sought: some authors who can be seen as representatives of the *Usus modernus Pandectarum* merit our attention. Reinhard Voppel[190] has examined a number of these authors for natural law – and in particular Grotian – influences on their doctrines of private law. For David Mevius (1609–1670) and his son-in-law Georg Engelbrecht the results are rather negative[191]. The first modest signs of such an influence are found in the works of Georg Adam Struve (1619–1692), in particular in his *Jurisprudentia Romano-Germanica forensis* (1670), where he follows more or less the order of Grotius' *Inleidinge tot de Hollandsche rechtsgeleerdheid* (deviating from the order of the Justinian Institutes)[192]. Although in the part concerning delict he cites the *Inleidinge* e.g. for the admissibility of "Schmerzensgeld"[193], he does not give any general formula for the obligation arising from wrong ("misdaed", *maleficium*)[194].

More important in this respect would seem a work by Johann Schilter (1632–1705), *Institutiones juris ex principiis juris naturae, gentium et civilis, tum Romani, tum Germanici, ad usum fori hodierni accommodatae* (1685)[195]. Here indeed a general formula for the obligation *ex maleficio* is given, which reminds us of Pufendorf and Grotius, both of whom are cited[196].

---

[189] *Benöhr* 222 ff., *Kiefer* 96 ff., *Kupisch* 142 f.; cf. also *von Mehren/Gordley* (above n. 3) 574–575, with an extended quotation from Wolff in English translation.

[190] *Voppel* (above n. 115) 125 ff.; cf. also *Kiefer* 58 ff., who for court decisions refers mainly to *Kaufmann* (above n. 104) 47 ff.

[191] *Voppel* 127–137.

[192] *Voppel* 137–140.

[193] See Deliktsrecht (above n. 1) 454 and n. 126 as well as Réparation (above n. 108) 420; cf. also *Kiefer* 71.

[194] *Voppel* 138. Struve also omits the categories of wrong used by Grotius (wrong against life, wrong against body etc.)

[195] Leipzig 1685. For this work see *Voppel* (above n. 115) 140–144, in particular 144: "In der gesamten Anlage und Durchdringung des Stoffes sind Schilters Institutionen durchaus mit der Inleidinge des Grotius zu vergleichen, wenn sie auch eher rezeptiven Charakter haben, während Grotius Neuland betrat". For our purposes Schilter's Institutiones are of greater importance than his Praxis iuris Romani in foro Germanico (first ed. under this title Jena 1698, but originally published as Exercitationes ad quinquaginta libros Digestorum, Jena 1675–1684), cf. *Voppel* 142; for our subject cf. Praxis, Exerc. 19 (ad D.9.2), § 59 ff.

[196] See Schilter, Institutiones, on Inst. 4,1 pr., num. 1 (ed. 1685, p. 520–521): "... Repetenda itaque haec est prima juris naturalis regula de altero non laedendo et de damno quod laesione fit reparando, cum alias vanum sit et humanae societati noxium, prohibere damnum nisi restitutio simul praecipitur. Omnis itaque transgressio

In the *Usus modernus Pandectarum* (1690) of Samuel Stryk (1640–1710)[197] – the work which gives its name to the period we are dealing with – there is also a passage in which the author hints at a general action for negligence: in the first paragraph of his commentary on Digest 9,2 Stryk says: "*Tituli praesentis usus amplissimus est, cum omnium damnorum reparatio ex hoc petatur, si modo ulla alterius culpa doceri possit*"[198]. Direct reminiscences of Grotius or Pufendorf, are, however not found here, although Stryk refers to Grotius' *Inleidinge* for a detail concerning *aestimatio deformitatis*[199].

After having dealt in some detail with the possible influence of Grotius' doctrine of liability for negligence on German authors – of the Natural Law School and of the *Usus modernus Pandectarum* – a few short remarks should suffice for such influence on the main German codifications of the end of the 18th and the beginning of the 19th century. In recent times German legal historians tend to warn against overrating the influence of natural law doctrines on these codifications, in particular as far as liability for negligence is concerned[200]. A distinction is made between the "schadensersatzrechtliche Generalklauseln" of the codifications and their detailed elaboration of liability problems: the former clearly show natural law inspiration, the latter in many particulars borrow from the *Usus modernus Pandectarum*. With this in mind, we can state that some of these "Generalklauseln" still show Grotian elements. This is notably the case[201] of the *Allgemeines Landrecht für die Preussischen Staaten* (1794), I,6,1 ("Schade heisst jede Verschlimmerung des Zustandes eines Menschen, in Ansehen seines Körpers, seiner Freiheit oder Ehre, oder seines Vermögens")[202] and, in a somewhat lesser degree, of the Austrian *Allgemeines Bürgerliches Gesetzbuch* (1811), § 1293 ("Schade heisst jeder Nachteil, welcher jemandem an Vermögen, Rechten oder seiner Person zugefügt worden ist")[203].

---

primae hujus legis naturalis et socialis est delictum. Laeditur autem vel res familiaris sive bona fortunae, vel fama et existimatio in societate civili, vel corpus ac vita …"

197 On this work in general see *Voppel* 153–155.

198 Continuatio usus moderni Pandectarum a libro VI usque ad XII (ed. Halle 1704) 146–147; cf. *Voppel* 155 n. 57.

199 On D.9,3, see *Voppel* 155 and n. 59.

200 See most recently *Schröder* (above n. 5) 156 and n. 46, referring in particular to *Benöhr* (statement 252; details 228 ff.) and to *Kiefer* (statement 162; details 137 ff.).

201 It is less clear for Codex Maximilianeus Bavaricus civilis 4,16,6 (for a partial quotation see my Vergelding (above n. 1) 46; for "4,6,6" read "4,16,6"); for details see *Benöhr* 228–229.

202 For details see other paragraphs of the title I,6 (for some quotations see my Vergelding 46–48). For the context and further details (also on the origins of this title of the ALR) see *Kiefer* 112–164; cf. *Benöhr* 229–233.

IV. Influence of Grotius' doctrine in France

The influence of Grotius' doctrine of liability for negligence is much more difficult to trace in France than in Germany. There is no lack of general statements[204] about the links between Grotius' doctrine and art. 1382 of the French Code civil ("Tout fait quelconque de l'homme, qui cause à autrui un dommage, oblige celui par la faute duquel il est arrivé, à le réparer"); details, however, are seldom given. Reference is made to passages in the works of Jean Domat (1625–1696) and Robert-Joseph Pothier (1699–1772), but in none of these texts is Grotius mentioned explicitly nor, with one possible exception[205], is the resemblance between their statements and those of Grotius so strong that direct Grotian influence is evident.

For Domat, who has been called "grand lecteur de Grotius"[206], the main text cited is *Les Loix civiles dans leur ordre naturel, Première partie,* II, 8,4,1[207]:

> Toutes les pertes et tous les dommages qui peuvent arriver par le fait de quelque personne, soit imprudence, legereté, ignorance de ce qu'on doit sçavoir, ou autres fautes semblables, si legeres qu'elles puissent être, doivent être réparées par celui dont l'imprudence ou autre faute y a donné lieu. Car c'est un tort qu'il a fait, quand même il n'auroit pas eu intention de nuire. Ainsi, celui qui jouant imprudemment au mail dans un lieu où il pouvoit y avoir du péril pour les passans, vient à blesser quelqu'un, sera tenu du mal qu'il aura causé.

This statement has to be read in its context[208]. It is not the opening paragraph of a discussion of "faute". Domat had started making a distinction between three categories of "faute": "celles qui vont à un crime ou à un

---

203 Compare also the details in other paragraphs; the texts are easily accessible. For the context and the origins cf. *Benöhr* 233–242.

204 Cf. e.g. *Parisi* (above n. 3) 151. He refers to *von Mehren/Gordley* (above n. 3) 573, who, however, do not mention Domat in this context (only Pothier).

205 See below at n. 218.

206 *M. Villey,* La formation de la pensée juridique moderne (1968) 633; he does not give references for this statement..

207 The part containing book II was first published in Paris 1691. I quote from the ed. Paris 1745, I, p. 180.

208 For this context and for the interpretation of Domat's texts on liability for negligence in general see *H.* and *L. Mazeaud / A. Tunc,* Traité théorique et pratique de la responsabilité civile délictuelle et contractuelle, I, 6th ed. (1965) 45–51, cf. also 55–57. In this work references are made to the unpublished thesis of *Y. Ranjard,* La responsabilité civile dans Domat (thèse droit Paris 1943) which I was able to consult through the kindness of my Paris colleague Mrs. Anne Lefebvre-Teillard.

Another (recent) unpublished thesis of some interest for our subject is: *Elisabeth Dandine,* La responsabilité civile devant le Parlement de Toulouse au XVIIIe siècle, Essai d'une théorie générale (thèse droit Toulouse 1997; the author kindly sent me a copy). It contains also some general statements on Domat (e.g. at 2–3, 96–97 and 435) but its main theme is the role of the practicians (at the Parlement de Toulouse

délit", "celles des personnes qui manquent aux engagements des conventions" and "celles qui n'ont point de rapports aux conventions et qui ne vont pas à un crime ni à un délit"[209]. It is clear that he is not using the general concept of *maleficium* we found in Grotius. While not mentioning the term *quasi-délit,* he is apparently following the tradition of a number of Romanists, who distinguished *delicta,* wrongs based on *dolus,* and *quasi delicta,* wrongs based on *culpa*[210]. It is only with the latter category, that he deals in title 8 of the second book devoted to "dommages causez par des fautes qui ne vont pas à un délit". In the first three sections of this title he discusses a number of Roman law texts which could be subsumed under this category and then continues with the text cited above as first paragraph of a fourth section "Des autres espèces de dommages causez par des fautes sans crime ni délit"[211]. This gives him the opportunity of classifying some other Roman law texts. We should not forget that the main purpose of his book was to put "les lois civiles" (the Roman law texts) in their "ordre naturel". He is not aiming at creating a new formula for liability for negligence, which would include a number of entirely new cases outside the Roman law [212]. The fact that this text among others was used by the makers of the Code civil for art. 1382[213] should not change our interpretation of Domat's treatise on this subject. In any case there is no sign of Grotian influence here[214].

---

and elsewhere) in developing the principle of article 1382 of the Code civil: they might have had as much influence as the "grands noms de la doctrine" (cf. 465).

209 Les loix civiles, 1e partie, II,8, introduction (ed. p. 175).

210 See above at n. 34.

211 In the first three sections of title II,8 he had dealt respectively with "De ce qui est jetté d'une maison ou qui en peut tomber et causer du dommage" (II,8,1), "Des dommages causés par des animaux" (II,8,2) and "Du dommage qui peut arriver de la chûte d'un bâtiment ou de quelque nouvelle oeuvre" (II,8,3).

212 According to *J.-L. Gazzaniga,* Notes sur l'histoire de la faute, in Droits, Revue française de théorie juridique 5 (1985) 17–28, at 25, Domat goes beyond Grotius in disengaging himself from the Roman law tradition and "paraît bien être le seul à avoir tenté de réduire, en quelques formules, la responsabilité civile". To me it would seem to be the other way round. In stating that Grotius' method "est restée très fidèle à la tradition romaine" (with reference to Djbap 2,17, written "sur le modèle de la loi Aquilia"), Gazzaniga completely distorts Grotius' discourse (and its sources). Cf. also the short statement in *Gazzaniga,* Introduction historique au droit des obligations (1992) 244.

213 For details see *Mazeaud/Tunc* and *Ranjard* (above n. 208).

214 It would seem that Domat is somewhat more congenial with Pufendorf when he mentions "l'engagement général de ne faire tort à personne", see Les loix civiles, 1e partie III, 5, introduction (ed. p. 225): "C'est une suite naturelle de toutes les espèces d'engagements particuliers et de l'engagement général de ne faire tort à personne, que ceux qui causent quelque dommage, soit pour avoir contrevenu à quelque engagement ou pour y avoir manqué, sont obligez de réparer le tort qu'ils ont fait". *Ranjard* uses this passage as the motto for his thesis; cf. *Mazeaud/Tunc*

As far as Pothier is concerned, Grotian influence is, in general, more probable. In another context I have stated [215] that in his *Pandectae Justinianae in novum ordinem redactae* (1748–1752) Pothier shows a strong preference for Vinnius (where he may have found some doctrines of Grotius) and that, on the other hand, in his *Traité des obligations* (1761), among the non-French works quoted, the standard works of Grotius, Pufendorf and Barbeyrac predominate. For Pothier's opinion on liability for negligence, the *Traité* would seem the more important of the two. In § 116 it has a rather short statement on that subject, which is often quoted[216]:

> Les délits sont la troisième cause qui produit les obligations, et les quasi-délits la quatrième.
>
> On appelle délit le fait par lequel une personne, par dol ou malignité, cause du dommage ou quelque tort à une autre.
>
> Le quasi-délit est le fait par lequel une personne, sans malignité, mais par une imprudence qui n'est pas excusable, cause quelque tort à une autre.

This statement would not seem to contain any Grotian element: we have seen that Grotius does not make the distinction between delict and quasi-delict in this – rather traditional – way[217]. There is, however, another passage in the *Traité des obligations* which is closer to Grotius' doctrine, § 123:

> La loi naturelle est la cause au moins médiate de toutes les obligations: car si les contrats, délits et quasi-délits produisent des obligations, c'est primitivement parce que la loi naturelle ordonne que chacun tienne ce qu'il a promis, et qu'il répare le tort commis par sa faute.

The expression "réparer le tort commis par sa faute" is reminiscent of the short formula used by Grotius in § 8 of the *Prolegomena* of his *De iure belli ac pacis* for one of the principles of natural law: *damni culpa dati reparatio*[218].

---

46. See also Les loix civiles, 1e partie, livre préliminaire, I,1,5 (ed. p. 2), where among "règles de l'équité naturelle" is mentioned "qu'il ne faut faire tort à personne"; cf. *Villey* (above n. 206) 633.

[215] *Feenstra/Waal* (above n. 120) 97.

[216] Traité des obligations (first edition 1761), in his Oeuvres complètes, I, Paris 1835, p. 427.

[217] See above at n. 34.

[218] Djbap, ed. 1939 (1993), p. 9. Grotius mentions there as the second and third of four principles of natural law: "promissorum implendorum obligatio, damni culpa dati reparatio" (for the first principle see Unjust enrichment (above n. 9) 208; the fourth principle is "poenae inter homines meritum"). *Villey* (above n. 206) 633 considers the quoted passage of Pothier (referred to as "I.1.3") as "l'âme du système de Grotius" (*Massetto* 1166 n. 651 wrongly ascribes this dictum to A.-J. Arnauld). In his Esquisse historique sur le mot responsable, in Archives de philosophie du droit

It might be worthwhile to look for Grotian influence on less prominent French authors than Domat and Pothier. One interesting example is given by Christian Chêne in his *L'enseignement de droit français en pays de droit écrit,* in which he devotes a small chapter to the opinions of three 18th century law professors on "dommage et responsabilité"[219]. One of these professors refers explicitly to Grotius' *De iure belli ac pacis,* book II, chapter 17, for a general statement on reparation and some examples[220]; another gives the essence of Grotius' rule on reparation in case of homicide but without reference[221].

V. Epilogue

The history of the doctrines of liability for negligence on the Continent during the 16th, 17th and 18th centuries which we have tried to analyse in the preceding pages could be summarized as follows.

In the 16th century we mainly find repeated by the civil lawyers the principle that besides a public *actio criminalis* there is always an *actio civilis* for the aggrieved person. The medieval Romanists would call this action an *actio civilis in factum.* There was, however, a tendency not to connect this action with the *actio legis Aquiliae.* The Legal Humanists of the 16th century would seem to ignore the developments this action had undergone in the practice of their time, but the systematization of the Roman law proper which was undertaken by Donellus, also in the field of the law of

22 (1977) 45–58, at 56, Villey states that the formula of what I have quoted as the third principle of Grotius "est passée dans le Code Napoléon: article 1382".

219 *Chr. Chêne,* L'enseignement du droit français en pays de droit écrit (1679–1793) (Travaux d'histoire éthico-politique 39; 1982) 307–314. Apart from the citations from the law professors he gives some interesting extracts from the dictionaries of this period.

220 Jean-Joseph Julien, Elémens de jurisprudence selon les loix romaines et celles du Royaume, livre 3, titre 14, no. 9 (first edition, Aix 1785, p. 380): "Soit qu'il s'agisse d'un délit privé ou d'un crime public, celui que le commet s'oblige à en faire la réparation. Grotius, de iure belli ac pacis, liv. 2, chap. 17 ... marque les diverses réparations qui sont dues aux diverses sortes de crimes". Cf. *Chêne* 312.

221 François de Boutaric, Les Institutes de l'Empereur Justinien conférées avec le droit françois (first edition 1738), ad Inst. 4,3 pr., Si quis alienum hominem occiderit (ed. Toulouse 1740, p. 523): "Si le dommage avoit été causé en la personne d'un homme libre, il seroit réparé également par la condamnation aux dommages et intérêts; nous les voyons adjuger tous les jours à une veuve qui a perdu son mari, à un fils qui a perdu son père, à un père qui a perdu son fils; les Lettres de Grâce accordées par le Prince ne faisant point obstacle à cette condamnation". Cf. *Chêne* 311: "c'est une des innovations importantes de Grotius que Boutaric, il est vrai, énonce comme un fait de pratique".

delict, opened the way for widening the group of *obligationes quae ex maleficio nascuntur*.

Apart from the civil lawyers the Moral Theologians – in particular in Spain – had worked out a fundamental text of Thomas Aquinas in this field.

It was Grotius' merit to make a fortunate synthesis of the doctrines of comtemporary moral theology and Donellus' systematical approach of the Roman law, adding elements from 16th century non-humanistic authors and from customary law. His general definition of liability for negligence would seem to be the most important innovation. It is in fact the oldest example of a „deliktsrechtliche Generalklausel". However, it is his formula for the obligation arising from homicide which gives the clearest evidence of its sources (Donellus on one side, the Moral Theologians at the other). This formula had more influence on later jurists of the 17th and 18th centuries than his „Generalklausel". By contrast, his concept of „wrong-by-construction-of law" as a civil law correction on the natural fault-principle, a concept which could have become a fruitful basis for rules on strict liability, elicited practically no response, even in his own country.

Among the Dutch jurists of the 17th and 18th centuries Vinnius, Groenewegen and Voet contributed most to the diffusion outside the Netherlands of Grotius' homicide formula. His „Generalklausel" has not had much influence even in the Netherlands, with a notable exception in the drafts of a „national" Dutch civil code shortly before and after 1800, just before the introduction of the French Code civil in the Netherlands.

In Germany Pufendorf was largely inspired by Grotius; even the tenor of his general rule on liability for negligence is not fundamentally at variance. In my opinion the originality of Pufendorf in this respect has been exaggerated. A synthesis of the Grotian and the Pufendorfian „deliktsrechtliche Generalklausel" is to be found in Johann Schilter's *Institutiones juris* (1685). An important innovation comes with Thomasius' *Larva legis Aquiliae detracta actioni de damno dato receptae in foris Germanorum* (1703). In this work Thomasius diverges from Grotius in many respects, in particular by abandoning the fault principle. He was not, however, followed by most of the 18th century German authors. The German codifications of the end of this century and the beginning of the 19th century still show a certain amount of Grotian influence.

In France Domat and Pothier were no doubt also inspired by Grotius in the field of delictual liability but they do not show this explicitly (at least not at the *sedes materiae*). Some less prominent 18th century French authors provide clearer evidence in this respect. This might strengthen the probability that the makers of the Code civil were indirectly influenced by Grotius in formulating article 1382.

PETER BIRKS

Negligence in the Eighteenth Century Common Law

When milk is spilled or a plate broken, every child's reflex is, 'It was an accident. I didn't mean to do it!' The parent is unimpressed: 'You weren't looking where you were going!' or, 'You should have been holding it with both hands!' The child intuitively identifies an accident as something to which no liability will attach and in the same breath defines accident as something which happens *contra voluntatem suam.* Instinctively, the child thus urges a liability for *dolus,* evil intent. The parent tacitly accepts the major but not the minor premise. There may indeed be something called an accident to which no liability, or a heavily reduced liability, attaches, but an accident is something which happens when conduct is not blameworthy. The parent's view is that the crucial line runs, as Alfenus Varus was already in the habit of saying in the first century BC, between *casus* and *culpa.*[1] Liability is not for *dolus* but for *culpa,* non-intentional fault, and an accident is not a disaster which happens unintentionally but one which happens without fault.

This kind of tussle to locate the line between liability and accident has to be conducted by every legal system. By the beginning of the eighteenth century English law had managed to establish that civil liability was not confined to *dolus.* Nor was it in general strict. There were cases of strict liability. Robert Eden, introducing Roman law with English parallels in the middle of the century, distinguished between crimes and private wrongs. He accepted that it was indeed true of *crimina majora* (major crimes, felonies) that one had to ask what the accused person desired and intended, but he then went out of his way to contradict the *Institutes'* position in relation to private wrongs by affirming, of trespass on the case, that it extended even to instances of strict liability: '*Hac etiam actione tenetur, qui per infortunium, et non dolo vel culpa alium laesit* (A person is liable under this action if he harms another by mischance and not through evil intent or by fault).'[2] There were such cases. But it is safe enough to say that liability

---

[1] D. 9.2.52.4; 10.3.26.

[2] Robert Eden, Jurisprudentia Philologica sive Elementa Juris Civilis (Oxford, 1744) 224, 229, contradicting Justinian, *Inst.* 4.3.2–3 and 14, which exclude liability for loss arising from *casus* (accident), without *dolus* or even *culpa.*

was, in general, fault-based. The defendant who caused the harm would be liable if he was blameworthy. However, this simple starting point has immediately to admit three related complications.

Substantive Uncertainty

The substantive matter in which we are interested is the basis of liability. As with other matters of substance, we expect the relevant issues to be explicated through analysis. We hope to find closely reasoned argument and detailed answers. It is an error to look for stable answers of that kind. In the early eighteenth century issues mostly went to the inscrutable decision of a jury in broad, unanalysed terms. What degree of fault would make you liable for harm? The answer is that what was required was as much fault as would satisfy a jury. What would be the measure of your liability, in money? As much, all things being considered including your degree of fault, as it seemed to the jury fair and good that you should pay. The common moral sense of the jury was in large measure the law. In our domestic example, the parent would be hard put to it to explain what precisely what would count as fault in any case or to propound abstract tests by which to predict the incidence of future liability. The same was true of the law. It had not thought its way through to general tests to answer analytically distinct questions.

But the century saw the common law begin to make advances in this respect. That is to say, by the end of the century some common lawyers had begun to insist on analysis and had tried to identify abstract tests applicable in diverse factual situations. Moreover, procedures had been introduced which made it easier to keep the jury within the railway lines so laid down.

The Forms of Action

The rules of procedure and pleading still dominated. The law, looked at as a whole, was no more than a list of actions. Some attempt will be made later to explain what this means.[3] The field of liability for harm was occupied by more than one form of action, and in the different actions fault arose and was handled in different ways. What might have been one story thus becomes a fragmented story, and the relations between the different actions tend to become its principal theme. Moreover, when the law is organized in this way, not every question comes easily to the surface. The truest account would probably confine itself to showing in what ways each

[3] Text from n. 12 below.

action would allow substantive questions as to the requirement of fault to be exposed. How did fault arise in the pleadings? To what extent could a court be compelled to analyse and define, so as to instruct a jury more closely and intelligibly or perhaps to correct a verdict already given? As the quest for greater substantive rationality gathered momentum, the forms of action fell into disrepute. Their abolition came in the nineteenth century. At the beginning of the eighteenth century they were still taken for granted.

The Language of Blameworthiness

This book examines the history of negligence. The word itself creates a difficulty. Nowadays we use it of almost all forms of fault less than malicious intent. In Latin the modern notion of 'negligence' is no longer *neglegentia* but *culpa,* which means 'fault' or 'blame'. Some examples of fault still cause us to hesitate. A disproportionate response, as where a person defends himself against a fist with a knife, may be blameworthy but is not quite 'negligent'. Still, with one or two such marginal awkwardnesses, we do think of the law of negligence as the law relating to non-intentional fault. In the eighteenth century a narrower core meaning was still dominant, though there was already a bridge between that core and the broad modern sense of the word. Although lawyers were happy enough to cross that bridge, the materials of the period cannot be safely approached without sensitivity to the strength of the core meaning.

Moreover, the tension between the earlier and the modern sense of the word makes it necessary to say rather carefully whether the task is to examine the nature and role of *culpa* in the eighteenth century or, more narrowly, the nature and role of negligence as then understood. The chapter is aimed at the broader of these two tasks. Broadly speaking, its argument is that by the end of the eighteenth century English law was still much in the position of the parent in the opening paragraph. It knew that liability was in general based on *culpa*. It had not yet mastered the business of analysing and defining quite what that meant. Its vision was still fragmented by the different forms of action. And its grip on detail was still weakened by habit of feeding large questions into the black box which was the jury. Nevertheless, it had embarked upon the process of defining more closely the questions which the jury should be answering. Albeit slowly, the demand for closer rationality was asserting itself, not only in matters of detail but in the intellectual organization of the law as a whole. By the end of the century there were still not many common lawyers who asked themselves where a figure such as negligence, wide or narrow, belonged on the map. Was it an independent wrong in a category of civil wrongs? Those who thought about such things would probably have answered that it was not, that it could only be an ingredient in a number of different wrongs which were themselves differentiated according to the nature of the interest alleged to have been infringed.

With this much by way of introduction, the chapter will deal first, briefly, with the meaning of 'negligence' in the eighteenth century. The meat of its story will then follow in its second part, which is devoted to the most important actions, the way in which fault arose for consideration within them, and the relations between them. The third and final part deals with the beginnings of systematization, a process which has never gone very far in the common law. Even though this was the century of Blackstone, the first professor of the common law in any university, the third part has rather little to offer.

I. The Word 'Negligence'

'Negligence' nearly always appeared in the pleadings in company with clusters of words all indicating fault, frequently one or more of 'improvidently,' 'incautiously,' 'carelessly,' 'improperly,' unskilfully,' 'ignorantly,' 'inexpertly'. It would be foolish to suppose that these were all distinctly differentiated in lawyer's minds. There was anyhow no practical need to examine the definition of each shade of blameworthiness. Nevertheless it is clear that 'negligence' and 'negligently' primarily indicated inactivity. As 'diligence' was active attentiveness to those things which ought to be done, so 'negligence,' the opposite of 'diligence', was inattentiveness to the call of duty, failure to act when one ought. The *Book of Common Prayer* requires us to seek forgiveness for doing those things which we ought not to have done and leaving undone those things which we ought to have done. In its core meaning, 'negligence' comprehended the sins of omission.

The famous chapter in Buller's *Nisi Prius* which is sometimes taken to be the root of the modern tort of negligence is called 'Of Injuries arising from Negligence or Folly'.[4] 'Folly' is not heavily used in the two pages devoted to this chapter, but it must have been thought necessary in order to cover active misconduct. Thus, where someone whips my horse which then bolts and runs down a third party, the third party has an action on the case against the whipper, 'for the whipping my Horse was an Act of Folly, and therefore he ought to be answerable for the Consequence of it.'[5] A little

---

[4] Francis Buller, An Introduction to the Law relative to Trials at Nisi Prius, 3rd edition (London, 1781) 25. All citations in this paper are to the 1781 edition. The first printed edition was in 1765, when Buller, who went to the KB at the age of 32, was only 19. The book is thought to derive from a manuscript collection of Buller's uncle, Lord Bathurst.

later the case is contemplated of a surgeon whose cure miscarries through his 'Negligence or Unskilfulness.'[6] Here the negligence is inattention or neglect, while unskilfulness covers blameworthy activity, in sub-standard cutting and binding and so on. One is entitled to think that this is not folly, any more than it is negligence. The chapter heading is thus put under stress by 'unskilfulness'.

Comyns' *Digest* reinforces the natural or core sense of 'negligence' as connoting a failure to act. It is, moreover, a failure to act which is not necessarily tied to any notion of fault. If one ought to act and did not, that would be negligence. But it might be case of strict liability. Negligence was, at its core, a not doing of one's duty. Whether that omission involved fault would depend on the design of the duty. Under the head of 'Action on the Case for Negligence' Comyns has dozens of examples of failure to do one's duty, whatever the origin of the duty, whether law, custom or undertaking. For example:

> 'So it lies against him, who neglects to do that, which by Law he ought to do: As, if a man is bound by prescription to pay Toll, and refuses Payment. Or, to provide Beer for the Beadle of the Hundred, and does not do it. So, if the Parson is bound by Prescription to find a Bull, and a Boar yearly, for the Increase of Cattle within his Parish, and does not do it. ... If a Man, who has an upper Room of a House does not repair it, to the Damage of him, who has the under Room. So if he, who has the under Room, does not under-pin, and support it. If a Man does not repair the Wall of his House, whereby his Privy annoys his Neighbour.'[7]

This core meaning of 'negligence' is well illustrated by an argument which cropped up from time to time in the cases in connection with the need to differentiate one action from another. For example, in *Ogle* v. *Barnes,* which will be discussed below, the plaintiff had brought an action of trespass on the case. The defendant moved in arrest of judgment that on the facts as set out in the pleadings the plaintiff ought to have brought trespass *vi et armis.* Counsel for the plaintiff retorted that the pleadings complained of negligence – that is, of a failure to act:

> 'But to support an action of Trespass *vi et armis* there must be some act by the defendant. Now in this case it does not appear that any act whatever was done by the defendants; on the contrary, it appears that the injury was occasioned by their negligence.'[8]

---

[5] Ibid.

[6] Ibid, 26.

[7] Sir John Comyns A Digest of the Laws of England vol. 1 (London 1762) 224–225. It might almost be said that 'negligence' is used synonymously with nonfeasance here, balancing the preceding head, which is 'Action on the Case for Misfeasance'. Also he appears to use 'neglect' and 'negligence' as synonyms.

The same can be seen, in the very different context of breach of trust. In *Caffrey* v. *Darby*[9] the plaintiffs claimed in Chancery that trustees make good from their own pockets a loss suffered by the trust. Contemplating remarriage the widow of an innkeeper made provision for her children by setting up a trust for them and then transferring the inn to her second husband on condition he paid the price of £800 in annual instalments to the trustees for the children, the trustees meanwhile being secured by a mortgage of the land. Business turned down and the second husband found it difficult to pay. Acting in good faith and confident of the sufficiency of their security the trustees did not demand payment. In the end the new husband became insolvent and, for unforeseeable reasons, the security proved insufficient. Sir William Grant MR said the trustees were entitled to give their debtor some leeway, but that their failure to call in the money or enforce their security had gone far beyond what was permissible. They would have to make good the fund because their omission to do their duty in the first place meant that they took the risk of the security later becoming insufficient, however unforeseeably. Their negligence – that is, their failure in their duty to call the money in when due – put the risk on them:

> '[I]f they have already been guilty of negligence, they must be responsible for any loss in any way to that property: for whatever may be the immediate cause, the property would not have been in a situation to sustain that loss, if it had not been for their negligence. If they had taken possession of the property, it would not have been in his possession. If the loss had happened by fire, lightning or any other accident, that would not be an excuse to them, if guilty of previous negligence.'[10]

The Bridge to Careless Misfeasance

Nowadays we have no difficulty in seeing a driver who drives too fast, or a doctor who follows a wrong procedure, as having acted negligently. For most of us most of the time, a negligent driver is one who drives in a blameworthy manner, and a negligent doctor is not only one who plays golf when he should be seeing his patients but also one who acts unskilfully. The bridge between the core 18th century meaning and this wider modern sense of negligence was always open. The very fact that 18th century declarations could allege that the defendant 'so negligently and impro-

---

[8] (1799) 8 TR 188, 189 (Erskine, Gibbs, Alderson). The same contrast between doing an act and negligence can be seen in the judgment of Lord Kenyon C J (191) and Lawrence J (192).

[9] (1801) 6 Ves. Jun. 488.

[10] (1801) 6 Ves Jun. 488, 496. It had long been established that a trustee was not normally liable for the loss of the trust fund, provided he had been keeping them 'as his own': *Morley* v. *Morley* (1678) 2 Ch Cas 2.

perly drove his carriage that ...' proves that legal usage could already travel across it.

The bridge is the notion that all blameworthy conduct is also a failure to take precautions. The old meaning of negligence is, to a degree, satisfied in the case of bad driving because that activity connotes a failure of a duty of care, a not-doing of a duty requiring positive action. Similarly, a person who attempts a surgical operation without the necessary skill or experience, or when he is too tired, is simultaneously doing a positive act of folly and at the same time neglecting his duty to reflect on the probable danger. Even nowadays, if a disproportionate response, as for instance excessive self-defence, remains blameworthy by reasonable standards, without quite being negligence, it is because the requirement of proportionality cannot easily be rendered as a duty broken by not doing.

The scruples we feel about using the word 'negligence' in that case are of the same kind as the eighteenth century lawyer may have felt with any use of the word in the context of action rather than inaction, misfeasance rather than nonfeasance. Nevertheless, it is clear that, though the dominant or core meaning of negligence in the eighteenth century was not doing when one should have done, the bridge to careless misfeasance was open and was crossed. We have already seen that Sir John Comyns' list of actions on the case for negligence starts with numerous cases of failure to do one's duty. Without any explicit warning the list shifts from failure to act to failure to take care while acting:

> 'So, if a Man lend his Horse, or other profitable Cattle, to another *gratis,* he [the borrower] is bound to a strict Care; and therefore, if he neglect to take due Care of it an Action on the Case lies: As, if he do not shut the Stable, and it is stolen ... Otherwise if it be stolen without his Default, or any Neglect. ... But, if there be not any Neglect in the Defendant, an action upon the Case does not lie against him, tho' he does not perform his undertaking: As, if he be disabled by Act of God: As if a Man promise to re-deliver a Horse upon Request, and the Horse dies, without his fault, before Request. ... So an Action upon the Case lies for Neglect in Taking Care of his Cattle, Dog, & c. As, if a Man ride an unruly Horse in *Lincoln's Inn Field* (or other publick Place of Resort,) to tame him, and he breaks loose, and strikes the Plaintiff. ... So it lies, if a Man permit a mad Bull to go at large, knowing he was mad, whereby the Plaintiff is gored.'[11]

As soon as the illustrations involve a duty of care, the examples slip round to instances which are or may be instances of positive conduct. In the midst of the list we find the man who thinks it right to break a young horse in Lincoln's Inn Fields or other public place of resort.[12] This was active

---

[11] Comyns (n. 7 above) 225.

[12] The case is *Mitchell* v. *Allestry* (1676) 3 Keb 650, 1 Vent 295, extracted with an additional manuscript report in *J H Baker* and *S F C Milsom,* Sources of English

misfeasance. It is listed as an example of negligence only because it was active misfeasance by one who did nothing to honour his duty to take care.

II. The Principal Actions

In the eighteenth century the law was still dominated by the forms of action, which is as much as to say by the list of claims claimable in the courts. An 'action' or 'form of action' is best thought of as a set of words, a winning proposition which the plaintiff undertakes to substantiate. The list of winning propositions was as it was thanks to all those processes, rational, opportunistic and accidental, which together made up the earlier history of the common law. As there were known forms of claims claimable, so also there were listable defences, or pleas (*exceptiones*). Knowing the law meant knowing the claims, knowing what pleas could be opposed to them, and knowing what facts would need to be proved in order to substantiate which claim and which defence. This last task made more difficult by the fact that over the years it had come about that many of the traditional sets of words no longer meant what they said. Some allegations, still invariably recited, did not have to be proved, others had to be proved by evidence of facts other than those which they appeared to rehearse.

It is broadly true that if one reviews all the actions known to the eighteenth century common law one can divide them between first generation actions and second generation actions. The first generation actions were those already known by the end of the beginning of the common law, say by death of Edward I in 1307. The second generation actions were those which began to be admitted later in the fourteenth century to fill gaps and remedy imbalances in the original list. These gap-fillers, originally called 'actions on the case' or 'trespass on the case', were at first confined to their supplementary role, but two centuries later most had escaped that restriction and were doing the work even of the actions which they had once supplemented. In relation to personal injuries and damage to property that transformation of the relationship between first generation action and action on the case came much later, not in the sixteenth but in the nineteenth century.

Legal History (London. 1986) 572. In fact it seems that the plaintiff had to amend his pleading in that case, precisely to take out 'negligently' and confine himself to other words of fault, as 'incautiosly' and 'improvidently': 'Coming to trial before my lord Hale, the evidence as to the negligence seeming against us, we were nonsuit. And my lord Hale did in a manner direct this action and [said] that it would lie without laying it to be done negligently' B&M 574. See too *M J Prichard, 'Scott* v. *Shepherd* (1773) and the Emergence of the Tort of Negligence' Selden Society Lecture for 1973 (London, 1976) 2–3.

At the beginning of the eighteenth century the standard action for injury and damage was still trespass *vi et armis*. Every such action looked on the face of its wording as though the plaintiff's complaint was that the defendant had intentionally attacked him or his property, for the action always said that the defendant had acted with force and arms. As we shall see, the reality was quite different. Force and arms did not have to be proved, and liability was not based on intent. It seems that liability was for *culpa*, with the onus on the defendant to show that he had not been at fault.

The supplementary actions on the case were diverse in nature, for trespass on the case was no more than a stable syntactical technique for complaining of almost any grievance. Negatively, trespass on the case made no mention of force and arms. Positively, the words alleged alleged that in one way or another the defendant had made himself responsible for some harm which the plaintiff had suffered. In alleging the defendant's responsibility the plaintiff would use words imputing fault to the defendant. In some cases the allegations would be of *dolus*, frequently of *culpa*. Just as the allegations in trespass were not to be taken at face value, so also in actions on the case it was necessary to know how the law handled the substantiation of the allegations. The fact that a recurrent declaration in trespass on the case recited fraud and malice did not necessarily mean that such *dolus* had to be proved. We will look first at trespass *vi et armis*.

1. The Principle of Liability in Trespass vi et armis

Declarations in trespass *vi et armis* stuck to a time-honoured traditional form. In *Gibbons* v. *Pepper* (1695)[13] what had actually happened was that the plaintiff had been run down by a horse which was being ridden by the defendant. But, if the defendant had simply taken the general issue 'Not Guilty' and let the matter go off to a jury, we would not know from the record what the real facts were. We know what happened because the defendant sought, unsuccessfully, to escape liability by entering a special defence. The plaintiff's complaint went like this, in time-honoured standard form:

> 'Thomas Gibbon complains of Thomas Pepper, in the custody of the marshal of the Marshalsea of the lord king and lady queen, being before the said king and queen themselves, for that the same Thomas Pepper on the first day of May [1694] ... at the parish of St Martin in the Fields in the aforesaid county of Middlesex, with force and arms etc., made assault upon him the said Thomas Gibbon and then and there beat, wounded and ill-treated him so that his life was despaired of, and inflicted other outrages upon the same Thomas Gibbon, against the

[13] (1695) 1 Ld Raym 38; 4 Mod 405, 2 Salk 638; record printed in *Baker* and *Milsom* (n. 12 above) 335.

peace of the said present lord king and lady queen, and to the damage of him the said Thomas Gibbon of £40.'[14]

Pepper could have said 'Not guilty' and thus taken the general issue to the jury, in which event the jury would have learned each side's version of the true facts in evidence given before it at *nisi prius*.[15] Instead, Pepper made a special plea. His defence required the true story to be told. He had been riding his master's horse, to take him to water, when something frightened the horse. The horse thereupon bolted. Pepper then shouted to warn people to get out of the way, but Gibbons did not get out of the way and, against Pepper's will, was knocked down by the horse. The plaintiff demurred to this plea, and the Kings Bench upheld the demurrer. The reason was that he ought to have taken the general issue. That is, on these facts it was proper simply to deny the allegations of trespass to the person. For if what the defendant said was true he had not done this battery. It was not his act. There is a fine line on some facts between two simple exculpations: 'I did not do it!' and 'Not my fault!' Here, if the horse bolted, the defendant did not do the deed. 'In the same manner, if A. takes the hand of B. and with it strikes C., A is the trespasser and not B.'[16] In one report it is said 'The reason of the judgment was because the defendant justified a trespass and does not confess it.'[17] That seems to mean that on the facts as he represented them there was not even a prima facie trespass. He was not saying, 'Yes, I did this prima facie unlawful deed, but ...' On the contrary, he was saying, 'I did not do this at all!' And that was matter for the general issue.

Though the two tend run together, and all the easier in a still unanalytical world, we are more interested in the case in which the defendant wanted to say, not 'I did not do it!' but 'It was not my fault!' It is that response which intuitively supposes that liability is for *culpa*. If 'Not my fault!' is once held to be in principle a good defence, the law will shortly have to confront the task of identifying the standard by which fault should be judged. It is frustrating that we cannot see a tidy development on those lines.

We have seen that the allegation of force and arms implied a deliberate attack. The first step in the articulation of the principle of liability was the rejection of a requirement of *dolus* (evil intent, malice). Human nature and the nature of the routine allegations in trespass *vi et armis* made it inevita-

[14] *Baker* and *Milsom* (n. 12 above) 335.

[15] The phrase *nisi prius*, meaning 'unless before', indicates 'at a trial on circuit, away from Westminster'. It derives from the fact that parties were called to be before the King's judges at Westminster on a given date 'unless before that date' the judges themselves came to the locality.

[16] (1697) 1 Ld Raym 38.

[17] 2 Salk 638.

ble that defendants would try to escape by saying 'I did not mean it! It happened against my will, *contra voluntatem meam*!' Nearly a century before our period, that was held to be an insufficient answer. Liability was not for *dolus* alone.

In *Weaver* v. *Ward* (1616)[18] the plaintiff had been shot and brought trespass *vi et armis*. The defendant pleaded that he and the plaintiff had been in training as soldiers and that in a practice skirmish his musket had gone off and had injured the plaintiff against his will. Though the case seems never to have reached judgment,[19] the court's opinion appears to have been, and was later taken to have been, that the defence was bad:

> 'And therefore no man shall be excused a trespass ... except it be utterly without his fault. As if a man by force take my hand and strike you. Or if here the defendant had said that the plaintiff ran across his piece when it was discharging, or had set forth the case with the circumstances so as it had appeared to the court that it had been inevitable and that the defendant had committed no negligence to give occasion to the hurt.'[20]

This ignores the distinction between 'I did not do it!' and 'It was not my fault!' but its first purpose is to say that a plea 'I did not mean it!' or 'I did not intend it!' was not good. Liability was not for *dolus* alone. At the other extreme, the court here also indicates that liability was not strict. The fair interpretation is that liability was for fault, *culpa,* but that the standard was more severe than that of the reasonable man. However, no standard is stated. We will return to the question of the standard, and the difficulty of managing without one, below.

At the end of the reign of Charles II, in *Lambert and Olliot* v. *Bessey* in1680, the Kings Bench had occasion to consider *Weaver* v. *Ward* in a case of allegedly innocent false imprisonment. There the court assembled with that case a number of other well-known examples, namely that in which thorns fall on a neighbour's land against the pruner's will, where a branch of a tree is lopped and falls on another against the lopper's will, where an archer shooting at the butts hits another person unawares, where willow which I cut falls into a river and clogs the flow of the water to your mill, or I work on my house and cause piece of timber to fall on your house, or I lift my staff in self-defence and unwillingly strike you standing behind me. This mixed bunch was taken to justify these generalizations:

> 'In all civil cases the law doth not so much regard the intent of the actor as the loss and damage of the party suffering. ... And the reason of all these cases is, because he that is damaged ought to be recompensed. But otherwise it is in criminal cases, for there *Actus non facit reum nisi mens sit rea*.'[21]

---

[18] (1616) Hobart 134, Moo KB 864, *Baker* and *Milsom* (n. 12 above) 331.

[19] *Baker* and *Milsom* (n. 12 above) 333.

[20] Hobart 134.

Taken in context this is not an affirmation of strict liability, nor indeed on its own terms. It once affirms that there is no requirement of *mens rea,* which here undoubtedly means *dolus.*

How should the defendant plead if he wanted to defend himself on the basis that he had been utterly without fault in the matter? If a defendant wanted to plead self-defence or defence of property, it was clear enough that he should enter a special plea in justification. It was then up to him to show the jury that he acted in self-defence and that the response was proportionate.[22] It is less clear what the defendant had to do where the defence was 'Not in any way at fault!'

Buller twice indicates that the defendant could choose either to take the general issue and put the matter to the jury or to make a special plea, which shows uncertainty as to the substantive consequence of his not being at fault, whether it negatived the trespass altogether or admitted a prima facie trespass. He does not say that the defendant must confess the battery and then avoid it,[23] only that he admits the fact, with a view to excusing it. He seems to mean that there is then not even a prima facie trespass, the fact but not the requisite element of fault:

> 'There are three Sorts of Defence to this Action. 1. Inficiation. 2. Matter of Excuse, 3. Justification. ... Matter of Excuse is Admission of the Fact: but saying that it was done accidentally and without any Default in the Defendant; and that (as I have already said) may be either pleaded or given in Evidence on the General Issue.'[24]

The first course involved making the general denial, *non culpabilis* (not guilty).[25] The general issue would then be taken to the jury. There is some evidence that, taking that course and putting the matter in evidence to the jury, the defendant who thought he had not been at fault might be able to persuade the jury to exonerate him or condemn him only for heavily reduced damages.[26] There seems to have been little sign that the plaintiff's recovery should reflect only his loss, as opposed to the culpability of the

---

21 (1680) Sir T Raym 421.

22 Buller (n. 4 above) 18.

23 Contrast cases of 'justification': 'Whenever the Defendant justifies a Battery, he must confess it, otherwise on a Demurrer the Plaintiff will have Judgment' ibid 19.

24 Ibid 17, cf 16.

25 The Latin can be translated as 'not to blame' or 'not blameworthy'. But there is no evidence that those words influenced matters, either as to the taking of the general issue or in not clearly distinguishing different grounds for being 'not to blame'.

26 *Angell* v. *Satterton* (1663) 1 Sid 108, *Baker* and *Milsom* (n. 12 above) 333; *Burford* v. *Dadwell* (1669) 1 Sid 433, *Baker* and *Milsom* 334.

defendant.[27] Buller says, paraphrasing *Weaver* v. *Ward* that if he took the other course, entering a special plea:

> '... he must set forth the Circumstances, so as to make it appear to the Court, that it was inevitable, and that he committed no Negligence to give Occasion to the hurt, for it is not enough to say, that he did it *casualiter et per infortunium, contra voluntatem suam,* for no Man shall be excused a Trespass, unless it may be justified intirely without his Default: and therefore it has been holden, that an Action lay where the Plaintiff, standing by to see the Defendant uncock his gun, was accidentally wounded.'[28]

Sir John Comyns, in a passage which in some respects adds to the confusion, in that it draws into the mixture even the invocation of necessity as justifying intentional harm, certainly comes down in favour of the availability of the special plea, though he does not deny the possibility of taking the general issue and putting the relevant matter to the jury.

> 'So the Defendant may plead, that he did it thro' inevitable Necessity against his will: As, that at a Muster he (being a Soldier) discharged his Musket, and the Plaintiff suddenly crost him, whereby he was inevitably struck. [There follows a reference over to a plea of saving passenger lives by throwing the plaintiff's goods from a sinking barge in the Thames, and another of extinguishing a fire by pulling down the plaintiff's house.] ... But the Plea is not good, if it does not appear to the Court that it was inevitable without the Defendant's Default or Negligence.'[29]

Despite the confusion of at least three ideas – 'I did not do it!', 'I was not at fault!', and 'I did it intentionally but to achieve a necessary purpose!' – the evidence of both Buller and Comyns is that they thought that a plea which denied all *culpa* on the part of the defendant was a good plea. In relation to an action on the case 'for so negligently managing his Barge that he ran down the Plaintiff's' Buller reports that Lee C J 'permitted the Defendant to produce every one of the Men on board his Vessel, to show that there was no Neglect, he being himself at that Time asleep on Board.'[30] It is impossible to believe that, whether under a plea or under the general issue, the same was not being done in cases of trespass *vi et armis*. If this is right, it follows that, though the onus is formally placed on the defendant, liability is for *culpa*. To the modern lawyer that proposition nonetheless bears a very uncertain meaning in the absence of a standard by

---

[27] Buller (n. 4 above) 25–26, where it is said that it is advisable, though not necessary, to put in evidence facts which made it probable that the plaintiff would be hurt, since such circumstances 'will have Weight in diminishing or increasing the *Quantum* of the Damages.' It is apparent that he is thinking chiefly of the culpability of the defendant.

[28] Ibid 16, which then cites *Underwood* v. *Hewson, Trin 10 Geo I,* Str 596.

[29] Comyns (n. 7 above) vol. 5 (1767) 321, sv 'Pleader'/ 'Trespass'.

[30] Buller (n. 4 above) 77, referring to a case decided at the Guildhall in 1744.

which to judge. The jury inscrutably embodied the standard. We will return to that later.

2. *Principles of Liability in Trespass on the Case*

In trespass on the case the situation is, at least at first sight, somewhat more straightforward. Actions on the case for injury and damage expressly alleged *dolus* or *culpa* as a basis for making the defendant liable. The syntactical structure of such actions generally consisted in one or more 'whereas' clauses, followed by a main sentence usually beginning 'nevertheless'. The form was, in barest, outline, 'why, whereas X, nevertheless Y.' The main sentence 'nevertheless Y' recited the actual wrong complained of. The 'whereas X' clause, or clauses, had the function of locating the wrong in a context which underlined the wrongfulness so as to put it beyond doubt that the plaintiff's complaint was and should be actionable. The 'whereas' clauses thus supplied relevant background and, in particular, advanced some basis for the defendant's being under a legal duty to the plaintiff to behave differently from the dreadful way in which the 'nevertheless' sentence then reveals that he did behave.

In actions on the case for injury and damage negligence is very frequently invoked to indicate fault on the part of the defendant and hence responsibility for the harmful outcome. On the other hand negligence never stands alone. It is always used in a cluster of overlapping language, indicating carelessness, want of foresight, want of skill, and so on.[31] The main sentence of the declaration is frequently on the lines, 'nevertheless the defendant so negligently, improvidently and unskilfully did such and such that such and such consequences followed, to the damage of the plaintiff.' The action thus attributes a blameworthy course of conduct to the defendant, which course of conduct brought it about that harm happened to the plaintiff. The allegation is typically, not, as it is in trespass *vi et armis,* that the plaintiff harmed the defendant, but that the defendant negligently, and in other respects faultily, brought it about that harm happened to the plaintiff.

A feature which distinguishes different groups of actions on the case for injury and damage is the nature of the 'whereas' clause or clauses which provide the context within which the court is invited to regard the harm as indubitably actionable. Three different kinds of 'whereas' clause require notice.

The first type alleges an *assumpsit*: 'whereas the defendant undertook to do treat the plaintiff's hand, nevertheless he so negligently and unskilful-

[31] Text from n. 4 above.

ly ... .' The second type alleges a common custom of the realm requiring care: 'whereas by the law and custom of the realm of England every man must keep his fire safely so that it does not for want of due keeping ..., nevertheless the defendant so negligently and improvidently ...'[32] The third type recites neither an undertaking nor a custom but simply states the factual background and assumes that the faulty conduct recited in the main sentence will attract liability.[33] It is tempting, but slightly anachronistic, to say that the first two forms assert a particular duty of care and that the third form simply supposes the existence of a duty of care. In fact what actions in the third form really assume is, less elaborately, that the bad doing of the activity in question must necessarily attract liability. Just as the action on the case for conversion assumes that it is actionably wrong to misappropriate another's things, so these actions on the case assume that bad riding or bad driving attracts liability. Typically, actions on the case of this third kind involve collisions on roads and waterways: 'whereas the defendant was driving his cart on the highway and whereas the plaintiff was driving his carriage on the same highway, yet the defendant so negligently ... managed his cart that it struck the plaintiff's carriage ... .'[34]

It might seem, therefore, that, in order to assess the range of liability for *culpa,* one would need only to comb through all examples of trespass on the case setting on one side those which made allegations of *dolus*. However, the words of these actions can also deceive. Whatever was intended when any particular action was first invented, it often came about that what the plaintiff actually had to prove was rather different from what was recited. Those who drafted a new action of this kind had their eyes chiefly a possible demurrer by the defendant. A demurrer was essentially the same as a modern application to strike out a statement of claim. A new action on the case had to look plausibly actionable; it must look an unlikely candidate for striking out. Just as we have seen that the words of the action for trespass *vi et armis* came to mean a good deal less than they said and could be substantiated even by a plaintiff who could not point to any violence, nor to arms or the evil intent implicit in an armed attack, so an action on the case, once it had established itself, might turn out to require less fault than its words suggested. In a logical world the words of the action would have been immediately modified to reflect rulings to that effect, but the process of modification was very slow. A gap thus opened up between what was routinely alleged and what the law required to be proved by a plaintiff seeking to substantiate those allegations.

---

[32] Examples 2 and 3 (second alternative) in the Appendix, below.

[33] Examples 1 and 3 (first alternative) in the Appendix, below.

[34] Compare examples 1 (collision on river) and 5 (conversion) in the Appendix below.

Many examples of this could be given. However, the clearest is perhaps the action on the case for conversion. This action, a full example of which is given in the appendix,[35] came into the law as a wrong requiring *dolus*. Abbreviated, it went like this:

> '... whereas the plaintiff was possessed of the cow Buttercup as of his own proper goods, and casually lost the same, and the defendant then came into possession of Buttercup by finding, nevertheless the defendant, knowing that Buttercup belonged to the plaintiff, and wickedly scheming to defraud and deceive the plaintiff, sold Buttercup and converted the price to his own use, to the plaintiff's damage ...'

This looks like a story of theft by a finder. But the allegation of loss and finding established itself as an all-purpose account of the defendant's possession of goods which the plaintiff had a right to possess. The defendant could not answer that it was not by finding that he acquired. He had to take the general issue, thus denying conversion of the plaintiff's goods. Nearer our present theme, he also could not enter a special defence to the effect that there had been no fraud or deceit on his part or, which is much the same, that he did not know that the goods were the plaintiff's, as for instance because he was an innocent buyer. Again, he had to take the general issue. It may be that he would then escape altogether, or pay much reduced damages, by persuading the jury of his innocence.

However, as these matters came to be more frequently taken out of the black box which was the jury and were more fully examined by the court, it became established that, despite the allegations of dishonesty, innocence was no defence. The only question was whether the defendant had converted the plaintiff's *res* to his own use. It made no difference that he honestly thought it was his own and had reasonable grounds for so thinking. Conversion thus became a tort of strict liability.[36] Once this was established, it was the business of the judge, at the trial, to tell the jury that the verdict must be for the plaintiff if the defendant converted the plaintiff's goods to his own use, however honestly and innocently he had done so. The allegations of *dolus* thus became as empty as the allegations of armed attack in trespass *vi et armis*.

---

35 Example 4 in the Appendix below.

36 It is not easy to pin down the moment at which the strict nature of liability for conversion became established. It is certainly the law from the mid-18th century: *Hartop* v. *Hoare* (1743) 2 Str 1187; *Cooper* v. *Chitty* (1756) 1 Burr 20. Blackstone 3 Commentaries 153, though brief, is to the same effect. But Buller, for all the surprising length of his treatment, appears to go no further than to deny the availability of any special plea, adding nothing as to the irrelevance of evidence of innocence under the general issue: *Nisi Prius* (n. 4 above) 48–49. So far as anything can be made of it, the much earlier *Vandrink* v. *Archer* (1590) 1 Leon 221 goes no further than to disallow the special plea. Cf *Gallyard* v. *Archer* (1789) *Baker* and *Milsom* (n. 12 above) 535.

This brief account of liability in conversion serves as a warning against the deceptive nature of declarations in trespass on the case, especially in relation to the requirements as to fault. Suspicion is the order of the day. Questions about the requirements as to fault can only be answered when courts rule on the real proposition which must be supported by the plaintiff's evidence to the jury or the effect in law of what may be loosely called mitigations put in evidence by the defendant. Unless and until the courts are induced to make such specific rulings, the jury remains the arbiter of the meaning of the words. In an unanalysed way, under those conditions the words retain their natural force and effect. The black box delays the development of stable detail, and the artificiality which is its inevitable concomitant.

The appendix includes an example of an action on the case for negligently keeping fire. Following the usual form, the plaintiff declares on a custom of the realm to the effect that 'every person in the same kingdom is bound to keep his fire safe and secure by day and night, so that no damage may any way happen to his neighbours, for want of good care of his fire'. Against that background the wrong alleged is that 'on the 10th day of August in the 36th year of the reign of the lord Charles the second, now king of England, &c. at St Martin in the Fields in the county of Middlesex aforesaid, so negligently and inconsiderately kept his fire, that for want of good care of that fire a mansion house of the said John Wallbanck [and all its elaborate contents] ... were burnt ...'

The history of this action shows that the words were not regarded as necessarily requiring the defendant to have been at fault at all, the negligence being no more than failure to keep the fire under control.[37] Late in the seventeenth century a softer position was taken in one famous case, though in language which vividly reveals the uncertainties inherent in the language of fault and risk.

In *Turberville* v. *Stamp* (1697) Holt CJ, Rokeby J, and Eyre J, first repeated that a man 'must at his peril take care that [his fire] does not, through his neglect, injure his neighbour.' These words seem to hover between strict and fault-based liability. But the court continued: 'If he kindle it at a proper time and place, and the violence of the wind carry it into his neighbour's ground and prejudice him, this is fit to be given in

[37] In 1401 Thirning C J said that a defendant must answer for a fire which spread by misfortune, drawing an analogy with homicide by misfortune, and Markham J appeared to agree with that, excepting only the case in which a stranger 'against my will' started a fire on my land and that fire spread: *Beaulieu* v. *Finglam* YB Pas 2 Hen IV, fo. 18, pl. 6; *Baker* and *Milsom,* (n. 12 above) 557–558. Cf. In 1610 Wray C J: '... you must at your own peril keep your fire so well that no damage ensues therefrom to anyone' Baker and Milsom 559.

evidence.'[38] That seems to indicate that the liability was ultimately fault-based, in that a defendant who had done everything as it ought to be done could take the general issue and expect to be exonerated by the jury.[39] However that may be, it was decided a decade later to prohibit by statute the bringing of any action in respect of damage from a fire accidentally started in the defendant's house or chamber.[40] Presumably the aim of the statute was to confine liability to those cases in which fault was proved.[41] If that is right, the words of the action, which to us seem to indicate a liability based on *culpa,* could not at the time of the statute be relied on to confine liability to fires attributable to the defendant's fault.

Morse v. *Slue* (1671),[42] which is discussed in *Coggs* v. *Bernard* (1703),[43] provides a vivid example of the same phenomenon. It was again a count based on a custom of the realm for the safe keeping of cargo carried by sea, alleging that the master nevertheless 'did so negligently keep them that, in default of sufficient care and custody of him and his said servants ... the same were totally lost out of the said ship'. The jury brought in a special verdict stating the real facts: while the ship lay in the Thames at London, a gang of eleven boarded and carried off the goods. The court clearly accepted that there had been no fault: 'If a carrier be robbed by an hundred men, he is never the more excused.' It would have been different if, but only if, the loss had been occasioned by enemies, pirates or acts of God. In *Coggs* v. *Bernard* Holt CJ explained this strict liability, limited only by these extreme exceptions, as based on sound policy, to ensure that common carriers of the various kinds would not undo those who dealt with them 'by combining with thieves, etc., and yet doing it in such a clandestine manner as would not be possible to be discovered.'[44]

These examples warn that allegations of negligence are compatible with a reality which amounts to strict liability. In so far as the language of negligence and neglect indicate inactivity or failure to take required steps, the words of the actions are not entirely contradicted by the reality. The defendant has been negligent: he has neglected the steps and measures which

[38] *Turberville* v. *Stamp* (1697) 12 Mod 152.

[39] The language is very close to that of Paul in D. 9.2.30.3.

[40] *An act for the better preventing mischiefs that may happen by fire* (1707) 6 Anne cap 31, section 6, made perpetual by (1711) 10 Anne cap 14, section 1.

[41] Although the wording of the statute is not easy, it seems that the defendant who thought the fire in question was 'accidental' was to take the general issue and that, if he won, the erring plaintiff would be penalized by an order that he pay triple costs.

[42] (1671) 1 Ventr 190 and 238.

[43] (1703) 2 Ld Raym 909.

[44] Ibid 917.

would have secured the end result which the law required. He failed to keep the fire in its place, to bring the goods to their destination, and so on.

3. *Standards*

The language of fault always supposes some standard by which to judge the matter, and if that standard is not made explicit, the speaker or writer's meaning is bound to be elusive. Where the milk is spilled at breakfast, I may counter the plea 'I didn't mean it!' with 'You should not have been fooling around!' That will do by way of bald assertion that there is punishable *culpa* beyond *dolus,* but it does not go far towards revealing the general nature of breakfast-time fault. In the same way, to say that a person shall not be excused a trespass 'except it may be adjudged utterly without his fault' is almost meaningless until we know what general standard to apply. The same is true when it is said that the defendant should have 'set forth the case with the circumstances so as it had appeared to the court that it had been inevitable and that the defendant had committed no act of negligence to give occasion to the hurt.'[45]

One is 'utterly without fault' if one passes the test suggested by the relevant standard. Similarly a disaster is 'inevitable' or 'irresistible' only according to a particular standard. One might judge by the 'any individual' test: could any individual have avoided or overcome the danger? Or one might judge by the 'this particular individual' test: could this particular individual have avoided or overcome the danger? There are numberless ways of modifying and supplementing the test to be applied. Should one add 'by taking any steps at all' or 'by taking reasonable steps'? And within what time frame should the question be asked? A disaster which is inevitable once it begins to happen might have been avoided by foresight the day before or the month before? To the modern mind the exasperating feature of earlier notions of blameworthiness is their seeming indifference to the need for stable and explicit standards. *Ad hoc* answers are given, much on the same level as 'You should not have been fooling around!' For example, Buller has this example of a disaster which was certainly inevitable from a certain moment:

> '[A]nd therefore in an Action against such a Carrier, where Goods were spoiled by the Water, the Defendant proving, that when the Goods were put on Board the Ship was tight, and that the Hole through which the Water came had been made by a Rat eating out the Oakum, was holden to be no Excuse.'[46]

---

[45] These quotations are taken from *Weaver* v. *Ward* (1616) Hobart 134, the case in which the defendant's musket went off during a training skirmish: text to n. 17 above.

Similarly, in another case against a carrier by water, where the defendant's boat had been blown by a squall into a bridge and so sunk, the defendant argued that the disaster had been irresistible, but the plaintiff immediately sought to take his stand at an earlier time. It could have been resisted by providing a stronger boat in the first place. But to that argument Pratt CJ gave the answer that a carrier was not bound to provide a new boat for every journey but only a boat which could cope with ordinary exigencies.[47] Again, no attempt to generalize.

The ultimate explanation of the absence of stable standards is dependence on the jury. The notion of *culpa* in the Roman texts on Aquilian liability is similarly imprecise, and for a similar reason. Some concrete guidance is given by the jurists, as for instance that want of skill must be treated as a form of fault, but by and large the law clearly relied on the lay *iudex* to decide whether the defendant had been at fault. The standard was to be supplied by the *iudex* himself: a person was blameworthy if a *iudex* thought that he was blameworthy. In much the same way, in eighteenth century England the law was broadly content with the proposition that people were liable if juries thought them liable. We find this disconcerting, even intellectually disreputable. We have grown so used to mediating inquiries into fault through the standard of the Clapham omnibus, that we cannot find our way about a landscape from which the reasonable man is still absent.

Advances were made in this respect, outside the courts and seemingly with only delayed influence. Thus, Buller himself took one of the three great commandments of the law – *alterum non laedere*[48] – and, anticipating Lord Atkin in *Donoghue* v. *Stevenson,*[49] injected into it the standard of reasonable care:

> 'Every Man ought to take reasonable Care that he does not injure his Neighbour; therefore wherever a Man receives any Hurt through the Default of another, though the same were not wilful, yet if it be occasioned by Negligence or Folly, the Law gives him an Action to recover Damages for the Injury so sustained.'[50]

It is impossible to tell whether this formulation was deliberately considered in the light of the intellectual condition of the law. It may have been

---

46 Buller (n. 4 above) 70. Oakum was sealing material based on the fibre obtained by unpicking old rope. The case was *Dale* v. *Hall* Mich 24 G 2 otherwise unreported.

47 *Amies* v. *Steven* (1719) Strange 45 and 129; Buller (n. 4 above) 70.

48 'The commandments of the law are these: to live honourably (*honeste vivere*), to harm nobody (*alterum non laedere,* lit. not to harm the other), to give everyone his due (*suum cuique tribuere*) J.Inst.1.1.3, taken from Ulpian: D. 1.1.10.

49 [1932] AC 562, 580.

50 Buller (n. 4 above) 25.

no more than a chance hit.[51] It cannot be said that the notion of 'reasonable care' is systematically worked into the many examples which Buller collects. There is no evidence that he seriously intended to invoke the standard of the reasonable man with a view to moderating the ambiguity and imprecision of the language of fault. Indeed in none of the three chapters in which one might expect to see it invoked does it ever recur.

In *Coggs* v. *Bernard* (1703) Holt CJ made a spirited attempt to sort out the bases on which different kinds of bailee might be made liable for damage to and loss of the thing bailed. For this purpose he imposed upon the generic notion of bailment, which comes from the French *bailler,* to deliver, and covers all temporary deliveries, a Roman or Romanesque classification, distinguishing six different kinds of bailment. His purpose was to show what degree of fault would render each bailee liable. His judgment as reported shows him at the end less than satisfied with his own efforts.[52] And, if he failed, it was for the usual reason, namely not stating stable standards by which to test for fault. Abstract adjectives do not help unless they suggest a standard. Holt CJ used 'reasonable care' once.[53] 'Gross neglect' and 'slight neglect', by contrast, suggest no standard and have no more meaning than 'neglect', until standards are stated.

Holt CJ's one seemingly accidental hit upon the phrase 'reasonable care' was taken up some years later in the Chancery. It had been established at least since *Morley* v. *Morley* (1678) that trustees were not strictly liable for the safety of the trust property.[54] In *Charitable Corporation* v. *Sutton* (1742) Lord Hardwicke LC had to consider the liability trustees for mismanagement of a fund. He invoked Domat's *Civil Law*[55] to support his view that the trustees' liability could attach to both misfeasance and non-feasance and then cited *Coggs* v. *Bernard* in support of his statement of the trustee's duty:

> 'By accepting a trust of this sort, a person is obliged to execute it with fidelity and reasonable diligence; and it is no excuse to say that they had no benefit from it, but that it was merely honorary.'[56]

---

[51] As is almost certainly the phrase 'reasonable care' the judgment of Holt C J in *Coggs* v. *Bernard* (1703) 2 Ld Raym 909, 918 (of bailees and factors); he uses 'ordinary care' of pawnees.

[52] *Coggs* v. *Bernard* (1703) 2 Ld Raym 909, 918.

[53] Ibid 918.

[54] (1678) 2 Ch Cas 2.

[55] Jean Domat, The Civil Laws in their Natural Order, tr W Strahan (London, 1722) Bk 2, Tit 3, Sec 1 and 2. The French original was published between 1689 and 1694.

[56] (1742) 2 Atk. 400, 406. Lord Hardwicke then addressed the argument that it was impossible for the court to attribute any loss to any individual's 'particular

This formula of 'reasonable diligence' evidently became habitual. A century later Lord Cottenham LC, distinguishing between management within the fiduciary's powers and excesses of those powers, used almost exactly the same phrase:

> 'It will be found to be the result of all the best authorities upon the subject, that although a personal representative, acting strictly within the line of his duty, and exercising reasonable care and diligence, will not be responsible for the failure or depreciation of the fund ... yet if that line of duty be not strictly pursued ... such personal representative will be liable to make [the loss] good, however unexpected the result, however little likely to arise from the course adopted ...'[57]

Whether or not it was Chancery which first adopted the regular use of the notion of reasonable care, the first person to insist on a scientific approach based on the necessity of on explicit standards, and the true inventor of the standard of the reasonable man, was Sir William Jones. Inspired, or provoked, by *Coggs* v. *Bernard* and drawing heavily on civilian writers, he composed a scholarly account of the law of bailment, in particular of the duties of care of different bailees. It was published in 1781.[58] If he has not been credited with the invention of the reasonable man, it is because the words he used were slightly different and less catchy. But his meaning was clear enough:

> '[B]y observing the different manners and characters of men, we may find a certain standard, which will greatly facilitate our inquiry; for, although some are excessively careless, and others excessively vigilant, and some through life, others only at particular times, yet we may perceive, that *the generality of rational men* use the same degree of diligence in the conduct of *their own* affairs; and this care, therefore, *which every person of common prudence and capable of governing a family* takes of *his own* concerns, is a proper measure of that, which would uniformly be required in the performing every contract, if there were not reasons for *exacting* in some of them a *greater,* and permitting in others a *less,* degree of attention.'[59]

---

neglect': if they were all guilty of 'supine negligence' they would all be liable for the loss.

57 *Clough* v. *Bond* (1838) 3 Mylne & C 490, 492.

58 William Jones. An Essay on the Law of Bailments (London, 1781). Sir William Jones (1746–1794) became a judge in Calcutta in 1783, but he was above all a scholar, the first to take seriously the study Hindu and Muslim law. His essay, which draws on these, as also on the Mosaic law, is a virtuoso performance, separating analysis, history, and synthesis, and showing his robustly independent intelligence underpinned by a quite extraordinary command of the both the common law and civilian authorities. His compliments were dangerous; they often concealed a dagger.

59 Jones (n. 58 above) 6.

He might at that point have christened his fixed standard of care 'reasonable care', but he did not. He decided on the word 'ordinary' instead, not meaning to diminish the standard by any pejorative overtone:

> 'The fixed mode or standard of diligence I shall (for want of an apter epithet) invariably call *ordinary*; although that word is equivocal, and sometimes involves a notion of degradation, which I mean wholly to exclude; but the unvaried use of the word in one sense will prevent the least obscurity.'[60]

Having fixed the standard of ordinary care, Jones scrupulously applied the same word to that kind of blameworthiness which consisted in the failure to adhere to that fixed standard. Hence, 'the omission of that care, *which every prudent man takes of his own property*' becomes 'ordinary default' or 'ordinary neglect'.[61]

For special cases in which it might be necessary to require more than ordinary care (and impose liability of less than ordinary neglect) he proposed the terms '*less* neglect' or '*slight* neglect', which was to consist in failure to show that care which 'a very cautious and vigilant man' takes of his own affairs. And at the other end of the spectrum he proposed the terms '*greater* neglect' or '*gross* neglect' which was to be judged by the standard '*of a man of common sense, however inattentive.*'[62]

If one source of confusion in the cases is the absence of clearly stated standards, another is the competition between different approaches to exculpation. One approach implies a standard, however inarticulate. The question is then whether the defendant was blameworthy. The other is to look for typified exculpations, as for instance by asking whether the disaster came about by Act of God or violence by the king's enemies or robbers. Ambiguous between the two approaches are phrases such as irresistible accident or inevitable accident, for the notion of inevitable accident can be defined in either way, by absence of fault or by typically irresistible irruptions. Loss by theft provides a context in which these two approaches commonly clash. That is, if the typified exculpation includes only Acts of God and violence, one who loses another's thing to clandestine theft remains liable, however careful he has been. Another point at which the two approaches clash, and one which we have encountered above,[63] is the case in which the violence or Act of God would not have been encountered but for the fault of the defendant, as where I would not have been robbed by brigands had I followed advice not to set out at dusk. The approach through typified exculpation then reveals itself as ultimately dependent on fault measured by a particular standard.

---

60 Ibid.

61 Ibid 8.

62 Ibid.

63 Text to n. 46 above.

Jones deals with these problems. He accepts that particular policy reasons may dictate exceptional rules, as for instance where the danger of secret collaboration between common carriers and criminals had to be met with a rule making the carrier liable even for loss through violence (robbery in the strict sense).[64] In the absence of any such exceptional policy, he makes fault, determined by the appropriate standard of care, the sole criterion. He achieves this by saying that the cases which impose liability for loss by non-violent theft are to be understood only as shifting the onus of proof by virtue of a presumption of want of care,[65] and by explicitly making exoneration by Act of God and other irresistible forces depend on conforming to the appropriate standard of care in the taking of precautions against encountering them.[66] In this way he not only makes fault intelligible by reference to stable standards but also overcomes the confusion in the cases arising from the clash between blameworthiness according to the facts and blameworthiness in the absence of typified exculpations.

Jones shows himself well aware of the artificiality of specifying just three standards, as also of the necessity of that artificiality. The practical exigencies of decision-making require robust standards. He also knows that it will often not be self-evident how standards apply to facts. At the very end of his essay he uses the case of *Mytton* v. *Cock*[67] to make a clear statement of the respective roles of the judge and the jury. In retrospect it seems elementary, but it represents a position to which English law, having for centuries been willing to leave very large questions to the jury, was only slowly approaching. In Jones's picture the judge, speaking for the law, must specify intelligible criteria of responsibility and, allowing a generous margin of appreciation, must retain ultimate control over its decision whether on the facts those criteria had been met:

> '[T]hus, when a painted *cartoon,* pasted in canvas, had been *deposited,* and the bailee kept it so near a damp wall, that it peeled and was much injured, the question "whether the depositary has been guilty of GROSS neglect" was properly left to the jury, and, on a verdict for the plaintiff with pretty large damages, the court refused to grant a new trial; but it was the judge, who determined, that the defendant was *by law* responsible for *gross* negligence *only*; and, if it had been proved, that the bailee had kept *his own* pictures *of the same sort* in the same place and manner, and that *they too* had been spoiled, a new trial would, I conceive, have been granted; and so, if no more than SLIGHT neglect had been committed, and the jury had, nevertheless, taken upon themselves to decide against law, that a bailee without reward was responsible for it.'[68]

---

[64] Jones (n. 58 above) 104.

[65] Jones (n. 58 above) 42–44, 66, 119.

[66] Jones (n. 58 above) 66–68, 95–98.

[67] (1739) 2 Str 1099.

4. The Limits of Liability

The earlier discussion drew attention to the examples in the Appendix which simply take for granted the actionable unlawfulness of the conduct complained of, without bothering to make the complaint more convincing by asserting an undertaking or a custom of the realm creating a primary duty not to misbehave in that particular way.[69] Reading models of that particular kind of action on the case, one is entitled to wonder why it took so long to achieve a generalized action for physical harm blameworthily brought about. It is easy enough to adapt the model to *Donoghue* v. *Stevenson* facts, in outline: 'Whereas the defendant was a maker of ginger beer sold in opaque glass bottles and whereas the plaintiff and other members of the public were accustomed from time to time to consume ginger beer of the plaintiff's manufacture, nevertheless the defendant so negligently and incautiously conducted the bottling of his ginger beer as to allow a snail to remain and decompose in a bottle the contents of which the said plaintiff drank, to the plaintiff's damage ...'

If such an action on the case had been drafted in, say, 1750, it might very well have slipped unobtrusively through. It might even have crept into an abridgment, becoming a model for others. Even an action for economic loss from negligent words might have succeeded, though one suspects that it would have been dressed up with allegations of deceit in the hope that evidence tending to show fault less than *dolus* would not persuade the jury to exonerate. There is no obvious reason why such actions should not have succeeded. They would have been within the words of Buller's proto-Atkinian principle.[70] One can only identify the hurdles they would have had to clear, without being at all certain that they would have fallen. Novelty was an objection in itself, though not a decisive one. Matthew Bacon's *Abridgment* begins its exemplification of the action on the case with a series of sentiments which on the one hand encourage innovation and on the other warn that novelty is dangerous: non-usage is a good interpreter of the law, meaning that things unfamiliar invite extirpation.[71] And Buller likewise

---

[68] Jones (n. 58 above) 122–123. These last examples reflect his conclusions summarised on 120, that a depositary without reward could not be liable for less than gross neglect and, even if guilty of gross neglect, could not be liable if, his character being known to the depositary, he he treated his own goods in the same way. Jones considers this point at 46–47.

[69] Appendix, below, examples 1 and 3 (first count).

[70] Text to n. 50 above.

[71] He starts on the other foot: 'Nor is it any Objection that such an Action was never brought before... [but, changing foot] ... no Action having been brought on the statute of Merton, it is to be presumed that no action will lie: and *Co.Lit. 81.b.* per Ld.Coke, Non-Usage is a good Interpreter of the Law. But [changing foot

both encourages and discourages. 'All these Cases,' he says, 'go upon this Principle, that every Man should so use his own as not to damnify another.'[72] But he immediately warns that this fine principle is restricted by a still inarticulate counter-principle hidden in the phrase *damnum absque iniuria* (loss without wrong): 'But if a new School be set up in a Town, where an ancient School had been Time out of Mind, by which the old School receives Damage, yet no Action lies, and this is founded upon public Convenience, and comes within the Description *Damnum sine Iniuria.*'[73]

An unfamiliar declaration would be very probably be challenged at once, by demurrer, or, after the verdict of the jury, by motion in arrest of judgment. In *Coggs* v. *Bernard* (1703) the declaration was challenged by motion: 'There has been a motion in arrest of judgment, that the declaration is insufficient, because the defendant is neither laid to be a common porter, nor that he is to have any reward for his labour.'[74] It will be recalled that the defendant *assumpsit,* undertook, to carry hogsheads of brandy and so negligently, etc., did the job that one was broken. The motion was, in modern terms, that there was no duty of care unless the defendant either was a common carrier (ie in the trade of carrying) or undertook to carry for a valuable consideration. But the answer was that even a private person was liable for blameworthy conduct in the actual execution of his gratuitous commission. That is, an executory promise to carry would not have been actionable but, despite the gratuitous nature of the commission, an action lay for damage done though want of care in the execution, the voluntary assumption of responsibility then being sufficient to ground the duty of care.[75]

Donoghue v. *Stevenson*[76] could have happened in the eighteenth century. There was no obvious obstacle. An action on the case could easily have been framed for the case in which a plaintiff had been made ill by food or drink supplied under a contract with a third party. If it had been, and if there had been a demurrer, the arguments would have resembled those of the majority and minority in 1932. It is impossible to say with confidence

again] *per* Holt Ch.Just. Wherever an Act of Parliament gives a Right, the common Law gives a Remedy; so where the Common Law gives a right, or makes a think an Injury, the same law gives a Remedy or Action. Salk.20, 21. 6 Mod.54' Matthew Bacon, A New Abridgment of the Law, vol. 1 (London 1768) 44.

[72] Buller (n. 4 above) 75. text to n. 50 above.

[73] Ibid 76. The case of the competing school is a recurrent example: Y B Hil 11 Hen IV, fo. 136v (1410), *Baker* and *Milsom* (n. 12 above) 613.

[74] (1703) 2 Ld Raym 909, 912, Holt C J.

[75] Cf text to n. 135 below.

[76] [1932] AC 562.

that the 1932 majority would not have won in 1750. Dr Ibbetson's chapter shows that the step which was taken in by Lord Atkin tried to happen several times before 1932.

5. *The Boundaries of Actions*

Blackstone and Buller, as we shall see, both approached wrongs in a manner which transcended, though it could not entirely escape, the boundary between trespass *vi et armis* and trespass on the case. In the courts that distinction could not be ignored. The line between the two kinds of action was not in all respects completely clear, even to the lawyers of the time. But it was certain that there were facts on which trespass *vi et armis* would not lie, though an action on the case might nonetheless do so. It was equally clear that a defendant might on occasion win a technical victory, against the merits, by arguing that the plaintiff's facts fell on the wrong side of the boundary an d could only substantiate the action which he had not brought.

That kind of technical argument, against the merits, would not run well before a jury. Technical points, if they were to come out at all, depended on the existence of procedural mechanisms for compelling judges to rule on the legal effect of the real facts, as opposed to the facts routinely recited in the forms of action. During the eighteenth century it became easier to do this, so that defendants could force courts to examine the limits of *trespass vi et armis*. A plaintiff who brought trespass *vi et armis* then had to be careful. His story must substantiate the particular proposition which he had made. It would do him no good to adduce facts which might substantiate some different allegation which could be advanced in an action on the case.

One fairly obvious way to avoid this danger was to not to bother with trespass *vi et armis* at all but to formulate the complaint from the outset as an action on the case. However, defence lawyers took the tactical game one stage further. As the boundaries of trespass *vi et armis* became clear, they began to use the same procedural mechanisms to argue that, within those boundaries, an action on the case could not be brought. Hence, just as a plaintiff who brought trespass *vi et armis* might find his defendant driving him back to an action on the case, so a plaintiff who brought an action on the case might face an argument that he should have brought trespass.

The end of our period echoes with arguments two centuries out of date designed to confine the action on the case to a supplementary role. Almost exactly a century before *Donoghue* v. *Stevenson,*[77] *Williams* v. *Holland*[78]

---

[77] [1932] AC 562.

[78] (1833) 10 Bing 112. See *David Ibbetson,* in this volume.

was the *Slade's Case*[79] of this story. The defendant had crashed his gig into the plaintiff's cart and injured the plaintiff's son and daughter who had been sitting in the cart. The plaintiff brought an action on the case which recited that 'through the carelessness, negligence, unskilfulness and improper conduct of the defendant' the defendant's gig and horse had broken his cart and injured his children, so that he lost the service of his son and incurred medical expenses. The defendant objected that the plaintiff ought to have brought trespass *vi et armis*. At the trial a verdict for plaintiff was given, but the objection to the form of action was reserved for the consideration of the court. The court's holding laid a foundation of the modern tort of negligence: where injury or damage had been negligent, as opposed to wilful, the availability of trespass was no bar to the bringing of an action on the case.

6. *Defining the Factual Boundary of Trespass* vi et armis

We will briefly return below to the end of the century story, but first we must look at the boundary of trespass *vi et armis*. There were three common fact-situations which would not substantiate an allegation that the defendant had with force and arms injured the plaintiff or damaged things belonging to him. The first was where the plaintiff had entrusted himself or his *res* to the defendant in such a way as to license physical contact, as where he went to a barber to have his hair cut, or to a doctor for treatment of a wound, or where he gave his horse to a farrier to be shoed, or a box to a carrier to be taken to London. Here the licence to touch excluded force and arms.

The other two cases were manifestations of 'I did not do it!' So, where the acts complained of had been done by the servant of the defendant but had not been specifically ordered by the defendant, it was not the master who did the relevant doings. If a master ordered his servant, driving his carriage, to run over the plaintiff's dog, the command of the master would make the act his own, and trespass *vi et armis* would lie. In the absence of the order, the action against the master would have to be trespass on the case.

The other example may loosely be called injury or damage, not done, but brought about. Here the defendant could say, 'I may have caused your injury, but I certainly did not do it.' This too was incompatible with the

---

[79] *Slade* v. *Morley* (1602) 4 Co Rep 92, now much more fully reported in *Baker* and *Milsom* (n. 12 above) 420–444. The case is taken to mark the collapse of the argument that trespass on the case, in the form of *assumpsit,* could not lie were Debt would lie, or, in other words, that a first generation action, here Debt, had a natural priority over the late-coming and supplementary action on the case.

allegation that the defendant had with force and arms beaten and mistreated the plaintiff or broken the plaintiff's chattels. If the injury or damage had happened merely consequentially upon some other doing of the defendant, it could not have been done by the defendant *vi et armis*. This requires further examination.

In 1726 in *Reynolds* v. *Clarke*[80] the plaintiff brought trespass *vi et armis,* charging the defendant with rotting his wall. The defendant had a right to use a privy at the back of the plaintiff's yard. In maintaining or repairing it he had brought it about that rainwater spouted over the plaintiff's wall. It was held that the plaintiff ought to have brought trespass on the case. Fortescue J said, *arguendo,* 'The difference between trespass and case is that in trespass the plaintiff complains of an immediate wrong, and in case of a wrong that is the consequence of another act.' And then, in giving his judgment, he amplified this, thus:

> 'Trespass will not lie for procuring another to beat me. If a man throws a log into the highway and in that act it hits me, I may maintain trespass, because it is an immediate wrong; but if as it lies there I tumble over it and receive an injury, I must bring an action upon the case; because it is only prejudicial *in consequence,* for which originally I could have no action at all.'[81]

Not always easy to apply to particular facts, this is the test which prevailed. However, it is evident from different formulations used by different judges that there was no completely clear answer. This is not surprising. It is difficult to draw such a line. Lord Raymond CJ, for instance, was reported to have mixed immediacy and initial unlawfulness:

> 'We must keep up the boundaries of actions, otherwise we shall introduce the utmost confusion. If the act in the first instance be unlawful, trespass will lie; but if the act is prima facie lawful (as it was in this case), and the prejudice to another is not immediate but consequential, it must be an action on the case; and this is the distinction.'[82]

This was taken up by others,[83] despite the fact that in his own report of the case he says nothing of the sort:

> 'The distinction in law is, where the immediate act itself occasions a prejudice, or is an injury to the plaintiff's person, house, land, & c, and where the act itself is not an injury, but the consequence from that act is a prejudicial to the plaintiff's person, house, land, &c. In the first case trespass *vi et armis* will lie; in last it will not, but the plaintiff's proper remedy is by an action on the case. ... and therefore, if it had been laid, the defendant poured the rain water into the plaintiff's yard, trespass would have lain, because the immediate act of pouring by the

---

80 (1726) 2 Ld. Raymond 1399, 1 Str 634.

81 1 Str 634, 635–636.

82 Ibid 635,

83 Text from n. 90 below.

plaintiff would have been a trespass. If J.S. lays a log of wood in the highway, and J.N. receives hurt by it, trespass will not lie, because the injury is only a consequence of the act done; but case will lie.'[84]

In the *Commentaries* Blackstone adhered to Fortescue J's approach and put the matter in this way:

> 'As to the damage that may be offered to things personal, while in the possession of their owner, as hunting a man's deer, shooting his dogs, poisoning his cattle, or in any wise taking from the value of any of his chattels, or making them in a worse condition than before, these injuries are too obvious to need explication. I have only therefore to mention the remedies given by the law to redress them, which are in two shapes; by an action of *trespass vi et armis,* where the act is in itself *immediately* injurious to another's property, and therefore necessarily accompanied with some degree of force; and by special action *on the case,* where the act is in itself indifferent, and the injury only *consequential,* and therefore arising without any breach of the peace'[85]

Lord Raymond C J's own report of *Reynolds* v. *Clarke* is also important for the clear position which it takes in relation to the remoter consequences of an act which was itself a trespass. His view was that, if the plaintiff had once suffered harm immediately from the act of the defendant, so as to entitle him to bring trespass *vi et armis,* he was entitled to recover damages not only for that immediate injury but for the consequences. Thus, discussing a case decided earlier by Holt C J, he says:

> '[B]ut he held, that if A. brought trespass against B. for entring his meadow, and mowing the grass there, *per quod* he lost the whole profit of his meadow; there the action of trespass *vi et armis* would be the proper action, and case would not lie; for the *per quod* would only be in aggravation of damages.'[86]

It is clear therefore that in his view an action of trespass *vi et armis* could reach the loss consequential on the immediate trespass. In *Scott* v. *Shepherd* Blackstone J interpreted this rather differently. He said that trespass *vi et armis* with a *per quod* of that kind should be regarded as a combination of an action of trespass and an action on the case, and, further, that a plaintiff could if he wished bring an independent action on the case for the consequential loss.[87] Buller has a chapter called '*Of Case for Consequential Damages*' which, though it ends with a repetition of the routine distinction between trespass and case, appears to regard case as suitable in all such instances.[88]

---

84 (1726) 2 Ld Raymond 1399, 1402–1403. In *Scott* v. *Shepherd* Blackstone J suggested that the report by Strange had put words into the Chief Justice's mouth: (1773) William Blackstone 892, 894.

85 Commentaries, 3.153. Cf. Buller (n. 4 aboe) 26, repeated at 79.

86 Ibid 1402. The earlier case was *Loveridge* v. *Hoskins* (1711) Mich 8 Ann BR.

87 (1773) 2 William Blackstone 892, 897.

88 Buller (n. 4 above) 74–79.

The dramatic facts of *Scott* v. *Shepherd,* in 1773, put the test of immediacy or directness under pressure.[89] The outcome demonstrates that it was as true then as it is now that a rule will often bend under the pressure of the merits. The jury stated a special case. That is, they stated the facts as they found them to be. A special case took the facts out of the black box and compelled the court to state the law as it applied precisely to that story. The plaintiff had lost his eye when, a week before Guy Fawkes Night, a firework blew up in his face. He brought trespass *vi et armis,* reciting that with force and arms the defendant had thrown the squib and burned his eye, so that he lost the sight of it. The true facts were that the defendant had indeed thrown the squib, but that he had thrown it into a market and that two stallholders had knocked it on before it reached the plaintiff's face. The defendant said that on those facts he could not be liable in trespass.

Blackstone J, agreeing that this could not be trespass, now restated from the Bench what he had said in his book. 'He took the settled distinction to be that, where the injury is *immediate,* an action of *trespass* will lie; where it is only *consequential,* it must be an action on the *case*.'[90] De Grey C J agreed with the principle so expressed but not with its application to the facts. While Blackstone J accepted that a trespasser guilty of a direct injury would also be liable for the natural consequences, De Grey C J thought all the natural consequences were themselves part of the defendant's own act, and that the injury was therefore to be regarded as immediate. Gould and Nares JJ agreed that trespass would lie, relying in part on Raymond C J's supposed view that initial unlawfulness, or the unlawfulness of the initial act, was the key to trespass *vi et armis*.

Another boundary was feebly proposed but rightly rejected, namely that trespass was confined, as it appeared on its face to be confined, to intentional injuries. We have seen that that reality was rejected in the seventeenth century. After *Williams* v. *Holland*[91] the rule became that, for injuries which were both immediate and wilful, only trespass *vi et armis* would lie. But by then the notion that trespass lay only for intentional injuries had been finally scotched by *Leame* v. *Bray* (1803).[92] In that case the plaintiff had brought trespass alleging that the defendant had with force and arms driven his single-horse chaise into his two-horse curricle. The defendant argued that the plaintiff should have brought an action on the case. The

---

[89] (1773) 2 William Blackstone 892. This account does not claim any advance from *M J Prichard, 'Scott* v. *Shepherd* (1773) and the Emergence of the Tort of Negligence' Selden Society Lecture for 1973 (London, 1976).

[90] Ibid 894.

[91] (1833) 10 Bing 112.

[92] (1803) 3 East 593.

Kings Bench under Lord Ellenborough C J rejected the notion that there could be no unintentional trespass and confirmed that the right test was that which had been applied, with different results, by De Grey C J and Blackstone J in *Scott* v. *Shepherd.*

In Blackstone J's analysis of the *Scott* v. *Shepherd* event Noel Swerdlow has detected an echo of Isaac Newton's first two laws of motion. Although Bentham's attacks on Blackstone tend to overshadow both the magnitude of his achievement and the depth of his learning, Swerdlow's discovery in fact fits perfectly with the true picture of Blackstone's energetic intellect.[93]

---

[93] *N. M. Swerdlow,* 'Blackstone's "Newtonian" Dissent' in I B Cohen, ed, The Natural Sciences and the Social Sciences (1994, Kluwer) 205–234, esp. 214–217. The principal passage which Swerdlow analyses is: 'The original act was, as against Yates (the first stallholder), a trespass; not as against Ryal (the second stallholder) or Scott. The tortious act was complete when the squib lay at rest upon Yates's stall. He, or any bystander, had, I allow, a right to protect themselves by removing the squib, but should have taken care to do it in such a manner as not to endamage others. But Shepherd, I think, is not answerable in an action of trespass and assault for the mischief done by the squib in the new motion impressed upon it, and the new direction given it, by either Willis or Ryal; who were both free agents, and acted upon their own judgment. This differed it from the cases put of turning loose a wild beast or a madman. They are only instruments in the hand of the first agent. Nor is it like diverting the course of an enraged ox, or of a stone thrown, or an arrow glancing against a tree; because there the original motion, the *vis impressa,* is continued, though diverted. Here the instrument of mischief was at rest, till a new *impetus* and a new direction are given to it, not once only but by two successive rational agents. But it is said that the act is not complete, nor the squib at rest, till after it is spent or exploded. It certainly has the power of doing fresh mischief, and so has a stone that has been thrown against my windows, and now lies still. Yet if any person gives that stone a new motion, and does further mischief with it, trespass will not lie against the original thrower'. Swerdlow observes, p. 214: 'It is remarkable that both in language and, with one bit of imprecision, in substance it is based squarely upon Newton's Fourth Definition and first two Laws of Motion from Book I of the *Principia.* The Fourth Definition is: An impressed force (*vis impressa*) is an action upon a body for the purpose of changing its state either of resting or of moving uniformly in a straight line.' Having noted the slight imprecision, Swerdlow, citing the First Law of Motion – Every body continues in its state of resting or moving uniformly in a straight line except in so far as it is compelled to change its state by impressed forces (*viribus impressis*) – continues ' Blackstone seems to have this in mind when he says that "the instrument of mischief was at rest, till a new *impetus* (which he appears to use synonymously with *vis impressa*), and a new direction are given to it." Further, the specification of a "new direction" as well as the earlier reference to "the new motion impressed upon it and the new direction given to it" are applications of the Second Law of Motion: The change of motion is proportional to the motive force impressed (*vi motrici impressae*) and takes place in the direction of the straight line in which the force is impressed.' Swerdlow cites Newton in translation using: Philosophiae naturalis principia mathematica, ed *A Koyré* and *I B Cohen* (Cambridge Mass 1972) 13.

Where did this notion that the injury must be immediate come from? Its refinement in the form given to it by Blackstone must owe a great deal to the Roman texts, which, in relation to wrongful loss, draw the same line between the action available under the lex Aquilia and actions *in factum* (on the case) granted by way of extension of Aquilian liability. The drawing of this line generated a good deal of Roman case law. The key text is D.9.2.7.6, where Ulpian reports Celsus as saying that an important difference is made between killing a slave and furnishing the cause of his death, because one who only furnishes the cause of a death, as for example one who supplies a poison instead of a medicine or puts a sword in the hand of a madman, is liable to an action *in factum,* not to the Aquilian action itself. In Justinian's *Institutes,* the most accessible of the Roman texts, the boundary of the Aquilian action is drawn thus: '*Ceterum placuit ita demum ex hac lege actionem esse si quis praecipue corpore suo damnum dederit* (However, it has been decided that the action only lies under this *lex* where a person has caused loss directly by his own body.)'[94]

However, if the refinement of the test was influenced by the Roman texts and ornamented by Blackstone's reading in Isaac Newton, the underlying reason why it was thrust unwanted on the law was both simpler and common to both systems. Liability under the *lex Aquilia* required the plaintiff to show that the defendant had killed, burned, broken, and so on. On some facts, as where I had pushed past a person who, forced to step into the road, was struck by an oncoming carriage, I could plausibly answer that I had no doubt behaved very badly but I had not done the killing, for, manifestly, the killing had been done by the oncoming carriage. If it once accepts, or is compelled to accept, the challenge of discriminating between killing or doing damage and causing death or damage to be done, the law is more or less bound to settle on the *corpore* test, however difficult it may be to apply on some facts and however amenable to distortion by the merits of particular parties.[95]

Trespass *vi et armis* required the plaintiff to say that the defendant had with force and arms beaten him, killed his cow, and so on. The recitations of force and arms and slings and swords and arrows became empty forms, but their last residue was that the plaintiff must have done the harm in

---

94 J.Inst. 4.3.16. The briefest acquaintance with the texts shows that 'by his body' means 'by his bodily force' or 'by his bodily acts', not 'by bodily contact'. The simplest cases which demonstrate this are those which contemplate liability where a slave is killed by a javelin thrown be the defendant or by something dropped by the defendant from above: J.Inst. 4.3.4,5.

95 Discussion at greater length: *P. Birks,* 'Doing and Causing to be Done' in: The Roman Law Tradition. edd. ADE Lewis and D. J. Ibbetson (Cambridge, 1994) 42–53.

question. So long as the jury remained a black box from which an inscrutable answer would emerge, it was neither necessary nor possible to examine the limits of doing. But once attention could be focused on this specific point, it was almost inevitable that the question would be answered in terms of immediate bodily force.

7. Trespass on the Case: Subsidiarity at the End of the Century

To have allowed trespass *vi et armis* outside its own factual limits would have made nonsense. To that extent Lord Raymond C J could quite rightly say, in *Reynolds* v. *Clarke,* 'We must keep up the boundaries of actions; otherwise we shall introduce the utmost confusion.'[96] One of the factors which precipitated the more careful delimitation of those boundaries was the relatively recent emergence of overlap. The boundaries between trespass *vi et armis* and trespass on the case did not need much keeping up so long as plaintiffs never thought of bringing case except on facts manifestly outside the scope of the older action. Trespass *vi et armis* was not weighed down by any obvious procedural disadvantage, such as trial by wager of law. There was not much reason for recourse to actions on the case as an alternative to it. For centuries, therefore, plaintiffs stuck to general trespass except on facts which it obviously could not reach.

In or shortly before our period the new notion asserted itself that there might indeed be an overlap or, in short, that even a plaintiff who could bring trespass might find advantages in bringing case instead. Where the plaintiff had been run over by horse or horse-drawn vehicle or, on water, had been the victim of a collision, there was some danger that in an action of trespass *vi et armis* the defendant might persuade the jury that he had not done the deed, as for instance because the horse bolted or the wind deprived him of control of the barge. Some plaintiffs thought it safer to frame their complaint as an action on the case, thus taking the initiative in asserting that it was not the defendant's doing that formed the burden of his complaint but rather his *culpa* in bringing it about that the disaster had happened.[97] This tactic would not ensure victory,[98] but it would help to prevent the jury's being sidetracked.

---

[96] (1726) 1 Str 634, 635.

[97] The pattern of such an action on the case is discussed above, text to nn. 32, 33, with examples there identified in the Appendix below.

[98] It might still be that the defendant would be found not to have been at fault, as in *Amies* v. *Steven* (1719) Str 45, 128, cited in Buller (n. 4 above) 69. That was not a case in which trespass could have been brought, but it illustrates the kind of exchange to be expected. The plaintiff's goods had perished after the defendant's barge had hit a bridge and sunk. In an action on the case the defendant said that a

It was logical, before the closer examination of its limits, that general trespass would not lie outside its own frontier, even though an action on the case might have rendered the defendant liable. It was an altogether different matter to assert that an action on the case would not lie simply because trespass *vi et armis* would. That objection was an ingenious try-on, a recrudescence of the old notion that actions on the case were by nature subsidiary or supplementary. The action on the case, being no more than a pattern of words adaptable to any complaint, had no natural limits. We have already noticed that the attempt to push into a purely subsidiary role was repudiated in 1833 in *Williams* v. *Holland.* The one case which had to be roughly overridden when that decision was made was *Day* v. *Edwards* (1794).[99]

Day v. *Edwards* itself was a demurrer to what appeared to be an action on the case. The plaintiff declared, in essence, that whereas he and the defendant were driving horse-drawn vehicles on the highway, nevertheless the defendant 'so furiously negligently and improperly' drove that 'through the furious, negligent and improper conduct ... his cart was then and there driven and struck with great force and violence upon [the plaintiff's carriage].' The demurrer was upheld and the declaration was quashed. Lord Kenyon CJ said that it was clear that where an injury was committed by the immediate act complained of the action must be trespass.[100] The court upheld the demurrer, evidently thinking that the syntax left no room for any factual inference other than that the defendant drove his vehicle into that of the plaintiff.

Provided that the language of the declaration avoided asserting that the defendant has done the harm in question and presented instead a story of his having incurred responsibility for it having happened, the declaration itself would be immune to objection. It might nevertheless come out in evidence at the trial that what had happened was 'a proper strict trespass'. The plaintiff then stood the risk of being nonsuited.[101] However, if the judge let the matter go to the jury and the plaintiff obtained a judgment, a

---

gust of wind had driven him into the bridge, but the plaintiff wanted to say that he was nonetheless responsible for using a barge susceptible to so slight a blow. But Pratt C J held the defendant not liable, 'the Damage being occasioned by the Act of God, which no Care of the Defendant could foresee or prevent.'

99 (1794) 5 TR 648.

100 Ibid 649.

101 *Haward* v. *Bankes* (1760) 2 Burr 1113, 1114: 'The Plaintiff describes, in his Declaration, a Fact which, as it comes out at the Trial, may, or may not, be a proper strict Trespass: It might, at the Trial, be proved to be either a Trespass, or Case; either One or the Other of them, according to the Evidence. And it appears, that it was here proved at the Trial, to be a Trespass upon the Case. If it has been proved to be Trespass *vi et armis* the Plaintiff must in that event, have been non-suited.'

subsequent challenge would not find the court astute to turn the plaintiff round to a different form of action.[102]

Thus, in 1799, in *Ogle* v. *Barnes* the plaintiff's action on the case said that the defendant so incautiously, negligently, and inexpertly managed steered and directed their ship, the *Actaeon,* that by reason of their negligence carelessness ignorance and unskilfulness the *Actaeon* with great violence and force sailed against and ran foul of the plaintiff's ship, the *Anne.*[103] Here the plaintiff obtained a verdict, but the defendant moved in arrest of judgment that the action should have been trespass *vi et armis.* Lord Kenyon CJ said that the plaintiff could not be driven back to trespass when the on the words of the pleadings the defendants had not been charged with any act at all but only with so negligently steering the vessel that, by reason of that negligence, their ship had struck the other.[104] And Lawrence J observed that, so far as the defendants' acts were concerned they might, compatibly with the declaration, have been doing all they possibly could not to hit the *Anne,* 'after having been guilty of the negligence which led to the mischief.'[105]

Anticipating the resolution of these problems which was to come in 1833, Lawrence and Grose JJ both said that the defendants' challenge would have been upheld if the evidence had shown that in fact the defendants had wilfully driven their ship into the defendants. Grose J said that they would then have been in the same situation as the plaintiff in *Tripe* v. *Potter* who, having brought an action on the case against the defendant for wilfully rowing into his fishing nets, submitted to a nonsuit but subsequently brought a new action in trespass *vi et armis,* and won.[106]

At the turn of the century, therefore, the position might be summed up in this way. An action on the case would be struck out if its wording alleged

102 They would not look 'with eagle eyes': *Slater* v. *Baker* (1767) 2 Wils KB 359. This leniency has, however, to be read in the light of Blackstone J's fiercer comments in *Scott* v. *Shepherd*: '*Slater* and *Baker* was a Motion for a new trial *after* Verdict. In our case the Verdict is suspended till the Determination of the Court. And though after Verdict the Court will not look with Eagle's Eyes to spy out a Variance; yet, when a question is put by the Jury upon such a Variance, and it is made the very point of the Cause, the Court will not wink against the Light, and say that Evidence, which at most is only applicable to an Action on the Case, will maintain an Action of Trespass' (1773) 2 William Blackstone 892, 897. He went on to say that *Slater* was anyhow an action on the case, evidently taking the view that there were many facts in which you could bring case instead of trespass, but not, *e converso,* trespass instead of case.

103 (1799) 8 TR 188.

104 Ibid 191.

105 Ibid 192.

106 (1767) 6 TR 128.

that the defendant had directly injured the plaintiff. If the wording suggested only a responsibility for an injury which had come about, but the evidence showed the defendant has actually done it, it was possible though unlikely that a challenge to the form of action might succeed after verdict. To this extent, ingenious defendants had managed to push the action on the case into a subsidiary role.

III. System

The aim of this part is to ask to what extent if at all eighteenth century lawyers saw negligence as an entity with a place in a map of the law. In the background is the continuing mystery of the modern common law's indifference to its own taxonomy. It leans heavily, but without thought, on the civilian system, itself derived ultimately from the second century jurist, Gaius. At least in the western legal tradition, Gaius' *Institutes,* mediated through the new edition commissioned by Justinian in the sixth century, has some claim to have been the most influential book ever written.[107]

The modern common law knows a law of civil wrongs, which still goes under the French name 'tort'. Neither its boundaries nor its internal subdivisions are agreed, but the practice of law schools assumes that in this law of wrongs negligence is one member of a list of wrongs and is indeed the dominant wrong. If it did not dominate, to the point, most of the time, of hiding all else, the tort of negligence would stick out as an obvious cuckoo in an alien nest, since, with the exception of deceit, the other wrongs are named more or less explicitly by reference to the interest infringed, interference with chattels, defamation, infringement of copyright, breach of confidence, interference with contractual relations, trespass to the person, and so on. It ought to be impossible, and in truth it is impossible, to mix torts named by kinds of fault with torts named by interests infringed, for the two categories must intersect. Is a negligent defamation two torts or one?[108]

In the eighteenth century the disorder was more overt. In the middle years the great Sir William Blackstone initiated an intellectual revolution. Using a scheme derived from Grotius[109] and more remotely from those to

---

[107] No manuscript of Gaius' *Institutes* was thought to have survived, until Niebuhr discovered an overwritten copy in Verona in 1816: *F de Zulueta,* The Institutes of Gaius, Part II (Commentary), (Oxford, 1953) 1–7. On the institutional system derived from Gaius through Justinian, and on the place of Justinian's *Institutes* in Justinian's new law library, see *P Birks* and *G McLeod,* Justinian's Institutes (London 1987) 7–18.

[108] *Spring* v. *Guardian Assurance Plc* [1995] 2 AC 296 appears to say two, much as a canary, being both yellow and an eater of seeds, must count as two birds.

[109] Further discussion, text to n. 121 below.

whom Grotius himself owed a debt, he showed that it was possible to give a coherent account of English law, its substance released from the tyranny of the forms of action. However, rather as Gaius himself made little immediate mark on the disorder of the Roman law library, so Blackstone's scheme stood outside the alphabetical chaos of the eighteenth century common law. In the world of the courts, the list of actions dominated, mixed with a rag-bag of more or less random headings suitable to a scrap-book. The best view of the law in this condition is to be seen from the last of the 'abridgments',[110] forerunners of *Halsbury's Laws of England,* in which the alphabet provides the only systematic, though unworthy of that name.

Thomas Wood

Thomas Wood, in 1722, hoped to impose some civilian order on 'this Heap of Good Learning'.[111] He aimed to apply to the common law the method and form of Justinian's *Institutes*. However, the reader who looks for sections equivalent to the Roman treatment of obligations will be disappointed, for the raw material relevant to that division of the Roman law is all pushed into his treatment of the law of actions. More accurately, since in Roman law itself the law of obligations was the product of deliberately removing the substance of all the actions *in personam* from its actional envelopes and then reclassifying it, we should say, not that Wood pushed this matter into the law of actions, but that he never attempted to remove it from the law of actions.

Even then some ordering might have been expected, and Wood does indeed begin promisingly enough:

> '*Personal* Actions are Those which the Plaintiff may have against the Defendant by Reason of any Debt or Contract for Goods and Chattels, or for Damage done to his Goods or to his Person.'[112]

---

[110] The best eighteenth century examples are the 23 volumes (1741–1756) compiled by Charles Viner, whose generosity established the Vinerian Chair of which Blackstone was the first holder, and the 5 volumes compiled by Matthew Bacon (1736–1766). Bacon died in 1759. The work was completed by others.

[111] Thomas Wood, An Institute of the Laws of England (London, 1722), who wrote in his preface: 'I entertained hopes that now it might not be impossible to sort, and put in some order, this heap of good learning; and that a general and methodical distribution, preparatory to a more large and accurate study of our laws, might now be made, as well as an Institute of Civil or Canon Law or of the laws of other nations; which were once too heap'd up together without beginning or end ...' (I have modernized the quotation only to the extent of eliminating the original capitalization and italicization.)

However, the alphabet almost immediately takes over: Account, Case, Detinue, Covenant, Debt, Trespass *vi et armis* (taken out of alphabetical order), Ejectment, Quare Impedit, Waste (likewise out of alphabetical order), Replevin. Looking for sub-classifications, one finds the inherently miscellaneous trespass on the case neatly divided: 'It lies For *Words* and For *Deeds*.'[113] But the treatment of the second limb is disappointing. The necessity of brevity releases the author from the painful task of finding a stable basis on which to classify the relevant deeds. In the result the material in which we are primarily interested – actions on the case for blameworthily bringing about harm – is omitted. Coming in his list to trespass *vi et armis* Wood divides it according as the wrong is directed either against the person or against property. But the treatment is very short and never touches the principle of liability.[114]

Robert Eden

Thomas Wood tried to order the common law with civilian help. The other way about, Robert Eden set himself the task of introducing Roman law with comparative reference to the common law. His picture is clear, but too small to reveal interesting detail. In 1744 his introduction to Roman law, coming to the law of delict, offered this brief comparison with the *Jus Anglicanum*:

> 'Trespass is a wide term. It comprehends every violation of the law. But those learned in our law reserve the name trespass solely for private wrongs. And these they divide as follows. Those which are accompanied with some degree of force they describe as trespasses proper. The rest they identify as trespasses arising from particular types of unlawful, albeit not violent, act, or (if I may use their own phrase) trespasses on the case. The form of action in respect of the former thus bears the words *vi et armis,* by force and arms, while that for the latter only says *contra pacem,* against the peace.'[115]

Two pages later he adds some further explanation of *transgressiones super casu*:

> 'A trespass of the kind called on the case either causes the victim loss and no more, or it makes him suffer contempt as well as loss. The authors of the civil law deal with the former under the title of the *lex Aquilia,* treating of the latter under the title *de injuriis.*

---

[112] Wood (previous note) 4.4, page 534. The base for this is his emulation of J.Inst. 4.6.1, distinguishing actions in rem and in personam.

[113] Ibid 535.

[114] Ibid 545.

[115] Robert Eden, Jurisprudentia Philologica sive Elementa Juris Civilis (Oxford, 1744) 227.

> Therefore, one commits a trespass on the case by making another's state or condition worse through one's wrongful act. However, the examples which might be given are infinitely various.'[116]

This needs to be glossed in two ways. First, what is here said of trespass on the case is no less true of general trespass, trespass *vi et armis*. Secondly, the generic trespass extended beyond the Roman delicts which he mentions and reached also the field of *furtum* and *rapina* (theft and violent attacks on goods). Eden felt compelled to lock trespass *vi et armis* within the Roman delict *rapina*.[117] He was not brave enough to sweep aside the recitations of violence as mere fictions. These difficulties do not conceal an important fact. For Eden and for the many English lawyers who knew their Roman law, at least to the level of the *Institutes* if no higher, actions of trespass, meaning both *vi et armis* and on the case, were perceived as the direct equivalent of the private law of delict.

William Blackstone

Two decades later, Blackstone is in an altogether different category. His classification transcends the actions. In the third book of the *Commentaries,* he writes under the title of 'Private Wrongs', but the language of injuries competes and sometimes seems to prevail. He treats 'wrong' and 'injury' as synonyms. His exposition is based on a principal distinction between wrongs to persons, to personal property, and to real property. In other words his classification is interest-based. His courageous decision to use a rational basis of classification of wrongs, ignoring the boundaries of actions, creates for him a new problem. How to keep in touch with the reality of the law as applied in the courts? His solution is to draw initial attention to the actional distinction between trespass and case, and then to issue periodic reminders:[118]

> 'But I must first beg leave to premise, that all civil injuries are of two kinds, the one *without force* or violence, as slander or breach of contract; the other coupled *with force* and violence, as batteries, or false imprisonment. ...And this distinction of private wrongs, into injuries *with* and *without* force, we shall find to run through all the variety of which we are to treat.'

He carries through the classification of wrongs by reference to the interest infringed very thoroughly. For example, injuries to persons are divided according as they affect personal security or personal liberty, and injuries to personal security are subdivided according as they affect life, limb (or

---

116 Ibid 229.

117 Ibid 227.

118 Sir William Blackstone, Commentaries on the Laws of England, Book 3 (London, 1768) 118–119; cf. 122–123, 152.

body), health, or reputation.[119] This is strongly reminiscent of the classification used in the late seventeenth century by Viscount Stair, in his title *'Reparation, where of Delinquences, and Damages thence arising.'*

> 'It shall in general suffice here to consider, that, according to our several rights and enjoyments, damages and delinquences may be esteemed. As, first, our life, members, and health; which though they be inestimable, and can have no price, yet they are therewith incident damages reparable. ... Next to life, is liberty: ... The third is fame, reputation and honour, ... The fourth interest, that may be damnified, is our content, delight and satisfaction; and especially by the singular affection to, or opinion of the value or worth of any thing that the owner hath... . The last damage is in goods and possessions; the redress whereof is more clear, because the things themselves are more valuable and estimable.'[120]

However, it is clear enough that both Blackstone and Stair derive their schemes from Grotius, whose treatment of delict departs quite dramatically from the Roman model which he had continually in his sights. In the *Introduction to the Jurisprudence of Holland* Grotius says that wrongs should be distinguished according as they affect life, body, personal liberty, honour, and property, and he then treats each of these one by one.[121] In his master work, *The Law of War and Peace,* the same interest-based approach can be seen.[122]

Had one been able to ask Blackstone whether he would number among the private wrongs the wrong of *culpa* (fault), he would almost certainly have denied that there could be any such wrong. His system commits him to the view that every wrong – that is to say, every injury to person, personal property, or real property – must in law require some level of culpability, either *dolus* (malice, evil intent) or *culpa* (fault short of intent). In other words malice and fault can only be an ingredient in liability for one of the interest-based wrongs. It is a disappointing fact that he does not go into this.

It is a symptom of the underdeveloped state of the law in this area, as also of it relative unimportance, that even Blackstone says nothing enlightening about the content of *culpa* or the standards to be applied, not even in relation to bailment,[123] where the discussion was raised to a compara-

---

119 Commentaries (previous note) 3.120–126.

120 Stair, The Institutions of the Law of Scotland (1681) 1.9.4.

121 Hugo Grotius, Introduction to the Jurisprudence of Holland (ed. and tr. RW Lee) 3.33–3.37. This was written during the imprisonment from which he escaped in 1618, though pubished in 1631.

122 Hugo Grotius, De iure belli et pacis (1625) 2.17.2. Very similar is Samuel Pufendorf, De iure naturae et gentium libri octo (The Law of Nature and Nations) (1672) 3.2.

123 His treatment of this subject, *Commentaries* (n. 118 above) 2.451–454, is thin and justly criticised by Sir William Jones: '... especially as our excellent Black-

tively prominent level by Holt C J early in the century.[124] Since authors whom he admired and used consider the question whether there can be liability without fault, and conclude that by natural reason there cannot, though in positive law examples are found and defended by the pursuit of a given policy objective,[125] it is curious to find him silent on the issue of strict liability and the nature of the line between *casus* and *culpa*.

Francis Buller

Francis Buller's *Nisi Prius* was closer in spirit to the abridgements. It had nothing of Blackstone's serious academic purpose. Nevertheless his book is not without taxonomic interest. He expressly used the distinction between contract and tort, albeit translated from obligations to actions. He called Part I 'Of Actions founded upon Torts' and Part II 'Of Actions founded upon Contract'. Then, subdividing Part I, and using the word 'injuries' rather than the 'torts' of its title, he divided that Part into three Books according to the interest injured: first injuries affecting the person, next injuries affecting personal property, and finally injuries affecting real property.[126]

Nevertheless, Buller does not carry through his plan as thoroughly as Blackstone, so that the chapters of his exposition are once again actional. The action on the case is not integrated in the purportedly interest-based approach. It has its own chapters. It catches the eye that one of these segregated chapters is entitled '*Of injuries arising from Negligence or Folly*'.[127] The two pages which follow have some importance in the later development of the law, but it would be wrong to suggest that Buller thought of himself as proposing the recognition of a distinct tort. The chapter is merely an opportunistic vehicle for making his initially interest-related classification reach out to some instances of trespass on the case.

Injuries from negligence or folly form a sub-head of Book I, which is itself entitled 'For what Injuries affecting the Person an Action may be brought.' In Book II, entitled 'For what Injuries affecting a Man's personal

---

stone, who of all men was best able to throw the clearest light on this, as on every other, subject, has comprised the whole doctrine in three paragraphs, which, without affecting the merit of his incomparable work, we may safely pronounce the least satisfactory part of it ...; and on the great question of responsibility for neglect, he speaks so loosely and indeterminately, that no fixed ideas can be collected from his words' *An Essay on the Law of Bailments* (London, 1781) 3.

124 Further discussion above, text from n. 52.

125 Grotius (n. 122 above) 3.11.4,8; Pufendorf (n. 122 above) 3.1.6.

126 Buller (n. 4 above) v–vi.

127 Buller (n. 4 above) 25.

Property, an Action may be brought', one might expect a parallel chapter. In fact there is no chapter on damage to property arising by negligence or folly. The matter which might have been so presented appears in a chapter called '*Of Case for Misbehaviour in Office, Trust or Duty*'.[128] The failure to carry negligence and folly through to the second relevant head suggests that he had no settled or serious purpose under the first. He had not really cracked the problem of elegantly sub-dividing the immensely diverse action on the case.

The protean action on the case is indeed the crux. Some particular actions on the case settled down, for most purposes, with names taken from some prominent word, such as *assumpsit* or conversion (a name which ultimately prevailed over its competitor, trover). But the action on the case remained an open-ended technique for complaining of grievances,[129] and many examples suggested no obvious label. Committing himself to an interest-related typology of wrongs, Buller nevertheless found himself faced at a certain level with this labelling problem. He solved the problem differently in different places. Many of the examples given under the title '*Of Case for Misbehaviour in Office, Trust or Duty*' in relation to injuries to personal property could have been put under a title '*Of injuries arising from Negligence or Folly*'. 'For Misbehaviour in a Trust or Duty, an Action on the Case will likewise lie; for whosoever undertakes to do a Thing for another ought to do it faithfully, else he is answerable for the Damages arising from his Negligence or Misbehaviour.'[130] This sentence, which itself reflects the structure of the wording of trespass on the case, suffices to reveal that the search for nomenclature might focus on the trust or duty or might descend to the *culpa* which caused the plaintiff's damage. In other words, the analyst might prefer to see the action as firing on the primary level (which, in the action of *assumpsit,* is what the very name prefers) or on the secondary level (on the wrong consisting in breach of a primary duty).

---

128 Ibid 64.

129 'After Verdict for the Plaintiff for 3000 *l.* Damages, it was moved in Arrest of Judgment, that this was an Action *primae impressionis.* But the Court said that every special Action on the Case was in itself a Novelty: no Action lies without Damages, and the *per quod* will not alone be sufficient, unless the Act be illicit; … yet the Jury under the Direction of the Judge are the Judges of the Legality: …' Buller (n. 4 above) reporting the Common Pleas in *Winsmore* v. *Greenbank* (1746) Mic.19 G.2 CB.

130 Buller (n. 4 above) 69.

Trespass, Case, and Tort

This discussion of the taxonomy or taxonomic consciousness of our period must conclude with one further caution. Events and inquiries which fall within our notion of tort or civil wrong could fall outside the generic category of trespass, and, *vice versa,* matter which we now exclude from the category of wrongs could fall within it. We have been trying to see to what extent eighteenth century lawyers saw their law of wrongs as a unity and, more particularly, whether they recognized a tort of negligence within it. Once within the field of trespasses (wrongs, *transgressiones*), whether general or on the case, the modern lawyer thinks he knows more or less where he is. However, the truth is distorted if we too easily accept the oversimplifying assumption that trespass and trespass on the case together made up the law of tort.

On the one hand, issues relating to liability for wrongful harm could sometimes arise in equity or in other actions. *Southcote* v. *Bennet,*[131] for instance, was a claim in Detinue, in which the plaintiff bailor demanded his goods, and the defendant bailee entered a plea that they had been stolen. The plaintiff's replication was that the alleged thief had been one of the defendant's own servants. The defendant demurred and lost. The larger point at issue was the principle of liability applicable to a depositee in the absence of express terms. In reaching judgment for the plaintiff, the court allowed itself to say that even robbery would not excuse, and Sir Edward Coke, in reporting the case, reinforced that incorrect opinion, which was corrected in *Coggs* v. *Barnard,* which preferred the Roman rule imposing liability on a bailee only for *dolus* and *culpa lata* (gross neglect).[132] Outside the forms of action altogether, equity had to face similar issues. A trustee was not an insurer for his beneficiary. So long as he stayed within his powers, his liability was fault-based.[133] We have therefore to be aware that wrongs and the inquiry into liability for *culpa* find only the bulk of their raw material in the actions of trespass and trespass on the case.

On the other hand, if wrongs and liability for *culpa* could be found outside trespass and trespass on the case, it is also true, and perhaps more important, that some not-wrongs had found their way inside. The success of trespass on the case took it outside its natural boundaries. By the beginning of the eighteenth century plaintiffs were complaining of wrongs (trespasses in the case) in circumstances in which a modern lawyer would certainly not regard their claim as arising in tort. And, even given that some such exam-

---

131 (1601) 4 Co Rep 83b, Cro Eliz 815.

132 (1703) 2 Ld Raym 909.

133 Brief discussion, text to n. 9 above.

ples might qualify as 'wrongs' even if not as 'torts', there were still some cases in which there was no wrong at all, and the use of trespass on the case could only be explained by the vicissitudes of the history of pleading.

Complications of this kind mostly arise in relation to the particular action on the case which settled down under the name *assumpsit* (he promised or undertook). The bare outline of an action of *assumpsit* was: 'why, whereas <'in consideration that ...'> the defendant undertook to ..., nevertheless he <wickedly broke his promise>, to the plaintiff's damage.' Most of the modern law of contract was worked out under this action. For example, the 'whereas' clause invited the law to say what counted as an actionable contract. Was it enough to say 'whereas he promised ...' or must one say 'whereas, in consideration that ..., he promised'? And, if the latter, how should the three dots be filled in? In other words, what counted as a good and sufficient consideration?

Although it inevitably entails some presuppositions as to remedial consequences, there is no fundamental objection a system's working out its law of contract in a context in which the ultimate focus is constantly on the wrong of breach of contract. The 'nevertheless' clause might recite a blameworthy breach: 'whereas the defendant undertook to cure the plaintiff's horse or a certain disease, nevertheless he so negligently and carelessly applied medicines that the horse died.'[134] It would not, at least at first, matter whether this claim for blameworthily causing the death of the horse arose in 'contract' or in 'tort'. Nevertheless it was inevitable that, as the law settled the factual conditions for a binding contract, a question would arise whether every *assumpsit*-based action for blameworthily bringing about damage had to satisfy those conditions. In other words, could liability for wrongful damage done within the context of a voluntary assumption of responsibility survive where the assumption of responsibility did not amount to a binding contract? The answer was that it could and did. For the action itself, this entailed a schism: a line had to be drawn between a pattern of words in which the alleged undertaking had to be supported by consideration and a pattern of words in which it did not.

Actions on both sides of this line were examples of trespass on the case. But those with recitations of sufficient consideration are actions in contract, not actions in tort. In *Coggs* v. *Barnard* (1703) the action on the case alleged, without making any mention of his getting anything for doing the job, that the defendant had undertaken to move barrels of brandy and had so negligently and improvidently managed the task that one barrel had been broken, so that the brandy had spilled out. It was held that this was not a

---

134 *Marshall's Case* (1441) YB Hil 19 Hen VI, fo. 49 pl. 5; *Baker* and *Milsom* (n. 12 above) 367.

case in which it was necessary to plead a consideration for the undertaking. Holt C J said that the *assumpsit* here signified 'an actual entry upon the thing, an taking the trust upon himself. And if a man will do that, and miscarries in the performance of his trust, an action will lie against him for that, though nobody could have compelled him to do the thing.'[135] In modern terms, *Coggs* v. *Barnard* is itself an action of *assumpsit,* and hence an action on the case, for tortious negligence. Most actions of *assumpsit,* equipped with an 'in consideration ...' clause, were not actions in tort but in contract and, so far as they rested on negligence, it was then negligence born of a purely contractual duty of care.

There is a different but related kind of difficulty in relation to *assumpsit.* By the use of fictions, it took over much of the work previously done by the action of debt, so that it was used to recover debts born of events which could not be construed as promises. *Assumpsit* brought to recover debts was known as *indebitatus assumpstit* (= having become indebted, he promised). Most of the English law of unjust enrichment was worked out within this sector of the action of *assumpsit.* It obtained its independence only in the late twentieth century.

The plaintiff in *indebitatus assumpsit* claimed a payment which generally could not plausibly be said to arise from any wrong at all. He was directly enforcing a primary obligation arising from the event which created the debt – the loan, sale, unjust enrichment, as the case might be. The action was accommodated within trespass on the case only by means of pleading fictions.[136] Blackstone himself nevertheless deals with the whole subject of breach of contract under the head of wrongs to personal property, and in amongst those wrongs he therefore necessarily dealt with the recovery of debts which ought never to have been caught up on the law of either contract or wrongs.[137] At this point he did not emancipate himself from the actions. Had he done so, he could have probably have saved the common law of non-contractual claims, especially claims in unjust enrichment, from a crippling error.

---

135 (1703) Ld Raym 909, 915.

136 In bare outline an *indebitatus assumpsit* went like this: 'Whereas D was indebted to P in such and such a sum for such and such a reason and, being so indebted, in consideration thereof subsequently promised to pay, nevertheless he wickedly did not pay, to P's damage.' The 'wrong' is stated in the 'nevertheless' sentence and is the wrong of breach of contract. But P had only to prove facts substantiating the earlier proposition, that D was indebted in so much money for such and such a reason.

137 Blackstone (n. 118 above) 3 *Commentaries* 153–165.

Conclusion

The first part showed that in our period the word 'negligence' primarily denoted inaction or omission in circumstances in which action was required. The bridge to the modern sense of carelessness or fault was the fact that active conduct could nonetheless be 'negligent' if the actor were conceived in his acting to have omitted to do that which was required, in particular had omitted to take care when care was due.

The second part began from the proposition that liability in trespass *vi et armis* was based on non-intentional fault (*culpa*). On the face of its wording it ought to have been for *dolus* only, but it was not. By contrast, liability in trespass on the case was on the face of things based on either *culpa* or *dolus,* depending on the words used in the particular example. 'Negligence' was one of many words, frequently used in clusters, to express *culpa.* However, once again the words which were used were not a sure guide to the principle of liability. Negligence, the omission of that which was required, could mean strict liability if the duty was construed as a duty to achieve a particular result, as for example to keep in a fire. In some instances a characteristic form of legal development took place through the courts' fictionalization of allegations in the pleadings, reducing some to empty assertions which did not have to be proved at all.

Even where it was clear that a liability was indeed intended to be based on *culpa* the law was slow to specify clear standards. Juries were left to apply their own. Their awards of damages reflected the degree of a fault found. The intellectual necessity of the now ubiquitous standard of the reasonable person or the person of ordinary prudence was asserted late in the century in the learned writing of Sir William Jones. Prior to his work it had made only fleeting appearances, although it may have been recurrently applied in chancery, where there was no jury.

Perhaps only because it was more easily raised in the available procedures, through demurrers and motions in arrest of judgment, the matter which appears to have dominated the reported cases was not the careful definition of the principle of liability but the more technical one, reminiscent of the sixteenth century, of the correct choice of action and the definition of the proper sphere of each. The principal line drawn between trespass *vi et armis* and trespass on the case was ultimately the Roman one, which Blackstone fitted out in the language of Newton's laws of motion. If the defendant did the injury or damage, trespass *vi et armis* lay; if his fault brought it about that the harm was done, the plaintiff's action was trespass on the case. But shortly after the end of our period, in the twilight of the forms of action, this discrimination broke down. After 1833 you could bring trespass on the case even against a plaintiff who did the harm, so long only as he had not done it intentionally.[138]

The third part turned to those exceptional few whose overview of the law went beyond the alphabet. Did they see 'negligence' or 'fault' as a tort with its own place in the map of the law? The answer is that they did not. Within a somewhat over-inclusive notion of civil wrongs, they pursued an interest-based classification, following the model adopted by Grotius. In a law of wrongs organized in that way, negligence could not be numbered among other particular wrongs. It could only be the basis upon which liability could attach in respect of wrongs viewed as harms to particular protected interests. Unfortunately none of these jurists, not even Blackstone, ventured into detailed consideration of the bases of liability for wrongs thus defined.

Appendix: Trespass and Trespass on the Case

These materials are taken from John Lilly, *A Collection of Modern Entries,* 5th edition (London, 1791). Their chief purpose is to show what an action on the case really was. One example of trespass *vi et armis* has been included. These 'entries' were taken from the court records. The records were kept in Latin. They were, in the words of the Preface, translated for the collection 'with the greatest care and exactness'. The exactness is sometimes bought at a price which the reader has to pay. Nevertheless, these primary materials are more interesting and informative than any amount of second-hand interpretation. I have added a very brief indication of the nature of each example. Also, by the use of italics I have tried to draw the reader's attention to the more essential and structural parts of each. By reading the italicized parts, the reader will immediately grasp the structure of the whole.

1. Browne v. Davis

This is an action on the case for damage to the plaintiff's boat resulting from a collision caused by the defendant's barge. It is an example of such an action which merely assumes the actionability of the conduct as alleged. It makes no attempt to suggest a duty arising from any custom or undertaking.

Midd', to wit, William Browne complains of John Davis in the custody of the marshal, &c. for this, to wit, that *whereas the said William* on the 6th day of March in the 4th year of the lady Anne now queen of England, &c. at the parish of Chelsea in the county aforesaid, *was lawfully possessed of a certain flat-bottomed boat then loaded with dung,* and riding at anchor

[138] *Williams* v. *Holland* (1833) 10 Bing 112; *D Ibbetson* in this volume, p. 229.

in the river Thames within the parish aforesaid, as of his own proper boat; *And the said John Davis then and there was the master and pilot of a certain barge* then sailing in the river Thames aforesaid towards the city of London; *yet the said John Davis then and there his barge so negligently, carelessly and unskilfully managed and steered, that the said barge,* for want of good and sufficient care and management thereof, in and upon the said boat of him the said William so as aforesaid loaded then and there fell foul, and *the said boat broke and sunk; and the said William by reason thereof not only his dung as aforesaid in the said boat totally lost,* but likewise lost the whole use, profit and benefit of the said boat for the space of six days then next following, and also expended and laid out great sums of money in and about the raising and repairing of his said boat; whereby the said William says that he is prejudiced, and hath damage to the value of 30*l*. And therefore he produces suit, &c.

2. *Wallbanck v. Bucknall and others*

This is an action on the case for damage done by fire. It exemplifies the express invocation of a custom of the realm as the basis for the defendant's liability

Midd', to wit, Ralph Bucknall late of London, esq.; John Bucknall late of London, esq; and William Hall late of London, gent. were attached to answer unto John Wallbanck, gent. in a plea of trespass on the case, &c. And whereon the said John Wallbanck by John Lilly his attorney complains, *why, whereas, according to the law and custom of the kingdom of the lord the king of England hitherto used and approved, every person in the same kingdom is bound to keep his fire safe and secure* by day and night, so that no damage may any way happen to his neighbours for want of good care of his fire, *the said Ralph* (<the other two should be named here or their names struck out above>) on the 10th day of August in the 36th year of the reign of the lord Charles the second, now king of England, &c. at St Martin in the Fields in the county of Middlesex aforesaid, *so negligently and inconsiderately kept his fire, that for want of good care of that fire a mansion-house of the said John Wallbanck in the parish of and county aforesaid,* being in the possession of the said John Wallbanck there, and of which the said John Wallbanck was then and there possessed for the residue of a term of eleven years, which said term began from the feast of St, Michael the archangel in the 31st year of the reign of the said lord the now king, *was by that fire burnt down, and sundry goods and chattels of the said John Wallbanck,* to wit, a study of books, one hundred and ten pictures, ten tables, four Turkey-work carpets, forty-three chairs, four couches, eight brass sconces, eight gilt sconces, eight brass locks with their keys, one bird-cage, twenty alabaster images, ten China basons, thirty-three brass pots, three brass kettles, sixty glass bottles, two hundred gallons of claret, three presses for books, twenty yards of silk sashes for windows, four guns, four pistols, six feather-beds, six bedsteads, ten trunks, thirty curtains, thirty blankets, ten coverlets, one hundred yards of lace, thirty pair of sheets, thirty table cloths, sixty napkins, one hundred yards of mohair cloth, six looking-glasses, six pair of tongs, six iron grates, six pokers, a jack, two clocks, six boxes, six stools, ten chests, six hogsheads of beer, ten hogsheads of ale, forty silver spoons, four pair of bellows, ten spits, three fire-shovels, three iron pots, four basters, six pair of andirons, twenty candlesticks, twenty pillows, thirty pillowbers, thirty towels, six hats, twelve shirts, twelve caps, twelve cravats, four pair of boots, four belts, four swords, four cloaks, ten coats, ten pair of breaches, four periwigs, three gowns, six pair of gloves, twenty pair of stockings, ten pair of shoes, six womens silk gowns, ten petticoats, ten stomachers, twelve shifts, twelve coifs, five hundred yards of woollen cloth, five hundred yards of linsey woolsy, five hundred ounces of silver plate, to the value of 1500*l.* of the said John Wallbanck in the same house then and there were burnt, to the great damage of the said John Wallbanck; whereby the said John Wallbanck says that he is prejudiced, and has damage to the value of 1500 *l.* And therefore he produces the suit, &c.

3. Hawbank v. Trim

This is an action on the case for causing the sinking of the plaintiff's vessel, the Herring. The defendant having failed to mark the position of the anchor of his own boat, the Herring had been holed by it at low tide. The action is drafted on two bases, once on the model of *Browne* v. *Davis,* above, and once alleging a custom of the realm, on the model of *Wallbanck* v. *Bucknall* above. But the action differs from both in alleging *dolus* rather than *culpa*.

Midd,' to wit. George Hawbank complains of Matthew Trim in the custody of the marshall, &c. for this, to wit, that *whereas the said George* on the 23rd day of September in the year of the lord 1697, at the parish of Stebunheath, otherwise Stepney in the county aforesaid, *was and yet is master of a ship called the Herring being then in the river of Thames* in the parish and county aforesaid, the said river then being a navigable river, and the king's common highway; which said ship was then and there moored ashore in the parish and county aforesaid: *And whereas the said Matthew* the same day and year, and before, *was and is master of a ship called the Robert and Samuel* then and there being in the river aforesaid near the said ship of him the said George, *the said Matthew, contriving and maliciously intending greatly to hurt and prejudice him the said George, a certain anchor* out of the ship aforesaid called the Robert and Samuel, and to the same ship with a rope fixed, *into the said river then and there threw,* and in the river aforesaid for the space of twetny-four hours then next continued, *and did not affix a buoy to the said anchor to shew where the said anchor was put, by reason whereof the ship aforesaid, called the Herring,* afterwards to wit the same day and year, at the parish aforesaid in the county aforesaid, in the ebbing of the tide, for want of fixing a buoy to the anchor aforesaid in the said river Thames in the parish and county aforesaid, fell upon the said anchor of him the said Matthew, *whereby that ship falling upon the said anchor through the neglect of him the said Mathew, and by reason thereof was so much broke that the said ship then and there sunk; and for this,* to wit, that *whereas by the custom of England from time immemorial used and approved, all masters of ships, whose ships are riding at anchor in any navigable river within this kingdom of England, used and for all the time aforesaid were accustomed and ought to fix a buoy to their anchors* holding their ships, whereby other ships being in that river by such buoy might avoid such anchors, so that they might not be damaged thereby, that whereas the said George on the 23rd day of September in the year last abovesaid, at the parish of Stebunheath, otherwise Stepney in the county aforesaid, was and yet is master of another ship called the *Herring* being then in the river of Thames in the parish and county aforesaid which said ship was moored ashore in the parish and county aforesaid: And whereas the said Matthew then and there was master of a certain other ship called the *Robert and Samuel,* riding at anchor in the said river Thames in the parish and county aforesaid near unto the said last mentioned ship of him the said George: *Nevertheless the said Matthew, contriving and intending greatly to hurt and prejudice him the said George, a certain anchor out of the ship aforesaid called the Robert and Samuel, and to the same ship with a rope fixed, into the said river then and there threw, and in said the river for the space of twenty hours then next following continued, and did not affix a buoy* to the said anchor of his last mentioned ship, to shew where the said anchor of the said last-mentioned ship of him the said Matthew was placed, *by reason whereof the last mentioned ship* of him the said George afterwards, to wit, the same day and year, at the parish aforesaid in the county aforesaid, in the ebbing of the tide, for want of fixing a buoy to the anchor aforesaid of the last mentioned ship of him the said Matthew last mentioned so as aforesaid placed in the said river Thames in the parish and county aforesaid, fell upon the said anchor of him the said Matthew, whereby the said ship of him the said ship of him the said George last mentioned loaden with sea-coals falling upon the anchor of him the said Matthew last mentioned, through the neglect of him the said Matthew, was so much broke that the said ship of him the said George last mentioned *then and there sunk, whereby the same George says that he is prejudiced, and hath damage to the value of 200 l.* And thereof he produced suit, &c.

4. Nurton v. Paris

This is an action on the case against a common waggoner for causing injury to the plaintiff, one of his passengers. On the journey the waggon had overturned and the plaintiff had fractured a collar bone and suffered other injuries. The wrong is set in the context of the defendant's being a common waggoner and having received the plaintiff into his waggon for the journey and having been paid to do so. The draftsman alleges negligent and careless driving, but he also includes allegations of dolus.

Midd.' to wit. Anne Nurton complains of Humphry Paris in the custody of the marshal, &c. for this, to wit, that *whereas the said Humphry* on the first day of July in the first year of the reign of the lord George, now king of Great Britain, &c. and for divers years then last past and ever since hitherto *was and yet is a common waggoner,* to wit, between the city of London and the town of Ailesbury in the county of Bucks: And *whereas the said Humphry* on the said first day of July in the year abovesaid, and long before and after *was used and accustomed to convey and carry by himself and his servants in a certain waggon of the said Humphry divers subjects of the said lord the king, for a reasonable salary* to him in that behalf to be paid from and between the city of London aforesaid and the said town of Ailesbury: *and whereas also the same Anne* the day and year abovesaid, at London in the parish of St.Sepulchre in the ward of Faringdon without, *at the special instance of the said Humphry enter'd into the said waggon* aforesaid, to be conveyed and carried safely and securely from the city of London aforesaid to the town of Ailesbury aforesaid for a reasonable salary by him the said Humphry of the same Anne therefore to be had: and that the said Humphry the day and year abovesaid, at London abovesaid, the said Anne to convey and carry from the city of London aforesaid in the waggon aforesaid had and received: *Nevertheless the said Humphry* contriving and intending to deceive and defraud the said Anne, did not convey and carry the said Anne from city of London aforesaid to the town of Ailesbury aforesaid, but the said waggon the day and year abovesaid *did so negligently and carelessly dispose, manage and drive, that the waggon aforesaid was overset and overturned, whereby the left collar bone of her the said Anne was broke, and the left shoulder bone of the said Anne was put out of joint,* and the left arm of the said Anne was bruised, bent and maimed; whereby she says that she is prejudiced, and has damage to the value of 100*l.* And therefore she produces suit, &c.

5. Wickam v. Sperring

This is an action on the case for conversion by personal representatives. The printed example is very long, with counts in respect of different items. This extract is confined to the last count. Some immaterial adjustments have had to be made in order to sever the one count.

And *whereas also the said William Wickham and Frances,* as administratrix of the said James Jeoffrey the elder, afterwards, to wit, the first day of September in the 35th year of the reign of the lord Charles the Second, now king of England, at the parish of St Clement Danes ... *were possessed of divers other goods and chattels,* to wit, of 20 chairs, a silver tankard, a clock, two silver bowls, two pieces of gold, five feather beds and five carpets, *as of the goods and chattels of the said William and Frances as administratrix of the said James Jeoffrey the elder; and being so thereof possessed the said William and Frances casually lost the said goods and chattels out of their hands and possession, which said goods and chattels so lost afterwards, to wit, the day aforesaid..., came by finding to the hands and possession of the said William Sperring: Nevertheless the said William Sperring ... knowing the goods and chattels aforesaid to be the goods and chattels of the said William Wickham and Frances as administratrix to the said James Jeoffrey the elder ... and contriving and fraudulently intending the said William Wickham and Frances ... of the goods and chattels aforesaid craftily and subtilly to deceive and defraud, the said several ... goods and chattels* aforesaid to the said William Wickham and Frances, although often required, &c. have not yet delivered, but those several ... goods and chattels aforesaid afterwards, to wit, the day aforesaid ..., at the parish of St Clement Danes aforesaid, in the county aforesaid, *to his own proper use converted and disposed, to the damage of the said William Wickham and Frances 350 l.* And therefore they produce suit, &c.

6. Harding v. Wood

This is trespass *vi et armis* for an assault and battery. The defendant justifies by alleging that he gently laid hands upon the plaintiff (*molliter manus imposuit*) as he lawfully might to remove him from his master's stable. The plaintiff denies,replying that it was by the defendant's own wrong that the battery happened.

Stafford, to wit. It is granted by the court here, that Jane Harding, widow, may prosecute for Charles Harding, who is under the age of 21 years, as the next friend of the said Charles, against Peter Wood, in a plea of trespass and assault.

Stafford, to wit. Peter Wood puts in his place Peter Cottingham his attorney against the said Charles Harding in the plea aforesaid.

Stafford, to wit. Be it remembered, that otherwise in Michaelmas term last past before the lady the queen at Westminster came Charles Harding, who is under 21 years, by Jane Harding his next friend, hereto by the court specially admitted, and produced in the court of the said lady the queen then there his certain bill against Peter Wood in the custody of the marshal, &c. in a plea of trespass and assault: and there are pledges to prosecute, to wit John Doe and Richard Roe; which said bill follows in these words, to wit, Stafford to wit, *Charles Harding,* who is under 21 years, by Jane Harding his next friend, hereto by the court specially admitted, *complains of Peter Wood in the custody of the marshal, &c. for this, that he* on the first day of October in the 6th year of the reign of the lady the now queen, *with force and arms, to wit, with swords and staves and knives, on him the said Charles, at Stone, in the county aforesaid, made and assault, and him beat, wounded and ill treated, so that his life was greatly despaired of; and other outrages on him then and there committed, against the peace* of the said lady the now queen, and to the damage of the said Charles 40*l*. And thereof he produces suit, &c.

And now on this day, to wit, Friday next after the octave of St.Hilary in this same term, until which day the said Peter had leave to imparl to the bill aforesaid, and then to answer, &c. before the lady the queen at Westminster comes as well the said Charles by his next friend aforesaid, as the said Peter Wood by Peter Cottingham his attorney; and *the said Peter Wood, as to the force and arms and anything that is against the peace of our lady the now queen, and also the wounding of him the said Charles, the said Peter says that he is not guilty thereof; and of this he puts himself on the country: and the said Charles likewise: and as to the residue of the trespass and assault aforesaid above supposed to be committed, the same Peter says, that the said Charles ought not to have or maintain his action aforesaid thereof against him, because* he says, that one Edward Minshull, esq; long before the said time when the trespass and assault aforesaid is supposed to be committed, and also at the said time when, &c., was possessed at a stable in Nantwich in the county of Chesrter, in which said stable the said Edward at the said time when, &c. kept his horses; and the same Edward so being thereof possessed, *the said Charles* at the same time when the trespass and assault aforesaid is supposed to be committed, to wit, on the said first day of October in the sixth year above said, at Nantwich aforesaid into the county aforesaid, *into the stable of him the said Edward, in and upon the possession of him the said Edward, with force and arms, and against the will of him the same Edward, entered and him the said Edward in quiet possession thereof disturbed, and certain horses of him the said Edward in the stable aforesaid then being disturbed, frightened and startled, whereupon the same Peter, then being the servant of the said Edward, and by the command of the said Edward his master, then having the care of the said stable and the said horses in the said stable, by his order at the said time, &c. went to the said Charles, then being in the said stable, and required him to go out of the same stable and to do no further damage in that stable; wherefore the said Peter at the said time when &c. as servant of the said Edward, and in defence of his possession of his stable aforesaid, and of his horses then being in the same stable, and to compel the said Charles to go out of that stable, then and there gently laid his hands on the said Charles, then being in the same stable, to put him the said Charles out of the stable aforesaid, as he lawfully might,* which is the same residue of the trespass and assault aforesaid whereof the said Charles above now complains; without that, that the same Peter is guilty of the trespass and assault aforesaid, at Stone aforesaid, or elsewhere, out of Nantwich aforesaid in the said county of Chester: and this he is ready to verify; wherefore he prays judgment if the said Charles ought to have or maintain his action aforesaid thereof against him, &c.

And *the said Charles says, that he* by any thing by the said Peter above in pleading alledged *ought not to be precluded from having his action aforesaid thereof against him, because he says, that the said Peter of his own wrong, and without such cause by him the said Peter above in pleading alledged, made an assault on him the said Charles,* and him the said Charles beat, wounded and ill-treated so that his life was greatly despaired of, and of this he puts himself on the country: and the said Peter likewise, &c. and because the several issues between the parties aforesaid above joined ought to be tried by the men of the county palatine of Chester, where the writ of our lady the queen doth not run, and not elsewhere; therefore let the record of the plea aforesaid be sent to the justices of the said lady the queen of the county of Chester aforesaid, so that the same justices, by the writ of the lady the queen of that county duly to be made, cause the sheriff of the same county to be commanded, that he cause to come before the same justices of the said lady the queen of the county of Chester aforesaid at the next sessions for that county, after the record aforesaid shall have been delivered to them, 12 free and lawful men of the body of the county palatine of Chester aforesaid, by whom &c. and who neither, &c. to recognize, &c. because as well, &c. And when the averment and those issues shall be made and tried, that the said justices do send the record of the plea aforesaid, with all that therein in the court of the said lady the queen there before them shall be done, to the lady the queen at Westminster on a certain day which the same justices of the county palatine of Chester aforesaid to the parties aforesaid in the same court there shall prefix, to hear thereon their judgment, &c. and the said Charles is ordered to prosecute with effect, at the peril, &c.

D. J. IBBETSON

The Tort of Negligence in the Common Law in the Nineteenth and Twentieth Centuries

I. The birth of the Tort of Negligence

The Common Law's Tort of Negligence[1] is a creation of the nineteenth century, though its tendrils reach back into the eighteenth century and before. Sir John Comyns' *Digest* (1762) under the title 'Action upon the Case for Negligence' had already brought together a range of situations in which a person might be liable for negligent conduct – negligence in a man's trust or in the performance of an office, neglect in doing that which the law demanded, neglect to perform an undertaking, and neglect in taking care of an animal or fire – though its focus was more on the imposition of liability for failure to do something that was required rather than for causing loss by doing something badly. It was not until the publication of the supplement to Petersdorff's *Abridgment of Common Law* in 1843 that we find the first unequivocal identification of there being an 'Action for Negligence' based on the failure to live up to a standard of care.[2] As Winfield pithily and accurately observed, 'One can no more seize upon any exact moment for the birth of the tort than one can paint a chameleon',[3] but we may safely see its emergence from the old law centred round the forms of action in the early part of the nineteenth century, and its consolidation around 1860.

From a formal standpoint, crucial to this development was the coalescence in the same form of pleading – the action of trespass on the case – of actions claiming damages for negligently caused harm. Though there had been moves in this direction in the eighteenth century,[4] as a matter of

---

[1] It is worth noting at the outset that the Tort of Negligence is very much a product of Anglo-American (and not just English) Law: there is considerable transnational citation of cases (see, for example, *Donoghue* v. *Stevenson* [1932] AC 562) and cross-fertilisation among academic writers. That the present paper concentrates on English material is the result of considerations of space rather than of any intellectual isolation of English Law.

[2] *P. Winfield,* The History of Negligence in the Law of Torts (1926) 42 LQR 184, 195.

[3] *P. Winfield,* Duty in Tortious Negligence (1934) 34 Col LR 41, 49.

theory trespass on the case was appropriate when the harm had been caused indirectly; when there was a direct causal link the correct action was the general action of trespass. For most of the eighteenth century the courts exercised some leeway in the operation of this, though in the last decade of the century the King's Bench began to insist on its strict observance.[5] This created very considerable practical difficulties,[6] and in *Williams* v. *Holland*[7] in 1833 the strict position was reversed. This involved the explicit recognition that where negligence was the basis of the claim the plaintiff might elect between the general action of trespass and the action of trespass on the case. There were a variety of procedural reasons for using trespass on the case in negligence-based actions;[8] moreover, if the general action of trespass was used in such situations there was no necessity for any allegation other than that the defendant had injured the plaintiff, so that even if negligence was in issue it was well-hidden behind the bland allegation of the causation of harm.[9] Consequently, we may say that after the decision in *Williams* v. *Holland* the action on the case certainly appeared to be and probably was the primary vehicle for the compensation of negligently caused harm. The way was now clear for the shift from Comyns' 'Action upon the Case for Negligence' to Petersdorff's 'Action for Negligence'.

II. The Idea of Negligence: Trinity and Unity

The basic notion of negligence in the nineteenth-century Common Law was that found in Francis Buller's *Nisi Prius,* probably derived from the writers of the continental Natural law tradition: 'Every man ought to take reasonable care that he does not injure his neighbour'.[10] The same idea is found in Jeremy Bentham's definition of the notions of 'heedlessness' and 'rashness' in terms of the failure to live up to the standard of behaviour of a person of ordinary prudence.[11] Behind these, and well-known to the lawyers of the time, was the bonus paterfamilias of the Roman lawyers. We

---

4 See Professor Birks' paper in the present volume.

5 *Day* v. *Edwards* (1794) 5 TR 648; *M. J. Prichard,* Trespass, Case, and the Rule in Williams v. Holland [1964] CLJ 234.

6 There was still doubt about the true boundary between trespass and case as late as 1831: P[arliamentary] P[apers] 1831 (92) X p. 7.

7 (1833) 10 Bing 112.

8 Most important were the rules relating to joinder of counts: *M. J. Prichard,* Scott v. Shepherd (1773) and the Emergence of the Tort of Negligence (1976), 19–22. There were also advantages from the point of view of costs.

9 Holmes v. *Mather* (1875) LR 10 Ex 261; *Stanley* v. *Powell* [1891] 1 QB 86; *Fowler* v. *Lanning* [1959] 1 QB 426.

10 1st ed. (1767), p. 35; later editions, p. 25. See Professor Birks' paper in the present volume.

may surmise that it was principally from a combination of these sources that the Common lawyers began to analyse liability in terms of the defendant's having caused loss through not having behaved as a 'reasonable man'.[12]

Alongside this, purportedly following the Roman classification, is the division into culpa lata ('gross negligence'), culpa levis ('ordinary negligence') and culpa levissima ('slightest negligence'). This tripartition is central to Sir William Jones' analysis of the liability of the bailee.[13] It was, indeed, perhaps useful in that it enabled a distinction to be drawn between the circumstances in which liability would be imposed on gratuitous bailees (for 'gross negligence', or culpa lata[14]) and on bailees for reward (ordinary negligence, or culpa levis[15]). When statute allowed carriers of goods to exclude liability for the loss of goods above a certain value, it was held that they could not exclude 'gross negligence'.[16] Perhaps unsurprisingly, given that a considerable proportion of early negligence actions did in fact involve bailees, it had some influence in the emergent tort. *Vaughan* v. *Menlove,*[17] for example, the most notable early case featuring the 'reasonable man', analogises directly from liability in commodatum (loan for use) to liability between neighbouring landowners; and an agent acting gratuitously was treated as being on a par with a gratuitous depositary.[18] The tenacity of the division is shown by the fact that some of the commentators of the later nineteenth century continue to discuss 'degrees of negligence',[19] though it is steadfastly ignored by others;[20] and in its original context in the law of bailment it survived at least until 1962.[21]

---

[11] Introduction to the Principles of Morals and Legislation (*J. H. Burns* and *H. L. A. Hart,* eds.) (1970), 90, 92.

[12] See in particular *Vaughan* v. *Menlove* (1837) 3 Bing NC 468.

[13] *W. Jones,* The Law of Bailments (1781), 6–7, 12–34 (on which see Professor Birks' paper in the present volume). See too *Coggs* v. *Barnard* (1703) 2 Lord Raym 909 (in *J. H. Baker* and *S. F. C. Milsom,* Sources of English Legal History (1986) 370). The close connexion between the law of bailment and the law of negligence is noted in *F. Wharton,* A Treatise on the Law of Negligence (Philadelphia, 1874), v.

[14] *Shiells* v. *Blackburne* (1789) 1 Hy Bl 158, 162, per Lord Loughborough; *Beauchamp* v. *Powley* (1831) 1 M & R 38; *Doorman* v. *Jenkins* (1834) 2 Ad & El 256. The same was true in America: *Tompkins* v. *Saltmarsh* (1826) 14 Serg & Rawle 275, 279 (Pennsylvania).

[15] *Cooper* v. *Barton* (1810) 3 Camp 5n; *Dean* v. *Keate* (1811) 3 Camp 4 (though confusingly referring to gross negligence); *Broadwater* v. *Blot* (1817) Holt NP 547.

[16] *Prichard,* Scott v. Shepherd (1773) and the Emergence of the Tort of Negligence, 29 (and note).

[17] (1837) 3 Bing NC 468.

[18] *Dartnall* v. *Howard* (1825) 4 B & C 345. See *H. Smith,* Negligence (1880), 147–148.

By the middle of the century the tripartite division was coming under attack. The American scholar Luther Stearns Cushing – a Common lawyer with a good knowledge of the Civil law – criticised it as a doctrine 'in vogue on the continent of Europe, at the middle of the last century' but subsequently abrogated;[22] even Francis Wharton, one of those who continued to apply an analysis in terms of degrees of negligence, abandoned culpa levissima on the grounds both that it was wholly un-Roman and that it had no roots in Anglo-American practice.[23] An unnamed American commentator in 1870 pointed to its analytical emptiness:[24] it made sense for the degree of care required by the law to vary according to the circumstances, but then negligence need be defined solely as a failure to live up to the standard of care required by the law.

At the same time as the division was coming under attack at a theoretical level, it was losing such grip as it had at a practical level. Even where the test of gross negligence had established some sort of a foothold the judges were never wholly comfortable with it. In *Hinton* v. *Dibbin* in 1842 Denman C. J. professed himself unable to understand it;[25] one year later, in *Wilson* v. *Brett,* Rolfe B. dismissed it cursorily as negligence with a 'vituperative epithet';[26] and in *Ronnenburg* v. *Falkland Islands Co*[27] the Court of Common Pleas got very close to holding firmly that a gratuitous bailee was liable for ordinary (non-gross) negligence. Crystallising the single standard of negligence was the crisp definition of Alderson B. in *Blyth* v. *Bimingham Waterworks* in 1856: 'Negligence is the omission to do something which a reasonable man, guided upon those considerations which ordinarily regulate the conduct of human affairs, would do, or something which a prudent and reasonable man would not do.'[28]

---

19 e.g. *Wharton,* Negligence, 25–75; *W. Beven,* Principles of the Law of Negligence (1889), 16–45.

20 e.g. *C. Addison,* The Law of Wrongs and their Remedies (1860); *F. Pollock,* The Law of Torts (1887).

21 *Houghland* v. *R. R. Low (Luxury Coaches) Ltd* [1962] 1 QB 694. See *N. Palmer,* Bailment, 53–54.

22 Introduction to the Study of Roman Law (Boston, 1854), 199; quoted by *M. H. Hoeflich,* Roman and Civil Law and the Development of Anglo-American Jurisprudence in the Nineteenth Century (Georgia, 1997), 89.

23 Negligence, 48–68. cf. his criticism of the scholastic divisions of the mediaeval and later writers, and his preference for the purity of 'business Rome' (preface, v–ix). Wharton's indebtedness to continental European scholarship is transparent in his discussion of *Hasse,* Die Culpa des Römischen Rechts, and *Mommsen,* Beiträge zum Obligationenrecht.

24 Degrees of Negligence (1870) 5 Amer Law Rev 38.

25 (1842) 2 QB 646, 661.

26 (1843) 11 M & W 113, 116.

27 (1864) 17 CBNS 1.

Especially significant in this regard – unexpectedly so – is the dissenting opinion of Sir Alexander Cockburn C. J. in the international arbitration between the United States and the United Kingdom arising out of the building of a number of ships, and the equipping of others, for the confederate navy in the American Civil War. After the end of the war, the victorious north sought compensation from the United Kingdom for losses which had been caused by these ships. By the Treaty of Washington the dispute was submitted to a panel of five arbitrators, including Cockburn as the nominee of the British government. The Treaty itself defined the duty of neutral states (inter alia) as a duty to use 'due diligence' to prevent the fitting out, arming, or equipping of belligerent ships within its jurisdiction. A significant part of the task of the arbitrators, therefore, required a consideration of the meaning of 'due diligence'. Only Cockburn essayed this in any degree of detail. His very lengthy opinion was published in a supplement to the London Gazette[29] and unsurprisingly attracted considerable comment in the press; more to the point, though, his reasoning on the meaning of 'due diligence' was reported and discussed in legal periodicals in both Britain and the United States.[30] He begins by referring to the traditional tripartite division of culpa (noting in passing that it did not find favour with Donellus). The French Code Civil, though, had discarded it in favour of a single test of the 'bon père de famille', the 'diligens paterfamilias' of Roman law. Other codes, including the Austrian, had followed the French. Modern scholars, such as Thibaud, von Lohr, Hasse ('in a most learned and able treatise, *Die Culpa des Römischen Rechts'*) and Mommsen (in 'his well-known work' *Beiträge zum Obligationenrecht*) had moved away from this scholastic division; and French authors (Duranton, Ducarroy, Troplong, Demolombe) agreed that the only appropriate standard was that of 'men of ordinary capacity, prudence, and care'. Perhaps carried away by this display of learning, he proceeds to quote from Mommsen, Rivier (in Holzendorff's *Rechtslexicon),* Windscheid, Unger and Stubenrauch (both on Austrian law), finishing with a passage from Story's (American) *Bailment*.[31] All of these pointed to a single standard of diligence based on the behaviour of the ordinary man.

> The same standard is, in practice, applied in the English law. The older authorities, indeed, speak of three degrees of negligence, and of 'gross' negligence being necessary in some cases to found liability; but the tendency of modern decisions

[28] (1856) 11 Ex 781, 784.

[29] 24th September 1872, 4115–4368; the section on 'due diligence' is at 4139–4142. The opinions of the other four arbitrators take up a total of only 79 pages.

[30] The Geneva Award – Sir Alexander Cockburn's Judgment (1872) 53 Law Times 382; Degrees of Negligence (1872) 6 Albany Law Journal 313.

[31] It is worth noting that Cockburn had taken a first in Civil Law at the University of Cambridge, and had been a fellow of Trinity Hall.

> has been to apply in all cases the sound practical rule that in determining the question of negligence, the true test is whether there has been, with reference to the particular subject matter, that reasonable degree of diligence and care which a man of ordinary prudence and capacity might be expected to exercise in the same circumstances.

English law for the future was to have a single test, that of the reasonable man. If Cockburn's opinion was the death-knell for the tripartite analysis, it is significant that it was sounded to the tune of German romanists and French commentators as part of a conscious attempt by an English judge at European syncretism.

III. The Structure of the Tort of Negligence

From a structural point of view, the developed nineteenth-century Tort of Negligence had three elements:

(1) there must have been an antecedent duty to take care owed by the defendant to the plaintiff;

(2) the defendant must have breached this duty; and

(3) loss must have been caused thereby to the plaintiff.

The most significant feature of this division is the separation between the first two elements, the duty of care and its breach. From an analytical point of view little is added by this: it does not differ materially from saying that in certain circumstances liability was imposed if one person carelessly caused loss to another.[32]

The early stirrings of the use of the duty of care in the analysis of negligence cases occurred towards the beginning of the nineteenth century. Plaintiffs who wished to stress that their action was not contractual in its nature began to assert that the defendant's conduct had been such as to impose a duty to take care.[33] The terminology is found in other contexts by the 1830s;[34] but it was in the 1860s that it finally established itself as an organising device.[35] As late as 1860 the general principle gets only the

---

[32] *W. W. Buckland,* The Duty ot Take Care (1935) 51 Law Quarterly Review 637, especially at 639; *Winfield,* Duty in Tortious Negligence (1934) 34 Col LR 41, 61–65.

[33] *Govett* v. *Radnidge* (1802) 3 East 62; *Ansell* v. *Waterhouse* (1817) 6 M & S 385; *Prichard,* Scott v. Shepherd (1773) and the Emergence of the Tort of Negligence, 31–32. For the need to draw a boundary between contract and tort, see infra, section 3(a)(ii).

[34] *Bird* v. *Holbrook* (1828) 4 Bing 628; *Daniels* v. *Potter* (1830) 4 C & P 262; *Drew* v. *New River Co* (1834) 6 C & P 754; *Vaughan* v. *Menlove* (1837) 6 Bing NC 468; *Langridge* v. *Levy* (1837) 2 M & W 519, 4 M & W 337.

briefest mention in the first edition of Charles Addison's *The Law of Wrongs and their Remedies.*[36] In 1862 a classic definition was given by Wilde B. in 1862 in *Swan* v. *North British Australasian Co* (not itself a case of negligence): 'The action for negligence proceeds from the idea of an obligation towards the plaintiff to use care, and a breach of that obligation to the plaintiffs injury'.[37] This was rapidly incorporated into Addison's second edition (1864), where the coy prefatory remarks of the first edition were expanded into a full-blooded introductory chapter.[38] By the time of the first substantial treatments of negligence liability in America, around 1870, the central function of the duty of care, and with it the classic structure of negligence, was clearly established.[39]

1. The Separation between Duty and Breach

However unnecessary in theory, the bifurcation between duty and breach had respectable antecedents. It is found already in Buller's Law of Nisi Prius in the middle of the eighteenth century, which seems to have drawn together elements from the writers of the Natural Law school of the seventeenth and eighteenth centuries. These – Grotius, Puffendorf, Barbeyrac, Burlamaqui – were as much concerned to elucidate the duties owed by human beings living within society as they were to detail the circumstances in which liability should be imposed in cases of shortcoming.[40] Similar notions were present in Aristotle's Ethics, and these too seem to have fed into the nineteenth-century foundations Tort of Negligence.[41]

To say that there were respectable antecedents for the bifurcatory analysis between duty and breach in no way explains why it was adopted. Eng-

---

[35] This is graphically visible from the cases cited by *Winfield,* The History of Negligence in the Law of Torts (1926) 42 LQR 184, 199.

[36] Preface, p. v.

[37] (1862) 7 H & N 603, 636. See too the definition of Willes J. in *Grill* v. *General Iron and Screw Collier Co* (1866) LR 1 CP 600, 612: 'the absence of such care as it was the duty of the defendant to use'.

[38] See especially pp. 13–16. The reference to *Swan* v. *North British Australasian Co* is at p. 15. Curiously the dicta of Wilde B. are misquoted: 'The action for negligence proceeds upon the idea of an obligation on the part of the defendant towards the plaintiff to use care and a breach of that obligation to the plaintiffs injury', a misquotation which remained uncorrected in subsequent editions of the work.

[39] *T. G. Shearman* and *A. A. Redfield,* Treatise on the Law of Negligence (New York, 1869), 4, 7 (I have used the second edition (New York, 1870; reprinted Buffalo, 1980)); *Wharton,* Negligence, 3, 18. There is a tolerably clear formulation of the idea, though not as yet generalised, in *Thomas* v. *Winchester* (1852) 2 Seld 397 (New York).

[40] Supra, section 2. See Professor Birks' paper in the present volume.

[41] *Pollock,* The Law of Torts (1887), 357.

lish Law had managed without it for several centuries, and it plays little part in the modern Tort of Negligence.[42] Four factors conduced to this:

(1) the analysis of negligence in terms of liability for omissions;

(2) the need to establish a boundary between contractual and tortious liability;

(3) the desire to establish boundaries of liability, allowing the courts to refuse liability in a range of situations notwithstanding that the defendant had carelessly caused loss to the plaintiff;

(4) the shifting balance between judge and jury.

a) Liability for Omissions

In the nineteenth century, as in the eighteenth,[43] liability for negligence might be framed in terms of the language of neglect, i.e. the failure to do something. This inexorably elevated the status of duty in analytical terms, for it was only where there was a duty to act that a failure to do so could be treated as culpable. Particularly important here were John Austin's *Lectures on Jurisprudence* first published in 1863. For Austin 'negligence' should be applied exclusively to 'breaches by omission of positive duties',[44] thus fixing in place the requirement of the duty. The inverse of negligence, which he termed 'heedlessness', was defined simply by inverting the definition, in terms of breaches of negative duties. Consequently, whether acts or omissions were in question liability was explained by reference to the breach of a duty.

The analysis from neglectful omissions to negligent acts, with the consequent centrality of the role of the duty, can be seen in nineteenth-century treatments of the emergent Tort of Negligence. For some, such as Francis Wharton and Thomas Beven, the debt to Austin was transparent and explicit.[45] For others, such as Robert Campbell (himself editor of Austin's lectures), it was more muted but none the less present.[46]

b) Contract and Tort[47]

The action of trespass on the case, as it had developed by the beginning of the nineteenth century, covered a wide range of situations. Some of

---

[42] See Professor Baker's paper in the present volume. Infra, section 6(d).

[43] Supra, section 1.

[44] Lectures on Jurisprudence (2nd ed. [1st thus]) 2.108.

[45] *Wharton,* Negligence; *Beven,* Negligence.

[46] The Law of Negligence (London, 1871), 2.

these – for example the torts of nuisance, defamation, and conversion – were essentially selfcontained and remained peripheral. The main core covered three situations: contractual non-performance (through the action of assumpsit);[48] contractual mis-performance; and the negligent causation of harm wholly outside contractual situations. At the one end the action was clearly contractual; at the other end it was clearly tortious; and in the middle it was clearly ambiguous.[49] For both practical and theoretical reasons, though, it was necessary to be able to distinguish between claims in contract and tort. This was achieved by defining the source of the defendant's duty.

Practical considerations were uppermost in this, especially before 1852 (when the rules were made more flexible by the Common Law Procedure Act). It was permissible to join together several claims in the same writ, but only if the claims were of the same type; in particular, a claim in contract could not be joined with a claim in tort.[50] Liability in tort was several, so that an action could be brought against any one of a group of alleged tortfeasors; liability in contract was joint, so that all contracting parties had to be sued together and a verdict in favour of any one of the defendants was fatal to the plaintiffs claim.[51] A joint contracting party might have a claim against fellow contractors for contribution; a joint tortfeasor might not.[52]

These issues were particularly acute in actions against carriers of goods and persons.[53] There was no doubt that a carrier might be sued in contract, counting specially on the agreement with the plaintiff. As an alternative, though, there was a standard-form count against a 'common' carrier, and it

---

47 This is identified as the prime motor for the development of the language of duty by *Winfield,* Duty in Tortious Negligence (1934) 34 Col LR 41.

48 *J. H. Baker,* Introduction to English Legal History (1990), 374–400.

49 *Addison,* Wrongs (2nd ed.), 12 (not in 1st edition); Pollock, Torts, 353–354, 429–446; *W. Markby,* Elements of Jurisprudence (Oxford, 1871), 87–91. The ambiguity is marked by references to the middle category as 'Tort founded on Contract' *(Addison,* Wrongs (2nd edition), 12) or 'Quasi-Torts' *(Underhill,* Torts, 25), or by analogising them to the Roman category of Quasi-Delicts (*M. de W. Howe,* ed., The Pollock-Holmes Letters (Cambridge, 1942), 1.4–5) (Pollock).

50 *Dickson* v. *Clifton* (1766) 2 Wils 314; *Prichard,* Scott v. Shepherd (1773) and the Emergence of the Tort of Negligence, 27.

51 *Ansell* v. *Waterhouse* (1817) 6 M & S 385; *Bretherton* v. *Wood* (1821) 3 Brod & B 54; *Prichard,* Scott v. Shepherd (1773) and the Emergence of the Tort of Negligence, 27–28.

52 *Merryweather* v. *Nixan* (1799) 8 TR 186; *Powell* v. *Layton* (1806) 2 B & P (NR) 367, 371; *Bretherton* v. *Wood* (1821) 3 Brod & B 54; *Prichard,* Scott v. Shepherd (1773) and the Emergence of the Tort of Negligence, 28.

53 *Prichard,* Scott v. Shepherd (1773) and the Emergence of the Tort of Negligence, 26–28.

was not clear whether this should be characterised as contractual or tortious. After some uncertainty, the Court of Exchequer Chamber held in *Bretherton* v. *Wood* (1821)[54] that it was to be regarded as tortious: 'A breach of this duty is a breach of the law, and for this breach an action lies founded on the common law, which action wants not the aid of a contract to support it.'[55] Behind this there lay a general principle that if the plaintiffs cause of action could be fully stated without reference to any special contract between the parties then it could properly to be regarded as tortious, and the plaintiff was able to take advantage of the favourable rules of joinder. In appropriate cases, therefore, the plaintiff would have the option of suing in either contract or tort.[56]

These practical considerations may have been responsible for the theoretical concern with the boundary between contract and tort. Whatever the explanation, it seems clear that the nineteenth century did witness an increasing recognition that the contract-tort division was the principal analytical division within the law of obligations. In the middle of the century Charles Addison wrote separate treatises on tort and contract, as did Frederick Pollock a generation later; and the near-definition of torts as 'wrongs independent of contract' was well-established by the Common Law Procedure Act of 1852.[57] Given this division some distinguishing criterion was essential, but since it cut across the traditional forms of action none could be found within the traditional Common Law. The most straightforward test was to analyse both contractual and tortious obligations as arising out of breaches of duties, and to say that the duty in contract arose out of the agreement of the parties while the duty in tort arose by operation of law. Whatever the analytical adequacy of this,[58] it provided a rough and ready workable distinction, and became entrenched in the literature of the law. More importantly for the present investigation it provided a further stimulus to conceive of liability in tort in general as deriving from the breach of a legal duty, and liability in negligence in particular as deriving from the breach of a duty of care.

---

54 3 Brod & B 54.

55 3 Brod & B 54, 62 per Dallas C. J.; cf. *Marzetti* v. *Williams* (1830) 1 B & Ad 415.

56 *Brown* v. *Boorman* (1844) 11 Cl & F 1, 44, per Lord Campbell. The overlapping of remedies is thoroughly explored by *Pollock,* Torts, 429–446.

57 No less important in locking in place the contract – tort division were the County Courts Acts of 1846 onwards: *P. Winfield,* The Province of the Law of Tort (Cambridge, 1931) 76–78.

58 See in particular the critical comments of *Markby,* Elements of Jurisprudence, 87–91.

c) Restrictions on Liability

The most popular, and oft-quoted, definition of negligence liability in the nineteenth century was that of Alderson B. in *Blyth* v. *Birmingham Waterworks,* failing to live up to the standards of the prudent and reasonable man.[59] Many writers were content simply to reproduce this definition without comment, but the more reflective ones accurately argued that if was excessively wide. Francis Wharton, for example, pointed to the range of situations where falling short of the behaviour of the prudent and reasonable man did not ground liability: 'extravagance, gambling, even wild speculation with manufacturing, and similar enterprises which involve the welfare of multitudes of employees'.[60] Frederick Pollock made the same point more briefly; after quoting the definition of Alderson B. he immediately introduced the qualification, 'provided, of course, that the party whose conduct is in question is *already* in a situation that brings him under a duty of taking care'.[61] For both of these writers the duty of care had an essential function in the demarcation of those areas within which negligent conduct would ground legal liability; it was the obverse of the ideas of policy and proximity found in the late twentieth century.[62]

Secondly, and no less importantly, the analysis of liability in terms of the breach of a duty to take care made it possible for the law to specify that not every person injured by a negligent act would necessarily be entitled to compensation. Liability would arise if and only if a duty was owed *to that person.*[63] Such a qualification was important where the duty was said to have arisen out of a contractual relationship, for here the duty would extend only as far as the parties to the contract. Thus in *George* v. *Skivington*[64] it was argued that where a man manufactured and sold goods to another, this raised a duty vis-a-vis the other but did not necessarily do so vis-a-vis the ultimate user of the goods.[65] It might be important where the defendant was under a statutory duty owed to a person other than the

[59] (1856) 11 Ex 781, 784; supra, section 2.

[60] Negligence, 1–2.

[61] Torts, 355 (emphasis added).

[62] Infra, section 6(b).

[63] *J. F. Clerk* and *W. H. B. Lindsell,* The Law of Torts (1889), 361–367. *Collis* v. *Selden* (1866) LR 3 CP 495, 16 WR 1170; *Thomas* v. *Quartermaine* (1887) 18 QBD 685, 695.

[64] (1869) LR 5 Ex 1 (infra, n. 159).

[65] *Pollock,* Torts, 448–449. This did not, of course, entail that there could not be an independent duty arising towards the ultimate user, as in *George* v. *Skivington* itself. The point is made very clearly in the New York case of *Thomas* v. *Winchester* (1852) 2 Seld 397.

person injured.[66] It might apply when the defendant was outside the foreseeable range of injury.

d) Law and Fact

Central to the entrenchment of the duty-breach analysis was the division between law and fact. Crudely speaking, whether there had been a breach of duty was a question of fact for the jury to decide, but its existence was a question of law. So long as the issue could be framed in terms of the duty-situation, therefore, it was removed from the sphere of jury discretion. According to one influential commentator it was this 'substitution of approximate standards of conduct for the unchecked determination of juries' which brought about the expansion and increasing complexity of the nineteenth-century tort of negligence.[67]

The nineteenth century witnessed an enormous growth in the legislative control of a host of professions and activities. This statutory regulation generated a panoply of detailed duties, breach of which would lead to legal liability. Though there was some argument that the breach of such a duty constituted an independent tort based on the wording of chapter 50 of the Statute of Westminster II (1285),[68] it was more normal to treat them as fixing concrete duty-situations within the tort of negligence.[69] These duties were fixed by law, and they were consequently wholly outside the sphere of jury discretion. Equally, as a matter of theory, they were immune from judicial control; but the fact that the judges had the power to interpret legislation meant that it was within their power to mould and adjust such statutory duties to fit the circumstances.

Outside these statutory contexts, too, the question whether or not there was a duty of care was in principle a matter for the judge, though more sophisticated commentators recognised that there was an intermingling of the functions of judge and jury.[70] It is telling that under the heading of 'Duty' in his commonplace book Parke B. notes only that it is a matter of

---

66 *Winfield,* Duty in Tortious Negligence (1934) 34 Col LR 41, 57. Cf. *Tonawanda Rail-Road Co* v. *Murger* (1848) 5 Denio 255, 266–267, per Beardsley C. J. (New York).

67 *Beven,* Negligence, 12. See too *Winfield,* Duty in Tortious Negligence (1934) 34 Col LR 41, 61 n. 92.

68 *Addison,* Wrongs (2nd edition), 34; *Couch* v. *Steel* (1854) 3 E & B 402, per Lord Campbell C. J. (disapproved by Lord Cairns L. C. in *Atkinson* v. *Newcastle Waterworks* (1877) 2 Ex D 441).

69 *Smith,* Negligence, 2, 7; *Underhill,* Law of Torts, 20; *Beven,* Principles of the law of Negligence, passim. See E. *Thayer,* Public Wrongs and Private Action (1914) 27 Harvard Law Rev 317.

law,[71] and hence for the judge to decide. This was no novelty of the nineteenth century, for it was inherent in the action of trespass on the case from its beginnings in the middle of the fourteenth century that its boundaries of application were questions of 'law' rather than questions of 'fact';[72] at an abstract level the only change in the nineteenth century was the relatively unimportant terminological shift to the use of the language of 'duty of care'. At a concrete level, though, even outside the sphere of statutory duties there was a marked increase in the degree of detail with which duty situations were formulated.[73] The more precisely delineated they became, the more firmly did the incidence of liability fall under the control of the judges.

2. *Generality and Specificity: Duties of Care or Duty of Care?*

Lawyers writing about the emergent tort of negligence might adopt one of two strategies. Those writing brief analyses (such as Saunders, Campbell and Underhill) tended to limit themselves to a brief statement of the duty to take care not to injure another, harking back to the moral authors of the eighteenth century and before.[74] At the opposite extreme were writers like Thomas Beven in England or Francis Wharton in America, whose aim was to give a more thorough – perhaps more practical – treatment of the subject; their treatment of duty-situations was consequently vastly more detailed and far more exhaustive. Beven, for example, followed Wharton in dividing the specific duties into those arising out of contractual relationships and those arising independent of contract; in the first edition of his *Principles of the Law of Negligence* (1889) the examination of the range of duty situations extends for some 700 pages. As one commentator noted in 1883, "The Law in regard to Negligence is the most uncultivated part of the 'wilderness of single instances' of which our law consists."[75]

---

[70] *Howe*, ed., The Pollock-Holmes Letters, 1.85 (Pollock), 1.92 (Holmes). Particularly penetrating is *Holmes* The Theory of Torts, reprinted at (1931) 44 Harvard Law Review 773, especially at 779.

[71] *Prichard*, Scott v. Shepherd (1773) and the Emergence of the Tort of Negligence, 43.

[72] See Professor Baker's paper in the present volume.

[73] Infra, section 3(b).

[74] See for example the works of Saunders, Campbell, and Underhill. Bigelow is explicit: the major part of litigation in negligence revolves around the question whether the facts submitted to the court make a case to be submitted to the jury, i.e. whether there is a duty of care; but 'to consider such questions would require a detailed examination of the authorities beyond the scope of this book' (Elements of the Law of Torts, 283).

[75] The Duty of Care towards One's Neigbour (1883) 18 Law Journal 618, 619.

The difference between these two extremes was not so much theoretical as pragmatic. Beyond it, though, there was a more abstract tension. On the one hand there were those who believed that there was a single tort of negligence based on a duty to take care not to injure others, whose precise topography was delineated by the multiplicity of duties of care;[76] on the other hand there were those who believed that 'negligence' described merely the level at which the defendant's conduct became culpable, and that when liability for negligence was discussed it was merely a convenient umbrella covering a whole range of innominate torts.[77] The debate between these two schools of thought continued well into the twentieth century.[78]

So far as the law in practice was concerned there was no such polarity between specificity and generality in the nineteenth century. Legal reasoning proceeded casuistically.[79] There were, it is true, cases such as *Blyth* v. *Birmingham Waterworks*[80] which hinged on the application of a general definition of negligence-liability; but the issue in these cases was not whether the defendant had owed a duty to the plaintiff – this would usually not be in question – so much as whether there was any evidence of breach of duty sufficient to leave the case to the jury. If there was nothing from which the jury could properly conclude that the defendant had failed to live up to the appropriate standard of care, it was open to the judge to withdraw the question from them.

The first attempt to apply a generalised duty of care in negligence occurred in *Heaven* v. *Pender* in 1883.[81] The defendant, a dock owner, provided staging on which the plaintiff, a painter not employed by the defendant, was to work. A rope supporting the staging broke and the plaintiff was injured. In giving judgment for the plaintiff, Brett M. R. applied a general principle of liability: 'Whenever one person is by circumstances placed in such a position with regard to another that every one of ordinary sense who did think would at once recognise that if he did not use ordinary care and skill in his own conduct with regard to those circumstances he would

---

[76] e.g. *Saunders,* Negligence, 1; *Pollock,* Torts, 22, 352.

[77] e.g. *Addison,* Wrongs (2nd edition), 15; *Bigelow,* Elements of the Law of Torts, 279 n. 1.

[78] *Winfield,* The History of Negligence in the Law of Torts (1926) 42 LQR 184, especially 196 n. 2.

[79] In addition, of course, statutory duties were inherently specific and not susceptible to any process of generalisation.

[80] (1856) 11 Ex 781; supra, section 2. Similar are *Vaughan* v. *Menlove* (1837) 3 Bing NC 468; *Vaughan* v. *Taff Vale Railway* (1860) 5 H & N 679; *Smith* v. *London and South Western Railway Co* (1870) LR 5 CP 98.

[81] (1883) 11 QBD 503. A similarly broad approach is visible one year earlier in America: *Devlin* v. *Smith* (1882) 89 NY 470 (on almost identical facts to *Heaven* v. *Pender).*

cause danger to the person or property of the other, a duty arises to use ordinary care and skill to avoid such danger'.[82] The other two members of the court were unwilling to support such a wide proposition;[83] but it was followed, and extended, five years later in *Cann* v. *Willson*[84] when an action was allowed to recover financial loss suffered as a result of a negligent representation in connexion with a mortgage. One year after this, though, the House of Lords held in *Derry* v. *Peek*[85] that no action would lie for a deceitful representation unless there was evidence of actual fraud. *Derry* v. *Peek* was not a case of negligence at all, and neither *Heaven* v. *Pender* nor *Cann* v. *Willson* was cited, but it was immediately treated as overruling *Cann* v. *Willson.*[86] Brett M. R., now Lord Esher, adopted the same approach in 1893 in *Le Lievre* v. *Gould,*[87] another mortgage case, restating the principle of *Heaven* v. *Pender* in its more limited form: 'If one man is near to another, or is near to the property of another, a duty lies upon him not to do that which may cause personal injury to another or may injure his property.'[88]

Even in this narrower form, restricted to personal injury and property damage, the proposition of Brett M. R. was not immediately followed, and for almost half a century English judicial practice followed the more conservative stream of academic opinion in its unwilingness to formulate any general duty of care.[89] It was not until 1932 that English (or Scottish) judicial opinion began to shift.[90]

---

[82] (1883) 11 QBD 503, 509. Later lawyers perhaps read such a general principle back into *George* v. *Skivington* (1869) LR 5 Ex I (infra, n. 159), but it is not really to be found there.

[83] (1883) 11 QBD 503, 516.

[84] (1888) 39 Ch D 39.

[85] (1889) 14 App Cas 337.

[86] *Scholes* v. *Brook* (1891) 63 LT (NS) 837 (where the judge, Romer J., had been the successful counsel *in Cann* v. *Willson*).

[87] [1893] 1 QB 491.

[88] [1893] 1 QB 491, 497. To the same effect, though more influential in their language, were the dicta of A L Smith L. J. at 504: '[A] duty to take due care did arise when the person or property of one was in such proximity to the person or property of another that, if do care was not taken, damage might be done by the one to the other.'

[89] The formulation of Brett M. R. was more favourably received in America: *MacPherson* v. *Buick Motor Co* (1916) 217 NY 382, 111 NE 1050, per Cardozo J., though in general the chronology of development in the American courts was not significantly different from that in England: S. *Donnelly,* The Fault Principle (1967) 18 Syracuse Law Rev 728, 740–746.

[90] Infra, section 6(b).

3. Breach of Duty and Remoteness of Damage

a) Breach of Duty

It was clear that it was the function of the judges to determine whether there was a duty of care. It was no less clear that it was the function of the jury to determine whether the duty had been breached. In principle the function of the judge was to direct the jury using the appropriate test of negligence, increasingly commonly the test of the reasonable man. This was given a slightly more precise definition in *Blyth* v. *Birmingham Waterworks*[91] in 1856. Unusually severe frosts had caused the defendants' water hydrants to freeze closed; as a result when the main water pipe ruptured a large quantity of water seeped into the plaintiffs cellar rather than being released through the hydrant. In an action against the water company the judge left to the jury the question whether the defendants had acted reasonably, and a verdict was given for the plaintiff. This was overturned by the Court of Exchequer. Such a severe frost was unforeseeable, and a reasonable person does not take steps to guard against unforeseeable possibilities.[92]

The role of the judges was to determine whether there was sufficient evidence on which the jury might properly make a finding of negligence; if there was not the trial judge might withdraw the question from the jury, or the court in banc might overturn a verdict given for the plaintiff (as occurred in *Blyth* v. *Birmingham Waterworks*). The result of this was that the judges' powers were limited to the most extreme cases; most cases fell within the grey area of jury discretion. The only circumstances in which the judges would themselves have to decide a case within this grey area were where the parties agreed the facts and presented a special case for the decision of the court,[93] or where the case was heard without a jury.[94]

From the 1860s there were moves by the judges to infiltrate themselves further into the determination of whether there had been a breach of duty. In *Bridges* v. *North London Railway* Company,[95] for example, B had been

---

91 (1856) 11 Ex 781; supra, section 2.

92 (1856) 11 Ex 781, 784 per Alderson B. The test of foreseeability was already found as a rule of remoteness of damage, and its translation from there marks the first step of its re-categorisation: infra, section 3(c)(ii).

93 *T. Chitty,* Archbold's Practice of the Court of Queen's Bench (9th edition, 1855), 1.422 (incorporating the changes introduced by the Common Law Procedure Act, 1854).

94 Trials without a jury were possible in the County Court from 1846, and later in the century in some cases in the High Court (infra, pp. 259–260).

95 (1871) LR 6 QB 377; (1874) LR 7 HL 213.

killed when alighting from a train. The evidence showed that he had been travelling on the train from Broad Street to Highbury; when the train stopped at Highbury it had failed to draw fully out of the dark tunnel into the lit station. The guard shouted the name of the station and B, who was in the last carriage and hence still in the tunnel, alighted. The platform extended some distance into the tunnel but at its end there was a mass of rubble and it was impossible to see where the one ended and the other began. Expecting a firm surface B put his foot down confidently, but fell over and was killed when it turned out not to be. His widow brought an action in negligence against the Railway Company. There was no doubt that there was a duty of care, but Blackburn J. was of the opinion that it had not been breached.[96] The jury strongly disagreed. The judge accordingly took their verdict for the plaintiff (to avoid the need for a new trial should he be held to have been wrong), but gave judgment for the defendants. The full Court of Queen's Bench agreed that he had been correct to withdraw the case from the jury, but this was reversed on appeal to the House of Lords and judgment finally given for the plaintiff. So long as there was some evidence on which the jury might hold that there had been a breach, it was the duty of the judge to leave the question to them: it was emphatically not his job to replace their judgement with his own.[97]

Bridges v. *North London Railway Company* might have been interpreted as allowing only a very limited function to the judge, but three years later, in *Metropolitan Railway Company* v. *Jackson*[98], the House of Lords (now including Lord Blackburn) stressed that they still had the responsibility to remove the case from the jury if there was insufficient evidence of the defendant's negligence.[99] This went some way (though by no means all the way) towards restoring the judicial power which Blackburn J. had claimed in *Bridges*.

b) Causation of Damage: Remoteness and Proximity

The final element of negligence liability, the causation of damage, was in principle as much a matter for the jury as was the question of breach. There was little problem with the question of factual causation, whether the defendant's act was a *causa sine qua non* of the plaintiffs injury; more controversial was the question of legal causation, whether the injury should

---

96 Perhaps surprisingly he did not shelter behind the argument of B's contributory negligence.

97 The general principle was established in *Ryder* v. *Wombwell* (1868) LR 4 Ex 32.

98 (1877) 3 App Cas 193.

99 See especially Lord Cairns at 197, and Lord Blackburn at 208.

properly be imputed to the defendant. For much of the century the determination of questions of causation was so firmly within the domain of the jury that we cannot be certain on what principles they acted, and even when the issue came before the judges by way of case stated after the facts had been found it is hard to avoid the impression that they dealt with it on a case-by-case basis.[100]

A rough and ready approach was to say the defendant should be liable for all the consequences of the negligent act. There was, however, a long tradition that liability would only exist for the 'proximate' consequences of the act; 'remote' consequences were too distant.[101] A similar idea had appeared in Buller's *Nisi Prius* (with overtones of natural law thinking[102]), that the wrongdoer should only be held liable for the foreseeable consequences of his act.[103] By the middle of the century it was being suggested that such a rule should be applied. This was propounded, with acute hesitation, by Pollock C. B. in 1850.[104]

> I entertain considerable doubt whether a person [who is guilty of negligence] is responsible for all the consequences which may under any circumstances arise, and in respect of mischief which could by no possibility have been foreseen, and which no reasonable person would have anticipated.[105]

Other similar formulations were found: the consequences had to be 'immedidiately and necessarily' flowing from the wrong, or 'the natural and reasonable result'.[106] Sir Frederick Pollock, in the first edition of his text-book on the law of torts, knitted these together masterfully:

> [T]hose consequences, and those only, are deemed 'immediate', 'proximate', or, to anticipate a little, 'natural and probable', which a person of average competence and knowledge, being in the like case with the person whose conduct is complained of, and having the like opportunities of observation, might be expected to foresee as likely to follow upon such conduct.[107]

The principle of foreseeability, however, by now had its place as an element determining whether the defendant was in breach of duty: the reason-

---

100 e.g. Hill v. *New River Co* (1868) 9 B & S 303; *Bailiffs of Romney Marsh* v. *Trinity House* (1868) LR 5 Ex 208, affirmed (1871) LR 7 Ex 247.

101 *F. Bacon,* Maxims of the Law (1598), reg. 1.

102 Cf. D. 9.2.31.

103 1st edition p. 36; subsequent editions p. 25.

104 *Rigby* v. *Hewitt* (1850) 5 Ex 240; *Greenland* v. *Chaplin* (1850) 5 Ex 243 (dissenting on this point from the other members of the court).

105 (1850) 5 Ex 243, 248. The words in brackets are omitted from the version of his judgment in 19 LJ Ex 295, with the result that he could subsequently be taken to have been referring only to torts other than negligence (infra, n. 112). This view was approved by Byles J. in *Hoey* v. *Felton* (1861) 11 CBNS 142, 143.

106 *J. D. Mayne,* Treatise on the Law of Damages (1856), 14–15.

107 Torts, 28; cf. the far more sophisticated analysis of *Wharton:* Negligence, 76–152.

able person does not guard against unforeseeable possibilities.[108] If the foreseeability of injury had already been dealt with it was hardly necessary to deal with it again under the heading of remoteness. This is implicit in the approach of Bramwell B. in *Blyth* v. *Birmingham Waterworks*[109] and *Cornman* v. *Eastern Counties Railway Co,*[110] and it is made absolutely explicit by Channell B. *in Smith* v. *London and South Western Railway Co:*

> [W]here there is no direct evidence of negligence, the question what a reasonable man might foresee is of importance in considering the question whether there is evidence for the jury of negligence or not ... but when it has once been determined that there is evidence of negligence, the person guilty of it is equally liable for its consequences, whether he could have foreseen them or not.[111]

Though the view of Pollock C. B., that foreseeability had an independent role as a test of remoteness, was not finally rejected until 1921,[112] in practice the decision in *Smith* v. *London and South Western Railway Co* locked in place the rule that the negligent defendant was liable for all the consequences of his act.

On the face of it, the effect of this was to abridge yet further the functions of the jury: where once they might have had to decide whether the injury was too remote, now their power was limited to saying whether it had been caused by the defendant. This would be too simplistic, however. All that has happened is that foreseeability has been moved from the rules of remoteness to the rules of breach. In all but the most exceptional circumstances there is no more than a semantic difference between saying that the defendant was not in breach of duty because the consequences were unforeseeable and saying that the defendant, though in breach of duty, should not be liable for the consequences because they were unforeseeable.

4. Duty, Breach and Remoteness

The combined effect of *Bridges* v. *North London Railway Company* (as explained in *Metropolitan Railway Company* v. *Jackson)* and *Smith* v. *London and South Western Railway* was that the power of the jury had been somewhat abridged, though perhaps not as far as the judges would have liked. Those who wanted to limit the power of the jury further than

---

108 Supra, n. 92.

109 (1856) 11 Ex 781, 785. The point appears more strongly in the variant versions of the judgment of Alderson B.: 25 LJ Ex 212, 213; 2 Jur (NS) 333.

110 (1859) 4 H & N 780, 786.

111 (1870) LR 6 CP 14, 21.

112 *re Polemis and Furness, Withy & Co* [1921] 3 KB 560; the ambiguity in the remarks of Pollock C. B. in *Greenland* v. *Chaplin* (supra, n. 105) was invaluable in allowing the court to reinterpret them.

this were constrained to do so by expanding the role of the duty of care, whose determination was more or less firmly within the judicial domain. It is no accident that it was only a few years after these cases that Brett M. R. began the movement to generalise the duty of care in terms of a requirement to take the care which would be taken by a reasonable man.[113] In this way the quintessential jury question of breach of duty – had the defendant acted as a reasonable man – could be transmuted into the judicial question whether there had been a duty in the first place. And in the course of this transmutation, foreseeability was further removed from its original home as a rule of remoteness, this time finding its niche in the very heartland of the tort of negligence, whether there was a duty of care in the first place.

IV. Liability without Personal Fault

The new-found negligence liability of the first half of the nineteenth century equated tortious liability with the actor's failure to live up to the standards reasonably to be expected of individuals in society. Legal liability, therefore, was significantly identified with personal moral shortcoming.[114] This moral dimension of the tort was peculiarly problematical for those situations in which one person was made responsible for the wrongul acts of another, cases of vicarious liability. The earlier Common law had dealt with these without any apparent difficulty: so long as the law could reflect popular ascriptions of responsibility legal liability could straightforwardly be imposed in those cases where it was considered appropriate, and there was no need for any soul-searching analysis to justify this.[115] In so far as lawyers put their minds to it it could be explained by a theory of identification, treating X's act in law as Y's, or by a notion of agency;[116] behind it, too, we could perhaps see a skeletal notion of enterprise liability.[117]

The shift of emphasis on to personal fault as the grounds of liability put an end to this, and from the 1790s there was an increasing awkwardness in the courts' attitude to such cases.[118] Just as the Natural lawyers had signally failed to integrate it into their theories, the Common lawyers in their

---

[113] *Heaven* v. *Pender* (1883) 11 QBD 503; supra, n. 81.

[114] Supra, section 2, section 3(a).

[115] *Hern* v. *Nichols* (1708) 1 Salk 289; *Jones* v. *Hart* (1698) 2 Salk 441; cp *Kingston* v. *Booth* (1685) Skinner 228.

[116] *Middleton* v. *Fowler* (1698) 1 Salk 282; *Turberville* v. *Stampe* (1697) 1 Ld Raym 264.

[117] *W. Blackstone,* Commentaries, 1.417–420; R. *Wooddesson,* Systematical View of the Laws of England (1792) 1.465–466.

[118] e.g. *Stone* v. *Cartwright* (1795) 6 TR 411; *Bush* v. *Steinman* (1799) 1 B & P 404.

turn began to treat vicarious liability as an exceptional situation to be justified (if at all[119]) by unprincipled, and relatively feeble, explanations in terms of the maxims *Respondeat Superior* and *Qui facit per alium facit per se*.[120] The truth of the matter was clearly seen by Joseph Story: it was a rule 'founded on public policy and convenience'.[121] Deprived of any principled basis, it rapidly settled down into a set of more or less arbitrary rules.

Its essence was expressed in terms of the liability of a 'master' for torts committed by a 'servant'. The corollary of this was that there was no liability for torts committed by an 'independent contractor'.[122] Exactly what these terms embraced was unclear: in the 1850s it could be held that vicarious liability attached to a man who gave five shillings to a 'common labourer' to clean out a drain,[123] but not to a railway company employing a surveyor at a salary of £250 per year.[124] The operator of a barge was liable for the negligence of a licensed waterman whom he had taken on board to navigate along the River Thames;[125] but the operator of a foreign ship was not liable for the negligence of a licensed pilot taken on board to navigate along the River Tyne,[126] nor was a butcher for the negligence of a a drover employed to take his bullock to market.[127] The servant had to be acting 'in the course of employment' and not 'on a frolic of his own'.[128] There was no clear boundary to any of these terms. It was for the jury to make as much sense of them as they could,[129] though by now judicial control over jury discretion was sufficiently strong that it was impossible for the judges to avoid the issues entirely. Nor was any explanation given why the law should have set the boundaries of liability here rather than at some other point.

Though the rules had the advantage of being easily stated, they floated free of any principled base and did not have the flexibility to deal with

---

119 See for example the strictures of Joseph Brown Q. C.: P. P. 1876 ix. 669, q. 942.

120 *Weyland* v. *Elkins* (1816) Holt NP 227 & note; *C. M. Smith,* Treatise on the Law of Master and Servant (1852), 151–152.

121 *J. Story,* Agency (London, 1839), 404 § 452.

122 *Milligan* v. *Wedge* (1840) 12 Ad & El 737; *Rapson* v. *Cubitt* (1842) 9 M & W 710; *Knight* v. *Fox* (1850) 5 Ex. 721.

123 *Sadler* v. *Henlock* (1855) 4 El & Bl 570.

124 *Knight* v. *Fox* (1850) 5 Ex 721.

125 *Martin* v. *Temperley* (1843) 4 QB 298.

126 *The Maria* (1839) 1 W Rob 95.

127 *Milligan* v. *Wedge* (1840) 12 Ad & El 737.

128 *Croft* v. *Alison* (1821) 4 B & Ald 491; *Huzzey* v. *Field* (1835) 4 C M & R 432; *Joel* v. *Morison* (1834) 6 C & P 501; *Mitchell* v. *Crassweller* (1853) 13 CB 237.

129 *Brady* v. *Giles* (1835) 1 Mo & Ro 494; *Randleson* v. *Murray* (1838) 8 Ad & El 109; *Fenton* v. *City of Dublin Steam Packet Co* (1838) 8 Ad & El 835.

cases which did not fit neatly within them. The courts adopted no consistent stance to cases where the wrongdoer was undoubtedly a 'servant', but one who had been hired out from his 'general' 'employer' to a 'special' employer.[130] Sometimes liability was attached to the former, sometimes the latter. There was no clear solution where the reality of economic organisation did not map neatly on to legal categories. In most dockyards, for example, porters were (casual) employees of warehousemen, who on ordinary principles would be vicariously liable for their negligence. In Liverpool there was a specialist cadre of independent master-porters, whose interposition meant that labouring porters were technically not employees of the warehousemen. It was argued, therefore, that in Liverpool the warehousemen should not be vicariously liable for porters' negligence, since they were technically not their employees. The Queen's Bench rejected this: it would have been quite irrational for the liability of the warehouseman to have varied from place to place depending on the vagaries of labour organisation.[131] Nor was there a clear solution where the servant was as a matter of law acting in breach of his contract (and hence could hardly be said legally to have been acting 'in the course of employment'), but as a matter of reality doing precisely what he was expected to do. In *Limpus* v. *London General Omnibus Company,*[132] the question was raised whether the Company would be vicariously liable to a person injured by a driver racing in contravention of the Company's rules, where there was some suggestion that the rules had been introduced as a cynical public relations ploy and that drivers thought that they were better off breaking the rules than obeying them.[133] The Court of Exchequer refused to let legal nicety get in the way of common sense, holding that the company should be vicariously liable.[134]

---

[130] *Laugher* v. *Pointer* (1826) 5 B & C 547; *Smith* v. *Lawrence* (1828) 2 Man & Ry 1; *Quarman* v. *Burnett (*1840) 6 M & W 499; *Dalyell* v. *Tyrer* (1858) El BI & El 899.

[131] *Randleson* v. *Murray* (1838) 8 Ad & El 109.

[132] (1862) 1 H & C 526.

[133] P. P. 1876 ix 669, q. 416 (C P Ilbert QC). Cf. *[London Transport],* London General (1956), 20–22; T. C. *Barker* and *M. Robbins,* History of London Transport (1975), 69–98. Racing had been endemic long before this: ibid, 34–35.

[134] The basis of the decision in some conception of public policy is hinted at in the judgment of Byles J.: 'If we were to hold [otherwise], a change, of course, at Nisi Prius would follow, and the consequence would be that in almost every case a driver would come forward and exaggerate his own negligence or misconduct, he not being worth one farthing, and say, 'I did it wilfully and unnecessarily,' and so the master would be absolved.' ((1862) 32 L J Ex. 34, 41 (fuller than I H & C 526, 541)). Willes J. was less diffident: 'There ought to be a remedy against some person capable of paying damages to those injured by improper driving.': (1862) 1 H & C 526, 539.

The real difficulty with the rules of vicarious liability, though, was not so much that they led to arbitrary decisions as that they excluded liability in some situations where it was thought that liability should lie. There was a clear argument through the first half of the century, for example, that special rules applied to occupiers of land, making them liable for the negligent acts of their independent contractors,[135] but this was firmly rejected in *Reedie* v. *London and North Western Railway* in 1849.[136] Shortly after this there was a spate of cases in which the courts made use of a range of strategies to achieve the same result notwithstanding the normal operation of the rules. Occupiers were made liable to (lawful) visitors to their premises injured by the negligence of independent contractors by a subtle reformulation of the duty of care: instead of saying there was a duty to take reasonable care not to injure the visitor it was said that the occupier had to take reasonable care to ensure that the visitor was not injured.[137] A related strategy, used for example in cases of statutory duties, was to say that the duty was non-delegable, so that a person could be held to be in breach of duty through the acts of another.[138] An employer of an independent contractor who had committed a public nuisance, as for example by leaving a pile of rubble in the highway, could be held liable as a joint wrongdoer.[139] Liability in private nuisance could be squeezed within the maxim *Sic utere tuo ut alienum non laedas.*[140] In a spectacular example of judicial constructivism, a reservoir owner was held liable for the negligent conduct of his

---

[135] *Bush* v. *Steinman* (1799) 1 B & P 404; *Sly* v. *Edgeley* (1806) 6 Esp 6; *Laugher* v. *Pointer* (1826) 5 B & C 547; *Rapson* v. *Cubitt* (1842) 9 M & W 710; *Rich* v. *Basterfield* (1847) 4 CB 783.

[136] (1849) 4 Ex 244, 20 LJ Ex 65, 13 Jur 659. The remarks of Parke B, not reported in 4 Ex 244, are briefly eloquent: 'Having an interest in the Northwestern Railway Company, I decline to take any part in these proceedings unless the counsel allow me. If they do, must say that I concur in the judgment which has been delivered.' His interest in the Company had not prevented him playing a full part in the argument of the case.

[137] *Pickard* v. *Smith* (1861) 10 CBNS 470; cf. *Indermaur* v. *Dames* (1866) LR 2 CP 311. The passive formulation can be seen earlier, but without anything depending on the shift of voice: *Daniels* v. *Potter* (1830) 4 C & P 262; *Proctor* v. *Harris* (1830) 4 C & P 337).

[138] *Hole* v. *Sittingbourne and Sheerness Railway Company* (1861) 6 H & N 488. The same strategy was used to impose liability in the case of 'hazardous activities': *Woodley* v. *Metropolitan Railway Company* (1877) 36 LTNS 419, 421. See too the judgment of Littledale J. in *Randleson* v. *Murray* as reported in (1838) 7 LJQB 132, 133.

[139] *Ellis* v. *Sheffield Gas Consumers Co* (1853) 2 El & Bl 767 (Queen's Bench); the Common Pleas was less convinced: *Overton* v. *Freeman* (1852) 11 CB 867; *Peachey* v. *Rowland* (1853) 13 CB 182.

[140] *Rich* v. *Basterfield* (1847) 4 CB 783, 802; *Reedie* v. *London and North Western Railway* (1849) 4 Ex 244, 257.

independent contractor by imposing a form of strict liability for the escape of dangerous things brought on to land.[141] And if all else failed it might still be possible to find personal negligence on the part of the employer.[142]

In all of these cases the judges were able to avoid the strictures of the newly developed rules of vicarious liability, but in doing so they added to the fragmentary and atomised nature of the law of tort(s) by setting in place a further set of near-arbitrary rules. The fundamental problem, brought into sharp relief by the problems generated by vicarious liability, was that the moral idea of liability for failing to take reasonable care not to cause foreseeable injury to one's neighbour was too narrow a principle to cover even the central core, let alone the whole, of the law of tort; but this was not to be recognised until well into the twentieth century.[143]

V. The Incidence of Liability

The casuistic nature of legal reasoning means that it is difficult, and dangerous, to draw too precise conclusions about the incidence of liability. None the less, it is important to make some general observations.

In the first place, it needs to be said that 'negligence' – the failure to take the care which would have been taken by a reasonable person – is an inherently narrower standard than 'fault'. This is well illustrated by the early case of *Flower* v. *Adam.*[144] The plaintiff's horse had been injured after it had been blinded by dust blown up from the defendant's pile of rubbish; Mansfield C. J. directed the jury that if the placing of the rubbish was no more than a person would do in the usual course of business, then the injury to the horse was a mere accident. There was no question of demanding a greater standard of care than was normally exercised. In such a case as *Blyth* v. *Birmingham Waterworks,*[145] therefore, however much the jury might have thought that liability should be imposed on the defendant company – in common parlance, that the damage was their fault – they

---

[141] *Rylands* v. *Fletcher* (1865) 3 H & C 774, (1866) LR I Exch 265, (1868) LR 3 HL 330.

[142] *Wanstall* v. *Pooley* (1841) 6 Cl & F 910n. (employment of drunken person).

[143] nb also the development of no-fault liability for employees' claims in respect of work-related injuries: Workmen's Compensation Act, 1897. Interestingly, only twenty years earlier the secretary of the Trades Union Congress Parliamentary Committee had regarded the possibility of such strict liability as 'preposterous': P. P. 1876 ix 669 q. 880. Similar sentiments are expressed by other workers' representatives in P. P. 1877 x 551, q. 345, qq. 2075–2076.

[144] (1810) 2 Taunt 314.

[145] (1856) 11 Ex 781; supra, section 2.

were exonerated by the law on the ground that they had done all that such a company would normally do: this was all that the law required of them.

Secondly, there is reason to believe that in at least some circumstances juries were more favourably inclined towards plaintiffs than judges would have been. It was a commonplace of the second half of the nineteenth century that juries were generally prejudiced against railway companies.[146] 'They generally go wrong,' asserted Baron Bramwell in evidence to the Scottish Law Courts Commission in 1869;[147] and in *Metropolitan Railway* v. *Jackson* Lord Cairns L. C. was quite explicit in his justification for reserving a power to the judge in determining whether the defendant had been in breach of duty:

> A company might might be unpopular, unpunctual, and irregular in its service; badly equipped as to its staff; unaccommodating to the public; notorious, perhaps, for accidents occurring on the line; and when an action was brought for the consequences of an accident, jurors, if left to themselves, might upon evidence of general carelessness, find a verdict against the company in a case where the company was really blameless.[148]

This was not just the view of judges (who were in any event criticised for being inclined against railway companies themselves[149]); even the most complacent apologists for the use of the jury in civil trials accepted that they were prejudiced in railway cases.[150] Other situations existed where judges and juries disagreed about where liability should fall, though without the explicit recognition that juries were simply prejudiced. It seems likely that juries were more inclined than judges would have been to favour plaintiffs in cases where the defendant was a commercial corporation,[151] and in cases where an employee sued an employer;[152] and Baron Bramwell thought that they displayed a strong bias against defendants in running-down case.[153] It followed that as the judges arrogated to themselves ever greater power in determining the outcome of cases of negligence – whether

---

[146] See generally *R. W. Kostal,* Law and English Railway Capitalism, 1825–1875 (Oxford, 1994), 290–291, 293–293, 303–306, 307–308.

[147] P. P. 1868–9 xxv q. 11,997. Contrast the view of Lord Justice Brett: 'They are generally right' (P. P. 1877 x 551 q. 1919). Bramwell's own views on negligence were notoriously pro-defendant (Lord Justice Bramwell on Actions of Negligence (1880) 24 Solicitors Journal 305), though in reality his position cannot be so easily characterised (compare for example, P. P. 1877 x 551, q. 1120).

[148] (1877) 3 App Cas 193, 197–198. See too the remarks of Lord Blackburn at 208.

[149] *Kostal,* Law and English Railway Capitalism, 292, 297, 312–313.

[150] e.g. *M. D. Chalmers,* Trial by Jury in Civil Cases (1891) 7 LQR 15, 18.

[151] P. P. 1913 xxx q. 2392–2396, 2433.

[152] P. P. 1876 ix 669, q. 504 (Joseph Brown. Q. C.).

[153] P. P. 1869–9 xxv q. 12,005.

by controlling the jury's discretion over questions of breach and remoteness or by recategorising issues in terms of the duty of care – the balance inevitably swung further in the direction of the defendants.

Thirdly we may point to areas where judicial choices can be seen to have brought about a very restricted scope of liability. Two examples will suffice: products liability and employers' liability to employees.

The question of the liability of a negligent supplier towards the person injured by his product was raised in *Winterbottom* v. *Wright* in 1842,[154] where the plaintiff had been injured when a wheel flew off a mail-coach supplied by the defendant to the Postmaster-General. The court held that the plaintiff could not sue the negligent defendant either in contract (since the doctrine of privity of contract meant that only the parties to the contract could sue or be sued on it) or in tort (because of the risk of the defendant's being subjected to unlimited and indeterminate liability). It would be wrong to be too hasty to condemn the court, though. The spectre of unlimited and indeterminate liability takes on a more substantial form in a world where loss-spreading is impracticable: nineteenth-century manufacturers were typically relatively small concerns, not large enough to distribute unpredictable losses amongst their customers; and liability insurance was as yet unknown.[155] This did not mean that the injured party would have no action at all: the assumption behind the arguments in *Winterbottom* v. *Wright* was that there would commonly be an action against somebody (though not necessarily somebody solvent), typically the person from whom the victim had bought the defective product or its user.[156] There were some limitations on the manufacturer's immunity in tort: liability would be imposed if the manufacturer had been fraudulent,[157] or if the product was 'dangerous in itself.'[158] Beyond this, though, the courts would hold the defendant liable only in the most extraordinary cases. *George* v. *Skivington*[159] was one such. A wife was injured by hair shampoo bought for her by her husband; it seems that she was present at the time of the sale, and may well have conducted the transaction herself. On the face of it this should have been a simple case, whether the action was framed in contract or tort, but

154 (1842) 10 M & W 109.

155 Infra, section 6(a).

156 Though on the facts of the case the Postmaster-General was immune from liability: 10 M & W 114.

157 *Langridge* v. *Levy* (1837) 2 M & W 519, (1838) 4 M & W 337.

158 e.g. *Farrant* v. *Barnes* (1862) 11 CB(NS) 553; *Mangan* v. *Atterton* (1866) LR I Ex 239. See generally *J. Charlesworth,* Liability for Dangerous Things (1922), 279–292.

159 (1869) LR 5 Ex 1, 21 LT(NS) 495, 39 LJ Ex 8. The brief report in *The Times,* 16th November 1869, assists in piecing together the story.

this was not so. A married woman was deemed to contract on behalf of her husband, who was therefore the principal contracting party. The rules of privity of contract had once applied relatively loosely to contracts made by one family member on behalf of another, and perhaps she might then have been joined as co-plaintiff; but the recent case of *Tweddle* v. *Atkinson*[160] had insisted on the rigorous application of the rules in such family contexts, and this route would have been available only if she had provided the purchase price out of her own money (which would normally not be the case because of the rule that 'her' property was treated as her husband's).[161] Mr George could undoubtedly sue in contract, but he could not recover damages for his wife's loss. Mrs George could not sue her husband (thereby causing him a loss which he might have been able to pass on to the defendant[162]) because of the procedural bar on actions between spouses. The only possible route was for Mrs George to sue in tort. On the authorities her claim should have failed, but by a feat of the most transparent legerdemain the Court of Exchequer equated fraud with negligence and allowed her to recover.[163] It was not a case that could easily be followed,[164] and it was not until 1932 that the courts finally began to allow a general remedy against the negligent manufacturer.[165]

The judicial approach to products liability indicates a stance favourable to emergent enterprises; such a stance is no less visible in their approach to employers' liability. For most of the nineteenth century it was held that the employee impliedly consented to all those risks ordinarily incidental to the work.[166] In most cases it was little more than a rhetorical flourish justifying

160 (1861) 1 B & S 393.

161 See *L. W. Cave,* ed., Addison on the Law of Contracts (6th ed., 1869), 753–755.

162 Addison on the Law of Contracts (6th ed., 1869), 1067–1068.

163 The court does seem to have gone unusually far out of its way to favour the plaintiff. The case was pleaded in contract, with Mrs George named as co-plaintiff, to which the defendant demurred. Plaintiffs' counsel said that he was willing to argue the claim in tort, and at the court's suggestion the declaration was amended to make Mr George sole plaintiff. Defendant's counsel was then required to argue in support of the demurrer, despite the amendment of the declaration and the shifting of the whole basis of the claim. The court then gave judgment without even hearing argument on the plaintiff's side.

164 For other examples of the courts' manipulation of rules in order to give judgment for an apparently deserving plaintiff, see *Francis* v. *Cockrell* (1870) 5 QBD 184; *Heaven* v. *Pender* (1883) 11 QBD 503; *Clarke* v. *Army and Navy Cooperative Stores* [1903] 1 KB 155. The strict rule is stated with impeccable certainty in *Blacker* v. *Lake and Elliot* (1912) 106 LT 533.

165 *Donoghue* v. *Stevenson* [1932] AC 562; infra, section 6(b).

166 *Clarke* v. *Holmes* (1862) 7 H & N 937, 943, per Cockburn C. J. A distinction could be drawn between those existing at the start of the work and those coming into existence subsequently.

the court's decision that there was no duty (or no evidence of breach to be left to the jury), though it did have an analytically independent function where the employer's duty was imposed by statute.[167] The maxim lost much of its importance – both rhetorically and analytically – from the 1870s when the courts began to stress that mere knowledge of a risk did not in itself prove consent, reversing their consistent anti-employee stance of the middle years of the century,[168] an approach which became fixed by the decision of the House of Lords in *Smith* v. *Baker.*[169] It was *Smith* v. *Baker* too which brought out into the open that the plaintiffs implied consent to run a risk was normally only the correlative of the defendant's not being in breach of duty.[170] A yet stronger indication of the pro-employer inclination of the judges is their invention of the 'fellow-servant' rule, the rule that an employer would not be vicariously liable if one employee negligently injured another employee.[171] This rule first appeared in England in 1850,[172] consciously borrowed from the decision of Shaw C. J. in the Massachusetts case of *Farwell* v. *Boston and Worcester Railroad,*[173] who in his turn claimed to have based his decision on the judgment of Lord Abinger C. B. in *Priestley* v. *Fowler.*[174] English lawyers had not themselves thought to interpret *Priestley* v. *Fowler* in this way; their doing so in 1850 was a transparent judicial choice to adopt the economic liberalism espoused by Shaw C. J. All depended on the 'implied terms' of the contract of employment and on the definition of 'fellow-servant'; both were treated as matters of law for the judges to decide, effectively neutralising what was perceived to be the pro-employee bias of jurors presented with such cases.[175] The rule came under attack in the 1870s – it was noted that it did not apply in France or Germany[176] – and its worst effects were removed by statute from

---

167 As in *Clarke* v. *Holmes* (last note) itself.

168 *Woodley* v. *Metropolitan District Railway Company* (1877) 2 Ex D 384, 393–394, per Mellish L. J.; *Thomas* v. *Quartermaine* (1877) 18 QBD 685. Compare the approach of Willes J. in *Saxton* v. *Hawksworth* (1872) 26 LT 85, quoted in *W. R. Cornish and G. de N. Clark,* Law and Society in England 1750–1950 (1989), 500.

169 [1891] AC 325.

170 There had already been a finding of no-negligence against the defendant, and no appeal lay against this under the terms of the County Courts Act 1888.

171 *Kostal,* Law and English Railway Capitalism, 254–279.

172 *Hutchinson* v. *York, Newcastle and Berwick Railway* (1850) 5 Ex 343. See too *Bartonshill Coal Company* v. *Reid* (1858) 3 Macq 266, where the rule was forced on the unwilling Scots.

173 (1842) 4 Metc 49.

174 (1837) 3 M & W 1. See *A. W. B. Simpson,* A Case of First Impression: *Priestley* v. *Fowler,* in: Leading Cases in the Common Law (1995), 100.

175 *Kostal,* Law and English Railway Capitalism, 274 n. 117.

176 P. P. 1876 ix 669 qq. 313–315 (C. P. Ilbert, Q. C.).

1880, though it was not until 1948 that it was finally eradicated from the law.[177]

It would be quite wrong to conclude from these two examples that the judges adopted a consistently pro-industrial policy.[178] At the same time as they were operating a tough policy against the imposition of liability in cases by railway employees against their employers, they were generous in giving actions in cases of injury or death of passengers;[179] in the first half of the century a higher standard of care was demanded of profit-making enterprises than those established for the public good, and when the liability rules shifted in 1866 it was in the direction of imposing the higher standard on public bodies than the lower standard on private ones;[180] there was a willingness to impose liability on the employers of independent contractors in a range of situations despite the narrowed field of application of the doctrine of vicarious liability;[181] and in *Rylands* v. *Fletcher*[182] they did not shrink from imposing strict liability where injury was caused by the escape of a dangerous thing brought on to the plaintiffs land. What is important, though, is that it was the judges who were making these decisions rather than the juries; and that by and large the judges were more favourable to industrial enterprises than the juries would have been.

VI. The Tort of Negligence in the Twentieth Century

The framework of the tort of negligence was firmly in place by the end of the nineteenth century, though there were as yet unanswered questions. The development which had begun then rapidly reached its culmination in the first half of the twentieth century. Already by 1900, though, there were

177 *P. W. J. Bartrip and S. Burman,* Wounded Soldiers of Industry (Oxford, 1983), 126–157. The first and last statutes were the Employers' Liability Act 1880 and the Workmen's Compensation Act 1948.

178 The allegedly pro-enterprise bias of judges has been most heavily studied for America. The opposite poles are best represented on the one hand by *M. Horwitz,* The Transformation of American Law, 1780–1860 (Cambridge, Mass., 1977), and on the other hand by *G. A. Schwartz,* Tort Law and the Economy in Nineteenth-Century America: a Reinterpretation (1981) 90 Yale Law Journal 1717 and The Character of Early American Tort Law (1989) 36 UCLA Law Rev 641. For the difficulties of seeing any consistent position in England, cf. *J. P. S. McLaren,* Nuisance Law and the Industrial Revolution (1983) 3 Oxford Journal of Legal Studies 155.

179 *Kostal,* Law and English Railway Capitalism, 279–321.

180 See in particular *Duncan* v. *Findlater* (1839) 6 Cl & F 894 (a Scots case, but decided on identical principles to English law), and the cases there cited; *Mersey Docks and Harbour Board* v. *Gibbs* (1866) LR 1 HL 93.

181 Supra, section 4.

182 (1865) 3 H & C 774, (1866) LR 1 Exch 265, (1868) LR 3 HL 330.

visible the seeds of destruction of the nineteenth-century tort; in the second half of the twentieth century these seeds took root, so that by the end of the century the process of decomposition can be seen to be far advanced.

1. Transformative Factors in the Twentieth-Century Tort of Negligence

From around the beginning of the twentieth century a number of factors combined to alter the nature and structure of negligence liability.

First of all, there were a number of economic chances which altered the whole basis on which negligence liability operated. Most obvious of these was the increasing preponderance of corporate defendants. This was, of course, not a new phonomenon, as the frequency of actions against railway companies in the nineteenth century amply demonstrates; but the increasingly corporate nature of industrial enterprise by the early twentieth century[183] meant that actions were ever more commonly brought against companies rather than individuals. This undoubtedly brought about a more plaintiff-centred approach to liability, equivalent to that found in actions by railway passengers after the 1850s. As well as the prejudice against wealthy defendants – the 'maxim of natural jurisprudence, "It is no sin to rob an apparently rich man"'[184] – large corporate defendants were undoubtedly better able to spread losses across their business and so pass them on to customers or shareholders than were individual capitalists or small partnerships. Moreover, in so far as the nineteenth-century legal thinking was built on a moral principle that individuals should only be liable for their own shortcomings, the justification for this in a world of corporate defendants was rather more difficult to see. Added to this there was the increasing availability of liability insurance. Whereas in the nineteenth century individuals might only insure against their losses, from the late nineteenth century it became possible to insure against legal liability;[185] and well into the twentieth century there were doubts about the legality of insuring against the consquence of one's own wrongdoing.[186] Moreover, as the cen-

183 *P. S. Atiyah,* The Rise and Fall of Freedom of Contract (Oxford, 1979), 596–601.

184 *C. Fairfield,* Memoir of Lord Bramwell (1898), 153.

185 *H. E. Raynes,* History of British Insurance (2nd edition, 1964), 289–308. The first employers' liability policy dates from 1880, the first third-party motor insurance from 1896.

186 *A. W. B. Welford,* Law Relating to Accident Insurance (1923) 428–436. Employers' insurance against liability was tacitly recognised by statute in 1906; the legality of motor car insurance was questioned for the first time (but admitted) in *Tinline* v. *White Cross Insurance* [1921] 3 KB 327.

tury progressed it became compulsory to take out such liability insurance in respect of certain activities, such as driving a motor vehicle. The same arguments came into play here as in the case of corporate defendants: as between an injured plaintiff and an anonymous (and wealthy) insurance company it was easy to have sympathy with the plaintiff, and losses could be spread widely and relatively painlessly rather than borne by the individual plaintiff or defendant.

Secondly, there was an intellectual shift. The acute individualism which had characterised Victorian England began to give way to a more communitarian approach: no longer was it obvious that an individual who caused harm to another while pursuing his own economic self-interest should be liable only if it could be shown that he had not taken reasonable care. Alongside this, legal commentators began to stress that negligence liability did not depend on a moral principle but on a social one; it was not based on something internal to the defendant but on a failure to live up to an external standard, and that external standard was something which could be determined by public policy. The American jurist Oliver Wendell Holmes was the principal proponent of this view,[187] and even before 1900 it had become so much part of common learning that it was being misunderstood by examination candidates.[188] As corporate and insured defendants became the norm judges and scholars, especially in America, came to formulate the principles of liability in wholly economic, non-moral, terms.[189]

Thirdly, this time affecting more the structure of liability than its incidence, the jury disappeared from the trial of negligence actions.[190] This occurred in three stages. First of all, the County Courts Acts provided that trial would be without jury in small cases, and might be without jury in other cases within the jurisdiction of the court (though either party had a right to demand a jury). In practice, jury trials in County Courts were very uncommon in any form of action, including negligence actions;[191] they were abolished in 1934.[192] Secondly, after the Judicature Acts of 1873–1875 it was possible for some negligence cases to be assigned to the Chan-

---

[187] Privilege, Malice, and Intent (1894) 8 Harv L R 1. For the contrary view see *J. Salmond,* Essays in Jurisprudence and Legal History (1891), 132.

[188] *Howe,* ed., Pollock-Holmes Letters, 1.46 (1893).

[189] Infra, section 6(d).

[190] There is a very substantial body of polemical literature relating to the abolition of jury trial. The arguments for its abolition are well put by Joseph Brown Q. C. in his address to the Social Science Association in 1882 (reprinted as Trial by Jury – Should it be Abolished? (1882) 74 Law Times 3, 23, 42). See too the First Interim Report of the Committee on Business of Courts (the Hanworth Committee) (P. P. 1932–1933 x 561).

[191] *R. M. Jackson,* The Incidence of Jury Trial During the Past Century (1937) 1 Modern Law Review 132, 144. (1933) 87 *Hansard* (House of Lords), col. 1050.

cery Division of the High Court; such cases would be heard without a jury.[193] Thirdly, and most significantly, after a prolonged stutter, the jury was to all intents and purposes abolished in actions brought in the King's (Queen's) Bench Division: trial by jury was made optional after the Judicature Acts of 1873–1875, though in actions sounding in tort the option generally appears to have been exercised;[194] temporary provisions restricting the right to trial by jury to a small number of situations (not including negligence) were in force from 1918 to 1925;[195] new rules of procedure were introduced in 1932;[196] and in 1933 the right to trial by jury in negligence actions was effectively abolished.[197] After this, practically all cases were tried by judge alone. In so far as the classic structure of the tort of negligence had largely been generated by the separation between judge and jury, the reintegration of the trial process brought about a reintegration of the elements of the tort of negligence.[198]

2. *The Structure of the Tort of Negligence*

So far as the structure of negligence liability was concerned, the fundamental question outstanding at the end of the nineteenth century was whether the multifarious duties of care could be knitted together into a single duty of care. Brett M. R. had begun the process of unification in *Heaven* v. *Pender* and *Le Lievre* v. *Gould,*[199] but had met with considerable judicial opposition. Through the first three decades of the twentieth century pressure – from academic lawyers rather than the judiciary[200] – built up for the recognition of such a test.

---

192 County Courts Act 1934, s. 91 (re-enacting County Courts (Amendment) Act 1934, s. 17).

193 Rules of the Supreme Court 1883, Order 36 rule 3.

194 Rules of the Supreme Court 1883, Order 36 rule 6. The graphs printed by Jackson (Incidence of Jury Trial (1937) 1 Modern Law Review 132, 134–135) conceal the differential incidence of jury trial in contractual and tortious actions. Information given to the Parliamentary Commission on Juries in 1913 suggests that actions in tort were still predominantly tried by jury: P. P. 1913 xxx q. 4568.

195 Juries Act 1918, s. 1; Administration of Justice Act 1920 s. 2; Jackson, Incidence of Jury Trial (1937) 1 Modern Law Review 132, 14 1. Jackson's graphs (134–135) indicate that jury trial (in all King's Bench cases) hovered around 10% between 1919 and 1922, rising to 30–35% after 1925.

196 Rules of the Supreme Court (New Procedure) 1932, introducing new Order 38A.

197 Administration of Justice (Miscellaneous Provisions) Act, s. 6, giving effect to the recommendations of the Hanworth Committee (supra, n. 190).

198 Infra, section 6(d).

199 (1883) 11 QBD 503, [1893] 1 QB 491; supra, section 3(b).

The turning point came with the well-known decision in *Donoghue* v. *Stevenson.*[201] The plaintiff's friend bought a bottle of ginger beer manufactured by the defendants, and gave it to the plaintiff. When she poured it over her ice cream, she discovered a decomposed snail at the bottom of the bottle, and suffered a strong physical and nervous reaction. She brought an action in negligence, and by a majority of three to two the House of Lords held that it was well-founded. In point of detail, this amounted substantially to a reversal of the line of cases stemming from *Winterbottom* v. *Wright*[202] and the approval of the decision (though hardly the reasoning) in *George* v. *Skivington;*[203] it was never afterwards doubted that the person injured by a defectively manufactured product might have an action against the negligent manufacturer.

There were three possible routes to this conclusion. Most minimally, it could simply have been said that the cases following *Winterbottom* v. *Wright* had been overruled, and that a duty of care was in fact owed by the manufacturer to the ultimate consumer. This would have been sufficient to explain the ultimate decision in the case. It would not, however, have involved any qualification of the traditional analysis in terms of a multiplicity of duties of care; nor would it have involved any qualification of the traditionally conservative 'incremental' approach to liability whereby the plaintiff was expected to demonstrate the existence of a duty of care by showing that the case fell within an already recognised duty situation or was very closely analogous to one. Such a minimalist approach was consistent with the speeches of Lord Thankerton and Lord Macmillan, and was the favoured interpretation of the case by contemporary commentators.[204] Most trenchant was the Oxford scholar P. A. Landon in the first post-*Donoghue* edition of *Pollock on Torts,* despite hints of a broader interpretation having begun to emerge; he expressed the hope that the case would be

---

200 See for example *Winfield,* History of Negligence in the Law of Torts (1926) 42 LQR 184; *Pollock,* Torts (13th edition, 1929), 21; *J. Salmond,* Torts (7th edition by W. T. S. Stallybrass, 1929), 63–70 (Excursus A).

201 [1932] AC 562. The issue arose on a preliminary issue, where the facts as alleged were assumed to be true. The case was a Scottish case, but the laws of England and Scotland were presumed to be the same. For the factual background of the case, see *A. Rodger,* Mrs Donoghue and Alfenus Varus [1988] Current Legal Problems 1.

202 (1842) 10 M & W 109; supra, n. 154.

203 (1869) LR 5 Ex 1; supra, n. 159.

204 See the notes on the case in (1932) 76 Solicitors' Journal 387; (1933) 5 Cambridge Law Journal 116; (1932) 173 Law Times 411 (though even this minimal interpretation was regarded as 'revolutionary'); (1932) 174 Law Times 399; (1932) 74 Law Journal 75; (1932) 10 Canadian Bar Review 478. See too *Farr* v. *Buttes Brothers* [1932] 2 KB 606, per Scrutton L. J.

regarded as 'an illustration of a new category of negligence and as nothing beyond that.'[205]

Secondly, *Donoghue* v. *Stevenson* could have been treated as accepting an approach based upon a multiplicity of duty situations, but without any requirement that new duty situations could be recognised only by very close analogy to duty situations which had previously been recognised. This was implicit in Lord Macmillan's speech, and in his central conclusion that 'The categories of negligence are never closed.'[206] Such an approach inevitably involved some element of generalisation, though Lord Macmillan himself was diffident about laying down any such principle.[207]

Finally, and most generally, *Donoghue* v. *Stevenson* might have involved the wholesale rejection of the analysis dependent upon a multiplicity of duties of care in favour of a single requirement of taking reasonable care. This was, famously, the approach of Lord Atkin:

> In English law there must be, and is, some general conception of relations giving rise to a duty of care, of which particular cases found in the books are instances. The liability for negligence, whether you style it as such or treat it as in other systems as a species of 'culpa', is no doubt based upon a general public sentiment of moral wrongdoing for which the offender must pay. But acts or omissions which any moral code would censure cannot in a practical world be treated so as to give a right to every person injured by them to demand relief In this way rules of law arise which limit the range of complainants and the extent of their remedy. The rule that you are to love your neighbour becomes, in law, you must not injure your neighbour; and the lawyer's question, Who is my neighbour? receives a restricted reply. You must take reasonable care to avoid acts or omissions which you can reasonably foresee would be likely to injure your neighbour. Who, then, in law is my neighbour? The answer seems to be – persons who are so closely and directly affected by my act that I ought reasonably to have them in contemplation as being so affected when I am directing my mind to the acts or omissions which are called in question.[208]

---

205 Torts (14th edition, 1939), vii, 344–347, especially 346 n.s. Pollock himself had cautiously welcomed a broader interpretation: (1933) 49 LQR 22. Oral tradition has it that Landon dismissed the case as 'the aberrant decision of a Celtic minority'.

206 [1932] AC 562, 619. The point was originally made specifically with reference to Scots law: *Rodger,* Lord Macmillan's Speech in Donoghue v. Stevenson (1992) 108 LQR 236, 242.

207 [1932] AC 562, 619: 'the law can refer only to the standards of the reasonable man in order to determine whether any particular relation gives rise to a duty to take care as between those who stand in that relation to each other.' The original version is even clearer: 'There is no absolute standard for determining this question, and no principle of law involved in it other than the principle of reasonableness' (*Rodger,* Lord Macmillan's Speech in Donoghue v. Stevenson (1992) 108 LQR 236, 258).

208 [1932] AC 562, 580.

This statement marks the quintessential generalisation of negligence in terms of the duty of care. The general definition of negligence, what would in the nineteenth century have been the principal question for the jury, is now bundled up as part of the duty; and foreseeability of harm, having made its move from the rules of remoteness in *Blyth* v. *Birmingham Waterworks in* 1856 has now found its home firmly in the definition of the duty of care.

In practice there was not a great deal of difference between the approaches of Lord Macmillan and Lord Atkin, for both of them allowed the law considerable flexibility to adapt to new situations. At a rhetorical level Lord Atkin's approach was particularly valuable, for it provided ready support for any conclusion which a judge wished to reach, and a useful starting-point for any academic analysis. As a matter of reality, though, it was Lord Macmillan's more careful approach that was followed.[209] Textbook writers, while paying lip-service to Lord Atkin's statement, still dealt with the law in terms of more or less discrete categories of duty-situation, albeit that they were couched at a more general level than they would have been in such a book as Beven's *Negligence in Law*.[210] Judges, too, although less hide-bound by previous precedents, did not expand the law into a whole range of new situations simply on the grounds that the defendant had carelessly caused foreseeable harm to the plaintiff.

Two types of case in particular stood in the way of the wholesale recognition of a general duty of care of the sort formulated by Lord Atkin: cases where a trespasser had been injured, and cases where financial loss had been suffered by reliance upon a negligent representation.

It had been accepted in the early nineteenth century that a negligent occupier should not normally be liable to an injured trespasser; but in a series of cases in which a trespassing person (or dog) had been injured or killed by a man-trap, spring-gun, or dog-spike (all contrivances designed to do harm to poachers and their dogs) it had been said that the law did not go so low as to permit such forms of inhumanity.[211] The specific issue in these cases was put to rest by statute,[212] so that the general principle was allowed to remain unquestioned. The courts were quick to allow the development of a number of legal mechanisms enabling them to treat trespassers in fact as licensees in law;[213] these narrowed down the sphere of applica-

---

209 *R. F. V. Heuston,* Donoghue v. Stevenson in Retrospect (1957) 20 Modern Law Review 1.

210 The last edition of Beven was published in 1928: by this time it had swelled to 1570 pages of text. The table of cases occupied a further 176 pages.

211 *Deane* v. *Clayton* (1817) 7 Taunt 489; *Ilott* v. *Wilkes* (1820) 3 B & Ald 304; *Bird* v. *Holbrook* (1828) 4 Bing 628.

212 Stat 7 & 8 Geo IV c. 18.

tion of the general principle without undermining it. More significant was the attack derived from *Donoghue* v. *Stevenson,* for so long as it was foreseeable that someone might trespass and foreseeable that they might be injured it could be argued that there was a duty of care imposed on the occupier. Such an argument did not meet with a warm reception in the 1950s,[214] but it was regarded more favourably in the 1960s, and was finally accepted by the House of Lords in 1971 when they introduced (or reintroduced) the rule that an occupier of land owed to a trespasser a duty of 'common humanity', no more than a reformulation of the duty to take reasonable (i. e. relatively low) care in the circumstances.[215]

After a brief flirtation in the wake of *Heaven* v. *Pender,* the Common Law had turned its face against allowing actions for negligent statements (as opposed to negligent acts or omissions).[216] The wider view of *Donoghue* v. *Stevenson,* though, contained no such limitation, and by the early 1950s it was being argued (unsuccessfully) that liability should be imposed.[217] As in the case of trespassers this was at first rejected, but in 1963 the House of Lords laid down that there was no relevant differences between causing loss by negligent statement and causing loss in some other way.[218] Thus an action was held to lie in principle against a bank which had negligently represented to the plaintiff that its customer was a good credit risk, as a result of which the plaintiff had allowed the customer's order to continue in place and had hence suffered loss.

Hedley Byrne v. *Heller* and *Herrington* v. *British Railways Board* removed the two largest obstacles to the acceptance of Lord Atkin's broad approach. By around 1970 the law of negligence was beginning to be conceptualised in terms of an ocean of liability for carelessly causing foreseeable harm, dotted with islands of non-liability,[219] rather than as a crowded archipeligo of individual duty-situations. Such an approach was first articulated by the courts in *Dorset Yacht Co* v. *Home Office,*[220] but its most sub-

---

213 e.g. *Lowery* v. *Walker* [1911] AC 10; *Pearson* v. *Coleman Bros* [1948] 2 KB 359; *Phipps* v. *Rochester Corporation* [1955) 1 QB 450.

214 See for example the astonished response of Glyn Jones J. to the suggestion: 'My God!' (*Cairns* v. *St Marylebone Borough Council* (1954) *The Times,* 8th December).

215 *Videan* v. *British Transport Commission* [1963] 2 QB 650; *Commissioner for Railways* v. *Quinlan* [1964] AC 1054; *British Railways Board* v. *Herrington* [1972] AC 877. See now the Occupiers Liability Act 1984.

216 Supra, section 3(b).

217 *Candler* v. *Crane Christmas & Co* [1951] KB I64.

218 *Hedley Byrne & Co Ltd* v. *Heller & Partners Ltd* [1964] AC 465.

219 For situations of non-liability, see for example *Rondel* v. *Worsley* [1969] 1 AC 191 (barrister); *Sirros* v. *Moore* [1975] QB 118 (judge); *Thorne* v. *University of London* [1966] 2 QB 237 (university examiners).

stantial formulation was by Lord Wilberforce in *Anns* v. *Merton London Borough Council:*

> [T]he question has to be approached in two stages. First, one has to ask whether, as between the alleged wrongdoer and the person who has suffered damage there is a sufficient relationship of proximity or neighbourhood such that, in the reasonable contemplation of the former, carelessness on his part may be likely to cause damage to the latter – in which case a prima facie duty of care arises. Secondly, if the first question is answered affirmatively, it is necessary to consider whether there are any considerations which ought to negative, or to reduce or limit the scope of the duty or the class of person to whom it is owed or the damage to which a breach of it gives rise.[221]

Liability in negligence arises from the careless causation of foreseeable harm, unless there is some reason of 'policy' to reject it.

Subsequently to the decisions in *Dorset Yacht* and *Anns,* there has been an apparent backlash. First, there has been some backtracking into the approach associated with Lord Macmillan in *Donoghue* v. *Stevenson,* requiring greater fidelity towards previous decisions than the general approach of Lord Atkin would demand. Thus, it has been said, the courts should not recognise whole new areas of liability at a single stroke; rather they should proceed 'incrementally' from previously-recognised duty situations.[222]

Secondly, the House of Lords has several times stressed that a duty-situation arises not merely from the foreseeability of harm, but that there is in addition a requirement of 'proximity'.[223] Such an idea was contained in the notion of 'neighbourhood' found in Lord Atkin's speech in *Donoghue* v. *Stevenson,* derived from *Heaven* v. *Pender* and *Le Lievre* v. *Gould*[224] (and, more distantly, in Buller's *Nisi Prius*); in truth, though, like the idea of 'foreseeability', it is the governing idea of remoteness of damage which had been translated into the definition of breach of duty (and the very idea of negligence)[225] in the nineteenth century, and further translated into the definition of the duty of care in the twentieth. It is doubtful whether it adds a great deal to the formulation in terms of prima facie liability, subject to exceptions grounded in 'policy'.[226] Both have the same function, the identification of situations where there is no liability in negligence notwithstand-

---

220 [1970] AC 1004, 1027.

221 [1978] AC 728, 751.

222 *Sutherland Shire Council* v. *Heyman* (1985) 157 CLR 424, 483; *Murphy* v. *Brentwood District Council* [1991] 1 AC 398.

223 *Peabody Donation Fund (Governors* of) v *Sir Lindsay Parkinson & Co* [1985] AC 210; *Caparo Industries plc* v. *Dickman* [1990] 2 AC 605; *Marc Rich* v. *Bishop Rock Marine* [1996] 1 AC 211.

224 Supra, section 3(b), section 6(b).

225 Supra, section 3(b).

ing that foreseeable harm has been caused,[227] the only difference seems to be that where the requirement of 'proximity' is used the onus is on the plaintiff to show why liability should arise, while where 'policy' is used it is for the defendant to show why it should not.[228]

3. *Kinds of Harm*

Before *Donoghue* v. *Stevenson,* it was essentially beyond question that the only type of harm compensated by the tort of negligence was physical injury to the person or property, though this was to a large extent concealed by the law's focus on the way in which injury was caused rather than the kind of injury. *Donoghue* v. *Stevenson* demanded no such limitation, though; and as the range of liability expanded in the 1960s and 1970s (in terms of liability to trespassers and for statements, for example) so too was it argued that the tort could extend to different kinds of harm, in particular psychiatric injury and purely economic loss.

Nineteenth-century law was heavily focused on physical injury to the person or to property. Mental illness was largely outside the legal domain, and it seems to have been felt that it was not a proper subject of legal remedy.[229] Equally, when the issue arose, there was reluctance to countenance claims for injury (whether mental or physical) brought about by shock rather than by physical impact.[230] In a series of cases from the end of the nineteenth century to the middle of the twentieth there was gradually (and very cautiously) laid down a set of guidelines for the recovery of illness brought about by shock.[231] In all of these cases the injury was almost

---

226 e.g. *M. H. McHugh,* Neighbourhood, Proximity and Reliance, in: *P. D. Finn,* ed., Essays on Torts (Sydney, 1989), 5. The point is well made by Lord Wilberforce in *McLoughlin* v. *O'Brien* [1983] AC 410, 420.

227 As well as the 'psychiatric injury' and 'pure economic loss' cases dealt with below, this tool has been particularly important in limiting the private-law liability of public bodies: e.g. *Yuen Kun Yeu* v. *Attorney-General of Hong Kong* [1988] AC 175; X v. *Bedfordshire County Council* [1995] 2 AC 633; *Stovin* v. *Wise* [1996] AC 923. The relevant point is made sharply by J. A. Weir, (1982) 2 Oxford Journal of Legal Studies 440.

228 *Stovin* v. *Wise* [1996] AC 923, 949, per Lord Hoffman.

229 *Lynch* v. *Knight* (1861) 9 HLC 577, 598 (not a case of negligence). See Mental Suffering as an Element of Damages in Actions of Negligence (1881) 24 Albany Law Journal 144. The discussion in *Beven,* Negligence (4th edition), 61–62 is particularly clear.

230 *Victorian Railway Commissioners* v. *Coultas* (1888) 13 App Cas 222 (see (1888) 23 Law Journal 390).

231 *Pugh* v. *London, Bristol and South Coast Railway Co* [1896] 2 QB 248; *Dulieu* v. *White* [1901] 2 KB 669; *Yates* v. *South Kirby Collieries* [1910] 2 KB 538; *Hambrook* v. *Stokes Bros* [1925] 1 KB 150; *Bourhill* v. *Young* [1943] AC 92.

undeniably physical; it was only the way in which it had been precipitated which was problematical. Only in one case was recovery allowed for the 'form of illness which is known as shock'.[232] In 1953 the cases of causation by shock began to be reinterpreted as cases where the shock – or severe emotional distress – was the injury complained of.[233] This process of reinterpretation culminated in the 1980s, as the apparently old-fashioned 'nervous shock' was abandoned in favour of the more up-to-date terminology of 'pychiatric injury'.[234] Most recently the House of Lords has held that where the plaintiff is the 'primary victim' there is no difference between psychiatric and physical injury (and that the carefully-crafted limitations derived from the causative analysis of 'nervous shock' should no longer apply), revealing the continued potency of the general principle of *Donoghue* v. *Stevenson* to expand the tort of negligence into hitherto excluded areas.[235]

More important was the extension to purely economic loss. When the nineteenth century judges were (briefly) willing to countenance liability for negligent statements it did not seem to concern them that the loss suffered was purely economic: nineteenth-century law was concerned with how loss was suffered than with the kind of loss. Nor was it a matter of concern to the House of Lords in *Hedley Byrne* v. *Heller*. In these cases the loss suffered by the plaintiffs was a genuine financial loss: as a result of the defendants' negligence they no longer had money that they had once had. 'Pure economic loss', however, was not in its nature so limited; it could, without much twisting be extended to include loss of expected commercial profits.[236] Restrictive rules of the law of contract, such as the doctrines of consideration and privity of contract, could be side-stepped by suing in negligence;[237] behind a poor or insolvent wrongdoer it would frequently be pos-

---

232 *Owens* v. *Liverpool Corporation* [1939] 1 KB 394. The case, involving a road accident in which a coffin was overturned during a funeral procession, was sufficiently anomalous that no great weight could be put on it.

233 *King* v. *Phillips* [1953] 1 KB 429. The antinomy physical injury – emotional shock is clearest in the judgment of Denning L. J. (at 438–439).

234 *McLoughlin* v. *O'Brien* [1983] AC 410; *Alcock* v. *Chief Constable of South Yorkshire* [1992] 1 AC 310. The equivalence of nervous shock and psychiatric illness is treated as axiomatic by the Law Commission: Report no. 249, Liability for Psychiatric Illness (1998), especially at p. 9.

235 *Page* v. *Smith* [1996] 1 AC 155.

236 Academic commentators have been curiously willing to discuss 'pure economic loss' without ever defining precisely what is meant (see for example *B. J. Stapleton,* 'Duty of Care and Economic Loss (1991) 107 LQR 249). Cf. Oliver L. J. in *The Aliakmon*. [1985] QB 350, 375, 377–378.

237 *Hedley Byrne* v. *Heller* [1964] AC 465 (no consideration); *Junior Books* v. *Veitchi* [1983] AC 520 (no privity). See generally *B. S. Markesinis,* An Expanding Tort Law – Price of a Rigid Contract Law (1987) 103 LQR 354.

sible to find an apparently wealthy business or public authority which, by taking more care, might have been able to prevent the damage occurring, and on whom liability could be fixed;[238] the take-over of a company whose financial health was less than had been expected might lead to an attempt to sue the auditors who had prepared the company's accounts;[239] commercial speculators might sue for loss of the profits which they might have made had their speculations been successful.[240] The extension into these areas was temporarily checked by the Court of Appeal in the early 1970s,[241] but after the decision in *Anns* v. *Merton* there was a short-lived expansive phase, firmly nipped in the bud by the House of Lords in 1991.[242] None the less, it has still been possible to hold a solicitor liable to intended beneficiaries when, as a result of the solicitor's negligence, a will was not drawn up before the death of the testator.[243]

4. Return to the Eighteenth Century: Decomposition of the Tort of Negligence

In the eighteenth century, the incidence of tortious liability was almost exclusively within the domain of the jury, so far as can be seen applying no criteria more sophisticated than that the defendant 'ought' to be liable for the harm suffered by the plaintiff. The characteristic structure of the nineteenth century – duty, breach, causation – was generated by the separation between judge and jury; as the jury came to be completely replaced by the judge so this structure broke down and the tort of negligence decomposed – or recomposed – into its eighteenth-century unity.

Already in the nineteeth century the process of decomposition of the tort of negligence was becoming visible. The definition of negligence and the question what constituted a breach of duty had already begun to move into the judicial domain of the duty of care; so too had the issue of remoteness of damage and foreseeability.[244] The generalising approach of *Donoghue* v. *Stevenson* accentuated this tendency; and with the disappearance of the jury after 1933 any need which had once existed to separate out the various elements of the tort of negligence had disappeared. So marked was the quest for homogeneity within the tort that the foreseeability of harm, translated

238 *Anns* v. *Merton London Borough Council* [1978] AC 728; *Murphy* v. *Brentwood District Council* [1991] 1 AC 398.

239 *Caparo* v. *Dickman* [1990] 2 AC 605.

240 *Muirhead* v. *Industrial Tank Specialities* [1986] QB 507.

241 *Spartan Steel* v. *Martin & Co* [1973] QB 27.

242 *Murphy* v. *Brentwood District Council* [1991] 1 AC 398.

243 *White* v. *Jones* [1995] AC 207.

244 Supra, section 3(b), section 3(c).

from the question of remoteness of damage into the question of duty in *Smith* v. *London and South Western Railway Co* in 1870, was reintegrated as the test for remoteness in 1961: it would have been irrational to allow foreseeability to determine whether there was a duty without at the same time laying down that only foreseeable damage could be recovered.[245] By the 1970s judges were beginning to admit that the elements of duty, breach, and remoteness were essentially interchangeable:

> The more I think about these cases, the more difficult I find it to put each into its proper pigeon-hole. Sometimes I say: 'There was no duty.' In others I say: 'The damage was too remote.' So much so that I think the time has come to discard those tests that have proved so elusive.[246]

> The truth is that all these three – duty, remoteness and causation – are all devices by which the courts limit the range of liability for negligence.[247]

By 1980 the 'wilderness of single instances' which had characterised the tort of negligence a century earlier[248] had been largely remoulded into the single principle formulated in Buller's *Nisi Prius* a century before that: 'Every man ought to take reasonable care that he does not injure his neighbour'.

The nineteenth-century tort had been based on the moral principle that a person should be liable – and only liable – for the failure to take reasonable care. This, as has been seen, was inherently narrower than the undifferentiated notion of 'fault', of which it was only one example. Gradually, around the beginning of the twentieth century, the moral base began to be abandoned. 'There is a strong and growing tendency,' observed Dean Roscoe Pound in 1914, 'where there is no blame on either side, to ask, in view of the exigencies of social justice who can best bear the loss, and hence to shift the loss by creating liability where there has been no fault.'[249] By mid-century, in America, the idea of negligence had been (or was being) emptied of all its moral content in favour of a value-neutral economic test.[250] While English law did not follow so far in the direction indicated by economics, the moral dimension of the tort none the less sub-

---

[245] *The Wagon Mound (No. 1)* [1961] AC 388. In practice there has been difficulty in holding to this impeccably logical position: see *Page* v. *Smith* [1996) 1 AC 155.

[246] *Spartan Steel* v. *Martin & Co* [1973] QB 27, 37, per Lord Denning M. R.

[247] *Lamb* v. *Camden Council* [1981] QB 625, 636, per Lord Denning M. R. (under the subheading, 'The Truth').

[248] Supra, section 3(b).

[249] The End of Law (1914) 27 Harvard Law Review 195, 233.

[250] See most notably *United States* v. *Carroll Towing* (1947) 159 F.2d 169 (Judge Learned Hand). This spawned further economic analysis: *G. Calabresi* and *J. T. Hirschoff*, Toward a Test for Strict Liability in Torts (1972) 81 Yale Law Journal 1055.

stantially disappeared. The judges have taken over the result-oriented approach with which Baron Bramwell castigated the jury.[251] Variable levels of liability, in no way necessarily connected to the care that could reasonably have been expected of the defendant, came to be imposed behind the facade of 'negligence'. A relatively low standard came to be demanded of the medical profession,[252] fuelled by fears about the risk of defensive medicine and the cost of health care if heavy damages were frequently awarded to the victims of doctors' misjudgements; liability of (compulsorily insured) car drivers became to all intents and purposes strict;[253] so too did the liability of the manufacturers of defective products, by a mixture of procedural and evaluative factors.[254] In Australia (though not yet in England) the strict liability associated with *Rylands* v *Fletcher* has been reabsorbed back into the main stream of negligence liability.[255] Moreover, the dissolution of the moral basis of negligence liability washed away the problems of justifying vicarious liability which had dogged the nineteenth century. Just as liability can be imposed on individuals independently of moral fault, it can equally be imposed on their employers: the only question is whether the (human) wrongdoer was acting as part of the defendant's organisation.[256] Vicarious liability (in the form of the liability of corporate defendants) has become the primary example of negligence liability (at least outside the field of (insured) motor accidents): no better witness is needed of the etching away of the moral base of liability[257].

---

[251] Supra, n. 153.

[252] *Whitehouse* v. *Jordan* [1981] 1 WLR 246. See *I. Kennedy and A. Grubb,* Medical Law (2nd edition, 1994), 397–565.

[253] *Roberts* v. *Ramsbottom* [1980] 1 WLR 823; see too *Nettleship* v. *Weston* [1971] 2 QB 691 (ruling out defence of consent despite consent of defendant); *Morgans* v. *Launchbury* [1973] AC 127 (special rules of vicarious liability, apparently to allow victim of a road accident to take advantage of owner's insurance policy. But see *Mansfield* v. *Weetabix* [1998] 1 WLR 1263.

[254] *Grant* v. *Australian Knitting Mills Ltd* [1936] AC 85 (reversal of burden of proof). See generally C. J. *Miller and P. A. Lovell,* Product Liability (1977) 171–190; the Common law has now been effectively superseded by explicitly strict liability: Consumer Protection Act 1987.

[255] *Burnie Port Authority* v. *General Jones* (1994) 120 ALR 42.

[256] *Cassidy* v. *Ministry of Health* [1951] 2 KB 343; *Roe* v. *Ministry of Health* [1954] 2 QB 66. It is curious to observe that most modern writers persist in reproducing nineteenth-century law.

[257] A paradoxical consequence of this has been that as vicarious/corporate liability has become the norm in actions for negligence, suffusing the whole of the tort, the analysis of vicarious liability as an independent topic has become fossilised in the nineteenth-century terminology of the liability of masters (sic) for the torts of their servants (sic).

In sum, we might conclude, all that remains of the divided structure and the moral individualism of the nineteenth-century tort of negligence is its language, though there is still some working out to be done in terms of the recoverability of pure economic loss. History, sadly, avoids neat closures.

HECTOR L. MACQUEEN and W. DAVID H. SELLAR[1]

History of Negligence in Scots Law

Introduction

Although something will be said of the earlier law, the main focus of this study is the period from 1795 until 1932. 1795 marks the date of the case of *Gardner* v. *Ferguson,*[2] generally regarded as the first case in the modern Scots law of negligence, while 1932 is the date of the decision of the House of Lords in the celebrated Scottish appeal of *Donoghue* v. *Stevenson,* the snail in the bottle case, in which Lord Atkin formulated the legal duty to take care not to injure another in terms of "neighbourhood" and "reasonable contemplation".[3]

Unlike English law, at the end of the eighteenth century the Scots law of negligence appeared to be developing in conformity with a recognisably Civilian pattern. A basis was provided by the Roman text on liability for property damage, the *lex Aquilia,* as developed in the medieval and early modern *ius commune* and by the Natural Lawyers to provide a compensatory remedy for any form of *damnum iniuria datum* (damage caused by wrongfulness). Wrongfulness might be either *dolus* (intentional wrongdoing) or *culpa* (fault), the latter of which had three degrees – *lata* (gross),

---

[1] Faculty of Law, University of Edinburgh. We are grateful to Ralph Riddiough and Murray Earle for research assistance in the preparation of this contribution, and to our Faculty and department for the financial assistance which made their employment possible. We are also indebted to the Faculty of Advocates, Edinburgh, for permission to consult the unpublished Session Papers and other material held in the Advocates' Library, and to Angus Stewart QC, Keeper of the Library, and Catherine Smith, Senior Librarian, for invaluable assistance with that research.

[2] Unreported. See further below, text at notes 55–59.

[3] 1932 SC (HL) 31; 1932 SLT 317; [1932] AC 562. For fuller accounts of this case which, it is said, has never been properly reported, see *A. F. Rodger,* Mrs Donoghue and Alfenus Varus, Current Legal Problems 41 (1988) pp. 1–22; *W. W. McBryde,* Donoghue v. Stevenson: the story of the "snail in the bottle" case, in Obligations in Context: Essays in Honour of David M. Walker, ed A. J. Gamble (Edinburgh, 1990), pp. 13–32; *P. T. Burns and S. J. Lyons* (eds), Donoghue v. Stevenson and the Modern Law of Negligence: The Paisley Papers (Vancouver, 1991); *A. F. Rodger,* Lord Macmillan's speech in Donoghue v. Stevenson, Law Quarterly Review 108 (1992) pp. 236–259. *J. D. Gordan III,* The American authorities in Donoghue v. Stevenson, Law Quarterly Review 115 (1999) pp. 183–186.

levis (small), or *levissima* (least or slightest). *Culpa* was to be measured by the standards of the diligent or prudent *paterfamilias*.[4] One hundred years later, however, Scots law appeared to be closer to the English Common law. By 1931 it was a matter of agreement between counsel in *Donoghue* v. *Stevenson* before the House of Lords that Scots law and English law were the same in the area of negligence in question, and the case proceeded on that basis. It is one of the objects of this paper to seek to explain this apparent shift in the orientation of Scots law from Civil to Common law.

One of the features which traditionally distinguishes the history of the Common law in this area from the Civil law tradition is the fact that the Common law remained until quite recently a law of torts, rather than a law of tort, whereas systems within the Civil law tradition had moved much earlier towards the concept of a general action for wrongs set within the wider framework of obligations – although this has not prevented the recognition of specific delicts. The development of the Common law has been founded on actions – notably those of trespass and case – rather than deduced from general principles. In this respect Scots law, both before and after 1795, and before and after *Donoghue,* has conformed more closely to the Civilian norm, rather than to the Common law. Scots law recognises a law of delict rather than a law of torts; and since at least the time of James Dalrymple, Viscount Stair, who published his *Institutions of the Law of Scotland* in 1681, it has distinguished between delict and contract in the context of a general scheme of obligations, recognising delict as an "obediential" obligation, and contract as the prime example of a "conventional" obligation. The word "tort" has, indeed, no meaning in Scots law, which knows neither "trespass" nor "case", nor a "tort" of "negligence". In Scots law the word "negligence" has not become a legal term of art, as in English law, but retains its sense in ordinary speech.

Another feature often said to mark a difference between the Common law and the Civilian tradition in the field of negligence is the recognition by the Common law of a "duty of care" as a prerequisite for a successful action. The notion of a duty of care emerged in English law as the nineteenth century progressed, the case of *Heaven* v. *Pender*[5] in 1883 being seen as an important milestone, and became firmly embedded in the jurisprudence of negligence early in the twentieth century. In this respect, however, modern Scots law is in line with English law: it too recognises a duty of care as an essential prerequisite for a successful action on negligence.[6] This recognition of the requirement of a duty of care, therefore, may pro-

---

4 On the *lex Aquilia* and its later development see *R. Zimmermann,* The Law of Obligations: Roman Foundations of the Civil Law (Cape Town, 1990; paperback edn, 1996), pp. 953–1049.

5 (1883) 11 QBD 503 (CA). See further below, text at notes 128–130.

vide a clue towards Scots law's apparent change of orientation. It has been suggested that the acceptance by Scots law of the concept of a duty of care came as the result of undue and unwelcome English influence.[7] This paper, however, raises the possibility that the concept came to be articulated in Scots law, not through the undue influence of English law, but as the result of a gradual convergence between the two systems.

The history of the law of delict in Scotland has attracted a good deal of scholarly attention over the last half-century, making the main lines of development fairly clear.[8] This scholarship makes it possible to divide that history into three major periods. The earliest of these lasts until the end of the seventeenth century and the first publication of Stair's *Institutions* in 1681, and can be characterised as being dominated by native customary law, albeit occasionally shot through with Civilian learning. Stair's *Institutions* inaugurated a second period in which Scots law came to engage more clearly with the Civilian tradition and the *lex Aquilia,* although the older customary law was by no means eliminated. Whereas the earlier law had been concerned primarily with the nature of the harm, in the eighteenth

---

[6] The duty of care appears at the beginning of all the standard modern expositions of negligence in Scots law: see e.g. *D. M. Walker,* The Law of Delict in Scotland, (1st edn, Edinburgh, 1966) (2nd edn, Edinburgh, 1981) ch. 7; *W. J. Stewart,* Delict (1st edn, Edinburgh, 1989, 2nd edn, Edinburgh, 1993), ch. 4; *J. M. Thomson,* Delictual Liability (2nd edn, Edinburgh, 1999), ch. 3; The Laws of Scotland: Stair Memorial Encyclopaedia, vol 15 (1996) paras. 252–310 (*K. M. Norrie*); *F. McManus* and *E. Russell,* Delict: a comprehensive guide to the law (London, 1998), chs. 2–8. See also *W. A. Wilson,* Introductory Essays in Scots Law (2nd edn, Edinburgh, 1984), whose analysis of negligence does not begin with a requirement of a duty of care and considers whether it is necessary, before concluding that the absence of such a duty is the best way of explaining cases where there is no liability (e.g. pure omissions, animals, financial damage and nervous shock) even though all other requirements are met.

[7] See in particular the third part of *R. Black,* A historical survey of delictual liability in Scotland for personal injuries and death, Comparative and International Law Journal of Southern Africa 8 (1975) pp. 46–70 (henceforth *Black I*), 189–211 (*Black II*), 318–343 (*Black III*), and 9 (1976) pp. 57–80 (*Black IV*).

[8] In addition to the materials already cited in note 3, and *Black I–IV* (note 7), see in particular *D. M. Walker,* The development of reparation, Juridical Review 64 (1952) pp. 101–34; *H. McKechnie,* Delict and quasi-delict, in Introduction to Scottish Legal History, ed. G. C. H. Paton (Stair Society, Edinburgh, 1958), pp. 265–279; *G. MacCormack,* Culpa tenet suos auctores: the application of a principle in Scots law, Juridical Review 18 (1973), pp. 159–172; *G. MacCormack,* Culpa in the Scots law of reparation, Juridical Review 19 (1974), pp. 13–29; *A. D. M. Forte,* Reparation for pure economic loss: an historical perspective of Scots law in the seventeenth and eighteenth centuries, Journal of Legal History 8 (1987) pp. 3–17; *D. W. McKenzie* and *R. Evans-Jones,* The development of remedies for personal injuries and death, in The Civil Law Tradition in Scotland, ed. R. Evans-Jones (Stair Society, Edinburgh, 1995), pp. 277–309.

century the focus shifted increasingly to the conduct which had led up to the harm. The third period begins with a series of court decisions between 1795 and 1812 which allowed an action based loosely on the *lex Aquilia* and the concept of *culpa* in respect of personal injuries and deaths arising from faults of omission. As the nineteenth century progressed, the Scottish courts came to be increasingly aware of developments in England, and in both jurisdictions the language of duty, reasonableness and foreseeability came to be employed. This was to culminate in 1932 with *Donoghue* v. *Stevenson*. Since that case, English decisions on negligence have been cited ever more freely in Scotland, and the Civilian roots of the concept of *culpa* have been largely forgotten.

The Early Law

Much of the early history of what we now call delict is obscure, and here we can only touch, with considerable risk of over-simplification, on those points which appear to have been significant in the later development of the law. The forms of action found in the medieval royal courts included one for breach of the king's protection which was closely analogous to the contemporary trespass action in England.[9] Under the action, damages were recoverable by the pursuer. By the fifteenth century, however, this general remedy seems to have broken down into a set of nominate actions dealing with particular types of situation. Also, although the medieval law distinguished between civil and criminal pleas, the distinction was not always a clear one. An example of particular importance is the action of assythment.[10] Here the claim was for compensation in respect of any homicide or other injury to the person. In the later law assythment was due only when the act causing death or injury was a crime, but in the earlier law the emphasis was on harm done rather than on motivation: all homicide was effectively regarded as criminal, at least as regards the requirement of compensation. In the mature sixteenth-century action the claim could be made in either the criminal or the civil courts. The kindred of the homicide victim, to whom the action was available, included, but was not limited to, spouses and children. The damages recoverable fulfilled the dual function of compensating the pursuers in respect of patrimonial loss suffered, and also the "pacifying of their rancor",[11] that is, assuaging the desire for

---

[9] *A. Harding,* The medieval brieves of protection and the development of the common law, Juridical Review 11 (1966), pp. 115–149; *H. L. MacQueen,* Common Law and Feudal Society in Medieval Scotland (Edinburgh, 1993), pp. 127–129.

[10] See *Black I* (note 7); also *J. Wormald,* Bloodfeud, kindred and government in early modern Scotland, Past and Present 87 (1980), pp. 54–97.

[11] The Practicks of Sir James Balfour of Pittendreich, ed. P. G. B. McNeill (2 vols, Stair Society, Edinburgh, 1962–3), ii, p. 516.

vengeance. This latter element was to have its effect in the development of the modern law as regards "*solatium*".[12] It is perhaps worth noting in passing that the word "assythment" also continued to be used in its original and primary meaning of "satisfaction" or "compensation" in general. This ambiguity in terminology was to cause some confusion in the nineteenth century.

The word "negligence" does appear in the early law, but as an element in some particular claim rather than as a general basis for liability.[13] A statute of 1426 in the Scots language provides an early example.[14] This requires magistrates in burghs to guard against the danger of fire. If they were "negligent in the execution hereof", they were to be fined [s. 1]. The same statute distinguishes between fire arising "of purpos", that is intentionally, and arising "of mysgovernance" [s. 5]. The statute also uses the language of foreseeability, setting out that there is to be no punishment if fire arises "of suddande case that may nocht be forsene" [s. 7]. There is later supporting evidence of the relevance of negligence in the two types of particular claim covered by the statute: in respect of damage by fire and breach of duty by officials. An especially interesting case in 1685 arising from fire damage is considered in the next section.[15] There is also material on negligence in the care of animals and ships; with regard to the latter, it was said by sixteenth-century writers that an action lay on the analogy of the *lex Aquilia* for allowing one vessel to collide with another.[16]

Stair and the Eighteenth Century

The point of departure for the development of the learned law relating to delictual liability in Scotland came with the *Institutions* of Stair, first published in 1681.[17] Stair's account should be set first within his general theory of law and especially his theory of the law of obligations. The *Insti-*

---

[12] See further below, text at notes 75–78.

[13] See *McKechnie* (note 8), pp. 266–70.

[14] Acts of the Parliaments of Scotland [APS], edd. T. Thomson and C. Innes (12 vols, Edinburgh, 1814–75), ii, p. 12 (ch. 23).

[15] See further below, text at note 50.

[16] On this and other early recognition of liability based on the *lex Aquilia*, see *McKechnie* (note 8), pp. 270–1. Further on liability for animals see *D. L. Carey Miller*, The Scottish institutional writers on animal liability: civilian or scienter? Juridical Review 19 (1974) pp. 1–12; *B. S. Jackson*, Liability for animals in Scottish legal literature: from the auld lawes to the sixteenth century, Irish Jurist 10 (1975), pp. 334–51; *B. S. Jackson*, Liability for animals in Scottish legal literature: from Stair to the modern law, Juridical Review 22 (1977) pp. 139–63.

[17] We have used the tercentenary or 6th edition (based on the 2nd of 1693) edited by D. M. Walker (Edinburgh, 1981).

tutions set out a systematic account of the private law of Scotland, strongly influenced by natural law theory and, in particular, by the *De Jure Belli et Pacis* of Grotius.[18] Stair drew on the Civil law, not as a direct source of Scots law, but for its equity and expediency (*aequum et bonum*). Equity lay at the root of the law, and was constituted by equality amongst persons, "from that general moral principle, *Quod tibi fieri non vis, alteri ne feceris*".[19] Where inequality arose, restitution – that is, restoration of the former equality – was required. The fourfold Roman division of obligations as *ex contractu, quasi ex contractu, ex maleficio* and *quasi ex maleficio* was rejected by Stair,[20] who replaced it with a distinction drawn from theology, that between "conventional obligations", based upon the "will, engagement and consent" of the parties, and "obediential obligations", "which are put upon men by the will of God, not by their own will, and so are most part natural, as introduced by the law of nature, before any addition made by engagement, and are such as we are bound to perform solely by our obedience to God".[21] Amongst the obediential obligations was to be placed the obligation of reparation, arising from delinquence, i.e. delict.[22] Stair elaborated his position as follows:

> That obligations of delinquence are introduced by the law of nature, the suffrage of all men and all nations will evince, who do everywhere acknowledge the reparation of damages, and punishment of crimes and injuries, ... The obligation of delinquence then ... is twofold: either that which relateth to God, or that which relateth to man ... the power of exaction of reparation of his damage is man's for himself, but the power of exacting punishment is in God ... It is manifest and agreed by all, that, though in all damages done to man there are also punishments which may be inflicted by God, yet where the matter is chiefly man's interest, and so reparable to him, none will think it is a duty, in all of these cases, to inflict vengeance on such ... But our purpose here being only to insist in private rights, we shall not follow these [*cases which involve punishment*] ... but shall return to the private rights of men, arising to them by delinquence, of exacting reparation of their damages inferred thereby.[23]

Stair went on to reject the Roman categories of delinquence, indicating that he would deal with obligations "as they are known by the terms in our law";[24] but as a preliminary he offered some generalisations about the

[18] On this influence see *W. M. Gordon,* Stair, Grotius and the sources of Stair's Institutions, in Satura Roberto Feenstra, edd. J. A. Ankum, J. E. Spruit and F. B. J. Wubbe (Freiburg, 1985), pp. 571–83.

[19] Institutions, 1.1.6.

[20] Ibid, I.3.2.

[21] Ibid, I.3.3.

[22] Ibid, I.9 (chapter entitled "Reparation, where, of Delinquences and Damages thence arising").

[23] Ibid, I.9.1–2.

[24] Ibid, I.9.4.

"several rights and enjoyments" by which "damages and delinquences may be esteemed".[25] The list of five interests which he gives – (1) life, members and health; (2) liberty; (3) fame, reputation and honour; (4) content, delight or satisfaction ("*pretium affectionis* in the civil law"); (5) in goods and possession – is clearly influenced by Grotius.[26] In language with an Aquilian echo, Stair defines damage as "*damnum, a demendo* because it diminisheth or taketh away something from another, which of right he had",[27] and concludes his generalisations with a comment on the content of the obligation of reparation: "Reparation is either by restitution of the same thing ... or where that cannot be, by giving the like value ... if none be found fitter, reparation must be by money".[28] His wording makes clear the extent to which Stair was indebted to the traditions of the *ius commune,* and in particular the Canon law, in his conceptualisation of the obligation of reparation.[29]

Stair next turns "to the obligations by delinquence, which are civilly cognoscible by our custom, according to their known names and titles in our law".[30] He goes on:

> These are either general, having no particular name or designation: and such are pursued under the general names of damage and interest. Which hath as many branches and specialties, as there can be valuable and reparable damages: besides those of a special name and nature, which are chiefly these, assythment, extortion, circumvention, spuilzie, intrusion, ejection, molestation, breach of arrestment, deforcement, contravention, forgery.[31]

The significance of this passage has been the subject of debate. The received wisdom until recently was that the innominate "general" action for compensation, (that is, for damage and interest), could not be seen as the origin in Scots law of a general principle of liability for negligence. McKechnie argued that for Stair reparation was primarily the civil aspect of crime, that all his nominate delicts concerned intentional injuries, and

---

25 Ibid.

26 See *R. Feenstra,* Grotius' doctrine of liability for negligence, in this volume. Grotius lists life, body, freedom, honour and property. This also corresponds closely to the list of protected interests later adopted in the BGB: see further *W. Ernst,* Negligence in 19th Century Germany, and *P. Mossler,* The discussion on general clause or numerus clausus during the preparation of the German Civil Code, both in this volume resp. p. 341–360 and 361–390.

27 Institutions, I.9.3. See further on this passage *Gordon* (note 18), pp. 577–8.

28 Institutions, I.9.4.

29 See in particular *J. Hallebeek,* Negligence in medieval Roman law, and *H. Dondorp,* Crime and punishment: negligentia for the canonists and moral theologians, both in this volume.

30 Institutions, I.9.5.

31 Ibid, I.9.6. By "damage and interest" Stair refers to the long established Civilian action for compensation for patrimonial loss.

that his work contained no general treatment of negligence; in particular, that no formulation was made of a general principle of liability for omissions, and that the only detailed treatment of personal injuries was under the head of assythment, where liability only arose if the perpetration of the injury was a crime. McKechnie concluded that one should not "read into a 17th century work the ideas of a later age".[32]

This argument has been countered, however, by Donna McKenzie and Robin Evans-Jones who take the view that Stair envisaged two separate actions for personal injury or death: assythment certainly, but also the general claim for damage and interest.[33] They make a number of convincing points in support of their position:

(1) While for Stair assythment arose from "slaughter" and "mutilation", he framed the right to reparation for injury to "life, members and health" in much more neutral terms.

(2) Assythment was available to the injured party or, in the case of death, to the wife, children or nearest of kin. Reparation for injury to life, members and health was available, more narrowly, to "those who were entertained and maintained by his life, as his wife and children".

(3) While assythment contained much that was penal, reparation for injury to life, members and health is compensatory only – "either *lucrum cessans* or *damnum emergens* ... the loss any man hath in the expense of his cure, or the loss of his labour, and industry in his affairs"...[34]

(4) The passage quoted earlier from Institutions I.9.6 draws an explicit distinction between assythment and the general action for damage and interest.

(5) As indeed McKechnie recognised,[35] Stair's contemporary Sir George Mackenzie also formulated a general principle of reparation arising from "committing malefices", which gave rise to a "reipersecutory"[36]) action "by which we pursue that *quod patrimonio nostro abest* – commonly called damage and interest".

We agree that Stair did indeed envisage a general action for reparation based upon liability for delinquence. It is not clear, however, just how far beyond the realm of the criminal and/or intentional he was prepared to take

---

32 *McKechnie* (note 8), pp. 273–4.

33 *McKenzie* and *Evans-Jones* (note 8), passim.

34 Again, note that this exemplification of the loss to be repaired as medical expenses and loss of earnings is drawn straight from the traditions of the canon law (see *Dondorp*, note 29, p. 109).

35 *McKechnie* (note 8), p. 274.

36 I.e, compensatory rather than penal.

the concept of "delinquence". Although there is no direct reference to the *lex Aquilia* in Stair's text, he does glancingly distinguish *culpa* from *dolus* (fraud),[37] and the influence of the contemporary Natural Law interpretation of Aquilian liability is clearly apparent. Stair seems to be saying that, consistently with Natural Law, the obligations of reparation stretch beyond the well-established nominate delicts of Scots law, but the precise basis and limits of this extension are not stated.

Nor is it clear how widely the courts and other writers applied the action for damage and interest in or after Stair's time. Even although, as McKenzie and Evans-Jones observe,[38] it was argued in a case of 1768 that "if a man, who is culpable only, be liable in damages, what doubt can there be of his being liable when the damages are occasioned by his being guilty of a flagrant crime",[39] there was no definitive judicial recognition of an action for personal injuries and death distinct from assythment until 1795.[40] Bankton, whose *Institutes* were published in 1751, treats of assythment as the only action for personal injuries and death. He recognises another action "called Damage" which concerns wrongs to goods or property,[41] and goes on:

> Damage is likewise a general term, but here it is particularly understood of that damage which arises from diminishing, spoiling or destroying one's goods, without any advantage to the offender. ... The damage here understood must be *damnum injuria datum* as it was called in the civil law, and was repaired by the *lex Aquilia*. ... The smallest fault or neglect of the offender subjects him to the damage thereby occasioned.[42]

"The smallest fault or neglect" in this passage clearly stands for the *culpa levissima* of the Civil law. "Diminishing, spoiling or destroying" echoes the developed understanding of the "*urere, frangere et rumpere*" of the *lex Aquilia,* as does Bankton's restriction of the action to property damage,[43] of which two major instances are given: damage caused by fire and damage caused by animals. Finally, Bankton departed from Stair by

---

37 Institutions, 1.9.11, where *dolus* (fraud) is distinguished from *culpa lata,* interestingly on the basis that fraud is "oftentimes by positive acts" whereas *culpa lata* is "by omission of that which the party is obliged to show".

38 *McKenzie* and *Evans-Jones* (above note 8), p. 302.

39 *Lady Leith Hall* v. *Earl of Fife* (1768) Mor 13904 at p. 13905.

40 See further below, text from note 55 on.

41 *Andrew McDouall, Lord Bankton,* An Institute of the Laws of Scotland in Civil Rights (Edinburgh, 1751), I.10.14. We have used the reprint of this, the only edition, published in the Stair Society series (vols 41–43, Edinburgh, 1993–5) together with an invaluable introduction by *W. M. Gordon.*

42 Ibid, I.10.40.

43 See *McKenzie* and *Evans-Jones,* (note 8), p. 278, *Zimmermann,* (note 4), pp. 983–7, 1022–4.

reinstating the distinction between delict and quasi-delict, delict being "where the crime or offence of one causes damage to another, which must be repaired by the offender to the person aggrieved", while quasi-delict "is not a delinquency in the proper sense, but has an affinity or resemblance to it, and which the law construes as a crime to a certain extent for the public good".[44]

Henry Home, Lord Kames, and John Erskine of Carnock, writing shortly after Bankton, both appear to have recognised a broad general principle of liability to make reparation following upon, in Kames' language, "culpable transgressions" and "the slightest fault",[45] (i.e. *culpa levissima*) or, in Erskine's, "not only from positive acts of trespass or injury, but from blameable omission or neglect of duty".[46] Erskine, having rejected the terminology of "delict" and "quasi-delict" to return to Stair's "obediential obligations", observes that the obligation of reparation arises from "every fraudulent contrivance or unwarrantable act by which another suffers damage", and continues:

> "No person ought to be subjected to the reparation of damage who has not by some culpable act or omission been the occasion of it".[47] [The pursuer is to be compensated only for] "the loss truly sustained ... estimated by its real worth, and not by the *pretium affectionis*, or imaginary value that the sufferer is pleased to set upon it, agreeably to the rule of the *lex Aquilia*, L. 33, *pr. Ad leg. Aquil.*; see *Spence*, 25 Jan 1687 ..."[48]

Kames too refers to the *lex Aquilia*, encompassing omissions within his concept of fault, and explains that not only must a man be careful for himself but also for those within his power such as servants, children, animals and things.[49] Kames' argument is, however, a very general one, not necessarily confined to Scots law, the context being his theoretical distinction between what might be appropriate in his ideal world to a court of "law", and what to a court of "equity".

One may say from the foregoing that in the late seventeenth and eighteenth centuries, initially under the influence of natural law ideas, Scottish

---

44 *Bankton,* Institutes, 1.4.25–27.

45 *Henry Home, Lord Kames,* Principles of Equity (3rd edn, 1778), i, pp. 44, 60. This was the last edition produced by Kames himself; a posthumous 4th edition appeared in 1800, and a 5th in 1825. On Kames see *I. S. Ross,* Lord Kames and the Scotland of his Day (Edinburgh, 1972).

46 *John Erskine of Carnock,* An Institute of the Law of Scotland (1st edn, 1773), III.1.13. We have used the 1989 reprint of the 8th edn of 1871. The reprint contains an introduction by *W. W. McBryde,* giving a valuable account of Erskine and his work.

47 Ibid.

48 Ibid, III.1.14. The case is *Spence and Watson* v. *Ormiston* (1687) Mor 3153.

49 Principles of Equity, i, pp. 60–65.

legal writers had certainly formulated the concept of a general liability to make reparation for harm caused by culpable conduct, including acts of omission, but had not done much to develop it further. Some distinguished *culpa* from *dolus* (fraud or intentional conduct), others between true delicts (crimes) and conduct treated as though it were a delict but for civil purposes only. Material was not forthcoming from the courts in any quantity, which may explain the continuing relative generality and opacity of the analyses. As already noted, there are no reported decisions on death or personal injury based on Aquilian liability, although a few cases about damage to property show that arguments based on Aquilian *culpa* were being put to the judges from the late seventeenth century on. In 1685, in the case of *Sir Robert Sibbald* v. *Lady Rosyth,* which concerned destruction of property by fire, the Court of Session was confronted with an argument that clearly distinguished between contract (*locatio conductio*), delict, and liability under the statute of 1426, and asserted that under the *lex Aquilia* Lady Rosyth was liable for the least fault (*culpa levissima*) of her servant. "Before answer to so dangerous a preparative", the Court ordained a proof to investigate, inter alia, "the way and manner of the rising of the fire, and what negligence was in it".[50] In another fire damage case in 1698 the pursuer's claim was based on *culpa* and the defender's failure to show the *diligentia* of a prudent *paterfamilias* in the conduct of his own affairs.[51] When a boat collided with another, the subsequent action in 1712 was based upon *culpa latissima.*[52] In 1765 defenders pleaded the *lex Aquilia* to escape responsibility for damage by fire to the pursuer's wood.[53] Finally in a defamation case in 1765 the Court noted that "An *actio injuriarum,* where there is no patrimonial loss, and where damages are awarded only in *solatium,* must be founded upon *dolus malus,* according to the opinion of all writers upon law; and so far it differs from damages awarded to repair a patrimonial loss, in which it is sufficient to specify even *culpa levissima.*"[54]

The Modern Law

The General Action

It has long been understood that the law on liability for personal injuries and death, which had earlier fallen within the preserve of assythment, was transformed on the basis of Aquilian *culpa* after the cases of *Gardner* v.

50 *Sibbald* v. *Rosyth* (1685) Mor 13978.

51 *Farquharson* v. *Gillanders* (1698) 4 Brown's Synopsis 400.

52 *Forfar and Moyes* v. *Stark* (1712) 4 Brown's Synopsis 888.

53 *Gordon* v. *Grant* (1765) Mor 7365.

54 *Graeme & Skene v Cunningham* (1765) Mor 13923.

Ferguson in 1795,[55] *Innes* v. *Magistrates of Edinburgh,*[56] decided in 1798 by a court "a good deal divided in opinion", and *Blacks* v. *Cadell,* decided by the Court of Session in 1804 and affirmed by the House of Lords in 1812.[57] All three cases concerned faults of omission: in each a person had fallen into a drain or a pit left inadequately fenced and guarded by the defenders.[58] In *Gardner* and *Innes,* the victim was injured; in *Blacks* he was killed and the action was raised by his twelve children. The pursuers' claim for damages succeeded in all three cases. The question of the criminality of the defender's conduct was not raised in *Gardner* and *Innes.* It was raised in *Black,* but was not regarded as crucial.

The pleadings in *Gardner* relied almost entirely upon the *lex Aquilia* for authority, and made no reference to assythment. The pursuer was at pains to say that the action was not based upon the defender's *dolus malus* or *animus injuriandi*:

> In the civil law, many very amusing cases are put in the title *Ad legem Aquiliam* ... In all of these cases, he is subjected in the damage who has been in the fault, though the mischief has arisen without any intention upon his part.

Ferguson, he argued, was guilty of "a very great *culpa,* because common sense and reason must have told him, that in all probability some person or other might very probably be very much injured by his operations". Interestingly, Ferguson's counsel made no attempt to controvert the principle upon which the pursuer's case rested; he simply argued that his client had shown the care required of a diligent *paterfamilias.*[59]

---

55 The case is not reported. Information about it is derived from the parties' unpublished pleadings, which may be consulted in the Advocates Library, Edinburgh: Session Papers, Hume Collection, vol. 87, no. 97; Campbell Collection, vol. 79, nos. 8 and 9.

56 (1798) Mor 13189 and 13967. The former is much the fuller report.

57 9 Feb 1804, FC; (1804) Mor 13905; (1812) 5 Paton 567. See also the unreported case of *Mary Sawers* v. *Patrick Graham* (1799) cited in Baron David Hume's Lectures 1786–1822, ed. G. C. H. Paton (6 vols, Stair Society, Edinburgh, 1939–58, henceforth Hume, Lectures), iii, p. 186 (successful claim for "damages and expense of cure" by woman who, having partaken of alcoholic refreshment at a wedding celebration, fell into an unfenced well under repair). The Session Papers for this case (Hume Collection, vol. 68, no. 36) reveal no reference to any authority, simply a debate as to whether or not the defender's conduct was "culpable" and amounted to "negligence".

58 *Gardner* arose out of the development of Edinburgh's New Town (for which see *A. J. Youngson,* The Making of Classical Edinburgh [Edinburgh, 1966]), the accident occurring just off St James Square. The pit in *Innes* had been dug in connection with the construction of the north-west corner of what is now known as Old College in the University of Edinburgh (for which see *A. Fraser,* The Building of Old College [Edinburgh, 1989], especially at pp. 114–5). The building is the working home of the authors of this article.

In *Innes* the pursuer's printed arguments were headed "*Magistratus Municipales, si damnum injuria dederint, posse, Aquilia teneri, D 9.2.29.7*". The basis of his claim was the liability of magistrates for the safety of the inhabitants of the town under the *lex Aquilia,* and indeed in England and in "every other civilized and well governed realm".[60] He argued that the accident could not have happened without some degree of negligence and culpable omission by the defenders, the Magistrates of Edinburgh, and the court, upholding the argument, observed, in language evocative of Aquilian ideas, that the magistrates were liable for "the smallest neglect of this duty [to keep the streets safe], and in this case, without some degree of *culpa* on their part, the pursuer could not have met with the misfortune".[61] The case appears in Morison's Dictionary in both the section headed "Public Police" and the section on "Reparation" entitled "Negligence in Office", and, therefore, could be considered as falling under that well recognised head of liability.[62] But the case could also be seen as pointing the way forward to a more general claim: the pursuer relied on *Gardner* v. *Ferguson,* which did not involve public officials,[63] and also argued that "by the common law of this and the sister kingdom [*i. e. England*], both the magistrates of a burgh, *and the individual inhabitants of the town,* by whose encroachments and *negligence* any accident happens to the lieges, are bound, and will be compelled by the courts of justice of the country, to repair to the utmost extent the damage sustained by their *fault*".[64] The pursuer also drew the distinction between delict and quasi-delict, recognising that while normally damages were available only in respect of delicts, there were exceptions where there was "such a degree of negligence and remissness in office, which, though properly speaking, not amounting to an actual delict, approaches so near it, that the law holds it sufficient to infer damages".[65]

Blacks was a rather different case. The action was raised by the children of the victim, and there was no question here of dereliction of duty on the part of public officials. The successful pursuers, terming their claim as one *quasi ex delicto,* drew on the Bible, the *lex Aquilia,* the precedent of *Innes,*

---

59 For the quotations see Session Papers, Campbell Collection, vol. 79, nos. 8 (pp. 18–22) and 9 (p.18) (also in Hume Collection, vol. 87 no. 97).

60 For the pleadings in *Innes,* see Session Papers, Campbell Collection, vol. 88, nos. 45–49. The quotation is in no. 49 at p. 19. Blackstone was cited as authority for the position in England (ibid, pp. 19–20).

61 (1798) Mor at 13189–90.

62 See above, text at notes 13–14.

63 There was nonetheless a strong element of "public police" in the pursuer's pleadings: see, for example, Session Papers, Hume Collection, vol 87, no. 97, p. 6.

64 Session Papers, Campbell Collection, vol. 88, no. 47, p. 19 (emphasis supplied).

65 Ibid, p. 31.

the rules of assythment in granting compensation to the victim's kindred, and also on Stair's observation that "The life of any person being taken away, the damage of those who were entertained and maintained by his life, as his wife and children, may be repaired".[66] The defenders, as appellants in the House of Lords, argued that, "This is the first action of the kind that appears in the records of the Court of Session",[67] and there may have been some truth in this claim. They argued further that the pursuers' case found no support in the action of assythment, or in actions for damages, or in Jewish or Roman law – the *lex Aquilia* and Vinnius being specifically mentioned. Nevertheless the House of Lords affirmed the judgement of the Court of Session awarding damages to the pursuers.

The new head of liability was only gradually recognised in legal writings, with a distinction being drawn between intentional and other wrongs and developed under the headings "delict" and "quasi-delict", previously rejected by Stair and Erskine, but evidently still in use as shown by the pleadings in *Innes* and *Blacks,* and also by its appearance in statute in 1819.[68] In his lectures on Scots law given at Edinburgh University between 1786 and 1822, David Hume (nephew of the philosopher of the same name) dealt first with "obligations *ex delicto*", which term was left undefined but under which were comprised most of the traditional nominate wrongs.[69] Then he turned to "obligations *quasi ex delicto*", in which he first treated briefly of cases where "a man is made liable, as a *quasi* delinquent for the consequences of his own negligence or inadvertency, which, where it is prejudicial to others, the law considers as approaching to or savouring of a delinquency".[70] The *Blacks* case was cited under this head. The lecture went on to deal with those situations in which the law imposed liability upon one for the fault of another "on considerations of expediency", the prime example being the liability of a master for the wrongs of his servant.[71] Hume's successor in the Edinburgh chair between 1822 and 1839, George Joseph Bell, made the distinction much more clear in his

---

[66] (1812) 5 Paton at p. 573, quoting *Stair,* Institutions, I.9.3. For the parties' pleadings in the Court of Session, see Session Papers, Campbell Collection, vol. 112, no. 40.

[67] (1812) 5 Paton at p. 570.

[68] See further below, text at note 87. The currency of the terminology probably also gained strength in the early nineteenth century from its use by Pothier, whose treatise on obligations was published in English translation in 1806, and from its use as the heading of ch. II in Book III, Title IV, of the French Civil Code of 1804.

[69] *Hume,* Lectures, iii, ch. XIV.

[70] Ibid, p. 186.

[71] The quotation is at ibid, p. 187. *Innes* is treated in this section, the magistrates being "considered as *quasi* delinquents in not sufficiently watching the conduct of builders" (ibid, p. 188).

Principles first published in 1829. For him a delict was "an offence committed with an injurious, fraudulent, or criminal purpose",[72] while a quasi delict was "gross negligence or imprudence ... held as a delict", "though it should bear no such character of fraud, malice, or criminal purpose as to subject the person to criminal cognizance".[73] *Innes* and *Blacks* were cited as authorities for the latter. Bell's equation of quasi-delict with *culpa* or negligence became the standard understanding of the term in Scots law.[74]

The right of action confirmed in *Blacks* developed rapidly in the courts. It was quickly established that the pursuer could recover, not just patrimonial, but also moral damage (*solatium doloris*) in respect of pain and suffering.[75] The availability of *solatium* was particularly important in the claim of the deceased victim's relatives, especially once the Court of Session held that it was not necessary to link the claim with one for patrimonial loss.[76] The recognition of *solatium* represented both a point of continuity with assythment and a development in line with Natural Law thinking.[77] But since the original *lex Aquilia* had not extended so far, a degree of confusion crept into the terminology of Scots law in the mid-nineteenth century which even now has not been completely eradicated: the description of the general action for damages in delict as an *actio injuriarum,* the Roman claim for contumelious insult under which *solatium* damages had been recoverable.[78]

---

[72] *G. J. Bell,* Principles of the Law of Scotland (1st edn, Edinburgh, 1829), § 544 (repeated in the 4th edn of 1839, the last published in Bell's lifetime, and still there in the 10th and final edition of 1899).

[73] Ibid, § 553. This definition too survived for the lifetime of the work. *P. Stein,* The actio de effusis vel dejectis and the concept of quasi-delict in Scots law, International and Comparative Law Quarterly 4 (1955) pp. 356–375 at 374–5, suggests that the immediate source of Bell's definitions was the 1822 Edinburgh edition of *Heineccius*' Elementa Iuris Civilis.

[74] For deconstruction of this terminology down to the present, see *W. J. Stewart,* Smith's question-mark, Walker's exhortation and quasi-delict, Juridical Review 35 (1990) pp. 71–82. One of the present writers has been examiner in Delict and Quasi-Delict for the Faculty of Advocates.

[75] *Brown* v. *Macgregor* 26 Feb 1813, FC.

[76] *Dow* v. *Brown* (1844) 6 D 534.

[77] See *Zimmermann,* (note 4), pp. 1026–7; also *R. Feenstra,* Réparation du dommage et prix de la douleur chez les auteurs du droit savant, du droit naturel et du droit romano-hollandais, in La Douleur et le Droit, edd. B. Durand, J. Poirier and J.-P. Royer (Paris, 1997), pp. 411–21.

[78] See *Eisten* v. *North British Railway Co* (1870) 8 M 980 at pp. 983–4 per Lord President Inglis, confirmed and reinforced by Lord President Dunedin in *Black* v. *North British Railway Co* 1908 SC 444 at p. 453. Given that the *actio injuriarum* of the medieval canon law extended to physical assault as well as the Roman insult (see *Dondorp,* [note 29], p. 109), the usage in Scotland may not be quite so heretical as more recent observers have thought. It was presumably in this extended

A good deal of litigation concerned the determination of which relatives might claim. *Blacks* had allowed the claim of children; the claim of a widower was allowed in 1844,[79] and those of a father[80] and mother[81] in 1842 and 1861. But in the mid-nineteenth century the court drew the line at collateral relatives, denying siblings first a claim to *solatium* in *Greenhorn* v. *Addie*,[82] and then to patrimonial loss in *Eisten* v. *North British Railway Co.*[83] The basis in legal principle for this limitation of the action was that claims would only be allowed to those with whom the deceased had had a mutual obligation of support in law (i.e. husband and wife, and those in the direct line of ascent and descent), the existence of *de facto* support being irrelevant. These cases, in particular *Eisten*, helped to draw a definitive distinction between the old action of assythment and the new general action for personal injuries and death. The latter was narrower in scope in terms of those who might enjoy its benefits but did not require the commission of a crime before the right of action arose. In fact, changes in society and in the criminal law had rendered the action of assythment well-nigh obsolescent by the mid-eighteenth century, although it was to enjoy a curious latter-day revival in the case of *M'Kendrick* v. *Sinclair* [84] in 1972.

The Jury Court

An important change in court structure and civil procedure which was to affect the subsequent development of the law of negligence was the re-introduction of trial by jury in civil causes to Scotland in 1815 on the English model.[85] The function of the jury was to try such issues of fact as were remitted to it. The Jury Trials Act 1815 established a Jury Court with the power, when directed by the Court of Session, to try issues and assess

---

sense that the phrase "*in omnimoda accione injuriarum*" appears in an act of 1318 which seems to have nothing to do with insult or affront. A later Scots translation rendered this as "in al maner of accione of wrang" (APS, i, p. 471, c. 17). For the best Latin text of this act see now Regesta Regum Scottorum VI: The Acts of Robert I 1306–1329, ed. A. A. M. Duncan (Edinburgh, 1988), p. 411.

79 *Dow* v. *Brown* (1844) 6 D 534.

80 *Hislop* v. *Durham* (1842) 4 D 1168.

81 *Weems* v. *Mathieson* (1861) 4 Macq 215.

82 (1855) 17 D 860.

83 (1870) 8 M 980.

84 1972 SC (HL) 25. Assythment was finally abolished by the Damages (Scotland) Act 1976, s. 8. See further *Black I* (note 7), at pp. 64–70.

85 On this development in general see *I. D. Willock*, The Origins and Development of the Jury in Scotland (Stair Society, Edinburgh, 1966) and *N. T. Phillipson*, The Scottish Whigs and the Reform of the Court of Session 1785–1830 (Stair Society, Edinburgh, 1990). See also *W. M. Gordon*, George Joseph Bell, Law Commissioner, in Obligations in Context (note 3), pp. 79–99.

damages in cases, among others, "wherein the Summons concludes for Reparation by Pecuniary Damages".[86] The Jury Trials Act 1819 set out a list of actions to be sent to the Jury Court, including "any Action founded on Delinquency, or *quasi* Delinquency of any kind, where the Conclusion shall be for Damages and Expences only".[87] In 1825 the list of enumerated causes (as they came to be called) appropriate to the Jury Court was further extended.[88] The Court consisted of three, later five, Lords Commissioners, the Chief Commissioner being William Adam.[89] In 1830 the Jury Court was merged into the Court of Session; the list of enumerated causes, however, remained unaltered, although all jury trials in civil cases were now to take place in the Court of Session.[90] Later legislation reduced the list of enumerated causes, and made more provision for trial by way of proof before a judge sitting alone, but until the end of the nineteenth century and beyond, trial by jury in actions for reparation remained the norm in Scotland.[91]

William Adam, who like Henry Brougham after him was a member of both the Scottish and English bars, held the office of Lord Chief Commissioner throughout the existence of the Jury Court as an independent body, and was instrumental in devising its procedure. He gave much attention to the proper framing and refining of the general issue which was to go before the jury, taking advice on this from, among others, Lord Ellenborough. Adam was determined that the form of issue adopted in the Jury Court should be sympathetic to the Scottish system of pleading by way of Condescendences and Answers, which set out clearly the facts relied on and the remedy sought, and avoided surprise. The Condescendences and Answers sent to the jury (at least under the 1825 Act) were to contain only pure averments of fact. The judges were to direct the jury as to the law, but only to comment on matters of fact.[92]

---

86 Jury Trials (Scotland) Act 1815, s. 5.

87 Jury Trials (Scotland) Act 1819, s. 1. See above, text at notes 68–74, on the distinction between delinquency and quasi-delinquency.

88 Court of Session Act 1825, s. 28.

89 William Adam (1751–1839) was the nephew of the famous architects Robert and Janes Adam. He was a friend and companion of both the Prince of Wales (later George IV) and Sir Walter Scott. For his remarkable career of over 60 years in public life see Dictionary of National Biography and *Willock* (note 85), pp. 258–62.

90 Court of Session Act 1830.

91 An enumerated cause may still be removed from the jury by consent of parties or on special cause being shown.

92 *W. Adam,* A Practical Treatise and Observations on Trial by Jury in Civil Causes (Edinburgh, 1836). For an account of Adam's tenure as Lord Chief Commissioner, and his skill and persistence as regards the proper framing of issues, see *Phillipson* (note 85), pp. 136–42 and 151–68.

Adam must be accounted outstandingly successful: the forms of issue which he designed, at least in the field of negligence, remained little changed until well into the twentieth century. The case of *Allan* v. *M'Leish* provides a good example of an early form of issue:[93]

> Whether, on or about the 25th day of July 1818, the Waterloo Coach, of which the defenders are proprietors or contractors, was overturned between North Queesferry and Inverkeithing, in consequence of the negligence or improper conduct of the coachmen or guard, whereby the pursuer, then a passenger in the said coach, suffered bodily harm, to the injury and damage of the pursuer?
>
> Damages laid at, for medical expenses, L.200
>
> Solatium, L.5000

By 1827 a settled form of issue had emerged:

> Whether the death of the said child was caused by fault, negligence, or want of skill, on the part of the said William Wilson, to the loss, injury, and damage of the pursuer. (*Miller* v. *Harvie*)

On this, Adam comments:[94]

> This instance of an issue arises out of an action by a father, in consequence of a cart running over his child on the highway. The action was brought against the master of the carter, as being responsible for the careful conduct of his servant, and liable in damages for a delinquency arising out of the servant's want of care. It is a general issue, preceded by an admission of fact, that the child was run over and killed.

This was "the ordinary form of issue" approved in *Morton (Cooley's Factor)* in 1845.[95] It is worth noting that the word *culpa* as such never seems to have been used in the form of issue, although the formula "... caused by the culpable, reckless and negligent conduct ..." does appear.[96] In *Morton* the issue was expressed thus:

> Whether the death of the said Thomas Cooley was caused by fault, negligence or want of skill, on the part of the defenders, or another, in their employment, and for whom they were, and are responsible, to the loss, injury, and damage of the said Mary Cooley and Thomas Cooley [junior], or either of them.

Lord Commissioner Adam was well aware of developments in English law, and prepared to follow them where he thought it was appropriate. The

---

93 *Adam* (note 92), p. 135. *Allan* is reported at (1819) 2 Murr 158. The verdict for the pursuer (at p. 164) awarded £200 for medical expenses and £1,000 "for damages and *solatium*".

94 *Adam* (note 92), pp. 138–9. For *Miller* v. *Harvie,* see (1827) 4 Murr 385.

95 (1845) 8 D 288, followed in *Dobie* (1855) 18 D 862, and approved again in *Black* v. *North British Ry Co* 1908 SC 444.

96 For another collection of forms of issue see *J. Guthrie Smith,* A Treatise on the Law of Reparation (Edinburgh, 1864), Appendix. See further *MacCormack,* Culpa in the Scots law of reparation (note 8).

case of *Anderson* v. *Pyper*[97] in 1820 involved the allegedly defective construction of a coach. On this Adam comments:[98]

> I stated to the jury that the owners were bound to find a sufficient vehicle; and that an accident arising from insufficiency, rendered them liable in damages to the sufferer. But I observed, at the same time, that if the insufficiency was of a hidden nature, not to be discovered by human inspection, – the inspectors being persons of skill in their business, – that this would relieve the owners.
>
> This was a case of first impression in this country [Scotland]. In England it had been laid down as I stated it, in a remarkable case, tried by Sir James Mansfield, Chief Justice of the Common Pleas. The fairness and good sense of the doctrine has established it in England; and I stated that it appeared to me that it should govern in such cases in this country, not because it had been adopted as doctrine in England, but because it was consonant to justice and sound sense.

Culpa, Negligence and Foreseeability

For most of the nineteenth century the judges emphasised that the basis of the action of damages for unintended injury was *culpa* without ever elaborating in great detail what precisely that concept meant. The maxim *culpa tenet suos auctores* was constantly mentioned as the first principle of the law.[99] Although at first, following the Civilian tradition, it was said that "the slightest fault", or *culpa levissima,* was enough to infer liability, the drawing of distinctions between different degrees of *culpa,* whether for purposes of establishing liability or for determining its extent, was eventually rejected, and an objective criterion – the standard of a reasonable man in the circumstances – was deployed to determine the existence of an obligation of reparation.[100] This standard could readily be equated with the *diligentia* of a prudent *paterfamilias* in the conduct of his own affairs. The words "negligence" and "fault" are commonly found as synonyms for "*culpa*". Their appearance in the standard form of issue used in the Jury Court has already been noted.[101]

---

[97] (1820) 2 Murr 261.

[98] *Adam* (note 92), pp. 137–8.

[99] *MacCormack,* Culpa tenet suos auctores, (note 8). See also the first textbook devoted specifically to the subject, *Guthrie Smith* (note 96), p. 25. Note also the translation of the *lex Aquilia* published in the Journal of Jurisprudence 14 (1870) pp. 592, 649, and 15 (1871), pp. 113, 292 and 410.

[100] See *MacCormack's* articles on *culpa* (note 8); *Black II* (note 7), pp. 195–6; *Guthrie Smith,* (note 96), pp. 60–63. In *Gray* v. *Brassey* (1852) 15 D 135, Lord Ivory said at p. 141: "If I am to lay down any general doctrine, I would hold with Lord Mackenzie in the case of *Sneddon,* that there must be *culpa* on the part of the master, but that *culpa levis* will do." In *Sneddon* v. *Addie* (1849) 11 D 1159 Lord Mackenzie had said (at p. 1161), "There is always implied some *culpa* – *culpa levis* would be enough".

[101] See above, text at notes 93–96.

The language of foreseeability was also used, closely linked to the degree of fault required. In *Anderson* v. *Pyper,*[102] when *culpa levissima* was still being put forward as the standard, the issue approved was "whether the defenders used the utmost care to which human foresight could reach". However, by 1857 it was held that what was expected was not "unusual foresight", but "ordinary foresight" and "proper skill".[103] Other formulations included "common sense, and ordinary reflection",[104] and "reasonable care".[105] In the first textbook devoted to the subject and published in 1864 under the title *A Treatise on the Law of Reparation,* John Guthrie Smith (1831–1895) summed up *culpa* in Aquilian language, nonetheless anticipating Lord Atkin's later "neighbour" test in *Donoghue*:[106]

> The measure of this *culpa* is found in the answer to the question, – How would a man of ordinary prudence and sagacity have acted in like circumstances; or rather in the circumstances as they must have appeared at the time to the person sought to be made liable? ... Negligence, or *culpa,* ... means the doing of a lawful act in an unlawful way, i.e. without that care and prudence which a person of common understanding placed in similar circumstances would have observed on the occasion. ... Responsibility for *culpa* rests on the one great principle, that in well-regulated communities every one must so govern his affairs and regulate his conduct, as not to be productive of injury to his neighbour ... It is our duty to ... manifest that care and circumspection which may be reasonably expected of us in the circumstances. Any failure in this duty ... in every case entitles the private party to be compensated for any injury he may have sustained in consequence.

Guthrie Smith's book is interesting for its division of wrongs, into those directly contrary to the law and requiring *dolus,* and those legal in themselves but illegally done where *culpa* or negligence or imprudence was required. This, he said, paralleled the delict and quasi-delict of Roman law. Before there could be a legal wrong or *injuria,* there had to be an unlawful act: "It is thus the *illegality* of the act out of which the obligation springs; and there can be no violation of the precept *alterum non laede* in any other way". Unlawfulness in this sense could arise in two ways: "by ... being carried on ... either for a malicious purpose, or without that care and prudence required of every one in order to maintain the safety of his neighbour". This analysis is very much that which had established itself in contemporary Europe,[107] and may well reflect Guthrie Smith's year studying

---

102 (1820) 2 Murr 261.

103 *Cook* v. *Bell* (1857) 20 D 137.

104 *Wm. Paton & Richard McNab* (1845) 2 Brown 525, discussed further below, text at notes 145–148.

105 *Grant* v. *Caledonian Railway Co* (1870) 9 M 258.

106 *Guthrie Smith* (note 96), pp. 8, 58–60.

107 See *E. J. H. Schrage,* The Dutch Civil Code of 1838; *Ernst, Mossler* (note 26), and *B. Auzary,* La responsibilite delictuelle dans l'ancien droit Français d'apres la

law at Heidelberg (presumably under the Pandektist C. A. von Vangerow) in 1854–55.[108]

Vicarious Liability

The need for *culpa* received its most extensive discussion in cases concerned with a master's liability for the *culpa* of his servants.[109] Despite the principle of *culpa tenet suos auctores,* it was established by the case of *Brown* v. *Macgregor* in 1813 that a master or employer was strictly liable for negligence on the part of his servant.[110] Hume,[111] Bell[112] and, later, Guthrie Smith[113] all accepted this as the basic position, albeit not without ambiguity. Examples of the application of the principle of vicarious liability can be found in the issues discussed above in the section on the Jury Court. In 1826 one of the judges in the Court of Session referred to the principle as part of "the general law of Europe".[114] The greatest difficulty was with cases of damage to property. Although the first such case, *Keith* v. *Keir,*[115] found the master liable "for every damage that had occurred", despite his servants acting in his absence and against his instructions, this was disapproved shortly afterwards.[116] The 1873 edition of Lorimer's *Handbook of the Law of Scotland* noted that, in contrast to the rule of common employment, where a third party, not being an employee, was

---

jurisprudence du parlement, (all in this volume) for the Netherlands, Germany and France respectively.

108 *G. Toepke and P. Hintzelmann* (eds.), Die Matrikel der Universität Heidelberg 1386–1870 (7 vols., Heidelberg, 1907, Kraus reprint, 1976), vi, p. 238 (no. 436). See generally *A. Rodger,* Scottish advocates in the nineteenth century: the German connection, Law Quarterly Review 110 (1994) pp. 563–591. Guthrie Smith's studies in Germany are mentioned at p. 565 but without an indication of which university he attended or when he did so. He also studied law at Edinburgh from 1851–1853 (Edinburgh University Library, University Matriculation Roll 1830–1853 transcribed by A. Morgan, pp. 1291 and 1308), and became a founder editor of the Journal of Jurisprudence in 1857. For further details of his career, see obituaries at Scots Law Times 3 (1895), p. 50, and Scottish Law Review 11 (1895), pp. 211–9.

109 *MacCormack,* Culpa tenet suos auctores (note 8).

110 *Brown* v. *Macgregor,* 26 Feb 1813, FC; *Smith* v. *Milne* (1814) 2 Dow 390 (HL); *Allan* v. *M'Leish* (1819) 2 Mur 158; *Gunn* v. *Gardner* (1820) 2 Mur 194; *Anderson* v. *Pyper* (1820) 2 Mur 261; *Baird* v. *Hamilton* (1826) 4 S 790; and see *Black II* (note 7) p.207 ff.

111 Lectures, iii, pp. 187–96.

112 Principles (1st edn, 1829), § 547, is not so clear, but observe the development of the paragraph by the time of the 4th edition in 1839.

113 Above note 96, p. 25, and see further chs. IV–VI.

114 *Baird* v. *Hamilton* (1826) 4 S 790, per Lord Alloway, at p. 792.

115 10 June 1812, FC.

116 *Linwood* v. *Hathorn* 14 May 1817, FC.

injured through the fault of a servant, the master was liable.[117] The fact that the servant had not had express orders as to how to act was no excuse, although it was different if the servant had been specially ordered not so to act. It made no difference whether the injury arose from negligence or unskilfulness. Only in 1877 were the last traces of *culpa* eliminated from vicarious liability.[118]

Liability for escapes from property

For a time it seemed that a proprietor might be strictly liable in respect of damage arising from operations on his property, but these cases were later distinguished, and it was made clear that there was no abstract principle that reparation was due, arising *ex dominio,* when damage was done in this way.[119] The most significant case asserting the need for *culpa* was *Laurent* v. *Lord Advocate,*[120] decided in 1869, just a year after the House of Lords in *Rylands* v. *Fletcher*[121] had affirmed strict liability in English law for the escape of dangerous things from one's land. Subsequent stray dicta and at least one decision of the House of Lords created some uncertainty as to the scope of *Rylands* in Scots law,[122] however, and this was not eliminated until the 1980s.[123]

Contributory Negligence

A further dimension of *culpa* concerned its concurrence in both defender and pursuer – what would become known as contributory negligence. Was

---

117 At pp. 645–650. For common employment, see text below at notes 159–162.

118 *Woodhead* v. *Gartness Mineral Co* (1877) 4 R 469. As late as 1880 Lord Shand could argue against vicarious liability in the pages of the Journal of Jurisprudence 24 (1880) pp. 1–18. See however the response at ibid, pp. 65–71.

119 See for the cases raising the doubts *Callendar* v. *Eddington* (1826) 4 Murr 108; *Douglas* v. *Monteith* (1826) 4 Murr 130; *Cleghorn* v. *Taylor* (1856) 18 D 664; *Kerr* v. *Earl of Orkney* (1857) 20 D 298. *Culpa* was reasserted in *M'Intosh* v. *Scott* (1859) 21D 364; *Campbell* v. *Kennedy* (1864) 3 M 121; *Mackintosh* v. *Mackintosh* (1864) 2 M 1357; and *Laurent* v. *Lord Advocate* (1869) 7 M 607.

120 Ibid, especially per Lord President Inglis.

121 (1868) LR 3 HL 330.

122 See e.g. *Chalmers* v. *Dixon* (1876) 3 R 461; *Eastern & South African Telegraph Co Ltd* v. *Cape Town Tramways Co Ltd* [1902] AC 381 per Lord Robertson at p. 394; *Reynolds* v. *Lanarkshire Tramways Co* (1908) 16 SLT 230; *Caledonian Railway Co* v. *Greenock Corporation* 1917 SC (HL) 56; *Western Silver Fox Ranch Ltd* v. *Ross & Cromarty County Council* 1940 SC 601.

123 *RHM Bakeries (Scotland) Ltd* v. *Strathclyde Regional Council* 1985 SC (HL) 17. It may still be the law that liability is strict where the defender has interfered with the course of a natural stream.

it a complete defence or merely a reason for diminishing the damages awarded to the pursuer? The early case law appeared to favour the latter view,[124] but the complete defence theory also had its early proponents[125] and came to hold the field by the middle of the century,[126] probably influenced by the English approach to the subject and by the fundamental principle of *culpa tenet suos auctores*. Only by statute passed in 1945 did contributory negligence become merely a ground for reducing the quantum of damages.[127]

The Language of Duty

It is sometimes asserted that the concept of duty of care in negligence, especially in a "particular" or "directional" sense, is an invention of English law, and an English imposition upon Scots law. These are deep and difficult matters. The seminal study on the origins of the concept of a duty of care in English law was written by Percy Winfield in 1934.[128] He pinpointed the contract/tort fallacy as the likely source of the doctrine, and suggested that, some remarks made *obiter* by Baron Parke in *Winterbottom* v. *Wright*[129] in 1842 on privity of contract and negligence, were "in a curiously roundabout way ... largely responsible for getting into our law [*i. e. English law*] something else which is still firmly rooted there, and that is the duty idea in negligence." Winfield thought, however, that the development of the idea of duty had been "fitful" and "hesitant and sluggish" until the case of *Heaven* v. *Pender*[130] in 1883, when Brett MR said that there could be no liability "unless the person charged with such want of ordinary care had a duty to the person complaining to use ordinary care in respect of the matter called in question." *Heaven* v. *Pender* for Winfield was the point at which duty "was clinched in the law of negligence".

---

124 *Allan* v. *M'Leish* (1819) 2 Murr 158; *Hislop* v. *Durham* (1842) 4 D 1168.

125 *McLachlan* v. *Wigtonshire Road Trs* (1827) 4 Murr 216; *Millar* v. *Road Trs* (1828) 4 Murr 563.

126 *McNaughton* v. *Caledonian Railway Co* (1858) 24 D 160; *Forbes* v. *Aberdeen Harbour Commissioners* (1888) 15 R 323; *Florence* v. *Mann* (1890) 18 R 247; *Guthrie Smith,* (note 96), ch. III (3).

127 Law Reform (Contributory Negligence) Act 1945.

128 *P. H. Winfield,* Duty in tortious negligence, Columbia Law Review 34 (1934) pp. 41–66; see also his The history of negligence in the law of torts, Law Quarterly Review 42 (1926) pp. 184–208. See further *D. J. Ibbetson,* The tort of negligence in the common law in the nineteenth and twentieth centuries, in this volume.

129 (1842) 10 M & W 109.

130 (1883) 11 QBD 503. For a contemporary Scottish reaction to the case, see Journal of Jurisprudence 27 (1883) pp. 113–24.

Whether or not Winfield's thesis holds good for English law, it is abundantly clear that the language of obligation and of duty – not merely moral duty, but legal duty also – has been regularly employed in Scotland for as long as the modern general action for negligence in delict has been recognised. In part this flows naturally from Stair's classification of obligations, noted above:[131] reparation in delict is an "obediential" obligation; and integral to an obediential obligation is the idea of duty. Scots lawyers certainly remained conscious of Stair's classification. Thus in the leading case of *Laurent* in 1869, Lord President Inglis described delinquency as "a wrong done to another in breach of an obediential obligation".[132] It is worth emphasising *en passant,* in view of the suggested origins of the concept of duty of care in English law,[133] that this classification of obligations into "obediential" and "conventional" meant that Scots lawyers were less likely than their English counterparts to be misled by the "contract/tort fallacy".[134] When one talks of "obligation", a natural synonym is "duty"; witness Guthrie Smith, who in 1864 talks frequently of "duty" and includes remarks such as the following:[135]

> As to the negative species of *culpa* – *culpa in non faciendo* – we may observe that, in order to make one legally answerable for his conduct, we must necessarily suppose a pre-existing obligation to do the contrary. The duty we are speaking of is a legal duty, or one enforceable by law.

We have already noted Erskine speaking of "neglect of duty" while deploying Stair's terminology of obligations in the eighteenth century,[136] and the words "duty" and "neighbour" appear in both pleadings and decisions in the earliest cases in the Court of Session. Thus in *Gardner* v. *Ferguson* the pursuer argued that "regard must be had to the safety, and even the comfort of our neighbours".[137] The pursuer in *Innes* v. *Edinburgh Magistrates* pleaded, and the Court held, that the magistrates had a "duty" to keep the streets safe;[138] the pursuer also referred to the need to avoid

---

131 See text at notes 18–22.

132 *Laurent* v. *Lord Advocate* (1869) 7 M 607 at p. 610.

133 See text above, at notes 128–130.

134 The "contract/tort fallacy" under which if A's negligent performance of a contract with B injured C, the last-named had no right of action against the first, might have been introduced into Scots law by the House of Lords in *Robertson* v. *Fleming* (1861) 4 Macq 167, but seems never to have commanded much support and was finally rejected in *Edgar* v. *Lamont* 1914 SC 277. See further *Black III* (note 7), at pp. 322–3, 326. In the second (1889) edition of his treatise on reparation (below, note 163), *Guthrie Smith* had no doubt that there could be "double liability – to one in contract, to another in delict" (pp. 56–58).

135 *Guthrie Smith* (note 96), p. 9. See also a very similar passage at ibid, p. 65.

136 See above, text at note 46.

137 Session Papers, Hume Collection, vol 87, no 97, p 21.

risk to "neighbours or fellow-creatures".[139] Again, in *Blacks* v. *Cadell* the pursuers' pleadings referred to "neglect or omission to fulfil what the rule of duty requires to be performed".[140] In the controversial case of *Linwood*[141] in 1817, arising from an employee on an estate cutting down a tree without permission so that it fell on the public highway, Lord Bannatyne referred to the need on the part of the defenders "to act with particular care", and their duty to avoid the tree falling on the high road. In *Brownlie* in 1854 one suggested issue was that the defenders had "culpably neglected their duty".[142] As Black has pointed out, the terminology of "duty" came to be employed regularly in the written pleadings in reparation cases in Scotland, the pursuer alleging at various points of his pleadings that it had been the defender's duty to act in such and such a way, and that he had failed to do so.[143] As already observed, Guthrie Smith's treatise of 1864 is also peppered with references to "duty" and "neighbours".[144]

The language of culpability and duty was also in regular use in the criminal law in Scotland at the same time in connection with the crime of culpable homicide, which was then interpreted very broadly. The *locus classicus* is Lord Justice-Clerk Hope's charge to the jury in *William Paton & Richard McNab* in 1845,[145] a criminal prosecution for culpable homicide arising from the use of a defective railway engine. Setting out the requirements for liability, he said:

> The general rule is, that every person, placed in a situation in which his acts may affect the safety of others, must take all precautions to guard against the risk of them arising from what he is doing ... Railway servants are not entitled to neglect any precaution necessary for the safety of others, whether laid down in the rules of the company or not; and if that has been omitted, which common sense, and ordinary reflection as to the situation of others required, which their duty to the law required for the safety of others, the guilt is clear ... They are not entitled to neglect any precaution which ordinary prudence and foresight ought to have recommended.[146]

As Sheriff Gordon comments, "Lord Hope's statement of the duty of care sounds very like Lord Atkin's famous statement of the law in *Dono-*

---

138 Session Papers, Campbell Collection, vol 88, no 47, pp. 5, 29; (1798) Mor 13189.

139 Session Papers, Campbell Collection, vol 88, no 47, p 18.

140 Session Papers, Campbell Collection, vol 112, no 40, p 13.

141 *Linwood* v. *Hathorn* 14 May 1817, FC.

142 *Brownlie* v. *Tennant* (1854) 16 D 998 at 999. For a later stage of the case see (1854) 17 D 422.

143 *Black III* (note 7), p. 321.

144 See e.g. pp 2–3, 59, 60, 63, 65, 66.

145 (1845) 2 Brown 525.

146 Ibid, at pp. 533–4.

ghue v. *Stevenson*".[147] *Paton & McNab* was the criminal counterpart of *Morton (Cooley's Factor)*, referred to above, which arose out of the same facts and settled the terms of the issue in negligence cases.[148]

In most cases, no doubt, the language of duty merely signifies that the defender had a duty in law to foresee the likely consequences of his acts or omissions. Thus in the appeal of *Cook* v. *Bell* in 1857, Lord President M'Neill, who had been the judge at the original jury trial, stated "I told the jury ... that it was the employer's duty (the breach of which is fault) ... to use ... ordinary foresight."[149] In some cases, as Black points out, the language is ambiguous, and may refer either to foreseeability or to a more policy-orientated approach.[150] Thus in the House of Lords case of *Weems* in 1861 it was argued that, "the summons is irrelevant. It does not allege any obligation, nor any negligence on the part of the master. It neither avers a duty nor an omission to perform it".[151] The headnote to the report begins "Obligation of Care cast upon the Master".

Sometimes, however, it is difficult to avoid the impression that the concept of duty is being used as an instrument of policy, particularly where liability was denied. This is particularly so in relation to occupiers' liability to trespassers and the doctrine of "common employment", which developed in Scotland in the second half of the nineteenth century. In these areas of the law, the presence of *culpa* as conduct foreseeably causing harm ceased to be sufficient for liability; instead, in parallel with developments in England, it came to be said that the occupier owed no duty to the trespasser and that an employee (and therefore his employer) owed no duty to his fellow-employee.[152]

Liability to trespassers

In *Lumsden* v. *Russel*[153] in 1856 a nine-year-old boy carried gunpowder to a works where his father was employed. The boy laid hold of a winding chain which was not sufficiently protected and was drawn into the machinery and killed. The Lord Ordinary, Lord Ardmillan, disposing of the case on relevancy, said:

---

147 *G. H. Gordon,* The Criminal Law of Scotland, 2nd edn (Edinburgh, 1978), p. 791.

148 See above, text at note 95.

149 (1857) 20 D 137 at p. 143.

150 *Black III* (note 7), pp. 320–1.

151 *Weems* v. *Mathieson* (1861) 4 Macq 215 at p. 220.

152 See generally *Black III* (note 7), pp 327–43.

153 (1856) 18 D 468.

In order to support the conclusion for damages, the pursuer must allege *culpa* ... and he must so connect the accident with the *culpa*, as to deduce clearly the liability which he seeks to enforce ... *It cannot be said to have been part of the duty of the defenders* to calculate on a child going instead of a man, and to guard against the possibility of an act so rash and so improbable as the laying hold of the winding chain.[154]

This should be read with the judgement of Lord Justice-Clerk Hope on appeal, which is in interesting contrast to his above-quoted exposition of the general rule as regards criminal liability in *Paton & McNab*. Lord Hope affirmed the judgement of the court below. He was concerned about "extending the law of liability in a most dangerous way". He considered that the whole blame lay with the father of the child. Parents had a duty to keep their children from danger. The child had been "where he had no lawful occasion to be".[155]

The following year the Second Division, including Lord Justice-Clerk Hope again, took the same line in the leading case of *Balfour* v. *Baird & Brown*.[156] Battens had been stored in piles on an unfenced piece of ground adjoining a roadway along a canal harbour, which if not technically public, had certainly long been used by the public. Some of the battens fell from the top of a pile and killed a ten-year-old boy who was between two of the piles. The Sheriff-Substitute and the Sheriff of Lanark both found for the pursuer, but the finding was overturned by the Division. Lord Justice-Clerk Hope was particularly unsympathetic:

That boys will frequent such a place in numbers, and often, as appears here, to the annoyance of people carrying on traffic, is to be expected. But boys have no business there. They are there only to amuse themselves. They have no right to be there. They come for idleness and amusement ... and though the resort of boys and other idlers cannot well be prevented, yet they are trespassers, who ought not to be there.[157]

Lord Cowan was concerned "that if we were to affirm the principle recognised by the Sheriffs in the Court below, we should open a wide door to litigation".[158] Admittedly the words "duty" and "foreseeability" do not appear to have been used in *Balfour* but, taking it with *Lumsden*, one gains

154 Ibid at p. 468 (emphasis supplied).

155 Ibid, at p. 470. *Guthrie Smith* (note 96), at p. 75, cited this case for the proposition that the injured trespasser was in an unfavourable position to make recovery but that he would fail to do so only if he was doing things which he had no right to do as well as being in a place where he had no right to be.

156 (1857) 20 D 238.

157 Ibid, at pp. 242–4.

158 Ibid, at p. 244. The case is in striking and direct contrast to the recent decision of Lord Nimmo Smith in *Galbraith's Curator* v. *Stewart (No 2)* 1998 SLT 1305.

the clear impression that a policy decision had been taken in regard to trespass, foreseeable or not, and that the language of duty was quite apt for the denial of liability.

Common employment

The acceptance of the doctrine of common employment, by which an employee (or "servant") injured through the fault of a fellow employee was barred from recovering against his employer (or "master") is generally reckoned, and probably justly, to be an example of the unwelcome anglicisation of Scots law. The rationale for the doctrine was that the employee, by the mere fact of his engagement, knowingly and willingly accepted the risk of injury through the negligence of a fellow employee. In English law the doctrine can be traced back to the case of *Priestley* v. *Fowler* in 1837.[159] In Scotland, although the matter was debated, the balance of opinion was against the introduction of such a rule. The matter came to a head in *Bartonshill Coal Co.* v. *Reid,*[160] appealed from Scotland to the House of Lords in 1858, when in a famous (or infamous) speech Lord Chancellor Cranworth held that

> in England the doctrine must be regarded as well settled; but if such be the law of England, on what ground can it be argued not to be the law of Scotland? The law, as established in England, is founded on principles of universal application, not on any peculiarities of English jurisprudence.[161]

This inequitable doctrine was substantially modified for both Scotland and England by the Employers Liability Act 1880, but was not finally abolished by statute until 1948.[162]

Duty as a requirement

By 1889, when Guthrie Smith published the second edition of his text on reparation, he could formulate a decidedly "directional" duty of care as one of the law's requirements for liability:

> It is sometimes forgotten that negligence is not a positive, but a negative word; it does not define the duty owing by one person to another, but expresses the breach of the duty; and the inquiry thus resolves in every case into a question strictly personal to the parties concerned, and liable to be modified by many con-

---

159 (1837) 3 M & W 1.

160 (1858) 3 Macq 266.

161 Ibid, at p. 285.

162 Law Reform (Personal Injuries) Act 1948, s. 1(1). With regard to the 1880 Act, the Faculty of Advocates would have preferred the legislation to use the word "fault" instead of "negligence": Journal of Jurisprudence 24 (1880), pp. 433–5.

> siderations depending on who the party is who complains that his safety has not been duly attended to; visitors, for instance, unacquainted with the premises, when the action is founded on the condition in which they were kept; workmen familiar with them; licencees who resort to them at their own risk; grown-up people who can take care of themselves; young persons who cannot; and young persons who had no business to be there at all. In every case, the point to be decided is, whether in a question, *not with the public, but with the particular individual injured,* the defender did all that he was bound to do, to prevent the mischief which happened.[163]

The requirement of a "duty" was articulated again in the next text to appear, *Glegg on Reparation* (1st edition 1892). Having quoted the judgment of Brett MR in *Heaven* v. *Pender,*[164] Glegg wrote of Scots law:

> It follows, from the nature of the obligation in delict, that mere proof of damage, though shown to be due to the act of the defender, is not sufficient to instruct liability. A duty must be set forth, and a breach of duty proved. ... Negligence is a breach, by omission, of a positive duty. ... An act is not negligent in itself, but only in respect that it is likely to cause injurious consequences to some determinate person, or one of a determinate class of persons ...[165]

When *Green's Encyclopaedia of the Law of Scotland* first appeared in 1898, Glegg contributed a short article on Negligence quite separate from the much longer one on Reparation, a structure retained in the second edition of 1914.[166] In each of these, negligence was founded upon a pre-existing duty of care between the parties. That duty was a requirement was definitively settled by the Court of Session in the early years of the twentieth century.[167] When in the 1920s the young Hector McKechnie, who was more aware than most of the Scottish legal tradition, came to contribute

---

163 *J. Guthrie Smith,* The Law of Damages: a Treatise on the Reparation of Injuries as Administered in Scotland (2nd edn, Edinburgh, 1889), pp. 23–4 (emphasis supplied). The change in title is symptomatic of a very substantial revision of the first edition which deserves more attention than it can be given here.

164 (1883) 11 QBD 503 (CA).

165 *A. T. Glegg,* A Practical Treatise on the Law of Reparation (1st edn, Edinburgh, 1892), pp. 8, 12, 34–5. At the second quoted sentence he cites *Austin's* Jurisprudence, Lecture 20. It may be noted here that Glegg thought "tort" the best name for his subject, "but it is unknown to Scotch legal nomenclature" (p. 3 note). His treatment of reparation none the less continued the basic distinction between wrongs where there was wrongful intention or malice and those where there was negligence.

166 See also the division of Negligence from Reparation in the Faculty Digest, which first appeared in 1922. The basis and utility of this division, still found in current legal digests, remain unclear.

167 *Black III* (note 7), pp. 319–27, citing *Kemp & Dougall* v. *Darngavil Coal Co* 1909 SC 1314 and *Clelland* v. *Robb* 1911 SC 253. *Black* singles out "that doughty angliciser" (p. 338), Lord Kinnear, as the judicial villain of the piece, with Lord President Dunedin guilty art and part.

articles on "Negligence" and "Reparation" to the Dunedin Encyclopaedia of 1926, he too accepted as axiomatic the directional duty of care in negligence. The concession made in *Donoghue* v. *Stevenson* that the laws of Scotland and England were the same on this matter was therefore firmly established as legal orthodoxy at the time.

Given the arguments and evidence adduced above, it is extremely unlikely that Winfield's theory provides any explanation of the origins of duty of care in Scots law. It is evident that the concept of a duty of care, whether or not indigenous to Scotland, fitted in quite readily with the development of Scots law in the mid to late nineteenth century. A further factor, common to both Scots and English law, which must have encouraged a tendency to regard the question of duty, so far as it related to policy, as a prerequisite for negligence, was the existence of trial by jury in both jurisdictions. In Scotland, certainly, it was natural to consider matters of policy as questions of law to be decided by the judge, in contrast to the issue of negligence which, as a matter of fact, would be decided by the jury.[168]

The Development of the Modern Law

How does one explain the rise and development of the modern Scots law of negligence? Much of the discussion to date has focused on the shift away from assythment, coupled with the demands of a new industrial age. For McKechnie, "Scots lawyers in fact invented a new form of process to meet the needs of building and transport developments".[169] Black argues that at the root of the development was the increasing emphasis in the criminal law on the requirement of *mens rea* or dole (wicked intent) which meant that many acts which caused harm ceased to be regarded as criminal, together with an increasing risk of harm concomitant with the "rapidly expanding urbanization and mechanization of society".[170] McKenzie and Evans-Jones disagree with Black, observing that negligent behaviour was not wholly de-criminalised in the nineteenth century. They propose instead that "the fundamental factor leading to the decline of assythment ... was the separation of private from public wrongs which is reflected in the changing conception of the function of the law of delict".[171] Punishment, with which assythment was linked, was for the state, compensation for the injured individual.

168 See e.g. *Guthrie Smith,*(note 96), p. 63, and text at notes 85–92, above.

169 *McKechnie* (note 8), at p. 276.

170 *Black II* (note 7), p. 189.

171 *McKenzie and Evans-Jones* (note 8), p. 298.

We do not find these explanations wholly convincing. It is true that the origin of the action of assythment is to be sought at a time before the emergence of a public criminal law as now understood. But the principle of the public prosecution of homicide had long been accepted in Scotland, the Criminal Justice Act of 1587 being particularly important in this regard;[172] and the significance of the mental element in the crime of homicide had also long been recognised.[173] Despite its revival in *M'Kendrick* v. *Sinclair,* the action of assythment was already in terminal decline by the mid-eighteenth century, some time before the rise of the modern law of delict. Too close a connection should not, therefore, be looked for between assythment and the modern law. In addition, an assythment-based explanation fails to take account of the European dimension. Assythment in its latter guise was distinctively Scottish, whereas it is clear that the rise of the modern law of delict was to a considerable extent a European phenomenon. Nevertheless, the long survival of the action of assythment, only formally abolished in 1976, alerts us to the slow evolution of the modern law of delict from what had gone before, and to the long overlap with earlier actions and patterns of thought; to the distinction long made between injury to the person and injury to property; to the change in focus from types of harm to questions of liability; to the movement from criminal law to civil, and from public to private.

As regards the argument based on the increasing mechanisation of society, we may observe that the accidents which led to *Gardner* v. *Ferguson, Innes* v. *Edinburgh Magistrates* and *Blacks* v. *Cadell* were not of a type peculiar to urban or industrialising society; probably people, whether or not with drink taken, have been falling into holes in the ground since the first distillation of alcohol and the invention of spades, both occurrences considerably pre-dating the Industrial Revolution. Increasing mechanisation, therefore, is only part of the answer.[174] However, it is clear that the social conditions of the early nineteenth century – burgeoning construction projects, the development of roads along which competing stage coaches raced, the arrival of the railway age, the use in mass employment contexts of massive and dangerous machinery – did much to accelerate the expansion of the law of *culpa* in the field of personal injuries and death.

---

172 APS, iii, p. 458 (c. 57).

173 *W. D. H. Sellar,* Forethocht felony, malice aforethought and the classification of homicide, in Legal History in the Making, edd. W. M. Gordon and T. D. Fergus (London and Ronceverte, 1991) pp. 43–59.

174 In particular it cannot explain the case of *Sawers* v. *Graham* in 1799, for which see note 57 above. *Blacks* involved a fall into a long-disused mine by the road between Bo'ness and the deceased's farm of Scotstoun near South Queensferry.

The Case for Convergence

At the beginning of this paper we raised the question: How does one explain the apparent shift in orientation of Scots law in the course of the nineteenth and twentieth centuries from the Civil to the Common law? The currently prevailing view, the most ardent proponents of which have been Sir Thomas Smith and Robert Black, is that the answer lies in the legal imperialism of an English-dominated House of Lords, coupled with the anglicising tendencies of at least some members of the Scottish bench. In particular, Black argues that the rules of *culpa* developed by the Scottish courts in the first three-quarters of the nineteenth century came thereafter to be overlaid by influence from the equally rapidly developing English law of negligence. He believes that the broad general standard of *culpa*, concerned essentially with the reasonableness of the conduct of the defender in the circumstances, was displaced by what he calls the "directional duty of care", in which the pursuer had to show, not just the unreasonableness of the defender's conduct, but that a duty was owed to him in particular. The breadth of *culpa* began to break up into categories in which a duty was or was not owed, a particular example being the long uncertainty over whether occupiers owed a duty to trespassers on their property, finally resolved in the negative by the House of Lords in an appeal as late as 1929.[175] In a curious way, therefore, while the Scottish appeal of *Donoghue* v. *Stevenson* in 1932 liberalised the English tort of negligence, the decision and Lord Atkin's famous formulation of the duty of care set Scots law on a rather more constrained path than it had enjoyed for most of the nineteenth century.[176]

We are not convinced by this analysis. That English legal imperialism played a part in the development of Scots law, there can be little doubt, a prime example being in respect of the doctrine of common employment.[177]

---

[175] See *Black III* (note 7), pp. 334–43, for the full story.

[176] It is however interesting to note that in an article published in the immediate aftermath of *Donoghue,* Lord Cooper, father figure of Scottish legal nationalism, criticised the decision, not as a departure from Scottish purity, but as judicial legislation: *T. M. Cooper,* The length of the Chancellor's foot, Juridical Review 45 (1933) pp. 145–50, reprinted in his Selected Papers 1922–1954 (Edinburgh, 1957), pp. 53–7. In the 1950s, as the full impact of *Donoghue* began to dawn, there was a revival of interest in *culpa,* but it led nowhere: *W. A. Elliott,* Reparation and the English tort of negligence, Juridical Review 64 (1952) pp. 1–11; *J. J. Gow,* Is culpa amoral?, Juridical Review 65 (1953) pp. 17–36; *W. A. Elliott,* What is culpa?, Juridical Review 66 (1954) pp. 6–36; and some of the work of *T. B. Smith,* Studies Critical and Comparative (Edinburgh, 1962), pp. 80–4, 103–15, 154–67. For a defence of the duty concept see *D. Brodie,* In defence of *Donoghue,* Juridical Review 42 (1997) pp. 65–75.

[177] See above, text at notes 159–162.

It is also clear from the pleadings in *Innes* that from the beginning of the development of negligence liability pleaders looked to English authority.[178] However, we believe that it can be argued that the apparent shift in direction of the Scots law of negligence in the last third of the nineteenth century was in large part the result of a gradual and unsurprising convergence between Scots and English law, not least in the matter of the concept of a duty of care. We have already touched on several of the factors which gave rise to this convergence.

One obvious factor is the common language of Scottish and English lawyers. Words such as "duty", "negligence", "foreseeability" and "reasonableness" thus occur naturally in both systems. We have noted that the word "negligence" appears already in 1426 in a Scots statute, as does the concept of foreseeability. Later, "negligence" was frequently seen as synonymous with, or as a translation of "*culpa*". Thus, for example, from the beginning of the Jury Court in 1815 the issues to be put to the jury were regularly expressed, not in the Latin form *culpa,* but in terms of the "fault, negligence and want of skill" of the defender. The familiarity of the word must have made it easy to turn to English cases as examples and authorities. Indeed some reverse traffic may have occurred, as English judges in the House of Lords dealt with the steady stream of Scottish appeals in reparation cases.[179]

The same may be said about the word "duty", but here the correspondence went further than the natural use of the word in ordinary speech. The concept of legal duty was part of the very fabric of the law of obligations, as expounded by Stair, and followed by later Scots lawyers. Whatever may be said of the use of the language of duty in English law, or the origins of the concept of a duty of care there, particular or otherwise, neither the word nor the concept can have appeared unfamiliar to Scots lawyers.

Again, the Scottish understanding of *culpa* was never authoritatively formulated in either text or judicial opinion. The Institutional and other writers up to and including Bell in the early nineteenth century provided little guidance or doctrine, and indeed frequently used ambiguous phrases like "culpable neglect" in their analyses. There was no Scottish textbook on the subject until 1864. At that point, it is probably fair to say that the law might well have taken another path, pursuing notions of wrongfulness or unlawfulness such as had established themselves on the Continent rather

---

178 See above, text at notes 60 and 64. Note also Adam's explanation for his reference to English authority, quoted above, text at note 98.

179 *R. Stevens,* Law and Politics: The House of Lords as a Judicial Body 1800–1976 (London, 1979) observes that with Scottish appeals greatly out-numbering English ones, "the House ... for much of the nineteenth century [was] ... predominantly a Scottish court" (at p. 323; see also pp. 15–19, 43 note and 51 note).

than the duty of care; but there was not a radical conceptual departure from tradition in the choice of the latter route.

Another factor which tended towards the convergence of the two systems and the emergence of a duty of care as a pre-requisite was the common system of trial by judge and jury. The jury remained master of the facts, but the judge might determine on relevancy that there was no case in law to answer and so assoilzie (absolve) the defender. The literature of the period discloses some criticism of juries as being biased in favour of the pursuer.[180] There may accordingly have been a tendency to treat questions as matters of law and so remove cases from the jury. So defining negligence more in terms of legal duties may have been a means of getting away from the essentially jury question of what is reasonable in the circumstances.

In addition, the problems with which the Scottish and English legal systems had to deal were similar – the liability of masters/employers to servants/employees, railway accidents, accidents to children and to people in places where they had no business to be. There may also have been a sense that in the single economy of a great imperial and industrial nation the same problems should be given the same answers.[181] We might speculate also about judicial perceptions that too much liability would inhibit enterprise and economic activity, perhaps particularly with regard to small businesses. The feeling that the policy issues were the same in Scotland and England must have been reinforced by legislation such as the Employers Liability Act 1880, which applied in both jurisdictions.

Conclusion

We would suggest, therefore, that the convergence between the Scots and English law of negligence in the course of the nineteenth century and beyond is unsurprising, indeed, almost natural, and that this, rather than English legal imperialism, is the main reason for the apparent shift in Scots law from the Civilian tradition towards the Common law. In fact, the shift may have been more apparent than real, for this was a two-way process: if the Scots law came closer to the English, it is undeniable that the English law, through the recognition and development of the tort of negligence, had come much very much closer to the Civil law. This may help to explain the essential paradox that the most famous case on the law of torts in the

---

180 See for example articles in the Journal of Jurisprudence 23 (1879) pp. 126–33, and 24 (1880), pp. 194–9.

181 See *A. F. Rodger,* Thinking about Scots law, Edinburgh Law Review, 1 (1996), pp. 3–24.

Common law world, *Donoghue* v. *Stevenson,* was a Scottish case, and not, therefore, strictly speaking, about torts at all. Reinhard Zimmermann's remark that, "It was in the famous case of *Donoghue* v. *Stevenson* in which the new tort of negligence came to be recognised unequivocally by the House of Lords …",[182] may seem uncontroversial, even a truism; yet no Scots lawyer could describe the result of the case in these terms, as Scots law recognises neither a law of torts, nor a tort of negligence. The concession made by counsel in *Donoghue* in the House of Lords that the case could proceed on the basis that Scots law and English law were the same may have been rightly made, and Alan Rodger is no doubt correct in taking this to suggest "that no substantial difference in the relevant law of the two jurisdictions could be detected by those experienced counsel",[183] yet the intellectual superstructure of the law in the two systems remained different. Scots law held and holds to the systematics of the law of obligations as laid down by Stair within the general tradition of the *ius commune*. Here there has been no shift towards the Common law. If anything, the shift has been in the other direction.[184]

---

182 *Zimmermann* (note 4), p. 911.

183 *Rodger,* Lord Macmillan's speech (note 3), p. 241. Perhaps however it might be said that neither could see any substantial *advantage* in taking up any differences between Scots and English law.

184 This article has also appeared in *K. Reid* and *R. Zimmermann* (eds.), A History of Private Law in Scotland (Oxford, 2000), vol. 2, pp. 517–547, by kind permission.

BERNADETTE AUZARY-SCHMALTZ

Liability in Tort in France before the Code Civil: The Origins of Art. 1382 ff. Code Civil*

Scholars[1] interested in the origins of the principle of tort liability contained in art. 1382 ff. Code civil have often noted that it was only after a long and hesitant evolution, starting at the beginning of the Middle Ages that the reparation granted to the victim was fully distinguished from the punishment inflicted on the guilty party, a subject which, according to Georges Chevrier[2] at the end of the 1950s, had been "too long confined in the abstraction of grand principles" when further consultation of our national history,[3] especially the customs and judicial decisions of lower courts as well as the Parlement de Paris, would have "given some life" to it.

His wishes have been met, at least in part. A team originally formed by Professor P.-C. Timbal has systematically exploited and extensively documented the remarkable records of the Parlement de Paris[4], the supreme court of the kingdom from the middle of the 13th to the middle of the fifteenth century, when the first provincial Parlement was created in Toulouse. A wealth of material has been unearthed by research done on the

---

* I am very grateful to Professor Tony Weir for his skillful translation.

[1] Among legal historians, see *J.-M. Carbasse,* Histoire du droit pénal et de la justice criminelle (PUF 2000), 280; *G. Chevrier,* Les origines de l'article 1382 du Code Civil français (manuscript notes of an unpublished lecture kindly furnished by Professor R. Feenstra), and Composition pécuniaire et réparation civile du délit dans la Bourgogne ducale du XIVe siècle au XVIe siècle, in Mémoire de la Société pour l'Histoire du Droit et des Institutions des anciens pays bourguignons, comtois et romands (Dijon 1960), 21st fasc.; *J.-L. Gazzaniga,* Introduction historique au droit des obligations (PUF 1992), 236 f.; *Ph. Godding,* Le droit privé dans les Pays-bas méridionaux du XIIe au XVIIIe siècle (Brussels, Académie Royale, 1987), 500. Among private lawyers, see *M. Mazeaud,* Répétitions écrites de droit civil approfondi et comparé, Les Cours de droit (1940–41), 47 f.; *A. Tunc,* La responsabilité civile (2nd ed. Paris 1989) 47–56; *G. Viney,* Traité de droit civil: Introduction à la responsabilité (2nd ed. Paris 1995), 6–20.

[2] Les origines de l'art. 1382 du Code civil (n. 1).

[3] In Germany and England, by contrast, medieval law has been much studied.

[4] In the Archives nationales, série X; for information, see *M. Langlois* in Guide des recherches dans les fonds judiciaires de l'Ancien Régime, Parlement de Paris, 65–160.

liability of the employer,[5] and the study methods worked out by Centre d'Etude d'Histoire Juridique (CEHJ)[6] have produced a collection more broadly based. These offer invaluable insights into the long and fluctuating evolution whereby customary practice and judicial decision adapted and extended the *lex Aquilia,* which reappeared in the twelfth century with the renaissance of Roman law.

This article considers first the general principle of liability for one's own act (art. 1382 Code civil) and then, as an example of liability for others, the liability of masters and employers (art. 1384(5) Code civil).

I.

The General Régime of Liability in Tort: Liability for One's Own Act (art. 1382 Code civil).

Two periods can be distinguished in the historical evolution which led to the emergence of the grand principles of tort which were to be laid down by the Code civil (art. 1382 ff.): first, a creative period full of innovations, followed by a more theoretical and less innovative phase which was the immediate precursor of the code of 1804.

First Period: Creative Evolution (Twelfth to Fourteenth Centuries)

The system of civil liability for damage caused began at the end of the twelfth century and its development during the thirteenth was confirmed and consolidated in the fourteenth. Thanks to recent analysis of decisions of the Parlement during this period we can now see how the law of liability managed to emancipate itself by distinguishing reparation from punishment. This distinction occurred at two levels, first in relation to monetary composition and secondly, within private law itself, when liability in tort was seen as differing from liability for breach of contract.

---

[5] See my doctoral thesis, under the direction of P.-C.Timbal, Préposé et commettant dans l'Ancien Droit français d'aprés la jurisprudence du Parlement de Paris (278 pp., typed, Paris II, 1981).

[6] CEHJ, a research unit of Paris II and the Archives nationales in association with CNRS (URA 2014), has drawn up significant records of civil decisions (série X^1A) for the period 1324 to 1380, with analytical files and indices of subject-matter and names. The oldest decisions of the Parlement, known as the Olim (1254–1318), have also been analysed on cards; the work started by Professor P.-C. Timbal is now being completed by J. Hilaire and B. Auzary-Schmaltz; finally the series of criminal records (Serie X^2A) has been added to the collection, currently under the direction of Professor J.-M. Carbasse.

Other developments relate to the evaluation of the reparation and how it was to be effected, innovations made possible largely because of the obsolescence of group responsibility.

1. The separation of reparation and punishment

a) In the early days, liability is barely distinguishable from monetary composition

The principle of monetary composition was very acceptable to the twelfth century, dominated as it was by the ideal of peace, promoted by Saint Bernard,[7] and the *pax privata* negotiated between the guilty party and the victim or his family had been endorsed by the Glossators.[8] When the author of the outrage more or less spontaneously offered the victim reparation for the harm the settlement had two aims, not only to indemnify the victim but also to achieve peace between the families. The terms used are highly indicative: in the oldest decisions the word *pax* keeps appearing.[9] But how were such practices thought compatible with the authority of the state, already being re-established in the thirteenth century? After all, public authority is weakened when antagonists settle their differences privately without its intervention. However, J.-M. Carbasse[10] has recently suggested that in the deeply Christianised Middle Ages the practice of composition would not seem shocking either to church or state: they could quite willingly adopt it, even as a central feature of their penal policy. Monetary composition, as provided for in the merovingian period and fixed in

---

[7] It remained strong in customary law as well as in "inferior justice", namely the practices just outside the courts, see *J.-M. Carbasse* and *B. Auzary-Schmaltz,* La douleur et sa réparation dans les registres du Parlement mediéval (XIIIe – XIVe siècles) in *B. Durand, J. Poirier* and *J.-P. Royer* (eds.), La douleur et le droit (PUF 1997), 430 ff. The same is true of Northern Italy: see *A. Padoa Schioppa,* Delitto e pace private nel pensiero dei legisti bolognesi, in Mélanges G. Fransen (= Studia Gratiana XX, 1976), 270–287.

[8] *R. Feenstra,* L'actio legis Aquiliae utilis en cas d'homicide chez les Glossateurs, in *Spruit* (ed.), Major XXV annis, Essays in commemoration of the 6th Lustrum of the Institute for Legal History of the University of Utrecht (Assen 1979), 57.

[9] Beugnot, Les Olim ou Registres des arrêts rendus par la Cour du roi sous les règnes de Saint Louis, Philippe le Hardi, Philippe le Bel, Louis le Hutin et Philippe le Long, (4 vol. Paris, 1829–1848), ii, 283 no. 5 (1288); iii(l), 297 no. 36 (1308), 626 no. 2 (1311); X^1A 18, fol. 1 (1363): *concordandi et pacificandi.*

[10] *J.-M. Carbasse,* Ne homines interficiantur: Quelques remarques sur la sanction mediévale de l'homicide, in *S. Dauchy, J. Montballyu* and *A. Wijffels* (eds.), Auctoritates: Xenia R. C. van Caenegem oblata. La formation du droit et ses auteurs, Juris scripta historica XIII (Brussels 1997), 168 f.

amount in the famous *lex Salica,* under the name *pactus legis Salicae,* had the enormous advantage for the kingdom of re-establishing peace between parties and clans and breaking the "blind chain of vendettas": furthermore, as the author also notes, the secular authorities which supported this system of resolving conflict were far from keen on the unduly harsh penal system of Roman law. In the light of this it appears perfectly understandable that monetary composition should be not only tolerated but actively promoted. Saint Louis himself, the very model of the sovereign-judge, nominated prelates to oversee a monetary composition between the count of Angoulême and the bishop on whom he had inflicted grievous bodily harm, and this even before the count had been found guilty in court.[11]

At the end of the thirteenth century and during the fourteenth we find the Court taking a more or less important part in refining the methods of resolving conflicts in accordance with the wishes of the parties, without necessarily entering directly into their negotiations.[12] The Court sometimes intervenes to take official note of agreements between the parties in relation to delicts of varying degrees of severity and to decide on the consequences, sometimes at the request of the parties, sometimes on its own motion. In 1288[13] a widow who had made "peace" with the tutor of the heirs of her husband's murderer sought and obtained the fulfilment of the promise to pay her 200 livres parisis.[14] In a similar case in 1346 the Court intervened again; the widow sought from Parlement the enforcement of a civil agreement with the person who had inflicted fatal injuries on her husband, the agreement being reached after letters of remission had been obtained.[15] Occasionally the Court records the agreement of the parties but pronounces only on the fine due to the king.[16] Thus Parlement made it clear in imposing a large fine payable to the king for damage done to a forest in breach of his rights that the victim was to receive no part of it;[17] it did likewise even when the composition was reached after the inquiry which established

11 Olim i, 93 no. 5 (1259).

12 *B. Auzary-Schmaltz* and *S. Dauchy,* L'assistance dans la résolution des conflits au civil devant le Parlement de Paris au Moyen Age, in Recueils de la Société Jean Bodin, lxiv: L'assistance dans la résolution des conflits (Brussels 1997), part 3, 41–83.

13 Olim ii, 283 no. 5 (1288).

14 The livre consisted of 20 sous, each of 12 deniers parisis (d.p.) or 15 deniers tournois (d.t.); 20 sous tournois (s.t.) were worth about one gold franc.

15 X^1A 10, 357 v° (24 April 1346); agreement of 28 June 1345 (X^1C 3, no. 187); the case is discussed in *P.-C. Timbal,* Les obligations contractuelles dans le droit français des XIIIe et XIVe siécles d'après la jurisprudence de Parlement (2 vols., Paris, 1973–1977), i, 328.

16 The expression is deliberate; it may seem pleonastic, but in fact in many decisions a "fine" is awarded to the victim, also called "amende a partie".

17 X^1A 6, fol. 364 (1334).

the circumstances of the wrong: the guilty party is merely fined.[18] The Court also intervenes to verify the legality of these extra-judicial transactions. Sometimes the agreement is examined by the *commissaires réformateurs*, officers charged by the king with supervising his officials with a view to ensuring good administration throughout the kingdom; thus the royal commissioners examined a composition (a *pax* concluded to indemnify the victim) said to have been unjustly imposed by the seneschal of Saintonge on a person charged with kidnapping, and after inquiry absolved the accused.[19]

In some cases composition was made with royal officials, and can comprise both a proposal that the defendant pay for the harm he caused and negotiation with the court as regards the penalty.[20] Thus Parlement enforced the terms of a composition between royal officials and those responsible for attacks on two sergeants of the king (on the occasion of gaol-breaking) even though a judicial inquiry was on foot, the *compositionis tractatu* covering both the indemnity for the victims and the fine payable to the king.[21] The Court is ready to respect the wishes of the antagonists even if the procedure is well under way when their willingness to settle becomes clear: for example, when the goods of a man guilty of rape and assault had been seized and he later compounded with the victim's relatives, the seizure was rescinded and the parties were allowed to withdraw from the case without any fine.[22]

Sometimes reference is made to a custom as justifying the practice of composition. Thus a case before Parlement in 1332[23] involved a composition between the officers of the baron of Montlaur in Vivarais and a merchant and his servant. The latter had been showing off a camel in their

---

18 X^1A 8, fol. 138 (1340).

19 Olim. iii, 297 no. 36 (1308).

20 Although not relating to liability in tort, it is worth mentioning a case which clearly evidences the royal preference for composition over punishment; in a decision of 3 December 1353 (X^2A 6, fol. 128), the king "par grâce spéciale" allowed the defendants, accused of counterfeiting royal coins, to compound for 2000 *florins d'or à l'écu* against a remission of any other penalty, civil or criminal. The decision is explicit: "Nos erga unumquemque subditorum nostrum et maxime officariorum et servitorum nostrorum misericorditer procedere graciamque et equitatem rigoris justicie preferi volentes ... attentis informacionibus predictis et aliis aliter contra ipsos et eorum quemlibet de rigore et justicia procedi facere potuissemus ad graciam, misericordiam at composicionem predictas in casu dubii et obscuro, ut est in case presenti, per presentes ..."

21 Olim, iii(2), 924, no. 86 (1314).

22 X^1A 18, fol. 1 (17 November 1363); the agreement is not to be found in the series X^1C, so one cannot discover the price of the young girl's virginity.

23 X^1A 6, fol. 220v (4 April 1332); see *J.-M. Carbasse,* Ne homines (n. 10), 178–181 on the use of the renascent Roman Law as a justification for compositions.

troupe and were arrested after a child trying to get a free look at the beast had had his eye put out by one of the merchant's staff. Their release on payment of 40 pounds (20 pounds per person) without prejudice to the claim of the injured child was justified "both in law and by the well-known custom of this part of the country (we are in the land of written law, where the *lex Aquilia* obtains) whereby in such a case one may compound for the penalty."[24]

When the legal system itself claimed to maintain the peace by repressing disorder the legality of these pacification agreements was questioned, and at the end of the thirteenth century the king deployed his powers against composition. First was an ordinance of 1280 whereby Philip III abolished the "bad customs" of Gascony which permitted murderers to avoid public sanction by paying a composition of 300 sous to the family of the victim.[25] This ordinance did nothing to curtail the practice of monetary composition, which obtained not only in Gascony but throughout the whole kingdom, as is demonstrated by decisions of Parlement. Slight though its practical effect was, we see here the emergence at the end of the thirteenth century of the idea that the public authorities are not bound by a transaction with a criminal, that because the malefactor has offended the public interest, direct dealings with him did not constrain the judge.[26] It is not till the middle of the fourteenth century that a royal ordinance of 1357 attempts to prohibit transactions in all "criminal and capital" cases;[27] but it may be thought that like most medieval legal prescriptions this ordinance was rather ignored in practice. Only ten years later the *procureur* of the king was objecting to a composition which he believed to be thwarting justice: in a case before the Grands Jours of Troyes a sergeant of the religious order of Moutiers en Der claimed that, despite his being under the protection of the king, the monks had extorted from him by "oppression de prison" an "obligation ou composition" of 15 francs, and when the defendants objected that no capital crime was involved the *procureur* riposted that "justice and the public good" had been blocked by the composition extracted from the complainant.[28]

---

[24] The justification for the composition according to the officials is given in the arguments of the lord of Montlaur: the accused were "men of humble estate" who had been in prison for some time for the theft of four chickens.

[25] *J.-M. Carbasse,* Philippe le Hardi et les "mauvaises coutumes" pénales de Gascogne, in Hommages à Gérard Boulvert (Nice 1987), 154.

[26] This view appears in the first great treatise on criminal law, by Albertus Gandinus; see *J.-M. Carbasse,* "La Ville saisie par la justice", in Justices (Paris, 1995), no. 2 p. 18, and on the maxim *Interest rei publicae ne maleficia remaneant impunita* see *J.-M. Carbasse,* Ne homines (n. 10), 178 and 180.

[27] Ordonnances des rois de France de la troisième race, iii, 130, art. 9.

[28] X^1A 9182, fol. 4 (14 September 1367); unfortunately the outcome of the case is unknown.

Furthermore, private composition might work against the victim's representatives: in a decision of 5 March 1368 the Parlement held that a composition between a murderer and his victim's widow barred the claim of the victim's brother as partie civile.[29]

Notwithstanding the legislation which sought to prohibit it, monetary composition long obtained in different parts of France: it is found in Burgundy in the 15th century,[30] round Autun at the beginning of the sixteenth,[31] and in Auvergne and Languedoc as late as the eighteenth.[32] In countries to the North monetary composition continued to be practised for a long time: in Brussels, indeed, so many capital crimes were the subject of conciliation or composition that capital punishment was ordained only seventeen times in the fifteenth century, and in Liège there are compositions for murder as late as the sixteenth century.[33]

b) In the field of civil liability, a distinction is drawn between liability for contractual and delictal fault

The first signs of this distinction can probably be found in the customs: the custom of Saint-Bauzeil near Pamiers in the Ariège (1278) allows the creditor who has been insulted by his debtor to sue him "tam in debito quam de alio foris facto sibi ab ipso injuriose illato".[34] P.-C. Timbal, a specialist in the area, has made a detailed study of the law of obligations in early law, and his work should be consulted.[35] He writes that "the law of civil liability is clear enough in the fourteenth century for the basic rules of the modern law to be discernible".[36] He notes that though the law was romanistic in form, it did not adopt the Roman system of degrees of fault: appreciation of the debtor's *culpa* depended on the particular facts of each case, and *custodia* denoted merely the possession and control of a thing belonging to the creditor. Analysis of decisions is particularly profitable when the archives contain not only the holdings but also the pleadings of the parties, which are often brimming over with the facts, and P.-C. Timbal

---

29 X^1A 28, fol. 146 (5 March 1378).

30 *J.-M. Carbasse* (n. 1), 161.

31 See *G. Chevrier,* Composition pecuniaire ... (n. 1), 137.

32 *J.-M. Carbasse* (n. 1), 18; see also, by way of comparison, the cases cited for the northern Low Countries in *R. C. van Caenegem,* La peine dans les anciens Pays-bas, in Recueils de la Société Jean Bodin, Ivi: La Peine (Brussels 1991), 118–141.

33 See *J.-M. Carbasse* (n. 1), 18.

34 Cited by *G. Chevrier* Les origines (n. 1).

35 *P.-C. Timbal* (n. 15).

36 *P.-C. Timbal* (n. 15), ii, 11.

has commented on a large number of such cases, many of which he has published. There is not much to add, but two cases from the end of the fourteenth century rate a mention here.

One involved a *mutuum,* the loan of 5,000 gold francs, the repayment of which presumably triggered the lawsuit. The contract contained a clause calling for a penalty of 5 francs per day of delay ("paines" in the text) and an impressive number of hostages (25 horsemen and 15 footmen) to be held until repayment. The terminology is inherently confusing,[37] but the penalty clause has the interesting feature of providing for the payment of half of the penalty to the court seised of any claim.[38] In its council decision of 16 July 1392[39] the Court awarded the creditor "for his principal and penalties converted into interest the sum of 13,000 francs, and to the king for his part of the penalty 3,000 francs", the creditor to be paid first. This global sum doubtless summarises the decision made at the hearing since in the decision as registered[40] the court distinguishes between the 5,000 francs lent and the penalties, which were reduced to 8,000 for the creditor and 3,000 francs for the *procureur* of the king.

The second case of interest to us involved a contract of lease whereby the scholars of the Sorbonne rented one of their houses on the rue de la Sorbonne to a royal counsellor, Jean de Folleville, the tenant to pay 30 livres tournois per annum and the owners to maintain the roof and walls. The tenant effected repairs valued at 40 francs, but the house burnt down. The owners sued Folleville, seeking a judgment that Folleville rebuild the house on the ground that the fire was due to his fault or the fault of one of his household for whom he was responsible, tenants being liable for *levi* and *levissima culpa.*[41] It is the last point which concerns us at present. Folleville obviously knew his business, for he replied first that when in occupation of the house he used "such care as a *bonus pater familias* would have shown" (a Roman notion which was to have a great future), and then that even if he were guilty of *levi culpa* he was excused by *cas fortuit;* the house having been burnt down by "cas de fortune", the loss must be borne by the owner. The Court accepted his arguments and required the scholars to reinstate the house for Folleville. One has to admire the astuteness of the

---

37 Ambiguity remains to this day in our use of the phrase "penalty clause".

38 This solution is beneficial to the plaintiff since the *procureur* of the king will join him to claim the half payable to him; this is a guarantee of success, given the zeal with which the *procureurs* acted in defence of the king's rights and profits.

39 X¹A 1476, fol. 234 v.

40 X¹A 39, fol. 229 (16 July 1392).

41 Reported by Jean Le Coq at question no. 128: "An dominus teneatur ratione combustionis per suum familiarem facte"; see *M. Boulet,* Questiones Johannis Galli (Paris 1944), p. 151 ff.

lawyer-tenant and take note of the modernity of the way the dispute was resolved.[42]

In the fourteenth century the classic exonerations of the contractual debtor were *cas fortuit* and *act of the prince.* To the many instances studied by P.-C. Timbal arising from all kinds of contract, including deposit, hire, lease and carriage,[43] one can add a case from 1418, remarkable in that both these defences were raised together in argument. The dispute was between a collector of duties at the Saint Jacques and Saint Martin gates of Paris and the *prévôté des marchands,* the municipal authority which had for three years granted him the rights of collection. The collector sought a reduction in the price payable on two grounds external to the original contract, first that one of these gates was kept closed to protect the city (this was during the Hundred Years War), and secondly that coal merchants were exempt from the duties.[44]

2. Problems relating to measure of damages and methods of reparation

Liability in tort tended to become an autonomous principle as it more or less successfully separated itself out from rather a confused background. This emerges from the *jurisprudence:* as collective responsibility waned from the end of the thirteenth century one can see greater precision in the methods of measuring damages and determining their incidents.

a) The waning of collective responsibility

Although collective responsibility was on the wane, instances of it can still be found, especially in urban communities; sometimes the judgment imposes a fine as well as exacting damages, as happened to the town of Sancoins, held liable in 1270 for a gaol-break effected by the citizenry *en masse,*[45] as well as to Provins in 1282, when a murder had taken place and

[42] According to the texts in the Code civil on the contract of lease one of the two main obligations of the tenant is "d'user de la chose louée en *bon père de famille* (art. 1728); in case of fire the tenant is liable unless he proves, *inter alia,* that "the fire occurred by *cas fortuit* or force majeure (art. 1733(l)).

[43] *P.-C. Timbal* (n. 15) ii, 40–52.

[44] Arguments dated 6 May 1418: X^{1}A 4792, fol. 46; interlocutory order 17 August 1418: X^{1}A 1480, fol. 142. The actual outcome is unknown, but the case is analysed by *B. Auzary,* Fluctuat nec mergitur. La prévôté des marchands et l'urbanisme parisien au XIVe siècle d'aprés la jurisprudence du Parlement (1380–1500), Ph. D. supervised by J. Favier (typed, Paris IV Sorbonne, 1989) 243 f.

[45] Olim i, 337 no. 7 (1270).

all the men then resident in the town were required to contribute to the global award.[46]

By contrast one finds Parlement rejecting all the rules suggested as being customary and providing for collective responsibility, whether for wrongs or not. In 1298 the Court rejected a custom alleged by the count of Hainault whereby all the relatives of a murderer were required to take an oath within the year that they had nothing to do with the murder, on pain of being themselves punished as murderers.[47] A century later Parlement rejected an attempt by the lord of Parthenay to make the inhabitants of Doux (now Deux-Sèvres) collectively liable for the non-payment by one of them of the *"hernaut"*, a kind of customs duty;[48] the arguments on each side are worth recounting, the inhabitants maintaining the moral view that "no one should be punished for the act of another" while the lord sought to legitimate his supposed right of *"hernaut"* on the analogy of a right of *marque*.

The latter was quite a good argument since letters of marque do indeed constitute, in a broad sense, a measure of reprisal,[49] for in respect of damage caused by a foreigner they authorise execution on the goods of any of his compatriots in the country. By allowing an individual to obtain payment due from a foreigner in default on a debt or as compensation for a wrong, letters of marque represent a legal remedy in the field of private international law. Thus, as P.-C. Timbal says,[50] letters of marque "represent an extension of private vengeance which, though now excluded in internal legal relations, reappears in international relations when the judicial sanction is unavailing; it is based on the solidarity which exists between the fellow-subjects of a prince, who are collectively responsible for the damage caused by their compatriot and which their national system of justice has not redressed." A similar solidarity existed between the inhabitants of communities in the south of France in respect of dark misdeeds.[51] However, these measures inhibited commerce and public opinion took against them,

---

[46] Olim. ii, 198 no. 7 (1282).

[47] Olim ii, 428 no. 34 (1298), cited by *Fr. Olivier-Martin,* Le roi de France et les mauvaises coutumes au Moyen Age, in ZSS (Germ.Abt.) 58, 120 (1938), and *J.-M. Carbasse,* (n. 1) 219, n. 25, who mentions that this rule was adopted by the charter of Hainault of 1323 despite its disapproval by Parlement.

[48] In the pleadings of 10 June 1389 (X^1A 1474, fol. 283 v) the *procureur* of the king argued that such a custom "would be contrary to good morals and the public interest"; Jean le Coq indicates that the custom was not accepted by the court (see M. Boulet (n. 41) Question no. 182).

[49] The letters are called *littere marche* or *littere represaliarum:* see *M.-Cl. Chavarot,* La pratique des lettres de marque d'après les arrêts du Parlement (XIIIe – début XIVe siècles), in Bibliothéque de l'école de Chartes 1991, vol. 149 p. 52.

[50] *P.-C. Timbal,* Les lettres de marque dans le droit de la France mediévale, in Recueil de la Société Jean Bodin, x: L'étranger (Brussels 1958), 109–138.

so they were replaced from the fifteenth century onwards by a different device, namely a tax *ad valorem* on goods emanating from the country whose citizens had caused the harm; in this way the money was raised indirectly and fairly from the exporters. This new device was used fairly frequently in the fourteenth and fifteenth centuries but letters of marque, as we shall see, disappeared only gradually. It should be noted, as does the author mentioned,[52] that the very existence of letters of marque exemplifies the containment of private vengeance by a legal institution subject to precise rules.

b) Measure of damages

aa) Civil damages distinguished from the fine payable to the court

At the end of the thirteenth century, compensation was included in the fine and the victim received part of the fine in respect of his harm.[53] In decisions at the beginning of the fourteenth century fine and damages are distinguished, though they may be sought together, with the victim sometimes demanding a fine for the king in addition to his damages,[54] and the *procureur* of the king sometimes claiming damages for the victim as well as the fine.[55]

Occasionally the payment of the fine is modified in favour of the damages. Thus when the defendants are impoverished, the fine may be remitted and the damages made payable in instalments.[56] Sometimes, too, part of the fine is allotted to the victim by way of compensation[57] or the fine is simply cancelled in order to allow the payment of the damages.[58]

---

51 *J.-M. Carbasse,* La responsabilité des communautés en cas de 'Méfaits clandestins' dans les coutumes du midi de la France', in Diritto commune e diritti locali nella storia dell'Europa (Milan 1980), 141–152.

52 *P.-C. Timbal* (n. 50) 113.

53 Olim i, 337 no. 7 (1270): fine of 100 pounds imposed for gaol-breaking, of which 20 pounds went to the royal officer who had been molested; Olim i, 911 no. 73 (1273): fine of 800 pounds, of which the injured bailiff received 200 *pro injuria sua.*

54 Olim iii(1), 605 no. 97 (1310).

55 Olim iii(1), 667 no. 32 (1315): citizens molested during an armed attack on a town in the Auvergne.

56 Olim iii(2), 1046 no. 94 (1315): the trial judge awarded damages of 30 livres parisis to the victims of personal injury and imposed a fine of 100 sous parisis to the king; on appeal the Court gave the defendants three years in which to pay the 30 pounds.

57 X^1A 5, fol. 479 (13 December 1326): after reducing to 100 pounds the fine of 2000 pounds ordained by the bailiff of Sens, the Court ordered it to be paid to the victims (judgment published by *P.-C. Timbal* (n. 15) i, 80; X^1A 5, fol. 597v

bb) The nature of the damage

(1) Damage to property

In a predominantly rural society property damage normally results from agrarian delicts, such as the destruction of mills or fishponds, burning of barns or silage, ruining crops, damage caused by marauding cattle,[59] infringements of hunting rights, improper seizure of animals (pigs, sheep, ewes or cattle). Not much need be said about such damage, which falls within the direct action under the *lex Aquilia* (D. 9.2). As to the extent of damage it is worth observing that in deference to the theory of *interesse* elaborated by the Glossators and Bartolists from the *id quod interest* in classical Roman law,[60] the courts also took *lucrum cessans* into account:[61] thus in 1266 when the men of the chapter of Langres whose lands had been devastated by the soldiers of the King of Navarre obtained compensation from Parlement, they were also indemnified for the fact that their lands remained fallow while they were in durance and for the dues they had been unable to collect on those lands.[62] Damages for personal injury raised more delicate problems.

(2) Damages for personal injury

Although in principle the *lex Aquilia* covered only physical damage to property *(damnum)*, the tendency in the Middle Ages was to extend it to all "acts" with economic consequences: the Glossators thus gave an *actio utilis* not only when a free man was injured in his body (cost of cure, loss of earning capacity), but also when a person was killed and his relatives suffered economic loss as a result.[63] Only damages for pain and suffering and

(17 September 1328): the *procureur* du roi having achieved the conviction of the Viscount of Meaux and his men for torturing and hanging one of the king's sergeants, the victim's widow was granted 140 livres tournois out of the fine *pro emenda, labore* and *expensis prosecutione cause.*

58 Olim iii(l), 319 no. 67 (1308): *Nulla facta est condempnacio pro rege quia de bonis condempnatorum non poterit exigi de quo leso satisfiat pro lesione, sumptibus et expensis.*

59 Olim i, 139 no. 5: a decision of 1261 involved *dampnum herbe.*

60 In the classical period Ulpian affirmed that in damages claims account was generally taken of what the plaintiff's interest would have been if the delict had not taken place (D. 9,2,21,2).

61 See C. 7,47,1 on "possibile est" *(interesse est damnum emergens et lucrum cessans).*

62 Olim i, 657 no. 19 (1266).

63 *R. Feenstra* (n. 8).

emotional harm were taken to be excluded by the Roman rule *liberum corpus nullam recipit aestimationem.*

This was so, for example, in the customary law of Burgundy: in assessing damages account was taken of the cost of medical care and amount of earnings lost.[64] In most cases the court fixes a global sum:[65] when a cleric claimed 300 livres tournois for medical expenses and the same amount by way of "damages and fines", the Court, eight years later, awarded a monetary "fine" to be determined in accordance with the wealth of the accused;[66] and when a Parisian assaulted and injured by a nightwatchman claimed 200 marks for the injuries he had suffered and 100 pounds for his damages and expenses, he received a total of 20 livres parisis.[67] Exceptionally in later decisions Parlement grants amounts specifically for the cost of cure: a priest who had been assaulted was granted 40 livres parisis by way of fine and 30 pounds to pay the surgeon.[68] There seems to have been a special regime for medical costs, although doctors and surgeons were not yet treated as privileged creditors.[69] In a case of 1350[70] the Court accepted a claim by doctors against the victim despite the victim's objection that in the pecuniary compensation he had negotiated with the parties responsible the latter had undertaken to pay the expenses and wages of the surgeons.

A vital distinction is clearly made in the pleadings of the victims: their claim is in two parts, separating the compensation they seek for the material damage (the *damnum),* to be indemnified by damages, and the wrong

---

64 *G. Chevrier* (n. 1) at 131 states that in this respect the Custom of Burgundy was in line with Roman law. *Contra, G. Rotondi,* Dalla Lex Aquilia all'art. 1151 Cod. civ., Ricerche storico-dogmatiche, Scritti Giuridici (Milan, 1922), ii, 537, where he states that medical costs are not special to Roman law, in as much as other systems grant such damages in the case of personal injury, as in Exodus xxi, 19 (cited by *Feenstra,* Théories sur la responsabilité civile en cas d'homicide et en cas de lésion corporelle avant Grotius, in Etudes offertes à P. Petot (Paris, 1959) 166, no. 19; see also *R. Vigneron,* La douleur vue par les jurisconsultes romains, in La douleur et le droit (n. 7) 39: the provincial governor has jurisdiction over the salaries of doctors.

65 See *J.-M. Carbasse* and *B. Auzary-Schmaltz* (n. 7) 436, where several examples are given.

66 Olim iii(l), 49 no. 16 (1300) and p. 319, no. 67 (1308).

67 Olim iii(l), 707, no. 70 (1311).

68 X^1A 10, fol. 184 (24 March 1345); alleging that the injury to his arm has disabled him, the priest sought an annuity of 50 pounds for the maintenance of a chaplain to look after his charges and a servant, but the expert report of the surgeon testified that the injury was relatively trivial (X^1A 11, fol. 69; 23 March 1345).

69 They became so privileged in the seventeenth century. See *S. Dauchy,* "Le jurisconsulte et le médecin. La douleur vue à travers les recueils d'arrêts (XVIe – XVIIIe s.), in La douleur et le droit (n. 7), 153.

70 X^1A 11, fol. 288 (6 March 1350).

done to them *(injuria,* i.e. the unlawful conduct), to be met by a fine, *(amende),* either *utile* or *honorable* or even both. The wording of the decisions of Parlement shows that the Court took account of this distinction: it regularly and systematically orders the defendant to "repair the damage" *(redere, restituere,* less often *solvere dampna)* and to "amend the injury" *(emandare injuria).* The fine is always sought separately by the victim *pro injuria sua*[71] and so can assuage emotional harm;[72] this the courts seem to allow only in cases of intentional wrongdoing.[73]

The *amende honorable,* as its name indicates, is designed to restore the victim's honour, so important in medieval life.[74] The court's sanction for wrongs which affect the victim's honour is to make the wrongdoer pay the penalty in the manner best adapted to counteract the dishonour. Here the place where the retraction is to be made is particularly important, whether the place of the wrong or the place of the victim's residence, whichever would give the greater publicity to the reparatory act. Thus in a case where the citizens of Orleans, by cries of "Death to the clergy", interrupted a congregation of the doctors and students who were promulgating a decretal on the conditions of study Parlement not only awarded the students a fine of 1,000 livres tournois but required two *procureurs* of the city to proceed along the main street of the city on Easter Sunday at six in the morning to the Church of the Preachers where the congregation had been held and there to make amends in the presence of six doctors and six students; for the actual harm done in the place of the congregation it awarded damages to the preacher brothers.[75] Likewise when insults and assaults were offered to the Mayor of Rouen and his clerk, it was in the place where the wrong was committed – the seat of the municipal tribunal – that the apology had to be made; this penalty, imposed in 1317[76] in addition to a fine for both the victim and the king, is exceptional in that it was applied to a nobleman, normally too dignified to be subjected to a sanction of infamy,[77] but the

71 Olim i, 911 no. 73 (1272); i, 337 no. 7 (1270), $X^{1}A$ 11, fol. 29v (1344); $X^{1}A$ 29, fol. 261 (11 May 1380).

72 $X^{1}A$ 9, fol. 206v (15 September 1341); 10,000 pounds for violiation of his mother's tomb.

73 $X^{1}A$ 7, fol. 61 (29 July 1335): the accused who swears on oath that he had no intention to cause the harm must make restitution and pay damages, but is relieved of the fine.

74 See *Cl. Gauvard,* De grace especial: Crime, Etat et société en France à la fin du Moyen Age (Paris, 1991) ii, 705–752: L'honneur blessé.

75 Olim, iii(1), 537, no. 37 (1310).

76 Olim, iii(2), 1153, no. 62 (1317).

77 The principle that a cleric could not be subjected to an *amende honorable* was generally admitted and is mentioned in several cases in Parlement: $X^{1}A$ 29, fol. 207v (6 October 1380): "religiosi ... ad proposita sue non erant admittenda

decision is doubtless explicable on the ground of the extreme gravity of the act and perhaps also of the determination of the courts to affirm their authority. The penalty may have to be discharged in several different places: the prévôt de Paris required a person who had defamed a married couple to discharge the honour fine, additional to a useful fine of 100 pounds, not only at the home of the victims but also at Notre-Dame de Pontoise.[78]

(3) The method of evaluation

Analysis of the cases shows that in line with the majority opinion among the Glossators and Roman law it was usually for the victim to estimate the harm. Various terms were employed, and were the subject of detailed discussion:[79] was it better to say "I swear that I would rather have *foregone* so much money than suffer this injury", or "I would rather have *lost* so much money than suffer this injury."? At the end of the thirteenth century, Guillaume de Ferrières suggested a formula which combined the *nolle* and the *velle*. Traces of the debate can be found in civil cases in Parlement: sometimes the victim swears that for so much money he would not have agreed to suffer such injuries[80] or that he would rather have lost such a sum,[81] and sometimes he uses the fuller formula and states that he would not have agreed to suffer such harm for such a sum of money and indeed would rather have lost a larger sum.[82]

---

maxime ad petendum quod dictus de Lessau, qui erat et est clericus, emendam honorabilem facere compelleretur"; X^1A 1474, fol. 273 (10 May 1389): the *procureur* of the king claims that the chief priest of Orleans "be publicly condemned ... to proclaim his wrongdoing, and, if he is not a cleric, subjected to an amende honorable (the pleadings are published by M. Boulet (n. 41) 214, Question no. 181).

78 Olim iii(2), 1379 no. 39 (1318): the defendant sought to have the judgement vacated because the victim claimed only a monetary penalty and it had been *ultra petita* for the judge to impose a *peine corporelle* (as he called the *amende honorable);* Parlement did vacate the judgement *quoad* the *amende honorable* and appointed commissioners to hear the case on remand.

79 The principal points are given in *J.-M. Carbasse* and *B. Auzary-Schmaltz* (n. 7) 432 ff.

80 Olim iii(l), 707 no. 70 (1311).

81 X^1A 11, fol. 48 (17 July 1344); X^1A 11, fol. 29v (20 March 1344); in a case of title deeds stolen by a half-brother, Gu. de Durban states that *litteras et processus ... noluisset pro mille* [livres parisis] *amisisse* [and] *in tanta summa erat bene dampnificatus.*

82 Olim iii(2), 1379 no. 39 (1318): *"quas injurias ... ipse noluisset eas sustinuisse pro centum libris parisiensibus, immo tantum et plus maluisset de suo proprio amisisse."* and X^1A 11, fol. 311 (26 June 1350): a priest alleged to be guilty of theft, homicide and sodomy maintained that "il n'aurait pas voulu subir ces injures pour [telle somme], mais aurait préféré perdre autant du sien."

In most cases, nevertheless, these formulae are missing and the victim is asked to swear to the global indemnity sought for his corporeal and material harm. More rarely, there is an inquiry into the amount, apparently only for damage to property (draining a pond,[83] burning a barn and its contents,[84] seizure of wine, corn[85] or hides)[86], possibly because the value of property could be ascertained by reference to the market. Finally, when the matter was more technical, the Court quite often has recourse to experts for an evaluation of the damage done.

cc) Modes of reparation

In ordering compensation the Court can include measures designed to give the victim the best chance of actually obtaining it. This is certainly the aim of certain conservatory measures automatically attaching to the sanction, such as the sequestration by the king of the wrongdoer's goods,[87] the obligation to furnish security[88] or a surety,[89] or even imprisonment.[90]

The victim's claim is often given the rank of a privileged debt;[91] and it tends to become the rule[92] that civil damages constitute a privileged debt taking priority over ordinary debts, and even confiscation orders.[93] Likewise it is accepted that the victim's damages are to be paid before the fine to the king.[94] The famous Parisian advocate Jean le Coq[95] who kept notes of cases which he argued or heard between 1383 and 1398 was extremely interested in the question of the priority of the victim's claim. In his notes, which are an invaluable resource for legal historians since they tell us what

[83] Olim i, 163 no. 10 (1262).

[84] Olim i, 170 no. 9 (1263).

[85] X^{1}A 5, fol. 39 v (20 June 1320).

[86] Olim i, 254 no. 14 (1267).

[87] This is the commonest measure: Olim iii, 587 no. 82 (1310); Olim iii(2), 1204 no. 9 (1317); X^{1}A 5, fol. 596 v (27 August 1327); X^{1}A 8, fol. 33 (20 February 1339); X^{1}A 11, fol. 182 (12 April 1348); X^{1}A 11, fol. 48 (17 July 1344).

[88] Olim iii(l), 47 no. 11 (1300); Olim iii(2), 858 no. 36 (1313).

[89] Olim iii(2),1153 no. 62 (1317).

[90] X^{1}A 13, fol. 358 v (16 June 1352).

[91] In the Customs of Thégra en Quercy (1266) and Clermont-Dessus in Lot et Garonne, as in the majority of medieval customs, one finds the clause *emenda prius facta damnum passo.*

[92] See, for example, Olim i, 257 no. 14 (1265).

[93] X^{1}A 5, fol. 599 v (7 May 1327).

[94] Olim iii(2), 858 no. 36 (1313); X^{1}A 10, fol. 184 (24 March 1345); X^{1}A 5, fol. 599 v (7 May 1327): restitution from the wrongdoer's goods before confiscation.

[95] It constitutes Question no. 265 in the edition of M. *Boulet* (n. 41) 314 ff.

kind of litigation took place before Parlement and let us witness the development of the legal methods of a contemporary practitioner, he collects all the cases under a rubric in the form of a question, here *Quando privatus in solutione perfertur regi.*

To facilitate the prior payment of the damages payment of the fine could be deferred,[96] or remitted as to half with the balance payable in instalments.[97] In one extreme case the Court refrained from imposing a fine to the king because the guilty party's assets were inadequate to satisfy the victim.[98] Furthermore Parlement often rendered defendants solidarily liable in order to help the victim.[99]

Sometimes reparation in kind is ordered in cases where this seems more appropriate, as when Parlement, in addition to awarding damages, ordered the return to Maurice de Belleville of a piece of jasper stolen from him along with other goods.[100] Even beans, vegetables and fodder[101] might have to be replaced, or a thorn hedge improperly removed, with power to substitute if need be.[102]

Contrary to the views of the Romanists, claims in tort were treated as transmissible both actively and passively from the thirteenth century onwards.[103] Under the influence of the canonists and in the interests of secondary victims the Court accepted that the victim's right to compensation passed to his relatives. In 1267 the widow was allowed to sue,[104] then the widow and minor son jointly,[105] and then more generally to the heirs.[106]

It was also under the influence of the canonists that the wrongdoer's heirs were held liable, notwithstanding the opposition of the Glossators who stuck to the contrary Roman principle. In a decision of 1288, the

---

96 X^1A 10, fol. 184 (24 March 1345).

97 Olim iii(1), 282 no. 13 (1308): the initial fine was of 1,000 livres tournois, the damages being of twice that sum.

98 Olim iii(1), 319 no. 67, cited above n. 66.

99 Olim iii(2), 818 no. 52 (1312); solidary liability might also be imposed for the fine: X^1A 5, fol. 80v (11 April 1320); X^1A 29, fol. 261 (11 May 1380).

100 Olim i, 259 no. 3 (1267); this semi-precious stone was thought to alleviate the pain of childbirth.

101 X^1A 8, fol. 19 (16 January 1339).

102 X^1A 11, fol. 352 (13 April 1351).

103 In classical Roman law liability under the lex Aquilia, still ruled by the typical formalities of penal actions, was extinguished by the death of the tortfeasor; under the Empire this was alleviated by allowing a claim against his heirs to the extent of their enrichment (D.9,2,23,8); see *P.-F. Girard,* Manuel élémentaire de droit romain (8th edn. Paris, 1929) i, 442.

104 Olim i, 257 no. 14 (1267).

105 Olim i, 290 no. 13 (1268).

106 Olim iii(1), 465 no. 73 (1309).

widow of the victim was awarded damages against the tutor of the deceased wrongdoer's minor children, the wrongdoer having entered into a settlement binding him to pay a penalty of 200 pounds for the maintenance of the victim's children.[107]

In all these examples from the decisions of Parlement we see a tendency to adopt, so far as possible, measures which conduce to compensation for the harm done. If legal procedures are exhausted, it can intervene in equity,[108] so as to "correct the result where experience showed that the mechanical application of principles would have consequences which were illogical or unconscionable."[109] Three cases in Parlement are particularly illuminating in this regard. In the first, from 1268,[110] the king intervened personally to award damages to a person whose claim had been rejected by the Court on the basis of an inquiry.[111] After royal justice gradually lost its feudal character and became more the justice of the state,[112] judgments in equity were issued by the Court itself: they were no longer the preserve of the king. In a case in 1313 where the Court had felt bound to nonsuit the claimant for a procedural error, it recognised the injustice of its decision and did not hesitate to revoke it; in the civil inquiry which it took upon itself to order it emerged that the defendant had used violence to extort promissory notes from the claimant, so it ordered him to pay compensation of 500 livres parisis and a fine to the king of 100 livres parisis.[113] The case shows that the flexibility which equity affords to the judge conduces at the same time to greater justice for the victim and more generally, by sanctioning illicit conduct, to the better administration of justice. In the third case, the Court modified the principle whereby no damages could be awarded to a party unless he had, to use a modern expression, constituted himself "partie civile":[114] in a decision of 21 July 1334 the procedure had been

---

[107] Olim ii, 283 no. 5 (1288).

[108] *G. Boyer,* in his article La notion d'équité et son rôle dans la jurisprudence des Parlements, in Mélanges Jacques Maury (Paris, 1962) i, 220–235, has shown that tort was one of the privileged areas in which equity operated.

[109] *G. Boyer* (n. 108), 222.

[110] Olim i, 265 no. 2: no reasons for the judgment are given, much less any explanation for the decision of the king: "Rex postmodum voluit quod dictus Lucas haberet centum solidos pro dampnis suis."

[111] See the article by *J. Hilaire,* Le Roi et Nous. Procédure et genèse de l'Etat aux XIIIe et XIVe siècles, in Histoire de la justice, no. 5 (1992), 3–18; at p. 14 the author cites two cases where the king intervened personally in a manner at odds with the *consuetudo curie* or equity.

[112] This is described in detail by J. *Hilaire* (n. 111) 11, who places the turning point around 1280.

[113] Olim iii(2), 858 no. 36 (1313).

[114] See *Y. Bongert,* Rétribution et réparation dans l'Ancien Droit français, in M.S.H.D.B. (45th fasc.) (1988), 59–107; the author mentions that the exceptions to

started by the *procureur* of the king alone without the victim, who had had his left hand mutilated, "being included in the procedure"; on appeal he was granted the favour of joining in with the *procureur* and was awarded an annuity of 15 livres tournois.[115]

One may tentatively conclude that in this period the law of tort made considerable progress. First, in the customs of the South and in many charters we see the emergence of a sort of general principle[116], stated after the enumeration of specific delicts, that the victims of delicts are entitled to reparation *("Damnum passo emendatio debetur").* This progress in the law is, as we have seen, by and large confirmed by the decisions rendered by the Parlement de Paris, the essential features being that the civil claim becomes distinct from the criminal prosecution and independent of it, that, as we have seen, damages may be awarded even to a party not constituted "partie civile" and, more generally, that rules develop which are very protective of those injured, for example, that when the king issued letters of remission, the pardon and dispensation from the penalty left the victim's claim and that of his family intact.

Second Period: Theorisation (Sixteenth and Seventeenth centuries)

Although the law of civil responsibility unquestionably made great progress during the thirteenth and fourteenth centuries, it still bore traces of old law which it is worth recalling; indeed, it remained handicapped by the past in some respects even when a general principle was formulated on the basis of the theorising work of great jurists from the sixteenth and seventeenth centuries onwards, such as Grotius, Domat and Pothier.

1. Survival of earlier principles

Even apart from the fact that in certain regions monetary composition was occasionally practised right up to the eighteenth century, as we have seen, civil liability was still not entirely distinct from criminal and collective liability.

---

this principle are of ancient date and cites Papon's reference to a case from 1397 (p. 67, no. 2).

[115] X^1A 6, fol. 401 (21 July 1334); thus exceptions made in favour of victims go further back than Papon believed.

[116] *G. Chevrier* Les origines (n. 1) cites a gloss of uncertain date on the custom of Châtillon en Dombes (1273) which states clearly that in all the cases specified by the custom (infringements of property rights, bodily integrity, reputation) whoever suffers an injury or damage is entitled to reparation.

a) Civil Liability retains certain penal elements

While the distinction between damages and civil reparation tends to disappear,[117] the former being purely compensatory as regards damage to property, traces of the criminal origins of civil liability can still be found in cases of personal injury or attacks on honour. According to G. Chevrier the idea of revenge survives, and an action in tort is spoken of as the price of avoiding vengeance; indeed, he maintains that the idea that it is "the price of blood" survived until the eighteenth century, the division of damages between the members of the family being reminiscent of the way in Frankish times wergeld was divided among members of the clan. This view is questionable: J.-M. Carbasse believes that one was not buying off revenge but purchasing peace.[118] Whatever the true nature of civil reparation, the widow and orphans are, according to Claude-Joseph de Ferrière, entitled to half the money payable for the killing. It is also common for those who fail to pay damages to be subjected to corporal punishment – an option open to poor defendants,[119] but denied by the Parlements to solvent defendants for fear of abuse.[120]

The liability of several wrongdoers or accomplices continues in practice to be solidary, and the rule indicated in the sixteenth century by Imbert[121] is taken up by Pothier. As we have seen, there is a tendency to require the victim to join in the prosecution in order to obtain damages.[122]

---

117 It never entirely disappears: see *Ph. Bornier,* Conférences des ordonnances de Louis XIV (Paris, 1737) ii, 166: "The practice of the Palace in criminal matters distinguishes damages from civil reparations ..."

118 *J.-M. Carbasse* (n. 10) 171.

119 *G. Boyer* (n. 108) 232, referring to Robert, De re judicata, 1.2C.15 (1599 edn.) 479 f., who cites Paris, 14 January 1586 and 12 June 1593.

120 Ibid., citing Paris 29 April 1595.

121 J. Imbert, Pratique judiciaire tant civile que criminelle (Geneva, 1625) iii, ch. 1.

122 On this point see *Y. Bongert* (n. 114) 64–67; she gives a list of those who may become partie civile and those who, for lack of means, are granted the privilege of intervening as complainants provided that their lack of funds is proved or notorious, a practice said by several authors to be old-established. For example, J. Papon in Recueils d'Arrets notables des Cours souveraines de France (Cologne, 1616) xxiv, title 1, Arrest premier, refers to a decision of 1397: "A person offended, though not a partie, could obtain a material and moral fine in the proceedings instituted by the *procureur* of the king alone. This was decided in Paris in 1397 in a case against ..." Compare the decision of 21 July 1334 (X^{1}A 6, fol. 401), cited n. 115. This practice, so favourable to victims, continued as long as the Parlements enjoyed the flexibility accorded to them by their power to decide in equity; in G. Berthon de Fromental's Décisions du droit civil, canonique et françois, par ordre alphabétique, avec observations sur l'ancienne et la nouvelle jurisprudence

Nevertheless these final traces of criminal liability tend to disappear: damages are no longer converted into corporal punishment, and Muyart de Vouglans has no hesitation in assimilating civil reparation and damages.[123]

b) Collective Responsibility gives way to Individual Liability

Certain archaic traces of collective responsibility remained in the law of the ancien régime, owing to incomplete analysis of delict as a whole. They tended, however, to disappear.

For a long time the family of a delinquent was held liable for his delicts, and this liability was sometimes extended to the whole community or parish. As examples one can cite decisions requiring one or more parishes to indemnify the victims of exactions by soldiers; under some Parlements inhabitants of places which were spared were made to pay their part of the loss;[124] by a decision of 4 April 1630 a company of archers was made to pay a person injured during archery practice, even though it was a pure accident.[125] Under the influence of Roman law, however, collective and family liability in tort yields to a strictly personal liability. The obligation to make the damage good binds the person responsible for the delictal conduct, and no longer bears on the social or familial group to which he belongs. Thus while the child was answerable for the damage done by his father until the sixteenth century, thereafter he was not.[126]

Only the victim himself and a limited number of his representatives may lay claim to damages. In the case of homicide the problem of determining the range of such representatives is acute. In principle only the widow and

---

des païs que se regissent par le droit écrit (Lyons, 1740), vo. Dommages, we find cited a decision by the Parlement de Toulouse to this effect, dated 23 March 1723.

123 The distinction is absent from his Les loix criminelles de France dans leur ordre naturel (Paris 1780) part i, book iii, Tit. III, ch. 1, XI, though it continues to appear in Guyot, Répertoire universel et raisonné ..., vo. Réparation civile.

124 *G. Boyer* (n. 108) 229.

125 Journal des audiences, vi., Suppl. c. 138, cited by *G. Boyer* (n. 108) 230.

126 The son's obligation of reparation was to be reintroduced in the eighteenth century: Berthon de Fromental (n. 122) cites a decision of the Parlement of Toulouse of December 1723 which held the heirs bound to repair the damage. This decision is in line with the view of A. Mornac, but contrary to that of Fr. Graverol, that "under Roman *jurisprudence* there could be no accessory without principal liability and the prosecution ended when the criminal died, so the claim for damages by the partie civile was also extinguished." Berthon de Fromental states in his commentary that "in this kingdom where the sovereign courts are readier to follow equity than strict law, the canon law is followed on this point, so that any property of the guilty party is subject to the damages claim of the partie civile, unless the heirs *purgent ... sa memoire*".

children share the damages, but the claim of the father or other ascendant is trickier. Though the father's claim is generally recognised, its juridical basis was debated. Several alternatives were put forward: sometimes it was based on *patria potestas,*[127] which made for problems where the victim was emancipated, sometimes on the right of aliment, which the father enjoyed as much as the widow and offspring.[128]

Another example of the survival of collective responsibility is provided by letters of marque, which found on the solidarity between compatriots and permit a victim injured by a foreigner to execute on the property of his fellow-citizens. Already less common in the sixteenth century, they gradually fall into disuse. The Assemblée Constituante discountenances them in 1791[129] and the Convention issued the last of them in 1793.[130]

2. *Doctrine*

Given the fragmentary nature of legal practice, as indicated by the collections of decisions and dictionaries of the Ancien droit,[131] what was the role of doctrine to be? Legal historians have often credited Grotius with being the first to enunciate a general principle of liability[132], but now, thanks to the researches of R. Feenstra,[133] we know that in founding the modern school of natural law he was very much influenced by the school of Salamanca. Domat, too, may be thought to have learnt much from the modern school of natural law, despite the hostility of the Jansenists to so purely rational an approach,[134] and his adoption and synthesis of the general principle[135] was to provide the basis for the draftsmen of the Code civil. He

---

127 Berton de Fromental (n. 122), vo. Grossesse, cites a decision of the Parlement of Toulouse of August 1729 which allowed the father to benefit from the provision ordered, at the expense of the rapist and his son, for his pregnant daughter.

128 Although Grotius was for long given the credit for it, it was really the theologian Domenico Soto of Salamanca who first allowed the widow, parents and children of the deceased to claim damages.

129 *M.-Cl. Chavarot* (n. 49) 89.

130 *P.-C. Timbal* (n. 50) 137.

131 The relatively few instances of liability in tort are always presented as decisions on the particular facts: there is no overview of the topic. Some general terms such as delicts, damages and so on may be defined, but this is done in a cursory manner with reference to cases; no principle is stated. On this see *J.-L. Gazzaniga* (n. 1) 247 f.

132 Grotius, Le droit de la Guerre et de la Paix (tr. Barbeyrac, Amsterdam 1724) ii, c. xvii, § 1: "when one is at fault in causing damage ..., one is naturally bound to make it good."

133 *R. Feenstra* (n. 64) 157–171.

134 On these influences see the very detailed work of *A.-J. Arnaud,* Les origines doctrinales du Code civil français (Paris 1969) 7–22 and 61–64.

not only rises to the level of general principle but also deals with its applications in practice, with examples given. Pothier's *Traité des obligations* proves him the heir of Domat, for he rejects the Roman system[136] and follows the natural law's emphasis on intention. On liability he refers to Domat: "When a person intentionally or by malice causes damage or a wrong to another we call this a delict. It is a quasi-delict when a person's unintentional but inexcusably careless conduct causes a wrong to another."[137] Here we find the distinction between delictal and quasi-delictal obligations and the acceptance of the principle that any fault which causes harm generates an obligation to repair it; for Pothier, however, like Domat, fault here includes breach of contract.

Important though the contributions of these two authors are, the medievalist cannot rest entirely content with this traditional picture. It is essential to study the texts of the customs. To a large extent they represent a doctrine much inspired by the Romanists, and though their area of application was restricted they were sometimes in the forefront of stating a general principle of liability: a gloss of uncertain date on the custom of Châtillon en Dombes of 1273, by a professional jurist clearly familiar with Roman law, states clearly that a person who has suffered injury or damage is entitled to "satisfaction", namely an indemnity in relation to the seriousness of the damage or injury.[138] This gloss is quite characteristic: many of the customs of the South take it up in similar formulae. In his *Somme rural,*[139] which summarises the customs of the North of France, Jean Boutillier categorically states the principle that damage must be repaired: "Pource que selon droict nul ne peut estre dommagé ne injurié par quelque voye que ce soit, qu'il n'en soit récompensé." At the end of the chapter he adds: "Peux

---

[135] J. Domat, Les lois civiles dans leur ordre naturel (Paris 1767) Part I, book ii, title VIII, s. iv, 1: "All the losses and all the damage that may arise from the act of another, whether imprudence, thoughtlessness, ignorance of what should be known, or other comparable faults, however slight, must be made good by the person whose imprudence or other fault has given rise to them. For he has done wrong, even if he had no intention of causing harm. Thus a person unwisely playing ball in a place where there was a risk of damage to passers-by will be held liable if he happens to injure someone."

[136] R. Pothier, Traité des obligations (Paris, 1768) no. 3: "The principles of Roman law on the different kinds of pacts and the distinction between contracts and mere pacts are not founded on natural law, and being very complicated, are not accepted in our law."

[137] Ibid. no. 116.

[138] "In omnibus autem casibus supra dictis et singulis, intellegimus et volumus quod passo injuriam sive damnum, secundum modum et quantitatem facti damni vel injuriae, satisfiat", cited by *G. Chevrier* Les Origines (n. 1).

[139] J. Boutillier, La Somme rural ou le Grand Coustumier de practique civil et canon (ed. Loys de Charondas le Caron, Lyons, 1621) tit. xxxvii.

et dois sçavoir ... que nul ne peut ne doit faire dommage a aucun ... sans amende et sans rendre." The *Très ancienne Coutume de Bretagne*[140] not only lays down the principle of just compensation but goes further and distinguishes reparation from punishment.

II.

Liability for the Acts of Others: The Special Case of Employers and Masters (art. 1384 of the Code civil).

Art. 1384(5) of the Code civil can be seen as the outcome of a tradition of case-law going back to the Middle Ages. The matter has been studied in detail,[141] but even a quick survey of the results of that research will show by the end of the fourteenth century the necessary link of dependence had already been largely realised, and that the solutions adopted by medieval judges, based on very diverse and fragmentary foundations, were highly original. It will show also that medieval legal practice contains the seeds of the rule in art. 1384, whose abstract terms are the product of theorising current at the time of Napoleon's codification.

a) Defining the relationship of subordination

No medieval text contains a definition of the requisite relationship, but judicial decisions permit us to identify certain factors. Though they sometimes overlap, they should be distinguished in order to give a fair reflection of the ingenuity of the arguments of defendants eager to establish that their role was a subordinate one which exempted them from liability.

The first and clearest example is when the superior avouches the relationship and thereby approves, ratifies and adopts the acts of the subordinate. "Avouchment" (a very characteristic medieval concept of feudal origin) is often used in conjunction with other cognate expressions: the superior "answers for his subordinate"[142], or is his "respondent"[143] or "takes the act upon himself".[144]

A second factor is when the superior implicitly authorises or ratifies the acts in question. The superior who is aware of his subordinate's conduct without having expressly commanded it is taken to have consented to it,

---

[140] Cited by *Y. Bongert* (n. 114) p. 80 n. 1.

[141] *B. Auzary,* Thesis (n. 5).

[142] X^2A 4, fol. 159 (8 June 1343); see Thesis (n. 5) 23–25.

[143] X^2A 4, fol. 102v (9 May 1343); ibid.

[144] Olim ii, 149 no. 31 (1279); ibid.

through the *scientia domini*. This is expressed in terms which show that the superior could have prevented the acts: *presente* or *sciente et vidente* or *ratum habente*.[145]

A third test turns on the status of the subordinate (official or servant), that is, whether his social standing indicates dependency. The subordinate will emphasise his dependent status as official (sergeant) or member of the household (servant) so that the master is held to account for what the subordinate actually or ostensibly did in his name.[146] The status of dependant seems to create a presumption favourable to the subordinate.

Finally, there is a subsidiary criterion, not enough by itself to establish the link of dependency: the subordinate may try to establish the intention with which his act was done, that it was for the benefit of someone else, namely his superior.[147]

By analysing the decisions of Parlement we can see the emergence of two notions which were to have a long future: the deference of the subordinate to the orders of the superior and his status as employee, subject to his authority. A third concept, also quite modern, appears, that the damage must have been caused in pursuance of the subordinate function. This is a dilatory exception which must be raised *in limine litis,* right at the beginning of the litigation, when the subordinate cites the master in whose service he committed the misdeeds.[148] Thereafter the suit lies against the master who can answer for the subordinate or refuse to defend.

The courts thus hit upon the three main characteristics of the relation of subordination which were to result in the liability of the superior. It is of interest to note that they are in line with the requirements of the law in force today in the great legal systems of the West: the BGB (§ 831), the Codice civile (art. 2049) and the Common Law.[149]

---

145 X²A 4, fol. 7 (3 August 1340); *B. Auzary* (n. 5) 24.

146 X¹A 19, fol. 58 (23 December 1364): ibid.

147 X¹A 21, fol. 307 (14 March 1368); ibid.

148 Stilus Curie parlamenti, published by F. Aubert (Paris 1909) p. 78 no. 20. Guillaume du Breuil, a famous advocate, wrote down the rules of procedure of the Parlement before which he practised at the beginning of the fourteenth century; among the dilatory pleas *pro garando* he mentions one for adjournment so as to allow the appearance of the superior cited by the officer who claimed to have acted "pour lui, sur son ordre et dans l'exercice de ses fonctions."

149 See *J. Baker,* An Introduction to English Legal History (3rd edn., London, 1990) 465: in addition to the master being liable for acts he had instructed the servant to carry out, the principle was accepted shortly before 1700 that there could be liability even in the absence of any instruction if the tort had been committed for the benefit of the master and as part of his work.

b) Distinctive features of the decisions of Parlement

When cited, the superior had a choice: he could "avouch" the acts of his subordinate and accept responsibility for them, that is, pay for the harm caused, or he could "disavow" the conduct, refuse to regard it as his own, and leave the liability to the subordinate.[150] It is the positive side of this which is of interest to us. Avouchment provisionally lets the subordinate out of the case, and the superior comes in to contest the claim. The inquiry will turn on the factors which allow the superior to be charged with the consequences of the act of the subordinate, namely the relationship of dependency and the misconduct constituting a "faute de service".

Given the sparsity and the diversity of the toeholds in the doctrine it is quite fair to describe the solutions of the Court of Parlement as original. Philippe de Beaumanoir, bailiff of Clermont-en-Beauvaisis at the end of the thirteenth century and writer on its customary law, lays down that in principle there can be no disavowal of acts done *justiciando.*[151] Boutillier, royal bailiff at the end of the fourteenth century and author of a private collection of the customs of Tournai and the Tournaisis, states that when a judgment is overturned, it is necessary to adjourn the proceedings for the attendance of both the officer who rendered the decision and his superior, since the latter may have to pay any monetary penalty;[152] Jean le Coq confirms that this principle was applied in practice.[153]

Beaumanoir also states that the subordinate is liable not only for disobeying orders but also for obeying orders which are unlawful.[154] Indeed, for the author of the custom of Beauvaisis the subordinate must obey only those orders which are given "selonc bonnes moeurs". Du Breuil also takes up the point that obedience has its limits: it cannot be invoked for intentional wrongs.[155]

The principal basis given for the liability of the superior is his own fault in choosing the subordinate or failing to supervise him properly. Beauma-

---

150 Thus while avowal amounts to a guarantee, disavowal corresponds to a denial or disowning, which reminds one of noxal abandonment, despite the differences: see *F. de Visscher,* La nature de l'abandon noxal, RHD 1930, 447 and 466, and Le système romain de la noxalité, in Etudes de droit romain public et privé (Milan, 1966) 356 f.

151 Ph. de Beaumanoir, Coutumes de Beauvaisis (reissue of the original edition of 1899–1900 by Am. Salmon, Paris, 1970) i, no. 803.

152 *Boutillier* (n. 139),16.

153 *M. Boulet* (n. 41) Qu. 374.

154 Ibid., no. 808: "Nus ne doit obeïr a fere autrui priere ou autrui mandement en vilain cas".

155 Du Breuil (n. 148) 77, no. 18: "cum eidem in talibus non tenetur obedire."

noir puts the master under an obligation to choose his inferiors properly[156] and the principle is taken up by Pothier in the eighteenth century who attributes it to the aim of "making masters take care to have good servants."[157]

The problem with private law at the end of the Ancien régime was that it was infinitely diverse and complex, indeed incoherent. Apart from contract law and commercial law, which were relatively well unified, the old law at the end of the eighteenth century was so complicated a patchwork that it was accessible only to lawyers. As Voltaire enjoyed saying, "in this country one changes legal systems as often as one changes horses." Ever since the sixteenth century, the country had been divided by a sinuous line running from the Ile d'Oléron to just North of Geneva, with customary law on the North and written law in the South, with Roman law playing a supplementary role in the former. Once the customs had been fixed in written form there were problems of adjustment to changing circumstances. Thus doctrinal writings and *jurisprudence* were of great importance. By 1789 there were twelve other Parlements in the kingdom in addition to the Parlement de Paris, which for two centuries had had no rival, so that there were at least thirteen sets of decisions, not always compatible; furthermore they were difficult to understand since the collections of decisions, which were unofficial, give a fragmentary and imperfect picture.[158] There were urgent demands for a simple legal system, one law for the whole of France.[159] The *philosophes* were enthusiasts for law, though they differed vociferously on the desirability of codification.[160] The urge to codify might not only have simplified but also radically reformed the law and given it a new basis and techniques, but most jurists at the end of the eighteenth century were not really minded for sweeping change of the rules. Their wishes were going to be met by the Revolution, or rather despite it, for the codification embarked on during the Revolution remained incomplete. Bonaparte succeeded where Cambacérès had failed, and the Code civil promulgated in

---

[156] Ibid. no. 803.

[157] R. Pothier, Traité des obligations (Paris, 1768) vol. i, no. 121.

[158] *S. Dauchy,* Les recueils privés de 'jurisprudence' aux Temps Modernes, in Case Law in the Making: The Techniques and Methods of Judicial Records and Law Reports (Berlin, 1997) i, 237–247.

[159] One should not forget the initiative of Louis XI who, in 1481, started on a code of private law for the whole kingdom; see *J. Krynen,* Voluntas domini regis in suo regno facit jus. Le roi de France et la coutume, in El dret comù i Catalunya (Barcelona, 1998) 64.

[160] Montesquieu was against it, and while Voltaire castigated the customs as barbaric, he never proposed a general codification; Diderot did propose such a code for Russia, and Rousseau, under the influence of the modern school of natural law, wanted three clear, short and precise codes, one on political rights, one on civil law and one on criminal law. See *J.-L. Halperin,* L'impossible Code civil (PUF 1992) 60 f.

1804 was a "veritable monument of Law, famous for its clarity and simplicity."[161] France was among the first countries in Europe to adopt a civil code, and its code has been uniquely admired and imitated: it long served as a model for legislation not only in Europe but also in much of Latin America, and when Japan opted for a code after the revolution of 1868, it was the Code civil, by reason of its modernity and the prestige given it by mimesis, which was preferred, at least at first, to the Common Law.[162] But although its façade is attractive, the monument is rather deceptive. The Code is rather short on innovation – "sobre de nouveautés", as Portalis, one of its draftsmen, coyly put it. It is agreed that much was adopted from the Ancien Régime. Those who wrote the Code of 1804 backed off markedly from the three drafts offered between 1793 and 1796 and "borrowed more from traditional law and the techniques of times past".[163] The bold legislation contained in earlier drafts was left aside, and revolutionary law is now relegated to the rank of "droit intermédiaire".[164]

In 1804, therefore, there was a compromise between the old law and the new, and art. 1382, which is of particular interest to us, represents in several respects a renunciation of certain advances proposed at the outset of the revolutionary period. It contains the whole principle of civil responsibility. There was virtually no debate on it in the Conseil d'Etat on 24 November 1803,[165] and this should not surprise us as its provisions seemed perfectly responsive to the spirit of the times. The now famous wording "Every act whatever of man obliges him by whose *fault* it occurs to repair it" appears in the final formulation in the Conseil d'Etat on 26 January 1804.[166] In presenting it to the Corps législatif[167] Teilhard was to say that a person's obligation to repair the damage he has caused is "the necessary consequence of his delict", and to conclude that the liability "so

---

161 *A.-J. Arnaud* (n. 134) 220.

162 *Y. Noda,* Gustave Boissonade, comparatiste ignoré, in Problèms contemporains de droit comparé (Tokyo, 1962), ii, 236: "in England some of the laws were formulated five or six centuries ago, and no complete code has been produced recently. ... Only France has a complete set of codes, drafted only 80 years ago." *T. Matsukama,* Le voyage de Monsieur Boissonade, in La révolution de la justice. Des lois du roi au droit moderne (Paris, 1989) 255–266.

163 *J.-L. Halperin* (n. 160) 289. See also *A.-J. Arnaud* (n. 134) 218: "The greatest novelties of the Code civil are not the work of one man but the product of generations of jurists."

164 *J.-L. Halperin* (n. 160) 13 believes that this legislation deserves better than to be bracketed as inferior.

165 The discussion of the Conseil d'Etat is reproduced in P. A. Fenet, Recueil complet des travaux préparatoires du Code civil (reproduction of the 1827 edition, Osnabruck, 1968) i, 450 f.

166 Id. at 460 f.

167 Id. at 467 f.

imposed is perfectly just". On its being officially communicated to the Tribunat on 6 February 1804,[168] Bertrand de Greuille observed that "the obligations resulting from the [tortious] act are simply natural equity" and that "these provisions are all drawn from reason, wisdom, natural equity and the principles of sound morals".[169] He justified the requirement of fault as contained in the new article 1382 as follows: "For damage to be reparable it must be the result of a fault or negligence on the part of another; if it cannot be so attributed, it is simply an accident of fate, a risk which all must accept."[170]

This requirement of fault is quite absent from the second (1794) draft of Cambacérès which provided simply that whoever caused damage must repair it.[171] The rule proposed by Cambacérès was no innovation, but reflected certain established practices. The Ancien Régime, after all, had a system of liability without fault, as one can see from the customs (see above) or from the earliest *jurisprudence* of the Parlement de Paris.[172] Both in the application of rural customs (in the case of damage caused by cattle) and in police regulations (the relationship of master and servant) there survived a system where liability was strict: and the particularist legislation of the Revolution on the municipal police (decree of 19–22 July 1791) contains a number of texts on liability for damage to goods where the emphasis is on the damage rather than the fault. There was thus an area of liability which escaped what Jean Carbonnier has called "the tyranny of the need to prove fault".[173]

Article 1382 is a *clausula generalis,* a fundamental principle governing liability in tort. In this respect French law differs from those legal systems which operate casuistically,[174] such as the Common Law, which has a range of specific torts with differing requirements (though the tort of negligence has recently become generalised up to a point), and the law of Ger-

---

[168] Id. at 469 f.

[169] Id. at 477.

[170] Id. at 488.

[171] Cited by *J. Carbonnier,* Droit civil iv (Les obligations) (PUF, 1995) 327.

[172] Olim, i, 942 no. 43 (1273): a farmer was held liable for damage done by his sheep even though the shepherds, his employees, were guilty of no fault in supervising the animals; had they been at fault, the farmer would have had to pay a fine as well as damages. With equal logic the Court modified the fine imposed on the superior for injuries wreaked by his employees on a royal sergeant, given that he himself was accepted to be free from fault (Olim ii, 141 no. 38 (1272)).

[173] See the observations of *Carbonnier* (n. 171) on "damage in the countryside" which could give rise to liability without any need to prove fault in the defendant.

[174] French law here is like the systems which have followed it – the Código civil of Spain (arts. 1902), the Codice civile (art. 2043) and the Swiss Code of Obligations (art. 41).

many, which lists the legal interests protected against invasion (§ 823 BGB), in addition to having some provisions which lend themselves to greater generalisation (§ 823 (1) and (2), § 826 BGB). There is another striking difference from other legal systems:[175] under article 1382 the basis of liability is fault. There are certain inconveniences in the French method: the abstraction of art. 1382, stamped with an intellectualism attributed to the school of natural law, has been severely criticised on both theoretical and practical grounds. The emphasis on fault has been deplored[176] on the ground that to tie liability to fault, as did the canonists and then the natural lawyers, only complicates the debate triggered by the ever-increasing number of instances of strict liability, above all in the area of vicarious liability where the idea of fault has to be abandoned in favour of objective liability. In this respect, perhaps it might have been preferable to look to the *lex Aquilia,*[177] with its idea of just reparation to undo the disturbance of a just equilibrium, though the imperfect reception of Roman law made this impossible.[178] By the end of the nineteenth century the system based exclusively on fault had proved inadequate; it was found increasingly unsatisfactory to deny compensation in cases where the damage was purely accidental. There were several reasons for this change of view: increasing mechanisation caused more and more accidents not imputable to human error, working classes emerged for whom bodily injury spelt penury, victims became less stoical and the uninjured more sympathetic, and the whole matter was accelerated by the introduction of liability insurance.[179] This development[180] involved a return to a less subjective liability, causal and independent of fault, and scholars and judges alike have had to face the task of maintaining the continuity of the Napoleonic code. If in the area of civil responsibility French law, in which fault still plays a considerable

---

175 German law certainly involves the notion of fault, but juxtaposes it to the notion of "unlawfulness", as in the Swiss Code of Obligations, art. 41 (see *G. Marty,* L'expérience française en matière de responsabilité civile et les enseignements du droit comparé, in Mélanges Maury (Paris, 1960) i, 178.

176 See *M. Villey,* Esquisse historique sur le mot responsable, in 22 Archives de philosophie du droit 45–48 (Paris, 1977).

177 In Roman law there were a range of special delicts with particular names *(injuria, dampnum injuria datum* etc.) rather than a general principle of liability for all cases of fault. The fact that the Germanic codes refer to unlawfulness, stemming from the *injuria* of the *lex Aquilia,* is attributable to the pandectist tradition.

178 See *M. Villey* (n. 176) 54 ff.

179 On accidents and insurance, see *P. Lecoq,* L'annonce faite au législateur par le préteur de la nécessité de règles protectrices nouvelles. Regards sur un siècle de jurisprudence du Conseil d'Etat (1895–1995) in *S. Dauchy, J. Montballyu* and *A. Wijffels* (eds.) (n. 10) 209–242; *J.-P. Nandrin,* La genèse du droit de travail en Belgique. Plaidoyer pour la chronologie", id. at 256–288.

180 On the present position see *A. Tunc* (n. 1) and G. Viney (n. 1).

part, still thrives under the flag of art. 1382 ff., it is essentially thanks to the fresh air breathed into it by the work of the courts, and it is that which, notwithstanding the differences of background, brings French law closer to that of other systems and particularly that of the Common Law.[181]

[181] *P. Catala* and *T. Weir,* Delict and torts: a study in parallel, 37 Tulane L. Rev. 577 (1962–63): "There is no clearly-marked frontier between the countries whose law is codified and the common law countries. Starting from a very narrow legal base, French judges have built up a theory which the legislator had not foreseen. They have done this while both respecting the fundamental principles of the written law, and displaying much ingenuity in adapting the law to new situations. In this respect, the study of 'delictal liability' ... constitutes the best bridge that can be built between the French legal system and the common law systems ..."

WOLFGANG ERNST

Negligence in 19th Century Germany

I. Introduction

Private law in19th century Germany was as diverse as Germany's political order. The *Ius Commune* coexisted with a multiplicity of older city- or county-statutes and more recent codifications. Among the latter were the Bavarian "Codex Maximilianeus Bavaricus Civilis" of 1756, the "Allgemeine Preußische Landrecht" of 1794, the Austrian "Allgemeines Gesetzbuch für die gesamten Erbländer der österreichischen Monarchie" of 1812 and the "Code Napoléon" of 1804/1807, which remained in force in a number of western territories and also, in the revised version of the "Badisches Landesrecht" (1809), in Baden. In 1865 the last of the territorial codifications, the " Sächsische Gesetzbuch", was enacted in Saxony. In the remaining parts of Germany, in the absence of statutes and codifications, the *Ius Commune* in the form of the *usus modernus pandectarum,* the "Gemeines Recht" or "Pandektenrecht", continued to be used as the primary source of law. Most of the older city- or county-statutes and some of the more recent codifications had also provided that the *Ius Commune* should be used as a subsidiary source of law. While we shall confine ourselves to the development of the "Gemeines Recht", it is necessary to take into account the coexistence of the French "Code Napoléon", the Austrian "Allgemeines Bürgerliches Gesetzbuch" and the Prussian "Allgemeines Landrecht". All these codifications had, in one form or another, a general clause stating that in principle there was a duty to compensate for damage (wilfully or) negligently caused[1]. These provisions were, of course, known

---

[1] § 1295 Austrian ABGB; art. 1382 French Code Civil; §§ 116, 773, 774 Saxon "Bürgerliches Gesetzbuch für das Königreich Sachsen"; on the Saxon Code, which borrowed to a remarkable extent from the Austrian Code, see *Chr. Ahcin,* Zur Entstehung des bürgerlichen Gesetzbuchs für das Königreich Sachsen von 1863/65 (1996). On the french Code Civil see *Coing,* Europäisches Privatrecht II – 19. Jahrhundert (1989) p. 516, and *H. P. Benöhr,* Zeitschrift der Savigny-Stiftung für Rechtsgeschichte [hereinafter ZRG] Rom. Abt. 93 (1976) p. 242 sequ.; on the Prussian code s. *Th. Kiefer,* Die Aquilische Haftung im Allgemeinen Landrecht für die preußischen Staaten (1989), and *Benöhr,* op. cit., p. 229 sequ.; on the Codex Maximilianeus Bavaricus Civilis see *Benöhr,* op. cit., p. 228 sequ.; on the Austrian ABGB again *Benöhr,* op. cit., p. 233 seq. and *U. Floßmann,* Österreichische Privat-

also to the legal scholars in the field of the "Gemeine Recht". While the codifications were drafted on the basis of the learned legal tradition and in turn inspired, in their respective territories, interpretations of a high standard, it was still the "Gemeines Recht", upon which most of the scholarly efforts concentrated. Even so, in the further interpretation and development of the "Gemeine Recht", authors quite often advocated solutions taken from the codifications. A good example is *Rudolf von Jhering*: Many of the theories he advanced, supposedly based on Roman law, were actually taken from the Prussian "Allgemeine Landrecht"[2]. On the other hand, traditional legal concepts formed in the development of the *Ius Commune* were indispensable for the scholarly interpretation of the codifications. Thus the codes and the *Ius Commune* were quite often brought into line both in doctrinal exposition and in practical application[3]. In sum, there were mutual exchange and interaction between the code-law and the learned "Gemeines Recht".

In the field of the *Ius Commune* we face a multiplicity of actions concerning delictual liability, including, to name only the most important, the *actio legis Aquiliae,* the *actio de dolo,* the *actio furti* and the *actio iniuriarum.* We shall focus mainly on the *actio legis Aquiliae* as applied in practice and as laid out in the scholarly literature. We shall not dwell on one aspect of the development, for it is collateral to the issue of liability for negligence: Roman actions which had originally been penal were stripped of their penal element and served only to compensate for losses actually suffered. For the *actio legis Aquiliae* this meant that punitive elements in the assessment of damages were disregarded in favour of a strict economic assessment of the loss suffered. The elimination of the penal factor remained unquestioned even under the impact of the historical school,

---

rechtsgeschichte (1983) p. 279 sequ., with further references. In Switzerland, Bluntschli's Zürcher Privatrechtliche Gesetzbuch (PRG) from 1854/56 has a twofold liability for criminal acts and for *dolus,* while the "Civil-Gesetzbuch für Stadt und Republik Bern" has a general clause (964. Satzung) in line with the Austrian ABGB; on both see *Eugen Bucher,* Der Einfluß des französischen Code Civil auf das Obligationenrecht, in: *P. Caroni* (ed.), Das Obligationenrecht 1883–1983 (1983) p. 162 sequ.

2 R. v. Jhering derived central features of his theory of risk from the Prussian code (s. *Ernst,* in: *W. Schön* [ed.], Gedächtnisschrift für Brigitte Knobbe-Keuk [1997] p. 69 sequ.), from which he also took his famous concept of *culpa in contrahendo,* s. *Flume,* Zeitschrift für Wirtschaftsrecht [ZIP] 1994, p. 337 N. 7.

3 For the Prussian ALR see *Kiefer* (supra N. 1) p. 189 sequ.; on the Bavarian and Austrian law as well as on the (basically french) law of Baden, see *J. Schröder,* Die zivilrechtliche Haftung für schuldhafte Schadenszufügung im deutschen *usus modernus,* in: *L. Vacca* (ed.), La responsabilità civile da atto illecito nella prospettiva storico-comparatistica (Turin 1995) p. 157 sequ.; *idem,* in: *M. Landfester* et al. (ed.), Der Neue Pauly – Enzyklopädie der Antike, vol. 13 – Rezeptions- und Wissenschaftsgeschichte (2000) s. v. "Delikt".

which, as we will now see, advocated a return to the actions in their Roman shape[4].

II. 19th Century Writers on Delictual Liability

a) The legal doctrine of the 19th century pandectists tended to cling quite closely to the texts of Roman law, even trying to purify the understanding of Roman law by undoing later, i.e. medieval and modern developments. With regard to this tendency the authors spoke of themselves as the historical school. The historical school had its forerunners in antiquarian scholars like Heinecius (1681–1741) and, especially Gustav Hugo (1764–1844) far back in the 18th century. Only with Friedrich Carl von Savigny (1779–1861), however, did it gain massive momentum. Since the older antiquarian scholars had already prepared the field, it is not surprising that the historical school was having an impact as early as the second decade of the 19th century. Although during the century purely historical research increasingly separated itself from the doctrinal work on the law in force[5], the "Gemeines Recht" kept its character as shaped by the historical school until it was superseded by the Bürgerliche Gesetzbuch (BGB) in 1900. Accordingly the various traditional Roman actions continued to form the basis for delictual liability throughout the 19th century, and although they were all modified in one way or another, there was not attempt to fuse them into a general law of torts. Even in its last edition *Windscheid's* Pandektenrecht, the book of authority of the second half of the 19th century, presented all delictual actions under a common heading ("Obligations from delicts and similar cases") but without any general introduction to a "law of torts"[6]. Somewhere in between the exposition of *Windscheid,* which knew no general law of torts, and the Bürgerliche Gesetzbuch (BGB) to come, which was to frame a general liability for illicit acts supported only by a few provisions for special torts, lies the so-called Dresdner Entwurf. The "draft of Dresden", the result of an unsuccessful attempt to unify the private law of obligations of the Deutsche Bund of the 1860s[7], contained

---

[4] Cf. *Coing* (supra N. 1), p. 518; *Jan Schröder,* Die zivilrechtliche Haftung (supra N. 3.), p. 160 sequ.: "Verdrängung der Privatstrafe". Among the 19th century authors, a comprehensive theoretical account can be found in *Binding,* Die Normen und ihre Übertretung, vol. I/1 (1872) p. 166 sequ., 213 sequ.

[5] In our field, the beginning of strictly historical research is marked by the publication of *A. Pernice,* Die Lehre von den Sachbeschädigungen nach römischem Rechte (1867).

[6] 3rd ed.1873 § 451, p. 640. Similar *Fr. L. v. Keller,* Pandekten (ed. *E. Friedberg,* 1861) p. 675 sequ., and *v. Vangerow,* Lehrbuch der Pandekten, 7th ed. 1876, vol. 3, p. 525 sequ. In *Windscheid*'s 9th ed. of 1906 (by *Th. Kipp*) the new law of the BGB was presented as an introduction to the law of torts, vol. 2, p. 947 sequ.

not only specific elaborate provisions for all kinds of special torts in the Roman tradition (art. 1007–1030) but also a general formula imposing liability for damages caused illicitly and negligently (art. 211, 212).

The reluctance to state a general formula for delictual liability is a striking feature of the 19th century doctrine[8] not only in comparison with the preceding period (due to its interaction with the ideas of natural law or law of reason), but also in comparison with the codifications of the 18th and early 19th century and the BGB to come. Here, however, we must put in a *caveat,* to which we will return later: The return to the system of special actions did not necessarily mean a restriction of liability, since a more general formula does not necessarily have to be a broader formula as well.

b) aa) In 1815 *Johann Christian Hasse* published "Die *culpa* des römischen Rechts", a work which may safely be attributed to the historical school[9]. (It has, for example, a distinct sally against Donellus, whose system of grades of *culpa* is said to be un-Roman[10].) In the 19th century the idea of *culpa* characteristically attracted most attention and in turn enhanced the concepts of delictual liability. The theory of *culpa* in a way made up for the lack of a fully worked-out theory or tort. According to *Hasse,* anybody who causes another person damage in an illegal way[11] is a *culpae reus,* but as he explains, there is no general obligation to avoid damaging other persons. It would be a mistake, *Hasse* writes, to assume that the whole issue can be summarized in the sentence: Whoever causes damage, has to compensate for it[12]. To consider each and every diminution of another's "Vermögen" as illegal would have incongruous consequences: Competition in commercial trading or industry, speculative transactions, which necessarily cause loss to one of the parties, would be illicit[13]. A diminuation of "Vermögen" is what nowadays is understood to be an economic loss. Even today, German scholars speak of "reiner Vermögensschaden"[14]. For *Hasse* the central need is to determine when the causing of

---

[7] On the Dresdner Entwurf see *W. Schubert's* introduction to: Protocolle der Commission zur Ausarbeitung eines allgemeinen Deutschen Obligationenrechts (Dresdner Protokolle), reprint 1984, vol. 1, p. XIII sequ.

[8] *Coing* (supra N. 1), p. 518 speaks of a return to the system of special actions.

[9] 2nd ed. by August Bethmann-Hollweg (1838).

[10] P. 110 sequ.

[11] "Endlich ist ... ganz allgemein ein jeder *culpae reus,* welcher dem anderen auf eine unerlaubt Art Schaden zuwege bringt", p. 11 (2nd ed. 1838; original display).

[12] "Wer hier mit dem allgemeinen Satz: wer Schaden thut, muß Schaden bessern, auszureichen glaubt, würde sich sehr täuschen"; p. 12.

[13] P. 12.

[14] Cf. *D. Mertens,* in: Münchener Kommentar zum Bürgerlichen Gesetzbuch vol. 5 (1997), no. 466 sequ. ad § 823.

damage is illicit. He refers us to statutory rules, the most relevant ones being, according to him, those of the *lex Aquilia.*

bb) To understand the relation between *Hasse*'s theory and the earlier writers, we must consider whether the *usus modernus pandectarum* had adopted a broad general clause of *neminem laedere,* according to which compensation was due for all damage negligently caused. From the perspective of the Roman texts, the alternative lay in the interpretation of the clause of the *lex Aquilia* requiring a *damnum iniuria datum*: Did the causation of damage – in the absence of a justification like self-defence – in itself constitute an *iniuria* or was it necessary that the act of causation be positively qualified as illegal? The answer to this question determines the attitude towards the problem of purely economic loss: According to the latter view, the causing of foreseeable economic loss must – at least in principle – create a liability. Modern doctrine poses the same alternative by asking whether illegality is presumed – "indiziert" – whenever damage is done to another person. If not, we speak, somewhat vaguely, of an "open concept" of illegality, since the illegality has to be positively asserted in a sometimes open process of a weighing of interests[15].

In a recent study, *Jan Schröder* has convincingly contended that – contrary to popular opinion[16] – the *usus modernus* did not acknowlege any such "allgemeines Schädigungsverbot"[17]. While a general prohibition to cause damage was quite often stated, the transformation of this principle (*neminem laede!*) into a hard-boiled liability was restricted by listing those rights and interests of which particular care must be taken. These rights and interests were precisely those which were traditionally protected by the Roman actions. No one held that another person's wealth called for such diligent attention that negligently to cause economic loss in itself led to a duty to compensate. According to *Schröder,* the authors of 18th century

[15] For a presentation of modern German doctrine see *Markesinis,* The German Law of torts (3rd ed. 1994) p. 42 sequ.; *Zimmermann,* Law of Obligations (1990) p. 1040 sequ. The champion of *neminem laedere* is *Picker,* Archiv für die civilistische Praxis (AcP) 1983, p. 369 sequ., *idem* Juristenzeitung (JZ) 1987, p. 1047 sequ., *idem,* Gutachterhaftung – Außervertragliche Einstandspflichten als innergesetzliche Rechtsfortbildung, in: *V. Beuthien/M. Fuchs/G. Schiemann/A. Wacke* (ed.), Festschrift für Dieter Medicus (1999) p. 397 sequ. The best renewal of the concept of illegality is *Michael Fraenkel,* Tatbestand und Zurechnung bei § 823 BGB (1979). Cf. also *Michael Börgers,* Von den "Wandlungen" zur "Restrukturierung" des Deliktsrechts (1992).

[16] *Coing* (supra N. 1) p. 518: According to *Coing,* the historical school did not continue the older *Ius Commune* but rather returned to Justinian's law; cf. also *Käppmann,* Die neuere dogmengeschichtliche Entwicklung der objektiven Tatbestände der §§ 823, 826 BGB, unpublished Diss. iur. Münster (1959) p. 34.

[17] *Jan Schröder,* Die zivilrechtliche Haftung (supra N. 3) p. 144 sequ.

usus modernus could therefore rightly confirm that their ideas of delictual liability were still in line with the Roman *actio legis Aequiliae*[18]. At that time one did not advocate liability in the absence of infringement of one of those specific rights or interests. Twenty years before *Johann Christian Hasse,* for example, *Adolph Dietrich Weber* had explained that all illicit acts, as determined by the statute books, required a wilful or negligent act (or omission) contrary to statutory laws or personal duties[19]. As further shown by *Jan Schröder* many – perhaps most – authors of the *usus modernus pandectarum* required a positive contravention against either statutory provisions or individual rights[20]. An especially clear exposition can be found already with Samuel Stryk's "De damno rebus alienis licite illato" (1684)[21].

cc) If such was the position of the 18th century writers, the changes brought about by the historical school rather seem to shrink. Insofar as there had been, in the *usus modernus pandectarum,* no breakthrough to a liability for purely economic loss under the catchword of *neminem laedere,* 19th century pandectists like *Hasse* did not have to revolt against their immediate precursors in order to uphold the main principles of the *lex Aquilia.* The 19th century writers of the historical school therefore do not, in comparison with their predecessors of the *usus modernus pandectarum,* re-restrict, in substance, delictual liability. It is simply that in the exposition of their doctrine they no longer mention the general all-encompassing principle of *neminem laedere* but confine themselves to describing the separate actions which govern the scope of liability now, just as they governed the scope of liability in the time of the *usus modernus* (and before). However, the 19th century jurists were not always as sure as *Jan Schröder* about whether or not the authors of the *usus modernus pandecatarum* had gone beyond Roman law: They sometimes assert that there was a tendency (which they find in the writings of Lauterbach or Höpfner) to extend the

---

18 *Schröder,* Die zivilrechtliche Haftung (supra N. 3.) p. 153 ff.

19 Es muß jemand "mit Vorsatz oder Fahrlässigkeit wider die Gesetze und seine Pflichten etwas unternommen oder unterlassen" haben, *Adolph Dietrich Weber,* Systematische Entwickelung der Lehre von der natürlichen Verbindlichkeit und deren gerichtlichen Wirkung (2nd ed. 1795) p. 104 sequ.

20 *Jan Schröder* also contends that even the so called natural-law-codifications were, by means of interpretation, brought in line with the *lex Aquilia,* Die zivilrechtliche Haftung (supra N. 3) p. 156 sequ. on the Bavarian, Austrian and the French code (as used in Baden). Similarily, on the Prussian law, *Kiefer* (supra N. 1) p. 189 sequ. For the Saxon "Bürgerliches Gesetzbuch für das Königreich Sachsen" see Oberappellationsgericht Dresden, judgement of 13/1/1893, Sächsisches Archiv für Bürgerliches Recht und Prozeß, vol. 3 (1893) p. 83: No liability for each and every negligently caused damage; there must be a contravention against specifically imposed duties.

21 For details, cf. *Schröder,* Die zivilrechtliche Haftung (supra N. 3) p. 152 sequ.

application of the *lex Aquilia* but that it had not prevailed[22]. To sum up, the extent of liability in the *usus modernus pandectarum* was and continued to be, in the time of the historical school, framed not by a general formula, but by the Roman actions. This shift in emphasis, away from a general theory towards the single actions and their particularities, is rather a matter of the doctrinal expositions of the "Lehrbücher des Pandektenrechts" than a matter of substance.

As we now see, the substantial issue, whether liability is incurred only by acts that must be considered illicit even in absence of detrimental effects, or whether negligently caused damage itself constitutes a wrong that incurrs liability, is not identical with the issue of whether or not to have a "general clause". In line with *Jan Schröder* one can argue that in overcoming many of the particularities of the Roman actions the authors of the 18th century *usus modernus pandectarum* established a general clause of a different kind: Each and every damage has to be compensated for, if it is caused by an illicit act[23]. The provisions of the *lex Aquilia* and of the other delictual actions were understood as merely particular instances of illegality. A general clause so phrased does not impose liability for all damage negligently caused and does not impose liability for purely economic loss.

c) We do not deny that in the 19th century there was, and continued to be, a rival tendency towards a broader concept, making the idea of *neminem laedere* the theoretical centre of delictual liability. However, such a theory, founding delictual liabiltiy on the principle of *neminem laedere* (and thereby introducing liability for purely economic loss) found no leading protagonists among the pandectists of the 19th century. This does not mean that the idea was completely forgotten. Though not overtly advocated, the concept of *neminem laedere* sometimes lurked in cloudy inconsistencies, as we shall now see with *Glück* and *Windscheid,* both books of authority of their time.

aa) Friedrich Wilhelm *Glück* in the tenth volume of his vast commentary "Ausführliche Erläuterung der Pandecten nach Hellfeld" (1808) requires, for the *actio legis Aquiliae,* illicit damage ("widerrechtlicher Schaden"). *Glück* proceeds, without evincing any doubt or hesitation and clearly without realising any inconsistency, to explain that the *actio legis Aquiliae* furthermore lies, wherever someone occupies himself with perfectly legal business and thereby wilfully or negligently causes harm to others[24]. The examples *Glück* gives are those which we today refer to as violations of

---

[22] Cf. *Dernburg,* Preußisches Privatrecht, 2nd ed. 1880, vol. 2, p. 828.

[23] This is also the concept adopted by the Bürgerliches Gesetzbuch (BGB), cf. *Mossler,* infra p. 385 f.

"Verkehrssicherungspflichten", duties of care arising from intensified social contacts: roofers dropping tiles on passers-by, riders unable to control their horse, games played on unsuitable grounds.

bb) The last book of authority, *Windscheid's* "Pandektenrecht", may be seen as riddled with a similar inconsistency: Dealing with the *lex Aquilia, Windscheid* too starts with the requirement of "Widerrechtlichkeit" (illicitness of the damaging act)[25]. For *Windscheid,* however, it seems that a damaging act is itself illicit, unless there is a positive justification like self-defence[26]. *Windscheid* then states the recognized extensions of the *lex Aquilia*[27]. The violation does not have to take place in the peculiar ways described in the *lex Aquilia*: Any physical harm will do, even if caused in an indirect way. But here *Windscheid* draws the line: The Roman law had not gone beyond physicial damage to corporeal things, that is it did not acknowledge compensation for purely economic loss[28]. In his exposition of the *actio de dolo, Windscheid* again expressely states that the Roman law did not recognize the rule that everyone must compensate for the damage he negligently causes[29]; it requires *dolus* to make someone liable, negligence is not sufficient. Given that where damage is inflicted with *culpa Windscheid* would impose liability unless there was some justification such as self-defence, it is hard to see how illicitness can still be upheld as a separate, indeed a crucial, prerequisite of liability[30].

d) In the second half of the century we find renewed attacks on the extensions of delictual liability based on the principle of *neminem laedere.* These efforts of defence come somewhat surprisingly, since there had been no outspoken attack on the pandectist doctrine either in the learned literature or – as we shall see – in the case law. However, the efforts to defend

---

[24] Those are (also) liable, who "zwar ein an sich erlaubtes Geschäft verrichten, aber dabey vorsätzlich, oder durch Unvorsichtigkeit und Ungeschicklichkeit Schaden thun", p. 320.

[25] § 455 Notes 10 sequ. (3rd ed. 1873) p. 655.

[26] Ibid. N. 11.

[27] Ibid. p. 653.

[28] Op. cit. § 455, p. 654, N. 6: "Weiter, d.h. über das Moment der Schadenszufügung an einer körperlichen Sache hinaus, ist man aber nicht gegangen, wie manche wohl aufgrund von §.16 I.h.t. [I. 4.3.16].und L.33 §.1 D.h.t. [D. 9.2.33.1: "In damnis, quae lege Aquilia non tenentur, in factum datur actio"] behauptet haben", p. 654, N. 6.

[29] "Das römische Recht hat nicht den Satz aufgestellt, daß Jeder den durch seine Schuld [...] entstandenen Schaden zu ersetzen verpflichtet sei", Op. cit. § 451, p. 640.

[30] On another occasion, *Windscheid* gives an exposition of what constitutes illicitness, especially in its relation to negligence, ibid. vol. 1, 9th ed., § 101, p. 519 sequ.

the traditional extent of liability may be taken as signs of a certain uneasiness.

aa) A thundering defence of the Gemeines Recht with its restricted liability was proffered by *Rudolf von Jhering* in 1861[31]. *Jhering* deals with cases of so-called *culpa in contrahendo,* arising from Roman texts such as those dealing with the sale of a free man as a slave, which held the seller liable although the sale of a free man cannot be valid. *Friedrich Mommsen* had sought to construe the seller's liability as an instance of extracontractual liability for *culpa*[32]. *Jhering* attacked him for this and, in order to advance his own theory of *culpa in contrahendo*[33], maintained that, contrary to *Friedrich Mommsen's* implication, there could be no extracontractual liability for *culpa (lata),* and that the *actio de dolo* could not be stretched to encompass cases of mere *culpa.* The consequences would be disastrous: A a careless remark or an information casually given could lead to a liability. Both commerce and conversation would be doomed. Six years later, *Jhering* had worked out this side remark into a lengthy study on "Das Schuldmoment im römischen Privatrecht"[34]. According to *Jhering* every advanced legal system is based on the idea of *culpa. Jhering* tries to interpret all the Roman actions as based on *culpa.* He concludes with the famous sentence: "It is not damage, that incurrs liability, but *culpa*"[35]. Without *culpa,* the loss must be seen as *casus. Jhering's* philosphy could therefore equally be summed up in the maxim: "losses must lie where they fall".

bb) While *Jhering* had expanded, in fact over-expanded, his doctrine to the whole range of actions both contractual and extra-contractual, we find, at the same time, a specific study on the nature of *damnum iniuria datum* by *Hefke,* a "minor poet" of his time[36]. *Hefke* lists definitions of *damnum*

---

[31] In: Jhering's Jahrbücher für die Dogmatik des heutigen römischen und deutschen Privatrechts (*C. F. v. Gerber, R. Jhering,* ed.) vol. 4 (1861) p. 12.

[32] Beiträge zum Obligationenrecht I, Die Unmöglichkeit der Leistung (1853) p. 122.

[33] On this theory, see *Byoung Jo Choe,* Culpa in contrahendo bei *Rudolph von Jhering* (1988) – reviewed by *K. Luig,* Zeitschrift für neuere Rechtsgeschichte (ZNR) 1990, p. 68 sequ.; *U. Diederichsen,* Jherings Rechtsinstitute im deutschen Privatrecht der Gegenwart, in: *O. Behrends* (ed.), Jherings Rechtsdenken – Theorie und Pragmatik im Dienste evolutionärer Rechtsethik, Abhandlungen der Akadademie der Wissenschaften in Göttingen, Phil.-Hist. Klasse, 3. Folge, vol. 216 (1996) p. 175 sequ., here 195 sequ.

[34] In: Festschrift für Birnbaum (1867), also in: *Jhering,* Vermischte Schriften (1879) p. 155 sequ.

[35] "Nicht der Schaden verpflichtet zum Schadensersatz, sondern die Schuld", ibid. p. 199.

[36] Das Wesen des damnum iniuria datum nach gemeinem Recht, in: *W. Heinzerling* (ed.), Archiv für die praktische Rechtswissenschaft, 3. Folge, vol. 3 (1886)

iniuria datum in "Lehrbüchern" as well as in monographs. He finds them mostly too vague and broad and advocates a return to the strict principle of the Roman *lex Aquilia*. It seems significant that *Hefke* cannot find a single champion of extended liability. Rather he is concerned about what seems to him a continuous erosion of the requirements of the Aquilian liability. Turning to the case law, we shall now see that in specific fields there was indeed a willingness to go beyond the Roman actions.

III. 19th Century Case Law

1. The Courts

Looking for 19th century case law one has to be aware of the multiplicity of jurisdictions. There was neither a supreme court for the whole of Germany nor even a court of last instance common to the different territories which shared the same private law, such as the "Gemeines Recht". Instead, there was a number of courts of appeal (Oberappellationsgerichte). These were courts of highest instance, which since the 17th century had been set up in single territories as the central Reichskammergericht lost parts of its jurisdiction[37]. In considering the decisions of these courts, one should keep in mind that in spite of their considerable reputation, their impact on the doctrinal development was relatively small[38]. Among the Oberappellationsgerichte, probably the Oberappellationsgericht Lübeck was held in highest regard, because its jurisdiction covered the coastal cities on the North Sea and the Baltic which had substantial foreign trade[39]. In 1869 the first federal court, the Bundesoberhandelsgericht, was set up, and it continued its jurisdiction after 1871 as the Reichsoberhandelsgericht. It was only in 1879, when the Reichsgericht was established, that a court with a general jurisdiction on all private law matters began to shape the development for all Germany.

---

p. 212 sequ., 321 sequ. Nothing on *Hefke* in *Stintzing/Landsberg*'s Geschichte der deutschen Rechtswissenschaft vol. III/2 (1910).

37 *E. Döhring,* Geschichte der deutschen Rechtspflege seit 1500 (1953) p. 26 sequ.

38 In the beginning of the 19th century, very few of the renowned "Lehrbücher des Pandektenrechts" bothered to take notice of court decisions at all, though there was an increasing willingness to do so during the century.

39 Set up in 1820 as the "Oberappellationsgericht der vier freien Städte Deutschlands zu Lübeck", i.e. a common court of highest instance for Bremen, Hamburg, Lübeck and Frankfurt, Frankfurt, having lost its status as a sovereign city to Prussia, in 1866 had to withdraw from the court which thereby lost his jurisdiction over Frankfurt.

2. The Cases

We have seen that in the learned literature there is no big clash between an adherence to the Roman actions and an effective extension according to a broad *neminem laedere*-clause. Similarily, in the case law the question of the extension of liability for negligence does not come up as a single, theoretical issue. Rather, there are quite specific situations which call for an extension of liability. In general, the fields where the traditional actions seemed to be insufficient, were later dealt with by the legislator, though by specific provisions, not by a basic shift towards a broad general clause.

a) Material Loss Due to Defamation

A first string of cases concerns the law of defamation. The underlying problem was that it was difficult to award proper damages on the basis of *actio iniuriarum,* for under the Roman texts the plaintiff could claim only a *poena aestimatoria,* i.e. exemplary damages (atonement money). How could a compensation be awarded, when the defamation had caused material damage?

aa) The Oberappellationsgericht Lübeck in a judgement of 13/10/1838[40] held against a captain who had, in a foreign port, denounced his mate as a criminal. The mate was arrested but cleared of the accusations in later proceedings. He claimed not only atonement money but also compensation for his pecuniary loss, which was granted on strength of the *actio iniuriarum*: The *aestimatio poena* should take pecuniary loss into account. The Oberappellationsgericht also considers the *actio legis Aquiliae* and on this occassion confirms the traditional view: The *actio legis Aquilia* is not a general action for each and every pecuniary loss. We have already seen in *Windscheid's* exposition the argument relied on by the Oberappellationsgericht: If there were a general action for each and every pecuniary loss, there would be no need and no room for the *actio de dolo.* The court quotes *Hasse, Wening-Ingenheim, Mühlenbruch* and *Seuffert* for support. Although no authors are named for the adverse opinion, the court warns that an extension of liability to the cases of extra-contractual *culpa* would have most dangerous consequences, without, however, spelling them out.

bb) During the 19th century, the *actio iniuriarum* was in a steady decline[41]. Legislation in various territories provided for the criminal prosecution of defamation, as did, from 1871 to 1877, the Reichsstrafgesetzbuch

---

[40] J. A. Seufferts Archiv für Entscheidungen der obersten Gerichte in den deutschen Staaten [hereinafter Seufferts Archiv], vol. 8. (1855) no. 137, p. 431 sequ.

and the corresponding code of criminal procedure. Parallel to this legislative activity, doubts were increasingly voiced whether the protection of honour by means of private law, i.e. by the *actio iniuriarum aestimatoria,* was still appropriate. To the spirit of the 19th century, private law seemed unfit to administer sanctions like the *poena aestimatoria* of the *actio iniuriarum.* And from the point of view of the historical school, the *actio iniuriarum* was not an *actio rei persequens* and therefore unsuited for the recovery of damages. Remaining doubts, whether the *actio iniuriarum aestmatoria* still existed, were silenced by the BGB, which expressly rejected compensation for non-pecuniary harm due to defamation. However, led by the Constitutional Court, courts in Germany have once more begun to grant exemplary damages for the so called infringement of the general right of personality since the 1950s. This is, as *Zimmermann* nicely puts it, a renaissance of the *actio iniuriarum (aestimatoria)* "in the guise and under the cover of the general right of personality"[42].

cc) The steady decline of the *actio iniuriarum aestimatoria* due to the activity of the 19th century legislators in the fields of criminal law and civil procedure undermined the possibility (as used by the Oberappellationsgericht Lübeck in 1838) of awarding, under the guise of the *poena aestimatoria,* compensation for material loss caused by a defamation[43]. It is not surprising that one increasingly turned to the *actio legis Aquiliae* in order to compensate for pecuniary loss caused by defamation. This extension of the *actio legis Aquiliae* was not totally new. Already in the 18th century material losses due to defamation had been compensated for on the strength of an *actio legis Aquiliae (in factum)*[44]. In 1864 the Oberappellationsgericht

---

[41] Cf. *Th. Moosheimer* Die actio injuriarum aestimatoria im 18. und neunzehnten Jahrhundert (1997); *Coing* (supra N. 1) p. 519; *Zimmermann* (supra N. 15) p. 1090 sequ., with a detailed account of the development of the *actio iniuriarum* in the time of the *usus modernus pandectarum,* which had already seen the *actio* under attack from the religious point of view, p. 1085 sequ. Cf. also *Jan Schröder,* Die zivilrechtliche Haftung (supra N. 3) p. 161 sequ.

[42] Supra N. 15, p. 1092.

[43] Beyond the protection of honour, the *actio iniuriarum* had found another economically important application, though not generally recognized, with regard to intellectual property; unlicensed reprints were seen, by some, as an *iniuria,* cf. *L. J. Neustetel,* Der Büchernachdruck nach römischem Recht betrachtet (1824, reprinted UFITA 124 [1994] p. 243 sequ.). See on the 19th century development, *E. Klingenberg,* ZRG Rom. Abt., vol. 96 (1979) p. 194 sequ.; *Elmar Wadle,* Festschrift Günther Jahr (1993) p. 517 sequ.; *Coing* (supra N. 1) p. 519 with references in N. 20.

[44] *Iustus Henning Böhmer,* Consultationes et decisionum iuris, Tom. 2 Pars 1, (Halle 1734) reports (as Responsum 396) the following case (p. 583 sequ.): The plaintiff, a lessee, had faced a termination of his lease due to the defendant's defamation: The Law Faculty of Halle granted the *actio legis Aquiliae in factum.* Cf. also *Jan Schröder,* Die zivilrechtliche Haftung (supra N. 3) p. 163 sequ.

Lübeck[45] granted the *actio legis Aquiliae (in factum)* based on the spreading of a defamatory rumour that the plaintiff was insolvent. The defendant's *culpa* alone was held to be sufficient to find against him. In this judgement we find a reference to the general clauses of the new codifications. In a judgement of 11/12/1868[46], the Oberappellationsgericht again granted damages for the harm done by defamatory advertisements. In a series of advertisements the defendants had wrongly denied the plaintiffs' assertion that in the world exhibition in Paris they had been awarded an international prize for their sewing machines. The court held the advertising to be illicit because any damaging act should be considered as illicit, if the acting person foresaw or should have foreseen the damaging effect.

While these decisions of the Oberappellationsgericht Lübeck, especially in their reasoning, seem to represent a fundamental departure from the traditional pandectist doctrine of the *actio legis Aquiliae,* this deviation is clearly limited to the field of defamation. 30 years later, the BGB expressly acknowledged the need for compensation, and accepted that pecuniary loss caused by wilful or negligent defamation must be compensated. However, the BGB provides for such compensation in § 824 quite separately from its main regulation of delictual liability (§ 823 BGB) and this has never exercised any influence on the general concepts of tort.

b) Damage Due to The Execution of Judgements Later Annuled

A notorious problem was posed by the execution of non-final judgements declared provisionally executable. If after execution such a judgement is annulled by a higher court, can the defendant recover damages for the harm suffered by the execution[47]? There was much debate on the issue[48]. Obviously the *actio de dolo* was available only where the plaintiff knew perfectly well that the judgement he had obtained was erroneous. Could the plaintiff be held liable if he was guilty of only *culpa,* mere negligence? In an elaborate judgement of 1890, the Reichsgericht, through its Third Civil Senate, discussed the issue in the broad context of all available actions[49],

[45] Judgement of 29/12/1864, Seufferts Archiv, vol. 21, no. 55.

[46] *Kierulff,* Sammlung der Entscheidungen des Ober-Appellationsgerichts der vier Freien Städte Deutschlands zu Lübeck, vol. 6 (1873) p. 63.

[47] The same problem arises where measures of execution can be invoked even before a judgement has been rendered in order to secure the future fulfillment of a possible judgement in favour of the plaintiff to be.

[48] Cf., with plenty of references, *Windscheid,* Pandektenrecht, 9th ed. (1906), § 451 N. 1 at p. 960.

[49] Judgement of 17/10/1890, Entscheidungen des Reichsgerichts in Zivilsachen [hereinafter: RGZ] vol. 26, p. 204 sequ.

considering in particular whether there is a general liability for economic loss caused by *culpa*[50]. Does the Roman *lex Aquilia* cover each and every case of economic loss or does the *lex Aquilia,* even if stretched to its very limits, still require damage to a corporeal asset? The Reichsgericht held that the question was unsettled, although all its references were in favour of the conservative, more restrictive point of view, but managed to avoid deciding the issue by finding that even negligence was not established against the defendant. Thus in 1890 it was clearly a matter for debate whether the *lex Aquilia* could be stretched so as to cover cases of economic loss negligently caused, but the idea of *culpa* still held good, and one could not possibly argue in favour of strict liability. A strict liability was, however, introduced to solve such cases by the Reichszivilprozeßordnung of 1877[51].

c) Liability for Negligent Statements?

In cases where bad advice had caused economic loss, the courts declined to grant the *actio legis Aquiliae.* The Reichoberhandelsgericht held that the *lex Aquilia,* even in its modern extensions, still required damage caused to a corporeal asset[52]. The *actio de dolo* requires *dolus,* and *culpa lata* was no substitute for it. The Roman texts which did allow *culpa lata* as a substitute were applied only within existing contractual relations[53], and very few voices were raised in favour of extending the *actio de dolo* to include cases of mere *culpa lata,* which would have extended delictual liability quite considerably[54]. The courts thus accepted liability for *culpa* outside contract

[50] Ibid., p. 207 sequ.

[51] Today: §§ 717, 745 ZPO.

[52] Judgement of 3/10/1873, Seufferts Archiv, vol. 29, no. 26, with references to precedents.

[53] There was a broad and increasing support for the view that within a contractual relation *culpa lata* was sufficient to constitute *dolus*; cf. *Windscheid,* supra N. 6, § 101 N. 10b, p. 524 with references. In the 1850ies the debate on this issue was immensely intensified due to the "Lucca-Pistoja-Actien-Streit". This controversy concerned the shares of a new corporation set up to build and run a railway between Lucca and Pistoja in Italy. Obviously due to mismangement, the enterprise ended in a desaster, avoiding bancrupcy only by a small margin. All over Europe, shareholders sued the sellers of the shares, mostly banks, for a return of the money invested. A learned opinion was given (to a banker and relative) and later published by *L. Goldschmidt,* Der Lucca-Pistoja-Actien-Streit (1859); hereto *Jhering,* Der Lucca-Pistoja-Eisenbahnstreit, Archiv für praktische Rechtswissenschaft, Neue Folge (new series) vol. 4 (1867) p. 225 sequ. We would today consider this as a case of pospectus liability.

[54] This view was taken by *Dernburg,* a prussian lawyer equally outstanding as a "Pandectist" and as a Commentator of the Prussian Allgemeine Landrecht, cf. his

only where damage had been done to a corporeal asset. The legal maxim "No liability for advice and recommendation" ("Keine Haftung für Rat und Empfehlung") was subsequently incorporated in terms into the Bürgerliche Gesetzbuch[55], but has been substantially eroded since then: Those giving "advice and recommendation" may now be held liable on the basis of a contract to give such advice, and professionals may even be held liable to a third party who becomes aware of such "advice and recommendation" and relies on it. This liability, however, is construed by the courts as contractual (contract with protective force for third parties)[56].

d) Contractual Positions Infringed by Third Parties

The remaining cases concern plaintiffs which one way or another have suffered economic loss because they could not fully enjoy a contractual position due to the negligent intervention of a third party. From today's perspective, this is the issue of the protection of – relative – contractual positions by means of the law of torts, considered sometimes to be the key issue of purely economic loss[57].

aa) We start with a judgement of the Oberappellationsgericht Celle of 1801[58]. A man who had claimed certain hunting rights had lost his case because his main witness had not shown up. He now brought a new suit against another defendant, whom he alledged of having negligently prevented this witness to appear. Since no physical damage was done to any specific corporeal asset we may treat this as case of purely economic loss. Nevertheless, the Oberappellationsgericht Celle awarded damages to the plaintiff, on the very general basis of the Gemeines Recht.

Pandektenrecht vol. II (3 rd ed. 1892) § 36 N. 6, p. 99. Against him *Windscheid*, op. cit. supra N. 53, with further references.

55 § 676 BGB.

56 Cf. *H. H. Seiler*, in: Münchener Kommentar, vol. 4, 3rd ed. (1997), ad § 676 BGB, esp. no. 12, 17. A highly debated case is Bundesgerichtshof [BGH] of 10/11/1994, in: Entscheidungen des Bundesgerichtshofes [BGHZ] vol. 127, p. 378 sequ., on which also *Picker*, in Festschrift Medicus (supra N. 15); for the most recent extension see BGH of 13/11/1997, in Neue Juristische Wochenschrift [NJW] 1998, 1059 sequ.

57 Cf., also with plenty of references to the historical development, *Christoph Becker*, Schutz von Forderungen durch das Deliktsrecht, in: Archiv für die civilistische Praxis [AcP] 196 (1996) p. 439 sequ.

58 *v. Bülow-Hagemann*, Praktische Erörterungen aus allen Theilen der Rechtsgelehrsamkeit III (1801) 46. Erörterung, p. 248 sequ. On this case see *J. Schröder*, Die zivilrechtliche Haftung (supra N. 3) p. 147 sequ.; on the 19th century case law cf. also *H. H. Seiler*, Römisches deliktisches Schadensersatzrecht in der obergerichtlichen Rechtsprechung, in: *D. Medicus, H.-J. Mertens, Knut Wolfgang Nörr* et al., ed., Festschrift f. Hermann Lange (1992) p. 245 sequ.

bb) Sometimes we find plaintiffs protected by an extended use of the *actio de dolo*. In 1846, some heirs had sold land, granting the buyer a contractual right of rescission. A countess challenged both the sale and the sellers' right to sell, and although her claim was totally without merit, even at first glance, the buyer was induced to rescind the contract. The sellers were able to resell only at a much lower price in 1850, by reason of the political upheavals of 1848. The Obertribunal Stuttgart made the countess pay damages[59]: She had made her claim frivolously, without even the slightest appearance of any right to do so. According to the court, "real" *dolus* was not required, nor was it necessary that she should have foreseen the damage she was causing.

cc) In 1864 the Oberappellationsgericht Wolfenbüttel[60] had to decide the following case: The plaintiff had leased a fishery. The defendant operated a sugar factory upstream, from which hot polluted water entered the river and killed the fish. The court held that the *actio legis Aquiliae* did not lie since no corporeal assets belonging to the plaintiff had been damaged, but nevertheless awarded damages on the basis of an *actio in factum,* holding this to be necessary to cover cases of illegal damage to the "Vermögen". The court does not bother to explain how, in the absence of regulations for the protection of the environment, the defendant's behaviour could be positively qualified as illegal.

dd) The Reichsgericht, however, maintained a strict line. A vessel had been damaged by another ship and the charterer of the damaged vessel brought a law suit against the owner of the ship which had caused the damage. In a long judgement the Reichsgericht held that neither the sources of the Roman Law nor the prevailing doctrine of the *Ius Commune* recognized the rule that there was liability for every *culpa*. The Reichsgericht does mention the new codifications and their general clauses and concedes that they may be in line with the modern idea of law ("Rechtsbewußtsein"): All this, the Reichsgericht found, did not carry enough weight to alter the law. To grant damages therefore would be *contra legem*[61]. Therefore, the wrongdoer who damages a physical thing is not liable to a person who does not own it but has only a contractual interest in its remaining undamaged. The Bürgerliche Gesetzbuch was drafted in line with this decision of the Reichsgericht[62].

---

[59] Judgement of 11/7/1854, Seufferts Archiv vol. 9 No. 25.

[60] 13/5/1864, Seufferts Archiv, vol. 17, no. 224.

[61] Judgement of 10/12/1883, RGZ 9, p. 158/162 sequ.

[62] *Mossler,* infra p. 386, *H.-P. Benöhr,* Die Redaktion der Paragraphen 823 und 826 BGB, in: R. Zimmermann (ed.) Rechtsgeschichte und Privatrechtsdogmatik (1999) p. 510 sub 3. On the legislative considerations, whether, as a consequence of an "Aquilian" damage to a corporeal asset, third parties can recover loss they have

Summing up both the doctrinal literature and the case law, we find a general willingness to defend the restrictions of liability inherent in the Roman actions. Indeed, while there are surprisingly many statements defending the traditional limits of liability, we find no explicit pleas for a general clause making liability turn on the negligent causing of damage. True, the codifications of France, Austria and Prussia had made the legal world acquainted with such a system – but even under such codifications there had been many attempts to re-restrict liability in line with Roman law. While it was not the idea of a general clause that made people question the traditional system, there were specific fields in which the traditional system came under real strain as being inadequate, the outstanding example being damage done by railways. These deficiencies were mostly made good by specific legislation. This legislation, however, did not impose extended liabilities for fault, but opted for strict liability right away[63]. It was perhaps only due to the introduction of a number of strict liabilites that the traditional system held good throughout the nineteenth century and was, indeed, taken over by the Bürgerliche Gesetzbuch.

IV. Vicarious Liability

a) "In the course of the 19th century, the principle that liability is based on fault, acquired a status of unquestionable, axiomatic truth" as *Zimmermann*[64] writes. Vicarious liability was therefore construed as liability for negligence in the choice, instruction or control of one's people[65]. The strict adherence to the fault principle was mellowed by a shift in the burden of proof: Already *Hasse*[66] and especially *Levin Goldschmid*[67] required the employer to prove that he was completely free from fault. With this modification we find the traditional, fault-oriented approach upheld by *Windscheid*[68]. Somewhat surprisingly, this point of view was brought into question by the laws imposing strict liabilities for railway and mining companies, for such liability, though primarily imposed because of the inherent

suffered because they depend, though "only" by way of a contractual relation, on the damaged asset, s. *M. Fraenkel,* (supra N. 15) p. 143 sequ.

63 A strict liability for railways was introduced in Prussia in 1838 by the "Preußisches Eisenbahn-Gesetz" (§ 25), cf. *Th. Baums,* ZRG Germ. Abt. vol. 104, (1987) p. 277 sequ. On the introduction of strict liabilities in the 19th century in general, see *R. Ogorek,* Untersuchungen zur Entwicklung der Gefährdungshaftung im 19. Jahrhundert (1975); *Coing* (supra N. 1) p. 524 sequ. with further references.

64 Supra N. 15, p. 1034. Cf. also *Coing* (supra N. 1) p. 521 sequ.

65 *Hasse* (supra N. 9) p. 411 sequ.

66 Op. cit., p. 411 sequ.

67 Zeitschrift für das gesamte Handelsrecht [ZHR], vol. 16 (1871), p. 322.

68 *Windscheid,* Pandektenrecht (3rd ed. 1873) vol. 2 (§ 455) p. 659 N. 27 and 12.

dangers of railway-transport and mining, incidentally also covered damage caused by the employees of such enterprises. It was, therefore, possible to ask whether all employers should not be subjected to the same liability as was imposed on railway companies and mining enterprises[69].

b) The case law of the 19th century already indicates some inadequacies in the traditional doctrine[70]. While in a judgement of 22/10/1860, the Oberappellationsgericht Munich continued to adhere to the traditional view of the Gemeines Recht[71], only a dozen years later, the Reichsoberhandelsgericht granted damages to the widow of a worker killed by a horse-drawn carriage negligently managed by an employee of the company sued[72]. The Reichsoberhandelsgericht noted that while "pure" Roman law did not acknowledge an extra-contractual liability for one's subordinates, there was a pan-German common law of vicarious liability which did so: Transport companies, and railways in particular, were subject to (strict) vicarious liability, be it for contractual or for "Aquilian" *culpa.* The court brought together cases decided by courts throughout Germany and Austria[73] and held that the law imposing strict liability on railway companies[74] simply codifies this customary liability evidenced in the widespread decisions. Cautiously, the Reichsoberhandelsgericht does not decide whether this customary law is general in its application or applies only to "the great transport companies"[75]. It requires also, in line with the French Code Civil (which is not quoted), that the employee must have acted within the scope of his functions.

c) Critical to the development of vicarious liability were the two sessions of the Deutsche Juristentag in 1884 and 1886, in which, in view of the forthcoming codification, the problem of vicarious liability was discussed. The "Deutsche Juristentag" is a private association of practising lawyers and teachers, the former being the dominating majority. We leave aside the question of contractual liability for the so-called "Erfüllungsgehilfe", i.e. a person who is used to perform a contractual duty. As far as

---

69 *Windscheid,* Pandektenrecht (9th ed. 1906) vol. 2 (§ 457) p. 985 N. 5a.

70 On the case law, cf. *Karl Irmscher,* Der privatrechtliche Schutz der Persönlichkeit in der Praxis des gemeinen und der partikulären Rechte des 19. Jahrhunderts, unpublished Diss. iur., Frankfurt/Main (1958) p. 53 sequ.; *Ursula Blankenburg,* Die Entwicklung der Haftung für Hilfspersonen in der höchstrichterlichen Rechtsprechung von etwa 1850 bis 1950, unpublished Diss. iur., Göttingen (1957).

71 Seufferts Archiv, vol. 14, no. 35.

72 Judgement of 17/12/1873, in: Entscheidungen des Reichs-Oberhandelsgerichts [ROHG-E], vol. 12 (1874) p. 78 sequ.

73 P. 80.

74 On the introduction of strict liability in the 19th century, see the references supra N. 63.

75 P. 79.

non-contractual liability is concerned, there was a heated debate whether strict vicarious liability should supersede the traditional system based on *culpa in eligendo*. The advocates of reform, among them *Otto Mayer,* later the pioneer of administrative law and then professor in Strassburg, tried to find support in art. 1384 of the French Code Civil. Art. 1384 cc states a strict liability of "maître et commettant" provided the employee's act is committed "dans les fonctions auxquelles ils les ont employés". Objections were voiced both to the theoretical construction and the practical consequences of art. 1384: The construction by early interpreters of art. 1384 as containing a *praesumtio iuris et de iure* for a *culpa in eligendo* of the employer was found to be artificial[76]. As far as the practical handling was concerned, one was afraid of a slippery slope: Was the requirement that the employee had to have acted within the scope of his duties an effective restriction of liability or would it lead to an overall liability for employees' "torts"? A French decision was cited as a warning: A servant living in his employer's home had disturbed the neighbours by blowing his trumpet at night, and the employer had been held liable, since domestic servants were constantly under their employers' control. The traditionalists wished to maintain the fault principle, subject only to a shift in the burden of proof. It was also argued that strict liabilities, as statutorily imposed on railways, had made strict vicarious liability superfluous in the fields where a need had made itself felt. The tradtitionalists seemed to have the upper hand in the battle of theories, notwithstanding a demand for the extension of vicarious liability on practical grounds, but when it came to the final vote, a majority – probably due to the mass of practitioners – opted for a strict liability for damage done by negligent employees acting in the scope of their duties. This recommendation was not, however, followed by the German legislator, who adhered to the more traditional rule[77, 78].

---

[76] *Enneccerus,* Verhandlung des 18. Deutschen Juristentages, vol. 2 (1886) p. 106.

[77] See *Mossler,* infra p. 388.

[78] I would like to thank Tony Weir, Cambridge, for his contributions to all the discussions in preparation of this volume and also for his linguistic improvements of this piece.

PATRICK MOSSLER

The discussion on general clause or numerus clausus during the preparation of the German Civil Code

Before one can understand the discussion that took place during the preparation of the German Civil Code (BGB), one must be aware of what the law of torts was in the nineteenth century, for it shows the alternatives open to the draftsmen. Thereafter we shall review the successive deliberations on §§ 823, 826 BGB, and see what considerations influenced the final draft of these paragraphs which have not been modified since their introduction and still form the basis of the German law of tort. Finally we shall consider in relation to their application by the courts whether the reasons and arguments raised during the discussions in the nineteenth century still have any validity today.

I. General clause and numerus clausus in the law of the nineteenth century[1]

Prior to the BGB there was no uniform law of torts in Germany. While the *gemeines Recht* was based upon the numerus clausus of Roman law, other parts of the country had adopted, under the influence of the *Vernunftsrecht* and the example of the French *Code civil,* a general clause for liability in tort.

1. The gemeines Recht

The doctrine of the *gemeines Recht,* in particular the doctrine of *Pandekten* in the nineteenth century, followed the model of Roman law as regards the legal consequences of torts. Instead of having a general clause, Roman law and the *gemeines Recht* had a limited number of specific bases for a claim.[2] In his *Lehrbuch des Pandektenrechts,* for example, *Windscheid,* a leading Pandectist, lists twelve different torts.[3]

---

[1] On this period see *W. Ernst's* chapter in the present volume.

[2] Cf. *M. Kaser,* Das römische Privatrecht, Erster Abschnitt, 2nd ed., München 1971.

These claims were admittedly extended by the courts in order to meet the need to protect person and property more comprehensively, but the scholars never really considered unifying the list of torts into one general rule.[4] This way, the *gemeines Recht* regulated the law of torts according to a strict numerus clausus, and refused to grant any claim outside the specific bases which were explicitly recognised.

2. *The general clause of the jus naturale*

Natural law brought about a striking change in the approach to delictual liability: Instead of tying compensation to a limited number of torts, it regarded the culpable infliction of damage as a ground of liability in itself. The proposition that one should be liable in damages for breach of general or particular human obligations was first stated by *Grotius* in 1625[5], and later adopted by several civil codes. The French *Code civil,* which was able to regulate the law of torts in a mere five articles, is the best-known of these. We proceed to a brief illustration of this alternative to the Roman numerus clausus.

a) The Code civil[6]

The basic general clause of the French law of torts can be found in art. 1382 and 1383 of the *Code civil*:

> Art. 1382 cc
>
> Every human act, whatever its nature may be, that causes damage to another person, obliges the person causing the damage by his fault to make it good.[7]
>
> Art. 1383 cc
>
> Everybody is liable for the damage he causes, whether through his acts or through his negligence or his carelessness.[8]

The separation of the two articles goes back to *Pothier* who distinguished between *délits* and *quasi-délits*. In French court practice a *délit*

---

[3] Cf. *B. Windscheid,* Lehrbuch des Pandektenrechts, Vol. II, 5th ed., Frankfurt a.M. 1882, §§ 451 ff.

[4] Cf. *Reichsgericht,* Entscheidungen des Reichsgerichts in Zivilsachen, Leipzig 1883, Vol. 9, pp. 163 ff.

[5] In: De Iure Belli ac Pacis; lib. II, cap. 17, § 1; see the chapter by *R. Feenstra* in the present volume.

[6] For a more detailed discussion of the law of negligence of the French *Code Civil* see the chapter by *B. Auzary* in the present volume.

[7] "Tout fait quelconque de l'homme, qui cause à l'autrui un dommage, oblige celui par la faute duquel il est arrivé, à le réparer."

[8] "Chacun est responsable du dommage qu'il a causé non seulement par son fait, mais encore par sa négligence ou par son imprudence."

under art. 1382cc is an act of "dol ou malignité"[9], i.e. an intentional act. Art. 1383cc, however, covers the conduct of a person causing a damage "sans malignité, mais par une imprudence qui n'est pas excusable"[10], i.e. negligence. In adopting so vague a general clause to describe the conditions of extracontractual liability, the legislator was ultimately leaving to the courts the decision as to what conduct should give rise to a claim for damages. Consequently, it was the case law that developed three conditions necessary for a claim for damages:

1. The plaintiff has suffered a damage (below aa.),
2. the defendant has committed a *faute*[11] (below bb.), and
3. the damage is a consequence of this *faute*.

aa) Damage

In contrast to German law, the damage does not have to be inflicted on an absolute right (*absolutes Recht*[12]) or a legally protected interest (*Rechtsgut*); mere economic loss is ipso jure indemnifiable. Furthermore, liability according to French law extends to non-material and indirect damages. But because the French courts obviously cannot award compensation for every remote damage, they have limited liability by requiring that there be a "lésion certaine d'un intérêt légitime juridiquement protégé"[13]. In applying this formula, the courts upheld claims for damages of close dependants of a person killed by the *faute* of the defendant.[14] Indeed a football club which incurred heavy transfer payments in order to procure a substitute for a player killed by the defendant was held entitled to compensation.[15]

bb) Faute (act that creates liability)

The most important constituent fact for liability is *faute*. From the German point of view, *faute* contains elements of both unlawfulness and

---

[9] Cf. *R.-J. Pothier*, Traité des obligations, Leiden 1873, Partie I, Chap. I, Sect. 2, § 2, p. 46.

[10] Cf. *Pothier* (above n. 9) p. 46.

[11] I.e. the act that creates the liability.

[12] A right that is enforceable against everyone, e.g. copyright, legal ownership.

[13] Cf. *H. Mazeaud/L. Mazeaud/A. Tunc*, Traité théorique et pratique de la responsabilité civile délictuelle et contractuelle, Vol. 1, 6th ed., Paris 1965, N. 275 ff., p. 361.

[14] Cf. *K. Zweigert/H. Kötz*, Introduction to Comparative Law, Vol. II: The Institutions of Private Law, 2nd ed., Oxford 1987, pp. 311 f.

[15] Cf. *Zweigert/Kötz* (above n. 14) p. 312.

fault. The prevailing doctrine in France assumes that two conditions must be met before *faute* gives rise to liability: *Culpabilité,* i.e. a culpable violation of an obligation, and *imputabilité,* i.e. guilt. We need to stress the fact that both of these conditions contain elements which the German doctrine considers to be elements of either unlawfulness or fault.

In determining the *culpabilité* of an act, the courts do not follow abstract standards (which are hardly definable[16]), but have developed the following categories:[17]

In the first place the violation of a written legal norm is culpable. Written legal norms include all substantive laws, e.g. administrative decrees and the *Code civil* itself. Here, the protection of the *Code civil* extends not only to absolute rights (*absolutes Recht*) and other objects of legal protection (*Rechtsgut*) but also to relative rights (*relatives Recht*[18]). This category covers the violation of penal norms as well.

It is also culpable to breach unwritten legal norms. Consequently, the violation of customary law, of prevailing practice, and of professional standards can result in tort liability. The contravention of moral obligations may also be culpable, at least if the conduct is immoral and the injury intentional.

Finally, a faute is any harmful act that differs from the conduct of a *personne avisée*: to ascertain culpability, the judge has to consider what would have been the conduct of a person of average diligence and understanding in a similar situation. Thus, the action of the defendant might be compared to the potential action of a conscientious expert (*comme un professionnel consciencieux*) or of any driver (*comme tout conducteur*).

The second condition is that the culpable act must be imputable. Following the above mentioned distinction between *délits* and *quasi-délits,* the fault can be a *faute délictuelle* (intent) or a *faute quasi-délictuelle* (negligence). Again the *imputabilité* is determined by referring to the *personne avisée*: to act as he would not have acted reveals a defect of intention, for he would have foreseen the consequences.

The parallel between *culpabilité* and *imputabilité* stresses once more the fact that the French doctrine does not distinguish as German doctrine does, between unlawfulness and fault. And the same can be observed in the treatment of grounds of justification (justifiable defence, necessity, consent,

---

[16] *M. Ferid,* Das französische Zivilrecht, Frankfurt a.M., Berlin 1971, Vol. 1, p. 830 = N. 2 M 49 f., comments on corresponding developments in the French doctrine.

[17] Cf. *Ferid* (above n. 16) pp. 833 ff. = N. 2 M 60 ff.

[18] A right that is effective only as related to a certain person.

etc.): There is no liability if the harmful act was justified. But while some authors state that the justification eliminates *culpabilité,* others consider this to be a question of *imputabilité.*

cc) The relation between liability in tort and contract

The application of a general clause of torts raises the question of whether in case of breach of a contract liability is created not only according to the law of contract but also according to the law of torts. First of all, it must be emphasised that such concurrence arises less frequently in French law than in German law, since in France "quasi-contractual liability" (*quasi-vertragliche Haftung*) in the form of the German *culpa in contrahendo*[19], *Vertrag mit Schutzwirkung zugunsten Dritter*[20], or parts of *positive Vertragsverletzung*[21] is not contractual at all. Accordingly concurrence in France could arise only when there is interference with the performance of an obligation. Even so, neither the courts nor the scholars have developed clear principles on this matter, so that sometimes French courts impose liability in tort when there is also contractual liability and sometimes consider the law of torts to be inapplicable in case of a breach of contractual duties.

This brief introduction into the practical application of a general clause reveals that it leads to a much wider liability for torts than the regime of §§ 823 ff. BGB. To distinguish conduct which leads to liability from conduct which does not, French courts have evolved abstract and concrete breach of duty as criteria.

b) Other codifications[22]

Other codes of the period also contain a general clause influenced by jus naturale. As early as 1794 the *Preußische Allgemeine Landrecht* laid down in §§ 8, 10 ALR I, 6:

> Whoever unlawfully causes damage to another person offends and insults this person.[23]
>
> Whoever intentionally or by gross negligence insults another person is obliged to compensate him in full.[24]

---

19 Breach of duty prior to contract.

20 Contract with protective effect for a third party.

21 Positive violation of contractual duty.

22 Cf. the summary in *H. Jentsch,* Die Entwicklung von den Einzeltatbeständen des Deliktsrechts zur Generalnorm und die Berechtigung einer solchen, Leipzig 1939, pp. 8 ff.

23 "Wer jemand ohne Recht Schaden zufügt, der kränkt und beleidigt denselben."

Following the example of the ALR the Austrian ABGB of 1809 likewise enacted a general clause in its § 1295[25]. Under the influence of these important natural law codes, the Saxon BGB (1863), the Draft of Dresden (Dresdner Entwurf, 1866), and the Swiss Law of Obligations (1881) all adopted a general clause.

The authors of the BGB began their deliberations against the background of these existing laws: The strict numerus clausus of the *gemeines Recht* on one hand, and the wide general clauses according to the law of nature on the other.

II. The deliberations on §§ 823, 826 BGB[26]

On December 4th, 1873, the *Bundesrat* approved of a proposal of the *Reichstag* that the constitution be changed so as to establish the competence of the *Reich* for civil law. Shortly afterwards the *Bundesrat* set up the *Vorkommission,* a commission of five jurists, to present proposals for the procedure of the formation of a German Civil Code.

The *Bundesrat* accepted their proposals, and its choice of members of the First Commission (*Erste Kommission*) reflected the different legal positions in Germany. Originally it included 6 judges, 3 government officials and 2 professors of law. Most of them, as was usual at the time, had been trained in Roman law.[27] Following the recommendations of the *Vorkommission,* the First Commission entrusted five of its members with the preparation of preliminary drafts of, respectively, a general part, property law, law of obligations, family law, and law of succession (*Redaktoren*). These drafts served as basis for the deliberations of the First Commission. The preliminary draft of the law of obligations was prepared by Judge *von Kübel.*

On October 10th, 1881, the deliberations of the First Commission began. The Minutes (*Protokolle*) of the proceedings[28] explain the motions that

---

24 "Wer einen anderen aus Vorsatz oder grobem Versehen beleidigt, muß demselben vollständige Genugtuung leisten."

25 "Jedermann ist berechtigt, von dem Beschädiger den Ersatz des Schadens, welchen dieser ihm aus Verschulden zugefügt hat, zu fordern; der Schade mag durch Übertretung einer Vertragspflicht, oder ohne Beziehung auf einen Vertrag verursacht worden sein."

26 On the formation of the BGB in general, cf. *W. Schubert,* Entstehungsgeschichte des Bürgerlichen Gesetzbuchs, in: *H. H. Jakobs/W. Schubert,* Die Beratung des Bürgerlichen Gesetzbuchs, Materialien zur Entstehungsgeschichte des BGB, Berlin, New York 1978, pp. 27 ff.

27 Cf. *Schubert* (above n. 26) pp. 36 ff. On the formation of §§ 823, 826 BGB see cf. *H.-P. Benöhr,* Die Redaktion der Paragraphen 823 und 826 BGB, in: R. Zimmermann (ed.) Rechtsgeschichte und Privatrechtsdogmatik (1999) p. 510 sub 3.

28 Quoted as Prot. I.

were submitted, name the member who presented them, and describe the course of the deliberations. They thus inform us of the most important considerations, but since they do not record the statements of individual members, we cannot trace the influence of any particular member on the decisions taken.

The deliberations on the five separate drafts lasted until the end of 1887. In 1888 the First Draft (*Erster Entwurf*) was published together with its motivations (*Motive*) in five volumes. The *Motive* were written by assistants of the *Redaktoren,* basing themselves on the minutes and the original motivations of the preliminary drafts. In part, the *Motive* are taken word for word from the minutes, in part dogmatic remarks are taken from the motives of the preliminary drafts. The *Motive* were not adopted by the First Commission, and while they can help us to a better understanding of the provisions of the BGB[29], they do nothing to clarify the course of the deliberations.

After the first draft was published it was subjected to criticism from professors, lawyers and judges in numerous articles; they denounced in particular its doctrinaire style and its general language. A majority of the critics, however, regarded it as a proper basis for an eventual civil code.

Before the members of the Second Commission were elected, the Pre-Commission of the Ministry of Justice (*Vorkommission des Reichsjustizamtes*) was founded.[30] The influence of its preparatory work on the deliberations of the Second Commission was not discovered until 1974 when *Kögler* showed that many decisions formerly attributed to the Second Commission were in fact rendered by this Pre-Commission.[31] The Pre-Commission had held its meetings since 1890 and continued its work when the Second Commission began its deliberations in April 1891. It ensured the influence of the Ministry of Justice on the further development of the BGB by constantly revising the different parts of the first draft prior to its discussion by the Second Commission. Representatives of the Ministry of Justice who were members of the Second Commission then introduced the revised drafts as their own motions, and their proposals were often approved by the Second Commission, in which government officials held the majority. As far as the law of torts is concerned, the Pre-Commission will be seen to have had an important influence on the second and final draft.

---

29 Yet one has to take into consideration that they illustrate the first draft which was revised again by the Second Commission.

30 On the Pre-Commission of the Ministry of Justice in general cf. *H. Schulte-Nölke,* Das Reichsjustizamt und die Entstehung des Bürgerlichen Gesetzbuchs, Frankfurt a.M. 1995; minutes of the deliberations of the Pre-Commission are quoted as Prot-RJA.

31 Cf. *P. Kögler,* Arbeiterbewegung und Vereinsrecht, Berlin 1974, pp. 78 f.

On December 4th, 1890, the *Bundesrat* chose a Second Commission to make a second draft of the BGB.[32] It consisted of 11 permanent and 13 non-permanent members. No judge in office was a member of the new commission, but seven of the eleven permanent members were government officials, who were thus able to preside over the meetings and dominate them. From April 1st, 1891, until March 27th, 1895, the Second Commission discussed alterations to the first draft, and – after another revision of their draft – on October 22nd, 1895, passed it on for debate in *Bundesrat* and *Reichstag*.

Only minor alterations were made by the parliamentary judicial committee of the *Bundesrat* and in the *Reichstag*, leaving the fundamentals and the total structure of the draft unchanged. After *Reichstag* and *Bundesrat* agreed to the draft in July 1896, the *Bürgerliches Gesetzbuch* took effect on January 1st, 1900.

1. The preliminary draft

The preliminary draft on the law of obligations was written by *Redaktor von Kübel*. Although the First Commission started its deliberations before work on the law of obligations was completed (so that it had to fall back in part on the Dresden draft of 1866), a partial draft on tort was already in existence.[33] The following basic rule was laid down in § 1 TE:

> A person who intentionally or by negligence causes damage to another by an unlawful act or omission is bound to compensate him for the damage.[34]

As explained in the motives of the preliminary draft, it was the intention of this partial draft to abandon the "restrictive position of Roman law"[35] with its specific claims, and to provide a unified rule as a general basis for tort liability, following the example of other modern codes.[36] In view of the general acceptance of the view that the enumeration of specific and discrete torts would not suffice[37], this fundamental decision of the preliminary draft was never challenged during the subsequent deliberations of the two commissions: they never considered laying down a strict numerus clausus like that of the *gemeines Recht*.

---

32 Minutes of the proceedings of the Second Commission quoted as Prot. II.

33 *Teilentwurf "Unerlaubte Handlungen"* of the preliminary draft to a BGB, quoted TE.

34 "Hat Jemand durch eine widerrechtliche Handlung oder Unterlassung aus Absicht oder aus Fahrlässigkeit einem Anderen Schaden zugefügt, so ist er diesem zum Schadensersatz verpflichtet."

35 Mot. VE, p. 4.

36 Cf. Mot. VE, p. 5.

37 Cf. e.g. *Denkschrift zur Reichstagsvorlage*, p. 100.

Nevertheless, the text of the preliminary draft already contained ambiguities which illustrate the matters that will dominate the ensuing discussion about general clause or numerus clausus.

According to § 1 TE, liability is created only if the damage was caused by an unlawful (*widerrechtlich*) act. Hence, one has to decide when an act is to be regarded as *widerrechtlich*: Does the violation of the law have to be established according to legal rules outside the law of torts or can the infliction of damage in itself be regarded as unlawful?

The doctrine of the *Pandektenwissenschaft* declared that the infliction of damage as such was not enough to establish the unlawfulness of an act. *Windscheid* and the doctrine of the *gemeines Recht* recognised two kinds of unlawfulness: The violation of a legal prohibition and the infringement of an (absolute) right (*absolutes Recht*) of another person.[38] Given that the number of prohibitions and absolute rights in the system was limited, this entailed a limitation of the number of torts as well. In this respect a regulation of this kind can be regarded as numerus clausus.[39]

Alternatively, the infliction of damage on another person can be regarded as unlawful *per se*, and that is why a general clause, based on the natural law principle of *neminem laedere*, poses a general obligation not to damage others. On this view, the liability of the damaging person is excluded only if the act or encroachment was especially authorised or justified. Here the creation of liability (*Haftungsbegründung*) is based on a general clause, stating that in principle every infliction of damage creates liability.

The motives of the preliminary draft do not make it clear what the position of the authors was on this matter or how they understood the condition of "widerrechtliche Handlung" (unlawful act). Certainly they show that *von Kübel* intended to reject the strict numerus clausus of Roman law and provide that there should be liability for infringing another's rights:

> According to civil law every act is prohibited through which somebody unlawfully, without authorisation encroaches on somebody else's sphere of rights. For the sphere of rights of every person has to be respected and left untouched by everyone; whoever violates this general rule of law without special justification thereby commits a tortious act.[40]

---

[38] Cf. *Windscheid* (above n. 3) Vol. I, § 101.

[39] The later discussion on numerus clausus or general clause was based on this understanding of numerus clausus only; cf. *M. Fraenkel,* Tatbestand und Zurechnung bei § 823 Abs. 1 BGB, Berlin 1979, p. 114.

[40] "Unerlaubt im civilrechtlichen Sinne ist jede Handlung, durch welche Jemand widerrechtlich, unbefugter Weise, in eine fremde Rechtssphäre verletzend eingreift. Denn die Rechtssphäre einer jeden Person muß von allen anderen Personen geachtet und unangetastet gelassen werden; wer gegen dieses allgemeine Rechtsgebot han-

The preliminary draft thus states the general legal obligation to respect and not to violate another person's sphere of rights. It is possible that in this context the author, contrary to traditional doctrine, regarded the infliction of damage itself as infraction of these rights.

The motives state two conditions that must be met to create liability: Besides the "objective infringement of a right" in terms of the above mentioned encroachment on somebody else's sphere of rights, the unlawfulness (*Widerrechtlichkeit*) of the act must be established. With reference to the second condition, the motives explain that an act is unlawful "if the author has no right or authority to commit it"[41], and this suggests that the infliction of damage is to be treated as unlawful if not explicitly justifiable.

This reading is supported by the wording of § 5 TE, which provides that one is not liable if, in self-defence, one damages the property or person of an aggressor. The rule seems to imply that every impairment of person or property meets the first condition (objective infringement of a right). *Schwitanski*[42] and *Fezer*[43] are consequently of the view that the aim of the preliminary draft was to establish a general clause on the principle that the infliction of damage entails liability: all damage caused to property or person was to constitute an infringement of rights because § 1 TE itself created a legal obligation not to cause damage to those interests.[44]

Yet, we also have to keep in mind that the author and other members of the First Commission had a traditional background in the *gemeines Recht*. Considering the importance of the question, it seems very improbable that *von Kübel* would have deviated from *Pandektenwissenschaft* without further explanation.[45] Furthermore, his introductory observations on the basis of delictual liability show that he did not intend to depart from the doctrine of *Windscheid* as regards the unlawfulness of conduct. Thus the motives to the preliminary draft state:

> Liability for damages is based on the fact that one person causes damage to another by unlawfully infringing the other person's interests, which the legal order deems to merit and need protection. (...) If the legal order recognises an interest as worthy of the protection of civil law, liability in damages arises if it is infringed and damage ensues, unless for some particular reason there is some specified exception.[46]

---

delt, ohne hierzu aus besonderen Gründen berechtigt zu sein, begeht ebendaher eine unerlaubte Handlung.", Mot. VE, p. 1.

41 Cf. Mot. VE, p. 13.

42 Cf. *H.-G. Schwitanski,* Deliktsrecht, Unternehmensschutz und Arbeitskampfrecht, Berlin 1986, p. 101.

43 Cf. *K.-H. Fezer,* Teilhabe und Verantwortung, München 1986, p. 475.

44 Cf. *Schwitanski* (above n. 42) p. 101.

45 Cf. likewise *Fraenkel* (above n. 39) p. 101.

These statements reveal that – regarding the determination of the unlawfulness of an act – the author of the preliminary draft followed the traditional doctrine of *Windscheid*. The First Commission came to share this view of the preliminary draft, and we can presume that as a member of the Commission, *von Kübel* would have clarified his standpoint if he had been misinterpreted in this respect by the other members.[47]

We may conclude, therefore, that *von Kübel* remained true to the *gemeines Recht* and did not regard the infliction of damage itself as infringement of somebody else's rights. According to this position the sphere of rights of the injured party is not simply defined by his person and property but has to be derived from the non-delictual rules of the legal order.[48]

Börgers[49], too, concludes that *von Kübel* started from the traditional view as regards the unlawfulness of conduct and thus abandoned the specific torts of Roman law without recommending a general clause of the natural law type. We do not, however, share *Börgers*' view that the only significant decision of policy was to abandon the specific torts of Roman law and that one can ignore the legal opinions that formed the basis of the condition "widerrechtliche Handlung". He is of the view that the courts could interpret § 1 TE as a general norm on the basis of their own interpretation of unlawfulness.

Doubtless it was only the text of the BGB as adopted by the legislator that was to have legal force[50], and if the BGB had adopted the wording of the preliminary draft the courts could have interpreted the notion of unlawfulness in a different and more extensive way.[51] The purpose of studying the preparation of the BGB, though, is to understand what its authors meant and intended by the texts in question, especially when the preliminary draft, on which the deliberations of the First Commission were based, is being analysed with a view to understanding the making of rules in force today.[52]

---

46 "Letztere (sc. die Schadensersatzpflicht) beruht darauf, daß eine Person widerrechtlich eine andere Person in einem von der Rechtsordnung als schutzwürdig und schutzbedürftig anerkannten Interesse verletzt und dadurch geschädigt hat. (...) Damit, daß ein Interesse von der Rechtsordnung als des privatrechtlichen Schutzes würdig anerkannt wird, ist auch im Falle seiner Verletzung und dadurch herbeigeführten Beschädigung der Anspruch auf Schadensersatz gegeben, wenn nicht aus besonderen Gründen eine positive Ausnahme gemacht wird.", Mot. VE, p. 4.

47 Cf. likewise *M. Börgers,* Von den "Wandlungen" zur "Restrukturierung" des Deliktsrechts?, Berlin 1993, p. 86, n. 84.

48 Cf. likewise *Fraenkel* (above n. 39) pp. 101 ff.

49 Cf. *Börgers* (above n. 47) pp. 71 ff.

50 Cf. Prot. I, p. 4.

51 On a similar development of the Dutch Civil Code see *E. J. H. Schrage's* chapter in the present volume.

It follows that the content of the preliminary draft is comparable to the regulation of today's § 823 BGB. "Unlawful acts" in § 1 TE comprise violations of a law[53] (*Gesetzesverletzungen*) corresponding to § 823 II BGB and infringements of a right (*Rechtsverletzungen*) corresponding to § 823 I BGB.

2. *The first draft (Erster Entwurf) and deliberations of the First Commission*

The first draft (E. I.) contains the following rules on tortious liability:

§ 704 E.I.[54]

Anyone who intentionally or negligently causes damage to another by unlawful conduct, act or omission, and foresaw or should have foreseen its occurrence is liable for that damage, whether or not its extent was foreseeable.

Anyone who intentionally or negligently infringes the rights of another by unlawful conduct is liable for the damage arising from the infraction, even if its occurrence was not foreseeable. Violation of another's life, body, health, freedom and honour count as infractions of a right under this provision.

§ 705 E.I.[55]

Also unlawful is any act contrary to good morals which inflicts damage on another, even if in itself it is permissible under the general freedom of action.

These provisions can only be understood in the light of the deliberations of the First Commission. For this purpose it is not enough just to glance at the *Motive* for their description of the considerations of the Commission is frequently incomplete or inexact[56]; they were formulated by the assistants

---

[52] Cf. *B. Schmiedel,* Deliktsobligationen nach deutschem Kartellrecht, Tübingen 1974, p. 14.

[53] In contrast to § 823 II BGB the preliminary draft covers the violation of any statutory prohibition not just protective laws.

[54] "Hat Jemand durch eine aus Vorsatz oder Fahrlässigkeit begangene widerrechtliche Handlung – Thun oder Unterlassen – einem Anderen einen Schaden zugefügt, dessen Entstehung er vorausgesehen hat oder voraussehen mußte, so ist er dem Anderen zum Ersatze des durch die Handlung verursachten Schadens verpflichtet, ohne Unterschied, ob der Umfang des Schadens vorauszusehen war oder nicht.

Hat Jemand aus Vorsatz oder Fahrlässigkeit durch eine widerrechtliche Handlung das Recht eines Anderen verletzt, so ist er den durch die Rechtsverletzung dem Anderen verursachten Schaden diesem zu ersetzen verpflichtet, auch wenn die Entstehung eines Schadens nicht vorauszusehen war. Als Verletzung eines Rechtes im Sinne der vorstehenden Vorschrift ist auch die Verletzung des Lebens, des Körpers, der Gesundheit, der Freiheit und der Ehre anzusehen."

[55] "Als widerrechtlich gilt auch die kraft der allgemeinen Freiheit an sich erlaubte Handlung, wenn sie einem Anderen zum Schaden gereicht und ihre Vornahme gegen die guten Sitten verstößt."

[56] Cf. likewise *Schmiedel* (above n. 52) pp. 23 ff.; *Börgers* (above n. 47) p. 77.

of the *Redaktoren* and never adopted by the Commission itself. In particular the discussion on general clause and numerus clausus can only be traced with the help of the minutes.

Two earlier studies on the preparation of the BGB reach contrary conclusions with regard to the position of the First Commission on the "general clause or numerus clausus?" question. They may serve as a basis for our analysis.

Schmiedel[57] claims that the First Commission intended to lay down a general clause. It is indeed quite true that during the first session on the law of torts the Commission took a vote on two fundamentally opposite positions. First there was the view of the preliminary draft as understood by the members of the Commission, that liability depends on the conduct being unlawful (*widerrechtliche Handlung*), unlawfulness having to be established by reference to the legal system as a whole and not inferable from the mere infliction of damage. On the other hand motions 1, 2 and 3 were introduced into the discussion. They were intended to lay down a general clause with the proposition that the infliction of "damage as such is a tortious act, provided the act is not authorised"[58]. The Commission actually voted by a majority of seven to four to support the general clause and adopted the following draft:

> A person who causes damage to another (knowingly or by his negligence) is bound to compensate him, unless he acted in exercise of a particular right or – consistent with good morals – in exercise of his natural freedom.[59]

This decision was based on the Commission's belief that the established law was insufficient for the protection of the victim. With reference to the problems of an extensive general clause, the Commission was confident that the judges could cope with the task. As the Commission never revisited this basic question in discussion or decision, it must be assumed that it was its intention to provide a general clause following the example of the natural law.

Yet, as we have seen, in its final version the first draft still contains the condition of unlawfulness and lists the three kinds of unlawful acts. *Schwi-*

---

57 Cf. *Schmiedel* (above n. 52) pp. 20 ff.

58 Die Schadensverursachung sei "schon an und für sich ein Delikt, sofern nicht die Handlung eine berechtigte war", Prot. I, p. 965 = *H. H. Jakobs/W. Schubert,* Die Beratung des Bürgerlichen Gesetzbuchs, Vol. 3.3: Recht der Schuldverhältnisse III, §§ 652–853, Berlin, New York 1983, p. 874.

59 "Wer (wissentlich oder fahrlässig) einem Anderen Schaden zufügt, ist diesem zum Schadensersatz verpflichtet, es sei denn, daß er in Ausübung eines besonderen Rechts oder in einer mit den guten Sitten übereinstimmenden Ausübung der natürlichen Freiheit gehandelt habe.", Prot. I, pp. 966 f. = *Jakobs/Schubert* (above n. 58) pp. 874 f.

tanski[60] believes that the resolution just mentioned retains unlawfulness as a condition of tortious liability, since it expressly safeguards the actor's interest in freedom of action. But in fact there is a great difference between a draft that treats such an interest as an exception from a general prohibition of damaging another's property and a draft that makes these elements preconditions of liability.[61] This difference was apparent to the First Commission as well:

> If the draft (i.e. the preliminary draft of *von Kübel*) considers unlawfulness a necessary condition to create liability, such unlawfulness must be established either through the violation of a legal prohibition or because the act has encroached on somebody's rights, protected according to other provisions of the legal order, and this must have led to damage. (...) Motions No 1, 2 and 3 (i.e. the motions of *Windscheid, Kurlbaum,* and *Planck*) differ in this respect: According to them the infliction of damage itself is considered a tortious act, unless justified.[62]

The adoption by the Commission of the modified motions in full awareness of this difference and after considering the need to restrict so extensive a clause constitutes a clear statement in favour of a general clause and against the numerus clausus.

Nevertheless, we agree with *Schwitanski* that several discrete grounds of tortious liability are contained in the first draft. While in substance §§ 704, 705 E.I. might comprise the same facts as the drafting adopted in the first session, in form they constitute a numerus clausus. Since conduct must be unlawful to generate tortious liability and the unlawfulness must result from the legal system as a whole – ensuing from the violation of a statutory prohibition, the encroachment on absolute rights, or from an "illoyal act" – we end up with a limited number of discrete torts, and this is true even if § 705 E.I. could let in claims for mere pecuniary loss.

This contradiction between the policy decision to adopt a general clause and the draft whose form entails a numerus clausus requires closer examination, for if the first meeting decided to treat damage as *per se* tortious

---

60 Cf. *Schwitanski* (above n. 42) pp. 106 ff.

61 *Börgers* is of a different opinion as well, arguing that this is only a difference in the wording (above n. 47) p. 82.

62 "Wird mit dem Entwurfe (sc. dem Vorentwurf *von Küblers*) die Widerrechtlichkeit für nöthig erachtet, so muß die letztere, damit die Verpflichtung zum Schadensersatze begründet werde, entweder durch eine Rechtsnorm verboten oder es muß durch die Handlung ein von dem Handelnden nach den Vorschriften der Rechtsordnung zu respektierendes Recht des Beschädigten verletzt und hieraus ein Schaden erwachsen sein. (...) Nach den Anträgen No 1, 2 und 3 verhält es sich anders: Ihnen zufolge ist die Schadensstiftung schon an und für sich ein Delikt, sofern nicht die Handlung eine berechtigte war.", Prot. I, p. 965 = *Jakobs/Schubert* (above n. 58) p. 874.

and abandon the condition of unlawfulness, this constituted a revolutionary about-turn from the principles of the traditional *gemeines Recht*. For according to this traditional point of view, unlawfulness as established from the rest of the legal order was at all times *conditio sine qua non* for liability in torts.

Schwitanski's reluctance to accept this about-turn is explained through the course of the following deliberations: During their later considerations, the members of the First Commission overlooked the scope of this early resolution.

After all, discussion of the law of tort could have been brought to an end by the adoption at the first meeting of the draft which combined art. 1382 and 1383 Code civil, with the provision "except if he acted in the exercise of a particular right or, consistently with good morals, in the exercise of his natural freedom" permitting the courts to limit liability where necessary. Nevertheless, the commission continued its deliberations on the law of torts two days later, considered the requirement of intention and negligence, and decided on this point to differentiate the cases of violation of statutory prohibition, encroachment on the rights of another and "illoyal conduct". Thus for the first time we find the distinction still drawn to this day in §§ 823, 826 BGB: The Commission decided that the fault has to be related

(1) (in principle) to the "objective unlawfulness" (!) of the act (= § 823 I BGB),

(2) to the damage in other cases of unlawful acts not involving encroachment on another's rights (= § 823 II BGB), and

(3) to the damage as well in case of "illoyal acts" (= § 826 BGB).[63]

Consequently during the later course of the deliberations we find this observation:

> The following remark was not contested: The resolution on illoyal acts taken during the previous meeting has created a distinct and specific tort requiring the occurrence of damage.[64]

Accordingly neither on that day nor subsequently was there any discussion or decision regarding any alteration on the substantial grounds of liability in damages, so we must assume that the Commission adhered to the idea of extensive liability on the basis of a general clause. In fact, however,

---

63 Cf. Prot. I, pp. 969 f. = *Jakobs/Schubert* (above n. 58) p. 876.

64 "Unbeanstandet blieb die Bemerkung: Durch den in der vorigen Sitzung über die Vertretung der illoyalen Handlungen gefaßten Beschluß sei ein besonderes oder spezielles Delikt geschaffen, zu dessen Thatbestand die Entstehung eines Schadens gehöre.", Prot. I, pp. 976 f. = *Jakobs/Schubert* (above n. 58) p. 878.

their views regarding fault are inconsistent with a general clause and involve a return to unlawfulness as the starting point of delictual liability.[65]

It is not possible to see a general clause in these later versions, or indeed, after the First Commission's deliberations, in the first draft[66], for the Commission's proposal results in having discrete grounds of liability in tort, including the violation of good morals as tortious act.

But as the reversion to the condition of unlawfulness, which was unintentional or at any rate not explicitly approved, results from the way the rule was formulated, it is quite possible that the inconsistency is due to the background in legal theory of the members of the Commission. Having been trained in Roman law they reverted to the traditional categories of unlawfulness in the *gemeines Recht* when attempting to draw distinctions within the realm of liability in tort. As they sought to integrate the more extensive liability already approved at their first meeting, they turned the infliction of damage "not in exercise of a particular right or – consistent with good morals – in exercise of natural freedom" into a category of unlawfulness labelled "illoyal acts".

In fact no such integration was possible consistently with a general clause. If liability for damage inflicted in an illoyal manner is perceived as a general clause which covers all conduct not in the exercise of a particular right or, consistently with good morals, in the exercise of natural freedom, it cannot be seen as coordinate with other forms of unlawfulness, for such a general clause would comprise every violation of a statutory prohibition and every encroachment on somebody else's rights and thus could not reasonably be seen as supplementing them.[67]

Nevertheless there are still authors in Germany who interpret § 704 I E.I. as a general clause[68], a position that is unquestionably mistaken.[69]

---

[65] The course of the following deliberations illustrates this clearly, cf. Prot. I, p. 982 = *Jakobs/Schubert* (above n. 58) p. 880.

[66] According to *Schmiedel,* however, the general clause was merely divided into two separate conditions, (above n. 52) p. 22.

[67] Likewise *F. v. Liszt,* Die Grenzgebiete zwischen Privatrecht und Strafrecht, Berlin, Leipzig 1889, p. 35; *G. Schmidt,* Das Schadensersatzrecht des Entwurfs, in: Gutachten aus dem Anwaltsstande über die erste Lesung des Entwurfs eines Bürgerlichen Gesetzbuchs, Berlin 1890, pp. 1194 f.

[68] Cf. e.g. *E. Deutsch,* Haftungsrecht, Vol. 1, Köln 1976, p. 107; *E. Picker,* Vertragliche und deliktische Schadenshaftung, in: Juristen Zeitung 1987, p. 1051; *M. Löwisch,* Der Deliktsschutz relativer Rechte, Berlin 1970, p. 7 n. 33 and p. 59; particularly erroneous *K. Larenz/C.-W. Canaris,* Lehrbuch des Schuldrechts, Vol. 2.2, 13th ed., München 1994, § 75 I, p. 354, claiming that § 704 I E.I. constitutes a "grand general clause" following the example of the French *Code Civil*! See also *B. S. Markesinis,* A Comparative Introduction to the German Law of Torts, 3rd ed., Oxford 1994, pp. 23 f.

Though the wording of the provision is ambiguous[70], even misleading for today's reader, the *Motive*[71] and minutes of the First Commission[72] reveal clearly that § 704 I E.I. only referred to the violation of statutory prohibitions, thus corresponding to and being slightly more extensive than § 823 II BGB. This is the sense in which the critics[73] and the Second Commission[74] understood this provision.

In conclusion it follows that the elaboration of today's §§ 823, 826 BGB goes back to the First Commission. It is true that liability according to the first draft was more extensive than liability according to the rules prevailing today, for the immoral infliction of damage by mere negligence is covered by § 705 E.I. but not by rules § 826 BGB, and § 704 I E.I. is more extensive than § 823 II BGB because it establishes liability in case of any violation of prohibitory rules and extends to harm which is remote.

The essential thing, however, is that the First Commission linked liability to encroachment on another's rights and sought to define those rights positively, thereby producing a system where liability is the consequence of acts rendered unlawful elsewhere in the legal system as encroachments on rights, violations of statutory prohibitions, and illoyal conduct in the sense of § 705 E.I.

---

69 Likewise *Schwitanski* (above n. 42) pp. 112 f.; *Fezer* (above n. 43) p. 478; *Schmiedel* (above n. 52) p. 14; *R. Reinhardt,* Das subjektive Recht in § 823 I BGB, in: Juristen Zeitung, 1961, p. 711; *H. Stoll,* Richterliche Fortbildung und gesetzliche Überarbeitung des Deliktsrechts, Heidelberg 1984, p. 27; *F. Keppmann,* Die neuere dogmengeschichtliche Entwicklung der objektiven Tatbestände der §§ 823, 826 BGB, Diss. Münster 1959, pp. 114 ff.

70 Likewise the Second Commission, cf. Prot. II, p. 2716 = *B. Mugdan,* Die gesamten Materialien zum Bürgerlichen Gesetzbuch für das Deutsche Reich, revised new print of the edition Berlin 1899, Vol. 2: Recht der Schuldverhältnisse, Aalen 1979, quoted as *Mugdan* II, p. 1075; *E. Meischeider,* Die alten Streitfragen gegenüber dem Entwurfe eines Bürgerlichen Gesetzbuches für das Deutsche Reich, Berlin, Leipzig 1889, p. 37.

71 Cf. Mot. II, pp. 725 ff. = *Mugdan* II, pp. 404 f.

72 Cf. Prot. I, p. 986 = *Jakobs/Schubert* (above n. 58) p. 882.

73 Cf. e.g. *Meischeider* (above n. 70) p. 36; *Fels,* Die außerkontraktliche Schadensersatzpflicht des Entwurfs eines bürgerlichen Gesetzbuchs, in: Beiträge zur Erläuterung des Deutschen Rechts, published by *Rassow* and *Küntzel,* 4th sequel, 5th year, Berlin 1891, p. 13; *V. Mataja,* Das Schadensersatzrecht im Entwurfe eines bürgerlichen Gesetzbuchs für das Deutsche Reich, in: Archiv für Bürgerliches Recht, Vol. 1, Berlin 1889, p. 269.

74 Cf. Prot. II, p. 2714 = *Mugdan* II, p. 1074.

3. Criticisms of the First Draft

None of the critics disapproved of the decision to abandon the specific torts of Roman law, a decision already taken by the preliminary draft. Yet many critics objected strongly to the rejection of a general clause. They realised that according to the first draft an act was not unlawful just because it did damage but that its unlawfulness depended on whether it invaded rights or contravened rules laid down elsewhere in the legal system. The basic justification for this resolution given in the *Motive* – "whatever is not unlawful is permitted"[75] – was rejected outright.

Von Liszt claims that this "profound proposition" is "as false as it could be"[76]. The draftsmen had failed to realise that the law of torts is also responsible for the protection of the legal order as a whole, and that in consequence it needed to be based on an extensive general clause following the example of modern codes.[77] The basic idea, he maintained, contrary to the *Motive,* must be that "encroachment on a third party's legally protected interests is prohibited unless justified for specific reasons"[78]: a general liberty to infringe the protected interests of other persons cannot be acknowledged. In this respect he assumes that rights in personam (*obligatorische Rechte*) are part of the protected interests as well.[79]

Likewise *Fels*[80] took exception to the postulate of the *Motive* that the infliction of damage is permitted if it is not explicitly prohibited and would have used art. 1382 f. Code civil as the basis for reforming the law of torts.[81] He would have accepted § 704 I E.I. as it stood provided it was not interpreted on the basis of the Commission's understanding of unlawfulness, preferring to follow French doctrine and proceed on the assumption that no damage is permitted unless the tortfeasor acts in exercise of a special right.[82] He doubted whether the loopholes in the first draft could be filled through an application of § 705 E.I., considering that the condition "against good morals" was too restrictive.

---

[75] Mot. II, p. 725 = *Mugdan* II, pp. 404 f.

[76] "So falsch wie nur möglich", *von Liszt* (above n. 67) p. 36.

[77] Cf. *F. v. Liszt,* Die Deliktsobligationen im System des Bürgerlichen Gesetzbuchs, Berlin 1898, pp. 3 ff.

[78] "die Verletzung fremder rechtlich geschützter Interessen ist verboten, soweit sie nicht ausnahmsweise aus besonderen Gründen erlaubt ist.", *v. Liszt* (above n. 67) p. 37.

[79] In this context it is very interesting how *v. Liszt* understands the final drafting of § 823 I BGB as a delictual clause of this extensiveness, (above n. 77) pp. 20 ff.

[80] Cf. *Fels* (above n. 73) pp. 6 ff.

[81] Cf. *Fels* (above n. 73) pp. 6 f.

[82] Cf. *Fels* (above n. 73) p. 15.

But *Schmidt*[83] regarded the provision of § 705 E.I. as important for this very reason: its application could close the loopholes that the positive definition of unlawfulness created in § 704 E.I. He, too, was of the view that in principle the infliction of damage itself should be deemed unlawful.

The same position was shared by *Mataja*[84] and *Menger*[85], who advocated better protection for the rights of the indigent social classes. For similar reasons *Gierke*[86] and *Meischeider*[87] rejected the proposals of the first draft, arguing that *relative Rechte* (claims arising from contract) of a creditor deserved delictual protection against third parties as well. Finally, even the *Kölner Handelskammer*[88] advocated adopting a general clause such as that of the *Code civil* and leaving its implementation up to court practice.

As against these views, *Bähr*[89] asserted that the first draft, and the text of § 705 E.I. in particular, went too far. He would leave it to the Criminal Code (StGB) to determine what acts should create liability, for he said that the highly developed criminal law covered all acts that needed to be treated as tortious, except negligent damage to property. The consequence of this position is a strict numerus clausus, differing from Roman law only in incorporating the specific delicts of criminal law.

The Pre-Commission of the Ministry of Justice (*Vorkommission des Reichsjustizamts*) and the Second Commission endeavoured to consider all these criticisms but, as we shall see, those in favour of a general clause failed to prevail.

4. The Pre-Commission of the Ministry of Justice (Vorkommission des Reichsjustizamts)

Without further discussion, the Pre-Commission of the Ministry of Justice based their deliberations on the first draft, with the result that the law of tort continued to turn on the unlawfulness of conduct, as established

---

83 Cf. *Schmidt* (above n. 67) pp. 1191 ff.

84 Cf. *Mataja* (above n. 73) p. 269.

85 Cf. *A. Menger,* Das bürgerliche Recht und die besitzlosen Volksklassen, Tübingen 1890, pp. 195 f.

86 Cf. *O. Gierke,* Der Entwurf eines bürgerlichen Gesetzbuchs und das deutsche Recht, Leipzig 1889, p. 263.

87 Cf. *Meischeider* (above n. 70) p. 37.

88 Cf. *Reichsjustizamt,* Zusammenstellung der gutachtlichen Äußerungen zu dem Entwurfe eines Bürgerlichen Gesetzbuchs, Vol. II, Osnabrück, reprint 1967 of the first print of 1890, quoted as Zusammenstellung der gutachtlichen Äußerungen, p. 400.

89 Cf. *O. Bähr,* Gegenentwurf zu dem Entwurfe eines bürgerlichen Gesetzbuches für das deutsche Reich, Kassel 1892, pp. 164 f.

elsewhere in the law: the alternative of a general clause was not taken into consideration.

With regard to the wording, the Pre-Commission disapproved of § 704 I E.I. in particular.[90] It went too far in making a person guilty of violating a statutory prohibition liable even for remote harm: only those whom the rule was intended to protect should have a claim in tort. On the other hand the damage need not have been anticipated by the tortfeasor.

Regarding § 705 E.I. the Pre-Commission asserted that – "in accordance with the dominant opinion in theory and practice"[91] – liability for immoral damage must be confined to deliberate acts and that no claim should lie where the damage was indirect. This statement shows that the members of the later commissions could not infer from the first draft and the *Motive* how this provision had been understood by the First Commission and in particular by the members who proposed it.

As we have seen above, the regulation of § 705 E.I. resulted from the decision of the First Commission taken in their first meeting that every infliction of damage creates liability, except if the act is performed in exercise of a particular right or – consistent with good morals – in exercise of natural freedom.[92] With regard to the specific rule of § 704 E.I. it would have covered all acts considered deserving liability except encroachment on rights and violation of prohibitions.

But the Pre-Commission and then the Second Commission misunderstood § 705 E.I. and took it for a continuation of liability for *dolus* as recognised in Roman law and the *gemeines Recht*.[93] In fact the wording of § 705 E.I. and the explications given in the *Motive* lead to the erroneous assumption that the First Commission wanted to codify the Roman *actio doli,* a claim for damages that is only awarded in case of intention.[94] Seeking to codify the law in force[95], the Pre-Commission thus limited liability under § 705 E.I. to deliberate acts.

Hence the Pre-Commission of the Ministry of Justice redrafted §§ 704, 705 E.I. as follows:

---

[90] Cf. Prot-RJA, p. 534 = *Jakobs/Schubert* (above n. 58) pp. 892 f.

[91] Prot-RJA, p. 535 = *Jakobs/Schubert* (above n. 58) p. 893.

[92] Cf. Prot. I, pp. 966 f. = *Jakobs/Schubert* (above n. 58) p. 875.

[93] Cf. e.g. *Windscheid* (above n. 3) Vol. II, § 451.

[94] Cf. *Windscheid* (above n. 3) Vol. II, § 451; *Reichsgericht* (above n. 4) pp. 163 ff.

[95] Cf. *Schulte-Nölke* (above n. 30) pp. 293 f.

§ 704 E.I.-RJA[96]

A person who intentionally or by his negligence unlawfully infringes the right of another or violates a prohibition intended to protect another is bound to compensate him for the damage arising therefrom.

Possession is one of the rights covered by this provision; violation of life, body, health, freedom and honour are also to be regarded as infringements of rights.

§ 705 E.I.-RJA[97]

A person who intentionally inflicts damage upon another person in a way that violates good morals is bound to compensate him for the damage, regardless of whether the extent of the damage was or was not foreseeable.

5. The Second Draft (Zweiter Entwurf) and deliberations of the Second Commission

The resolutions passed during the (secret!) deliberations of the Pre-Commission were not officially the basis for the discussions of the Second Commission. The Pre-Commission's versions were introduced as motions, and those relating to §§ 704, 705 E.I. became motion no. 1. Actually, during its deliberations on the law of torts the Second Commission never reverted to the wording of the first draft – "Neither side took the standpoint of the first draft."[98]

Nevertheless, the Second Commission found the opportunity to discuss the question of numerus clausus or general clause. In addition to the Pre-Commission's draft filed by *Struckmann*[99], professor *von Cuny,* referring to art. 50 of the Swiss Code of obligations, proposed (motion 6a):

to provide in § 704:

A person who unlawfully inflicts damage upon another, wilfully or by his negligence, is bound to compensate him.[100]

---

96 "Wer vorsätzlich oder aus Fahrlässigkeit widerrechtlich das Recht eines Anderen verletzt oder gegen ein den Schutz eines Anderen bezweckendes Gesetz verstößt, ist ihm zum Ersatze des dadurch entstandenen Schadens verpflichtet.

Zu den Rechten im Sinne dieser Vorschrift gehört auch der Besitz; als Verletzung eines Rechtes gilt auch die Verletzung des Lebens, des Körpers, der Gesundheit, der Freiheit und der Ehre."

97 "Wer in einer gegen die guten Sitten verstoßenden Weise vorsätzlich einem Dritten einen Schaden zufügt, ist diesem zum Ersatze des Schadens verpflichtet, ohne Unterschied ob der Umfang des Schadens vorauszusehen war oder nicht."

98 Prot. II, p. 2716 = *Mugdan* II, p. 1075.

99 "Vortragender Rat im Reichsjustizamt", cf. *R. Jahnel,* Kurzbiographien der Verfasser des Bürgerlichen Gesetzbuchs, in: *Jakobs/Schubert* (above n. 26) pp. 107 f.

100 "Wer einem Anderen widerrechtlich Schaden zufügt, sei es aus Vorsatz, sei es aus Fahrlässigkeit, ist ihm zum Ersatze verpflichtet.", Prot. II, p. 2710 = *Mugdan* II, p. 1073.

He substantiated his proposal[101] claiming that the wording of the first draft and the other motions was too imprecise and would lead to misinterpretation. It should be left to the judge's discretion and to the doctrine to delimit liability in individual cases and to further develop the law of torts. The practical application of the Prussian and French law in Germany proved that a general clause produced equitable decisions. Though "unlawfulness" reappears in his motion, in substance he postulated a general clause following the example of the Prussian ALR and the French *Code civil,* and leaving it to judge and doctrine to further develop the notion of unlawfulness.

Responding to the motion of *von Cuny,* the supporters of the Pre-Commission's proposal took an explicit position against a general clause of torts.[102]

They pointed out that regulating the law of torts this way only meant shifting the remaining difficulties on to the judge without solving them. To leave such challenges to be solved by the courts complied neither with the trend of legal doctrine nor with "the German people's prevailing conception of the position of the judiciary"[103]. Rather the law had to find the solution, providing objective criteria for the judge's decision. Furthermore, it was not clear that "German court practice might not produce excesses similar to those evidenced in numerous decisions of French courts."[104]

Von Cuny's motion was rejected by a narrow majority, there being ten votes to eight in favour of the RJA's motion.[105] With regard to the other modifications proposed in the RJA's motion, the Second Commission shared the standpoint of the Pre-Commission: Only the violation of a law intended to protect the victim created liability. On the other hand, the Commission considered that liability could not depend on the question of whether the tortfeasor could foresee the damage.[106] The Second Commission further agreed to limit liability under § 705 E.I. to deliberate acts "because in this respect there is no need to deviate from the law in force."[107] Ultimately, the Second Commission adopted the draft of the Pre-Commission (and its grounds), with the amendment that the exercise of a right – even if against good morals – does not create liability. We may therefore conclude that the fundamental changes made to the first draft were due to the proposals of the Pre-Commission.

---

101 Cf. Prot. II, pp. 2716 f. = *Mugdan* II, p. 1075.
102 Cf. Prot. II, pp. 2717 f. = *Mugdan* II, pp. 1075 f.
103 Prot. II, p. 2718 = *Mugdan* II, p. 1075.
104 Prot. II, p. 2718 = *Mugdan* II, p. 1075.
105 Cf. Prot. II, p. 2711 = *Mugdan* II, p. 1073.
106 Cf. Prot. II, p. 2719 = *Mugdan* II, p. 1076.
107 Prot. II, p. 2729 = *Mugdan* II, p. 1079; also see above.

Accordingly the second draft reads:

§ 746 E.II.[108]

A person who, intentionally or by his negligence, infringes the right of another in an unlawful way or violates a prohibition intended to protect another is bound to compensate him for any damage arising therefrom. If the law by its terms can be violated without fault, liability exists only in case of fault.

Necessity is no defence to a claim for damages.

§ 749 E.II.[109]

A person who intentionally and otherwise than in the exercise of a right vested in him inflicts damage upon another person in a way that violates good morals is bound to compensate him for the damage.

Once more the deliberations of the Second Commission on general clause and numerus clausus illustrate the conflicting interests that have to be balanced.[110] As the statement accompanying the proposal to the *Reichstag*[111] clearly shows, the authors wanted the protection by the law of torts to be comprehensive: the specific grounds of liability in Roman law had proved to be incomplete. On the other hand the commission wished to tie the judge to distinct legal rules rather than allow him to decide what conduct should entail liability.

All objectives considered, the First Commission relied on the judge's abilities and favoured a general clause. In contrast, the Second Commission concluded that it was necessary to provide objective criteria for the judge's decision and therefore voted against a general clause. Still, the different positions of the commissions with regard to legal policy cannot conceal the fact that the rules we have today stem from the inconsistent systematic approach of the First Commission[112], which enabled the Second Commission to feel that on this basic question it was at one with the First Commission.

---

[108] "Wer vorsätzlich oder fahrlässig ein Recht eines Anderen widerrechtlich verletzt oder wer gegen ein den Schutz eines Anderen bezweckendes Gesetz verstößt, ist dem Anderen zum Ersatze des dadurch entstandenen Schadens verpflichtet. Ist nach dem Inhalte des Gesetzes ein Verstoß gegen dasselbe auch ohne Verschulden möglich, so tritt die Ersatzpflicht nur im Falle des Verschuldens ein.

Die Schadensersatzpflicht wird nicht dadurch ausgeschlossen, daß die schädigende Handlung im Nothstande begangen ist."

[109] "Wer durch eine Handlung, die er nicht in Ausübung eines ihm zustehenden Rechtes vornimmt, in einer gegen die guten Sitten verstoßenden Weise einem Anderen vorsätzlich Schaden zufügt, ist dem Anderen zum Ersatze des Schadens verpflichtet."

[110] On this cf. *Schwitanski* (above n. 42) pp. 121 ff.

[111] Cf. Denkschrift zur Reichstagsvorlage, p. 100.

[112] Likewise *Schwitanski* (above n. 42) p. 119.

6. Editorial department (Redaktionskommission), Bundesrat, Reichstag

The *Redaktionskommission* provided the final drafting of the regulations. So in § 746 I E. II. it inserted:

> A person who, intentionally or by his negligence, violates the life, body, health, freedom, property or other rights of another ...[113]

This was a mere drafting change, quite in line with the editorial department's terms of reference and the intention of the proposal. All the drafts clearly covered the infringement of any absolute right, and the First Commission's only hesitation was whether the legally protected interests in life, health, and freedom could properly be regarded as rights.[114] That is why they provided in § 704 II E. I.:

> In terms of this proposition the violation of life, body, health, freedom, and honour is also considered infringement of a right.[115]

The Second Commission regarded this as too didactic and unnecessary because such interests were covered by protective laws.[116] In § 747 E. II. a separate regulation provided for the only loophole – negligent violations of freedom. Finally, the editorial department returned to an enumeration of the objects of legal protection and integrated it into § 746 I E. II.[117]

We need to stress the fact that the enumeration in § 823 I BGB is relevant only as providing that the violation of legally protected interests entails liability, regardless of whether they are deemed to be absolute rights.[118] § 823 I BGB constitutes a numerus clausus because it refers to absolute rights, of which our legal system recognises only a limited number, not because it enumerates life, body, health, freedom, and property as objects of legal protection. Thus the approach of § 823 BGB is sometimes characterised as a compromise solution[119]: Its limitation results from referring to (a limited number of) non-delictual provisions rather than from providing a limited number of torts like Roman law did.

---

113 "Wer vorsätzlich oder fahrlässig das Leben, den Körper, die Gesundheit, die Freiheit, das Eigenthum oder ein sonstiges Recht eines Anderen ..."

114 Cf. Prot. I, pp. 2848 f. = *Jakobs/Schubert* (above n. 58) p. 908.

115 "Als Verletzung eines Rechtes im Sinne der vorstehenden Vorschrift ist auch die Verletzung des Lebens, des Körpers, der Gesundheit, der Freiheit und der Ehre anzusehen."

116 Cf. Prot. II, pp. 2723 f. = *Mugdan* II, pp. 1076 f.

117 Cf. Prot. II, p. 8494 = *Mugdan* II, p. 1078.

118 Cf. *Stoll* (above n. 69) p. 27; *Reinhardt* (above n. 69) p. 711.

119 Cf. *Börgers* (above n. 47) p. 98; *Reinhardt* (above n. 69) p. 711.

As regards content, the *Reichstag* amended § 749 E. II., providing that the abusive exercise of inherent rights likewise creates liability.

Thus the enacted provisions read:

§ 823 BGB[120]

A person who, intentionally or by his negligence, unlawfully violates the life, body, health, freedom, property or other rights of another is bound to compensate him for any damage arising therefrom.

The same obligation applies to a person who violates a prohibition intended to protect another. If the law by its terms can be violated without fault, liability exists only in case of fault.

§ 826 BGB[121]

Whoever intentionally inflicts damage upon another person in a way that violates good morals is bound to compensate that person for the damage.

III. Conclusion

The basic objective throughout the deliberations on the law of torts was to provide a unified rule for non-contractual liability. Consequently, the considerations evolve from the idea that liability is created by an unlawful damaging act. The question of legal policy is whether it should be left to the judge to decide which acts create liability and which do not, or whether the law itself should make the distinction clear. Relying on the judge's abilities, the First Commission favoured the first alternative, but later reverted to the prevailing concept of unlawfulness according to which the unlawfulness results from the violation of a (definable) sphere of rights of another. In consequence, even in the first draft this sphere of rights figures as the basic condition of liability.

It fell to the Second Commission to adopt the system of the first draft as a matter of policy, explicitly stating its intention to establish by law the conditions for unlawfulness in accordance with the prevailing doctrine. The intent of the law of torts, as the Second Commission saw it, was to protect the sphere of rights of the individual, and they regarded the definition of this sphere as their task.[122] Consequently, the German law of torts lists a

---

120 "Wer vorsätzlich oder fahrlässig das Leben, den Körper, die Gesundheit, die Freiheit, das Eigentum oder ein sonstiges Recht eines anderen widerrechtlich verletzt, ist dem anderen zum Ersatze des daraus entstehenden Schadens verpflichtet.

Die gleiche Verpflichtung trifft denjenigen, welcher gegen ein den Schutz eines anderen bezweckendes Gesetz verstößt. Ist nach dem Inhalte des Gesetzes ein Verstoß gegen dieses auch ohne Verschulden möglich, so tritt die Ersatzpflicht nur im Falle des Verschuldens ein."

121 "Wer in einer gegen die guten Sitten verstoßenden Weise einem anderen vorsätzlich Schaden zufügt, ist dem anderen zum Ersatze des Schadens verpflichtet."

limited number of categories of unlawfulness: the encroachment on another's absolute rights, the violation of a statutory prohibition and the intentional and immoral infliction of damage. Unlike the Dutch Civil Code of 1838[123], the BGB did not permit the courts to redefine the notion of unlawfulness so as to extend the scope of liability.

The practice of German courts since 1900 reveals that the positive definition of the sphere of rights in § 823 BGB fails to cover every individual case in which liability seems equitable. Thus "quasi-contractual" liability[124] is just like delictual liability in being based on a legal rule independent of the will of the parties[125], so that when the German courts uphold claims for mere pecuniary loss in cases of *Sonderbeziehungen*[126] ("special legal relations", e.g. *culpa in contrahendo*[127], *Vertrag mit Schutzwirkung zugunsten Dritter*[128], *culpa in contrahendo mit Schutzwirkung zugunsten Dritter*[129] etc.) they are really transgressing the BGB's system of torts.

The question therefore arises today whether we would now define the sphere of rights more broadly or adopt a quite different approach to unlawfulness. Often the decisive condition is whether there was a breach of duty, with liability being incurred if the act was contrary to the tortfeasor's abstract and concrete duty. This condition is comparable with the French notion of *faute*[130], which developed from the interplay of the needs of legal practice with an extensive general clause.

IV. Appendix: Vicarious liability – The deliberations on § 831 BGB

Vicarious liability according to § 831 BGB is liability for fault. The principal is held liable because of his own *culpa* in selecting or supervising his employee. This restrictive position appeared to have been overcome during

---

122 Cf. Prot. II, pp. 2711 f. = *Mugdan* II, pp. 1073 f.; Denkschrift zur Reichstagsvorlage, p. 100.

123 See *E. J. H. Schrage's* chapter on the Dutch Civil Code in the present volume.

124 Cf. *E. v. Caemmerer,* Wandlungen des Deliktsrechts, in: Festschrift zum 100jährigen Bestehen des Deutschen Juristentages 1860–1960, Vol. II, Karlsruhe 1960, pp. 56 ff.

125 Cf. *Picker* (above n. 68) p. 1044.

126 Cf. *Picker* (above n. 68) pp. 1053 ff.

127 Breach of duty prior to contract.

128 Contract with protective effect for a third party.

129 *Culpa in contrahendo* with protective effect for a third party.

130 Thus the "sphere of rights" of the injured party cannot be defined positively but results as reflex from the duties of the other party.

the nineteenth century[131], so we must inquire why the authors of the BGB reverted to a mere liability for fault.

The preliminary draft provided from the outset that breach of a duty of supervision gives rise to a claim for damages if the supervised person causes damage (§ 9 TE). The official motivations for the preliminary draft explain that the duty of supervision exists not only towards the person under supervision but also towards third parties. So, according to general principles, neglect of this duty gives rise to a claim for damages if the neglect was culpable and caused the damage. The official motivations recognise that strict vicarious liability might be provided in special regulations for particular situations but it is not adopted as a general principle.[132]

This view was uncontested throughout the deliberations of the First Commission. The First Commission's draft even restricts liability with regard to the burden of proof.[133] *Seiler* supposes that the conservative position of the First Commission, that claimed to be in accordance with Roman law, can largely be attributed to *Windscheid* and his view of the *gemeines Recht.*[134] The Pre-Commission of the *Reichsjustizamt* left the draft unchanged in this respect, having considered and rejected the strict vicarious liability of art. 1384 *Code civil*: The principal's only obligation was to carefully select and supervise the assistant, and any more extensive liability had to remain the exception, provided in specific rules.[135]

The Second Commission considered the alternative of strict vicarious liability in more detail. By different motions strict vicarious liability was advocated for representatives, mandataries, employees of commercial enterprises, or for any assistant.[136] The argument was that modern practice had shown the need for strict liability. Given that modern (large-scale) enterprises generated unforeseen dangers and took advantage of progressive division of labour, it was just and economically sound to impose the burden of liability in the principals as well. It was inequitable that the liability of someone able to afford servants to do his work for him should be less severe than that of an individual or sole trader. The majority's doubts as to whether "some industries in need of protection and small agriculture could shoulder this heavy burden"[137] were rejected with reference to the practice of the *Code civil*, the Italian and the Anglo-American law.

---

[131] See *W. Ernst's* chapter in the present volume.

[132] Cf. Mot. VE, pp. 40, 43 f.

[133] Cf. infra.

[134] Cf. *H. H. Seiler*, Die deliktische Gehilfenhaftung in historischer Sicht, in: Juristen Zeitung 1967, p. 528.

[135] Cf. Prot-RJA, pp. 545 f. = *Jakobs/Schubert* (above n. 58), p. 941.

[136] Cf. Prot II, pp. 2774 ff. = *Mugdan* II, pp. 1091 ff.

Nevertheless, the majority retained vicarious liability as a liability for fault. Arguing from a doctrinaire point of view, the majority stressed that the servant is only entrusted to legally permitted tasks on behalf of the principal.[138] Strict liability should only be provided if particular situations require specific regulations. These members of the commission maintained the general rule that liability is based on fault, and regarded the reversal of the burden of proof as sufficient to protect the interests of the victim. Thus the enacted provision reads:

§ 831 BGB[139]

A person who employs another to do any work is bound to compensate for damage which the other unlawfully causes to a third party in the performance of his work. The duty to compensate does not arise if the employer has exercised ordinary care in the choice of the employee, and, where he has to supply appliances or equipment or to superintend the work, has also exercised ordinary care as regards such supply or superintendence, or if the damage would have arisen notwithstanding the exercise of such care.

The same responsibility attaches to a person who takes over the charge of any of the affairs specified in para. 1, sentence 2, by contract with the employer.

Again we follow *Seiler* who gives two main reasons for this outcome[140]: The members of the Second Commission were government officials and other jurists of advanced age who in their formation were very much influenced by the nineteenth century doctrine of the *Pandektenrecht*. They were not very likely to give up the traditional position. Secondly, commercial enterprise and agriculture naturally supported a restrictive regulation of vicarious liability. Finally, *Seiler* supposes that the members of the Second Commission might have regarded it as a question of national pride not to incorporate the regulation of the French *Code civil*.

With regard to the breach of duty of careful selection and supervision of the employee, § 831 BGB provides a reversal of the burden of proof. The principal has to prove that he has exercised care in selecting and supervis-

137 Prot. II, p. 2785 = *Mugdan* II, p. 1094.

138 Cf. Prot. II, p. 2784 = *Mugdan* II, p. 1094.

139 "Wer einen anderen zu einer Verrichtung bestellt, ist zum Ersatz des Schadens verpflichtet, den der andere in Ausführung der Verrichtung einem Dritten widerrechtlich zufügt. Die Ersatzpflicht tritt nicht ein, wenn der Geschäftsherr bei der Auswahl der bestellten Person und, sofern er Vorrichtungen oder Gerätschaften zu beschaffen oder die Ausführung der Verrichtung zu leiten hat, bei der Beschaffung oder der Leitung die im Verkehr erforderliche Sorgfalt beobachtet oder wenn der Schaden auch bei Anwendung dieser Sorgfalt entstanden sein würde.
Die gleiche Verantwortlichkeit trifft denjenigen, welcher für den Geschäftsherrn die Besorgung eines der im Absatz 1 Satz 2 bezeichneten Geschäfte durch Vertrag übernimmt."; translation taken from *Markesinis* (above n. 68) p. 13.

140 Cf. *Seiler* (above n. 134) pp. 528 f.

ing the servant or that the damage would have occurred even if he had done so. This provision of the Pre-Commission of the *Reichsjustizamt,* while in line with the doctrine of the *gemeines Recht,* reversed the First Commission's claim that it "corresponded to established principles of law to impose all burden of proof on the injured party"[141], i.e. the proof that the defendant has neglected his duty of supervision and the proof of its causation for the damage.

Today's court practice has circumvented the restrictive regulation of § 831 BGB either by assuming a (quasi-) contractual relationship and applying § 278 BGB – a strict liability for persons engaged to perform one's contractual duties – or by inventing new obligations of the principal that entail liability under § 823 I BGB.[142]

[141] Prot. I, p. 1013 = *Jakobs/Schubert* (above n. 58) p. 935.

[142] Cf. *U. Stein,* in: Münchener Kommentar zum Bürgerlichen Gesetzbuch, Vol. 5, 3rd ed., München 1997, § 831, N. 3 f., 8 = pp. 1780 ff.; *Markesinis* (above n. 68) pp. 685 ff.

ELTJO J. H. SCHRAGE

Negligence in the discussion during the preparation of the Dutch Civil Code of 1838

During the French Revolution the need for codification was felt in the Low Countries just as much as in other parts of Europe. Codification was expressly provided for in the Constitution *(Staatsregeling)* of 1798, and a committee was forthwith set up under the presidency of Hendrick Constantijn Cras, professor in Amsterdam. The law of obligations was entrusted to J. L. Farjon, whose draft, produced in 1800, is preserved in the Algemeen Rijksarchief in the Hague. Most of it derives from the doctrines of Hugo Grotius. This is so, for example, of Farjon's description of the sources of obligations, which he divides into three categories: the natural relations of persons, inequality and promise. Under the heading of inequality he places the law of tort as well as the law of restitution: inequality generates obligations either because a benefit is acquired at the expense of another in violation of his rights or because damage is inflicted by conduct for which the defendant is legally responsible, a tort or negligence. The general statement is followed by examples, clearly not designed to be exhaustive.

The draft had little success. Indeed, the committee as a whole seems not even to have discussed it.

In 1807 Louis Napoleon, King of Holland during the French Revolution, invited the Amsterdam advocate Johannes van der Linden to prepare a civil code. His draft, which was ready within the year, had a chapter (3.13) on obligations arising from torts and quasi-torts which likewise was strongly influenced by Hugo Grotius. This draft was never enacted, for in 1809 the *Wetboek Napoleon, ingerigt voor het Koningrijk Holland* - the French Code civil, adapted to the Kingdom of Holland - was brought into force. It remained in force until 1 March 1811 when the Code civil itself was introduced following the annexation by France of the Low Countries as a whole.

After the fall of Napoleon and the re-establishment of independence the French legislation remained in force. This was only provisional, however, for in 1814 the sovereign of the United Netherlands entrusted a small committee with the task of codifying private law. The draft offered to the King by the president of this committee, J. M. Kemper, in 1816 was rather verbose. As to the law of tort, it was quite different from the Code civil. In

Book 3 Title 26, under the heading "Of Obligations arising from culpability and omission" (*van verplichting uit benadeling door schuld en verzuim*) we find rules applicable both to non-performance of contracts and to tort. This structure is due to Hugo Grotius, and perhaps even more to Domat.

Torts in general are defined in article 3531: "any acts, whatever their quality or nature, which cause damage to another makes the person who causes the damage liable to make compensation." This is to cover damage due not only to positive acts but also to the omission of anything that should have been done (art. 3535), and applies not only to damage intentionally inflicted but also that caused inattentively, carelessly or negligently (art. 3536). The undue breadth of this is narrowed by the provision (itself deriving from the Digest) that "damage" does not include the effect of lawful conduct, authorised by statute or other institution. This includes conduct authorised by contract. It is expressly laid down that liability is not incurred under these articles for acts (*benadeling uit schuld*) or omissions of children under the age of ten or by lunatics.

This draft of Kemper's never reached the stage of legislation, and a second draft bearing his name which appeared in 1820 was likewise unproductive, as was the new draft of 1830 (*Ontwerp 1830*). But whereas the second draft hardly differed from the first as regards the law of tort, the 1830 draft was largely based in this area on article 1382 of the Code civil, subject to a very important modification. Instead of "tout fait quelconque" was substituted "any unlawful act" (*elke onrechtmatige daad*). This addition of the word "unlawful" was certainly deliberate, as the Preliminary Report shows: "This adjective is added on purpose, in order to put an end to the manifold disputes which have been caused by art. 1382 of the French civil code. It goes without saying that a claim for compensation cannot arise from every act which causes damage: it is only the unlawfulness of the conduct which crates the cause of action." Here we come very close to the wording actually adopted in articles 1401 and 1402 of Civil Code of 1838 (BW):

Art. 1401: Every unlawful act which causes damage to another makes the person whose fault caused the damage liable to make compensation.

Art. 1402: Everyone is liable not only for the damage he causes by his actions, but also for the damage he causes by way of omission or negligently."

Subsequent articles were slightly modified after the split between Belgium and the Netherlands in 1830, as can be seen from articles 1406 to 1416 BW. The government draft of 1833 contained a number of specific provisions regarding intentional or negligent homicide, offences or injuries done to free persons (articles 1406 and 1407), and defamation (articles 1408 to 1416).

The dominant opinion in those days regarding the addition of the word "unlawful" (onrechtmatig) to the translation of art. 1382 Code civil was that its principal purpose was to make it clear that a person acting in accordance with his rights should not be liable for any damage caused thereby: lawful conduct does not give rise to any cause of action, unlawful conduct does.

Thus the nineteenth century was faced with the question, when is conduct unlawful? How did they then decide whether particular conduct was unlawful or not? The case-law suggests that the judiciary were with the scholars in adopting a very narrow view of what was unlawful: conduct was only unlawful if it conflicted with a statute. Many decisions confirm this picture. In 1883 the Dutch Supreme Court decided that there was liability under articles 1401 and 1402 BW only if the act or omission in question was in breach of the defendant's legal duty or an invasion of the plaintiff's rights, and indicated that whether there were a duty or a right depended on written provisions. In short: "unlawful" was taken to mean "illegal", where "illegal" signifies "contrary to written statutory provisions."

Towards the end of the nineteenth century, however, serious cracks began to appear in this picture. To say that "unlawful" means "illegal" is simply to shift the problem, for one must ask when conduct is "illegal". The answer depends on one's interpretation of written provisions and legal rights: on a narrow interpretation there will rarely be a violation, whereas if they are interpreted broadly, liability will be more easily incurred and imposed.

It has recently been maintained that the approach adopted in the nineteenth century generally reached satisfying results. For example, according to continental civil law the tenant has a right only against his landlord: he has no right in the land he rents. If the tenant's enjoyment of the land is invaded, he can sue only the landlord who has guaranteed that enjoyment. The nineteenth century judges were, however, able to qualify the tenant's right as a legal right in the sense given above, so that infringements of this right counted as torts. Such reasoning was followed in 1881 and 1882: tenants were held able to sue when the pressure created by a recently erected railway embankment caused landslides.

Extension of the notion of legal rights was not the only way in which it was possible to reach satisfactory results in the nineteenth century. Articles other than article 1401 could be invoked and relied on. Here an important role was played by article 1402, virtually a literal translation of article 1383 of the Code civil, without the addition of the word "unlawful". Could one infer that in certain circumstances even a lawful act could ground a cause of action? A few early writers did adopt this position in order to avoid the unfortunate consequences of an unduly rigid interpretation of the notion of "unlawful" in article 1401. Thus when the civil code was still in draft in 1825, Barthlemy, a Member of Parliament, stated of the relation between articles 1401 and 1402: "If, however, a person who acts lawfully on the basis of his rights nevertheless negligently or incautiously causes damage to another, he makes himself liable, not so much by reason of the act itself, but because of his negligence or carelessness in acting."

After 1838, however, legal literature pays strikingly little attention to the interpretation of article 1402. Lipman was one of the few who saw the connection between articles 1401 and 1402. He treated them as translating into Dutch the French distinction between *délit* and *quasi-délit,* which came into the Code civil from Pothier. In Lipman's view article 1401 BW codified *obligationes ex delicto,* the *délits,* while article 1402 codified the Dutch law of obligations arising from *obligationes quasi ex delicto,* the *quasi-délits* of French law. Schüller expressed himself similarly, as if it were obvious. To elucidate the notion of negligence (*onvoorzigtigheid*) he referred to a text in the *Digest*: "one who creates the opportunity for damage to occur is taken to have caused it." In his view the mere fact of causing damage is a ground of liability, without any need further to qualify the act as unlawful.

This was a minority opinion. The dominant opinion came to be that the BW had distanced itself from Roman law by adopting a general action in tort, by article 1401, in place of the various actions with which Roman law had endowed legal culture: article 1401 contained the general action and subsequent articles merely added specifics. Indeed, in the second half of the nineteenth century several writers treated article 1402 as simply explaining and clarifying article 1401. One of these was C. W. Opzoomer (1821-1892), a professor in Utrecht whose name is almost mentioned in the same breath as that of Diephuis, his colleague in Groningen. On article 1402 Opzoomer wrote: "The only purport of this article is to elucidate the words of the previous article, particularly the word "act", which can be used in a broad or a narrow sense. In article 1401 the word is used in the broad sense, to include not only acts which should not have been committed but also to failures to act, to negligence in omitting to do what should have been done. This is the sole meaning of article 1402."

Omissions can be subsumed under the notion of act in article 1401 only because article 1402 renders such an extensive interpretation possible. But for article 1402 there would be the question whether article 1401 should be restrictively or extensively interpreted.

The restrictive view of the general action in tort is not to be found in the writings of the influential Groningen Professor Diephuis. He treated the two articles together and stated that article 1402 provided a basis for imposing liability for careless conduct even if the conduct in itself could not be classified as unlawful.

Nor, at any rate until the end of the century, did the case-law of the Dutch Supreme Court share the view that the only purpose of article 1402 in referring to omission and negligence (*nalatigheid en onvoorzigtigheid*) was to explain the concept of "act" in article 1401. On the contrary. In 1853 the Supreme Court rules that it emerges from articles 1401 and 1402, taken both jointly and severally, that even where an act is lawful and permissible there may be liability if it is done negligently or carelessly. The case involved a constable who had made an official report that the plaintiff had taken part in serious disturbances, with the result that the judge ordered him to be imprisoned. It later appeared that the plaintiff was not only totally innocent of participation in the riots, but had not even been present. It was careless of the constable to give the plaintiff's name, whether by error or on the basis of false information. Article 1402 was taken to mean much more than that "act" includes "omission".

Ten years later a ship was damaged one night when the lockkeeper, following instructions and the order of his superior, lowered the water level in the lock. Since no law forbade the lowering of the water-level at night, the Supreme Court held that the lockkeeper's act could not be qualified as a delict. There remained the question whether the damage was due to any omission or negligence on his part, in particular in failing to warn the owner of the ship. The Supreme Court ruled that while the lockkeeper was under an ethical obligation to warn the shipowner, this was insufficient to constitute an unlawful act of negligence, given that no such obligation was inferable from his instructions or other provisions. The lockkeeper was held not liable for the damage to the vessel.

Given the facts already related, one can conclude that in the first part of last century, contrary to the traditional view that case-law and doctrine were restrictive of liability, the results were satisfyingly broad, given the extensive interpretation of legal rights under article 1401 and the benevolent interpretation of article 1402 as an independent course of liability. Indeed the observation of G. Belinfante in 1865 gives a distinctly modern impression: "The true sense of our articles 1401 and 1402 is consequently the following: a person who causes damage to another by an act for which he is responsible or an omission to do something which, as a careful and honest member of society it was his obligation to do, is liable to make compensation for the damage due to his fault."

Doubtless the traditional picture is largely determined by what happened in the final quarter of the century. The Court of Eindhoven on 11 December 1976 ruled that there was no legal rule against publishing inaccurate data, and in 1883 the Supreme Court interpreted article 1402 in a manner which was significantly novel. The plaintiff, who was minded to buy a seagoing vessel, asked the defendant solicitor whether it were encumbered by any privileged rights. The defendant replied that it was not, but thereafter the buyer was evicted when execution was levied on the vessel for a debt already in existence at the time of the sale. The plaintiff argued that under article 1402 there could be liability for negligence and carelessness even if there was no violation of legal duty or infringement of right, whereas the defence was that there was no statutory duty to give information about the existence of debts. The Supreme Court held for the defendant, ruling "that for the application of these two articles the unlawfulness of the act or omission is a necessary condition. Article 1402 is merely supplementary to article 1401, simply making it clear that the omission to do what the law requires has the same consequences as acts positively unlawful. Consequently both articles are applicable only when the act or omission is contrary to the defendant's legal obligations or infringes another's right."

Did this signal a much narrower conception of tort than previously? The answer is not immediately obvious, for in several cases after 1883 the Supreme Court imposed liability on the state for damage it had caused, negligently, carelessly, or by omission, in the course of constructing installations in public harbours. But around the turn of the century a change of direction can be noted.

In those days competition was often unfair, and the lower courts varied in their attitude, sometimes holding it unlawful, sometimes not. The Supreme Court gave its first decision in this area in 1905. From a shop which carried in its window a large sign saying "Singer" a man called Ivens sold sewing machines which he described as "improved Singer sewing machines" (*Verbeterde Singer naaimachines*), and which bore the name Singer on the front and the word "improved" in small letters on the back. In fact the machines were not made by Singer at all, but either by the German firm Seidel und Naumann or Gritzner. Since the public was being misled as to the origin of the machines, the Singer Manufacturing Company sued Ivens for unfair competition, and obtained judgment in tort in the Court of Appeal. The Supreme Court reversed. It held that it was irrelevant whether or not it was unethical to advance one's own interests by misleading the public as to the origin of the products one was selling, for the applicability of articles 1401 and 1402 BW depended on whether the act or omission infringed the defendant's legal duties or the plaintiff's legal rights. The Supreme Court held that no legal right of the plaintiff was infringed, and that therefore Ivens had committed no tort.

This decision met with very general criticism from scholars, but scholars and judges are different, and this narrow interpretation of article 1401 met with acceptance in the courts, and not only in unfair competition cases. One well-known case is that of the "Zutphen tap". Mrs. de Vries lived in an apartment above a warehouse in Zutphen. In the apartment was a stopcock which controlled the flow of water to the whole building. In freezing weather a waterpipe burst, and the occupant of the warehouse asked Mrs. de Vries to turn off the stopcock. She refused to do so, and as a result the warehouse was flooded and the leather goods stored there were soaked and rendered unsaleable. The occupier sued Mrs. de Vries in tort for her failure to close the tap, but the Supreme Court rejected the claim: the conduct of Mrs. de Vries might be unethical and antisocial but that was not enough to render it tortious: articles 1401 and 1402 were applicable only where the act or omission infringed the defendant's legal duties or the plaintiff's legal rights.

The reasoning is clear and has the charm of simplicity: only illegal conduct is unlawful. No law required Mrs. de Vries to turn off the stopcock. Her refusal to do so was consequently not unlawful, though even the Supreme Court admitted that it was unethical and antisocial. Such an attitude met with little support in public opinion, even in commercial circles, for it opened the floodgates to unfair competition, and resistance to this restrictive interpretation of articles 1401 and 1402 BW increased. Molengraaff, the most influential professor the Netherlands has ever had, was particularly critical of the Supreme Court. It was time for the legislator to intervene. In order to widen the interpretation of "unlawful act" the government brought in a bill, named after the Minister of Justice Regout: it provided that an act or omission should constitute a tort (*onrechtmatige daad*) if the actor was at fault and his conduct contravened public order, good morals and customs, or fell short of the care of a *bonus paterfamilias*. This provision ran into criticism for using three different concepts in one provision, so two years later an amended bill, drafted by Heemskerk and closely following the terminology proposed by Molengraaff, was brought in: "Unlawful act includes an act or omission which either infringes the rights of another or contravenes the actor's legal duties or runs counter to good customs and morals or falls short of the duty of care which one owes in society to another person or his assets."

The Heemskerk government fell in 1913 and the First World War broke out, so the draft was never discussed in Parliament. While waiting for legislation to be put in place the Supreme Court initially maintained its narrow ruling. This can be seen in the case of the mendacious prospectus issued in Arnhem. The Court maintained its distinction between conduct which violates another's rights or infringes one's duties, which is tortious, and conduct which is merely unethical, which is not. It may be unethical to make careless misrepresentations in a prospectus, but there is no law against it, so a deceptive prospectus does not give rise to a cause of action.

Eventually, however, the Supreme Court changed its view, and in its decision of 31 January 1919, influenced by the draft originating in 1911, did what the legislator should long since have done. The *Lindenbaum-Cohen* case is the most famous case in Dutch legal history.

The facts were simple enough. Cohen and Lindenbaum were commercial printers. Cohen bribed one of Lindenbaum's employees to supply him with a list of Lindenbaum's clients and the terms on which he dealt with them. This enabled Cohen to underbid Lindenbaum. The Amsterdam High Court gave judgment for Lindebaum, but the Court of Appeal reversed, referring to the distinction so frequently drawn by the Supreme Court between unethical and unlawful conduct, that is, conduct in breach of a legal duty. Certainly employees are forbidden to disclose secret information, but this is a duty owed only to the employer. Since the Court of Appeal could find no provision rendering it illegal for Cohen to suborn his competitor's staff, it dismissed the claim.

The Supreme Court reversed, holding "that the decision of the Court of Appeal gave a very restrictive interpretation to the notion of *onrechtmatige daad* (tort), namely that it covers only such acts which are rendered unlawful by statutory texts, so that if no such text is directly applicable, the conduct is not tortious even if it contravenes social customs and morals. Such a restrictive interpretation of the notion of tortious conduct is not, however, inevitable, either on the wording of the article or its legislative history. The word "onrechtmatig" in article 1401 is not defined as meaning "contravening statutory provision". The history of the article shows that the only reason for replacing "tout fait quelconque de l'homme" with the term "onrechtmatige daad" was to make an explicit exception for acts in the exercise of the actor's rights, provided they were not negligently or carelessly executed."

The Supreme Court thereby adopted the extensive definition originating with Molengraaff and taken over into the Heemskerk draft proposal of 1911, given above. Accordingly it was clearly tortious of Cohen to bribe a competitor's employee into divulging his employer's professional secrets, and the deserving plaintiff had his remedy.

The general remedy in tort, as broadly interpreted, certainly gives effective protection to the interests of citizens, but the decision provoked an ever-increasing stream of claims. No article of the Civil Code of 1838 was quoted more frequently by litigants and courts than article 1401, and although the new Civil Code of 1992 effected many modifications, the practice remains constant.

List of Authors

Auzary-Schmaltz, Bernadette, Mme Dr, Centre d'Études d'Histoire Juridique c/o Archives Nationales, 60 Rue des France Bourgeois, 75141 Paris Cedex, France

Baker, John, Prof. St. Catherine's College, CB2 1TQ Cambridge, England

Birks, Peter, Prof. All Souls College, OX1 4AL, Oxford

Dondorp, Harry, Dr. Noorderkade 20, 8356 DD Blokzijl, the Netherlands

Ernst, Wolfgang, Prof. Dr., Institut für Römisches Recht der Rheinische Friedrich-Wilhelms-Universität, Adenauerallee 24–42, 53113 Bonn, Germany

Feenstra, Robert, Prof. Dr. Dr. h.c. mult., Van Slingelandtlaan 3, 2334 CA Leiden, the Netherlands

Hallenbeek, Jan J., Prof. Dr., Faculteit der Rechtsgeleerdheid Vrije Universiteit, De Boelelaan 1105, 1081 HV Amsterdam, the Netherlands

Ibbetson, David, Prof., Corpus Christi College, CB2 1RH Cambridge, England

MacQueen, Hector, Prof., Old College, South Bridge, EH8 9YL Edinburgh, Scotland

Mossler, Patrick, Ulmenstraße 62, 40476 Düsseldorf

Sellar, David, Dr. Old College, South Bridge, EH8 9YL Edinburgh, Scotland

Schrage, Eltjo J. H., Prof. Dr., Koningin Emmalaan 51, 1191 BL Ouderkerk aan de Amstel, the Netherlands

MIX
Papier aus verantwortungsvollen Quellen
Paper from responsible sources
FSC® C105338

Printed by Libri Plureos GmbH
in Hamburg, Germany